KEYBOARD SCAN CODES

The following keyboard scan codes may be retrieved either by calling INT 16h or by calling INT 21h for keyboard input a second time (the first keyboard read returns 0). All codes are in hexadecimal:

FUNCTION KEYS

Key	Normal	With Shift	With Ctrl	With Alt
F1	3B	54	5E	68
F2	3C	55	5F	69
F3	3D	56	60	6A
F4	3E	57	61	6B
F5	3F	58	62	6C
F6	40	59	63	6D
F7	41	5A	64	6E
F8	42	5B	65	6F
F9	43	5C	66	70
F10	44	5D	67	71
F11	85			
F12	86			

Key	Alone	With Ctrl Key
Home	47	77
End	4F	75
PgUp	49	84
PgDn	51	76
PrtSc	37	72
Left arrow	4B	73
Rt arrow	4D	74
Up arrow	48	
Dn arrow	50	
Ins	52	
Del	53	
Back tab	0F	
Gray +	4E	
Gray –	4A	

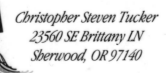

Christopher Steven Tucker
23560 SE Brittany LN
Sherwood, OR 97140

Assembly Language for Intel-Based Computers

Fourth Edition

Kip R. Irvine
Florida International University

Prentice
Hall

Pearson Education, Inc.
Upper Saddle River, NJ 07458

Library of Congress Cataloging-in-Publication Data

Irvine, Kip R.
    Assembly language for Intel-based computers--4th edition / Kip R. Irvine.
    CIP DATA AVAILABLE.

Vice President and Editorial Director, ECS: *Marcia Horton*
Executive Editor: *Petra Recter*
Editorial Assistant: *Renee Makras*
Vice President and Director of Production and Manufacturing, ESM: *David W. Riccardi*
Executive Managing Editor: *Vince O'Brien*
Assistant Managing Editor: *Camille Trentracoste*
Production Editor: *Irwin Zucker*
Manufacturing Manager: *Trudy Pisciotti*
Manufacturing Buyer: *Lisa McDowell*
Director of Creative Services: *Paul Belfanti*
Creative Director: *Carole Anson*
Art Director: *Jayne Conte*
Cover Designer: *KIWI Design*
Cover Art: *Photograph of Shell, Dorling Kindersley Media Library*
Executive Marketing Manager: *Pamela Shaffer*
Marketing Assistant: *Barrie Reinhold*

The author and publisher of this book have used their best efforts in preparing this book. These efforts include the development, research, and testing of the theories and programs to determine their effectiveness. The author and publisher make no warranty of any kind, expressed or implied, with regard to these programs or the documentation contained in this book. The author and publisher shall not be liable in any event for incidental or consequential damages in connection with, or arising out of, the furnishing, performance, or use of these programs.

TRADEMARK INFORMATION
TextPad is a trademark of Helios Software Solutions.
TASM and Turbo Debugger are trademarks of Borland International.
Microsoft Assembler (MASM),Windows NT, Windows Me, Windows 95, Windows 98, Windows 2000, Windows XP, MS-Windows, PowerPoint, Win32, DEBUG, WinDbg, MS-DOS, Visual Studio, Visual C++, and CodeView are registered trademarks of Microsoft Corporation.

Printed in the United States of America

10 9 8 7 6 5 4 3 2 1

ISBN 0-13-091013-9

Pearson Education Ltd., *London*
Pearson Education Australia Pty. Limited, *Sydney*
Pearson Education Singapore Pte. Ltd.
Pearson Education North Asia Ltd. *Hong Kong*
Pearson Education Canada Inc., *Toronto*
Pearson Educacíon de Mexico, S.A. de C.V.
Pearson Education—Japan, Inc., *Tokyo*
Pearson Education—Malaysia Pte. Ltd.
Pearson Education Inc., *Upper Saddle River, New Jersey*

To Jack and Candy Irvine

Contents

2   IA-32 Processor Architecture   31

3   Assembly Language Fundamentals   63

7   Integer Arithmetic 227

17 Advanced Topics

Chapter 17 is an additional chapter provided as a PDF file on the CD-ROM accompanying this book.

Preface

Assembly Language for Intel-Based Computers, Fourth Edition is based on the Intel IA-32 Processor architecture, seen from a programmer's point of view. It is appropriate as a text in the following types of college courses for computer science majors:

- Assembly Language Programming
- Fundamentals of Computer Systems
- Fundamentals of Computer Architecture

Although this book was originally designed as a programming textbook for community college students, it has gradually developed into much more. Currently, many universities use the book for their introductory computer architecture courses. At Florida International University, for example, this book is used in a course named *Fundamentals of Computer Systems*, which leads to a more comprehensive course in Computer Architecture.

The present edition includes topics that lead naturally into subsequent courses in computer architecture, operating systems, and compiler writing:

- Virtual machine concept
- Elementary boolean operations
- Instruction execution cycle
- Memory access using clock cycles
- Interrupts and polling
- Multi-stage pipeline
- Superscalar architecture
- Multitasking
- Loading and executing programs
- Floating-point binary representation

Other topics relate specifically to Intel IA-32 architecture, using information gained from its manuals:

- IA-32 Protected Memory addressing and paging
- Memory segmentation in Real-address mode
- Interrupt handling
- Direct hardware I/O
- Instruction encoding

Certain examples presented in the book lend themselves to courses that occur later in a computer science curriculum:

- Searching and sorting algorithms
- High-level language structures
- Finite-state machines
- Code optimization examples

There are a number of new features in this edition that relate to programming:

- A more comprehensive and logical explanation of data definition.
- A more careful explanation of addressing modes.
- A simplified link library that requires fewer input parameters for nearly all procedures. There are new procedures to dump the CPU registers and sections of memory, as well as a delay timer.
- An explanation and demonstration of top-down program design.
- Use of flowcharts as code-generation tools.
- Even more thorough coverage of assembly language directives, macros, and operators. For example, the PROC, PROTO, and INVOKE directives are thoroughly explained and demonstrated.
- More complete coverage of structures, including nested structures and arrays of structures.
- Block-structured IF, WHILE, and REPEAT statements (an advanced feature of MASM).
- Introduction to video graphics, using both BIOS and direct-memory mapping techniques.
- Mouse programming.
- Win32 Console programming, using calls to the Kernel32 Windows library.
- More array manipulation examples.

Still a Programming Book   It is important to note that this book is still focused on its original mission: to teach students how to write and debug programs at the machine level. It will never replace a complete book on computer architecture, but it does give students the first-hand experience of writing software in an environment that teaches them how the computer really works. The value of this cannot be underestimated, because they will retain a great deal more theoretical knowledge by having immediate contact with the machine. In an engineering course, students construct prototypes; in a software course, students write programs. In both cases, they have a memorable experience that gives them the confidence to work in any OS/machine-oriented environment.

Real Mode and Protected Mode   Many professors have indicated a desire to move to 32-bit programming, using Intel's protected memory model. This edition primarily emphasizes 32-bit Protected mode, but it still has three chapters devoted exclusively to Real-mode programming. For example, there is an entire chapter on BIOS programming for the keyboard, video display (including graphics), and mouse. There is another chapter exclusively on MS-DOS programming using interrupt (function) calls. It is very beneficial for students to have some experience programming directly for firmware and hardware.

The examples in the first part of the book are nearly all presented as 32-bit text-oriented applications running in Protected mode using the flat memory model. This is extremely straight-forward. No longer do students have to deal with segment-offset addressing. There are specially marked paragraphs and popup boxes that note the small differences between Protected mode and Real-mode programming. Most of the differences are hidden away in the book's two link libraries.

Link Libraries   There are two versions of the link library that students use for basic input-output in this book. The 32-bit version (*Irvine32.lib*) works in Win32 Console mode, under any version of MS-Windows. The 16-bit version (*Irvine16.lib*) works under MS-DOS, MS-Windows, and a Linux DOS emulator. In later chapters, all the functions in these two libraries are exposed, and readers can modify the libraries as they wish. It is important to realize that the link libraries are there only for convenience, not to prevent students from learning how to program input-output themselves.

Included Software and Examples   All the example programs have been tested with the Microsoft Macro Assembler Version 6.15. For the most part, the programs will assemble with Borland TASM 4.0 and 5.0, but there are some features that Borland does not fully support.

Web Site Information   Updates and corrections to this book may be found at the book's Web site, including additional programming projects for professors to assign at the ends of chapters:

```
http://www.nuvisionmiami.com/books/asm
```

If for some reason you cannot access this site, information about the book and a link to its cur-rent Web site can be found at **www.prenhall.com** by searching for the book title or for the full author name "Kip Irvine." The author's e-mail address is **kip@nuvisionmiami.com**

Overall Goals

Each of the following goals of this book is designed to broaden the student's interest and knowl-edge in topics related to assembly language:

- The Intel IA-32 processor architecture and programming
- Assembly language directives, macros, operators, and program structure
- Programming methodology, showing how to use assembly language to create both system-level software tools and application programs
- Computer hardware manipulation
- Interaction between assembly language programs, the operating system, and other applica-tion programs

One of my goals is to help students approach programming problems with a machine-level mind set. It is important to think of the CPU as an interactive tool, and to learn to monitor each of its actions as directly as possible. A debugger is a programmer's best friend, not only for catching errors, but as an educational tool that teaches about the CPU and operating system. I encourage students to look beneath the surface of high-level languages, and to realize that most programming languages are designed to be portable and, therefore, independent of their host machines.

In addition to the short examples, *Assembly Language for Intel-Based Computers* contains more than 115 ready-to-run programs that demonstrate instructions or ideas as they are presented in the text. Reference materials, such as guides to MS-DOS interrupts and instruction mnemonics, are available at the end of the book. There is a comprehensive link library that makes the user interface much more accessible for students writing their first programs. The macro library included with the book may also provide inspiration for further development by professors and students.

Required Background   The reader should already be able to program confidently in at least one other programming language, preferably Pascal, Java, C, or C++. One chapter goes into C++ interfacing in some depth, so it is very helpful to have a compiler on hand. I have used this book in the classroom with majors in both computer science and management information systems, and it has been used elsewhere in engineering courses. I used Microsoft Visual C++ 6.0 and Borland C++ 5.0 for the examples that deal with high-level language interfacing.

Features

Complete Program Listings   A companion CD-ROM contains all the source code from the examples in this book. Additional listings are available on the author's Web page. An extensive link library is supplied with the book, containing more than 30 procedures that simplify user input-output, numeric processing, disk and file handling, and string handling. In the beginning stages of the course, students can use this library to enhance their programs. Later, they can create their own procedures and add them to the library. Students are given the complete source code for the 16-bit and 32-bit link libraries.

Programming Logic   Two chapters emphasize boolean logic and bit-level manipulation. A conscious attempt is made to relate high-level programming logic to the low-level details of the machine. This helps students to create more efficient implementations and to better understand how language compilers generate object code.

Hardware and Operating System Concepts   The first two chapters introduce basic hardware and data representation concepts, including binary numbers, CPU architecture, status flags, and memory mapping. A survey of the computer's hardware and a historical perspective of the Intel processor family helps students to better understand their target computer system.

Structured Programming Approach   Beginning with Chapter 5, procedures and module decomposition are strongly emphasized. Students are given more complex programming problems that require the ability to carefully structure their code and to deal with complexity.

Disk Storage Concepts Students learn the fundamental principles behind the disk storage system on the PC, from both hardware and software points of view.

Creating Link Libraries Students are free to add their own procedures to the book's link library and can create libraries of their own. They learn to use a toolbox approach to programming and to write code that is useful in more than one program.

Macros and Structures A chapter is devoted to creating structures, unions, and macros, which are important in both assembly language and high-level languages. Conditional macros with advanced operators serve to make the macros more professional.

Interfacing to High-Level Languages A chapter is devoted to interfacing assembly language to C and C++. This is an important job skill for students who are likely to find jobs programming in high-level languages. They can learn to optimize their code and see actual examples of how C++ compilers optimize code.

Instructional Aids All the program listings are available on disk and on the Web. Instructors are provided a test bank, answers to all review questions, solutions to programming exercises, and a Microsoft PowerPoint slide presentation for each chapter.

Presentation Sequence

Chapters 1–8 represent the basic foundation of assembly language and should be covered in sequence. A great deal of effort went into making these chapters flow smoothly.

1. **Basic Concepts:** Applications of assembly language, basic concepts, machine language, and data representation.
2. **IA-32 Processor Architecture:** Basic microcomputer design, instruction execution cycle, IA-32 processor architecture, IA-32 memory management, components of a microcomputer, and the input-output system.
3. **Assembly Language Fundamentals:** Introduction to assembly language, linking and debugging, and defining constants and variables.
4. **Data Transfers, Addressing, and Arithmetic:** Simple data transfer and arithmetic instructions, assemble-link-execute cycle, operators, directives, expressions, JMP and LOOP instructions, and indirect addressing.
5. **Procedures:** Linking to an external library, description of the book's link library, stack operations, defining and using procedures, flowcharts, and top-down structured design.
6. **Conditional Processing:** Boolean and comparison instructions, conditional jumps and loops, high-level logic structures, and finite state machines.
7. **Integer Arithmetic:** Shift and rotate instructions with useful applications, multiplication and division, extended addition and subtraction, and ASCII and packed decimal arithmetic.
8. **Advanced Procedures:** Stack frames, local variables, parameter declarations, recursion, and advanced parameter passing.

Chapters 9–16 may be covered in any order, giving instructors the opportunity to choose topics that are most relevant to their courses.

9. **Strings and Arrays:** String primitives, manipulating arrays of characters and integers, two-dimensional arrays, sorting, and searching.

10. **Structures and Macros:** Structures, macros, conditional assembly directives, and defining repeat blocks.

11. **32-Bit Windows Programming:** Protected mode memory management, and using the Microsoft Windows API to display text and colors on the console.

12. **High-Level Language Interface:** Parameter passing conventions, inline assembly code, and linking assembly language modules to C/C++ programs.

13. **16-Bit MS-DOS Programming:** Calling MS-DOS interrupts for both console and file input-output.

14. **Disk Fundamentals:** Disk storage systems, sectors, clusters, directories, file allocation table, handling MS-DOS error codes, and drive and directory manipulation.

15. **BIOS-Level Programming:** Keyboard input, video text and graphics programming, and mouse programming.

16. **Expert MS-DOS Programming:** Custom-designed segments, runtime program structure, and Interrupt handling.

17. **Advanced Topics (on the enclosed CD-ROM):** Hardware control using I/O ports, instruction encoding, floating-point binary representation, and floating-point arithmetic.

- **Appendix A:** Installing and Using the Assembler
- **Appendix B:** The Intel Instruction Set
- **Appendix C:** BIOS and MS-DOS Interrupts
- **Appendix D:** MASM Reference

Reference Materials

In my own assembly course, I rely heavily on instructional materials such as tutorials, review questions, electronic slide shows, and workbooks. In that spirit, I have tried to provide ongoing support for instructors. If you find that something important is missing, please contact me and I may be able to provide it. The following reference information is included either in the book, on the accompanying CD-ROM, or on my Web site.

Assembly Language Workbook   An interactive workbook is included on the attached CD-ROM, covering such important topics as number conversions, addressing modes, register usage, Debug programming, and floating-point binary numbers. The content pages are HTML documents, making it easy for students and professors to add their own customized content. This workbook is also available on my Web site.

Debugging Tools   Tutorials on using Microsoft CodeView, Microsoft Visual Studio, and Microsoft Windows Debugger (WinDbg).

BIOS and MS-DOS Interrupts   Appendix C contains a brief listing of the most often-used INT 10h (video), INT 16h (keyboard), and INT 21h (MS-DOS) functions.

Instruction Set   Appendix B lists most nonprivileged instructions for the IA-32 processor family. For each instruction, we describe its effect, show its syntax, and show which flags are affected.

PowerPoint Presentations   A complete set of Microsoft PowerPoint presentations taken from my own classroom lectures is available on the instructor Web site.

Answers to Review Questions   Answers to all the odd-numbered review questions are available on the book's Web site. Answers to the even-numbered questions are available via the instructor Web site.

Acknowledgments

Special thanks are due to Petra Recter, Senior Computer Science Editor at Prentice Hall, who provided friendly, helpful guidance during the writing of the fourth edition. Irwin Zucker did a terrific job as production editor, constantly keeping track of numerous minute details. Bob Englehardt was a great help when preparing the book's CD-ROM. Camille Trentacoste was the book's managing editor.

I offer my special thanks and gratitude to the following three professors who boosted my morale, gave me great pedagogical tips, and tirelessly examined the entire book:

- **Gerald Cahill** from Antelope Valley College, who offered numerous excellent suggestions and corrections. A great many of his ideas became reality in this book.
- **James Brink** of Pacific Lutheran University gave me many great suggestions. His own 32-bit link library inspired me to create one for this book.
- **Maria Kolatis** of the County College of Morris provided incisive, in-depth reviews of my chapters that forced me to rethink the presentation of many topics.

In addition, three people contributed a great deal of their time either by proofreading my book or developing examples that inspired me:

- **Tom Joyce**, Chief Engineer at Premier Heart, LLC.
- **Jeff Wothke** of Purdue Calumet University.
- **Tim Downey** of Florida International University.

Several of my top students at Florida International University read the manuscript and made valuable suggestions: Sylvia Miner, Eric Kobrin, Jose Gonzalez, Ian Merkel, Pablo Maurin, and Hien Nguyen. Andres Altamirano wrote excellent solutions for many programming exercises.

Proofreaders   Many thanks to the following individuals for proofreading individual chapters. Unless otherwise noted, all are teaching faculty:

- Courtney Amor, a mathematics student at UCLA
- Ronald Davis, Kennedy-King College
- Ata Elahi, Southern Connecticut State University
- Leroy Highsmith, Southern Connecticut State University
- Sajid Iqbal, Faran Institute of Technology
- Charles Jones, Maryville College
- Vincent Kayes, Mount St. Mary College, Newburgh, New York
- Barry Meaker, Design Engineer, Boeing Corporation
- M. Nawaz, OPSTEC College of Computer Science
- Kam Ng, Chinese University of Hong Kong
- Ernie Philipp, Northern Virginia Community College
- Boyd Stephens, UGMO Research, LLC
- Zachary Taylor, Columbia College
- Virginia Welsh, Community College of Baltimore County
- Robert Workman, Southern Connecticut State University
- Tianzheng Wu, Mount Mercy College
- Matthew Zukoski, Lehigh University

Microsoft generously provided its Macro Assembler software for inclusion with this book. Helios Software Solutions Inc. permitted me to include an evaluation copy of the TextPad editor.

Basic Concepts

1

1.1 Welcome to Assembly Language

This book, entitled *Assembly Language for Intel-Based Computers*, focuses on programming Intel microprocessors, specifically members of the Intel IA-32 processor family. The IA-32 family began with the Intel 80386, and continues on through the current Pentium 4. Assembly language is the oldest programming language, and of all languages, it bears the closest resemblance to the native language of a computer. It provides direct access to a computer's hardware, making it necessary for you to understand a great deal about your computer's architecture and operating system.

Educational Value   Why do you have to read this book? Perhaps you're taking a college course whose name is similar to one of these:

- Microcomputer Assembly Language
- Assembly Language Programming
- Introduction to Computer Architecture

- Fundamentals of Computer Systems
- Embedded Systems Programming

In fact, these are names of actual courses at colleges and universities that used the third edition of this book. You will probably find that this book contains more assembly language techniques, reference information, and examples than you can possibly digest in a single semester.

If you are in a course whose name includes either the word *architecture* or *fundamentals*, this book will give you some basic principles about computer architecture, machine language, and low-level programming that will stay with you for years to come. You will learn enough assembly language to test your knowledge on today's most widely used microprocessor family. You won't be learning to program a "toy" computer using a simulated assembler; this is the real thing, the same one used by the professionals. You will learn the architecture of the Intel IA-32 processor family from the programmer's point of view.

If you are in doubt about the value of spending endless hours studying the low-level details of computer software and hardware, perhaps you can find inspiration in the following quote from a lecture given by one of the greatest computer scientists of our time, Donald Knuth:

> "Some people [say] that having machine language, at all, was the great mistake that I made. I really don't think you can write a book for serious computer programmers unless you are able to discuss low-level detail."[1]

Web Site   Before you go any farther, visit the book's Web site to see the extra support information and workbook exercises you can use:

```
http://www.nuvisionmiami.com/books/asm
```

There are always new workbook tutorials, interesting example programs, corrections to errors in the text, and so on. If for some reason the given URL is not available, you can reach the book's Web site through Prentice Hall's URL (www.prenhall.com). Search for "Kip Irvine".

1.1.1   Some Good Questions to Ask

Maybe we can answer some of your questions about this book and how it can be used.

What background should I have?   Before reading this book, you should have completed a single college course or its equivalent in computer programming. Most students learn C++, C#, Java, or Visual Basic. Other languages will work, provided they have similar features.

What is an assembler?   An *assembler* is a program that converts source-code programs from assembly language into machine language. The assembler can optionally generate a source listing file with line numbers, memory addresses, source code statements, and a cross-reference listing of symbols and variables used in a program. A companion program, called a *linker,* combines

---

[1]   Donald Knuth: *MMIX, A RISC Computer for the New Millennium,* Transcript of a lecture given at the Massachussetts Institute of Technology, December 30, 1999.

individual files created by an assembler into a single executable program. A third program, called a *debugger,* provides a way for a programmer to trace the execution of a program and examine the contents of memory. Two of the most popular assemblers for the Intel family are MASM (Microsoft Assembler) and TASM (Borland Turbo Assembler).

What hardware and software do I need?   You need a computer with an Intel386, Intel486, or one of the Pentium processors. All of these belong to the IA-32 processor family, as Intel calls it. Your operating system may be some version of Microsoft Windows, MS-DOS, or even Linux running a DOS emulator. The following are either required or recommended:

- *Editor:* You need a simple text editor that can create assembly language source files. You can use TextPad by Helios Software, which is supplied on the CD-ROM with this book. Or you can use NotePad (free with Windows), or the Microsoft Visual Studio editor (used with Visual C++). Any other editor that produces plain ASCII text files will do also.
- *Assembler:* You need Microsoft Assembler (MASM) Version 6.15, supplied free with this book on a CD-ROM. Update patches, as they become available, can be downloaded from the Microsoft Web site.
- *Linker:* You need a linker utility to produce executable files. We supply two linkers on the CD-ROM with this book: The Microsoft 16-bit linker, named LINK.EXE, and the Microsoft 32-bit linker, named LINK32.EXE.
- *Debugger:* Strictly speaking, you don't need a debugger, but you will probably want one. For MS-DOS programs, MASM supplies a good 16-bit debugger named *CodeView.* TASM supplies one named *Turbo Debugger.* For 32-bit Windows Console programs, our preferred debugger is Microsoft Visual Studio (msdev.exe), part of Microsoft Visual C++.

What types of programs will I create?   You will create two basic types of programs:

- *16-Bit Real-Address Mode:* If you're running either pure MS-DOS or a DOS emulator, you can create 16-bit Real-address mode programs. Most of the programs in this book can be adapted to run in Real-address mode. There are notes throughout the book with tips about programming in Real-address mode, and two chapters are exclusively devoted to color and graphics programming under MS-DOS.
- *32-Bit Protected Mode:* If you're using Microsoft Windows, you can create 32-bit Protected mode programs that display both text and graphics.

What do I get with this book?   You get a lot of printed paper. On the CD attached to the book, you get a complete copy of the Microsoft Assembler, version 6.15. You get a collection of example programs on the CD. Best of all, you get a whole lot of information on the author's Web site, including:

- Updates to the example programs. No doubt some of the programs will be improved and corrected.
- The *Assembly Language Workbook,* a constantly expanding collection of practice exercises covering topics from all over the book.

- Complete source code for the book's link libraries. One library is for 32-bit Protected mode under MS-Windows; the other library is for Real-address mode programming under MS-DOS or a DOS emulator. (*Note:* MS-Windows can also run Real-address mode programs.)
- Corrections to the book. Hopefully there won't be too many of these!
- Helpful hints on installing the assembler and configuring different editors to run it. Two editors I currently use are Microsoft Visual C++ and *TextPad* by Helios Software.
- Frequently asked questions. In the previous edition, there were about 40 of these.
- Additional topics on MS-Windows programming, graphics programming, and so on, that could not be included in the printed book for lack of space.
- E-mail access to the author for corrections and clarifications directly related to the book. But don't ask me to help you debug your programming projects. That's your professor's job.
- Solutions to programming exercises. In the previous editions, only professors were given access to solution programs, but this turned out to be somewhat controversial. I was continually fending off e-mail requests for solutions by individuals who (said they) were self-studying assembly language. (There will be additional suggested programming assignments posted on the instructor Web site, which will *absolutely, positively* be available only to registered college instructors.)

What will I learn?   Here are some of the ways this book will make you better informed about computer architecture, programming, and computer science:

- You will learn some basic principles of computer architecture, as applied to the Intel IA-32 processor family.
- You will learn some basic boolean logic and how it applies to programming and computer hardware.
- You will learn about how IA-32 processors manage memory, using real mode, protected mode, and virtual mode.
- You will learn how high-level language compilers (such as C++) translate statements from their language into assembly language and native machine code.
- You will learn how high-level languages implement arithmetic expressions, loops, and logical structures at the machine level.
- You will learn about data representation, including signed and unsigned integers, real numbers, and character data.
- You will improve your machine-level debugging skills. Even in C++, when your programs have errors due to pointers or memory allocation, you can dive to the machine level and find out what really went wrong. High-level languages purposely hide machine-specific details, but sometimes these details are important when tracking down errors.
- You will learn how application programs communicate with the computer's operating system via interrupt handlers, system calls, and common memory areas. You will also learn how the operating system loads and executes application programs.

- You will learn how to interface assembly language code to C++ programs.
- You will gain the confidence to write new assembly language programs without having to ask anyone for help.

How does assembly language relate to machine language? First, *machine language* is a numeric language that is specifically understood by a computer's processor (the CPU). Intel processors, for example, have a machine language that is automatically understood by other Intel processors. Machine language consists purely of numbers.

Assembly language consists of statements that use short mnemonics such as ADD, MOV, SUB, and CALL. Assembly language has a *one-to-one* relationship with machine language, meaning that *one* assembly language instruction corresponds to *one* machine-language instruction.

How do C++ and Java relate to assembly language? High-level languages such as C++ and Java have a one-to-many relationship with both assembly language and machine language. A single statement in C++, for example, expands into multiple assembly language or machine instructions.

Let's find out first-hand how C++ statements expand into machine code. Most people cannot read raw machine code, so we will show its closest relative, assembly language, instead. The following C++ statement carries out two arithmetic operations and assigns the result to a variable. Assume that X and Y are integers:

```
X = (Y + 4) * 3;
```

Following is the statement's translation to assembly language. Note that the translation requires multiple statements because assembly language works at a detailed level:

```
mov eax,Y         ; move Y to the EAX register
add eax,4         ; add 4 to the EAX register
mov ebx,3         ; move 3 to the EBX register
imul ebx          ; multiply EAX by EBX
mov X,eax         ; move EAX to X
```

(Registers are named storage locations inside the CPU which are often used for intermediate results of operations.)

The point in this example is not to show that C++ is "better" or more powerful than assembly language, but to show how assembly language implements a statement in a high-level language. The assembly language statements have a one-to-one correspondence with the computer's native machine language, which is a set of coded numbers with special meaning to the processor.

We? Who's that? Throughout this book, you're going to see constant references to *we*. Authors of textbooks and academic articles often use *we* as a formal reference to themselves. It just seems too informal to say, "I will now show you how to" do such-and-such. If it helps, think of *we* as a reference to the author, his reviewers (who really helped him a lot), his publisher (Prentice-Hall), and his students (thousands).

Is assembly language portable?   An important distinction between high-level languages and assembly language has to do with portability. A language whose source programs can be compiled and run on a wide variety of computer systems is said to be *portable*. A C++ program, for example, should compile and run on just about any computer, unless it makes specific references to library functions that only exist under a single operating system. A major feature of the Java language is that compiled programs run on nearly any computer system.

Assembly language, on the other hand, makes no attempt to be portable. It is tied to a specific processor family, so there are a number of different assembly languages widely used today. Each is based on either a processor family or a specific computer, with names such as Motorola 68x00, Intel IA-32, SUN Sparc, Vax, and IBM-370. The instructions in assembly language match the computer's instruction set architecture. For example, the assembly language taught in this book works only on processors belonging to the Intel IA-32 family.

Why learn assembly language?   Why not just read a good book on computer hardware and architecture, and avoid having to learn assembly language programming?

- You may be working toward a degree in computer engineering. If so, there is a strong likelihood that you will write *embedded systems* programs. Such programs are written in C, Java, or assembly language, and downloaded into computer chips and installed in dedicated devices. Some examples are automobile fuel and ignition systems, air-conditioning control systems, security systems, flight control systems, hand-held computers, modems, printers, and other intelligent computer peripherals.
- Many dedicated computer game machines have stringent memory restrictions, requiring programs to be highly optimized for both space and runtime speed. Game programmers are experts at writing code that takes full advantage of specific hardware features in a target system. They frequently use assembly language as their tool of choice because it permits total control over the creation of machine code.
- If you are working toward a degree in computer science, assembly language will help you gain an overall understanding of the interaction between the computer hardware, operating system, and application programs. Using assembly language, you can apply and test the theoretical information you are given in computer architecture and operating systems courses.
- If you're working as an application programmer, you may find that limitations in your current language prevent you from performing certain types of operations. For example, Microsoft Visual Basic doesn't handle character processing very efficiently. Programmers generally rely on DLL *(dynamic link libraries)* written in C++ or assembly language to perform character operations such as data encryption and bit manipulation.
- If you work for a hardware manufacturer, you may have to create device drivers for the equipment you sell. *Device drivers* are programs that translate general operating system commands into specific references to hardware details. Printer manufacturers, for example, create a different MS-Windows device driver for each model they sell. The same is true for Mac OS, Linux, and other operating systems.

Are there any rules in assembly language?   Yes, there are a few rules, mainly due to the physical limitations of the processor and its native instruction set. Two operands used in the same instruction, for example, must be the same size. But assembly language is far less restricting than C++.

Assembly language programs can easily bypass restrictions characteristic of high-level languages. For example, the C++ language does not allow a pointer of one type to be assigned to a pointer of another type. Ordinarily, this is a good restriction because it helps avoid logic errors in programs. An experienced programmer can find a way around this restriction but in doing so may end up writing code that is overly tricky. Assembly language, in contrast, has no restriction regarding pointers. The assignment of a pointer is left to the programmer's discretion. Of course, the price for such freedom is high: an assembly language programmer spends a lot of time debugging programs at the machine level.

1.1.2   Assembly Language Applications

In the early days of programming, most application programs were written partially or entirely in assembly language because programs had to fit in a small area of memory and had to run as efficiently as possible. As computers became more powerful, programs became longer and more complex; this demanded the use of high-level languages such as C, FORTRAN, and COBOL that contained a certain amount of structuring capability to assist the programmer. More recently, object-oriented languages such as C++, C#, Visual Basic, and Java have made it possible to write complex programs containing millions of lines of code.

It is rare to see large application programs written completely in assembly language because they would take too much time to write and maintain. Instead, assembly language is used to optimize certain sections of application programs for speed and to access computer hardware. Assembly language is also used when writing embedded systems programs and device drivers. Table 1-1 compares the adaptability of assembly language to high-level languages in relation to various types of computer programs.

Table 1-1   Comparison of Assembly Language to High-Level Languages.

Type of Application	High-Level Languages	Assembly Language
Business application software, written for single platform, medium to large size.	Formal structures make it easy to organize and maintain large sections of code.	Minimal formal structure, so one must be imposed by programmers who have varying levels of experience. This leads to difficulties maintaining existing code.
Hardware device driver.	Language may not provide for direct hardware access. Even if it does, awkward coding techniques must often be used, resulting in maintenance difficulties.	Hardware access is straightforward and simple. Easy to maintain when programs are short and well documented.

Table 1-1 Comparison of Assembly Language to High-Level Languages. (Continued)

Type of Application	High-Level Languages	Assembly Language
Business application written for multiple platforms (different operating systems).	Usually very portable. The source code can be recompiled on each target operating system with minimal changes.	Must be recoded separately for each platform, often using an assembler with a different syntax. Difficult to maintain.
Embedded systems and computer games requiring direct hardware access.	Produces too much executable code, and may not run efficiently.	Ideal, because the executable code is small and runs quickly.

C++ has the unique quality of offering a compromise between high-level structure and low-level details. Direct hardware access is possible but completely non-portable. Most C++ compilers have the ability to generate assembly language source code, which the programmer can customize and refine before assembling into executable code.

1.1.3 Section Review

1. How do the assembler and linker work together?
2. How will studying assembly language enhance your understanding of operating systems?
3. What is meant by a *one-to-many relationship* when comparing a high-level language to machine language?
4. Explain the concept of *portability* as it applies to programming languages.
5. Is the assembly language for the Intel 80x86 processor family the same as those for computer systems such as the Vax or Motorola 68x00?
6. Give an example of an *embedded systems* application.
7. What is a device driver?
8. Is type checking on pointer variables stronger in assembly language or in C++?
9. Name two types of applications that would be better suited to assembly language than a high-level language.
10. Why would a high-level language not be an ideal tool for writing a program that directly accesses a particular brand of printer?
11. Why is assembly language not usually used when writing large application programs?
12. *Challenge:* Translate the following C++ expression to assembly language, using the example presented earlier in this chapter as a guide: X = (Y * 4) + 3

1.2 Virtual Machine Concept

A most effective way to explain how a computer's hardware and software are related is called the *virtual machine concept*. Our explanation of this model is derived from Andrew Tanenbaum's book, *Structured Computer Organization*.[2] To explain this concept, let us begin with the most basic function of a computer, that of executing programs.

A computer is ordinarily constructed in such a way that it directly executes programs written in what may be called its *machine language*. Each instruction in this language is simple enough that it can be executed using a relatively small number of electronic circuits. For simplicity, we will call this language **L0**.

But programmers would have a difficult time writing programs in L0 because it is enormously detailed and consists purely of numbers. If a new language, **L1**, could be constructed that was easier to use, programs could be written in L1. There are two ways to achieve this:

- *Interpretation:* As the L1 program is running, each of its instructions could be decoded and executed by a program written in language L0. The L1 program begins running immediately, but each instruction has to be decoded before it can execute.
- *Translation:* The entire L1 program could be converted into an L0 program by an L0 program specifically designed for this purpose. Then the resulting L0 program could be executed directly on the computer hardware.

Virtual Machines   Rather than thinking purely in terms of languages, Tanenbaum suggests thinking in terms of a hypothetical computer, or *virtual machine*, at each level. The virtual machine **VM1**, as we will call it, can execute commands written in language L1. The virtual machine **VM0** can execute commands written in language L0, as shown below:

| Virtual Machine VM1 |
| Virtual Machine VM0 |

Each virtual machine can be constructed of either hardware or software. People can write programs for virtual machine VM1, and if it is practical to implement VM1 as an actual computer, programs can be executed directly on the hardware. Or, programs written in VM1 can be interpreted/translated and executed on machine VM0.

Machine VM1 cannot be radically different from VM0 because the translation or interpretation would be too time-consuming. What if the language VM1 supports is still not programmer-friendly enough to be used for useful applications? Then another virtual machine, VM2, can be designed which is more easily understood. This process can repeat itself until a virtual machine VMn can be designed that supports a powerful, easy-to-use language.

---

[2] Andrew S. Tanenbaum. *Structured Computer Organization*, 4th Edition. 1999, Prentice Hall.

The Java programming language is based on the virtual machine concept. A program written in the Java language is translated by a Java compiler into *Java byte code*. The latter is a low-level language that is quickly executed at run time by a program known as a *Java virtual machine* (*JVM*). The JVM has been implemented on many different computer systems, making Java programs relatively system-independent.

Specific Machines   Let us relate this to actual computers and languages, using names like **Level 1** for VM1, and **Level 0** for VM0, shown in Figure 1-1. Let us assume that a computer's digital logic hardware represents machine Level 0, and that Level 1 is implemented by an interpreter hard-wired into the processor called *microarchitecture*. Above this is Level 2, called the *instruction set architecture*. This is the first level at which users can typically write programs, although the programs consist of binary numbers.

Microarchitecture (Level 1)   Computer chip manufacturers don't generally make it possible for average users to write microinstructions. The specific microarchitecture commands are often a proprietary secret. It might require three or four microinstructions to carry out a primitive operation such as fetching a number from memory and incrementing it by 1.

Instruction Set Architecture (Level 2)   Computer chip manufacturers design into the processor an *instruction set* that can be used to carry out basic operations, such as move, add, or multiply. This set of instructions is also referred to as *conventional machine language*, or simply *machine language*. Each machine-language instruction is executed by several microinstructions.

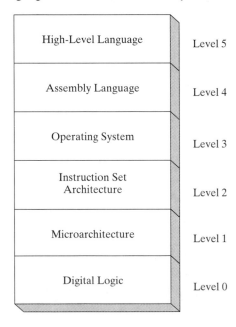

Figure 1-1   Virtual Machine Levels 0 through 5.

Operating System (Level 3)   As computers evolved, additional virtual machines were created to enable programmers to be more productive. A Level 3 machine understands interactive commands by users to load and execute programs, display directories, and so forth. This is known as the computer's *operating system*. The operating system software is translated into machine code running on a Level 2 machine.[3]

Assembly Language (Level 4)   Above the operating system level, programming languages provide the translation layers that make large-scale software development practical. Assembly language, which appears at Level 4, uses short mnemonics such as ADD, SUB, and MOV that are easily translated to the instruction set architecture level (Level 2). Other assembly language statements, such as Interrupt calls, are executed directly by the operating system (Level 3). Assembly language programs are usually translated (*assembled*) in their entirety into machine language before they begin to execute.

High-Level Languages (Level 5)   At Level 5 are languages such as C++, C#, Visual Basic, and Java. Programs in these languages contain powerful statements that often translate into multiple instructions at Level 4. Most C++ debuggers, for example, have the option to view a window that lists the assembly language translation of your code. In Java, you would look at a symbolic listing of *Java byte code* to see the same sort of translation. Level 5 programs are usually translated by compilers into Level 4 programs. They usually have a built-in assembler that immediately translates the Level 4 code into conventional machine language.

> The Intel IA-32 processor architecture supports multiple virtual machines. Its *virtual-86* operating mode emulates the architecture of the Intel 8086/8088 processor, used in the original IBM Personal Computer. The Pentium can run multiple instances of the virtual 86 machine at the same time, so that independent programs running on each virtual machine seem to have complete control of their host computer.

1.2.1   The History of PC Assemblers

There is no universal assembly language specification for Intel processors. What has emerged over the years is a *de facto* standard, established by Microsoft's popular MASM Version 5 assembler. Borland International established itself as a major competitor in the early 1990s with TASM (Turbo Assembler). TASM added many enhancements, producing what was called *Ideal Mode*, and Borland also provided a *MASM compatibility mode* which matched the syntax of MASM Version 5.

Microsoft released MASM 6.0 in 1992, which was a major upgrade with many new features. Since that time, Microsoft has released minor upgrades in versions 6.11, 6.13, 6.14, and 6.15, to keep up with changes to each new Pentium instruction set. The assembler syntax has not

---

[3]   Its source code might have been written in C or assembly language, but once compiled, the operating system is simply a Level 2 program that interprets Level 3 commands.

changed since version 6.0. Borland released 32-bit TASM 5.0 in 1996, which matches the
MASM 6.0 syntax.

There are other popular assemblers, all of which vary from MASM's syntax to a greater or
lesser degree. To name a few, there are: NASM (Netwide Assembler) for both Windows and
Linux, MASM32, a shell built on top of MASM, Asm86, and GNU assembler, distributed by the
Free Software Foundation.

1.2.2   Section Review

1. In your own words, describe the *virtual machine* concept.
2. Why don't programmers use the native language of a computer to write application programs?
3. (*True/False*): When an interpreted program written in language L1 runs, each of its instructions is decoded and executed by a program written in language L0.
4. Explain the technique of translation when dealing with languages at different virtual machine levels.
5. How does the Intel IA-32 processor architecture demonstrate an example of a virtual machine?
6. What software permits compiled Java programs to run on almost any computer?
7. Name the six virtual machine levels named in this section, from lowest to highest.
8. Why don't programmers write applications in microcode?
9. Conventional machine language is used at which level of the virtual machine shown in Figure 1-1?
10. Statements at the assembly language level of a virtual machine are translated into statements at which other level(s)?

1.3   Data Representation

Before we can begin to discuss computer organization and assembly language, we need a common mode of communication with numbers. Specifically, computer data can be represented in a variety of ways. Because we are dealing with the computer at the machine level, it is necessary to examine the contents of memory and registers. Computers are constructed from digital circuits that have only two states: *on* and *off*. At times, we will use binary numbers to describe the contents of computer memory; at other times, decimal and hexadecimal numbers will be used. You must develop a certain fluency with number formats, and have the ability to translate numbers from one format to another.

Each numbering format, or system, has a *base*, or maximum number of symbols that can be assigned to a single digit. Table 1-2 shows the possible digits for the numbering systems used most commonly in computer literature. In the last row of the table, hexadecimal numbers use the digits 0 through 9, and then continue with the letters A through F to represent decimal values 10 through 15. It's quite common to use hexadecimal numbers when showing the contents of computer memory and machine-level instructions.

Table 1-2 Binary, Octal, Decimal, and Hexadecimal Digits.

System	Base	Possible Digits
Binary	2	0 1
Octal	8	0 1 2 3 4 5 6 7
Decimal	10	0 1 2 3 4 5 6 7 8 9
Hexadecimal	16	0 1 2 3 4 5 6 7 8 9 A B C D E F

1.3.1 Binary Numbers

A computer stores instructions and data in memory as collections of electronic charges. Representing these entities with numbers requires a system geared to the concepts of *on* and *off* or *true* and *false*. *Binary numbers* are base 2 numbers in which each binary digit (called a *bit*) is either a 0 or a 1.

Bits are numbered starting at zero on the right side, and increasing toward the left. The bit on the left is called the *most significant bit* (MSB), and the bit on the right is the *least significant bit* (LSB). The MSB and LSB bit numbers of a 16-bit binary number are shown in the following figure:

```
MSB                          LSB
1 0 1 1 0 0 1 0 1 0 0 1 1 1 0 0
15                            0
```

Binary integers can be either signed or unsigned. A signed integer can be either positive or negative. An unsigned integer can only be positive, including zero. Through special encoding schemes, binary numbers can even represent real numbers. For now, we begin with the simplest type of binary numbers, unsigned integers.

1.3.1.1 Unsigned Binary Integers

Starting with the least significant bit, each bit in an unsigned binary integer represents an increasing power of 2. The following figure contains an 8-bit binary number, showing how the powers of two increase from right to left:

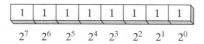

Table 1-3 lists the decimal values of 2^0 through 2^{15}.

Table 1-3   Binary Bit Position Values.

2^n	Decimal Value	2^n	Decimal Value
2^0	1	2^8	256
2^1	2	2^9	512
2^2	4	2^{10}	1024
2^3	8	2^{11}	2048
2^4	16	2^{12}	4096
2^5	32	2^{13}	8192
2^6	64	2^{14}	16384
2^7	128	2^{15}	32768

1.3.1.2   Translating Unsigned Binary Integers to Decimal

Weighted positional notation represents a convenient way to calculate the decimal value of an unsigned binary integer having *n* digits:

$$dec = (D_{n-1} \times 2^{n-1}) + (D_{n-2} \times 2^{n-2}) + ... + (D_1 \times 2^1) + (D_0 \times 2^0)$$

D indicates a binary digit. For example, binary 00001001 is equal to 9. We calculate this value by leaving out terms equal to zero:

$$(1 \times 2^3) + (1 \times 2^0) = 9$$

This is also shown in the following figure:

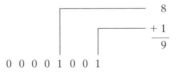

1.3.1.3   Translating Unsigned Decimal Integers to Binary

To translate an unsigned decimal integer into binary, repeatedly divide the decimal value by 2, saving each remainder as a binary digit. Here is an example of how we would translate decimal 37. The remainder digits, starting from the top row, are the binary digits D_0, D_1, D_2, D_3, D_4, and D_5:

Division	Quotient	Remainder
37 / 2	18	1
18 / 2	9	0

Division	Quotient	Remainder
9 / 2	4	1
4 / 2	2	0
2 / 2	1	0
1 / 2	0	1

Collecting the binary digits in the remainder column in reverse order produces binary 100101. Because we are used to working with binary numbers whose lengths are multiples of 8, we can fill the remaining two digit positions on the left with zeros, producing 00100101.

1.3.2   Binary Addition

When adding two binary integers, you must proceed bit by bit, beginning with the lowest order pair of bits (on the right side). Each bit pair is added. There are only four ways to add two binary digits, as shown below:

0 + 0 = 0	0 + 1 = 1
1 + 0 = 1	1 + 1= 10

In one case, when adding 1 to 1, the result is 10 binary. (You can also think of this as the decimal value 2.) The extra digit generates a carry to the next-highest bit position. In the following figure, for example, we add binary 00000100 to 00000111:

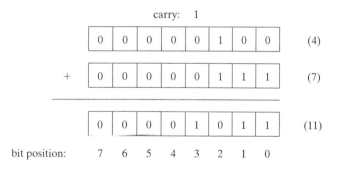

Beginning with the lowest bit in each number (bit position 0), we add 0 + 1, producing a 1 in the bottom row. The same happens in the next highest bit (position 1). In bit position 2, we add 1 + 1, generating a sum of zero and a carry of 1. In bit position 3, we add the carry bit to 0 + 0, producing 1. The rest of the bits are zeros. You can verify the addition by adding the decimal equivalents shown on the right side of the figure (4 + 7 = 11).

1.3.3 Integer Storage Sizes

The basic storage unit for all data in an IA-32-based computer is a *byte*, containing 8 bits. Other storage sizes are *word* (2 bytes), *doubleword* (4 bytes), and *quadword* (8 bytes). In the following figure, the number of bits is shown for each size:

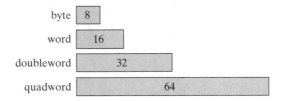

Table 1-4 shows the range possible values for each type of unsigned integer.

Table 1-4 Ranges of Unsigned Integers.

Storage Type	Range (low–high)	Powers of 2
Unsigned byte	0 to 255	0 to $(2^8 - 1)$
Unsigned word	0 to 65,535	0 to $(2^{16} - 1)$
Unsigned doubleword	0 to 4,294,967,295	0 to $(2^{32} - 1)$
Unsigned quadword	0 to 18,446,744,073,709,551,615	0 to $(2^{64} - 1)$

Large Measurements   A number of large measurements are used when referring to both memory and disk space:[4]

- One *kilobyte* is equal to 2^{10}, or 1,024 bytes.
- One *megabyte* (MB) is equal to 2^{20}, or 1,048,576 bytes.
- One *gigabyte* (GB) is equal to 2^{30}, or 1024^3, or 1,073,741,824 bytes.
- One *terabyte* (TB) is equal to 2^{40}, or 1024^4, or 1,099,511,627,776 bytes.
- One *petabyte* is equal to 2^{50}, or 1,125,899,906,842,624 bytes.
- One *exabyte* is equal to 2^{60}, or 1,152,921,504,606,846,976 bytes.
- One *zettabyte* is equal to 2^{70}.
- One *yottabyte* is equal to 2^{80}.

1.3.4 Hexadecimal Integers

Large binary numbers are cumbersome to read, so hexadecimal digits are usually used by assemblers and debuggers to represent binary data. Each digit in a hexadecimal integer represents four binary bits, and two hexadecimal digits together represent a byte.

---

[4] Source: www.webopedia.com.

A single hexadecimal digit can have a value from 0 to 15, so the letters A to F are used, as well as the digits 0-9. The letter A = 10, B = 11, C = 12, D = 13, E = 14, and F = 15. Table 1-5 shows how each sequence of four binary bits translates into a decimal or hexadecimal value.

Table 1-5 Binary, Decimal, and Hexadecimal Equivalents.

Binary	Decimal	Hexadecimal	Binary	Decimal	Hexadecimal
0000	0	0	1000	8	8
0001	1	1	1001	9	9
0010	2	2	1010	10	A
0011	3	3	1011	11	B
0100	4	4	1100	12	C
0101	5	5	1101	13	D
0110	6	6	1110	14	E
0111	7	7	1111	15	F

In the following example, we can see that the binary integer 0001011010100011110010100 is represented by hexadecimal 16A794:

1	6	A	7	9	4
0001	0110	1010	0111	1001	0100

It is often useful to display binary integers with a space between each group of four bits. Translation from binary to hexadecimal becomes that much easier.

1.3.4.1 Converting Unsigned Hexadecimal to Decimal

In hexadecimal, each digit position represents a power of 16. This is helpful when calculating the decimal value of a hexadecimal integer. First, let's number the digits in a 4-digit hexadecimal integer with subscripts as $D_3D_2D_1D_0$. The following formula calculates the number's decimal value:

$$dec = (D_3 \times 16^3) + (D_2 \times 16^2) + (D_1 \times 16^1) + (D_0 \times 16^0)$$

This can be generalized for any n-digit hexadecimal number:

$$dec = (D_{n-1} \times 16^{n-1}) + (D_{n-2} \times 16^{n-2}) + ... + (D_1 \times 16^1) + (D_0 \times 16^0)$$

For example, hexadecimal 1234 is equal to $(1 \times 16^3) + (2 \times 16^2) + (3 \times 16^1) + (4 \times 16^0)$, or decimal 4,660. Similarly, hexadecimal 3BA4 is equal to $(3 \times 16^3) + (11 * 16^2) + (10 \times 16^1) + (4 \times 16^0)$, or decimal 15,268. The following figure shows this last calculation:

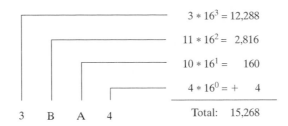

$$3 * 16^3 = 12,288$$
$$11 * 16^2 = 2,816$$
$$10 * 16^1 = 160$$
$$4 * 16^0 = + \quad 4$$

3   B   A   4   Total: 15,268

Table 1-6 lists the powers of 16, from 16^0 to 16^7.

Table 1-6   Powers of 16, in Decimal.

16^n	Decimal Value	16^n	Decimal Value
16^0	1	16^4	65,536
16^1	16	16^5	1,048,576
16^2	256	16^6	16,777,216
16^3	4096	16^7	268,435,456

1.3.4.2   Converting Unsigned Decimal to Hexadecimal

To convert an unsigned decimal integer to hexadecimal, repeatedly divide the decimal value by 16, and keep each remainder as a hexadecimal digit. For example, in the following table, we convert decimal 422 to hexadecimal:

Division	Quotient	Remainder
422 / 16	26	6
26 / 16	1	A
1 / 16	0	1

If we collect the digits from the remainder column in reverse order, the hexadecimal representation is **1A6**. You may recall that we used the same algorithm for binary numbers back in Section 1.3.1. It works for any number base, just by changing the divisor.

1.3.5   Signed Integers

As we said earlier, signed binary integers can be either positive or negative. In general, the most significant bit (MSB) indicates the number's sign. A value of 0 indicates that the integer is positive, and 1 indicates that it is negative. For example, the following figure shows examples of both negative and positive integers stored in a single byte:

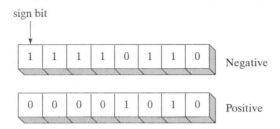

1.3.5.1 Two's Complement Notation

Negative integers are represented using what is called *two's complement* representation. The two's complement of an integer is simply its additive inverse. (You may recall that when a number's *additive inverse* is added to the number, their sum is zero.)

Two's complement representation is useful to processor designers because it removes the need for separate digital circuits to handle both addition and subtraction. For example, if presented with the expression $A - B$, the processor can simply convert it to an addition expression: $A + (-B)$:

The two's complement of a binary integer is formed by reversing its bits and adding 1. Using the 8-bit binary value 00000001, for example, its two's complement turns out to be 11111111, as can be seen below.

Starting value	00000001
Step 1: reverse the bits	11111110
Step 2: add 1 to the value from Step 1	11111110 +00000001
Sum: two's complement representation	11111111

Therefore, 11111111 is the two's complement representation of −1. The two's complement operation is reversible, so if you form the two's complement of 11111111, the result is 00000001.

Two's Complement of Hexadecimal   To form the two's complement of a hexadecimal integer, reverse all bits and add 1. An easy way to reverse the bits of a hexadecimal digit is to subtract the digit from 15. Here are several examples of hexadecimal integers converted to their two's complements:

```
6A3D --> 95C2 + 1 --> 95C3
95C3 --> 6A3C + 1 --> 6A3D
```

```
21F0 --> DE0F + 1 --> DE10
DE10 --> 21EF + 1 --> 21F0
```

Converting Signed Binary to Decimal   Suppose you would like to determine the decimal value of a signed binary integer. Here are the steps to follow:

- If the highest bit is a 1, it is currently stored in two's complement notation. You must form its two's complement a second time to get its positive equivalent. Then you can convert this new number to decimal as if it were an unsigned binary integer.
- If the highest bit is a 0, you can convert it to decimal as if it were an unsigned binary integer.

For example, signed binary 11110000 has a 1 in the highest bit, indicating that it is a negative integer. First we form its two's complement, then we convert the result to decimal. Here are the steps in the process:

Starting value	11110000
Step 1: reverse the bits	00001111
Step 2: add 1 to the value from Step 1	00001111 + 1
Step 3: form the two's complement	00010000
Step 4: convert to decimal	16

Remembering that the original integer (11110000) was negative, we infer that its decimal value was **−16**.

Converting Signed Decimal to Binary   Suppose you would like to determine the binary representation of a signed decimal integer. Here are the steps to follow:

- Convert the absolute value of the decimal integer to binary.
- If the original decimal integer was negative, form the two's complement of the binary number from the previous step.

For example, −43 decimal can be translated to binary as follows:

- The binary representation of unsigned 43 is 00101011.
- Because the original value was negative, we form the two's complement of 00101011, which is 11010101. This is the representation of −43 decimal.

Converting Signed Decimal to Hexadecimal   To convert a signed decimal integer to hexadecimal, do the following:

- Convert the absolute value of the decimal integer to hexadecimal.
- If the decimal integer was negative, form the two's complement of the hexadecimal number from the previous step.

Converting Signed Hexadecimal to Decimal   To convert a signed hexadecimal integer to decimal, do the following:

- If the hexadecimal integer is negative, form its two's complement; otherwise, retain the integer as is.
- Using the integer from the previous step, convert it to decimal. If the original value was negative, attach a minus sign to the beginning of the decimal integer.

> You can tell if a hexadecimal integer is positive or negative by inspecting its most significant (highest) digit. If the digit is >= 8, the number is negative; if the digit is <= 7, the number is positive. For example, hexadecimal 8A20 is negative, and 7FD9 is positive.

1.3.5.2   Maximum and Minimum Values

A signed integer of n bits can only use $n-1$ bits to represent the number's magnitude. Table 1-7 shows the minimum and maximum values for signed bytes, words, doublewords, and quadwords.

Table 1-7   Storage Sizes and Ranges of Signed Integers.

Storage Type	Range (low–high)	Powers of 2
Signed byte	−128 to +127	-2^7 to $(2^7 - 1)$
Signed word	−32,768 to +32,767	-2^{15} to $(2^{15} - 1)$
Signed doubleword	−2,147,483,648 to 2,147,483,647	-2^{31} to $(2^{31} - 1)$
Signed quadword	−9,223,372,036,854,775,808 to +9,223,372,036,854,775,807	-2^{63} to $(2^{63} - 1)$

1.3.6   Character Storage

Assuming that a computer can only store binary data, one might wonder how it could also store characters. To do this, it must support a certain *character set*, which is a mapping of characters to integers. Until a few years ago, character sets used only 8 bits. Because of the great diversity of languages around the world, the 16-bit *Unicode* character set was created to support thousands of different character symbols.[5]

When running in character mode (such as MS-DOS), IBM-compatible microcomputers use the *ASCII* (pronounced "askey") character set. ASCII is an acronym for *American Standard Code for Information Interchange*. In ASCII, a unique 7-bit integer is assigned to each character.

Because ASCII codes use only the lower 7 bits of every byte, the extra bit is used on various computers to create a proprietary character set. On IBM-compatible microcomputers, for example, values 128–255 represent graphics symbols and Greek characters.

---

[5]   You can read about the Unicode Standard at http:// www.unicode.org.

ASCII Strings   A sequence of one or more characters is called a *string*. An ASCII string is stored in memory as a succession of bytes containing ASCII codes. For example, the numeric codes for the string "ABC123" are 41h, 42h, 43h, 31h, 32h, and 33h. A *null-terminated* string is a string of characters followed by a single byte containing zero. The C and C++ languages use null-terminated strings, and many of the MS-DOS and MS-Windows functions require strings to be in this format.

Using the ASCII Table   There is a convenient table on the inside back cover of this book that lists all of the ASCII codes when running in MS-DOS mode. To find the hexadecimal ASCII code of a character, look along the top row of the table and find the column containing the character that you want to translate. The most significant digit of the hexadecimal value is in the second row at the top of the table; the least significant digit is in the second column from the left. For example, to find the ASCII code of the letter **a**, find the column containing the **a**, and look in the second row: The first hexadecimal digit is 6. Next look to the left along the row containing **a** and note that the second column contains the digit 1. Therefore, the ASCII code of **a** is 61 hexadecimal. This is shown below in simplified form:

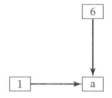

MS-Windows programs use a variety of different character sets, so it is not possible to use just a single lookup table. (You can read the Microsoft documentation on Windows fonts to see how characters translate into numeric codes.)

Terminology for Numeric Data Representation   It is important to use precise terminology when describing the way numbers and characters are represented in memory and on the display screen. Let's use decimal 65 as an example: stored in memory as a single byte, its binary bit pattern is 01000001. A debugging program would probably display the byte as "41," which is the hexadecimal notation for this bit pattern. But if the byte were moved to the video display area of memory by a running program, the letter **A** would appear onscreen. This is because 01000001 is the ASCII code for the letter **A**. In other words, the interpretation of numbers on a computer depends greatly on the context in which the number appears.

In this book, we use a naming method for numeric data representation that is reasonably general to avoid conflicts with terminology you might encounter from other sources.

- A *binary number* is a number stored in memory in its raw format, ready to be used in a calculation. Binary integers are stored in multiples of 8 bits (8, 16, 32, 48, or 64).
- An *ASCII digit string* is a string of ASCII characters, such as "123" or "65," which is made to look like a number. This is simply a representation of the number and can be in any of the formats shown for the decimal number 65 in Table 1-8:

Table 1-8 Types of Numeric Strings.

Format	Value
ASCII binary	"01000001"
ASCII decimal	"65"
ASCII hexadecimal	"41"
ASCII octal	"101"

1.3.7 Section Review

1. Explain the term LSB.
2. Explain the term MSB.
3. What is the decimal representation of each of the following unsigned binary integers?

    a. 11111000
    b. 11001010
    c. 11110000

4. What is the decimal representation of each of the following unsigned binary integers?

    a. 00110101
    b. 10010110
    c. 11001100

5. What is the sum of each pair of binary integers?

    a. 00001111 + 00000010
    b. 11010101 + 01101011
    c. 00001111 + 00001111

6. What is the sum of each pair of binary integers?

    a. 10101111 + 11011011
    b. 10010111 + 11111111
    c. 01110101 + 10101100

7. How many bytes are in each of the following data types?

    a. word
    b. doubleword
    c. quadword

8. How many bits are in each of the following data types?

    a. word
    b. doubleword
    c. quadword

9. What is the minimum number of binary bits needed to represent each of the following unsigned decimal integers?

   a. 65
   b. 256
   c. 32768

10. What is the minimum number of binary bits needed to represent each of the following unsigned decimal integers?

    a. 4095
    b. 65534
    c. 2134657

11. What is the hexadecimal representation of each of the following binary numbers?

    a. 1100 1111 0101 0111
    b. 0101 1100 1010 1101
    c. 1001 0011 1110 1011

12. What is the hexadecimal representation of each of the following binary numbers?

    a. 0011 0101 1101 1010
    b. 1100 1110 1010 0011
    c. 1111 1110 1101 1011

13. What is the binary representation of the following hexadecimal numbers?

    a. E5B6AED7
    b. B697C7A1
    c. 234B6D92

14. What is the binary representation of the following hexadecimal numbers?

    a. 0126F9D4
    b. 6ACDFA95
    c. F69BDC2A

15. What is the unsigned decimal representation of each hexadecimal integer?

    a. 3A
    b. 1BF
    c. 4096

16. What is the unsigned decimal representation of each hexadecimal integer?

    a. 62
    b. 1C9
    c. 6A5B

17. What is the 16-bit hexadecimal representation of each signed decimal integer?

    a. -26
    b. -452

18. What is the 16-bit hexadecimal representation of each signed decimal integer?

    a. -32
    b. -62

19. The following 16-bit hexadecimal numbers represent signed integers. Convert to decimal.

    a. 7CAB
    b. C123

20. The following 16-bit hexadecimal numbers represent signed integers. Convert to decimal.

    a. 7F9B
    b. 8230

21. What is the decimal representation of the following signed binary numbers?

    a. 10110101
    b. 00101010
    c. 11110000

22. What is the decimal representation of the following signed binary numbers?

    a. 10000000
    b. 11001100
    c. 10110111

23. What is the 8-bit binary (two's complement) representation of each of the following signed decimal integers?

    a. -5
    b. -36
    c. -16

24. What is the 8-bit binary (two's complement) representation of each of the following signed decimal integers?

    a. -72
    b. -98
    c. -26

25. What are the hexadecimal and decimal representations of the ASCII character capital X?
26. What are the hexadecimal and decimal representations of the ASCII character capital M?
27. Why was Unicode invented?
28. *Challenge:* What is the largest value you can represent using a 256 bit *unsigned* integer?
29. *Challenge:* What is the largest positive value you can represent using a 256-bit *signed* integer?

1.4 Boolean Operations

In this section we introduce a few fundamental operations of *boolean algebra*, the algebra that defines a set of operations on the values **true** and **false**. This algebra was invented by George Boole, a mid-nineteenth-century mathematician who never saw a working computer. When early computers were designed, it was discovered that his algebra could be used to describe the design of digital circuits. At the same time, boolean expressions are used in programming to express logical operations.

Boolean Expression   A boolean expression involves a boolean operator and one or more operands. Each boolean expression implies a value of true or false. The set of operators includes:

- NOT: notated as ¬ or ~ or `
- AND: notated as ∧ or •
- OR: notated as ∨ or +

The NOT operator is unary, and the other operators are binary. The operands of a boolean expression can also be boolean expressions. The following are examples:

Expression	Description
¬X	NOT X
X ∧ Y	X AND Y
X ∨ Y	X OR Y
¬X ∨ Y	(NOT X) OR Y
¬(X ∧ Y)	NOT (X AND Y)
X ∧ ¬Y	X AND (NOT Y)

NOT   The NOT operation reverses a boolean value. It can be written in mathematical notation as ¬X, where X is a variable (or expression) holding a value of true (T) or false (F). The following *truth table* shows all the possible outcomes of NOT using a variable **X**. Inputs are on the left side, and outputs (shaded) are on the right side:

X	¬X
F	T
T	F

A truth table can just as easily be constructed using 0 for false and 1 for true.

AND   The Boolean AND operation requires two operands, and can be expressed using the notation X ∧ Y. The following truth table shows all the possible outcomes (shaded) for the values of X and Y:

X	Y	X ∧ Y
F	F	F
F	T	F
T	F	F
T	T	T

Note that the output is true only when both inputs are true. This corresponds to the logical AND used in compound boolean expressions in programming languages such as C++ and Java.

OR   The Boolean OR operation requires two operands, and can be expressed using the notation **X ∨ Y**. The following truth table shows all the possible outcomes (shaded) for the values of X and Y:

X	Y	X ∨ Y
F	F	F
F	T	T
T	F	T
T	T	T

Note that the output is false only when both inputs are false. This corresponds to the logical OR used in compound boolean expressions in programming languages such as C++ and Java.

Operator Precedence   In a boolean expression involving more than one operator, the issue of precedence is important. As shown in the following table, the NOT operator has the highest precedence, followed by AND and OR. To avoid any ambiguity, use parentheses to force the initial evaluation of an expression:

Expression	Order of Operations
¬X ∨ Y	NOT, then OR
¬(X ∨ Y)	OR, then NOT
X ∨ (Y ∧ Z)	AND, then OR

1.4.1   Truth Tables for Boolean Functions

A *boolean function* receives boolean inputs and produces a boolean output. A truth table can be constructed for any boolean function that shows all possible inputs and outputs. The following are truth tables representing boolean functions having two inputs named X and Y. The shaded column on the right side is the function's output:

Example 1:   ¬X ∨ Y

X	¬X	Y	¬X ∨ Y
F	T	F	T
F	T	T	T
T	F	F	F
T	F	T	T

Example 2:   X ∧ ¬Y

X	Y	¬Y	X ∧ ¬Y
F	F	T	F
F	T	F	F
T	F	T	T
T	T	F	F

Example 3:   (Y ∧ S) ∨ (X ∧ ¬S)

X	Y	S	Y ∧ S	¬S	X ∧ ¬S	(Y ∧ S) ∨ (X ∧ ¬S)
F	F	F	F	T	F	F
F	T	F	F	T	F	F
T	F	F	F	T	T	T
T	T	F	F	T	T	T
F	F	T	F	F	F	F
F	T	T	T	F	F	T
T	F	T	F	F	F	F
T	T	T	T	F	F	T

This boolean function describes a *multiplexer*, a digital component that uses a selector bit (S) to select one of two outputs (X or Y). If S = false, the function output (Z) is the same as X. If S = true, the function outputs is the same as Y. Here is a diagram of such a device:

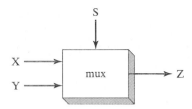

1.4.2 Section Review

1. Describe the following boolean expression: $\neg X \vee Y$.
2. Describe the following boolean expression: $(X \wedge Y)$.
3. What is the value of the boolean expression $(T \wedge F) \vee T$?
4. What is the value of the boolean expression $\neg(F \vee T)$?
5. What is the value of the boolean expression $\neg F \vee \neg$?
6. Create a truth table to show all possible inputs and outputs for the boolean function described by $\neg(A \vee B)$.
7. Create a truth table to show all possible inputs and outputs for the boolean function described by $(\neg A \wedge \neg B)$.
8. *Challenge:* If a boolean function has four inputs, how many rows would be required for its truth table?
9. *Challenge:* How many selector bits would be required for a four-input multiplexer?

1.5 Chapter Summary

This book, entitled *Assembly Language for Intel-Based Computers*, focuses on programming Intel microprocessors, specifically members of the Intel IA-32 processor family.

This book will give you some basic principles about computer architecture, machine language, and low-level programming. You will learn enough assembly language to test your knowledge on today's most widely used microprocessor family.

Before reading this book, you should have completed a single college course or its equivalent in computer programming.

An assembler is a program that converts source-code programs from assembly language into machine language. A companion program, called a linker, combines individual files created by an assembler into a single executable program. A third program, called a debugger, provides a way for a programmer to trace the execution of a program and examine the contents of memory.

You will create two basic types of programs: 16-Bit Real-address mode programs, and 32-bit Protected mode programs.

You will learn the following concepts from this book: Basic computer architecture applied to Intel IA-32 processors; elementary boolean logic; how IA-32 processors manage memory; how high-level language compilers translate statements from their language into assembly language and native machine code; how high-level languages implement arithmetic expressions, loops, and logical structures at the machine level; the data representation of signed and unsigned integers, real numbers, and character data.

Assembly language has a one-to-one relationship with machine language, meaning that one assembly language instruction corresponds to one machine-language instruction. Assembly language is not portable, because it is tied to a specific processor family.

It is important to understand how languages are simply tools that can be applied to various types of applications. Some applications, such as device drivers and hardware interface routines, are more suited to assembly language. Other applications, such as multi-platform business applications, are suited to high-level languages.

The virtual machine concept is an effective way of showing how each layer in a computer architecture represents an abstraction of a machine. Layers can be constructed of hardware or software, and programs written at any layer can be translated or interpreted by the next-lowest layer. The virtual machine concept can be related to real-world computer layers, including digital logic, microarchitecture, instruction set architecture, operating system, assembly language, and high-level languages.

Binary and hexadecimal numbers are essential notational tools for programmers working at the machine level. For this reason, it is vital that you understand how to mainpulate and translate between each of the number systems. It is also important to understand how character representations are created by computers.

The following boolean operators were presented in this chapter: NOT, AND, and OR. A boolean expression combines a boolean operator with one or more operands. A truth table is an effective way to show all possible inputs and outputs of a boolean function.

2

IA-32 Processor Architecture

2.1 General Concepts

This chapter describes the architecture of the Intel IA-32 processor family and its host computer system from a programmer's point of view. As we pointed out in the first chapter, assembly language is a great tool for learning how a computer works. This chapter is an essential part of the learning process, because you need to learn the basics of system architecture before assembly language can be useful.

We try to strike a balance between concepts that apply to all microcomputer systems and specific information about the IA-32 processor family. It is impossible to know what type of computer systems you will use in the future, so it would be a mistake for you to only learn about the IA-32. On the other hand, a generalized, superficial knowledge of computer processors might leave you with an empty feeling, not having had enough experience with a single CPU and its assembly language to do anything useful. To use an imperfect analogy, people don't become great cooks by reading cookbooks. They learn to cook a few dishes well, and then build on their experience.

> After reading this chapter, you may want to delve further into the IA-32's design. You can begin by reading Intel's well-written and authoritative manual: *IA-32 Intel Architecture Software Developer's Manual, Volume 1: Basic Architecture.* You can download it for free from the Intel Web site (www.intel.com). Far from being a dry, dull reference, this manual can keep your attention for days or weeks. But don't forget about the book you're holding in your hands—it still has a lot to offer you!

2.1.1 Basic Microcomputer Design

Figure 2-1 shows the basic design of a hypothetical microcomputer. The *central processor unit* (CPU) is where all the calculations and logic operations take place. It contains a limited number of storage locations called *registers*, a high-frequency *clock*, a *control unit*, and an *arithmetic logic unit*.

- The clock synchronizes the internal operations of the CPU with other system components.
- The control unit (CU) coordinates the sequencing of steps involved in executing machine instructions.
- The arithmetic logic unit (ALU) performs arithmetic operations such as addition and subtraction, and logical operations such as AND, OR, and NOT.

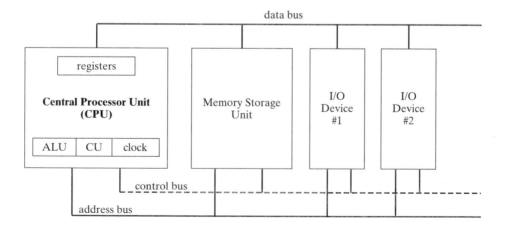

Figure 2-1 Block Diagram of a Microcomputer.

The CPU is attached to the rest of the computer via pins attached to the CPU socket. Most of these pins connect to the data bus, the control bus, and the address bus.

The *memory storage unit* is where instructions and data are held while a computer program is running. The storage unit receives requests for data from the CPU, transfers data from random access memory (RAM) to the CPU, and transfers data from the CPU into memory.

A *bus* is a group of parallel wires that transfer data from one part of the computer to another. The system bus of a computer usually consists of three different busses: the data bus, the control bus, and the address bus. The *data bus* transfers instructions and data between the CPU and memory. The *control bus* uses binary signals to synchronize the actions of all devices attached to the system bus. The *address bus* holds the addresses of instructions and data when the currently executing instruction transfers data between the CPU and memory.

Clock   Each operation involving the CPU and the system bus is synchronized by an internal clock that repeatedly pulses at a constant rate. The most basic unit of time for machine instructions is called the *machine cycle* (or *clock cycle time*), which is the time required for one complete clock pulse. In the following figure, one clock pulse is depicted as the time between one falling edge and the next:

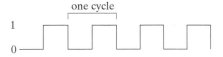

The duration of a clock cycle is the reciprocal of the clock's speed, measured in oscillations per second. A clock that oscillates 1 billion times per second (1 GHz), for example, produces a clock cycle with a duration of one billionth of a second (1 nanosecond).

A machine instruction requires at least one clock cycle to execute, and a few require in excess of 50 clocks (the multiply instruction on the 8088 processor, for example). Instructions requiring memory access often have empty clock cycles called *wait states* because of the differences between the speed of the CPU, the system bus, and memory circuits. (Recent research suggests that in the near future we may abandon the synchronized computing model in favor of a type of asynchronous operation that would not require a system clock.)

2.1.2   Instruction Execution Cycle

The execution of a single machine instruction can be divided into a sequence of individual operations called the *instruction execution cycle*. When the CPU executes an instruction using a memory operand, it must calculate the address of the operand, place the address on the address bus, wait for memory to get the operand, and so on.

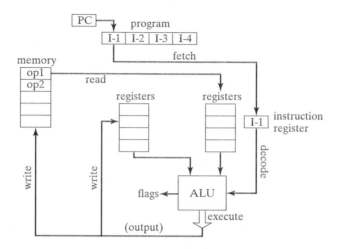

Figure 2-2 Instruction Execution Cycle.

Before it executes, a program must be loaded into memory. In Figure 2-2, the *program counter* is a register that contains the address of the next instruction about to be executed. The *instruction queue* is a holding area inside the microprocessor into which one or more instructions are copied just before they execute. When the CPU executes a single machine instruction, three primary operations are always necessary: *fetch, decode,* and *execute.* Two more steps are required when the instruction uses a memory operand: *fetch operand*, and *store output operand.* In other words, as many as five operations may be required by instructions that access memory.

- *Fetch:* The control unit fetches the instruction, copying it from memory into the CPU and increments the program counter (PC).
- *Decode:* The control unit determines the type of instruction to be executed. It passes zero or more operands to the arithmetic logic unit (ALU) and sends signals to the ALU that indicate the type of operation to be performed.
- *Fetch operands:* If a memory operand is used, the control unit initiates a read operation to retrieve the input operand from memory.
- *Execute:* The arithmetic logic unit executes the instruction, sends its data to the output operand, and updates status flags providing information about the output.
- *Store output operand:* If the output operand is in memory, the control unit initiates a write operation to store the data.

2.1.2.1 Multi-Stage Pipeline

Each step in the instruction cycle takes at least one tick of the system clock, called a *clock cycle.* But this doesn't mean that the processor must wait until all steps are completed before beginning to process the next instruction. The processor can execute the steps in parallel, a technique known as *pipelining.* The IA-32 processor (beginning with the Intel386) is a pipelined processor with a six-stage execution cycle. The six stages and the parts of the processor that carry them out are listed here:

1. *Bus Interface Unit* (BIU): accesses memory and provides input-output.
2. *Code Prefetch Unit:* receives machine instructions from the BIU and inserts them into a holding area named the *instruction queue.*
3. *Instruction Decode Unit:* decodes machine instructions from the prefetch queue and translates them into microcode.
4. *Execution Unit:* executes the microcode instructions produced by the instruction decode unit.
5. *Segment Unit:* translates logical addresses to linear addresses and performs protection checks.
6. *Paging Unit:* translates linear addresses into physical addresses, performs page protection checks, and keeps a list of recently accessed pages.

Example Let's assume that each execution stage in the processor requires a single clock cycle. Figure 2-3 uses a grid to represent a six-stage *non-pipelined* processor, the type used by Intel prior to the Intel486. When instruction I-1 has finished stage S6, instruction I-2 begins. Twelve clock cycles are required to execute the two instructions. In other words, for k execution stages, n instructions require $(n * k)$ cycles to process.

Of course, Figure 2-3 represents a major waste of CPU resources because each stage is used only one-sixth of the time.

If, on the other hand, a processor supports pipelining, as in Figure 2-4, a new instruction can enter stage S1 during the second clock cycle. Meanwhile, the first instruction has entered stage S2. This enables the overlapped execution of the two instructions. Two instructions, I-1 and I-2, are shown progressing through the pipeline. I-2 enters stage S1 as soon as I-1 has moved to stage S2. As a result, only seven clock cycles are required to execute the two instructions. When the pipeline is full, all six stages are in use all the time.

In general, for k execution stages, n instructions require $k + (n - 1)$ cycles to process. Whereas the non-pipelined processor we showed earlier required 12 cycles to process 2 instructions, the pipelined processor can process 7 instructions in the same amount of time.

Stages

	S1	S2	S3	S4	S5	S6
1	I-1					
2		I-1				
3			I-1			
4				I-1		
5					I-1	
6						I-1
7	I-2					
8		I-2				
9			I-2			
10				I-2		
11					I-2	
12						I-2

Cycles

Figure 2-3   Six-Stage Non-Pipelined Instruction Execution.

Stages

	S1	S2	S3	S4	S5	S6
1	I-1					
2	I-2	I-1				
3		I-2	I-1			
4			I-2	I-1		
5				I-2	I-1	
6					I-2	I-1
7						I-2

Cycles

Figure 2-4   Six-Stage Pipelined Execution.

2.1.2.2   Superscalar Architecture

A *superscalar* processor has two or more execution pipelines, making it possible for two instructions to be in the execution stage at the same time. In order to better understand why a superscalar processor would be useful, let's consider the preceding pipelined example, in which we assumed that the execution stage (S4) required a single clock cycle. That was an overly simplistic approach. What would happen if stage S4 required two clock cycles? Then a bottleneck would occur, shown in Figure 2-5. Instruction I-2 cannot enter stage S4 until I-1 has completed the stage, so I-2 has to wait one more cycle before entering stage S4. As more instructions enter the pipeline, wasted cycles occur (shaded in gray). In general, for k stages (where one stage requires 2 cycles), n instructions require $(k + 2n - 1)$ cycles to process.

When a superscalar processor design is used, multiple instructions can be in the execution stage at the same time. For n pipelines, n instructions can execute during the same clock cycle. The Intel Pentium, which had two pipelines, was the first superscalar processor in the IA-32 family. The Pentium Pro processor was the first to use three pipelines.

Let's introduce a second pipeline into our 6-staged pipeline and assume that stage S4 requires two cycles. In Figure 2-6, odd-numbered instructions enter the *u-pipeline* and even-numbered instructions enter the *v-pipeline*. This removes the wasted cycles, and it is now possible to process n instructions in $(k + n)$ cycles.

Stages
exe

	S1	S2	S3	S4	S5	S6
1	I-1					
2	I-2	I-1				
3	I-3	I-2	I-1			
4		I-3	I-2	I-1		
5			I-3	I-1		
6				I-2	I-1	
7				I-2		I-1
8				I-3	I-2	
9				I-3		I-2
10					I-3	
11						I-3

Cycles

Figure 2-5   Pipelined Execution Using a Single Pipeline.

Stages
┌── S4 ──┐

	S1	S2	S3	u	v	S5	S6
1	I-1						
2	I-2	I-1					
3	I-3	I-2	I-1				
4	I-4	I-3	I-2	I-1			
5		I-4	I-3	I-1	I-2		
6			I-4	I-3	I-2	I-1	
7				I-3	I-4	I-2	I-1
8					I-4	I-3	I-2
9						I-4	I-3
10							I-4

Cycles

Figure 2-6   Superscalar 6-Stage Pipelined Processor.

2.1.3   Reading from Memory

Memory access is an important factor when understanding the speed of a program. The CPU clock might be capable of running at 1 or 2 GHz, for example, but access to memory over the system bus is far slower. This forces the CPU to wait one or more clock cycles until operands have been fetched from memory before instructions can execute. These wasted clock cycles are called *wait states*.

Several steps are required when reading instructions or data from memory, controlled by the processor's internal clock. Figure 2-7 shows the processor clock (CLK) rising and falling at regular time intervals. In this example, a clock cycle begins as the clock signal changes from high to low. These changes are called *trailing edges*, and they indicate the time taken by the transition between states.

The following is a simplified description of what happens during each clock cycle as memory is read:

Cycle 1: The address bits of the memory operand are placed on the address bus (ADDR).

Cycle 2: The Read Line (RD) is set low (0) to notify memory that a value is to be read.

Cycle 3: The CPU waits one cycle to give memory time to respond. During this cycle, the memory controller places the operand on the data bus (DATA).

Cycle 4: The Read Line (RD) goes to 1, signaling that the CPU can now read the values on the data bus.

Cache Memory   Because conventional memory is so much slower than the CPU, microcomputers have high-speed *cache memory* that holds the most recently used instructions and data. Whenever possible, the CPU reads from cache memory, giving programs a noticeable boost in performance. There are two types of cache memory in an IA-32 system: *Level-1 cache* is inside the processor itself, and *Level-2 cache* is located on separate high-speed memory chips next to the CPU. Level-1 cache is faster and more expensive than Level-2 cache.

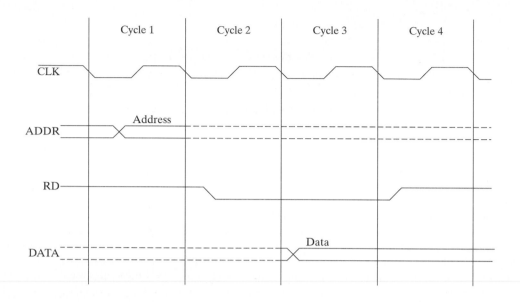

Figure 2-7 Memory Read Cycle.

2.1.4 How Programs Run

2.1.4.1 Load and Execute Process

When you tell the computer's operating system (OS) to load and run a program, the following things happen (in sequence):

- The user issues a command to run a certain program. This might be done by typing the program's filename at a command prompt (as in MS-DOS or Linux), or by clicking on an icon or shortcut that identifies the program (as in MS-Windows or Mac OS).
- The OS searches for the program's filename in the current disk directory. If it cannot find the name there, it searches a predetermined list of directories (called *paths*) for the filename. If the OS fails to find the program filename, it issues an error message.
- If the program's filename is found, the OS retrieves basic information about the program's file from the disk directory, including the file size and its physical location on the disk drive. (This process might involve several steps, but they are transparent to the user.)
- The OS determines the next available location in memory, and loads the program file into memory. It allocates a certain block of memory to the program and enters information about the program's size and location into a table (sometimes called a *descriptor table*). Additionally, the OS may adjust the values of pointers within the program so they contain the correct addresses of program data.
- The OS executes a branching instruction that causes the CPU to begin execution of the program's first machine instruction. As soon as the program begins running, it is called a

process. The OS gives the process an identification number (*process ID*) that makes it possible to keep track of the process while it is running.

- The process runs by itself. It is the OS's job to track the execution of the process and to respond to its requests for system resources. Examples of resources are memory, disk files, and input-output devices.
- When the process ends, its handle is removed and the memory it used is released so it can be used by other programs.

> If you're using Windows NT or 2000, press *Ctrl-Alt-Delete* and click on the *Task Manager* button. There are tabs labeled *Applications*, and *Processes*. Applications are the names of complete programs currently running, such as Windows Explorer or Microsoft Visual C++. When you click on the *Processes* tab, you see 30 or 40 names listed, often with names you might not recognize. Each of those processes is a small program running independently of all the others. Note that each has a PID (program ID), and you can continuously track both the amount of CPU time and the amount of memory used by the program. Most of these run in the background without any visible element. If you know what you're doing, you can shut down a process that was somehow left running in memory by mistake. Of course, if you shut down the wrong process, your computer may stop running, and you'll have to reboot.

2.1.4.2 Multitasking

When an operating system is able to run multiple tasks at the same time, it is said to be *multitasking* (or *preemptive multitasking*). A moment ago we were talking about processes, and now we're talking about tasks. A process may optionally contain multiple tasks (or *threads of execution*) that are more or less independent of each other. A game program, for example, with several animated graphics moving independently of each other, might assign each graphic to a separate task. Some processes consist of only a single task.

Most modern operating systems have to simultaneously run tasks that communicate with hardware, display user interfaces, do background file processing, and so on. The CPU can only execute one instruction at a time, so a component of the operating system called the *scheduler* allocates a small portion of CPU time (called a *time slice*) to each task. During a single time slice, the CPU will execute a block of instructions, stopping when the time slice has ended.

By rapidly switching tasks, the OS gives the illusion that loaded tasks are running simultaneously. One type of scheduling used by the OS is called *round-robin scheduling*. In Figure 2-8, nine tasks are active. Suppose the *scheduler* arbitrarily assigned 11 milliseconds to each task, and activated them in sequence. One full circuit of the tasks would require a little over 100 milliseconds, which includes time to switch from task to task.

A multitasking OS must run on a processor that supports *task switching*, which means that the processor saves the state of each task before switching to a new one. A task's *state* consists of the contents of the processor registers, the task's variables, and its program counter. A multitasking OS will usually assign varying priorities to tasks, giving them relatively larger or smaller time slices.

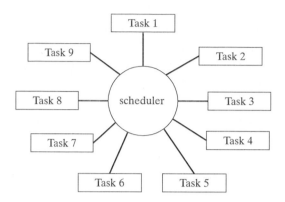

Figure 2-8   Round-Robin Scheduler.

2.1.5   Section Review

1. The central processor unit (CPU) contains registers and what other basic elements?
2. The central processor unit is connected to the rest of the computer system using what three buses?
3. Why does memory access take more machine cycles than register access?
4. What are the three basic steps in the instruction execution cycle?
5. Which two additional steps are required in the instruction execution cycle when a memory operand is used?
6. During which stage of the instruction execution cycle is the program counter incremented?
7. Define *pipelined execution*.
8. In a 5-stage non-pipelined processor, how many clock cycles would it take to execute 2 instructions?
9. In a 5-stage single-pipelined processor, how many clock cycles would it take to execute 8 instructions?
10. What is a *superscalar processor*?
11. Suppose that a 5-stage dual-pipelined processor has one stage that requires two clock cycles to execute, and there are two pipelines for that stage. How many clock cycles would be required to execute 10 instructions?
12. When a program runs, what information does the OS read from the filename's disk directory entry?
13. After a program has been loaded into memory, how does it begin execution?
14. Define *multitasking*.
15. What is the function of the OS scheduler?
16. When the processor switches from one task to another, what values in the first task's state must be preserved?

2.2   IA-32 Processor Architecture

In this section we detail many aspects of the IA-32 processor architecture. Although we mentioned this in Chapter 1, it is worth repeating that IA-32 refers to a family of processors beginning with the Intel386 and continuing up to the latest 32-bit processor, the Pentium 4. Although many enhancements have been made to the processor's performance and implementation, these differences are hidden behind the IA-32 standard. From the programmer's point of view, the IA-32 architecture has not changed substantially since the Intel386. The primary exception is the introduction of a set of high-performance instructions that improve multimedia processing.

2.2.1   Modes of Operation

IA-32 processors have three basic modes of operation: Protected mode, Real-address mode, and System Management mode. In addition, the Virtual-8086 mode is a special case of Protected mode.

Protected Mode   Protected mode is the native state of the processor, in which all instructions and features are available. Programs are given separate memory areas (called *segments*), and the processor detects any attempt by a program to reference memory outside its assigned segment.

Virtual-8086 Mode   While in Protected mode, the processor can directly execute Real-address mode software such as MS-DOS programs in a safe multitasking environment. In other words, even if an MS-DOS program crashes, it will not affect other programs running at the same time. (This feature is often called *Virtual-8086 mode* even though it is not really a separate processor mode.)

Real-address Mode   Real-address mode implements the programming environment of the Intel 8086 processor with a few extra features, such as the ability to switch into the other two modes. This mode is available in Windows 98, for example, if you need to run an MS-DOS program that seizes control of the computer's hardware. Old computer games often do this. All Intel processors boot in Real-address mode. After that, the host operating system may switch to another mode.

System Management Mode   System Management mode (SSM) provides an operating system with a mechanism for implementing such functions as power management and system security. These functions are usually implemented by computer manufacturers who want to customize the processor for a particular system setup.

2.2.2   Basic Execution Environment

2.2.2.1   Address Space

In Protected mode, IA-32 processors can access up to 4GB of memory. This is because 32-bit registers can have values between 0 and $2^{32} - 1$. In Real-address mode, a maximum of 1MB of memory can be accessed. If the processor is in Protected mode and running multiple programs in virtual-8086 mode, each program can access its own separate 1MB area of memory.

2.2.2.2   Basic Program Execution Registers

Registers are high-speed storage locations directly inside the CPU, designed to be accessed at much higher speed than conventional memory. When a processing loop is optimized for speed, for example, registers are used inside the loop rather than variables.

Figure 2-9 shows the *basic program execution registers* (as Intel calls them). There are eight general-purpose registers, eight segment registers, a register that holds processor status flags (EFLAGS), and an instruction pointer (EIP).

General-Purpose Registers   The *general-purpose registers* are primarily used for arithmetic and data movement. As shown in the following figure, each register can be addressed as either a single 32-bit value or a 16-bit value:

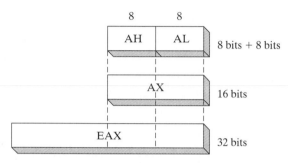

Some 16-bit registers can be addressed as two separate 8-bit values. For example, the EAX register is 32 bits. Its lower 16 bits are also named AX. The upper 8 bits of AX are named AH, and the lower 8 bits are named AL.

32-bit General-Purpose Registers

EAX		EBP
EBX		ESP
ECX		ESI
EDX		EDI

16-bit Segment Registers

EFLAGS		CS		ES
		SS		FS
EIP		DS		GS

Figure 2-9   IA-32 Basic Program Execution Registers.

This overlapping relationship exists for the EAX, EBX, ECX, and EDX registers:

32-bit	16-bit	8-bit (high)	8-bit (low)
EAX	AX	AH	AL
EBX	BX	BH	BL
ECX	CX	CH	CL
EDX	DX	DH	DL

The remaining general-purpose registers have separate names for their lower 16 bits, but cannot be divided further. The 16-bit registers shown here are usually used only when writing programs that run in Real-address mode:

32-bit	16-bit
ESI	SI
EDI	DI
EBP	BP
ESP	SP

Specialized Uses   Some general-purpose registers have specialized uses:

- EAX is automatically used by multiplication and division instructions. It is often called the *extended accumulator* register.
- The CPU automatically uses ECX as a loop counter.
- ESP addresses data on the stack (a system memory structure). It should never be used for ordinary arithmetic or data transfer. It is often called the *extended stack pointer* register.
- ESI and EDI are used by high-speed memory transfer instructions. They are sometimes called the *extended source index* and *extended destination index* registers.
- EBP is used by high-level languages to reference function parameters and local variables on the stack. It should not be used for ordinary arithmetic or data transfer except at an advanced level of programming. It is often called the *extended frame pointer* register.

Segment Registers   The *segment registers* are used as base locations for preassigned memory areas called *segments*. Some segments hold program instructions (code), others hold variables (data), and another segment called the *stack segment* holds local function variables and function parameters.

Instruction Pointer   The EIP, or *instruction pointer* register contains the address of the next instruction to be executed. Certain machine instructions manipulate this address, causing the program to branch to a new location.

EFLAGS Register   The EFLAGS (or just *Flags*) register consists of individual binary bits that either control the operation of the CPU or reflect the outcome of some CPU operation. There are machine instructions that can test and manipulate the processor flags.

> A flag is *set* when it equals 1; it is *clear* (or reset) when it equals 0.

Control Flags.   Individual bits can be set in the EFLAGS register by the programmer to control the CPU's operation. Examples are the *Direction* and *Interrupt* flags. We will cover these on an as-needed basis later in the book.

Status Flags.   The Status flags reflect the outcomes of arithmetic and logical operations performed by the CPU. They are the Overflow, Sign, Zero, Auxiliary Carry, Parity, and Carry flags. Their abbreviations are shown immediately after their names:

- The **Carry** flag (CF) is set when the result of an *unsigned* arithmetic operation is too large to fit into the destination.
- The **Overflow** flag (OF) is set when the result of a *signed* arithmetic operation is too wide (too many bits) to fit into the destination.
- The **Sign** flag (SF) is set when the result of an arithmetic or logical operation generates a negative result.
- The **Zero** flag (ZF) is set when the result of an arithmetic or logical operation generates a result of zero.
- The **Auxiliary Carry** flag is set when an arithmetic operation causes a carry from bit 3 to bit 4 in an 8-bit operand.
- The **Parity** flag sums the number of bits that are set in a number, and indicates whether the sum is odd or even.

2.2.3   Floating-Point Unit

The IA-32 has a *floating-point unit* (FPU) that is used expressly for high-speed floating-point arithmetic. At one time a separate coprocessor chip was required for this, but beginning with the Intel486, it was integrated into the main processor chip.

There are eight floating-point data registers in the FPU, named ST(0), ST(1), ST(2), ST(3), ST(4), ST(5), ST(6), and ST(7). The remaining control and pointer registers of the FPU are shown in Figure 2-10.

2.2.3.1   Other Registers

In passing, we will mention two other sets of registers used for advanced multimedia programming:

- Eight 64-bit registers for use with the MMX instruction set
- Eight 128-bit XMM registers used for single-instruction, multiple-data (SIMD) operations

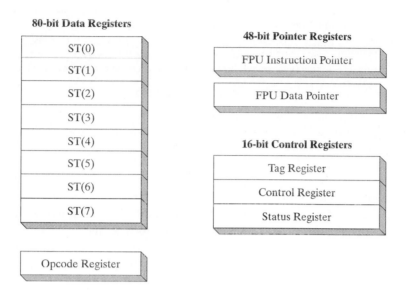

Figure 2-10   Floating-Point Unit Registers.

2.2.4   Intel Microprocessor History

In this chapter, you're about to get another dose of history from someone (me) who really was around when the first IBM-PC was released, in the dark days when they had 64K of RAM and no hard drives.

> Senior programmers love to talk about history and legends because a lot of them were actually around when the history was being written. One of my professors worked on the Mark I computer at Harvard University during World War II. He was given a single register from the Mark I when it was dismantled. (The register was about 2 feet high and weighed 20 pounds!)

Intel 8086   The Intel 8086 processor (created in 1978) marks the beginning of the modern Intel Architecture family. The primary innovations of the 8086 over earlier processors were that it had 16-bit registers and a 16-bit data bus, and used a segmented memory model that allowed programs to address up to 1MB of RAM. This greater access to memory made it possible to write complex business applications. The IBM-PC, introduced around 1980, contained an Intel 8088 processor, which was identical to the 8086 except that it had an 8-bit data bus, making it slightly less expensive to produce. Today, the Intel 8088 is primarily used in low-cost microcontrollers and costs only a few dollars.

> *Downward Compatibility.* It should be noted that each new processor introduced into the
> Intel family has always been downward-compatible with earlier generations. This has
> made it possible for the same software to run on the newer computers without modifica-
> tion. Newer software eventually appeared, however, that required the features of the more
> advanced processors.

Intel 80286   The Intel 80286 processor, first used in the IBM-PC/AT computer, quickly set a
new standard of speed and power. It was the first Intel processor to run in Protected mode. The
80286 could address up to 16MB of RAM using a 24-bit address bus.

2.2.4.1   IA-32 Processor Family

The Intel386 processor featured 32-bit registers and a 32-bit address bus and external data path.
This was the first member of the IA-32 family, which also includes the Intel486 and various Pentium processors. They support a new way of addressing virtual memory that is larger than the
computer's physical memory. Each program was given a 4GB linear address space.

Intel486   Continuing the IA-32 family, the Intel486 processor features an instruction set
microarchitecture using *pipelining* techniques that permit multiple instructions to be processed
at the same time.

Pentium   The Pentium processor added many performance improvements, including a *superscalar* design with two parallel execution pipelines. This permitted two instructions to be
decoded and executed simultaneously. The Pentium also introduced a 32-bit address bus and 64-
bit internal data path.

2.2.4.2   P6 Processor Family

In 1995, the P6 family of processors was introduced, based on a new micro-architecture design
that improved execution speed. At the same time, it extended the basic IA-32 architecture. This
family includes, among others, the Pentium Pro, Pentium II, and Pentium III. The Pentium Pro
introduced advanced techniques to improve the way instructions were executed. The Pentium II
added MMX technology to the P6 family. The Pentium III introduced SIMD (streaming extensions) into the IA-32 architecture, with special 128-bit registers designed to move large amounts
of data quickly.

Pentium 4   At the time of this writing, the Pentium 4 is the newest IA-32 processor. It introduced the *NetBurst* micro-architecture that permits the processor to operate at much higher
speeds than previous IA-32 processors. It appears to be oriented primarily toward high-performance multimedia applications.

2.2.4.3   CISC and RISC

The earliest Intel processors for the IBM Personal Computer were based on what is called a
Complex Instruction Set (CISC) approach. The Intel instruction set includes powerful ways to

address data, and instructions that are relatively high-level complex operations. The philosophy was that high-level language compilers would have less work to do if individual machine-language instructions were powerful. A major disadvantage to the CISC approach is that complex instructions require a relatively long time for the processor to decode and execute. An interpreter program inside the CPU written in a language called *microcode* decodes and executes each machine instruction. Once Intel committed to a complex instruction set, it was necessary for all subsequent Intel processors to be compatible with the first one. Software written for the original IBM Personal Computer can still run on today's latest Pentium.

A completely different approach to microprocessor design is called *Reduced Instruction Set* (RISC). A RISC machine language consists of a relatively small number of short, simple instructions that can be executed very quickly. Rather than using a microcode interpreter to decode and execute machine instructions, a RISC processor directly decodes and executes instructions using hardware. High-speed engineering and graphics workstations have been built using RISC processors for many years. Unfortunately, these systems have been expensive because the processors were produced in small quantities.

Because of the huge popularity of IBM-PC compatible computers, Intel was able to lower the price of its processors and thus dominate the microprocessor market. At the same time, Intel recognized many advantages to the RISC approach and found a way to use RISC-like features (such as pipelining and superscalar) in its Pentium processors. Meanwhile, the IA-32 instruction set continues to be enormously complex and constantly expanding.

2.2.5   Section Review

1. What are the IA-32 processor's three basic modes of operation?
2. Name all eight 32-bit general-purpose registers.
3. Name all six segment registers.
4. What special purpose does the ECX register serve?
5. Besides the stack pointer (ESP), which other register points to variables on the stack?
6. Name at least four CPU status flags.
7. Which flag is set when the result of an *unsigned* arithmetic operation is too wide to fit into the destination?
8. Which flag is set when the result of an *signed* arithmetic operation is too wide to fit into the destination?
9. Which flag is set when an arithmetic or logical operation generates a negative result?
10. Which part of the CPU performs floating-point arithmetic?
11. How many bits long are the FPU data registers?
12. Which Intel processor was the first member of the IA-32 family?
13. Which Intel processor first introduced superscalar execution?
14. Which Intel processor first used MMX technology?

15. Describe a CISC instruction set.

16. Describe a RISC instruction set.

2.3   IA-32 Memory Management

The IA-32 manages memory according to the basic modes of operation that we discussed earlier in Section 2.2.1.

In *Real-address* mode, only 1MB of memory can be addressed, from hexadecimal 00000 to FFFFF. The processor can run only one program at a time, but it can momentarily interrupt that program to process requests (called *interrupts*) from peripherals. Application programs are permitted to read and modify any area of RAM (random-access memory), and they can read but not modify any area of ROM (read-only memory). The MS-DOS operating system runs in Real-address mode, and Windows 95 and 98 can be booted into this mode.

In *Protected* mode, the processor can run multiple programs at the same time. It assigns each process (running program) a total of 4GB of memory. Each program can be assigned its own reserved memory area, and programs are prevented from accidentally accessing each other's code and data. MS-Windows and Linux both run in Protected mode.

In *Virtual-8086* mode, the computer runs in Protected mode and creates a virtual 8086 machine with its own 1MB address space that simulates an 80x86 computer running in Real-address mode. Windows NT and 2000, for example, creates a virtual 8086 machine when you open a *Command* window. You can run many such windows at the same time, and each is protected from the actions of the others. Some MS-DOS programs that make direct references to computer hardware will not run in this mode under Windows NT and 2000.

In the next two sections (Section 2.3.1 and Section 2.3.2), we will explain details of both Real-address mode and Protected mode. If you want to study this subject in more detail, a good source is the three-volume *IA-32 Intel Architecture Software Developer's Manual*. You can read or download it from Intel's Web site (www.intel.com).

2.3.1   Real-address Mode

In Real-address mode, the IA-32 processor can access 1,048,576 bytes of memory (1MB) using 20-bit addresses in the range 0 to FFFFF hexadecimal. The basic problem that Intel engineers had to solve was that the original 8086 processor had only 16-bit registers, so it was impossible to directly represent a 20-bit address. They came up with a scheme known as *segmented memory*. All of memory is divided into 64-kilobyte units called *segments*, shown in Figure 2-11.

An analogy might be a large building, where the *segments* represent the floors of the building. A person can ride the elevator to a particular floor, get off, and then begin following the room numbers to locate a single room. The *offset* of a room can be thought of as the distance from the elevator to the room.

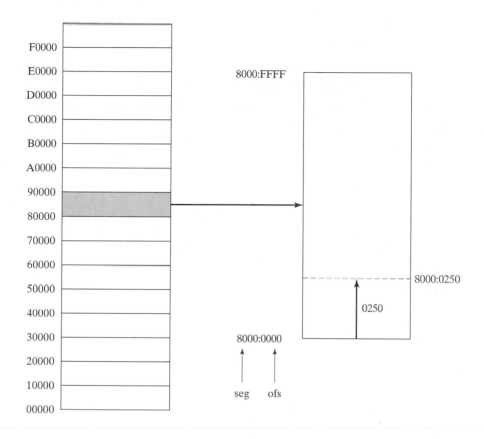

Figure 2-11   Segmented Memory Map, Real-address Mode.

Looking again at Figure 2-11, note that each segment begins at an address having a zero for its last hexadecimal digit. Because of this, when segment values are stated, the last zero is dropped. A segment value of C000, for example, refers to the segment that begins at address C0000.

In the same figure, we see an expansion of the segment beginning at 80000. To reach any of the bytes in this segment, we need a 16-bit offset value (0 to FFFF) that can be added to the segment's base location. An example is 8000:0250, which represents an offset of 250 inside the segment beginning at address 80000. The linear address is 80250h.

2.3.1.1   20-bit Linear Address Calculation

An *address* is a number that refers to a single location in memory. In Real-address mode, the *linear* (or *absolute*) address is 20 bits, ranging from 0 to FFFFF hexadecimal. But programs cannot use linear addresses directly, so they express addresses using two 16-bit numbers, which are together called a *segment-offset* address:

- A 16-bit **segment** value, placed in one of the segment registers (CS, DS, ES, SS).
- A 16-bit **offset** value.

When addresses are expressed this way, the CPU automatically does some arithmetic and converts the segment-offset address to a 20-bit linear address.

Example. Suppose that a variable's hexadecimal segment-offset address is 08F1:0100. The CPU multiplies the segment value by 10 hexadecimal and adds this to the variable's offset:

```
08F1 * 10 = 08F10            (adjusted segment value)

Adjusted Segment value:          0  8  F  1  0
Add the offset:                     0  1  0  0
Linear address:                  0  9  0  1  0
```

A typical program has three segments: code, data, and stack. Three segment registers, CS, DS, and SS, contain the base locations of a program's code, data, and stack segments:

- CS contains the 16-bit code segment address.
- DS contains the 16-bit data segment address.
- SS contains the 16-bit stack segment address.
- ES, FS, and GS can point to alternate data segments.

2.3.2   Protected Mode

Now let's turn our attention to Protected mode, the more powerful "native" processor mode. When the processor is running in Protected mode, each program can address up to 4GB of memory, from 0 to FFFFFFFF hexadecimal. This use of a flat address space is also called the *flat memory model* by the Microsoft Assembler. From the programmer's point of view, the flat memory model is very simple to use because it only requires a single 32-bit integer to hold the address of any instruction or variable. The operating system does quite a bit of background work to preserve the illusion of simplicity, aided by the processor's built-in capabilities. The segment registers (CS, DS, SS, ES, FS, GS) point to *segment descriptor tables* that the operating system uses to define the locations of individual program segments.

A typical Protected-mode program has three segments: code, data, and stack. Three segment registers are used all the time:

- CS references the descriptor table for the code segment.
- DS references the descriptor table for the data segment.
- SS references the descriptor table for the stack segment.

2.3.2.1   Flat Segmentation Model

In the flat segmentation model, all segments are mapped to the entire 32-bit physical address space of the computer. You have to create at least two segments, one for program code and one for data. Each segment is defined by a *segment descriptor*, a 64-bit value stored in a table known as the *global descriptor table* (GDT). Figure 2-12 shows a segment descriptor whose *base address* field points to the first available location in memory (00000000). The *segment limit* field can optionally indicate the amount of physical memory in the system. In the current figure, the segment limit is 0040. The *access* field contains bits that determine how the segment can be used.

> Suppose a computer had 265MB of RAM. The segment limit field would contain 0040 hexadecimal, because its value is implicitly multiplied by 1000 hexadecimal, producing 40000 hexadecimal (256 MB).

2.3.2.2   Multi-Segment Model

In the multi-segment model, each program is given its own table of segment descriptors, called a *local descriptor table* (LDT). Each descriptor points to a segment which can be distinct from all segments used by other processes. Each segment is a separate address space. Figure 2-13 shows that each entry in the LDT points to a different segment in memory. Each segment descriptor specifies the exact size of its segment. For example, the segment beginning at 3000 has size 2000 hexadecimal, which is computed as (0002 * 1000 hexadecimal). The segment beginning at 8000 has size A000 hexadecimal.

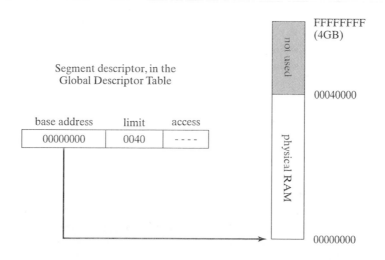

Figure 2-12   Flat Segmentation Model.

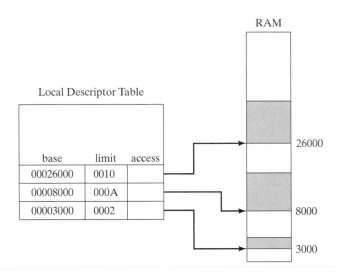

Figure 2-13   Multi-Segment Model.

2.3.2.3   Paging

The IA-32 supports a feature called *paging*, which permits a segment to be divided into 4096-byte blocks of memory called *pages*. Paging permits the total memory used by all programs running at the same time to be much larger than the computer's actual (physical) memory. Sometimes the complete collection of pages is called *virtual memory*. An operating system will usually include a program called a *virtual memory manager*.

Paging is an important solution to a vexing problem for software and hardware designers. A program must be loaded into main memory before it can run, but memory is expensive. Users want to be able to load numerous programs into memory and switch between them at will. Disk storage, on the other hand, is cheap and plentiful. Paging provides the illusion that memory is almost unlimited in size. Of course, disk access is much slower than main memory access.

When a task is running, parts of it can be stored on disk if they are not currently in use. We say that part of the task has been *paged* (swapped) to disk. Other parts of the task, which are actively executing code, can be in memory. When the CPU needs to execute the part of the task that is currently on disk, it issues a *page fault*, causing the page or pages containing the required code or data to be loaded back into memory. To see how this works, find a computer with somewhat limited memory (32MB or 64MB), and run 5 or 10 large applications at the same time. You should notice a delay when switching from one program to another, because the OS has to transfer parts of each program into memory from disk. A computer runs faster when more memory is installed becase large application files and programs can be kept entirely in memory. This reduces the amount of paging.

2.3.3   Section Review

1. What is the range of addressable memory in Protected mode?
2. What is the range of addressable memory in Real-address mode?
3. The two ways of describing an address in Real-address mode are segment-offset and _____.
4. In Real-address mode, convert the following segment-offset address to a linear address: 0950:0100.
5. In Real-address mode, convert the following segment-offset address to a linear address: 0CD1:02E0.
6. In the flat memory model used by the Microsoft Assembler, how many bits are used to hold the address of an instruction or variable?
7. In Protected mode, which register references the descriptor for the stack segment?
8. In Protected mode, which table contains pointers to the various segments used by a single program?
9. In the flat segmentation model, which table contains pointers to at least two segments?
10. What is the main advantage to using the paging feature of IA-32 processors?
11. *Challenge:* Can you think of a reason why MS-DOS was not designed to support Protected-mode programming?
12. *Challenge:* In Real-address mode, demonstrate two segment-offset addresses that point to the same linear address.

2.4   Components of an IA-32 Microcomputer

This chapter introduces you to the architecture of IA-32 computers from several points of view. First, the hardware (physical parts of the computer) can be viewed on the *macro* level, looking at peripherals. Then we can look at the internal details of the Intel processor, called the *central processing unit* (CPU). Finally, we look at the software architecture, which is the way the memory is organized, and how the operating system interacts with the hardware.

2.4.1   Motherboard

The heart of any microcomputer is its motherboard. This is a flat board onto which are placed the computer's CPU, supporting processors, main memory, input-output connectors, power supply connectors, and expansion slots. The various components are connected to each other by a *bus*, a set of wires etched directly on the motherboard. Literally dozens of motherboards are available on the PC market. Although they vary in expansion capabilities and speed, they have a number of elements in common:

- CPU socket: Within the IA-32 family, the socket can be different sizes, depending on the type of processor.
- External cache memory slot: For high-speed cache memory that is used by the CPU to reduce its access to slower conventional RAM.

- Slots to add main memory: Called SIMMs or DIMMs, the memory chips are on small boards that plug into available memory slots.
- BIOS (*basic input-output system*), which is software that has been loaded into a computer chip. Many BIOS chips can be upgraded as the need arises by copying the software from a file supplied by the computer manufacturer. They use a type of memory called *static RAM*.
- IDE cable connectors: For internal fixed disk and CD-ROM drives.
- Sound synthesizer.
- Parallel, serial, USB, video, keyboard, joystick, and mouse ports.
- Network adapter.
- PCI bus connectors for sound cards, graphics cards, data acquisition boards, and other I/O devices.

The following are some of the more important support processors in a typical IA-32 system:

- The Floating-Point Unit (FPU) handles floating-point and extended integer calculations.
- The 8284/82C284 *Clock Generator*, known simply as the *clock,* oscillates at a constant speed. The clock generator synchronizes the CPU and the rest of the computer.
- The 8259 *Programmable Interrupt Controller* (PIC) handles external interrupts from hardware devices, such as the keyboard, system clock, and disk drives. These devices interrupt the CPU and make it process their requests immediately.
- The 8254 *Programmable Interval Timer/Counter* interrupts the system 18.2 times per second, updates the system date and clock, and controls the speaker. It is also responsible for constantly refreshing memory, as RAM memory chips can remember their data for only a few milliseconds.
- The 8255 *Programmable Parallel Port* transfers data to and from the computer using the IEEE Parallel Port interface. This port is commonly used for printers, but it can be used with other input-output devices as well.

2.4.1.1   PCI Bus Architecture

The **PCI** (*Peripheral Component Interconnect*) bus was developed by Intel in 1992 to provide a convenient upgrade path for increasingly fast Pentium processors. It is still the dominant bus in today's Pentium systems. The PCI specification supports both 32-bit and 64-bit motherboards. The PCI motherboard provides a connecting bridge between the CPU's local 64-bit bus and the system's external bus.

2.4.1.2   Motherboard Chipset

Most motherboards contain an integrated set of microprocessors and controllers called a *chipset*. The chipset largely determines the capabilities of the computer. The names you see listed here are by Intel, but many motherboards use compatible chipsets from other manufacturers:

- The Intel 8237 Direct Memory Access (DMA) controller transfers data between external devices and RAM, without requiring any work by the CPU.

- The Intel 8259 Interrupt Controller handles requests from the hardware to interrupt the CPU.
- The 8254 Timer Counter handles the system clock that ticks 18.2 times per second, the memory refresh timer, and the time of day clock.
- Microprocessor local bus to PCI bridge.
- System memory controller and cache controller.
- PCI bus to ISA bus bridge.
- Intel 8042 keyboard and mouse microcontroller.

2.4.2 Video Output

The video adapter controls the display of text and graphics on IBM-compatibles. It has two components: the video controller and video display memory. All graphics and text displayed on the monitor are written into video display RAM, where it is then sent to the monitor by the video controller. The video controller is itself a special-purpose microprocessor, relieving the primary CPU of the job of controlling video hardware.

CRT video monitors use a technique called *raster scanning* to display images. A beam of electrons illuminates phosphorus dots on the screen called *pixels*. Starting at the top of the screen, the gun fires electrons from the left side to the right in a horizontal row, briefly turns off, and returns to the left side of the screen to begin a new row. *Horizontal retrace* refers to the time period when the gun is off between rows. When the last row is drawn, the gun turns off (called the *vertical retrace*) and moves to the upper left corner of the screen to start all over.

A direct digital LCD monitor receives a digital bit stream directly from the video controller and does not require raster scanning.

2.4.3 Memory

Several basic types of memory are used in PCs: ROM, EPROM, Dynamic RAM (DRAM), Static RAM (SRAM), Video RAM (VRAM), and CMOS RAM:

- **ROM** (read-only memory) is memory that is permanently burned into a chip and cannot be erased.
- **EPROM** (erasable programmable read-only memory) can be erased slowly with ultraviolet light, and reprogrammed.
- **Dynamic RAM** is where programs and data are kept when a program is running. It must be refreshed within less than a millisecond or it loses its contents. Because it is inexpensive, it is used for a computer's main memory. Some systems use ECC memory (error checking and correcting), which is memory that is able to detect multiple-bit errors and correct single-bit errors.
- **Static RAM** is the type of RAM chip used primarily for expensive, high-speed cache memory that greatly improves system performance. It keeps its value without having to be constantly refreshed.

- **Video RAM** is used exclusively for storing data that appears on a video display. It is usually located on a video controller board, and is optimized for storing color pixels. Whereas DRAM has only one access port, VRAM is dual-ported, allowing one port to continuously refresh the display while the other port writes data to the display.
- **CMOS RAM** is used on the system motherboard to store system setup information. It is refreshed by a battery, so its contents are retained even when the computer's power is turned off.

2.4.4 Input-Output Ports

USB Port   The Universal Serial Bus (USB) port provides an intelligent, high-speed connection between a computer and USB-supported devices. USB ports support data transfer speeds (at present) of up to 12 megabytes per second. You can connect either single-function units (mice, printers) or compound devices that have more than one peripheral sharing the same USB port. A USB hub, shown in Figure 2-14, is a compound device that can be connected to several other devices, including hubs. Each USB cable has two types of connectors (A = upstream), and (B = downstream).

When a device is attached to the computer via USB, the computer queries the device to get its name, device type, and the type of device driver it supports. This process is called *enumeration*. The computer can suspend power to individual devices and put devices in a suspended state.[1]

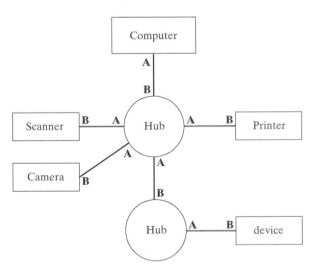

Figure 2-14   USB Hub Configuration.

---

[1] For more information, read *An Introduction to USB Development*, by Jack G. Ganssle. Embedded Systems Programming (www.embedded.com).

Parallel Port   Most printers connect to a computer via a *parallel port*. By "parallel" we mean that 8 or 16 data bits can travel simultaneously from the computer to the printer. Data can be transferred very quickly over short distances, usually no more than 10 feet. MS-DOS automatically recognizes three parallel ports: LPT1, LPT2, and LPT3. Parallel ports can be *bidirectional*, allowing the computer to both send data to and receive information from a device. The 8255 controller chip is used to program the parallel port.

Serial Port   An *RS-232 serial port* sends binary bits one at a time, resulting in slower speeds than the parallel and USB ports, but with the ability to send over larger distances. It can be used to connect a mouse, a modem, or any other serial device to the computer system. The chip that controls the serial ports is the 16550 UART (*Universal Asynchronous Receiver Transmitter*), which is located either on the motherboard or on an adapter card.

2.4.5   Section Review

1. Describe *external cache memory*.
2. Which Intel processor was behind the creation of the PCI bus?
3. In the motherboard chipset, what task does the Intel 8259 perform?
4. Where is the memory used by the video display located?
5. Describe raster scanning on a CRT video monitor.
6. Name four types of RAM mentioned in this chapter.
7. Which type of RAM is used for Level-2 cache memory?
8. What advantages does a USB device offer over a standard serial or parallel device?
9. What are the names of the two types of USB connectors?
10. Which processor chip controls the serial port?

2.5   Input-Output System

Perhaps you have dreamed of writing computer games. Games are very memory and I/O intensive, and often push their host computers to their absolute limit. Programmers who excel at this know a great deal about video and sound hardware, because they write their code in such a way that it takes advantage of particular hardware design features. You can write hardware-specific code in C++, but usually only after you have learned how to do it in assembly language.

2.5.1   How It All Works

An application program routinely reads input from the keyboard and from files, and it writes output to the screen and to files. This is accomplished not by directly accessing the computer's hardware, but by calling functions in the computer's operating system. Input-output is accomplished via different access levels, similar to the virtual machine concept shown in Chapter 1.

- A high-level programming language such as C++ or Java contains functions that perform input-output. These functions are designed to work on a variety of different computer systems.
- The OS (operating system) is at the next level. It deals with high-level operations, such as writing entire strings and records to files, reading strings from the keyboard, and allocating blocks of memory for application programs.
- The BIOS (Basic Input-Output System) is a collection of functions that communicate directly with hardware devices. The BIOS is installed by the computer's manufacturer, and must be tailored to fit the computer's exact configuration down to the selection of specific chips on the motherboard. Any operating system installed in the computer must be able to work with the computer's BIOS.

Device Drivers   What happens if a new device is installed in a computer that is unknown to the BIOS? When the operating system boots, it loads a device driver (program) that contains functions designed to communicate with the device. The device driver works much like the BIOS, providing input-output functions for the device. An example of such a driver is CDROM.SYS, which enables MS-DOS to read CD-ROM drives. It is loaded using a command such as:

```
DEVICE=CDROM.SYS
```

Figure 2-15 shows what happens when an application program displays a string of characters on the screen in a particular color. The following steps are involved:

1. A statement in the application program calls a library function that writes the string to standard output.
2. The library function (Level 3) calls an operating system function, passing a string pointer.

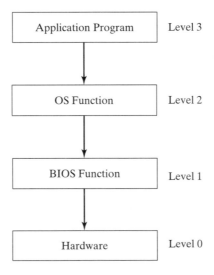

Figure 2-15   Access Levels for Input-Output Operations.

3. The operating system function (Level 2) repeatedly calls a function in the BIOS, passing it the ASCII code and color of each character. The OS calls another BIOS function to advance the cursor to the next position on the screen.

4. The BIOS function (Level 1) receives each character, maps it to a particular system font, and sends the character to a hardware port attached to the video controller card.

5. The video controller card (Level 0) generates timed hardware signals to the video display that control the raster scanning and displaying of pixels.

Programming at Multiple Levels   Assembly language programmers have a great deal of power and flexibility when it comes to input-output programming. As shown in Figure 2-16, an assembly language program can choose from the following access levels:

- Level 3: Call library functions to perform generic text I/O and file-based I/O. We supply such a library with this book, for instance.
- Level 2: Call operating system functions to perform generic text I/O and file-based I/O. If the OS uses a graphical user interface, it has functions to display graphics in a device-independent way.
- Level 1: Call BIOS functions to control device-specific features such as color, graphics, sound, keyboard input, and low-level disk I/O.
- Level 0: Send and receive data from hardware points, having absolute control over specific devices.

What are the tradeoffs? Control versus portability is the primary one. Level 2 (OS) works on any computer that runs the same OS. If the particular I/O device lacks certain capabilities, the OS will do its best to compromise. Level 2 is not particularly fast because each I/O call must go through several layers before it executes.

Level 1 (BIOS) works on all systems that have a standard BIOS, but will not necessarily produce the same results on all systems. For example, two computers might have video displays with different resolution capabilities. The programmer at Level 1 would have to write code to detect the user's hardware setup and adjust the output format to match. Level 1 runs faster than Level 2, because it is only one level above the hardware.

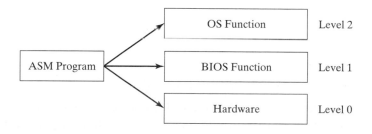

Figure 2-16   Assembly Language Access Levels.

Level 0 (hardware) works either with generic devices such as serial ports, or with specific I/O devices produced by known manufacturers. Programs using this level must extend their coding logic to handle variations in I/O devices. Real-mode game programs are prime examples, because they usually take over all operation of the computer. Programs at this level execute as quickly as the hardware will permit.

Suppose, for example, that you wanted to play a WAV file using an audio controller device. At the OS level, you would not have to know what type of device was installed, and probably would not be concerned overly much about the card's features. At the BIOS level, you would query the sound card (using its installed device driver software) and find out whether it belonged to a certain class of sound cards having known features. And finally, at the hardware level, you would fine-tune the program for certain brands of audio cards, to take advantage of each card's special features.

Finally, we must point out that not all operating systems permit user programs to directly access system hardware. Such access is reserved for the operating system itself and specialized device driver programs. This is the case with Windows NT, 2000, and XP, where vital system resources are shielded from application programs. MS-DOS, on the other hand, has no such restrictions.

2.5.2 Section Review

1. Of the three levels of input/output in a computer system, which is the most universal and portable?
2. What distinguishes the BIOS level of input/output?
3. Why are device drivers necessary, given that the BIOS already has code that communicates with the computer's hardware?
4. In the example regarding displaying a string of characters, which level exists between the operating system and the video controller card?
5. A which level(s) can an assembly language program manipulate input/output?
6. Why do game programs often send their sound output directly to the sound card's hardware ports?
7. *Challenge:* Is it likely that the BIOS for a computer running MS-Windows would be different from that used by a computer running Linux?

2.6 Chapter Summary

The central processor unit is where all the calculations and logic take place. It contains a limited number of storage locations called *registers*, a high-frequency clock to synchronize its operations, a control unit, and the arithmetic logic unit. The memory storage unit is where instructions and data are held while a computer program is running. A *bus* is a series of parallel wires that transmit data between various parts of the computer.

The execution of a single machine instruction can be divided into a sequence of individual operations, called the *instruction execution cycle*. The three primary operations are fetch, decode, and execute. Each step in the instruction cycle takes at least one tick of the system clock, called a *clock cycle*.

The *load and execute* sequence describes how a program is located by the operating system, loaded into memory, and executed by the operating system.

Pipelined execution greatly improves the throughput of multiple instructions in a CPU by permitting the overlapped execution of multi-stage instructions. A *superscalar* processor is a pipelined processor with multiple execution pipelines. This is particularly useful when one of the execution stages requires more than a single clock cycle.

A *multitasking* operating system is able to run multiple tasks at the same time. It must run on a processor that supports task switching, which means that the processor saves the state of each task before switching to a new one.

IA-32 processors have three basic modes of operation: Protected mode, Real-address mode, and System Management mode. In addition, the Virtual-8086 mode is a special case of Protected mode.

Registers are named locations within the CPU that can be accessed very quickly. The following are brief descriptions of register types:

- The general-purpose registers are primarily used for arithmetic, data movement, and logical operations.
- The segment registers are used as base locations for preassigned memory areas called segments.
- The EIP (instruction pointer) register contains the address of the next instruction to be executed.
- The EFLAGS register consists of individual binary bits that either control the operation of the CPU or reflect the outcome of ALU operations.

The IA-32 has a floating-point unit (FPU) that is expressly for the execution of high-speed floating-point arithmetic.

The Intel 8086 processor marks the beginning of the modern Intel Architecture family. The Intel386 processor, the first of the IA-32 family, featured 32-bit registers and a 32-bit address bus and external data path. The P6 processor family (Pentium Pro onward) is based on a new micro-architecture design that improves execution speed.

The earliest Intel processors for the IBM Personal Computer were based on the *complex instruction set* (CISC) approach. The Intel instruction set includes powerful ways to address data, and instructions that are relatively high-level complex operations. A completely different approach to microprocessor design is the *reduced instruction set* (RISC). A RISC machine language consists of a relatively small number of short, simple instructions that can be executed quickly by the processor.

In the IA-32's Real-address mode, only 1MB of memory can be addressed, from hexadecimal 00000 to FFFFF. In Protected mode, the processor can run multiple programs at the same time. It assigns each process (running program) a total of 4GB of memory. In Virtual-8086 mode, the computer runs in Protected mode and creates a virtual 8086 machine with its own 1MB address space that simulates an 80x86 computer running in Real-address mode.

In the flat segmentation model, all segments are mapped to the entire physical address space of the computer. In the multi-segment model, each task is given its own table of segment descriptors, called a local descriptor table (LDT). The IA-32 supports a feature called paging, which permits a segment to be divided into 4096-byte blocks of memory called pages. Paging permits the total memory used by all programs running at the same time to be much larger than the computer's actual (physical) memory.

The heart of any microcomputer is its motherboard, holding the computer's CPU, supporting processors, main memory, input-output connectors, power supply connectors, and expansion slots. The PCI (Peripheral Component Interconnect) bus provides a convenient upgrade path for Pentium processors. Most motherboards contain an integrated set of several microprocessors and controllers, called a chipset. The chipset largely determines the capabilities of the computer.

The video adapter controls the display of text and graphics on IBM-compatibles. It has two components: the video controller and video display memory.

Several basic types of memory are used in PCs: ROM, EPROM, Dynamic RAM (DRAM), Static RAM (SRAM), Video RAM (VRAM), and CMOS RAM.

The Universal Serial Bus (USB) port provides an intelligent, high-speed connection between a computer and USB-supported devices. A parallel port transmits 8 or 16 data bits simultaneously from one device to another. An RS-232 serial port sends binary bits one at a time, resulting in slower speeds than the parallel and USB ports.

Input/output is accomplished via different access levels, similar to the virtual machine concept. The operating system is at the highest level. The BIOS (Basic Input-Output System) is a collection of functions that communicate directly with hardware devices. Programs can also directly access input/output devices.

Assembly Language Fundamentals

3

3.1   Basic Elements of Assembly Language

Chapter 2 gave you some essential basics of computer hardware as well as specific knowledge of the IA-32 architecture. Now it's time to get practical and apply that knowledge. If you were a cook, I would now be showing you around the kitchen, explaining how to use mixers, grinders, knives, stoves, and saucepans. We're going to take the ingredients of assembly language, mix them together, and come up with working programs.

Assembly language programmers absolutely must first know their data backwards and forwards before writing executable code. Part of that goal was accomplished in Chapter 1, where you learned about various number systems and the binary storage of integers and characters. In this chapter, you will learn how to define and declare variables and constants, using Microsoft Assembler (MASM) syntax. Then you will get to see a complete program, which we dissect line by line. You can expand and modify the programs in this chapter as much as you wish, using the new knowledge you've gained.

3.1.1   Integer Constants

An *integer constant* (or integer literal) is made up of an optional leading sign, one or more digits, and an optional suffix character (called a *radix*) indicating the number's base:

```
[{+|-}]  digits  [radix]
```

> Microsoft syntax notation is used throughout this chapter. Elements within square brackets [..] are optional, and elements within braces {..} require a choice of one of the enclosed elements (separated by the | character). Elements in *italics* denote items which have known definitions or descriptions.

The *radix* may be one of the following (uppercase or lowercase):

h	hexadecimal	r	encoded real
q/o	octal	t	decimal (*alternate*)
d	decimal	y	binary (*alternate*)
b	binary		

If no radix is given, the integer constant is assumed to be decimal. Here are some examples using different radixes:

26	decimal	42o	octal
26d	decimal	1Ah	hexadecimal
11010011b	binary	0A3h	hexadecimal
42q	octal		

A hexadecimal constant beginning with a letter must have a leading zero to prevent the assembler from interpreting it as an identifier.

3.1.2   Integer Expressions

An *integer expression* is a mathematical expression involving integer values and arithmetic operators. The expression must evaluate to an integer which can be stored in 32 bits (0 – FFFFFFFFh). The arithmetic operators are listed in Table 3-1 according to their precedence order, from highest (1) to lowest (4).

Table 3-1   Arithmetic Operators.

Operator	Name	Precedence Level
( )	parentheses	1
+, -	unary plus, minus	2
*, /	multiply, divide	3
MOD	modulus	3
+, -	add, subtract	4

Precedence refers to the implied order of operations when an expression contains two or more operators. The order of operations is shown for the following expressions:

```
4 + 5 * 2          multiply, add
12 - 1 MOD 5       modulus, subtract
-5 + 2             unary minus, add
(4 + 2) * 6        add, multiply
```

The following are examples of valid expressions and their values:

Expression	Value
16 / 5	3
-(3 + 4) * (6 - 1)	-35
-3 + 4 * 6 - 1	20
25 mod 3	1

> It's a good idea to use parentheses in expressions to clarify the order of operations. Then you don't have to remember the precedence rules.

3.1.3   Real Number Constants

There are two types of real number constants: decimal reals and encoded (hexadecimal) reals. A *decimal real* constant contains a sign followed by an integer, a decimal point, an integer that expresses a fraction, and an exponent:

```
[sign] integer.[integer] [exponent]
```

This is how we describe the sign and exponent:

```
sign        {+,-}
exponent    E[{+,-}]integer
```

The sign is optional, and the choices are + or −. Following are examples of valid real constants:

```
2.
+3.0
-44.2E+05
26.E5
```

At the very least, there must be a digit and a decimal point. Without the decimal point, it would just be an integer constant.

Encoded Reals   You can specify a real constant in hexadecimal as an *encoded real* if you know the exact binary representation of the number. The following, for example, is the encoded 4-byte real representation of decimal +1.0:

```
3F800000r
```

(We will delay the discussion of IEEE real number formats until Chapter 17, stored on the book's CD-ROM.)

3.1.4   Character Constants

A *character constant* is a single character enclosed in either single or double quotes. The assembler converts it to the binary ASCII code matching the character. Examples are:

```
'A'
"d"
```

A complete list of ASCII codes is printed on the inside back cover of this book.

3.1.5   String Constants

A *string constant* is a string of characters enclosed in either single or double quotes:

```
'ABC'
'X'
"Goodnight, Gracie"
'4096'
```

Embedded quotes are permitted when used in the manner shown by the following examples:

```
"This isn't a test"
'Say "Goodnight," Gracie'
```

3.1.6   Reserved Words

Assembly language has a list of words called *reserved words*. These have special meaning and can only be used in their correct context. Reserved words can be any of the following:

- Instruction mnemonics, such as MOV, ADD, or MUL, which correspond to built-in operations performed by Intel processors.
- Directives, which tell MASM how to assemble programs.
- Attributes, which provide size and usage information for variables and operands. Examples are BYTE and WORD.
- Operators, used in constant expressions.
- Predefined symbols, such as @data, which return constant integer values at assembly time.

A complete list of MASM reserved words will be found in Appendix D.

3.1.7   Identifiers

An *identifier* is a programmer-chosen name. It might identify a variable, a constant, a procedure, or a code label. Keep the following in mind when creating identifiers:

- They may contain between 1 and 247 characters.
- They are not case-sensitive.
- The first character must be either a letter (A..Z, a..z), underscore (_), @, or $. Subsequent characters may also be digits.

- An identifier cannot be the same as an assembler reserved word.

> You can make all keywords and identifiers case-sensitive by adding the –Cp command line switch when running the assembler.

Avoid using a single @ sign as the first character, because it is used extensively by the assembler for predefined symbols. Here are some valid identifiers:

```
var1              Count             $first

_main             MAX               open_file

@@myfile          xVal              _12345
```

Common sense suggests that you should make identifier names descriptive and easy to understand.

3.1.8 Directives

A *directive* is a command that is recognized and acted upon by the assembler as the program's source code is being assembled. Directives are used for defining logical segments, choosing a memory model, defining variables, creating procedures, and so on.

Directives are part of the assembler's syntax, but are not related to the Intel instruction set. Various assemblers may generate identical machine code for the Intel processor, but their sets of directives need not be the same.

Different capitalizations of the same directive are assumed to be equivalent. For example, the assembler does not recognize any difference between **.data**, **.DATA**, and **.Data**.

Examples   The .DATA directive identifies the area of a program that contains variables:

```
.data
```

The .CODE directive identifies the area of a program that contains instructions:

```
.code
```

The PROC directive identifies the beginning of a procedure. *Name* may be any identifier:

```
name PROC
```

It would take a very long time to learn all the directives in MASM, so we will necessarily concentrate on the the few that are most essential. Appendix D contains a complete reference to all MASM directives and operators.

3.1.9 Instructions

An *instruction* is a statement that is executed by the processor at runtime after the program has been loaded into memory and started. An instruction contains four basic parts:

- Label (optional)
- Instruction mnemonic (required)
- Operand(s) (usually required)
- Comment (optional)

Source code lines may consist only of labels or comments. The following diagram shows the standard format for instructions:

| Label : | Mnemonic | Operand(s) | ; Comment |

Let's explore each part separately, starting with the *label* field, which is optional.

3.1.9.1 Label

A *label* is an identifier that acts as a place marker for either instructions or data. In the process of scanning a source program, the assembler assigns a numeric address to each program statement. A label placed just before an instruction implies the instruction's address. Similarly, a label placed just before a variable implies the variable's address.

Why use labels at all? We could directly reference numeric addresses in our program code. For example, the following instruction moves a 16-bit word from memory location 0020 to the AX register:[1]

```
mov ax,[0020]
```

But when new variables are inserted in programs, the addresses of all subsequent variables automatically change. A reference such as [0020] would have to be modified manually. Clearly, this would create a headache for programmers, and is not worth the effort. Instead, if location 0020h is assigned a label, the assembler automatically matches the label to the address. Now the same MOV instruction can be written as:

```
mov ax,myVariable
```

Of course, we're getting ahead a bit ahead of ourselves. Variable definitions will be explained in Section 3.4.2, and the MOV instruction will be explained in Section 3.2.3.

Code Labels A label in the code area of a program (where instructions are located) must end with a colon (:) character. In this context, labels are often used as targets of jumping and looping instructions. For example, the following JMP (jump) instruction transfers control to the location marked by the label named **target**, creating a loop:

```
target:
    mov ax,bx
    ...
    jmp target
```

---

[1] Don't try to assemble this instruction. It is only here for illustrative purposes.

A code label can share the same line with an instruction, or it can be on a line by itself:

```
target: mov ax,bx
target:
```

Data Labels   If a label is used in the data area of a program (where variables are defined), it cannot end with a colon. Here is an example that defines a variable named **first**:

```
first BYTE 10
```

Label names are created using the rules for identifiers already shown in Section 3.1.7. Data label names must be unique within the same source file. If, for example, you have a label named **first**, then you cannot have another label named **first** anywhere in the same source code file.

3.1.9.2   Instruction Mnemonic

An *instruction mnemonic* is a short word that identifies the operation carried out by an instruction. In the English dictionary, a mnemonic is generally described as a *device that assists memory.* That is why instruction mnemonics have useful names such as mov, add, sub, mul, jmp, and call:

mov	move (assign) one value to another
add	add two values
sub	subtract one value from another
mul	multiply two values
jmp	jump to a new location
call	call a procedure

3.1.9.3   Operands

An assembly language instruction can have between zero and three operands, each of which can be a register, memory operand, constant expression, or I/O port. We discussed register names in Chapter 2, and we discussed constant expressions in Section 3.1.2. (We will leave the discussion of I/O ports for a later chapter.) A memory operand is specified either by the name of a variable or by a register that contains the address of a variable. A variable name implies the address of the variable, and instructs the computer to reference the contents of memory at the given address, as shown in the following table:

Example	Operand Type
96	constant (*immediate value*)
2 + 4	constant expression
eax	register
count	variable name

Following are some examples of assembly language instructions with various numbers of operands. The STC instruction, for example, has no operands:

```
stc                     ; set Carry flag
```

The INC instruction has one operand:

```
inc   ax                ; add 1 to AX
```

The MOV instruction has two operands:

```
mov count,bx            ; move BX to count
```

3.1.9.4 Comments

Comments, as you probably know, are an important way for the writer of a program to communicate information about how the program works to a person reading the source code. The following information is typically included at the top of a program listing:

- A short description of the program's overall purpose.
- The name of the programmer(s) who has written and/or revised the program.
- The date the program was written, along with revision dates.

Comments can be specified in two ways:

- Single-line comments, beginning with a semicolon character (;). All characters following the semicolon on the same line are ignored by the assembler and may be used to comment the program.
- Block comments, beginning with the COMMENT directive and a user-specified symbol. All subsequent lines of text are ignored by the assembler until the same user-specified symbol appears. For example:

```
COMMENT   !
    This line is a comment.
    This line is also a comment.
!
```

We can also use any other symbol:

```
COMMENT   &
    This line is a comment.
    This line is also a comment.
&
```

3.1.10   Section Review

1. List the valid suffix characters that may be used in integer constants.
2. *(Yes/No):* Is A5h a valid hexadecimal constant?
3. *(Yes/No):* Does the multiply sign (*) have a higher precedence than the divide sign (/) in integer expressions?

4. Write a constant expression that divides 10 by 3 and returns the integer remainder.

5. Show an example of a valid real number constant with an exponent.

6. *(Yes/No):* Must string constants be enclosed in single quotes?

7. Reserved words can be instruction mnemonics. attributes, operators, predefined symbols, and _____.

8. What is the maximum length of an identifier?

9. *(True/False):* An identifier cannot begin with a numeric digit.

10. *(True/False):* Assembly language identifiers are (by default) case-insensitive.

11. *(True/False):* Assembler directives execute at run time.

12. *(True/False):* Assembler directives can be written in any combination of uppercase and lowercase letters.

13. Name the four basic parts of an assembly language instruction.

14. *(True/False):* MOV is an example of an instruction mnemonic.

15. *(True/False):* A code label is followed by a colon (:), but a data label does not have a colon.

16. Show an example of a block comment.

17. Why would it not be a good idea to use numeric addresses when writing instructions that access variables?

3.2   Example: Adding Three Integers

3.2.1   Program Listing

Now it's time to look at that first working program we promised you in the chapter introduction. It's really trivial—it just adds and subtracts three integers, using CPU registers. At the end, the registers are displayed on the screen:

```
TITLE Add and Subtract              (AddSub.asm)

; This program adds and subtracts 32-bit integers.

INCLUDE Irvine32.inc
.code
main PROC

    mov eax,10000h                  ; EAX = 10000h
    add eax,40000h                  ; EAX = 50000h
    sub eax,20000h                  ; EAX = 30000h
    call DumpRegs                   ; display registers

    exit
main ENDP
END main
```

3.2.2   Program Output

The following is a snapshot of the the program's output, generated by the call to the **DumpRegs** procedure:

```
EAX=00030000   EBX=7FFDF000   ECX=00000101   EDX=FFFFFFFF
ESI=00000000   EDI=00000000   EBP=0012FFF0   ESP=0012FFC4
EIP=00401024   EFL=00000206   CF=0   SF=0   ZF=0   OF=0
```

The first two rows show the hexadecimal values of the 32-bit general-purpose registers. Notice that EAX equals 00030000h, the value produced by the ADD and SUB instructions in the program. The third row shows the values of the EIP (extended instruction pointer) and EFL (extended flags) registers, as well as the values of the Carry, Sign, Zero, and Overflow flags.

3.2.3   Program Description

Let's go through the program line by line. In each case, the program code appears before its explanation:

```
TITLE Add and Subtract          (AddSub.asm)
```

The TITLE directive marks the entire line as a comment. You can put anything you want on this line.

```
; This program adds and subtracts 32-bit integers.
```

All text to the right of a semicolon is ignored by the assembler, so we use it for comments.

```
INCLUDE Irvine32.inc
```

The INCLUDE directive copies necessary definitions and setup information from a text file named *Irvine32.inc*, located in the assembler's INCLUDE directory. (The file is described in Chapter 5.)

```
.code
```

The **.code** directive marks the beginning of the *code segment*, where all executable statements in a program are located.

```
main PROC
```

The PROC directive identifies the beginning of a procedure. The name chosen for the only procedure in our program is **main**.

```
mov eax,10000h                  ; EAX = 10000h
```

The MOV instruction moves (copies) the integer 10000h to the EAX register. The first operand (EAX) is called the *destination operand*, and the second operand is called the *source operand*.

```
add eax,40000h                  ; EAX = 50000h
```

The ADD instruction adds 40000h to the EAX register.

```
sub eax,20000h                  ; EAX = 30000h
```

The SUB instruction subtracts 20000h from the EAX register.

```
        call DumpRegs                    ; display registers
```

The CALL statement calls a procedure that displays the current values of the CPU registers. This can be a useful way to verify that a program is working correctly.

```
        exit
    main ENDP
```

The **exit** statement (indirectly) calls a predefined MS-Windows function that halts the program. The ENDP directive marks the end of the **main** procedure. Note that **exit** is not a MASM keyword; instead, it's a command defined in *Irvine32.inc* that provides a simple way to end a program.

```
    END main
```

The END directive marks the last line of the program to be assembled. It identifies the name of the program's *startup* procedure (the procedure that starts the program execution).

Segments   Programs are organized around segments, which are usually named code, data, and stack. The *code* segment contains all of a program's executable instructions. Ordinarily, the code segment contains one or more procedures, with one designated as the *startup* procedure. In the **AddSub** program, the startup procedure is **main**. Another segment, the *stack* segment, holds procedure parameters and local variables. The *data* segment holds variables.

Coding Styles   You may be wondering at this point whether you should capitalize any particular keywords in assembly language programs. Because assembly language is case-insensitive, you are free to decide how to capitalize your programs, unless your instructor has specific requirements. Here are some varied approaches to capitalization that you can try:

- Capitalize nothing, except perhaps the initial letters of identifiers. C++ programmers often feel comfortable with this approach, since all their keywords are in lowercase. This approach makes the typing of source code lines fairly rapid.
- Capitalize everything: This approach was used in pre-1970 mainframe assembler programs, when computer terminals often did not support lowercase letters. It has the advantage of overcoming the effects of poor-quality printers and less-than-perfect eyesight.
- Use capital letters for all assembler reserved words, including instruction mnemonics and register names. This makes it easy to distinguish between user-defined names and assembler reserved words.
- Capitalize assembly language directives and operators. Leave everything else in lowercase. This is the approach used in the example programs throughout this book, except that .code and .data are lowercase.

3.2.3.1   Alternative Version of AddSub

You may have looked at the **AddSub** program and wondered exactly what was inside the *Irvine32.inc* file. To make your coding more convenient, we hide quite a few details that will be covered later in the book. Understandably, you (or your instructor) may prefer to create programs that do not depend on include files. The following version of AddSub hides nothing:

```
TITLE Add and Subtract                  (AddSubAlt.asm)

; This program adds and subtracts 32-bit integers.

.386
.MODEL flat,stdcall
.STACK 4096
ExitProcess PROTO, dwExitCode:DWORD
DumpRegs PROTO

.code
main PROC

    mov eax,10000h                  ; EAX = 10000h
    add eax,40000h                  ; EAX = 50000h
    sub eax,20000h                  ; EAX = 30000h
    call DumpRegs

    INVOKE ExitProcess,0
main ENDP
END main
```

Several lines in the program are different from the original version. As before, we show each line of code followed by its explanation:

```
.386
```

The .386 directive identifies the minimum CPU required for this program (Intel386).

```
.MODEL flat,stdcall
```

The .MODEL directive instructs the assembler to generate code for a Protected mode program, and STDCALL enables the calling of MS-Windows functions.

```
ExitProcess PROTO, dwExitCode:DWORD
DumpRegs PROTO
```

Two PROTO directives declare procedures used by this program: **ExitProcess** is an MS-Windows function that halts the current program (called a *process*), and **DumpRegs** is a procedure from the Irvine32 link library that displays registers.

```
INVOKE ExitProcess,0
```

The program ends by calling the **ExitProcess** function, passing it a return code of zero. INVOKE is an assembler directive that calls a procedure or function.

3.2.4 Program Template

Assembly language programs have a simple structure, with some small variations. When you begin to write and assemble your own programs, it helps to start with an empty shell program that has all the basic elements in place. You can avoid redundant typing by filling in the missing parts and saving the file under a new name. The following Protected-mode program (*Template.asm*) can easily be customized. Note that comments have been inserted, marking the points where your own code should be added:

```
TITLE Program Template                 (Template.asm)

; Program Description:
; Author:
; Creation Date:
; Revisions:
; Date:              Modified by:

INCLUDE Irvine32.inc
.data
    ; (insert variables here)

.code
main PROC
    ; (insert executable instructions here)

    exit
main ENDP

    ; (insert additional procedures here)
END main
```

Use Comments   Several comment fields have been inserted at the beginning of the program. It's a very good idea to include a program description, the name of the program's author, creation date, and information about subsequent modifications.

Documentation of this kind is useful to anyone who reads the program listing (including you, months or years from now). Many programmers have discovered, years after writing a program, that they must become reacquainted with their own code before they can modify it. If you're taking a programming course, your instructor may insist on additional information.

3.2.5 Section Review

1. In the AddSub program (Section 3.2), what is the meaning of the INCLUDE directive?
2. In the AddSub program, what does the .CODE directive identify?
3. What are the names of the segments in the AddSub program?
4. In the AddSub program, how are the CPU registers displayed?
5. In the AddSub program, which statement halts the program?
6. Which directive begins a procedure?
7. Which directive ends a procedure?

8. What is the purpose of the identifier in the END statement?

9. What does the PROTO directive do?

3.3   Assembling, Linking, and Running Programs

In earlier chapters we saw examples of simple machine-language programs, so it is clear that a source program written in assembly language cannot be executed directly on its target computer. It must be translated, or *assembled* into executable code. In fact, an assembler is very similar to a *compiler*, the type of program you would use to translate a C++ or Java program into executable code.

The assembler produces a file containing machine language called an *object file*. This file isn't quite ready to execute. It must be passed to another program called a *linker*, which in turn produces an *executable file*. This file is ready to execute from the MS-DOS/Windows command prompt.

3.3.1   The Assemble-Link-Execute Cycle

The process of editing, assembling, linking, and executing assembly language programs is summarized in Figure 3-1. Following is a detailed description of each step:

Step 1:   A programmer uses a **text editor** to create an ASCII text file named the *source file*.

Step 2:   The **assembler** reads the source file and produces an *object file,* a machine-language translation of the program. Optionally, it produces a *listing file*. If any errors occur, the programmer must return to Step 1 and fix the program.

Step 3:   The **linker** reads the object file and checks to see if the program contains any calls to procedures in a link library. The **linker** copies any required procedures from the link library, combines them with the object file, and produces the *executable file*. Optionally, the linker can produce a *map file*.

Step 4:   The operating system **loader** utility reads the executable file into memory, branches the CPU to the program's starting address, and the program begins to execute.

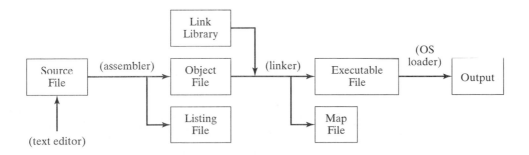

Figure 3-1   Assemble-Link-Execute Cycle.

Assembling and Linking 32-Bit Programs   To assemble and link a Protected mode assembly language program, execute the following command at the MS-DOS prompt:

```
make32 progname
```

Progname is the base name of your assembly language source file, with no extension. For example, the *AddSub.asm* program would be assembled and linked with the following command:

```
make32 AddSub
```

> The make32.bat file must be located either in the same directory as your ASM file or on the system path. Consult your operating system's documentation to find out how to add a directory to the system path. Refer to Appendix A for instructions on setting up your computer.

Assembling and Linking 16-Bit Programs   If you are programming in Real-address mode, use the **make16** command to assemble and link. Using the *AddSub* program as an example, the command would be the following:

```
make16 AddSub
```

3.3.1.1   Listing File

A *listing* file contains a copy of the program's source code, suitable for printing, with line numbers, offset addresses, translated machine code, and a symbol table. Let's look at the listing file for the **AddSub** program we created in Section 3.2:

```
Microsoft (R) Macro Assembler Version 6.15.8803    10/26/01 13:50:21
Add and Subtract                   (AddSub.asm)                Page 1 - 1

                          TITLE Add and Subtract            (AddSub.asm)

                          ; This program adds and subtracts 32-bit integers.

                          INCLUDE Irvine32.inc
               C          ; Include file for Irvine32.lib (Irvine32.inc)
               C          INCLUDE SmallWin.inc

00000000                  .code
00000000                  main PROC

00000000  B8 00010000       mov eax,10000h      ; EAX = 10000h
00000005  05 00040000       add eax,40000h      ; EAX = 50000h
0000000A  2D 00020000       sub eax,20000h      ; EAX = 30000h
0000000F  E8 00000000E       call DumpRegs

                              exit
0000001B                  main ENDP
                          END main

Structures and Unions: (omitted)
```

```
Segments and Groups:

N a m e                          Size     Length    Align    Combine Class
FLAT . . . . . . . . . . . . GROUP
STACK  . . . . . . . . . . . 32 Bit   00001000  DWord    Stack   'STACK'
_DATA  . . . . . . . . . . . 32 Bit   00000000  DWord    Public  'DATA'
_TEXT  . . . . . . . . . . . 32 Bit   0000001B  DWord    Public  'CODE'

Procedures,  parameters and locals (list abbreviated):

N a m e                  Type    Value     Attr
CloseHandle . . . . . . P Near  00000000  FLAT   Length=00000000 External STDCALL
ClrScr . . . . . . . . P Near  00000000  FLAT   Length=00000000 External STDCALL
.
.
.
main . . . . . . . . . P Near  00000000 _TEXT  Length=0000001B Public STDCALL

Symbols (list abbreviated):

N a m e                            Type    Value      Attr
@CodeSize . . . . . . . . . . . Number  00000000h
@DataSize . . . . . . . . . . . Number  00000000h
@Interface . . . . . . . . . . Number  00000003h
@Model . . . . . . . . . . . . Number  00000007h
@code  . . . . . . . . . . . . Text                _TEXT
@data  . . . . . . . . . . . . Text                FLAT
@fardata? . . . . . . . . . . Text                FLAT
@fardata . . . . . . . . . . . Text                FLAT
@stack . . . . . . . . . . . . Text                FLAT
.
.
.
exit . . . . . . . . . . . . . Text    INVOKE ExitProcess,0
                     0 Warnings
                     0 Errors
```

3.3.1.2 Files Created or Updated by the Linker

Map File   A *map* file is a text file (extension MAP) that contains information about the segments contained in a program being linked. It contains the following information:

- The EXE module name, which is the base name of the file.
- The timestamp from the program file header (not from the file system).
- A list of segment groups in the program, with each group's start address, length, group name, and class.
- A list of public symbols, with each address, symbol name, flat address, and module where the symbol is defined.
- The address of the program's entry point.

Program Database File   When you assemble a program with the −Zi option (debugging), MASM creates a *program database file* (extension PDB). During the link step, the linker reads the PDB file and updates it. Then, when you run your program using a debugger, the latter is able to display the program's source code and provide supplemental information about the program.

3.3.2   Section Review

1. What types of files are produced by the assembler?
2. *(True/False):* The linker extracts copies of compiled procedures from the link library file.
3. *(True/False):* When a program's source code is modified, it must be assembled and linked again before it can be executed with the changes.
4. What is the name of the part of the operating system that reads the executable file and starts its execution?
5. What types of files are produced by the linker?

Read Appendix A before answering the following questions:

6. What command line option tells the assembler to produce a listing file?
7. What command line option tells the assembler to add debugging information?
8. What does the linker's /SUBSYSTEM:CONSOLE option signify?
9. *Challenge:* List the names of at least four functions in the kernel32.lib file.
10. *Challenge:* Which linker option lets you specify the program's entry point?

3.4   Defining Data

3.4.1   Intrinsic Data Types

MASM defines various intrinsic data types, each of which describes a set of values that can be assigned to variables and expressions of the given type. A DWORD variable, for example, can hold any 32-bit integer value. Some types are slightly more restrictive, such as REAL4, which can only be initialized by a real number constant. In Table 3-2, all data types pertain to integers except the last three. In those, the notation "IEEE" refers to standard real number formats published by the IEEE Computer Society.

Table 3-2   Intrinsic Data Types.

Type	Usage
BYTE	8-bit unsigned integer
SBYTE	8-bit signed integer

Table 3-2   Intrinsic Data Types. (Continued)

Type	Usage
WORD	16-bit unsigned integer (can also be a Near pointer in Real-address mode)
SWORD	16-bit signed integer
DWORD	32-bit unsigned integer (can also be a Near pointer in Protected mode)
SDWORD	32-bit signed integer
FWORD	48-bit integer (Far pointer in Protected mode)
QWORD	64-bit integer
TBYTE	80-bit (10 byte) integer
REAL4	32-bit (4 byte) IEEE short real
REAL8	64-bit (8 byte) IEEE long real
REAL10	80-bit (10 byte) IEEE extended real

3.4.2   Data Definition Statement

A *data definition statement* sets aside storage in memory for a variable and may optionally assign a name to the variable. We use data definition statements to create variables based on the assembler's intrinsic types (Table 3-2). Each data definition has the same syntax:

```
[name] directive initializer [,initializer]...
```

Initializers   At least one *initializer* is required in a data definition, even if it is the **?** expression, which does not assign a specific value to the data. Additional initializers, if any, are separated by commas. For integer data types, *initializer* is an integer constant or expression that matches the size implied by the type (BYTE, WORD, etc.) Integer constants were explained in Section 3.1.1, and integer expressions were discussed in Section 3.1.2.

All initializers, regardless of their number format, are converted to binary data by the assembler. That is why initializers such as 00110010b, 32h, and 50d all produce the same binary value.

3.4.3   Defining BYTE and SBYTE Data

The BYTE (define byte) and SBYTE (define signed byte) directives, used in data definition statements, allocate storage for one or more unsigned or signed values. Each initializer must be an 8-bit integer expression or character constant. For example:

```
value1 BYTE   'A'          ; character constant
value2 BYTE    0           ; smallest unsigned byte
value3 BYTE   255          ; largest unsigned byte
```

```
value4 SBYTE -128              ; smallest signed byte
value5 SBYTE +127              ; largest signed byte
```

(We're capitalizing the BYTE and SBYTE keywords here for emphasis, but you can just as easily code them in lowercase letters.)

A variable can be left uninitialized by using a question mark for the initializer. This implies that the variable will be assigned a value at runtime by executable instructions:

```
value6 BYTE ?
```

Variable Name   A *variable name* is a label that marks the offset of a variable from the beginning of its enclosing segment. For example, suppose that **value1** was located at offset 0 in the data segment and consumed one byte of storage. Then **value2** would be located at offset 1:

```
.data
value1 BYTE 10h
value2 BYTE 20h
```

DB Directive   Earlier versions of the assembler used the DB directive to define byte data. You can still use DB, but it permits no distinction between signed and unsigned data:

```
val1 DB 255                    ; unsigned byte
val2 DB -128                   ; signed byte
```

3.4.3.1   Multiple Initializers

If multiple initializers are used in the same data definition, its label refers only to the offset of the first byte. In the following example, assume that the label **list** is at offset 0. If so, the value 10 is at offset 0, 20 is at offset 1, 30 is at offset 2, and 40 is at offset 3:

```
.data
list BYTE 10,20,30,40
```

The following illustration shows **list** as a sequence of bytes, each with its own offset:

Offset	Value
0000:	10
0001:	20
0002:	30
0003:	40

Not all data definitions require labels. If we wanted to continue the array of bytes begun with **list**, for example, we could define additional bytes on the next lines:

```
list BYTE 10,20,30,40
     BYTE 50,60,70,80
     BYTE 81,82,83,84
```

Within a single data definition, its initializers can use different radixes. Also, character and string constants can be freely mixed. In the following example, **list1** and **list2** have the same contents:

```
list1 BYTE 10, 32, 41h, 00100010b
list2 BYTE 0Ah,20h, 'A', 22h
```

3.4.3.2 Defining Strings

To create a string data definition, enclose a sequence of characters in quotation marks. The most common type of string ends with a null byte, a byte containing the value 0. This type of string is used by C/C++, by Java, and by Microsoft Windows functions:

```
greeting1 BYTE "Good afternoon",0
```

Each character uses a byte of storage. Strings are an exception to the rule that byte values must be separated by commas. Without that exception, **greeting1** would have to be defined as

```
greeting1 BYTE 'G','o','o','d'....etc.
```

which would be exceedingly tedious.

A string can be spread across multiple lines without the necessity of supplying a label for each line, as the next example shows:

```
greeting1 BYTE "Welcome to the Encryption Demo program "
  BYTE "created by Kip Irvine.",0dh,0ah,
  BYTE "If you wish to modify this program, please "
  BYTE "send me a copy.",0dh,0ah,0
```

As a reminder, the hexadecimal bytes 0Dh and 0Ah are called either CR/LF (explained in Chapter 1) or *end-of-line characters*. When written to standard output, they move the cursor to the left column of the line following the current line.

MASM's line continuation character (\) may be used to concatenate two lines into a single program statement. The \ symbol may only be placed at the end of a line. In other words, the following statements are equivalent:

```
greeting1 BYTE "Welcome to the Encryption Demo program "
```

and

```
greeting1 \
BYTE "Welcome to the Encryption Demo program "
```

3.4.3.3 Using the DUP Operator

The DUP operator generates a repeated storage allocation, using a constant expression as a counter. It is particularly useful when allocating space for a string or array, and can be used with both initialized and uninitialized data definitions:

```
BYTE 20 DUP(0)            ; 20 bytes, all equal to zero
BYTE 20 DUP(?)            ; 20 bytes, uninitialized
BYTE  4 DUP("STACK")      ; 20 bytes: "STACKSTACKSTACKSTACK"
```

3.4.4 Defining WORD and SWORD Data

The WORD (define word) and SWORD (define signed word) directives create storage for one or more 16-bit integers. Here are some examples:

```
word1   WORD    65535        ; largest unsigned value
word2   SWORD   -32768       ; smallest signed value
word3   WORD    ?            ; uninitialized, unsigned
```

Older versions of the assembler used the DW directive to define both signed and unsigned words. You can still use DW:

```
val1    DW 65535             ; unsigned
val2    DW -32768            ; signed
```

Array of Words   You can create an array of word values either by explicitly initializing each element or by using the DUP operator. Here is an array containing specific values:

```
myList   WORD 1,2,3,4,5
```

Following is a diagram of the array in memory, if we assume that **myList** starts at offset 0. Notice that the addresses increment by 2:

Offset	Value
0000:	1
0002:	2
0004:	3
0006:	4
0008:	5

The DUP operator provides a convenient way to initialize multiple words:

```
array WORD 5 DUP(?)            ; 5 values, uninitialized
```

3.4.5 Defining DWORD and SDWORD Data

The DWORD (define doubleword) and SDWORD (define signed doubleword) directives allocate storage for one or more 32-bit integers. For example:

```
val1 DWORD    12345678h       ; unsigned
val2 SDWORD  −2147483648      ; signed
val3 DWORD    20 DUP(?)       ; unsigned array
```

Older versions of the assembler used the DD directive to define both unsigned and signed doublewords. You can still use DD:

```
val1 DD 12345678h                ; unsigned
val2 DD −2147483648              ; signed
```

Array of Doublewords You can create an array of doubleword values either by explicitly initializing each element or by using the DUP operator. Here is an array containing specific unsigned values:

```
myList DWORD 1,2,3,4,5
```

Shown below is a diagram of the array in memory, assuming that **myList** starts at offset 0. Notice that the offsets increment by 4:

Offset	Value
0000:	1
0004:	2
0008:	3
000C:	4
0010:	5

3.4.6 Defining QWORD Data

The QWORD (define quadword) directive allocates storage for 64-bit (8 byte) values. Here is an example:

```
quad1 QWORD 1234567812345678h
```

You can also use DQ, for compatibility with older assemblers:

```
quad1 DQ 1234567812345678h
```

3.4.7 Defining TBYTE Data

The TBYTE (define tenbyte) directive creates storage for 80-bit integers. This data type is primarily for the storage of binary-coded decimal numbers. Manipulating these values requires special instructions in the floating-point instruction set:

```
val1 TBYTE 1000000000123456789Ah
```

You can also use DT, for compatibility with older assemblers:

```
val1 DT 1000000000123456789Ah
```

3.4.8 Defining Real Number Data

REAL4 defines a 4-byte single-precision real variable. REAL8 defines an 8-byte double-precision real, and REAL10 defines a 10-byte double extended-precision real. Each requires one or more real constant initializers that can fit into the assigned storage:

```
rVal1     REAL4  -2.1
rVal2     REAL8   3.2E-260
```

```
rVal3        REAL10  4.6E+4096
ShortArray REAL4   20 DUP(0.0)
```

The following table describes each of the standard real types in terms of their minimum number of significant digits and approximate range:

Data Type	Significant Digits	Approximate Range
Short real	6	1.18×10^{-38} to 3.40×10^{38}
Long real	15	2.23×10^{-308} to 1.79×10^{308}
Extended-precision real	19	3.37×10^{-4932} to 1.18×10^{4932}

Programs written under earlier versions of the assembler used DD, DQ, and DT to define real numbers; these directives can still be used:

```
rVal1 DD  -1.2
rVal2 DQ   3.2E-260
rVal3 DT   4.6E+4096
```

3.4.9 Little Endian Order

Intel processors store and retrieve data from memory using what is referred to as *little endian* order. This means that the least significant byte of a variable is stored at the lowest address. The remaining bytes are stored in the next consecutive memory positions.

Consider the doubleword 12345678h. If placed in memory at offset 0, 78h would be stored in the first byte. 56h would be stored in the second byte, and the remaining bytes would be at offsets 3 and 4, as the following diagram shows:

```
                        0000: | 78 |
                        0001: | 56 |
        Little endian
                        0002: | 34 |
                        0003: | 12 |
```

Some other computer systems use *big endian* order (high to low). The following figure shows an example of 12345678h stored in big endian order at offset 0:

```
                        0000: | 12 |
                        0001: | 34 |
        Big endian:
                        0002: | 56 |
                        0003: | 78 |
```

3.4.10   Adding Variables to the AddSub Program

Let's return for a moment to the **AddSub** program we wrote in Section 3.2. Using the information we've developed regarding data definition directives, we can easily add a data segment containing several variables. The revised program is named **AddSub2**:

```
TITLE Add and Subtract, Version 2          (AddSub2.asm)

; This program adds and subtracts 32-bit unsigned
; integers and stores the sum in a variable.

INCLUDE Irvine32.inc
.data
val1  DWORD 10000h
val2  DWORD 40000h
val3  DWORD 20000h
finalVal DWORD ?

.code
main PROC
    mov  eax,val1            ; start with 10000h
    add  eax,val2            ; add 40000h
    sub  eax,val3            ; subtract 20000h
    mov  finalVal,eax        ; store the result (30000h)
    call DumpRegs            ; display the registers
    exit
main ENDP
END main
```

How does it work? First, the integer inside the variable **val1** is moved to EAX:

```
mov eax,val1                 ; start with 10000h
```

Next, the integer inside **val2** is added to EAX:

```
add eax,val2                 ; add 40000h
```

Next, the integer inside **val3** is subtracted from EAX:

```
sub eax,val3                 ; subtract 20000h
```

Finally, the integer in EAX is copied into the variable **finalVal**:

```
mov finalVal,eax             ; store the result (30000h)
```

3.4.11   Declaring Uninitialized Data

The .DATA? directive can be used to declare uninitialized data. It is particularly useful for large blocks of uninitialized data because it reduces the size of a compiled program. For example, the following code is declared efficiently:

```
.data
smallArray DWORD 10 DUP(0)        ; 40 bytes
```

```
.data?
bigArray DWORD 5000 DUP(?)              ; 20000 bytes
```

The following code, on the other hand, produces a compiled program that is 20,000 bytes larger:

```
.data
smallArray DWORD 10 DUP(0)              ; 40 bytes
bigArray DWORD 5000 DUP(?)              ; 20000 bytes
```

Mixing Code and Data   The assembler lets you switch back and forth between code and data in your programs. This can be convenient when you want to declare a variable that will be used only within a localized area of your program. In the following example, we create a variable named **temp** by inserting it directly within our code:

```
.code
mov eax,ebx
.data
temp DWORD ?
.code
mov temp,eax
. . .
```

Although it appears as if **temp** would interrupt the flow of executable instructions in this example, it turns out that the assembler places **temp** in the data segment along with all the other variables. The variable **temp** has *file scope,* making it visible to every statement within the same source code file.

3.4.12   Section Review

1. Create an uninitialized data declaration for a 16-bit signed integer.
2. Create an uninitialized data declaration for an 8-bit unsigned integer.
3. Create an uninitialized data declaration for an 8-bit signed integer.
4. Create an uninitialized data declaration for an 64-bit integer.
5. Which data type can hold a 32-bit signed integer?
6. Declare a 32-bit signed integer variable and initialize it with the smallest possible negative decimal value. (*Hint:* refer to integer ranges in Chapter 1.)
7. Declare an unsigned 16-bit integer variable named **wArray** that uses three initializers.
8. Declare a string variable containing the name of your favorite color. Initialize it as a null-terminated string.
9. Declare an uninitialized array of 50 unsigned doublewords named **dArray**.
10. Declare a string variable containing the word "TEST" repeated 500 times.
11. Declare an array of 20 unsigned bytes named **bArray** and initialize all elements to zero.
12. Show the order of individual bytes in memory (lowest to highest) for the following double-word variable:

```
val1 DWORD 87654321h
```

3.5 Symbolic Constants

A *symbolic constant* (or *symbol definition*) is created by associating an identifier (a symbol) and either an integer expression or some text. Unlike a variable definition, which reserves storage, a symbolic constant does not use any storage. Symbols are used only during the assembly of a program, so they cannot change at runtime. The following table summarizes their differences:

	Symbol	Variable
Uses storage?	no	yes
Value changes at run time?	no	yes

In the next section, we will show how to use the equal-sign directive (=) to create symbols that represent integer constants. After that, we will use the EQU and TEXTEQU directives to create symbols that represent arbitrary text.

3.5.1 Equal-Sign Directive

The *equal-sign* directive associates a symbol name with an integer expression (see Section 3.1.2). The syntax is:

```
name = expression
```

Ordinarily, *expression* is a 32-bit integer value. When a program is assembled, all occurrences of *name* are replaced by *expression* during the assembler's preprocessor step. For example, if the assembler reads the following lines,

```
COUNT = 500
mov   al,COUNT
```

it generates and assembles the following statement:

```
mov   al,500
```

Why Use Symbols?   We might have skipped the COUNT symbol entirely and simply coded the MOV instruction with the literal 500, but experience has shown that programs are easier to read and maintain if symbols are used. Suppose COUNT were used ten times throughout a program. At a later time, it could be increased to 600 by altering only a single line of code:

```
COUNT = 600
```

When the program was assembled again, all instances of the symbol COUNT would automatically be replaced by 600. Without this symbol, the programmer would have to manually find and replace every 500 with 600 in the program's source code. What if one occurrence of 500 were not actually related to all of the others? Then a bug would be caused by changing it to 600.

Keyboard Definitions   Programs often define symbols for important keyboard characters. For example, 27 is the ASCII code for the Esc key:

```
Esc_key = 27
```

Later in the same program, a statement is more self-describing if it uses the symbol rather than an immediate value. Use this,

```
    mov   al,Esc_key              ; good style
```

rather than this:

```
    mov   al,27                   ; poor style
```

Using the DUP Operator   Section 3.4.3.3 showed how to use the DUP operator to create storage for arrays and strings. It is good coding style to combine a symbolic constant with DUP because it simplifies program maintenance. In the next example, if COUNT has already been defined, it can be used in the following data definition:

```
array COUNT DUP(0)
```

Redefinitions   A symbol defined with = can be redefined any number of times. The following example shows how the assembler evaluates COUNT each time it changes value:

```
COUNT = 5
mov al,COUNT                   ; AL = 5
COUNT = 10
mov al,COUNT                   ; AL = 10
COUNT = 100
mov al,COUNT                   ; AL = 100
```

The changing value of a symbol such as COUNT has nothing to do with the runtime execution order of statements. Instead, the symbol changes value according to the sequential processing of your source code by the assembler.

3.5.2   Calculating the Sizes of Arrays and Strings

Often when using an array, we would like to know its size. In the following example, we create a constant named **ListSize** and manually count the bytes in **list**:

```
list BYTE 10,20,30,40
ListSize = 43
```

But this is not good practice if this code must be later modified and maintained. If we were to add more bytes to **list**, **ListSize** would also have to be corrected or a program bug would result. A better way to handle this situation would be to let the assembler automatically calculate **List-Size** for us. MASM uses the $ operator (*current location counter*) to return the offset associated

with the current program statement. In the following example, **ListSize** is calculated by subtracting the offset of **list** from the current location counter ($):

```
list BYTE 10,20,30,40
ListSize = ($ - list)
```

It is important for **ListSize** to follow immediately after **list**. The following, for example,
would produce too large a value for **ListSize** because of the storage used by **var2**:

```
list BYTE 10,20,30,40
var2 BYTE 20 DUP(?)
ListSize = ($ - list)
```

String lengths are time consuming to calculate manually, so you can let the assembler do
the job for you:

```
myString  BYTE "This is a long string, containing"
          BYTE "any number of characters"
myString_len = ($ – myString)
```

Arrays of Words and DoubleWords   If each element in an array contains a 16-bit word, the
array's total size in bytes must be divided by 2 to produce the number of array elements:

```
list   WORD   1000h,2000h,3000h,4000h
ListSize = ($ – list) / 2
```

Similarly, each element of an array of doublewords is 4 bytes long, so its overall length must be
divided by 4 to produce the number of array elements:

```
list   DWORD   10000000h,20000000h,30000000h,40000000h
ListSize = ($ –list) / 4
```

3.5.3   EQU Directive

The EQU directive associates a symbolic name with either an integer expression or some arbitrary text. There are three formats:

```
name EQU expression
name EQU symbol
name EQU <text>
```

In the first format, *expression* must be a valid integer expression (see Section 3.1.2). In the second format, *symbol* is an existing symbol name, already defined with = or EQU. In the third format, any text may appear within the brackets <...>. When the assembler encounters *name* later in
the program, it substitutes the integer value or text for the symbol.

EQU can be useful when defining any value that does not evaluate to an integer. A real
number constant, for example, can be defined using EQU:

```
PI EQU <3.1416>
```

Example   We can associate a symbol with a character string. Then a variable can be created using the symbol:

```
pressKey EQU <"Press any key to continue...",0>
.
.
.data
prompt  BYTE    pressKey
```

Example   Suppose we would like to define a symbol that calculates the number of cells in a 10-by-10 integer matrix. We will define symbols two different ways, first as an integer expression, and second as a text expression. The two symbols are then used in data definitions:

```
matrix1   EQU   10 * 10
matrix2   EQU   <10 * 10>
.data
M1 WORD matrix1
M2 WORD matrix2
```

The assembler will produce different data definitions for **M1** and **M2**. The integer expression in **matrix1** is evaluated and assigned to **M1**. On the other hand, the text in **matrix2** is copied directly into the data definition for **M2**:

```
M1 WORD  100
M2 WORD  10 * 10
```

No Redefinition   Unlike the = directive, a symbol defined with EQU cannot be redefined in the same source code file. This may be seen as a restriction, but it also prevents an existing symbol from being inadvertently assigned a new value.

3.5.4 TEXTEQU Directive

The TEXTEQU directive, introduced in MASM Version 6, is very similar to EQU. It creates what Microsoft calls a *text macro*. There are three different formats: the first assigns text; the second assigns the contents of an existing text macro, and the third assigns a constant integer expression:

```
name TEXTEQU <text>
name TEXTEQU textmacro
name TEXTEQU %constExpr
```

For example, the **prompt1** variable uses the **continueMsg** text macro:

```
continueMsg TEXTEQU <"Do you wish to continue (Y/N)?">
.data
prompt1 BYTE continueMsg
```

Text macros can easily build on each other. In the next example, **count** is set to the value of an integer expression involving **rowSize**. Next, the symbol **move** is defined as **mov**. Then **setupAL** incorporates the values of **move** and **count**:

```
rowSize = 5
count    TEXTEQU   %(rowSize * 2)     ; same as: count TEXTEQU <10>
move     TEXTEQU   <mov>
setupAL  TEXTEQU   <move al,count>
; same as: setupAL TEXTEQU <mov al,10>
```

Unlike the EQU directive, a symbol defined with TEXTEQU can be redefined later in the program.

Compatibility Note: TEXTEQU was first introduced in MASM version 6. If you're writing assembler code that must be compatible with various assemblers including earlier versions of MASM, you should use EQU rather than TEXTEQU.

3.5.5   Section Review

1. Declare a symbolic constant using the equal-sign directive that contains the ASCII code (08h) for the Backspace key.
2. Declare a symbolic constant named **SecondsInDay** using the equal-sign directive and assign it an arithmetic expression that calculates the number of seconds in a 24-hour period.
3. Show how to calculate the number of bytes in the following array and assign the value to a symbolic constant named **ArraySize**:

```
myArray WORD 20 DUP(?)
```

4. Show how to calculate the number of elements in the following array and assign the value to a symbolic constant named **ArraySize**:

```
myArray DWORD 30 DUP(?)
```

5. Use a TEXTEQU expression to redefine "PROC" as "PROCEDURE."
6. Use TEXTEQU to create a symbol named **Sample** for a string constant, and then use the symbol when defining a string variable named **MyString**.
7. Use TEXTEQU to assign the symbol **SetupESI** to the following line of code:

```
mov esi,OFFSET myArray
```

3.6   Real-Address Mode Programming (*Optional*)

If you are programming for MS-DOS or for Linux's DOS Emulation feature, you can easily code your programs as 16-bit applications to run in Real-address mode. We will assume that you are using an Intel386 or later processor. When we call this a *16-bit* application, we refer to the use of 16-bit segments, also known as *Real-address mode* segments.

3.6.1   Basic Changes

There are only a few changes you must make to the 32-bit programs presented in this chapter to transform them into 16-bit programs:

- The INCLUDE directive references a different library:

  ```
  INCLUDE Irvine16.inc
  ```

- Two additional instructions must be inserted at the beginning of the startup procedure (main). They initialize the DS register to the starting location of the data segment, identified by the predefined MASM constant **@data**:

  ```
  mov ax,@data
  mov ds,ax
  ```

- The batch file that assembles and links your programs is named **make16.bat** (we will show an example later).
- Offsets (addresses) of data and code labels are 16 bits rather than 32 bits.

> You cannot move @data directly into DS because the Intel instruction set does not permit a constant to be moved directly to a segment register.

3.6.1.1   The AddSub2 Program

Here is a listing of the *AddSub2.asm* Program, revised to run in Real-address mode. New lines are marked by comments:

```
TITLE Add and Subtract, Version 2    (AddSub2.asm)

; This program adds and subtracts 32-bit integers
; and stores the sum in a variable.
; Target: Real-address mode.

INCLUDE Irvine16.inc        ; new
.data
val1     DWORD 10000h
val2     DWORD 40000h
val3     DWORD 20000h
finalVal DWORD ?

.code
main PROC
    mov ax,@data            ; initialize DS
    mov ds,ax               ; new

    mov eax,val1            ; get first value
    add eax,val2            ; add second value
    sub eax,val3            ; subtract third value
    mov finalVal,eax        ; store the result
    call DumpRegs           ; display registers
```

```
    exit
main ENDP
END main
```

3.7 Chapter Summary

An integer expression is a mathematical expression involving integer constants, symbolic constants, and arithmetic operators. Precedence refers to the implied order of operations when an expression contains two or more operators.

A character constant is a single character enclosed in either single or double quotes. The assembler converts a character to the binary ASCII code matching the character. A string constant is a string of characters enclosed in either single or double quotation marks, possibly ending with a null byte.

Assembly language has a list of reserved words, shown in Appendix D, that have special meanings and can only be used in their correct contexts. An identifier is a programmer-chosen name that can identify a variable, a symbolic constant, a procedure, or a code label. It cannot be a reserved word.

A directive is a command that is recognized and acted upon by the assembler as the program's source code is assembled. An instruction is a statement that is executed by the processor at runtime. An instruction mnemonic is a short assembler keyword that identifies the operation carried out by an instruction. A label is an identifier that acts as a place-marker for either instructions or data.

An assembly language instruction can have between zero and three operands, each of which can be a register, memory operand, constant expression, or I/O port.

Programs contain logical segments named code, data, and stack. The code segment contains executable instructions. The stack segment holds procedure parameters, local variables, and return addresses. The data segment holds variables.

A source file is a text file containing assembly language statements. A listing file contains a copy of the program's source code, suitable for printing, with line numbers, offset addresses, translated machine code, and a symbol table. A map file contains information about a program's segments. A source file is created with a text editor. The assembler (MASM) is a program that reads the source file, producing both object and listing files. The linker reads the object file and produces an executable file. The latter can be executed by the operating system.

MASM recognizes intrinsic data types, each of which describes a set of values that can be assigned to variables and expressions of the given type:

- BYTE and SBYTE define 8-bit variables.
- WORD and SWORD define 16-bit variables.
- DWORD and SDWORD define32-bit variables.
- QWORD and TBYTE define 8-byte and 10-byte variables, respectively.
- REAL4, REAL8, and REAL10 define 4-byte, 8-byte, and 10-byte real number variables, respectively.

A data definition statement sets aside storage in memory for a variable and may optionally assign a name to the variable. If multiple initializers are used in the same data definition, its label refers only to the offset of the first byte. To create a string data definition, enclose a sequence of characters in quotation marks. The DUP operator generates a repeated storage allocation, using a constant expression as a counter. The current location counter operator ($) can be used in an expression that calculates the number of bytes in an array.

Intel processors store and retrieve data from memory using little endian order. This means that the least significant byte of a variable is stored at the lowest memory address.

A symbolic constant (or symbol definition) is created by associating an identifier (a symbol) with an integer or text expression. There are three directives that create symbolic constants:

- The equal-sign directive associates a symbol name with an integer expression.
- The EQU and TEXTEQU directives associate a symbolic name with either an integer expression or some arbitrary text.

It is easy to switch between writing 32-bit Protected mode and 16-bit Real mode programs, if you keep in mind a few differences. The book is supplied with two link libraries containing the same procedure names for both types of programs.

3.8   Programming Exercises

The following exercises can be done in either Protected mode or Real-address mode.

1. Subtracting Three Integers

Using the **AddSub** program from Section 3.2 as a reference, write a program that subtracts three 16-bit integers using only registers. Insert a **call DumpRegs** statement to display the register values.

2. Data Definitions

Write a program that contains a definition of each data type listed in Section 3.4. Initialize each variable to a value that is consistent with its data type.

3. Symbolic Integer Constants

Write a program that defines symbolic constants for all of the days of the week. Create an array variable that uses the symbols as initializers.

4. Symbolic Text Constants

Write a program that defines symbolic names for several string literals (characters between quotes). Use each symbolic name in a variable definition.

4

Data Transfers, Addressing, and Arithmetic

4.1   Data Transfer Instructions

4.1.1   Introduction

In this chapter, you're going to be exposed to a surprising amount of detailed information. You will encounter a major difference between assembly language and high-level languages: In assembly language, you can (and must) control every detail. You have ultimate power, and along with it, enormous responsibility.

When you took your first programming course (probably C++ or Java), you noticed that the compiler performed strict type checking on variables and assignment statements. While you might have found it to be annoying at first, the compiler probably turned out to be your best friend when it came to preventing logic errors relating to mismatching data. An assembler, on the other hand, gives you an enormous amount of freedom when declaring and moving data. It performs little error checking, and it supplies operators and addressing expressions that let you do just about anything. What price must you pay for this power? You must master a significant number of details before writing meaningful programs.

If you take the time to thoroughly learn the material presented in this chapter, you will enjoy much smoother sailing later on. In particular, as the example programs become more complicated, you will rely on your mastery of the fundamental tools presented here. You may be happy to learn that near the end of this chapter you can begin using loops and arrays.

4.1.2   Operand Types

There are only three types of instruction operands presented in this chapter: *immediate*, *register*, and *memory*. Of these, only the third is in the least way complicated. Table 4-1 lists a simple notation for operands that has been freely adapted from the Intel Pentium manual. We will use it from this point on to describe the syntax of individual Intel instructions.

Table 4-1   Instruction Operand Notation.

Operand	Description
r8	8-bit general-purpose register: AH, AL, BH, BL, CH, CL, DH, DL
r16	16-bit general-purpose register: AX, BX, CX, DX, SI, DI, SP, BP
r32	32-bit general-purpose register: EAX, EBX, ECX, EDX, ESI, EDI, ESP, EBP

Table 4-1   Instruction Operand Notation. (Continued)

Operand	Description
reg	any general-purpose register
sreg	16-bit segment register: CS, DS, SS, ES, FS, GS
imm	8-, 16-, or 32-bit immediate value
imm8	8-bit immediate byte value
imm16	16-bit immediate word value
imm32	32-bit immediate doubleword value
r/m8	8-bit operand which can be an 8-bit general register or memory byte
r/m16	16-bit operand which can be a 16-bit general register or memory word
r/m32	32-bit operand which can be a 32-bit general register or memory doubleword
mem	an 8-, 16-, or 32-bit memory operand

4.1.3   Direct Memory Operands

Section 3.4 in Chapter 3 showed that variable names are simply references to offsets within the data segment. For example, the following declaration indicates that a byte containing the number 10h has been placed in the data segment:

```
.data
var1 BYTE 10h
```

Suppose **var1** were located at offset 10400h. Then a machine-level instruction referencing this data would be assembled as:

```
mov al,[00010400]
```

The right-hand operand is a 32-bit hexadecimal reference to a memory location. The brackets around the number indicate that when the instruction executes, the CPU dereferences the offset and obtains the contents of memory. (To *dereference* something means to look up the information it implies.)

While it might be possible to write programs that used numeric addresses as operands, it is much easier to use symbolic names such as **var1**. The assembler automatically converts a name such as **var1** to its numeric offset and then dereferences the offset:

```
mov  al,var1
```

> **Alternative Notation.** Some programmers prefer to use the following notation with direct operands because the brackets imply a dereference operation:
>
> ```
> mov  al,[var1]
> ```
>
> MASM permits this notation, so you can use it in your own programs if you want. Because so many programs (including those from Microsoft) are printed without the brackets, we will only use them in this book when an arithmetic expression is involved:
>
> ```
> mov  al,[var1 + 5]
> ```
>
> (This is called a direct-offset operand, a subject discussed at length in Section 4.1.8.)

4.1.4   MOV Instruction

The MOV instruction copies data from a source operand to a destination operand. Known as a *data transfer* instruction, it is used in virtually every program. Its basic format shows that the first operand is the destination and the second operand is the source:

```
MOV destination,source
```

The destination operand's contents change, but the source operand is unchanged. The right to left movement of data is similar to the assignent statement in C++ or Java:

```
dest = source;
```

(In nearly all assembly language instructions, the left-hand operand is the destination and the right-hand operand is the source.)

MOV is very flexible in its use of operands, as long as the following rules are observed:

- Both operands must be the same size.
- Both operands cannot be memory operands.
- CS, EIP, and IP cannot be destination operands.
- An immediate value cannot be moved to a segment register.

Here is a list of the general variants of MOV, excluding segment registers:

```
MOV reg,reg
MOV mem,reg
MOV reg,mem
MOV mem,imm
MOV reg,imm
```

Segment registers can be used only when the program is running in Real-address mode. The following options are available, with the exception that CS cannot be a target operand:

```
MOV r/m16,sreg
MOV sreg,r/m16
```

Memory to Memory   A single MOV instruction cannot be used to move data directly from one memory location to another. Instead, you can move the source operand's value to a register before moving it to the destination operand:

```
.data
var1 WORD ?
var2 WORD ?
.code
mov  ax,var1
mov  var2,ax
```

You must consider the minimum number of bytes required by an integer constant when copying it to a variable or register. For unsigned integer constants, refer to Table 1-4 in Chapter 1. For signed integer constants, refer to Table 1–7, also in Chapter 1.

4.1.5   Zero/Sign Extension of Integers

4.1.5.1   Copying Smaller Values to Larger Ones

We have already pointed out that if you try to use the MOV instruction to copy an integer from a smaller operand to a larger one, an error results. But sometimes you really have to make such a move. For example, suppose **count** (unsigned, 16-bits) must be moved to ECX (32 bits). A simple solution is to set ECX to zero and then move **count** to CX:

```
.data
count WORD 1
.code
mov ecx,0
mov cx,count
```

What happens if we try the same approach with a signed integer equal to −16?

```
.data
signedVal SWORD -1          ; FFF0h  (-16)
.code
mov ecx,0
mov cx,signedVal            ; ECX = 0000FFF0h  (+65520)
```

The value in ECX (+65520) is completely different from −16. On the other hand, if we had filled ECX first with FFFFFFFFh and then copied **signedVal** to CX, the final value would have been correct:

```
mov ecx,0FFFFFFFFh
mov cx,signedVal            ; ECX = FFFFFFF0h  (-16)
```

This presents a problem when dealing with signed integers: we don't want to have to check their values to see if they are positive or negative before deciding how to fill destination operands. Fortunately, the engineers at Intel noticed this problem when designing the Intel386 processor, and introduced the MOVZX and MOVSX instructions to deal with both unsigned and signed integers.

4.1.5.2   MOVZX Instruction

The MOVZX instruction (move with zero-extend) copies the contents of a source operand into a destination operand and zero-extends the value to either 16 or 32 bits. This instruction is only used with unsigned integers. There are three variants:

```
MOVZZ   r32,r/m8
MOVZX   r32,r/m16
MOVZX   r16,r/m8
```

(Operand notation was explained in Table 4-1.) In each of the three variants, the first operand is the destination and the second is the source. The destination must be a register. The following figure shows an 8-bit source operand zero-extended into a 16-bit destination:

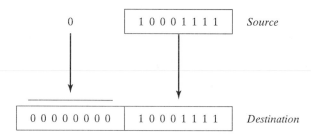

The following examples use registers for all operands, showing all the size variations:

```
mov     bx,0A69Bh
movzx   eax,bx          ; EAX = 0000A69Bh
movzx   edx,bl          ; EDX = 0000009Bh
movzx   cx,bl           ; CX  = 009Bh
```

The following examples use memory operands for the source and produce the same results:

```
.data
byte1 BYTE 9Bh
word1 WORD 0A69Bh
.code
movzx   eax,word1       ; EAX = 0000A69Bh
movzx   edx,byte1       ; EDX = 0000009Bh
movzx   cx,byte1        ; CX  = 009Bh
```

> If you plan to run and test the book's examples in Real-address mode, don't forget to INCLUDE Irvine16.lib and insert the following lines at the beginning of the main procedure:
>
> ```
> mov ax,@data
> mov ds,ax
> ```

4.1.5.3   MOVSX Instruction

The MOVSX instruction (move with sign-extend) copies the contents of a source operand into a destination operand and sign-extends the value to either 16 or 32 bits. This instruction is only used with signed integers. There are three variants:

```
MOVSX  r32,r/m8
MOVSX  r32,r/m16
MOVSX  r16,r/m8
```

An operand is sign-extended by taking the smaller operand's highest bit and repeating (replicating) the bit throughout the extended bits in the destination operand. For example, if an 8-bit value of 10001111b is moved to a 16-bit destination, the lowest 8 bits are copied as is. Next, as shown in the following figure, the highest bit of the source is copied into each of the high 8 bit positions of the destination:

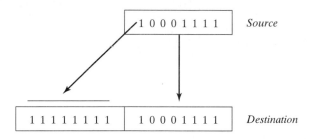

The following examples use registers for all operands, using all the size variations:

```
mov    bx,0A69Bh
movsx  eax,bx                 ; EAX = FFFFA69Bh
movsx  edx,bl                 ; EDX = FFFFFF9Bh
movsx  cx,bl                  ; CX  = FF9Bh
```

4.1.6   LAHF and SAHF Instructions

The LAHF (load status flags into AH) instruction copies the low byte of the EFLAGS register into AH. The following flags are copied: Sign, Zero, Auxiliary Carry, Parity, and Carry. Using this instruction, you can easily save a copy of the flags in a variable for safekeeping:

```
.data
saveflags BYTE ?
.code
lahf                          ; load flags into AH
mov saveflags,ah              ; save them in a variable
```

The SAHF (store AH into status flags) instruction copies AH into the low byte of the EFLAGS register. For example, you can retrieve the values of flags saved earlier in a variable:

```
mov ah,saveflags              ; load saved flags into AH
sahf                          ; copy into Flags register
```

4.1.7   XCHG Instruction

The XCHG (exchange data) instruction exchanges the contents of two operands. There are three variants:

```
XCHG reg,reg
XCHG reg,mem
XCHG mem,reg
```

The rules for operands in the XCHG instruction are the same as those for the MOV instruction, explained in Section 4.1.3.

In array sorting applications, XCHG provides a simple way to exchange two array elements. Here are a few examples using XCHG:

```
xchg   ax,bx               ; exchange 16-bit regs
xchg   ah,al               ; exchange 8-bit regs
xchg   var1,bx             ; exchange 16-bit mem op with BX
xchg   eax,ebx             ; exchange 32-bit regs
```

To exchange two memory operands, use a register as a temporary container and combine MOV with XCHG:

```
mov   ax,val1
xchg  ax,val2
mov   val1,ax
```

4.1.8   Direct-Offset Operands

You can add a displacement to the name of a variable, creating a direct-offset operand. This lets you access memory locations that may not have explicit labels. Let's begin with an array of bytes named **arrayB**:

```
arrayB   BYTE 10h,20h,30h,40h,50h
```

If we use MOV with **arrayB** as the source operand, we automatically move the first byte in the array:

```
mov al,arrayB                   ; AL = 10h
```

We can access the second byte in the array by adding 1 to the offset of **arrayB**:

```
mov al,[arrayB+1]               ; AL = 20h
```

The third byte is accessed by adding 2:

```
mov al,[arrayB+2]               ; AL = 30h
```

An expression such as **arrayB+1** produces what is called an *effective address* by adding a constant to the variable's offset. When we surround an effective address with brackets, it is to show that the expression is dereferenced to obtain the contents of its target memory location. The brackets are not required by MASM, so you can also write:

```
mov al,arrayB+1
```

Range Checking   MASM has no built-in range checking for effective addresses. If we execute the following statement, the assembler just retrieves a byte of memory outside the array. This creates a hard-to-find logic bug, so programmers try to be extra careful when checking array references:

```
mov al,[arrayB+20]                    ; AL = ??
```

Word and Doubleword Arrays   If you're using an array of 16-bit words, remember that the offset of each array element is two bytes beyond the previous one. That is why we add 2 to **ArrayW** in the next example to reach the second element:

```
.data
arrayW WORD 100h,200h,300h
.code
mov ax,arrayW                         ; AX = 100h
mov ax,[arrayW+2]                     ; AX = 200h
```

Similarly, the second element in a doubleword array is four bytes beyond the first one:

```
.data
arrayD DWORD 10000h,20000h
.code
mov eax,arrayD                        ; EAX = 10000h
mov eax,[arrayD+4]                    ; EAX = 20000h
```

4.1.9   Example Program (Moves)

The following program demonstrates most of the data movement examples shown in Section 4.1:

```
TITLE Data Transfer Examples              (Moves.asm)

INCLUDE Irvine32.inc
.data
val1  WORD 1000h
val2  WORD 2000h
arrayB  BYTE  10h,20h,30h,40h,50h
arrayW  WORD  100h,200h,300h
arrayD  DWORD 10000h,20000h

.code
main PROC

;   MOVZX
    mov    bx,0A69Bh
    movzx  eax,bx                     ; EAX = 0000A69Bh
    movzx  edx,bl                     ; EDX = 0000009Bh
    movzx  cx,bl                      ; CX  = 009Bh
```

```
;   MOVSX
    mov    bx,0A69Bh
    movsx eax,bx                    ; EAX = FFFFA69Bh
    movsx edx,bl                    ; EDX = FFFFFF9Bh
    movsx cx,bl                     ; CX  = FF9Bh

;   Memory-to-memory exchange:
    mov    ax,val1                  ; AX = 1000h
    xchg ax,val2                    ; AX = 2000h, val2 = 1000h
    mov    val1,ax                  ; val1 = 2000h

;   Direct-Offset Addressing (byte array):
    mov al,arrayB                   ; AL = 10h
    mov al,[arrayB+1]               ; AL = 20h
    mov al,[arrayB+2]               ; AL = 30h

;   Direct-Offset Addressing (word array):
    mov ax,arrayW                   ; AX = 100h
    mov ax,[arrayW+2]               ; AX = 200h

;   Direct-Offset Addressing (doubleword array):
    mov eax,arrayD                  ; EAX = 10000h
    mov eax,[arrayD+4]              ; EAX = 20000h

    exit
main ENDP
END main
```

This program generates no screen output, but you can (and should) run it using a debugger. Please refer to the tutorial on the book's Web site that shows how to use the Microsoft Visual Studio debugger. In Chapter 5 (Section 5.3) you will learn how to display integer values on the screen by making calls to a function library supplied with this book.

4.1.10 Section Review

1. What are the three basic types of operands?
2. *(True/False):* The destination operand of a MOV instruction cannot be a segment register.
3. *(True/False):* In a MOV instruction, the second operand is known as the *destination* operand.
4. *(True/False):* The EIP register cannot be the destination operand of a MOV instruction.
5. In the operation notation used by Intel, what does *r/m32* indicate?
6. In the operation notation used by Intel, what does *imm16* indicate?

Use the following variable definitions for the remaining questions in this section:

```
.data
var1 SBYTE -4,-2,3,1
var2 WORD 1000h,2000h,3000h,4000h
```

```
var3 SWORD -16,-42
var4 DWORD 1,2,3,4,5
```

7. For each of the following statements, state whether or not the instruction is valid:

```
a. mov ax,var1
b. mov ax,var2
c. mov eax,var3
d. mov var2,var3
e. movzx ax,var2
f. movzx var2,al
g. mov ds,ax
h. mov ds,1000h
```

8. What will be the hexadecimal value of the destination operand after each of the following instructions executes in sequence?

```
mov AL,var1                    ; a.
mov AH,var1+3                  ; b.
```

9. What will be the value of the destination operand after each of the following instructions executes in sequence?

```
mov ax,var2                    ; a.
mov ax,var2+4                  ; b.
mov ax,var3                    ; c.
mov ax,var3-2                  ; d.
```

10. What will be the value of the destination operand after each of the following instructions executes in sequence?

```
mov edx,var4                   ; a.
movzx edx,var2                 ; b.
mov edx,var4+4                 ; c.
movsx edx,var1                 ; d.
```

4.2 Addition and Subtraction

Integer addition and subtraction are two of the most fundamental operations that a CPU can perform. In this section, we explore instructions that perform binary addition and subtraction: INC (increment), DEC (decrement), ADD, SUB, and NEG (negate).

4.2.1 INC and DEC Instructions

The INC (increment) and DEC (decrement) instructions, respectively, add 1 and subtract 1 from a single operand. The syntax is:

```
INC reg/mem
DEC reg/mem
```

Following are some examples:

```
.data
myWord WORD 1000h
.code
inc myWord                    ; 1001h
mov bx,myWord
dec bx                        ; 1000h
```

4.2.2   ADD Instruction

The ADD instruction adds a source operand to a destination operand of the same size. The syntax is:

```
ADD dest,source
```

Source is unchanged by the operation, and the sum is stored in the destination operand. The set of possible operands is the same as for the MOV instruction (see Section 4.1.4). Here is a short code example that adds two 32-bit integers:

```
.data
var1 DWORD 10000h
var2 DWORD 20000h
.code
mov eax,var1
add eax,var2                  ; 30000h
```

Flags   The Carry, Zero, Sign, Overflow, Auxiliary Carry, and Parity flags are changed according to the value of the destination operand. We will elaborate on flag values in Section 4.2.6.

4.2.3   SUB Instruction

The SUB instruction subtracts a source operand from a destination operand. The set of possible operands is the same as for the ADD and MOV instructions (see Section 4.1.4). The syntax is:

```
SUB dest,source
```

Here is a short code example that subtracts two 32-bit integers:

```
.data
var1 DWORD 30000h
var2 DWORD 10000h
.code
mov eax,var1
sub eax,var2                  ; 20000h
```

The CPU performs subtraction by first negating and then adding. For example, 4 − 1 is really 4 + (−1). Recall that two's complement notation is used for negative numbers, so −1 is represented by 11111111, as shown below:

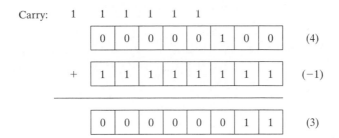

This addition generated a carry out of the highest bit position, but the carry bit is ignored for all signed arithmetic.

Flags   The Carry, Zero, Sign, Overflow, Auxiliary Carry, and Parity flags are changed according to the value of the destination operand. We will elaborate on this in Section 4.2.6.

4.2.4   NEG Instruction

The NEG (negate) instruction reverses the sign of a number by converting the number to its two's complement. The following operands are permitted:

```
NEG reg
NEG mem
```

Recall that the two's complement of a number can be found by reversing all the bits in the destination operand and adding 1.

Flags   The Carry, Zero, Sign, Overflow, Auxiliary Carry, and Parity flags are changed according to the value of the destination operand. We will elaborate on this in Section 4.2.6.

4.2.5   Implementing Arithmetic Expressions

Armed with the ADD, SUB, and NEG instructions, you now have the means to implement arithmetic expressions involving addition, subtraction, and negation in assembly language. In other words, we can simulate what a C++ compiler might do when reading an expression such as:

```
Rval = -Xval + (Yval - Zval);
```

The following signed 32-bit variables will be used:

```
Rval SDWORD ?
Xval SDWORD 26
Yval SDWORD 30
Zval SDWORD 40
```

When translating an expression, it is useful to evaluate each term separately and combine the terms at the end. First, we negate a copy of **Xval**:

```
; first term: -Xval
    mov   eax,Xval
    neg   eax                  ; EAX = -26
```

Then **Yval** is copied to a register and **Zval** is subtracted from it:

```
; second term: (Yval - Zval)
   mov   ebx,Yval
   sub   ebx,Zval            ; EBX = -10
```

Finally, the two terms (in EAX and EBX) are added:

```
; add the terms and store:
   add   eax,ebx
   mov   Rval,eax            ; -36
```

4.2.6   Flags Affected by Arithmetic

Whenever a program performs arithmetic, there is a possibility of errors caused by overflow (values either too small or too large). High-level languages generally do not detect integer overflow, leading to hard-to-catch bugs in program execution. In assembly language, on the other hand, you have a good deal of control over overflow errors because you can check the values of the CPU status flags after each operation.

Our discussion of the status flags in this section applies to the ADD, SUB, INC, and DEC instructions. Two other status flags, Auxiliary Carry and Parity, are less important and will be deferred until later.

You can display the values of the CPU status flags in your programs by inserting a call to the DumpRegs procedure, shown in Chapter 3.

4.2.6.1   Zero and Sign Flags

The Zero flag is set when the destination operand of an arithmetic instruction is assigned a value of zero. For example:

```
mov cx,1
sub cx,1                     ; CX = 0, ZF = 1
mov ax,0FFFFh
inc ax                       ; AX = 0, ZF = 1
inc ax                       ; AX = 1, ZF = 0
```

The Sign flag is set when the result of an arithmetic operation is negative. For example:

```
mov cx,0
sub cx,1                     ; CX = -1, SF = 1
add cx,2                     ; CX = 1, SF = 0
```

4.2.6.2   Carry Flag (unsigned arithmetic)

The Carry flag is significant only when the CPU performs unsigned arithmetic. If the result of an unsigned addition operation is too large (or too small) for the destination operand, the Carry flag is set. For example, the next ADD instruction sets the Carry flag because the sum will not fit into AL, an 8-bit register:

```
mov al,0FFh
add al,1                    ; CF = 1,  AL = 00
```

The following diagram shows what happens at the bit level when we add 1 to 0FFh. The carry out of the highest bit position of AL is automatically placed in the Carry flag:

| Carry: | 1 | 1 | 1 | 1 | 1 | 1 | 1 | 1 |

	1	1	1	1	1	1	1	1
+	0	0	0	0	0	0	0	1

| 0 | 0 | 0 | 0 | 0 | 0 | 0 | 0 |

On the other hand, if we add 1 to 00FFh in AX, the sum easily fits into 16 bits and the Carry flag is cleared:

```
mov ax,00FFh
add ax,1                    ; CF = 0,  AX = 0100h
```

If we add 1 to FFFFh in the AX register, a Carry is generated out of the high bit of AX:

```
mov ax,0FFFFh
add ax,1                    ; CF = 1, AX = 0000h
```

If we subtract a larger unsigned integer from a smaller one, the Carry flag is set and the value in AL is invalid:

```
mov al,1
sub al,2                    ; CF = 1
```

> The INC and DEC instructions do not affect the Carry flag.

4.2.6.3   Overflow Flag (signed arithmetic)

The Overflow flag is relevant only when performing signed arithmetic. Specifically, it is set when an arithmetic operation generates a signed result that cannot fit in the destination operand. For example, the largest signed value that may be stored in a byte is +127; if we add 1 to this, the Overflow flag is set:

```
mov   al,+127
add   al,1                  ; OF = 1
```

Similarly, the smallest negative byte value is −128. If we subtract 1 from this, the Overflow flag is set:

```
mov  al,-128
sub  al,1                        ; OF = 1
```

The Addition Test   There is a very easy way to tell if signed overflow has occurred when adding two operands. Overflow has occurred if:

- Two positive operands were added and their sum is negative.
- Two negative operands were added and their sum is positive.

Overflow never occurs when the signs of two addition operands are different.

The CPU Knows   The CPU detects signed overflow in a mechanical way. It compares the Carry flag to the bit that is carried into the sign bit of the destination operand. If they are unequal, the Overflow flag is set. For example, when adding the binary values 10000000 and 11111110, there is no carry from bit 6 to bit 7, but there is a carry from bit 7 into the Carry flag. Overflow has occurred, as shown in the following figure:

```
                             No carry from bit 6 to 7
                             7 6 5
        CF = 1  ◄─────── 1 0 0 0 0 0 0 0
                     +   1 1 1 1 1 1 1 0
                     =   0 1 1 1 1 1 1 0
```

A slightly more technical way of explaining overflow is to say that the Carry flag is assigned the result of exclusive-ORing the carry out of bit 7 with the carry out of bit 6. The exclusive-OR operation only returns a 1 when its two input bits are different.

NEG Instruction   The NEG instruction can produce an invalid result if the destination operand cannot be stored correctly. For example, if we move −128 to AL and try to negate it, the value +128 cannot be stored in AL. This causes the Overflow flag to be set, and an invalid value to be moved to AL:

```
mov al,-128              ; AL = 10000000b
neg al                   ; AL = 10000000b, OF = 1
```

On the other hand, if +127 is negated, the result is valid and the Overflow flag is clear:

```
mov al,+127              ; AL = 01111111b
neg al                   ; AL = 10000001b, OF = 0
```

Students often ask how the CPU knows whether a number is signed or unsigned. One can only give what seems to be a dumb answer: The CPU doesn't know—only the programmer knows. The CPU sets all the status flags after an operation, not knowing which of the flags will be important to the programmer. The programmer chooses which flags to interpret, and which flags to ignore.

4.2.7   Example Program (AddSub3)

Let's look at a simple example program that demonstrates the ADD, SUB, INC, DEC, and NEG instructions, and shows how the CPU status flags are affected:

```
TITLE Addition and Subtraction        (AddSub3.asm)

INCLUDE Irvine32.inc
.data
Rval    SDWORD ?
Xval    SDWORD 26
Yval    SDWORD 30
Zval    SDWORD 40

.code
main PROC
    ; INC and DEC
    mov ax,1000h
    inc ax                      ; 1001h
    dec ax                      ; 1000h

    ; Expression: Rval = -Xval + (Yval - Zval)
    mov   eax,Xval
    neg   eax                   ; -26
    mov   ebx,Yval
    sub   ebx,Zval              ; -10
    add   eax,ebx
    mov   Rval,eax              ; -36

    ; Zero flag example:
    mov cx,1
    sub cx,1                    ; ZF = 1
    mov ax,0FFFFh
    inc ax                      ; ZF = 1

    ; Sign flag example:
    mov cx,0
    sub cx,1                    ; SF = 1
    mov ax,7FFFh
    add ax,2                    ; SF = 1

    ; Carry flag example:
    mov al,0FFh
    add al,1                    ; CF = 1,   AL = 00
```

```
; Overflow flag example:
mov   al,+127
add   al,1                          ; OF = 1
mov   al,-128
sub   al,1                          ; OF = 1

      exit
main ENDP
END main
```

4.2.8 Section Review

Use the following data for the next several questions:

```
.data
val1 BYTE   10h
val2 WORD   8000h
val3 DWORD  0FFFFh
val4 WORD   7FFFh
```

1. Write an instruction that increments **val2**.
2. Write an instruction that subtracts **val3** from EAX.
3. Write one or more instructions that subtract **val4** from **val2**.
4. If **val2** is incremented by 1 using the ADD instruction, what will be the values of the Carry and Sign flags?
5. If **val4** is incremented by 1 using the ADD instruction, what will be the values of the Overflow and Sign flags?
6. Where indicated, write down the values of the Carry, Sign, Zero, and Overflow flags after each instruction has executed:

```
mov ax,7FF0h
add al,10h                  ; a. CF =      SF =      ZF =      OF =
add ah,1                    ; b. CF =      SF =      ZF =      OF =
add ax,2                    ; c. CF =      SF =      ZF =      OF =
```

7. Implement the following expression in assembly language: AX = (−val2 + BX) − val4.
8. *(Yes/No):* Is it possible to set the Overflow flag if you add a positive integer to a negative integer?
9. *(Yes/No):* Will the Overflow flag be set if you add a negative integer to a negative integer and produce a positive result?
10. *(Yes/No):* Is it possible for the NEG instruction to set the Overflow flag?
11. *(Yes/No):* Is it possible for both the Sign and Zero flags to be set at the same time?
12. *Challenge:* Write a sequence of two instructions that set both the Carry and Overflow flags at the same time.

4.3   Data-Related Operators and Directives

Operators and directives, as we said earlier, are not part of the Intel instruction set. They are only understood by the assembler (in this case, Microsoft MASM). Various assemblers have differing syntaxes for operators and directives, because there is no single defined standard. The various assembler makers often seem to be competing with each other, in fact, by providing more and more sophisticated features.

MASM has a number of operators that are effective tools for describing and addressing variables:

- The OFFSET operator returns the distance of a variable from the beginning of its enclosing segment.
- The PTR operator lets you override a variable's default size.
- The TYPE operator returns the size (in bytes) of each element in an array.
- The LENGTHOF operator returns the number of elements in an array.
- The SIZEOF operator returns the number of bytes used by an array initializer.

In addition, the LABEL directive provides a way to redefine the same variable with different size attributes. The operators and directives in this chapter represent only a small subset of the operators supported by MASM. You may want to view the complete list in Appendix D.

> MASM 5 used slightly different operator names: LENGTH (rather than LENGTHOF), SIZE (rather than SIZEOF). Avoid using the old names, because they have slightly different meanings.

4.3.1   OFFSET Operator

The OFFSET operator returns the offset of a data label. The offset represents the distance, in bytes, of the label from the beginning of the data segment. In Protected mode, an offset is always 32 bits long. In Real-address mode, offsets are only 16 bits. To illustrate, the following figure shows a variable named **myByte** inside the data segment:

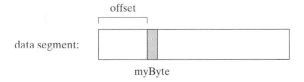

4.3.1.1   OFFSET Example

In the next example, we declare three different types of variables:

```
.data
bVal   BYTE   ?
```

```
wVal   WORD   ?
dVal   DWORD  ?
dVal2  DWORD  ?
```

If **bVal** were located at offset 00404000 (hexadecimal), the OFFSET operator would return the following values:

```
mov   esi,OFFSET bVal                     ; ESI = 00404000
mov   esi,OFFSET wVal                     ; ESI = 00404001
mov   esi,OFFSET dVal                     ; ESI = 00404003
mov   esi,OFFSET dVal2                    ; ESI = 00404007
```

The OFFSET operator can also be used with a direct-offset operand. Suppose that **myArray** contains five 16-bit words. The following MOV instruction obtains the offset of **myArray**, adds 4, and moves the sum to ESI:

```
.data
myArray WORD 1,2,3,4,5
.code
mov esi,OFFSET myArray + 4
```

4.3.2   ALIGN Directive

You can use the ALIGN directive to align a variable on a byte, word, doubleword, or paragraph boundary. The syntax is:

ALIGN *bound*

bound can be 1, 2, or 4. If it equals 1, the next variable or byte is aligned on a 1-byte boundary (the default). If bound is 2, the next variable is aligned on an even-numbered address, and if bound is 4, the next address is a multiple of 4. If necessary, the assembler inserts one or more empty bytes before the variable. Why bother aligning data? Because the CPU can process data stored at even-numbered addresses more quickly than those at odd-numbered addresses.

Revising our example from Section 4.3.1.1, we know that **bVal** is automatically at an even-numbered offset. Then, if we insert the ALIGN 2 before **wVal**, it is assigned an even-numbered offset. To illustrate, we can arbitrarily locate the first variable at offset 00404000:

```
bVal   BYTE   ?              ; 00404000
ALIGN 2
wVal   WORD   ?              ; 00404002
bVal2  BYTE   ?              ; 00404004
ALIGN 4
dVal   DWORD  ?              ; 00404008
dVal2  DWORD  ?              ; 0040400C
```

Note that **dVal** would have been at offset 00404005, but the ALIGN 4 directive bumped it back to offset 00404008.

4.3.3   PTR Operator

You can use the PTR operator to override the default size of an operand. This is only necessary when you're trying access the variable using a size attribute that's different from the one used to declare the variable.

Suppose, for example, that you would like to move the lower 16 bits of a doubleword variable named **myDouble** into AX. The assembler will not permit the following move because the operand sizes do not match:

```
.data
myDouble   DWORD   12345678h
.code
mov ax,myDouble                 ; error
```

But the WORD PTR operator makes it possible to move the low-order word (5678h) to AX:

```
mov ax,WORD PTR myDouble
```

Why wasn't 1234h moved into AX? That has to do with the *little endian* storage format used by the Intel CPU, which we first discussed in Section 3.4.9. In the following figure, the memory layout of **myDouble** is shown three ways: first as a doubleword, then as two words (5678h, 1234h), and finally as four bytes (78h, 56h, 34h, 12h):

doubleword	word	byte	offset	
12345678	5678	78	0000	myDouble
		56	0001	myDouble + 1
	1234	34	0002	myDouble + 2
		12	0003	myDouble + 3

The CPU can access memory in any of these three ways, independent of the way a variable was defined. For example, if **myDouble** begins at offset 0000, the 16-bit value stored at that address is 5678h. We could also retrieve 1234h, the word at location **myDouble+2** using the following statement:

```
mov    ax,WORD PTR [myDouble+2]    ; 1234h
```

Similarly, we could use the BYTE PTR operator to move a single byte from **myDouble** to BL:

```
mov    bl,BYTE PTR myDouble        ; 78h
```

Note that PTR must be used in combination with one of the standard assembler data types: BYTE, SBYTE, WORD, SWORD, DWORD, SDWORD, FWORD, QWORD, or TBYTE.

Moving Smaller Values into Larger Destinations   We might want to move two smaller values from memory to a larger destination operand. In the next example, the first word is copied to the lower half of EAX, and the second word is copied to the upper half. The DWORD PTR operator makes this possible:

```
.data
wordList WORD 5678h,1234h
.code
mov eax,DWORD PTR wordList        ; EAX = 12345678h
```

4.3.4   TYPE Operator

The TYPE operator returns the size, in bytes, of a single element of a variable. For example, the TYPE of a byte equals 1, the TYPE of a word equals 2, the TYPE of a doubleword is 4, and the TYPE of a quadword is 8. Here are examples of each:

```
.data
var1 BYTE   ?
var2 WORD   ?
var3 DWORD  ?
var4 QWORD  ?
```

The following table shows the value of each TYPE expression:

Expression	Value
TYPE var1	1
TYPE var2	2
TYPE var3	4
TYPE var4	8

4.3.5   LENGTHOF Operator

The LENGTHOF operator counts the number of elements in array, defined by the values appearing on the same line as its label. We will use the following data as an example:

```
.data
byte1    BYTE   10,20,30
array1   WORD   30 DUP(?),0,0
array2   WORD   5 DUP(3 DUP(?))
array3   DWORD 1,2,3,4
digitStr BYTE   "12345678",0
```

The following table lists the values returned by each LENGTHOF expression:

Expression	Value
LENGTHOF byte1	3
LENGTHOF array1	30 + 2

Expression	Value
LENGTHOF array2	5 * 3
LENGTHOF array3	4
LENGTHOF digitStr	9

Note that when nested DUP operators are used in an array definition, LENGTHOF returns the product of the two counters.

If you declare an array that spans multiple program lines, LENGTHOF only regards the data from the first line as part of the array. In the following example, LENGTHOF myArray returns the value 5:

```
myArray BYTE 10,20,30,40,50
        BYTE 60,70,80,90,100
```

Alternatively, you can end the first line with a comma and continue the list of initializers onto the next line. In the following example, LENGTHOF myArray returns the value 10:

```
myArray BYTE 10,20,30,40,50,
             60,70,80,90,100
```

4.3.6 SIZEOF Operator

The SIZEOF operator returns a value that is equivalent to multiplying LENGTHOF by TYPE. For example, **intArray** has TYPE = 2 and LENGTHOF = 32. Therefore, SIZEOF **intArray** equals 64:

```
intArray WORD 32 DUP(0)       ; SIZEOF = 64
```

4.3.7 LABEL Directive

The LABEL directive lets you insert a label and give it a size attribute without allocating any storage. Any of the standard size attributes can be used with LABEL, such as BYTE, WORD, DWORD, QWORD or TBYTE.

One common use of LABEL is to provide an alternative name and size attribute for some existing variable in the data segment. In the following example, we declare a label just before **val32** named **val16** and give it a WORD attribute:

```
.data
val16 LABEL WORD
val32 DWORD 12345678h
.code
mov  ax,val16                 ; AX = 5678h
mov  dx,val16+2               ; DX = 1234h
```

val16 is just an alias for the same storage location named **val32.** The LABEL directive itself uses no storage.

Example   Sometimes we need to construct a larger integer from two smaller integers. In the next example, a 32-bit value is loaded into EAX from two 16-bit variables:

```
.data
LongValue LABEL DWORD
val1   WORD   5678h
val2   WORD   1234h
.code
mov eax,LongValue                    ; EAX = 12345678h
```

4.3.8   Section Review

1. *(True/False):* In 32-bit Protected mode, the OFFSET operator returns a 16-bit value.
2. *(True/False):* The PTR operator returns the 32-bit address of a variable.
3. *(True/False):* The TYPE operator returns a value of 4 for doubleword operands.
4. *(True/False):* The LENGTHOF operator returns the number of bytes in an operand.
5. *(True/False):* The SIZEOF operator returns the number of bytes in an operand.

Use the following data definitions for the next seven exercises:

```
.data
myBytes BYTE 10h,20h,30h,40h
myWords WORD 3 DUP(?),2000h
myString BYTE "ABCDE"
```

6. Insert a directive in the given data that will align **myBytes** on an even-numbered address.
7. Indicate the value of EAX after each instruction executes:

```
mov eax,TYPE myBytes             ; a.
mov eax,LENGTHOF myBytes         ; b.
mov eax,SIZEOF myBytes           ; c.
mov eax,TYPE myWords             ; d.
mov eax,LENGTHOF myWords         ; e.
mov eax,SIZEOF myWords           ; f.
mov eax,SIZEOF myString          ; g.
```

8. Write a single instruction that moves the first two bytes in **myBytes** to the DX register. The resulting value will be 2010h.
9. Write an instruction that moves the second byte in **myWords** to the AL register.
10. Write an instruction that moves all four bytes in **myBytes** to the EAX register.
11. Insert a LABEL directive in the given data that will permit **myWords** to be moved directly to a 32-bit register.
12. Insert a LABEL directive in the given data that will permit **myBytes** to be moved directly to a 16-bit register.

4.4   Indirect Addressing

You've probably noticed already that direct addressing is completely impractical for array processing. We would never provide a different label name for every element of an array, nor would we use constant offsets to address more than a few array elements. The only practical way to handle an array is to use a register as a pointer and find ways to manipulate the register's value. This is called *indirect addressing*. A register holding an address is called an *indirect operand*.

4.4.1   Indirect Operands

An indirect operand can be any 32-bit general-purpose register (EAX, EBX, ECX, EDX, ESI, EDI, EBP, and ESP) surrounded by brackets. The register is assumed to contain the offset of some data. For example, ESI contains the offset of **val1**:

```
.data
val1 BYTE 10h
.code
mov esi,OFFSET val1
```

If a MOV instruction uses the indirect operand as the source, the pointer in ESI is dereferenced and a byte is moved to AL:

```
mov al,[esi]                    ; AL = 10h
```

Or, if the indirect operand is the destination operand, a new value is placed in memory at the location pointed to by the register:

```
mov [esi], BL
```

Real-address Mode   In Real-address mode, it is usual to use a 16-bit register to hold the offset of a variable. If the register is used as an indirect operand, it may only be SI, DI, BX, or BP. Generally, we avoid BP because it addresses the stack rather than the data segment. In the next example, we use SI to reference **val1**:

```
.data
val1 BYTE 10h
.code
main proc
    startup
    mov si,OFFSET val1
    mov al,[si]                 ; AL = 10h
```

General Protection Fault   In Protected mode, if the effective address points to an area outside your program's data segment, the CPU executes a *general protection (GP) fault*. This happens even when an instruction does not modify memory. For example, if ESI were uninitialized, the following instruction would probably generate a general protection fault:

```
mov ax,[esi]
```

Of course, the best way to avoid of this type of error is to carefully initialize registers used for indirect addressing. The same applies to high-level language programming with subscripts and pointers. General protection faults do not occur in Real-address mode.

Using PTR with Indirect Operands   The size of an operand is often not clear from the context of an instruction. Consider the following instruction, which would cause the assembler to generate an "operand must have size" error message:

```
inc [esi]                          ; error: operand must have size
```

The assembler doesn't know whether ESI points to a byte, word or doubleword. The PTR operator makes the operand size clear:

```
inc BYTE PTR [esi]
```

4.4.2 Arrays

Indirect operands are particularly useful when dealing with arrays because an indirect operand's value can easily be modified. Similar to an array subscript, an indirect operand can point to different array elements. For example, **arrayB** contains three bytes. We can increment ESI and make it point to each byte, in order:

```
.data
arrayB  BYTE 10h,20h,30h
.code
mov esi,OFFSET arrayB
mov al,[esi]                  ; AL = 10h
inc esi
mov al,[esi]                  ; AL = 20h
inc esi
mov al,[esi]                  ; AL = 30h
```

If we use an array of 16-bit integers, we add 2 to ESI to address each subsequent array element:

```
.data
arrayW  WORD 1000h,2000h,3000h
.code
mov esi,OFFSET arrayW
mov ax,[esi]                  ; AX = 1000h
add esi,2
mov ax,[esi]                  ; AX = 2000h
add esi,2
mov ax,[esi]                  ; AX = 3000h
```

Suppose that **arrayW** is located at offset 10200h. The following illustration shows ESI in relation to the array data:

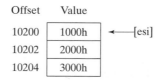

Example: Adding 32-Bit Integers   The following program excerpt adds three doublewords. A displacement of 4 must be added for each subsequent array value because doublewords are 4 bytes long:

```
.data
arrayD DWORD 10000h,20000h,30000h
.code
    mov esi,OFFSET arrayD
    mov eax,[esi]                       ; first number
    add esi,4
    add eax,[esi]                       ; second number
    add esi,4
    add eax,[esi]                       ; third number
```

If **arrayD** were located at offset 10200h, the following illustration would show ESI in relation to the array data:

Offset	Value	
10200	10000h	◄ [esi]
10204	20000h	◄— [esi] + 4
10208	30000h	◄— [esi] + 8

4.4.3   Indexed Operands

An *indexed operand* adds a constant to a register to generate an effective address. Any of the 32-bit general-purpose registers may be used as index registers. There are different notational forms permitted by MASM (the brackets are part of the notation):

```
constant[reg]
[constant + reg]
```

The first notational form combines the name of a variable with a register. The variable name is a constant that represents the variable's offset. Here are examples that show both notational forms:

arrayB[esi]	[arrayB + esi]
arrayD[ebx]	[arrayD + ebx]

As you probably guessed by looking at the notation, indexed operands are ideally suited to array processing. The index register should be initialized to zero before accessing the first array element:

```
.data
arrayB BYTE 10h,20h,30h
.code
mov  esi,0
mov  al,[arrayB + esi]          ; AL = 10h
```

In the last statement above, ESI is added to the offset of **arrayB**. The address generated by the expression (**arrayB + ESI**) is dereferenced, and the byte in memory is copied to AL.

Earlier, we presented an array processing example with indirect operands. Another way to implement that example would be to add a displacement to a register when accessing the second and third numbers of the array. This eliminates the need to use separate instructions to increment ESI:

```
.data
arrayW  WORD 1000h,2000h,3000h
.code
mov esi,OFFSET arrayW
mov ax,[esi]                    ; AX = 1000h
mov ax,[esi+2]                  ; AX = 2000h
mov ax,[esi+4]                  ; AX = 3000h
```

Using 16-Bit Registers   It is usual to use 16-bit registers as indexed operands in Real-address mode. In that case, you are limited to using SI, DI, BX, or BP:

```
mov al,arrayB[si]
mov ax,arrayW[di]
mov eax,arrayD[bx]
```

As with indirect operands, avoid using BP except when addressing data on the stack.

4.4.4 Pointers

A variable that contains the address of another variable is called a *pointer variable* (or *pointer*). Pointers are essential when manipulating with arrays and data structures. High-level languages such as C++ and Java purposely hide the implementations of pointers, because such details are not portable across different machine architectures. In assembly language, because we deal with a single implementation, we examine and use pointers at the physical level. This helps to remove some of the mystery surrounding pointers.

Intel-based programs use two basic types of pointers, NEAR and FAR. Their sizes are affected by the processor's current mode (16-bit Real, or 32-bit Protected), as shown in Table 4-2:

Table 4-2   Pointer Types in 16- and 32-Bit Modes.

	16-Bit Mode	32-Bit Mode
NEAR pointer	16-bit offset from the beginning of the data segment	32-bit offset from the beginning of the data segment
FAR pointer	32-bit segment-offset address	48-bit segment-offset address

The Protected-mode programs in this book use near pointers, so they are stored in double-word variables. Here are two examples: **ptrB** contains the offset of **arrayB**, and **ptrW** contains the offset of **arrayW**:

```
arrayB BYTE   10h,20h,30h,40h
arrayW WORD   1000h,2000h,3000h
ptrB   DWORD arrayB
ptrW   DWORD arrayW
```

Optionally, you can use the OFFSET operator to make the relationship clearer:

```
ptrB   DWORD OFFSET arrayB
ptrW   DWORD OFFSET arrayW
```

4.4.4.1   Using the TYPDEF Operator

The TYPDEF operator lets you create a user-defined type which has all the status of a built-in type when defining variables. TYPDEF is ideal for creating pointer variables. For example, the following declaration creates a new data type PBYTE that is a pointer to bytes:

```
PBYTE TYPEDEF PTR BYTE
```

This declaration would usually be placed near the beginning of a program, before the data segment. Then, variables could be defined using PBYTE:

```
.data
arrayB BYTE 10h,20h,30h,40h
ptr1   PBYTE ?                ; uninitialized
ptr2   PBYTE arrayB           ; points to an array
```

Example Program: Pointers   The following program (*pointers.asm*) uses TYPDEF to create three pointer types (PBYTE, PWORD, PDWORD). It creates pointer variables, and dereferences them at runtime to retrieve data from the arrays:

```
TITLE Pointers                          (Pointers.asm)

INCLUDE Irvine32.inc

; Create user-defined types.
PBYTE   TYPEDEF PTR BYTE        ; pointer to bytes
PWORD   TYPEDEF PTR WORD        ; pointer to words
PDWORD TYPEDEF PTR DWORD        ; pointer to doublewords

.data
arrayB BYTE   10h,20h,30h
arrayW WORD   1,2,3
arrayD DWORD 4,5,6

; Create some pointer variables.
ptr1 PBYTE   arrayB
ptr2 PWORD   arrayW
ptr3 PDWORD arrayD
```

```
.code
main PROC
; Use the pointers to access data.
    mov esi,ptr1
    mov al,[esi]                     ; 10h
    mov esi,ptr2
    mov ax,[esi]                     ; 1
    mov esi,ptr3
    mov eax,[esi]                    ; 4
    exit
main ENDP
END main
```

4.4.5 Section Review

1. *(True/False):* Any 16-bit general-purpose register can be used as an indirect operand.
2. *(True/False):* Any 32-bit general-purpose register can be used as an indirect operand.
3. *(True/False):* The BX register is usually reserved for addressing the stack.
4. *(True/False):* A general-protection fault occurs in Real-address mode when an array subscript is out of range.
5. *(True/False):* The following instruction is invalid: inc [esi]
6. *(True/False):* The following is an indexed operand: array [esi]

Use the following data definitions for the remaining questions in this section:

```
myBytes   BYTE 10h,20h,30h,40h
myWords   WORD 8Ah,3Bh,72h,44h,66h
myDoubles DWORD 1,2,3,4,5
myPointer DWORD myDoubles
```

7. Fill in the requested register values on the right side of the following instruction sequence:

```
    mov esi,OFFSET myBytes
    mov al,[esi]                     ; a. AL =
    mov al,[esi+3]                   ; b. AL =
    mov esi,OFFSET myWords + 2
    mov ax,[esi]                     ; c. AX =
    mov edi,8
    mov edx,[myDoubles + edi]        ; d. EDX =
    mov edx,myDoubles[edi]           ; e. EDX =
    mov ebx,myPointer
    mov eax,[ebx + 4]                ; f. EAX =
```

8. *Challenge:* Fill in the requested register values on the right side of the following instruction sequence:

```
    mov esi,OFFSET myBytes
    mov ax,WORD PTR [esi]            ; a. AX =
```

```
mov eax,DWORD PTR myWords        ; b.  EAX =
mov esi,myPointer
mov ax,WORD PTR [esi+2]          ; c.  AX =
mov ax,WORD PTR [esi+6]          ; d.  AX =
mov ax,WORD PTR [esi-4]          ; e.  AX =
```

4.5   JMP and LOOP Instructions

The CPU automatically loads and executes programs sequentially. As each instruction is decoded and executed, the CPU has already incremented the instruction pointer to the offset of the next instruction; it has also loaded the instruction into its internal queue. But real-life programs are not that simple. What about IF statements, gotos, and loops? They clearly require programs to transfer control to different locations within the programs.

A *transfer of control, or branch*, is a way of altering the order in which statements are executed. All programming languages contain statements to do this. We divide such statements into two categories:

- **Unconditional Transfer:** The program branches to a new location in all cases; a new value is loaded into the instruction pointer, causing execution to continue at the new address. The JMP instruction is a good example.
- **Conditional Transfer:** The program branches if a certain condition is true. Intel provides a wide range of conditional transfer instructions that can be combined to make up conditional logic structures. The CPU interprets true/false conditions based on the contents of the ECX and Flags registers. LOOP is a good example.

4.5.1   JMP Instruction

The JMP instruction causes an unconditional transfer to a target location inside the code segment. The location must be identified by a code label, which is translated by the assembler into an address. The syntax is:

```
JMP targetLabel
```

When the CPU executes this instruction, the offset of *targetLabel* is moved into the instruction pointer, causing execution to immediately continue at the new location. Ordinarily, you can only jump to a label inside the current procedure, unless the label has been specially designated as *global* (see Section 5.5.2.3 in Chapter 5 for details).

Creating a Loop   The JMP instruction provides an easy way to create a loop, simply by jumping to a label at the top of the loop:

```
top:
    .

    .
    jmp top                     ; repeat the endless loop
```

JMP is unconditional, so the loop will continue endlessly unless some other way is found to exit the loop (there is, but we haven't explained it yet).

4.5.2 LOOP Instruction

The LOOP instruction provides a simple way to repeat a block of statements a specific number of times. ECX is automatically used as a counter and is decremented each time the loop repeats. Its syntax is:

```
LOOP destination
```

The execution of the LOOP instruction involves two steps: First, it subtracts 1 from ECX. Next, it compares ECX to zero. If ECX is not equal to zero, a jump is taken to the label identified by *destination*. Otherwise, if ECX equals zero, no jump takes place and control passes to the instruction following the loop.

> In Real-address mode, CX is used as the default loop register rather than ECX. In any mode, the LOOPD instruction uses ECX as the loop counter, and the LOOPW instruction uses CX as the loop counter.

In the following example, we add 1 to AX each time the loop repeats. When the loop ends, AX = 5 and ECX = 0:

```
        mov   ax,0
        mov   ecx,5
L1:
        inc   ax
        loop L1
```

A common programming error is to inadvertently initialize ECX to zero before beginning a loop. If this happens, the LOOP instruction decrements ECX to FFFFFFFFh, and the loop repeats 4,294,967,296 times! Or, if CX is the loop counter (in Real-address mode), it repeats 65,536 times.

The loop destination must be within −128 to +127 bytes of the current location. Machine instructions have an average size of about 3 bytes, so a loop might contain, on average, a maximum of 42 instructions. Following is an example of an error message generated by MASM because the target label of a LOOP instruction was too far away:

```
error A2075: jump destination too far : by 14 byte(s)
```

If you modify ECX inside the loop, the LOOP instruction may not work properly. In the following example, ECX is incremented within the loop. It never reaches zero, and the loop never stops:

```
top:
        .
        .
```

```
        inc   ecx
        loop top
```

If you run out of registers and must use ECX for some other purpose, save it in a variable at the beginning of the loop and restore it just before the loop instruction:

```
.data
count DWORD ?
.code
     mov   ecx,100          ; set loop count
top:
     mov   count,ecx        ; save the count
     .
     mov   ecx,20           ; modify ECX
     .
     mov   ecx,count        ; restore loop count
     loop top
```

Nested Loops   When you must create a loop inside another loop, the problem arises of what to do with the counter in ECX. Saving the outer loop count in a variable is a good solution:

```
.data
count DWORD ?
.code
     mov   ecx,100          ; set outer loop count
L1:
     move count,ecx         ; save outer loop count
     mov   ecx,20           ; set inner loop count
L2:
     .
     .
     loop L2                ; repeat the inner loop
     mov   ecx,count        ; restore outer loop count
     loop L1                ; repeat the outer loop
```

As a general rule, avoid loops that are nested more than two levels deep. Otherwise, managing the loop counts becomes more trouble than it's worth. If the algorithm you're using requires more loop nesting, the inner loop(s) can be moved into called procedures. (We cover procedures in Chapter 5.)

4.5.3 Summing an Integer Array

To calculate the sum of an array of integers, follow these steps:

1. Set an index register to the offset of the array. This will be used as an indexed operand.
2. Set ECX to the number of elements in the array (CX in Real-address mode).
3. Set a register to zero that will accumulate the sum.
4. Create a label to mark the beginning of the loop.

5. In the loop body, use indirect addressing to add a single array element to the register holding the sum.
6. Point the index register to the next array element.
7. Use a LOOP instruction to repeat the loop from the beginning label.

(Steps 1–3 may be performed in any order.)

SumArray Program Example   The following **sumArray** program calculates the sum of an array of words:

```
TITLE Summing an Array                (SumArray.asm)

INCLUDE Irvine32.inc
.data
intarray WORD 100h,200h,300h,400h

.code
main PROC
    mov   edi,OFFSET intarray      ; address of intarray
    mov   ecx,LENGTHOF intarray    ; loop counter
    mov   ax,0                     ; zero the accumulator
L1:
    add   ax,[edi]                 ; add an integer
    add   edi,TYPE intarray        ; point to next integer
    loop L1                        ; repeat until ECX = 0

    exit
main ENDP
END main
```

4.5.4   Copying a String

A very common operation involving arrays and strings is that of copying large blocks of data. Compiler writers always try to produce code that performs copy operations as quickly as possible. Let's see how this can be done in assembly language, by creating a loop that copies a string. Indexed addressing works well for this type of operation because the same index register can reference both strings. The only requirement is that the target string have enough available space to receive the copied characters, including the null byte at the end:

```
TITLE Copying a String                     (CopyStr.asm)

INCLUDE Irvine32.inc
.data
source  BYTE  "This is the source string",0
target  BYTE  SIZEOF source DUP(0),0

.code
main PROC
    mov  esi,0                     ; index register
```

```
        mov   ecx,SIZEOF source        ; loop counter
L1:
        mov   al,source[esi]           ; get a character from source
        mov   target[esi],al           ; store it in the target
        inc   esi                      ; move to next character
        loop L1                        ; repeat for entire string

        exit
main ENDP
END main
```

Of course, the MOV instruction cannot have two memory operands, so each character is moved from the source string to AL, then from AL to the target string.

> When programming in C++ or Java, beginning programmers often do not realize how often background copy operations take place. In Java, for example, if you exceed the existing capacity of an ArrayList when adding new element, the runtime system allocates a block of new storage, copies the existing data to a new location, and deletes the old data. (The same is true when using a C++ vector). If a large number of copy operations take place, they can have a significant effect on a program's execution speed.

4.5.5 Section Review

1. *(True/False):* A JMP instruction can only jump to a label inside the current procedure, unless the label has been designated *global*.
2. *(True/False):* The JMP instruction is a conditional transfer instruction.
3. If ECX is initialized to zero before beginning a loop, how many times will the LOOP instruction repeat? (Assume that ECX is not modified by any other instructions inside the loop.)
4. *(True/False):* The LOOP instruction first checks to see if ECX is greater than zero; then it decrements ECX and jumps to the destination label.
5. *(True/False):* The LOOP instruction does the following: It decrements ECX; then, if ECX is greater than zero, the instruction jumps to the destination label.
6. In Real-address mode, which register is used as the counter by the LOOP instruction?
7. In Real-address mode, which register is used as the counter by the LOOPD instruction?
8. *(True/False):* The target of a LOOP instruction must be within 256 bytes of the current location.
9. *(Challenge):* What will be the final value of EAX in this example?

```
        mov eax,0
        mov ecx,10               ; outer loop counter
L1:
        mov eax,3
        mov ecx,5               ; inner loop counter
```

```
L2:
    add eax,5
    loop L2                    ; repeat inner loop
    loop L1                    ; repeat outer loop
```

10. Revise the code from the preceding question in such a way that the outer loop counter is not erased when the inner loop is started.

4.6 Chapter Summary

MOV, a data transfer instruction, copies a source operand to a destination operand. The MOVZX instruction zero-extends a smaller operand into a larger one. The MOVSX instruction sign-extends a smaller operand into a larger one.

The XCHG instruction exchanges the contents of two operands. At least one operand must be a register.

The following types of operands are presented in this chapter:

- A *direct* operand is the name of a variable, and represents the variable's address.
- A *direct-offset* operand adds a displacement to the name of a variable, generating a new offset. This new offset can be used to access data in memory.
- An *indirect* operand is a register containing the address of data. By surrounding the register with brackets (as in [esi]), a program can dereference the address and retrieve the memory data.
- An *indexed* operand combines a constant with an indirect operand. The constant and the register value are added together, and the resulting address is dereferenced. For example, [array + esi] and array[esi] are indexed operands.

The following arithmetic instructions are important to remember:

- The INC instruction adds 1 to an operand.
- The DEC instruction subtracts 1 from an operand.
- The ADD instruction adds a source operand to a destination operand.
- The SUB instruction subtracts a source operand from a destination operand.
- The NEG instruction reverses the sign of an operand.

It's easy to convert simple arithmetic expressions to assembly language. When doing this, you must follow standard operator precedence rules when selecting which expressions to evaluate first.

The following CPU status flags are affected by arithmetic operations:

- The Sign flag is set when the outcome of an arithmetic operation is negative.
- The Carry flag is set when the result of an unsigned arithmetic operation is too large for the destination operand.
- The Zero flag is set when the outcome of an arithmetic operation is zero.

- The Overflow flag is set when the result of an signed arithmetic operation is too large for the destination operand. Further, the CPU detects overflow by exclusive-ORing the carry out of bit 6 with the carry out of bit 5.

After reading this chapter, you should know how to use the following operators:

- The OFFSET operator returns the distance of a variable from the beginning of its enclosing segment.
- The PTR operator lets you override a variable's default size.
- The TYPE operator returns the size (in bytes) of a single variable, or of a single element in an array.
- The LENGTHOF operator returns the number of elements in an array.
- The SIZEOF operator returns the number bytes used by an array initializer.
- The TYPEDEF operator creates a user-defined type.

The JMP and LOOP instructions are useful when creating counting loops. In 32-bit mode, the LOOP instruction uses ECX as the loop counter. In 16-bit mode, CX is used rather than ECX. In both 16 and 32-bit modes, the LOOPD (loop double) instruction uses ECX as a counter.

4.7 Programming Exercises

The following exercises can be done in either Protected mode or Real-address mode:

1. Carry Flag
Write a program that uses addition and subtraction to set and clear the Carry flag. After each instruction, insert the **call DumpRegs** statement to display the registers and flags. Using comments, explain how (and why) the Carry flag was affected by each instruction.

2. INC and DEC
Write a short program demonstrating that the INC and DEC instructions do not affect the Carry flag.

3. Zero and Sign Flags
Write a program that uses addition and subtraction to set and clear the Zero and Sign flags. After each addition or subtraction instruction, insert the **call DumpRegs** statement to display the registers and flags. Using comments, explain how (and why) the Zero and Sign flags were affected by each instruction.

4. Overflow Flag
Write a program that uses addition and subtraction to set and clear the Overflow flag. After each addition or subtraction instruction, insert the **call DumpRegs** statement to display the registers and flags. Using comments, explain how (and why) the Overflow flag was affected by each instruction. *Optional:* include an ADD instruction that sets both the Carry and Overflow flags.

5. Direct-Offset Addressing

Insert the following variables in your program:

```
.data
Uarray WORD 1000h,2000h,3000h,4000h
Sarray SWORD -1,-2,-3,-4
```

Write instructions that use direct-offset addressing to move the four values in **Uarray** to the EAX, EBX, ECX, and EDX registers. When you follow this with a **call DumpRegs** statement, the following register values should display:

```
EAX=00001000   EBX=00002000   ECX=00003000   EDX=00004000
```

Next, write instructions that use direct-offset addressing to move the four values in **Sarray** to the EAX, EBX, ECX, and EDX registers. When you follow this with a **call DumpRegs** statement, the following register values should display:

```
EAX=FFFFFFFF   EBX=FFFFFFFE   ECX=FFFFFFFD   EDX=FFFFFFFC
```

6. Fibonacci Numbers

Write a program that uses a loop to calculate the first seven values in the *Fibonacci* number sequence { 1,1,2,3,5,8,13 }. Place each value in the EAX register and display it with a **call DumpRegs** statement inside the loop.

7. Arithmetic Expression

Write a program that implements the following arithmetic expression:

$$EAX = -val2 + 7 - val3 + val1$$

Use the following data definitions:

```
val1 SDWORD 8
val2 SDWORD -15
val3 SDWORD 20
```

In comments next to each instruction, write the hexadecimal value of EAX. Insert a **call DumpRegs** statement at the end of the program.

8. Copy a String Backwards

Write a program using the LOOP instruction with indirect addressing that copies a string from **source** to **target**, reversing the character order in the process. Use the following variables:

```
source   BYTE   "This is the source string",0
target   BYTE   SIZEOF source DUP(0)
```

Insert the following statements immediately after the loop. They will display the hexadecimal contents of the target string:

```
mov   esi,OFFSET target          ; offset of variable
mov   ebx,1                       ; byte format
```

```
    mov   ecx,SIZEOF target-2          ; counter
    call  DumpMem
```

If your program works correctly, you will see the following sequence of hexadecimal bytes on the screen when the program runs:

```
67  6E  69  72  74  73  20  65  63  72  75  6F  73  20  65  68
74  20  73  69  20  73  69  68  54
```

(The DumpMem procedure is explained in Chapter 5, Section 5.3.2.)

5

Procedures

5.1 Introduction

There are several good reasons why you should read this chapter:

- You need to learn how to do input-output in assembly language.
- You need to learn about the *runtime stack*, how it is the fundamental mechanism that makes it possible to call and return from functions (we call them *procedures*).
- Your programs will grow to the point where you will need to begin logically dividing them into procedures.

- You will learn how to draw *flowcharts*, which are graphing tools that portray program logic.
- Your professor might give you a test on this chapter.

5.2   Linking to an External Library

If you wanted to spend the time, you could learn to write all the detailed code required for performing even the simplest input-output. It would be about like assembling your car's engine every time you wanted to go for a ride. Interesting, but time-consuming. Much later in this book, in Chapter 11, you will get a chance to see how input-output is handled in MS-Windows Protected mode. It is great fun, and a new world will open up to you when you see the kinds of tools that are available.

For now, however, input-output should be fairly easy while you are just getting acquainted with assembly language. The first section of this chapter shows how to call procedures from a library supplied with this book named **Irvine32.lib**. The full source code of this library is available on the CD-ROM attached to the book, and is regularly updated on the book's Web site.

> If you are writing 16-bit programs in Real-address mode, the **Irvine16.lib** link library contains the same procedures as Irvine32.lib.

5.2.1   Background Information

A *link library* is a file containing procedures that have been assembled into machine code. The code in a library begins as one or more source files containing procedures, constants, and variables. The source files are assembled into object files, and the object files are inserted into the library.

Suppose you wanted your program to display a string on the console by calling a procedure named **Writestring**. Your program would have to contain a PROTO directive that names the procedure to be called. The following directive is found in the *Irvine32.inc* file:

```
WriteString PROTO
```

Next, a CALL instruction would execute the **Writestring** procedure:

```
call WriteString
```

When your program was assembled, the assembler would leave the target address of the CALL instruction blank, knowing that it would be filled in later by the linker. The linker would look for the **WriteString** name in the link library, and copy the appropriate machine instructions from the library into your program's executable file. Also, it would insert **Writestring**'s address into the CALL instruction.

If you try to call a procedure that is not in the link library, the linker issues an error message and does not generate an executable file.

Linker Command Options   The linker program combines your program's object file with one or more object files and link libraries. The following command, for example, links hello.obj to the irvine32.lib and kernel32.lib libraries:

```
link32 hello.obj irvine32.lib kernel32.lib
```

The batch file (*make32.bat* or *make16.bat*) you have been using to assemble and link the programs in this book uses nearly the same command. The only difference is that a replaceable parameter (%1) is used in place of "hello.obj". This allows the batch file to link any program:

```
link32 %1.obj irvine32.lib kernel32.lib
```

Overall Structure   You may be wondering where kernel32.lib fits into the picture. This file is supplied with the Microsoft Windows Platform *Software Development Kit*. It contains linking information for operating system functions stored inside another file named kernel32.dll. The latter is one of the fundamental parts of the MS-Windows operating system, and is called a *dynamic link library*. It contains executable functions that perform character-based input-output. You might think of kernel32.lib as a bridge to kernel32.dll, as shown in the following figure:

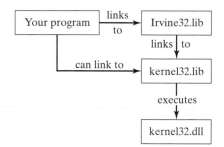

Using what you learn in this chapter, your programs link to Irvine32.lib. Later, in Chapter 11, you will learn how to link your programs directly to kernel32.lib.

5.2.2   Section Review

1. *(True/False):* A link library consists of assembly language source code.
2. Use the PROTO directive to declare a procedure named **MyProc** in an external link library.
3. Write a CALL statement that calls a procedure named **MyProc** in an external link library.
4. What is the name of the 32-bit link library supplied with this book?
5. Which library contains functions called from Irvine32.lib?
6. What is kernel32.dll?
7. What is the name used for the replaceable filename parameter in the **make32.bat** file?

5.3   The Book's Link Library

5.3.1   Overview

Table 5-1 is a quick reference to the procedure names in the Irvine32 link library. (Some additional procedures will be introduced in later chapters.) First, a few terms must be explained:

- **console:** A 32-bit console window, running in color text mode in MS-Windows. By default, there are 80 columns and 25 rows.
- **standard input:** The standard input device is the keyboard, although it can be redirected from the Command prompt to read from a file or serial port.
- **standard output:** The standard output device is the video display, although it can be redirected from the Command prompt to write to a file, printer, or serial port.

Table 5-1   Procedures in the Link Library.

Procedure	Description
Clrscr	Clears the console and locates the cursor at the upper left corner.
Crlf	Writes an end of line sequence to standard output.
Delay	Pauses the program execution for a specified *n* millisecond interval.
DumpMem	Writes a block of memory to standard output in hexadecimal.
DumpRegs	Displays the EAX, EBX, ECX, EDX, ESI, EDI, EBP, ESP, EFLAGS, and EIP registers in hexadecimal. Also displays the Carry, Sign, Zero, and Overflow flags.
GetCommandtail	Copies the program's command-line arguments (called the *command tail*) into an array of bytes.
GetMseconds	Returns the number of milliseconds that have elapsed since midnight.
Gotoxy	Locates the cursor at a specific row and column on the console.
Random32	Generates a 32-bit pseudorandom integer in the range 0 to FFFFFFFFh.
Randomize	Seeds the random number generator with a unique value.
RandomRange	Generates a pseudorandom integer within a specified range.
ReadChar	Reads a single character from standard input.
ReadHex	Reads a 32-bit hexadecimal integer from standard input, terminated by the Enter key.

Table 5-1 Procedures in the Link Library. (Continued)

Procedure	Description
ReadInt	Reads a 32-bit signed decimal integer from standard input, terminated by the Enter key.
ReadString	Reads a string from standard input, terminated by the Enter key.
SetTextColor	Sets the foreground and background colors of all subsequent text output to the console. *Not available in Irvine16.lib.*
WaitMsg	Displays a message and waits for the Enter key to be pressed.
WriteBin	Writes an unsigned 32-bit integer to standard output in ASCII binary format.
WriteChar	Writes a single character to standard output.
WriteDec	Writes an unsigned 32-bit integer to standard output in decimal format.
WriteHex	Writes an unsigned 32-bit integer to standard output in hexadecimal format.
WriteInt	Writes a signed 32-bit integer to standard output in decimal format.
WriteString	Writes a null-terminated string to standard output.

5.3.2 Individual Procedure Descriptions

Clrscr   The Clrscr procedure clears the screen. This is typically done at the beginning and ending of a program. If you call it at other times during a program's execution, remember to pause the program (by calling WaitMsg) before calling Clrscr. This will allow the user to view the information already on the screen before it is erased. Example:

```
call Clrscr
```

Crlf   The Crlf procedure advances the cursor to the beginning of the next line of standard output. It does this by writing a string containing two bytes, 0Dh and 0Ah. Example:

```
call Crlf
```

Delay   The Delay procedure pauses the program for a specified time interval. When calling this function, set EAX to the desired interval, in milliseconds. Example:

```
mov  eax,1000                 ; 1 second
call Delay
```

(The Irvine16.lib version of this procedure does not work under Windows NT, 2000, or XP.)

DumpMem   The DumpMem procedure writes a range of memory to standard output in hexadecimal. When you call it, pass the starting address in ESI, the number of units in ECX, and the unit size in EBX (1 = byte, 2 = word, 4 = doubleword). For example, the following statements display an array of eleven doublewords named **array**:

```
.data
array DWORD 1,2,3,4,5,6,7,8,9,0Ah,0Bh
.code
main PROC
    mov  esi,OFFSET array          ; starting OFFSET
    mov  ecx,LENGTHOF array        ; number of units
    mov  ebx,TYPE array            ; doubleword format
    call DumpMem
```

The following output is produced by DumpMem, using the given data:

```
00000001  00000002  00000003  00000004  00000005  00000006
00000007  00000008  00000009  0000000A  0000000B
```

DumpRegs   The DumpRegs procedure displays the EAX, EBX, ECX, EDX, ESI, EDI, EBP, ESP, EIP, and EFL (EFLAGS) registers in hexadecimal. It also displays the values of the Carry, Sign, Zero, and Overflow flags. The following is a sample:

```
EAX=00000613  EBX=00000000  ECX=000000FF  EDX=00000000
ESI=00000000  EDI=00000100  EBP=0000091E  ESP=000000F6
EIP=00401026  EFL=00000286  CF=0  SF=1  ZF=0  OF=0
```

The displayed value of EIP is the offset of the instruction that follows the call to DumpRegs. DumpRegs can be useful when debugging programs because it lets you display a snapshot of the CPU state while the program is running. It has no input parameters and no return value.

GetCommandtail   The GetCommandtail procedure copies the program's command line into a null-terminated string. If the command line was found to be empty, the Carry flag is set; otherwise, the Carry flag is cleared. This procedure is useful because it permits the user of a program to pass information on the command line.

For example, suppose a program named **Encrypt** reads an input file named **file1.txt**, and produces an output file named **file2.txt**. The user can pass both filenames on the command line when running the program:

```
Encrypt file1.txt file2.txt
```

When it starts up, the Encrypt program can call **GetCommandtail** and retrieve the two filenames.

When calling GetCommandtail, EDX must contain the offset of an array of at least 129 bytes:

```
.data
cmdTail BYTE 129 DUP(0)          ; empty buffer
.code
mov edx,OFFSET buffer
call GetCommandtail              ; fills the buffer
```

GetMseconds The GetMseconds procedure returns the number of milliseconds that have elapsed since midnight. This procedure can be useful when you want to measure the time between events. The return value is in EAX. There are no input parameters. In the following example, we call the function once, and store the value it returns. Next, a loop executes. Finally, we call GetMseconds again, and subtract the two times. We now know the approximate duration of the loop, in milliseconds:

```
.data
startTime DWORD ?
.code
call GetMseconds
mov  startTime,eax
L1:
    ; (execute a loop here...)
    Loop L1
call GetMseconds
sub  eax,startTime          ; EAX = loop time, in milliseconds
```

Gotoxy The Gotoxy procedure locates the cursor at a given row and column on the screen. By default, the console window's X-coordinate range is 0–79, and the Y-coordinate range is 0–24. When you call Gotoxy, pass the Y-coordinate (row) in DH and the X-coordinate (column) in DL. Example:

```
mov dh,10                   ; row 10
mov dl,20                   ; column 20
call Gotoxy                 ; locate cursor
```

Random32 The Random32 procedure generates a 32-bit random integer and returns it in EAX. When called repeatedly, Random32 generates a simulated random sequence in which each number is called a *pseudorandom integer*.[1] The numbers are created using a simple function having an input called a *seed*. The function uses the seed in a formula to generate the first random value. The next random value is generated using the previous random value as its seed. Generally, we use the term *random* to imply pseudorandom. Example:

```
.data
randVal DWORD ?
.code
call Random32
mov  randVal,eax
```

Randomize The Randomize procedure initializes the seed of the random-number formula used by both the Random32 and RandomRange procedures. The seed equals the time of day, accurate

---

[1] If you would like to read more about random number generators, see Donald Knuth, *The Art of Computer Programming* (Vol. 2), Addison-Wesley, 1997.

to 1/100 of a second. This virtually ensures that each time you run a program, the starting random integer will be different, and any sequence of random numbers will also be unique. You need only call Randomize once at the beginning of a program. In the following example, we produce ten random integers:

```
call Randomize
mov ecx,10
L1: call Random32
    ; use or display random value in EAX here...
    Loop L1
```

RandomRange   The RandomRange procedure produces a random integer within the range of 0 to (n−1), where n is an input parameter passed in the EAX register. The random integer is returned in EAX. For example, the following statements generate a single random integer between 0 and 4999 and place it in EAX:

```
.data
randVal DWORD ?
.code
mov  eax,5000
call RandomRange
mov  randVal,eax
```

ReadChar   The ReadChar procedure reads a single character from standard input and returns the character in the AL register. The character is not echoed on the screen. The following is a sample call:

```
.data
char BYTE ?
.code
call ReadChar
mov  char,al
```

ReadHex   The ReadHex procedure reads a 32-bit hexadecimal integer from standard input and returns the value in EAX. No error checking is performed for invalid characters. You can use both uppercase and lowercase letters for the digits A through F. A maximum of eight digits may be entered. Leading spaces are not permitted. Example:

```
.data
hexVal DWORD ?
.code
call ReadHex
mov  hexVal,eax
```

ReadInt   The ReadInt procedure reads a 32-bit signed integer from standard input and returns the value in EAX. The user can type an optional leading plus or minus sign, and the rest of the number can only consist of digits. ReadInt will set the Overflow flag and display an error message if the value entered cannot be represented as a 32-bit signed integer (range: $-2,147,483,648$ to $+2,147,483,647$). The following is a sample call:

```
.data
intVal SDWORD ?
.code
call ReadInt
mov  intVal,eax
```

ReadString   The ReadString procedure reads a string from standard input, stopping when the user presses the Enter key. It returns a count of the number of bytes read in the EAX register. Before calling ReadString, set EDX to the offset of an array of bytes where the input characters will be stored, and set ECX to the maximum number of characters to read.

The following statements call **ReadString**, passing ECX and EDX. Notice that we subtract 1 from the buffer size to save a byte at the end of the string for the null terminator:

```
.data
buffer BYTE 50 DUP(0)                 ; holds the characters
byteCount DWORD ?                     ; holds counter
.code
mov  edx,OFFSET buffer                ; point to the buffer
mov  ecx,(SIZEOF buffer) - 1          ; specify max characters
call ReadString                       ; input the string
mov  byteCount,eax                    ; number of characters
```

ReadString automatically inserts a null terminator at the end of the string. The following is a hexadecimal and ASCII dump of the first eight bytes of **buffer** after the user has entered the string "ABCDEFG":

```
41 42 43 44 45 46 47 00              ABCDEFG
```

The variable **byteCount** equals 7.

SetTextColor   The SetTextColor procedure sets the current foreground and background colors for text output. The following color constants are predefined and can be used for both the foreground and background:

black = 0	red = 4	gray = 8	lightRed = 12
blue = 1	magenta = 5	lightBlue = 9	lightMagenta = 13
green = 2	brown = 6	lightGreen = 10	yellow = 14
cyan = 3	lightGray = 7	lightCyan = 11	white = 15

These color constants are defined in *Irvine32.inc* (and *Irvine16.inc*). The background color must be multiplied by 16 before being added to the foreground color.[2] The following constant, for example, indicates yellow characters on a blue background:

```
yellow + (blue * 16)
```

Before calling **SetTextColor**, move the desired color to EAX:

```
mov  eax,white + (blue * 16)                    ; white on blue
call SetTextColor
```

(If you would like to read more about video colors, see Section 15.3.2. **SetTextColor** is not available in the Irvine16 link library.)

WaitMsg   The WaitMsg procedure displays the message "Press [Enter] to continue...", and waits for the user to press the Enter key. This procedure is useful when you want to pause the screen display before data scrolls off and disappears. It has no input parameters. An example call is:

```
call WaitMsg
```

WriteBin   The WriteBin procedure writes an integer to standard output in ASCII binary format. When you call WriteBin, pass the integer in EAX. The binary bits are displayed in groups of 4 for easy reading. For example:

```
mov  eax,12346AF9h
call WriteBin
; displays: "0001 0010 0011 0100 0110 1010 1111 1001"
```

WriteChar   The WriteChar procedure writes a single character to standard output. Place the character (or its ASCII code) in AL before calling the procedure:

```
mov  al,'A'
call WriteChar            ; displays: "A"
```

WriteDec   The WriteDec procedure writes a 32-bit unsigned integer to standard output in decimal format with no leading zeros. Before calling it, place the integer in EAX:

```
mov  eax,295
call WriteDec             ; displays: "295"
```

WriteHex   The WriteHex procedure writes a 32-bit unsigned integer to standard output in 8-digit hexadecimal format. Leading zeros are inserted if necessary. Before calling it, place the integer in EAX:

```
mov  eax,7FFFh
call WriteHex             ; displays: "00007FFF"
```

---

[2] This amounts to shifting the bits left 4 positions, which you will read about in Chapter 7.

WriteInt   The WriteInt procedure writes a 32-bit signed integer to standard output in decimal format with a leading sign and no leading zeros. Before calling it, place the integer in EAX:

```
mov  eax,216543
call WriteInt                    ; displays: "+216543"
```

WriteString   The WriteString procedure writes a null-terminated string to standard output. When calling it, place the string's offset in EDX. For example:

```
.data
prompt BYTE "Enter your name: ",0
.code
mov  edx,OFFSET prompt
call WriteString
```

5.3.2.1   The Irvine32.inc Include File

The following is a partial listing of the *Irvine32.inc* include file. It contains a prototype for each library procedure, as well as color constants, structures, and symbol definitions. This file will change over time, so be sure to get the latest copy from the book's Web site:

```
; Include file for Irvine32.lib           (Irvine32.inc)
INCLUDE SmallWin.inc
.NOLIST
;----------------------------------------
; Procedure Prototypes
;----------------------------------------
ClrScr PROTO
Crlf PROTO
Delay PROTO
DumpMem PROTO
DumpRegs PROTO
GetCommandtail PROTO
GetMseconds PROTO
Gotoxy PROTO
Randomize PROTO
RandomRange PROTO
Random32 PROTO
ReadInt PROTO
ReadChar PROTO
ReadHex PROTO
ReadString PROTO
SetTextColor PROTO
WaitMsg PROTO
```

```
WriteBin PROTO
WriteChar PROTO
WriteDec PROTO
WriteHex PROTO
WriteInt PROTO
WriteString PROTO

;----------------------------------
; Standard 4-bit color definitions
;----------------------------------
black         = 0000b
blue          = 0001b
green         = 0010b
cyan          = 0011b
red           = 0100b
magenta       = 0101b
brown         = 0110b
lightGray     = 0111b
gray          = 1000b
lightBlue     = 1001b
lightGreen    = 1010b
lightCyan     = 1011b
lightRed      = 1100b
lightMagenta  = 1101b
yellow        = 1110b
white         = 1111b
.LIST
```

The .NOLIST directive at the top of this file prevents these lines from being shown in source listings created by the assembler. At the end of this file, the .LIST directive enables listing of source lines again. The INCLUDE directive at the beginning of this file causes another include file (*SmallWin.inc*) to be included in the text stream passed to the assembler. The *SmallWin.inc* file contains function prototypes, constants, and data structures required when directly calling MS-Windows functions. They will be discussed in Chapter 11.

5.3.3 Library Test Program

Let's take a look at a short program that tests selected procedures in the book's link library. Comments have been inserted in the program listing that describe each step:

```
TITLE Testing the Link Library          (TestLib.asm)

; Testing the Irvine32 Library.
```

```
INCLUDE Irvine32.inc
CR = 0Dh                               ; carriage return
LF = 0Ah                               ; line feed

.data
str1 BYTE "Generating 20 random integers between "
     BYTE "0 and 990:",CR,LF,0
str2 BYTE "Enter a 32-bit signed integer: ",0
str3 BYTE "Enter your name: ",0
str4 BYTE "The following key was pressed: ",0
str5 BYTE "Displaying the registers:",CR,LF,0
str6 BYTE "Hello, ",0

buffer   BYTE 50 dup(0)
dwordVal DWORD ?

.code
main PROC
; Set text color to black text on white background:
    mov  eax,black + (white * 16)
    call SetTextColor
    call Clrscr             ; clear the screen
    call Randomize          ; reset random number sequence

; Generate 20 random integers between 0 and 990.
; Include a 500 millisecond delay.
    mov  edx,OFFSET str1    ; display message
    call WriteString
    mov  ecx,20             ; loop counter
    mov  dh,2               ; screen row 2
    mov  dl,0               ; screen column 0

L1: call Gotoxy
    mov  eax,991            ; indicate top of range + 1
    call RandomRange        ; EAX = random integer
    call WriteDec           ; display in unsigned decimal
    mov  eax,500
    call Delay              ; pause for 500 milliseconds
    inc  dh                 ; next screen row
    add  dl,2               ; move 2 columns to the right
    Loop L1
```

```
    call Crlf; new line
    call WaitMsg                ; "Press [Enter]..."
    call Clrscr                 ; clear screen

; Input a signed decimal integer and redisplay it in
; various formats:
    mov  edx,OFFSET str2     ; "Enter a 32-bit..."
    call WriteString
    call ReadInt                ; input the integer
    mov  dwordVal,eax           ; save in a variable
    call Crlf                   ; new line
    call WriteInt               ; display in signed decimal
    call Crlf
    call WriteHex               ; display in hexadecimal
    call Crlf
    call WriteBin               ; display in binary
    call Crlf

; Display the CPU registers:
    call Crlf
    mov  edx,OFFSET str5             ; "Displaying the registers:"
    call WriteString
    call DumpRegs                    ; display registers and flags
    call Crlf

; Display a memory dump:
    mov  esi,OFFSET dwordVal         ; starting OFFSET
    mov  ecx,LENGTHOF dwordVal       ; number of units in dwordVal
    mov  ebx,TYPE dwordVal           ; size of a doubleword
    call DumpMem                     ; display memory
    call Crlf                        ; new line
    call WaitMsg                     ; "Press [Enter]..."

; Ask the user to input their name:
    call Clrscr                      ; clear screen
    mov  edx,OFFSET str3             ; "Enter your name: "
    call WriteString
    mov  edx,OFFSET buffer           ; point to the buffer
    mov  ecx,SIZEOF buffer - 1       ; max. number characters
```

```
        call  ReadString              ; input the name
        mov   edx,OFFSET str6         ; "Hello, "
        call  WriteString
        mov   edx,OFFSET buffer       ; display the name
        call  WriteString
        call  Crlf

        exit
    main ENDP
    END main
```

Sample Output   Here is a sample of the program's output. The integers are randomized, so your own output screen will display different numbers:

After you press Enter, the program displays the following:

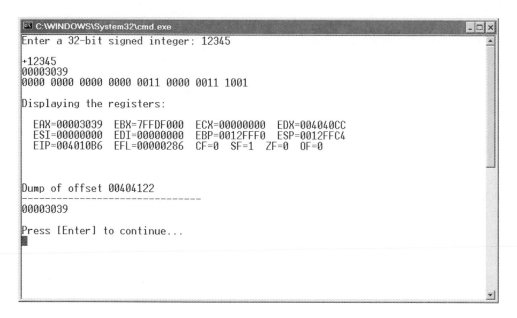

When you enter your name, it is redisplayed by the program. (The final "Press any key" message was not generated by the program.):

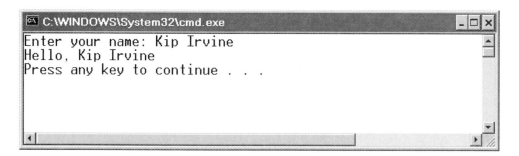

5.3.4   Section Review

1. Which procedure in the link library generates a random integer within a selected range?
2. Which procedure in the link library displays "Press [Enter] to continue..." and waits for the user to press the Enter key?
3. Write statements that cause a program to pause for 700 milliseconds.
4. Which procedure from the link library writes an unsigned integer to standard output in decimal format?

5. Which procedure from the link library places the cursor at a specific console window location?

6. Write the INCLUDE directive that is required when using the Irvine32 library.

7. What types of statements are inside the *Irvine32.inc* file?

8. What are the required input parameters for the **DumpMem** procedure?

9. What are the required input parameters for the **ReadString** procedure?

10. Which processor status flags are displayed by the **DumpRegs** procedure?

11. *Challenge:* Write statements that prompt the user for an identification number and input a string of digits into an array of bytes.

5.4   Stack Operations

If you were to stack ten dinner plates on top of each other as in the illustration shown below, you would be creating a *stack*. If the plates were extremely heavy, it would make sense to have a rule that you cannot pull a plate out from the middle of the stack, but you can remove plates from the top. New plates should only be added to the top of the stack, never to the bottom or middle:

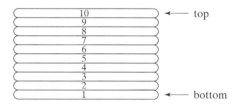

A stack is also called a *LIFO structure* (last-in, first-out), because the last value put into the stack is always the first value taken out. (LIFO is a well-known accounting term, but I prefer plates because they remind me of food.)

A *stack data structure* follows the same principle: new values are added to the top of the stack, and existing values are removed from the top. Stacks in general are useful structures for a variety of programming applications, and they can easily be implemented using object-oriented programming methods. If you have taken a programming course that used data structures, you have worked with the *stack abstract data type*.

In this chapter, however, we concentrate on what is called the *runtime stack*. It is supported directly by hardware in the CPU, and it is an essential part of the mechanism for calling and returning from procedures. Most of the time, we just call it *the stack*.

5.4.1   Runtime Stack

The runtime stack is a memory array that is managed directly by the CPU, using two registers: SS and ESP. In Protected mode, the SS register holds a segment descriptor and is not modified by user programs. The ESP register holds a 32-bit offset into some location on the stack. We rarely manipulate ESP directly; instead, it is indirectly modified by instructions such as CALL, RET, PUSH, and POP.

The stack pointer register (ESP) points to the last integer to be added to, or *pushed* on, the stack. To demonstrate, let's begin with a stack containing one value. In the following illustration, the ESP (extended stack pointer) contains hexadecimal 00001000, the offset of the most recently pushed value (00000006):

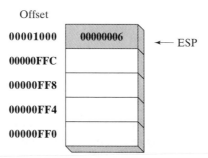

Each stack location in this figure contains 32 bits, which is the case when a program is running in Protected mode. In Real-address mode, each stack location is 16 bits, and the SP register points to the most recently pushed value.

5.4.1.1 Push Operation

A 32-bit *push* operation decrements the stack pointer by 4 and copies a value into the location in the stack pointed to by the stack pointer. In the following figure, we push 000000A5 on the stack:

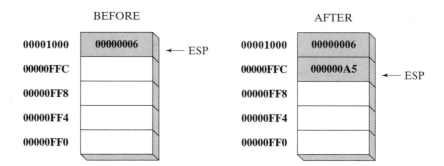

You have probably just noticed that the foregoing figure shows the stack order opposite to that of the stack of plates we saw at the beginning of this section. There's no reason why the runtime stack could not grow upward in memory, but the Intel designers decided that it would grow downward. Regardless of the direction it which it grows, a stack still follows the same last-in first-out principle.

Before the push, ESP = 00001000h, and after the push, ESP = 00000FFCh. The following illustration shows the same stack after pushing two more integers:

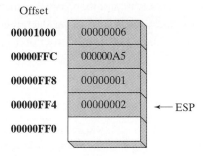

5.4.1.2   Pop Operation

A *pop* operation removes a value from the stack and places it in a register or variable. After the value is popped from the stack, the stack pointer is incremented to point to the next-highest location in the stack. The following diagram shows the stack before and after the value 00000002 is popped from the stack:

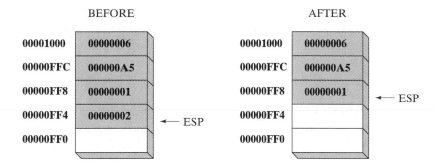

The area of the stack below ESP is *logically empty*, and will be overwritten the next time the current program executes any instruction that pushes a value on the stack.

5.4.1.3   Stack Applications

There are several important uses of stacks in programs:

- A stack makes a convenient temporary save area for registers when they are used for more than one purpose. After they are modified, they can be restored to their original values.
- When the CALL instruction executes, the CPU saves the current procedure's return address on the stack.
- When calling a procedure, we often pass input values called *arguments*. These can be pushed on the stack.
- Local variables inside a procedure are created on the stack and are discarded when the procedure ends.

5.4.2 PUSH and POP Instructions

5.4.2.1 PUSH Instruction

The PUSH instruction first decrements ESP and then copies either a 16- or 32-bit source oper-
and into the stack. A 16-bit operand causes ESP to be decremented by 2. A 32-bit operand
causes ESP to be decremented by 4. There are three instruction formats:

```
PUSH  r/m16
PUSH  r/m32
PUSH  imm32
```

> If your program calls procedures from the Irvine32 library, you should always push 32-bit values; other-
> wise, the Win32 Console functions used by this library will not work correctly. If your program calls pro-
> cedures from the Irvine16 library (in Real-address mode), you can push both 16-bit and 32-bit values.

Immediate values are always 32 bits in Protected mode. In Real-address mode, immediate
values default to 16 bits, unless the .386 processor (or higher) directive is used. (The .386 directive was introduced in Section 3.2.3).

5.4.2.2 POP Instruction

The POP instruction first copies the contents of the stack element pointed to by ESP into a 16- or
32-bit destination operand and then increments ESP. If the operand is 16 bits, ESP is incremented by 2; if the operand is 32 bits, ESP is incremented by 4:

```
POP  r/m16
POP  r/m32
```

5.4.2.3 PUSHFD and POPFD Instructions

The PUSHFD instruction pushes the 32-bit EFLAGS register on the stack, and POPFD pops the
stack into EFLAGS:

```
pushfd
popfd
```

> Real-Address mode programs use the PUSHF instruction to push the 16-bit
> FLAGS register on the stack and POPF to pop the stack into FLAGS.

There are times when it is useful to make a backup copy of the flags so you can restore
them to their former values later. One way to do this is to just enclose any block of code within
PUSHFD and POPFD:

```
pushfd                          ; save the flags
;
; any sequence of statents here...
;
popfd                           ; restore the flags
```

When using pushes and pops of this type, you must be very careful that the program's execution path does not skip over the POPFD. When a program is modified (and hopefully improved) over time, it can be tricky to remember where all the pushes and pops are located. A less error-prone way to do the same thing is to save the flags in a variable:

```
.data
saveFlags DWORD ?
.code
pushfd                     ; push flags on stack
pop  saveFlags             ; copy into a variable
```

The following statements restore the flags from the same variable:

```
push saveFlags             ; push saved flag values
popfd                      ; copy into the flags
```

5.4.2.4   PUSHAD, PUSHA, POPAD, and POPA

The PUSHAD instruction pushes all of the 32-bit general-purpose registers on the stack in the following order: EAX, ECX, EDX, EBX, ESP (original value), EBP, ESI, and EDI. The POPAD instruction pops the same registers off the stack in reverse order. Similarly, the PUSHA instruction, introduced with the 80286 processor, pushes the 16-bit general-purpose registers (AX, CX, DX, BX, SP original value, BP, SI, DI) on the stack in the order listed. The POPA instruction pops the same registers in reverse order.

If you write a procedure that modifies a number of 32-bit registers, use PUSHAD at the beginning of the procedure and POPAD at the end to save and restore the registers. The following code fragment is an example:

```
MySub PROC
    pushad                     ; save general-purpose registers
    .
    .
    mov eax,...
    mov edx,...
    mov ecx,...
    .
    .
    popad                      ; restore general-purpose registers
    ret
MySub ENDP
```

5.4.2.5   Example: Reversing a String

The *RevString.asm* program loops through a string and pushes each character on the stack. It then pops the letters from the stack (in reverse order) and stores them back into the same string variable. Because the stack is a LIFO (*last-in, first-out*) structure, the string is displayed in reverse:

```
TITLE Program Template                 (RevString.asm)
```

```
INCLUDE Irvine32.inc
.data
aName BYTE "Abraham Lincoln",0
nameSize = ($ - aName) - 1

.code
main PROC
; Push the name on the stack.
    mov ecx,nameSize
    mov esi,0

L1:movzx eax,aName[esi]            ; get character
    push eax                        ; push on stack
    inc esi
    Loop L1

; Pop the name from the stack, in reverse,
; and store in the aName array.
    mov ecx,nameSize
    mov esi,0

L2: pop eax                        ; get character
    mov aName[esi],al               ; store in string
    inc esi
    Loop L2

; Display the name.
    mov edx,OFFSET aName
    call Writestring
    call Crlf
    exit
main ENDP
END main
```

5.4.3   Section Review

1. Which two registers (in Protected mode) manage the stack?
2. How is the runtime stack different from the stack abstract data type?
3. Why is the stack called a LIFO structure?
4. When a 32-bit value is pushed on the stack, what happens to ESP?
5. *(True/False)* Only 32-bit values should be pushed on the stack when using the Irvine32 library.
6. *(True/False)* Only 16-bit values should be pushed on the stack when using the Irvine16 library.
7. *(True/False)* Local variables in procedures are created on the stack.
8. *(True/False)* The PUSH instruction cannot have an immediate operand.
9. Which instruction pushes all of the 32-bit general purpose registers on the stack?
10. Which instruction pushes the 32-bit EFLAGS register on the stack?
11. Which instruction pops the stack into the EFLAGS register?

12. *Challenge:* Another assembler (called NASM) permits the PUSH instruction to use specific registers. Why might this approach be better than the PUSHAD instruction in MASM? Here is an example:

```
PUSH EAX EBX ECX
```

5.5 Defining and Using Procedures

If you've already studied a high-level programming language, you know how useful it can be to divide programs into logical units called *functions*. Any complicated problem must be broken into a series of tasks before it can be understood, implemented, and tested effectively. In assembly language, we typically use the more general term *procedure* to mean the same thing.

If your orientation is toward object-oriented programming, you might think of all the functions in a single class as being roughly equivalent to a collection of procedures and data in the same assembly language source code module. Assembly language was created long before object-oriented programming, of course, so it doesn't have the formal structure found in C++, Java, and similar languages. It's up to you to impose whatever formal structure on your programs you deem necessary.

5.5.1 PROC Directive

5.5.1.1 Defining a Procedure

Informally, we can define a *procedure* as a named block of statements that ends in a return statement. A procedure is declared using the PROC and ENDP directives. It must be assigned a name (a valid identifier). Each program we've written so far contains a procedure named **main**, for example:

```
main PROC
.
.
main ENDP
```

When you create a procedure other than your program's startup procedure, end it with a RET instruction. It forces the CPU to return to the location from where the procedure was called:

```
sample PROC
    .
    .
   ret
sample ENDP
```

The startup procedure (**main**) is a special case because it ends with the **exit** statement. When you use the INCLUDE *Irvine32.inc* statement, **exit** is an alias for a call to **ExitProcess**, a MS-Windows function call that terminates the program:

```
INVOKE ExitProcess,0
```

(In Section 8.3.1 we introduce the INVOKE directive, which can call a procedure and pass arguments.)

> If you use the INCLUDE *Irvine16.inc* statement, **exit** is translated to the **.EXIT** assembler directive. The latter causes the assembler to generate the following two instructions:
>
> ```
>     mov ah,4Ch        ; call MS-DOS function 4Ch
>     int 21h           ; terminate program
> ```

5.5.1.2   Example: Sum of Three Integers

Let's create a procedure named **SumOf** that calculates the sum of three 32-bit integers. We will assume that relevant integers are assigned to EAX, EBX, and ECX before the procedure is called. The procedure returns the sum in EAX:

```
SumOf PROC
    add   eax,ebx
    add   eax,ecx
    ret
SumOf ENDP
```

5.5.1.3   Documenting Procedures

A good habit to cultivate is that of adding clear and readable documentation to your programs. The following are a few suggestions for information that you can put at the beginning of each procedure:

- A description of all tasks accomplished by the procedure.
- A list of input parameters and their usage, labeled by a word such as **Receives.** If any input parameters have specific requirements for their input values, list them here.
- A description of any values returned by the procedure, labeled by a word such as **Returns.**
- A list of any special requirements, called *preconditions,* that must be satisfied before the procedure is called. These can be labeled by the word **Requires.** For example, for a procedure that draws a graphics line, a useful precondition would be that the video display adapter must already be in graphics mode.

> The descriptive labels we've chosen, such as Receives, Returns, and Requires, are not absolutes; other useful names are often used.

With these ideas in mind, let's add appropriate documentation to the **SumOf** procedure:

```
;-----------------------------------------------------------
SumOf PROC
;
; Calculates and returns the sum of three 32-bit integers.
; Receives: EAX, EBX, ECX, the three integers. May be
;           signed or unsigned.
```

```
; Returns:   EAX = sum, and the status flags (Carry,
;            Overflow, etc.) are changed.
;--------------------------------------------------------
    add   eax,ebx
    add   eax,ecx
    ret
SumOf ENDP
```

5.5.2   CALL and RET Instructions

The CALL instruction calls a procedure by directing the processor to begin execution at a new memory location. The procedure uses a RET (return from procedure) instruction to bring the processor back to the point in the program where the procedure was called. Mechanically speaking, the CALL instruction pushes its return address on the stack and copies the called procedure's address into the instruction pointer. When the procedure is ready to return, its RET instruction pops the return address from the stack into the instruction pointer. The CPU always executes the instruction in memory pointed to by EIP, the instruction pointer register (or IP, in 16-bit mode).

5.5.2.1   Call and Return Example

Suppose that in **main**, a CALL statement is located at offset 00000020. Typically, this instruction requires five bytes of machine code, so the next statement (a MOV in this case) is located at offset 00000025:

```
          main PROC
00000020    call MySub
00000025    mov  eax,ebx
```

Next, suppose that the first executable instruction in **MySub** is located at offset 00000040:

```
          MySub PROC
00000040    mov eax,edx
              .
              .
            ret
          MySub ENDP
```

When the CALL instruction executes, the address following the call (00000025) is pushed on the stack and the address of **MySub** is loaded into EIP, as shown here:

All the instructions in **MySub** execute up to its RET instruction. When the RET instruction executes, the value in the stack pointed to by ESP is popped into EIP. As the next figure illustrates, this causes the processor to resume execution at offset 00000025, the location of the instruction following the procedure call:

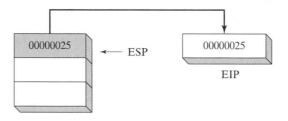

5.5.2.2   Nested Procedure Calls

A *nested procedure call* occurs when a called procedure calls another procedure before the first procedure returns. Suppose that **main** calls a procedure named **Sub1**. While **Sub1** is executing, it calls the **Sub2** procedure. While **Sub2** is executing, it calls the **Sub3** procedure. The process is shown in the next figure:

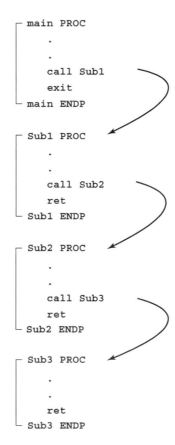

When the RET instruction at the end of **Sub3** executes, it pops the value at stack[ESP] into the instruction pointer. This causes execution to resume at the instruction following the **call Sub3** instruction. The following diagram shows the stack just before the return from **Sub3** is executed:

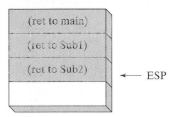

After the return, ESP points to the next-highest stack entry. When the RET instruction at the end of **Sub2** is about to execute, the stack appears as follows:

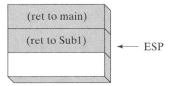

Finally, when **Sub1** returns, stack[ESP] is popped into the instruction pointer, and execution resumes in **main**:

Clearly, the stack proves itself a useful device for remembering information, including nested procedure calls. Stack structures, in general, are used in situations where programs must retrace their steps in a specific order.

5.5.2.3 Local Labels and Global Labels

By default, a code label (followed by a single colon) has *local scope*, making it visible only to statements inside its enclosing procedure. This prevents you from jumping or looping to a label outside the current procedure. In the unlikely event that you really must transfer control to a label outside the current procedure, the label name must be declared *global*. To do this, follow the label name with two colons. For example:

```
GlobalLabel::
```

In the following program excerpt (see *Jumps.asm*), the jump to **L2** from **main** generates a syntax error because **L2** is local to the **sub2** procedure. The jump to **L1** from **sub2**, on the other hand, is legal because **L1** is defined as a global label:

```
main PROC
    jmp L2                          ; error!
L1::                                ; global label
    exit
main ENDP

sub2 PROC
L2:                                 ; local label
    jmp L1                          ; ok
    ret
sub2 ENDP
```

5.5.2.4   Passing Register Arguments to Procedures

If you write a procedure that performs some standard operation such as calculating the sum of an integer array, it's not a good idea to include references to specific variable names inside the procedure. If you were to do that, the procedure could never be used with more than one array. A much better approach is to pass the offset of an array to the procedure, and pass an integer specifying the number of array elements. We call these *arguments* (or *input parameters*). In assembly language, it is common to pass arguments inside general-purpose registers.

In the preceding section we created a simple procedure named **SumOf** that added the integers in the EAX, EBX, and ECX registers. In **main**, before calling **SumOf**, we assign values to EAX, EBX, and ECX:

```
data
theSum  DWORD   ?
.code
main PROC
    mov   eax,10000h                ; argument
    mov   ebx,20000h                ; argument
    mov   ecx,30000h                ; argument
    call  SumOf                     ; EAX = (EAX + EBX + ECX)
    mov   theSum,eax                ; save the sum
```

After the CALL statement, we have the option of copying the sum in EAX to a variable.

5.5.3   Example: Summing an Integer Array

A very common type of loop that you may have already coded in C++ or Java is one that calculates the sum of an integer array. This is very easy to implement in assembly language, and it can be coded in such a way that it will run as fast as possible. For example, one can use registers rather than variables inside a loop.

Let's create a procedure named **ArraySum** that receives two parameters from a calling program: a pointer to an array of 32-bit integers, and a count of the number of array values. It calculates and returns the sum of the array in EAX:

```
;---------------------------------------------------
ArraySum PROC
;
; Calculates the sum of an array of 32-bit integers.
; Receives: ESI = the array offset
;           ECX = number of elements in the array
; Returns:  EAX = sum of the array elements
;---------------------------------------------------
    push esi                    ; save ESI, ECX
    push ecx
    mov  eax,0                  ; set the sum to zero

L1:
    add  eax,[esi]              ; add each integer to sum
    add  esi,4                  ; point to next integer
    loop L1                     ; repeat for array size

    pop  ecx                    ; restore ECX, ESI
    pop  esi
    ret                         ; sum is in EAX
ArraySum ENDP
```

Nothing in this procedure is specific to a certain array name or array size. It could be used in any program that needs to sum an array of 32-bit integers. Whenever possible, you should also create procedures that are flexible and adaptable.

Calling ArraySum   Following is an example of calling **ArraySum**, passing the address of **array** in ESI and the array count in ECX. After the call, we copy the sum in EAX to a variable:

```
.data
array  DWORD  10000h,20000h,30000h,40000h,50000h
theSum DWORD  ?
.code
main PROC
    mov  esi,OFFSET array       ; ESI points to array
    mov  ecx,LENGTHOF array     ; ECX = array count
    call ArraySum               ; calculate the sum
    mov  theSum,eax             ; returned in EAX
```

5.5.4 Flowcharts

A *flowchart* is a well-established way of diagramming program logic. Each shape in a flowchart represents a single logical step, and lines with arrows connecting the shapes show the ordering of the logical steps. Figure 5-1 shows the most common flowchart shapes.

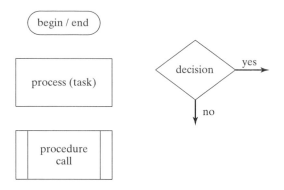

Figure 5-1   Basic Flowchart Shapes.

Text notations such as *yes* and *no* are added next to *decision* symbols to show branching directions. There is no required position for each arrow connected to a decision symbol. Each process symbol can contain one or more closely related instructions. The instructions need not be syntactically correct. For example, we could add 1 to CX using either of the following process symbols:

$$\boxed{cx = cx + 1} \qquad \boxed{add\ cx,1}$$

Let's use the **ArraySum** procedure from the preceding section to design a simple flowchart, shown in Figure 5-2. Note that it uses a decision symbol for the LOOP instruction, because LOOP must determine whether or not to transfer control to a label (based on the value of CX). A code insert shows the original procedure listing.

5.5.5   Saving and Restoring Registers

You may have noticed in the **ArraySum** example that ECX and ESI were pushed on the stack at the beginning of the procedure and popped at the end. This is typical of most procedures that modify registers. Always save and restore registers that are modified by a procedure, so that the calling program can be sure that none of its own register values will be overwritten.

5.5.5.1   USES Operator

The USES operator, coupled with the PROC directive, lets you list the names of all the registers modified within a procedure. This tells the assembler to do two things: First, generate PUSH instructions that save the registers on the stack at the beginning of the procedure. Second, generate POP instructions that restore the register values at the end of the procedure. The USES operator immediately follows PROC, and is itself followed by a list of registers on the same line separated by spaces or tabs (not commas).

ArraySum Procedure

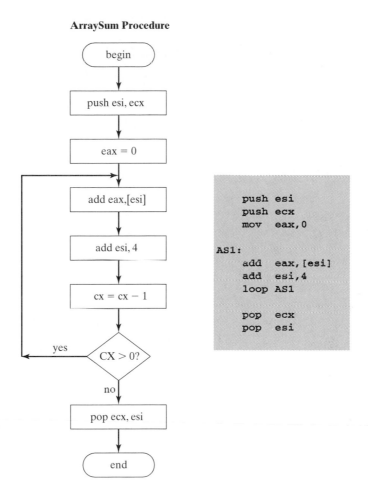

Figure 5-2   Flowchart for the **ArraySum** Procedure.

Let's modify the **ArraySum** procedure from Section 5.5.3. It used PUSH and POP instructions to save and restore ESI and ECX because these registers were modified by the procedure. Instead, we can let the USES operator do the same thing:

```
ArraySum PROC USES esi ecx
    mov eax,0                   ; set the sum to zero

L1:
    add eax,[esi]               ; add each integer to sum
    add esi,4                   ; point to next integer
    loop L1                     ; repeat for array size
```

```
    ret                         ; sum is in EAX
ArraySum ENDP
```

The following code would be generated by the assembler:

```
ArraySum PROC
    push esi
    push ecx
    mov eax,0                   ; set the sum to zero

L1:
    add eax,[esi]               ; add each integer to sum
    add esi,4                   ; point to next integer
    loop L1                     ; repeat for array size

    pop ecx
    pop esi
    ret
ArraySum ENDP
```

> *Debugging Tip:* If you're using a debugger such as Microsoft Visual Studio, you can view the hidden machine instructions generated by MASM's advanced operators and directives. Select *Debug Windows* from the *View* menu, and select *Dissassembly*. This window shows both your program's source code and all hidden machine instructions generated by the assembler.

Exception   There is an important exception to our standing rule about saving registers that applies when a procedure uses a register to return a value. In this case, the return register should not be pushed and popped. For example, in the **SumOf** procedure, if we were to push and pop EAX, the procedure's return value would be lost:

```
SumOf PROC                      ; sum of three integers
    push eax                    ; save EAX
    add   eax,ebx               ; calculate the sum
    add   eax,ecx               ; of EAX, EBX, ECX
    pop   eax                   ; lost the sum!
    ret
SumOf ENDP
```

5.5.6 Section Review

1. *(True/False)* The PROC directive begins a procedure and the ENDP directive ends a procedure.
2. *(True/False)* It is possible to define a procedure inside an existing procedure.
3. What would happen if the RET instruction was omitted from a procedure?
4. How are the words *Receives* and *Returns* used in the suggested procedure documentation?

5. *(True/False)* The CALL instruction pushes the offset of the CALL instruction on the stack.

6. *(True/False)* The CALL instruction pushes the offset of the instruction following the CALL on the stack.

7. *(True/False)* The RET instruction pops the stack into the instruction pointer.

8. *(True/False)* Nested procedure calls are not permitted by the Microsoft assembler unless the NESTED operator is used in the procedure definition.

9. *(True/False)* In Protected mode, each procedure call uses a minimum of four bytes of stack space.

10. *(True/False)* The ESI and EDI registers cannot be used when passing parameters to procedures.

11. *(True/False)* The **ArraySum** procedure (Section 5.5.3) can receive a pointer to any array of doublewords.

12. *(True/False):* The USES operator lets you name all registers that are modified within a procedure.

13. *(True/False):* The USES operator only generates PUSH instructions, so you must code POP instructions yourself.

14. *(True/False):* The register list in the USES directive must use commas to separate the register names.

15. Which statement(s) in the **ArraySum** procedure (Section 5.5.3) would have to be modified so it could work with an array of 16-bit words? Demonstrate.

5.6   Program Design Using Procedures

Any programming application beyond the trivial tends to involve a number of different steps. It is possible to write all of the program code in a single procedure, but one quickly finds that such a program is difficult to read and maintain. Instead, we divide up the various program tasks into separate procedures. The procedures may all be in the same source code file, or they may be spread out over multiple files.

When you begin to write a program, it is helpful to already have a set of specifications that list exactly what the program is supposed to do. They will often be the result of careful analysis of a real-world problem that needs to be solved. Using the specifications as a starting point, you can design your program.

A standard design approach is to divide an overall problem into discrete tasks, each of which can be coded in a single procedure. This process of dividing up a problem into tasks is often called *functional decomposition*, or *top-down design*. Here are some assumptions implied by this approach:

- A large problem may be more easily divided into small tasks.
- A program is easier to maintain if each procedure can be tested separately.
- A top-down design lets you see how procedures are related to each other.

• When you are sure of the overall design, you can more easily concentrate on details, writing code that implements each procedure.

In the next section, we use the top-down approach to design and implement the solution to a fairly simple problem (adding integers). The same approach could be used to design much more complex programs.

5.6.1 Integer Summation Program (Design)

The following are specifications for a simple program that we will call **Integer Summation**:

> Write a program that prompts the user for one or more 32-bit integers, stores them in an array, calculates the sum of the array, and displays the sum on the screen.

The following pseudocode shows how we might divide the specifications into tasks:

```
Integer Summation Program
    Prompt user for three integers
    Calculate the sum of the array
    Display the sum
```

In preparation for writing a program, let's assign a procedure name to each task:

```
Main
    PromptForIntegers
    ArraySum
    DisplaySum
```

In assembly language, input-output tasks often require detailed code to implement. To reduce some of this detail, we can call procedures that clear the screen, display a string, input an integer, and display an integer:

```
Main
    Clrscr                      ; clear screen
    PromptForIntegers
        WriteString             ; display string
        ReadInt                 ; input integer
    ArraySum                    ; sum the integers
    DisplaySum
        WriteString             ; display string
        WriteInt                ; display integer
```

Structure Chart   The following diagram, called a *structure chart*, describes the program's structure. Procedures from the link library are shaded:

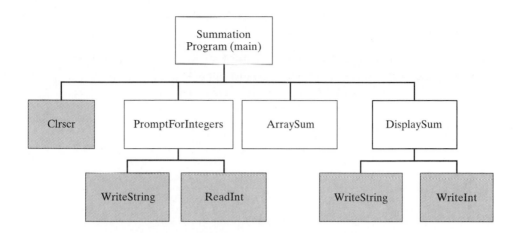

Stub Program   Let's create a minimal version of the program called a *stub program*. It contains only empty (or nearly empty) procedures. The program assembles and runs, but does not actually do anything useful:

```
TITLE Integer Summation Program    (Sum1.asm)

; This program inputs multiple integers from the user,
; stores them in an array, calculates the sum of the
; array, and displays the sum.

INCLUDE Irvine32.inc
.code
main PROC
; Main program control procedure.
; Calls: Clrscr, PromptForIntegers,
;        ArraySum, DisplaySum

    exit
main ENDP

;----------------------------------------------------
PromptForIntegers PROC
;
; Prompts the user for an array of integers, and
; fills the array with the user's input.
; Receives: ESI points to an array of
;   doubleword integers, ECX = array size.
; Returns: nothing
; Calls: ReadInt, WriteString
;----------------------------------------------------
    ret
PromptForIntegers ENDP
```

```
;------------------------------------------------------
ArraySum PROC
;
; Calculates the sum of an array of 32-bit integers.
; Receives: ESI points to the array, ECX = array size
; Returns:  EAX = sum of the array elements
;------------------------------------------------------
    ret
ArraySum ENDP


;------------------------------------------------------
DisplaySum PROC
;
; Displays the sum on the screen.
; Recevies: EAX = the sum
; Returns: nothing
; Calls: WriteString, WriteInt
;------------------------------------------------------
    ret
DisplaySum ENDP
END main
```

A stub program gives you the chance to map out all procedure calls, study the dependencies between procedures, and possibly improve the structural design before coding the details. You definitely should use comments in each procedure to explain its purpose and parameter requirements.

5.6.1.1 Integer Summation Implementation

It's time to complete the summation program. An array of integers is declared in the data segment, using a symbol name for the array size:

```
IntegerCount = 3
array DWORD IntegerCount DUP(?)
```

A couple of strings are used as screen prompts:

```
prompt1 BYTE "Enter a signed integer: ",0
prompt2 BYTE "The sum of the integers is: ",0
```

The **main** procedure clears the screen, passes an array pointer to the **PromptForIntegers** procedure, calls **ArraySum**, and calls **DisplaySum**:

```
    call Clrscr
    mov  esi,OFFSET array
    mov  ecx,IntegerCount
    call PromptForIntegers
    call ArraySum
    call DisplaySum
```

- **PromptForIntegers** calls **WriteString** to prompt the user for an integer. It then calls **ReadInt** to input the integer from the user, and stores the integer in the array pointed to by ESI. A loop executes these steps multiple times.
- **ArraySum** calculates and returns the sum of an array of integers.
- **DisplaySum** displays a message on the screen ("The sum of the integers is:") and calls **WriteInt** to display the integer in EAX.

Complete Program Listing   The following listing shows the completed Summation program:

```
TITLE Integer Summation Program          (Sum2.asm)

; This program inputs multiple integers from the user,
; stores them in an array, calculates the sum of the
; array, and displays the sum.

INCLUDE Irvine32.inc

IntegerCount = 3                    ; array size

.data
prompt1 BYTE   "Enter a signed integer: ",0
prompt2 BYTE   "The sum of the integers is: ",0
array   DWORD  IntegerCount DUP(?)

.code
main PROC
    call Clrscr
    mov   esi,OFFSET array
    mov   ecx,IntegerCount
    call PromptForIntegers
    call ArraySum
    call DisplaySum
    exit
main ENDP

;-----------------------------------------------------
PromptForIntegers PROC
;
; Prompts the user for an array of integers, and fills
; the array with the user's input.
; Receives: ESI points to the array, ECX = array size
; Returns:  nothing
;-----------------------------------------------------
    pushad                          ; save all registers

    mov   edx,OFFSET prompt1        ; address of the prompt

L1:
    call WriteString                ; display string
    call ReadInt                    ; read integer into EAX
    call Crlf                       ; go to next output line
```

```
    mov   [esi],eax              ; store in array
    add   esi,4                  ; next integer
    loop L1

    popad                        ; restore all registers
    ret
PromptForIntegers ENDP

;------------------------------------------------------
ArraySum PROC
;
; Calculates the sum of an array of 32-bit integers.
; Receives: ESI points to the array
;           ECX = number of elements in the array
; Returns:  EAX = sum of the array elements
;------------------------------------------------------
    push  esi              ; save ESI, ECX
    push  ecx
    mov   eax,0            ; set the sum to zero

L1:
    add   eax,[esi]        ; add each integer to sum
    add   esi,4           ; point to next integer
    loop L1               ; repeat for array size

    pop   ecx             ; restore ECX, ESI
    pop   esi
    ret                   ; sum is in EAX
ArraySum ENDP

;------------------------------------------------------
DisplaySum PROC
;
; Displays the sum on the screen
; Recevies: EAX = the sum
; Returns:  nothing
;------------------------------------------------------
    push edx

    mov   edx,OFFSET prompt2    ; display message
    call WriteString
    call WriteInt              ; display EAX
    call Crlf

    pop  edx
    ret
DisplaySum ENDP
END main
```

5.6.2   Section Review

1. What is the name given to the process of dividing up large tasks into smaller ones?
2. Which procedures in the Summation program design (Section 5.6.1) are located in the Irvine32 library?
3. What is a *stub program*?
4. *(True/False):* The **ArraySum** procedure of the Summation program (Section 5.6.1.1) directly references the name of an array variable.
5. Which lines in the **PromptForIntegers** procedure of the Summation program (Section 5.6.1.1) would have to be modified so it could handle an array of 16-bit words? Demonstrate.
6. Draw a flowchart for the **PromptForIntegers** procedure of the Summation program (flowcharts were introduced in Section 5.5.4).

5.7   Chapter Summary

This chapter introduces the book's link library, to make it easier for you to process input-output in assembly language applications.

Table 5-1 lists most of the procedures from the Irvine32 link library. The most up-to-date listing of all procedures is available on the book's Web site.

The *library test program* in Section 5.3.3 demonstrates a number of input-output functions from the Irvine32 library. It generates and displays a list of random numbers, a register dump, and a memory dump. It displays integers in various formats, and demonstrates string input/output.

The *runtime stack* is a special array that is used as a temporary holding area for addresses and data. The ESP register holds a 32-bit OFFSET into some location on the stack. The stack is called a LIFO structure (*last-in, first-out*), because the last value placed in the stack is the first value taken out. A *push* operation copies a value into the stack. A *pop* operation removes a value from the stack and copies it to a register or variable. Stacks often hold procedure return addresses, procedure parameters, local variables, and registers used internally by procedures.

The PUSH instruction first decrements the stack pointer and then copies a source operand into the stack. The POP instruction first copies the contents of the stack pointed to by ESP into a 16- or 32-bit destination operand and then increments ESP.

The PUSHAD instruction pushes the 32-bit general-purpose registers on the stack, and the PUSHA instruction does the same for the 16-bit general-purpose registers. The POPAD instruction pops the stack into the 32-bit general-purpose registers, and the POPA instruction does the same for the 16-bit general-purpose registers.

The PUSHFD instruction pushes the 32-bit EFLAGS register on the stack, and POPFD pops the stack into EFLAGS. PUSHF and POPF do the same for the 16-bit FLAGS register.

The *RevString* program, presented in Section 5.4.2.5, uses the stack to reverse a string of characters.

A *procedure* is a named block of code, declared using the PROC and ENDP directives. A procedure always ends with the RET instruction. The **SumOf** procedure, shown in Section 5.5.1.2, calculates the sum of three integers. The CALL instruction executes a procedure by inserting the procedure's address into the instruction pointer register. When the procedure finishes, the RET (return from procedure) instruction brings the processor back to the point in the program from where the procedure was called. A *nested procedure call* occurs when a called procedure calls another procedure before it returns.

By default, a code label (followed by a single colon) is considered local to its enclosing procedure. A code label followed by :: is a global label, making it accessible from any statement in the same source code file.

The **ArraySum** procedure, shown in Section 5.5.3, calculates and returns the sum of the elements in an array.

The USES operator, coupled with the PROC directive, lets you list all registers modified by a procedure. The assembler generates code that pushes the registers at the beginning of the procedure and pops the registers before returning.

A program of any size should be carefully designed from a set of clear specifications. A standard approach is to use functional decomposition (top-down design) to divide the program into procedures (functions). First, determine the ordering and connections between procedures, and later fill in the procedure details.

5.8 Programming Exercises

1. Draw Text Colors
Write a program that displays a string in four different colors, using the **SetTextColor** procedure from the book's link library.

2. Integer Array Input
Write a program that uses a loop to input ten signed 32-bit integers from the user, stores the integers in an array, and redisplays the integers.

3. Simple Addition (1)
Write a program that clears the screen, locates the cursor near the middle of the screen, prompts the user for two integers, adds the integers, and displays their sum.

4. Simple Addition (2)
Use the solution program from the preceding exercise as a starting point. Let this new program repeat the same steps three times, using a loop. Clear the screen after each loop iteration.

5. Random Integers
Write a program that generates and displays 50 random integers between −20 and +20.

6. Random Strings

Write a program that generates and displays twenty random strings, each consisting of ten capital letters {A..Z}.

7. Random Screen Locations

Write a program that displays a single character at 100 random screen locations. *Optional:* use a randomized delay between characters, between 10 and 300 milliseconds.

8. Color Matrix

Write a program that displays a single character in all possible combinations of foreground and background colors ($16 \times 16 = 256$). The colors are numbered from 0 to 15, so you can use a nested loop to generate all possible combinations.

6

Conditional Processing

6.1   Introduction

In the preceding chapters, you may have felt very restricted by not being able to include any decision-making in your programs. We've managed to create counting loops, procedures, data definitions, and array processing, while carefully avoiding decision making. This was by design, of course, because IF statements and conditional processing are a little more complicated in assembly language than in high-level languages.

After reading this chapter, you will be able to answer such questions as:

* How can I use the boolean operations introduced in Chapter 1 (AND, OR, NOT)?
* How do I write an IF statement in assembly language?
* How are nested-IF statements translated by compilers into machine language?
* How can I set and clear individual bits in a binary number?
* How can I do simple binary encryption of data?
* How do I tell the computer I'm comparing signed numbers versus unsigned numbers?
* What's a Finite State Machine?
* Isn't there any way to create the kinds of IF - ELSE - ENDIF structures in assembly language that I'm used to using in C++ and Java?
* Is GOTO really considered harmful?

This chapter follows a *bottom-up* approach, where you are first shown the binary foundations behind programming logic. Next, you will see how the CPU compares instruction operands, using the CMP instruction and the processor status flags. Finally, we put it all together and show how to use assembly language to implement logic structures characteristic of high-level languages.

6.2   Boolean and Comparison Instructions

We're going to begin the study of conditional processing by working at the binary level, using the four basic operations from boolean algebra: AND, OR, XOR, and NOT. These operations are used in the design of computer hardware and software.

The IA-32 instruction set contains the AND, OR, XOR, NOT, TEST, and B*Top* instructions, which directly implement boolean operations between bytes, words, and doublewords (see Table 6-1).

Table 6-1   Selected Boolean Instructions.

Operation	Description
AND	Boolean AND operation between a source operand and a destination operand.
OR	Boolean OR operation between a source operand and a destination operand.

Table 6-1   Selected Boolean Instructions. (Continued)

Operation	Description
XOR	Boolean exclusive-OR operation between a source operand and a destination operand.
NOT	Boolean NOT operation on a destination operand.
TEST	Implied boolean AND operation between a source and destination operand, setting the CPU flags appropriately.
BT, BTC, BTR, BTS	Copy bit *n* from the source operand to the Carry flag and complement/reset/set the same bit in the destination operand (covered in Section 6.3.5).

6.2.1   The CPU Flags

Each instruction in this section affects the CPU flags. You may recall from Chapter 4 that the Zero, Carry, and Sign flags show the results of boolean and comparison instructions.

- The Zero flag is set when the result of an operation equals zero.
- The Carry flag is set when an instruction generates a result that is too large (or too small) for the destination operand.
- The Sign flag is a copy of the high bit of the destination operand, indicating that it is negative if *set* and positive if *clear.*
- The Overflow flag is set when an instruction generates an invalid signed result.
- The Parity flag is set when an instruction generates an even number of 1 bits in the low byte of the destination operand.

6.2.2   AND Instruction

The AND instruction performs a boolean (bitwise) AND operation between each pair of matching bits in two operands and places the result in the destination operand:

```
AND   destination,source
```

The following operand combinations are permitted:

```
AND  reg,reg
AND  reg,mem
AND  reg,imm
AND  mem,reg
AND  mem,imm
```

The operands can be 8, 16, or 32 bits, and they must be the same size. For each matching bit in the two operands, the following rule applies: If both bits equal 1, the result bit is 1; otherwise, it is 0. The following truth table from Chapter 1 labels the input bits x and y. The third column shows the value of the expression **x** ∧ **y**:

x	y	x ∧ y
0	0	0
0	1	0
1	0	0
1	1	1

The AND instruction is often used to clear selected bits and preserve others. In the following example, the upper four bits are cleared and the lower four bits are unchanged:

```
                00111011
        AND     00001111
cleared ──────┤0000│1011├──── unchanged
```

The following instructions carry out this operation:

```
mov al,00111011b
and al,00001111b
```

The lower four bits might contain useful information, while we don't care about the upper four bits. It is useful to think of this technique as *bit extraction* because the lower four bits are "pulled" from AL.

Flags   The AND instruction always clears the Overflow and Carry flags. It modifies the Sign, Zero, and Parity flags according to the value of the destination operand.

6.2.2.1   Converting Characters to Upper Case

The AND instruction provides an easy way to translate a letter from lowercase to uppercase. If we compare the ASCII codes of capital **A** and lowercase **a**, it becomes clear that only bit 5 is different:

```
0 1 1 0 0 0 0 1 = 61h ('a')
0 1 0 0 0 0 0 1 = 41h ('A')
```

The rest of the alphabetic characters have the same relationship. If we AND any character with 11011111 binary, all bits are unchanged except for bit 5, which is cleared. In the following example, all characters in an array are converted to uppercase:

```
.data
array BYTE 50 DUP(?)
.code
    mov ecx,LENGTHOF array
    mov esi,OFFSET array
```

```
L1:
    AND  byte ptr [esi],11011111b            ;clear bit 5
    inc  esi
    loop L1
```

6.2.3   OR Instruction

The OR instruction performs a boolean OR operation between each pair of matching bits in two operands and places the result in the destination operand:

```
OR   destination,source
```

The OR instruction uses the same operand combinations as the AND instruction:

```
OR   reg,reg
OR   reg,mem
OR   reg,imm
OR   mem,reg
OR   mem,imm
```

The operands can be 8, 16, or 32 bits, and they must be the same size. For each matching bit in the two operands, the output bit is 1 when at least one of the input bits is 1. The following truth table (from Chapter 1) describes the boolean expression $\mathbf{x} \lor \mathbf{y}$:

x	y	x ∨ y
0	0	0
0	1	1
1	0	1
1	1	1

The OR instruction is often used to set selected bits and preserve others. In the following figure, 3Bh is ORed with 0Fh. The lower four bits of the result are set and the high four bits are unchanged:

```
                    00111011
              OR    00001111
unchanged ——[0011|1111]—— set
```

The OR instruction can be used to convert a byte containing an integer between 0 and 9 into an ASCII digit. To do this, you must set bits 4 and 5. If, for example, AL = 05h, you can OR it with 30h to convert it to the ASCII code for the digit 5 (35h):

```
            00000101      05h
   OR  00110000          30h
            00110101      35h, '5'
```

The assembly language instructions to do this are as follows:

```
   mov dl,5                    ; binary value
   or  dl,30h                  ; convert to ASCII
```

Flags   The OR instruction always clears the Carry and Overflow flags. It modifies the Sign, Zero, and Parity flags according to the value of the destination operand. For example, you can OR a number with itself (or zero) to obtain certain information about its value:

```
   or  al,al
```

The values of the Zero and Sign flags indicate the following about the contents of AL:

Zero Flag	Sign Flag	Value in AL is . . .
clear	clear	greater than zero
set	clear	equal to zero
clear	set	less than zero

6.2.4 XOR Instruction

The XOR instruction performs a boolean exclusive-OR operation between each pair of matching bits in two operands, and stores the result in the destination operand:

```
   XOR   destination,source
```

The XOR instruction uses the same operand combinations as the AND and OR instructions. The operands can be 8, 16, or 32 bits. For each matching bit in the two operands, the following applies: If both bits are the same (both 0 or both 1) the result is 0; otherwise, the result is 1. The following truth table describes the boolean expression $x \oplus y$:

x	y	$x \oplus y$
0	0	0
0	1	1
1	0	1
1	1	0

Note from this table that any bit exclusive-ORed with 0 retains its value, and any bit exclusive-ORed with 1 is toggled (complemented).

A special quality of XOR is that it reverses itself when applied twice to the same operand. The following truth table shows that when bit *x* is exclusive-ORed with bit *y* twice, it reverts to its original value:

x	y	x $\oplus$ y	(x $\oplus$ y) $\oplus$ y
0	0	0	0
0	1	1	0
1	0	1	1
1	1	0	1

As we will find out in Section 6.3.4.3, this "reversible" property of XOR makes it an ideal tool for a simple form of data encryption.

Flags   The XOR instruction always clears the Overflow and Carry flags. It modifies the Sign, Zero, and Parity flags according to the value of the destination operand.

Checking the Parity Flag   The Parity flag indicates whether the *lowest byte* of the result of a bitwise or arithmetic operation has an even or odd number of 1 bits. The flag is is set when the parity is even, and it is clear when the parity is odd. One way to check the parity of a number without changing its value is to exclusive-OR the number with all zeros:

```
mov al,10110101b              ; 5 bits = odd parity
xor al,0                      ; Parity flag clear (PO)
mov al,11001100b              ; 4 bits = even parity
xor al,0                      ; Parity flag set (PE)
```

(Debuggers often use PE to indicate even parity, and PO to indicate odd parity.)

16-Bit Parity   You can check the parity of a 16-bit register by performing an exclusive-OR between the upper and lower bytes:

```
mov ax,64C1h                  ; 0110 0100 1100 0001
xor ah,al                     ; Parity flag set (PE)
```

Think of the 1 bits in each register as being members of an 8-bit set. The XOR instruction eliminates any bits that represent the intersection between the two sets. XOR also forms the union between the remaining bits. The parity of this union will be the same as the parity of the entire 16-bit integer.

What about 32-bit values? If we number the bytes from B_0 through B_3, the parity can be calculated as: B_0 XOR B_1 XOR B_2 XOR B_3.

6.2.5   NOT Instruction

The NOT instruction toggles all bits in an operand. The result is called the *one's complement*. The following operand types are permitted:

```
NOT reg
NOT mem
```

For example, the one's complement of F0h is 0Fh:

```
mov   al,11110000b
not   al                         ; AL = 00001111b
```

Flags   No flags are affected by the NOT instruction.

6.2.6   TEST Instruction

The TEST instruction performs an implied AND operation between each pair of matching bits in two operands and sets the flags accordingly. The only difference between TEST and AND is that TEST does not modify the destination operand. The TEST instruction permits the same operand combinations as the AND instruction. TEST is particularly valuable for finding out if individual bits in an operand are set.

Example: Testing Multiple Bits   The TEST instruction can check several bits at once. Suppose we want to know if either bit 0 or bit 3 is set in the AL register. We can use the following instruction to find this out:

```
test al,00001001b                ; test bits 0 and 3
```

From the following example data sets, we can infer that the Zero flag is set only when all tested bits are clear:

```
0 0 1 0 0 1 0 1  <- input value
0 0 0 0 1 0 0 1  <- test value
0 0 0 0 0 0 0 1  <- result: ZF = 0

0 0 1 0 0 1 0 0  <- input value
0 0 0 0 1 0 0 1  <- test value
0 0 0 0 0 0 0 0  <- result: ZF = 1
```

Flags   The TEST instruction always clears the Overflow and Carry flags. It modifies the Sign, Zero, and Parity flags in the same way as the AND instruction.

6.2.7   CMP Instruction

The CMP (compare) instruction performs an implied subtraction of a source operand from a destination operand. Neither operand is modified:

CMP *destination,source*

CMP uses the same operand combinations as the AND instruction.

Flags The CMP instruction changes the Overflow, Sign, Zero, Carry, Auxiliary Carry, and Parity flags according to the value the destination operand would have had if the SUB instruction were used. For example, as shown below, when two operands are compared, the Zero and Carry flags indicate the relation between operands:

CMP Results	ZF	CF
destination < source	0	1
destination > source	0	0
destination = source	1	0

If the two operands being compared are assumed to be signed, the Sign, Zero, and Overflow flags indicate the following relations between operands:

CMP Results	Flags
destination < source	SF ≠ OF
destination > source	SF = OF
destination = source	ZF = 1

CMP is valuable because it provides the basis for most conditional logic structures. When you follow a CMP with a conditional jump instruction, the result is the assembly language equivalent of an IF statement.

Examples Let's look at three code fragments that show how the flags are affected by the CMP instruction. When we put 5 in AX and compare it to 10, the Carry flag is set because subtracting 10 from 5 requires a borrow:

```
mov   ax,5
cmp   ax,10             ; CF = 1
```

Comparing 1000 to 1000 sets the Zero flag because subtracting the source from the destination produces zero:

```
mov   ax,1000
mov   cx,1000
cmp   cx,ax             ; ZF = 1
```

Comparing 105 to 0 clears both the Zero and Carry flags because 105 is greater than 0:

```
mov   si,105
cmp   si,0              ; ZF = 0 and CF = 0
```

6.2.8 Setting and Clearing Individual CPU Flags

My students often ask: What is the easiest way to set or clear the Zero, Sign, Carry, and Overflow flags? There are a number of simple ways to change these flags, most of which require modifying the destination. To set the Zero flag, AND any operand with Zero; to clear the flag, OR the operand with 1:

```
and al,0                 ; set Zero flag
or  al,1                 ; clear Zero flag
```

To set the Sign flag, OR the highest bit of an operand with 1. To clear the sign flag, AND the highest bit with 0:

```
or  al,80h               ; set Sign flag
and al,7Fh               ; clear Sign flag
```

To set the Carry flag, use the STC instruction; to clear the Carry flag, use CLC:

```
stc                      ; set Carry flag
clc                      ; clear Carry flag
```

To set the Overflow flag, add two positive byte values that produce a negative sum. To clear the Overflow flag, OR an operand with 0:

```
mov al,7Fh               ; AL = +127
inc al                   ; AL = 80h (-128), OF=1
or eax,0                 ; clear Overflow flag
```

6.2.9 Section Review

1. In the following instruction sequence, show the changed value of AL where indicated, in binary:

```
mov al,00001111b
and al,00111011b         ; a.
mov al,6Dh
and al,4Ah               ; b.
mov al,00001111b
or  al,61h               ; c.
mov al,94h
xor al,37h               ; d.
```

2. In the following instruction sequence, show the changed value of AL where indicated, in hexadecimal:

```
mov al,7Ah
not al                   ; a.
mov al,3Dh
and al,74h               ; b.
mov al,9Bh
```

```
or   al,35h             ; c.
mov al,72h
xor al,0DCh             ; d.
```

3. In the following instruction sequence, show the values of the Carry, Zero, and Sign flags where indicated:

```
mov al,00001111b
test al,2               ; a. CF=    ZF=    SF=
mov al,6
cmp al,5                ; b. CF=    ZF=    SF=
mov al,5
cmp al,7                ; c. CF=    ZF=    SF=
```

4. Write a single instruction that clears the high 8 bits of AX and does not change the low 8 bits.

5. Write a single instruction that sets the high 8 bits of AX and does not change the low 8 bits.

6. Write a single instruction that reverses all the bits in EAX (do not use the NOT instruction).

7. Write instructions that set the Zero flag if the 32-bit value in EAX is even, and clear the Zero flag if EAX is odd.

8. *Challenge:* Write instructions that calculate the parity of the 32-bit memory operand, *Hint:* use the formula presented earlier in this section: B_0 XOR B_1 XOR B_2 XOR B_3

6.3 Conditional Jumps

6.3.1 Conditional Structures

There are no high-level logic structures in the IA-32 instruction set, but you can implement any logic structure, no matter how complex, using a combination of comparisons and jumps. Two steps are involved in executing a conditional statement: First, an operation such as CMP, AND, or SUB modifies the CPU flags. Second, a conditional jump instruction tests the flags and causes a branch to a new address. Let's look at a couple of examples.

Example 1 The CMP instruction compares AL to Zero. The JZ (jump if Zero) instruction jumps to label **L1** if the Zero flag was set by the CMP instruction:

```
        cmp    al,0
        jz     L1               ; jump if ZF = 1
        .
        .
    L1:
```

Example 2 The AND instruction performs a bitwise AND on the DL register, affecting the Zero flag. The JNZ (jump if not Zero) instruction jumps if the Zero flag is clear:

```
        and    dl,10110000b
        jnz    L2                          ; jump if ZF = 0
          .
          .
    L2:
```

6.3.2   J*cond* Instruction

A conditional jump instruction branches to a destination label when a flag condition is true. If the flag condition is false, the instruction immediately following the conditional jump is executed. The syntax is:

    Jcond destination

cond refers to a flag condition, identifying the state of one or more flags. For example:

jc	jump if carry (Carry flag set)
jnc	jump if not carry (Carry flag clear)
jz	jump if zero (Zero flag set)
jnz	jump if not zero (Zero flag clear)

We have already seen that flags are set by arithmetic, comparison, and boolean instructions. Each conditional jump instruction checks one or more flags, returning a result of true or false. If the result is true, the jump is taken; otherwise, the program skips the jump and continues to the next instruction.

Limitations   By default, MASM requries the *destination* of the jump to be a label within the current procedure (we mentioned this with JMP in Chapter 5). To get around this restriction, you can declare a global label (followed by ::):

```
        jc MyLabel
          .
          .
    MyLabel::
```

Also, the jump must be within −128 to +127 bytes from the offset of the next instruction. When a conditional jump is encoded as a machine instruction, the destination operand is represented as an 8-bit displacement.

Using the CMP Instruction   Suppose we want to jump to location **L1** when AX and BX are equal. In the next example, CMP sets the Zero flag because AX = BX, and the JE instruction jumps because the Zero flag is set:

```
        mov ax,5
        cmp ax,5
        je  L1                          ; jump if equal
```

On the other hand, the following jump is taken because AX is less than 6:

```
mov ax,5
cmp ax,6
jl  L1                          ; jump if less
```

In the following example, the jump is taken because AX is greater than 4:

```
mov ax,5
cmp ax,4
jg  L1                          ; jump if greater
```

6.3.3   Types of Conditional Jump Instructions

Most people are surprised when they find out how many different types of conditional jump instructions are available. Some instruction names are redundant, in that they simply provide a different name for an existing instruction. But the sheer variety of jumps provides for the full range of conditional statements programmers might want to invent. It is convenient to partition the conditional jump instructions into four groups:

- Based on specific flag values.
- Based on equality between operands, or the value of (E)CX.
- Based on comparisons of unsigned operands.
- Based on comparisons of signed operands.

Table 6-2 shows a list of jumps based on specific CPU flag values: Zero, Carry, Overflow, Parity, and Sign.

Table 6-2   Jumps Based on Specific Flag Values.

Mnemonic	Description	Flags
JZ	Jump if zero	$ZF = 1$
JNZ	Jump if not zero	$ZF = 0$
JC	Jump if carry	$CF = 1$
JNC	Jump if not carry	$CF = 0$
JO	Jump if overflow	$OF = 1$
JNO	Jump if not overflow	$OF = 0$
JS	Jump if signed	$SF = 1$
JNS	Jump if not signed	$SF = 0$
JP	Jump if parity (even)	$PF = 1$
JNP	Jump if not parity (odd)	$PF = 0$

6.3.3.1   Equality Comparisons

Table 6-3 lists jump instructions based on evaluating either the equality of two operands or the values of CX and ECX. In the table, the notations *leftOp* and *rightOp* refer to the left (destination) and right (source) operands in a CMP instruction:

```
CMP leftOp,rightOp
```

These operand names reflect the ordering of operands for relational operators in algebra. For example, in the expression X < Y, X can be called *leftOp* and Y called *rightOp*.

Table 6-3   Jumps Based on Equality.

Mnemonic	Description
JE	Jump if equal (*leftOp* = *rightOp*)
JNE	Jump if not equal (*leftOp* ≠ *rightOp*)
JCXZ	Jump if CX = 0
JECXZ	Jump if ECX = 0

6.3.3.2   Unsigned Comparisons

Jumps based specifically on comparisons of unsigned integers are shown in Table 6-4. This type of jump is useful when comparing unsigned values, such as 7FFFh and 8000h, where the former is smaller than the latter.

Table 6-4   Jumps Based on Unsigned Comparisons.

Mnemonic	Description
JA	Jump if above (if *leftOp* > *rightOp*)
JNBE	Jump if not below or equal (same as JA)
JAE	Jump if above or equal (if *leftOp* >= *rightOp*)
JNB	Jump if not below (same as JAE)
JB	Jump if below (if *leftOp* < *rightOp*)
JNAE	Jump if not above or equal (same as JB)
JBE	Jump if below or equal (if *leftOp* <= *rightOp*)
JNA	Jump if not above (same as JBE)

6.3.3.3   Signed Comparisons

Table 6-5 displays a list of jumps based on signed comparisons. These are used when the numbers you're comparing can be interpreted as signed values. For example, when the processor compares 80h to 7Fh, the interpretation is quite different depending on whether JA or JG is used:

```
mov   ax,80h            ; (80h or -128)
cmp   ax,7Fh            ; (7Fh or +127)
ja    IsAbove           ; no: 7F not > 80h
jg    IsGreater         ; yes: +127 > -128
```

The JA instruction does not jump, because unsigned 7Fh is smaller than unsigned 80h. The JG instruction, on the other hand, jumps because +127 is greater than −128.

Table 6-5 Jumps Based on Signed Comparisons.

Mnemonic	Description
JG	Jump if greater (if *leftOp* > *rightOp*)
JNLE	Jump if not less than or equal (same as JG)
JGE	Jump if greater than or equal (if *leftOp* >= *rightOp*)
JNL	Jump if not less (same as JGE)
JL	Jump if less (if *leftOp* < *rightOp*)
JNGE	Jump if not greater than or equal (same as JL)
JLE	Jump if less than or equal (if *leftOp* <= *rightOp*)
JNG	Jump if not greater (same as JLE)

6.3.4 Conditional Jump Applications

6.3.4.1 Testing Status Bits

Instructions such as AND, OR, NOT, CMP, and TEST are quite useful when followed by conditional jump instructions that use the status flag values to alter the program flow. For example, let's assume that an 8-bit memory operand named **status** contains status information about a machine connected to an interface board. The following instructions jump to a label if bit 5 is set, indicating that the machine is offline:

```
mov   al,status
test  al,00100000b            ; test bit 5
jnz   EquipOffline
```

Or, we might want to jump to a label if either bit 0, 1, or 4 is set:

```
mov   al,status
test  al,00010011b            ; test bits 0,1,4
jnz   InputDataByte
```

Finally, we might jump to a label if bits 2, 3, and 7 are all set. This requires both the AND and CMP instructions:

```
mov    al,status
and    al,10001100b        ; preserve bits 2,3,7
cmp    al,10001100b        ; all bits set?
je     ResetMachine        ; yes: jump to label
```

Larger of Two Integers   The following code compares the unsigned integers in AX and BX and moves the larger of the two to DX:

```
mov    dx,ax               ; assume AX is larger
cmp    ax,bx               ; if AX is >= BX then
jae    L1                  ;    jump to L1
mov    dx,bx               ; else move BX to DX
L1:                        ; DX contains larger integer
```

Smallest of Three Integers   The following instructions compare the unsigned values in the three variables V1, V2, and V3, and move the smallest of the three to AX:

```
.data
V1 WORD ?
V2 WORD ?
V3 WORD ?
.code
    mov    ax,V1           ; assume V1 is smallest
    cmp    ax,V2           ; if ax <= V2 then
    jbe    L1              ;    jump to L1
    mov    ax,V2           ; else move V2 to ax
L1: cmp    ax,V3           ; if ax <= V3 then
    jbe    L2              ;    jump to L2
    mov    ax,V3           ; else move V3 to ax
L2:
```

6.3.4.2   Application: Scanning an Array

A common task in many programming applications is to search for values in an array that meet some criteria. When the first matching value is found, it is common to either display its value or return a pointer to its location. Let's show how easily this is accomplished using an array of integers. The *ArryScan.asm* program looks for the first nonzero value in an array of 16-bit integers. If it finds one, it displays the value; otherwise, it displays a message stating that a value could not be found:

```
TITLE Scanning an Array              (ArryScan.asm)

; Scan an array for the first nonzero value.
INCLUDE Irvine32.inc

.data
intArray  SWORD  0,0,0,0,1,20,35,-12,66,4,0
```

```
;intArray SWORD    1,0,0,0          ; alternate test data
;intArray SWORD    0,0,0,0          ; alternate test data
;intArray SWORD    0,0,0,1          ; alternate test data
noneMsg  BYTE "A non-zero value was not found",0
```

> Note that the program contains alternate test data that are currently commented out.
> You can uncomment these lines to test the program with different data configurations.

```
.code
main PROC
     mov    ebx,OFFSET intArray     ; point to the array
     mov    ecx,LENGTHOF intArray   ; loop counter

L1:
     cmp    WORD PTR [ebx],0        ; compare value to zero
     jnz    found                   ; found a value
     add    ebx,2                   ; point to next
     loop   L1                      ; continue the loop
     jmp    notFound                ; none found

found:                              ; display the value
     movsx eax,WORD PTR[ebx]
     call   WriteInt
     jmp    quit

notFound:                           ; display "not found" message
     mov    edx,OFFSET noneMsg
     call   WriteString

quit:
     call   crlf
     exit
main ENDP
END main
```

6.3.4.3 Application: String Encryption

In Section 6.2.4 we saw that the XOR instruction has a unique quality—it reverses its effects on a number when applied twice. This provides an easy way to perform simple data encryption, in which a message (called *plain text*) entered by the user is transformed into an unintelligible string (called *cipher text*) using another string called a *key*. The cipher text can be stored or transmitted to a remote location without unauthorized persons being able to read it. The intended viewer uses a program to decrypt the cipher text and produce the original plain text.

Example Program   The program we are about to look at uses a process called *symmetric encryption*, which means that the same key is used for both encryption and decryption. The following steps occur, in order:

- The user enters the plain text.

- The program uses a repeated single-character key to encrypt the plain text, producing the cipher text, which is displayed on the screen.
- The program decrypts the cipher text, producing and displaying the original plain text.

Here is the output from a sample execution of the program:

```
Enter the plain text:   Attack at dawn.

Cipher text:            «¢¢Äîä-Ä¢-ïÄÿü-Gs

Decrypted:              Attack at dawn.
```

Program Listing   Here is a complete listing of the program:

```
TITLE Encryption Program                 (Encrypt.asm)

INCLUDE Irvine32.inc
KEY = 239                          ; any value between 1-255
BUFMAX = 128                       ; maximum buffer size

.data
sPrompt  BYTE  "Enter the plain text: ",0
sEncrypt BYTE  "Cypher text:        ",0
sDecrypt BYTE  "Decrypted:          ",0
buffer   BYTE   BUFMAX dup(0)
bufSize  DWORD  ?

.code
main PROC
    call InputTheString          ; input the plain text
    call TranslateBuffer         ; encrypt the buffer
    mov  edx,OFFSET sEncrypt     ; display encrypted message
    call DisplayMessage
    call TranslateBuffer         ; decrypt the buffer
    mov  edx,OFFSET sDecrypt     ; display decrypted message
    call DisplayMessage

    exit
main ENDP

;------------------------------------------------------
InputTheString PROC
;
; Asks the user to enter a string from the
; keyboard. Saves the string and its length
; in variables.
; Receives: nothing
; Returns: nothing
;------------------------------------------------------
```

```
    pushad
    mov   edx,OFFSET sPrompt        ; display a prompt
    call WriteString
    mov   ecx,BUFMAX                ; maximum character count
    mov   edx,OFFSET buffer         ; point to the buffer
    call ReadString                 ; input the string
    mov   bufSize,eax               ; save the length
    call Crlf
    popad
    ret
InputTheString ENDP

;------------------------------------------------------
DisplayMessage PROC
;
; Displays the encrypted or decrypted message.
; Receives: EDX points to the message
; Returns:  nothing
;------------------------------------------------------
    pushad
    call WriteString
    mov   edx,OFFSET buffer         ; display the buffer
    call WriteString
    call Crlf
    call Crlf
    popad
    ret
DisplayMessage ENDP

;------------------------------------------------------
TranslateBuffer PROC
;
; Translates the string by exclusive-ORing each
; byte with the same integer.
; Receives: nothing
; Returns: nothing
;------------------------------------------------------
    pushad
    mov   ecx,bufSize               ; loop counter
    mov   esi,0                     ; index 0 in buffer
L1:
    xor   buffer[esi],KEY           ; translate a byte
    inc   esi                       ; point to next byte
    loop L1

    popad
    ret
TranslateBuffer ENDP
END main
```

Public Key Encryption

Encryption is a hot topic in computer science today. The encryption technique shown in this section is very simple and could easily be broken. A much stronger form of encryption is called *public key encryption*. It is both convenient and difficult to break because it uses two key values, one public, the other private. A person wishing to receive messages makes available a public key to anyone who requests it. Anyone sending mail to this person can use the public key to encrypt the message text. The message can only be decoded by a second, private key, known only to the receiver of the message. The public key and private key are mathematically related to each other by a "one-way" function. A good analogy is a typical phone book: If you know a person's name you can easily find their phone number. But it is nearly impossible to find their name if you just know their phone number. If you want to read more about public key encryption, visit www.pgp.com and www.pgpi.org.

6.3.5 Bit Testing Instructions (Optional)

The BT, BTC, BTR, and BTS instructions can be collectively called *bit testing* instructions. They are important because they perform multiple steps within a single atomic instruction. This has implications for multithreaded programs, in which it is often very important for flag bits (called *semaphores*) to be tested, cleared, set, and complemented without any danger of interruption by another program thread. See our Web site for an example that describes a simple multi-threading scenario.

6.3.5.1 BT Instruction

The BT (bit test) instruction selects bit *n* in the first operand and copies the bit into the Carry flag:

```
BT bitBase,n
```

The first operand, called the *bitBase*, is not changed. BT permits the following types of operands:

```
BT r/m16,r16
BT r/m32,r32
BT r/m16,imm8
BT r/m32,imm8
```

In the following example, the Carry flag is assigned the value of bit 7 in the variable named **semaphore**:

```
.data
semaphore WORD 10001000b
.code
BT semaphore,7              ; CF = 1
```

Before the BT instruction was introduced into the Intel instruction set, we would have to copy the variable into a register and shift bit 7 into the Carry flag:

```
mov ax,semaphore
shr ax,8                   ; CF = 1
```

(The SHR instruction here shifts all bits in AX eight positions to the right. This causes bit 7 to be shifted into the Carry flag. SHR is covered in Chapter 7, in Section 7.2.3.)

6.3.5.2   BTC Instruction

The BTC (bit test and complement) instruction selects bit *n* in the first operand, copies the bit into the Carry flag, and complements (toggles) bit *n*:

```
BTC bitBase,n
```

BTC permits the same types of operands as BT. In the following example, the Carry flag is assigned the value of bit 6 in AX, and the same bit is complemented in AX:

```
.data
semaphore WORD 10001000b
.code
BTC semaphore,6            ; CF = 0, sempahore=11001000b
```

Without the BTC instruction, we would have to execute the following instructions:

```
mov ax,semaphore          ; copy the semaphore
shr ax,7                  ; shift bit 6 into Carry flag
xor semaphore,1000000b    ; complement bit 6
```

6.3.5.3   BTR Instruction

The BTR (bit test and reset) instruction selects bit *n* in the first operand, copies the bit into the Carry flag, and resets (clears) bit *n*:

```
BTR bitBase,n
```

BTR permits the same types of operands as BT and BTC. In the following example, the Carry flag is assigned the value of bit 7 in semaphore, and the same bit is cleared:

```
.data
semaphore WORD 10001000b
.code
BTR semaphore,7           ; CF = 1, semaphore=00001000b
```

6.3.5.4   BTS Instruction

The BTS (bit test and set) instruction selects bit *n* in the first operand, copies the bit into the Carry flag, and sets bit *n*:

```
BTS bitBase,n
```

BTS permits the same types of operands as BT. In the following example, the Carry flag is assigned the value of bit 6 in semaphore, and the same bit is then set:

```
.data
semaphore WORD 10001000b
.code
BTS semaphore,6           ; CF = 0, semaphore=11001000b
```

6.3.6   Section Review

1. Which conditional jumps are based on unsigned comparisons?
2. Which conditional jumps are based on signed comparisons?
3. Which conditional jump instruction is based on the contents of ECX?
4. *(Yes/No):* Are the JA and JNBE instructions equivalent?
5. *(Yes/No):* Are the JB and JL instructions equivalent?
6. Which jump instruction is equivalent to the JA instruction?
7. Which jump instruction is equivalent to the JNGE instruction?
8. *(Yes/No):* Will the following code jump to the label named **Target**?

```
mov ax,8109h
cmp ax,26h
jg Target
```

9. *(Yes/No):* Will the following code jump to the label named **Target**?

```
mov ax,-30
cmp ax,-50
jg Target
```

10. *(Yes/No):* Will the following code jump to the label named **Target**?

```
mov ax,-42
cmp ax,26
ja Target
```

11. Write instructions that jump to label L1 when the unsigned integer in DX is less than or equal to the integer in CX.
12. Write instructions that jump to label L2 when the signed integer in AX is greater than the integer in CX.
13. Write instructions that clear bits 0 and 1 in AL. If the destination operand is equal to zero, jump to label L3. Otherwise, jump to label L4.

6.4   Conditional Loop Instructions

6.4.1   LOOPZ and LOOPE Instructions

The LOOPZ (loop if zero) instruction permits a loop to continue while the Zero flag is set and the unsigned value of ECX is greater than zero. The destination label must be between –128 and +127 bytes from the location of the following instruction. The syntax is:

```
LOOPZ destination
```

The LOOPE (loop if equal) instruction is equivalent to LOOPZ because they share the same circuitry. This is the execution logic of LOOPZ and LOOPE:

```
ECX = ECX - 1
if ECX > 0 and ZF = 1, jump to destination
```

Otherwise, no jump occurs and control passes to the next instruction.

A program running in Real-address mode uses CX as the default loop counter in the LOOPZ instruction. If you want to force ECX to be the loop counter, use the LOOPZD instruction instead.

6.4.2 LOOPNZ and LOOPNE Instructions

The LOOPNZ (loop if not zero) instruction is the counterpart of LOOPZ. The loop continues while the unsigned value of ECX is greater than zero and the Zero flag is clear. The syntax is:

```
LOOPNZ destination
```

The LOOPNE (loop if not equal) instruction is equivalent to LOOPNZ because they share the same circuitry. This is the execution logic of LOOPNZ and LOOPNE:

```
ECX = ECX - 1
if ECX > 0 and ZF = 0, jump to destination
```

Otherwise, no jump occurs and control passes to the next instruction.

Example   The following code excerpt (from *Loopnz.asm*) scans each number in an array until a positive number is found (when the sign bit is clear):

```
.data
array   SWORD   -3,-6,-1,-10,10,30,40,4
sentinel SWORD  0
.code
    mov esi,OFFSET array
    mov ecx,LENGTHOF array

next:
    test WORD PTR [esi],8000h           ; test sign bit
    pushfd                              ; push flags on stack
    add esi,TYPE array
    popfd                               ; pop flags from stack
    loopnz next                         ; continue loop
    jnz quit                            ; none found
    sub esi,TYPE array                  ; ESI points to value
quit:
```

If a positive value is found, ESI is left pointing at it. If the loop fails to find a positive number, it stops when ECX equals zero. In that case, the JNZ instruction jumps to label **quit**, and ESI points to the sentinel value (0) just after the array.

6.4.3   Section Review

1. (*True/False*): The LOOPE instruction jumps to a label when (and only when) the Zero flag is clear.

2. (*True/False*): The LOOPNZ instruction jumps to a label when ECX is greater than zero and the Zero flag is clear.

3. (*True/False*): The destination label of a LOOPZ instruction must be no farther than −128 or +127 bytes from the instruction immediately following LOOPZ.

4. Modify the LOOPNZ example in Section 6.4.2 so that it scans for the first negative value in the array. Change the data declaration accordingly so it begins with positive values.

5. *Challenge:* The LOOPNZ example in Section 6.4.2 relies on a sentinel value to handle the possibility that a positive value might not be found. What would happen if we removed the sentinel?

6.5   Conditional Structures

In this section we will examine a few of the more common conditional structures used in high-level programming languages. You will see how each structure can easily be translated into assembly language. Let's consider a *conditional structure* to be one or more conditional expressions that trigger a choice between different logical branches. Each branch causes a different sequence of instructions to execute.

> An important area of study in computer science is *compiler construction*. Most trained computer scientists can design a simple programming or markup language and write a program that translates programs in their language to another language. The methods you learn in this section should be helpful to you later when you study compiler construction and code optimization techniques.

6.5.1   Block-Structured IF Statements

In most high-level languages, an IF statement implies that a boolean expression is followed by two lists of statements: one performed when the expression is true, and another performed when the expression is false:

```
if( expression )
   statement list 1
else
   statement list 2
```

The **else** portion of the statement is optional. The flowchart in Figure 6-1 shows the two branching paths in a conditional IF structure, labeled *true* and *false*.

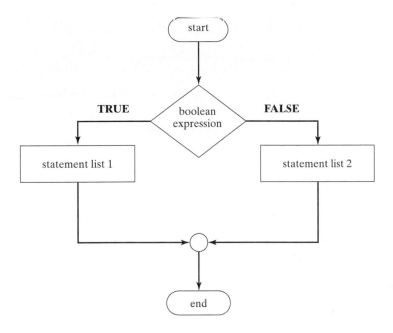

Figure 6-1 Flowchart of an IF Structure.

Example 1 Using Java/C++ syntax, two assignment statements are executed if **op1** is equal to **op2**:

```
if( op1 == op2 )
{
    X = 1;
    Y = 2;
}
```

A high-level language compiler might translate the preceding IF statement into a CMP instruction followed by one or more conditional jumps to labels. Assuming that **op1** and **op2** are memory operands, one of them must be moved to a register before executing CMP. The following code implements the IF statement:

```
    mov   eax,op1
    cmp   eax,op2                  ; compare EAX to op2
    je    L1                       ; jump if equal to L1
    jmp   L2                       ; otherwise, jump to L2
L1:
    mov   X,1
    mov   Y,2
L2:
```

It's important to realize that the same high-level language code can be translated into assembly language in multiple ways. When examples of compiled code are shown in this chapter, they represent only what a hypothetical compiler might produce.

Example 2 In the FAT32 file system used under MS-Windows, the disk cluster size depends on the disk's overall capacity. In the following pseudocode, we set the cluster size to 4,096 if the disk size (in the variable named **gigabytes**) is less than 8 GB. Otherwise, we set the cluster size to 8,192:

```
clusterSize = 8192;
if( gigabytes < 8 )
  clusterSize = 4096;
```

Here's how one might implement this structure in assembly language:

```
    mov clusterSize,8192    ; assume larger cluster
    cmp gigabytes,8         ; larger than 8 GB?
    jae next
    mov clusterSize,4096    ; switch to smaller cluster
next:
```

(Disk clusters are described in Section 14.2.)

6.5.2   Compound Expressions

6.5.2.1   Logical AND Operator

You can implement a boolean expression that uses the local AND operator in at least two ways. Consider the following compound expression, written in pseudocode:

```
if (al > bl) AND (bl > cl)
{
    X = 1
}
```

We will assume that the values are unsigned. The following is a straightforward implementation using JA (jump if above):

```
    cmp al,bl                       ; first expression...
    ja  L1
    jmp next
L1:
    cmp bl,cl                       ; second expression...
    ja  L2
    jmp next
L2:                                 ; both are true
    mov X,1                         ; set X to 1
next:
```

But this seems like entirely too much assembly code for such a simple problem. We can simplify the code if we reverse the JA condition and use JBE instead. This amounts to a *short-circuit* (or *early exit*) evaluation, where the second expression is not evaluated if the first expression is false:

```
      cmp al,bl              ; first expression...
      jbe next               ; quit if false
      cmp bl,cl              ; second expression
      jbe next               ; quit if false
      mov X,1                ; both are true
next:
```

The 29% reduction in code size (seven instructions down to five) results from letting the CPU fall through to the second CMP instruction if the first JBE is not taken. In general, high-level language compilers use short-circuit evaluation by default.

6.5.2.2   Logical OR Operator

When multiple expressions occur in a compound expression using the logical OR operator, the expression is automatically true as soon as any one expression is true. Let's use the following pseudocode as an example:

```
      if (al > bl) OR (bl > cl)
         X = 1
```

In the following implementation, the code branches to L1 if the first expression is true; otherwise, it falls through to the second CMP instruction. The second expression reverses the > operator and uses JBE instead:

```
      cmp al,bl              ; 1: compare AL to BL
      ja  L1                 ; if true, skip second expression
      cmp bl,cl              ; 2: compare BL to CL
      jbe next               ; false: skip next statement
L1:   mov X,1                ; true: set X = 1
next:
```

For any given compound expression, there are at least several ways the expression can be implemented in assembly language.

6.5.3   WHILE Loops

The WHILE structure tests a condition first before performing a block of statements. As long as the loop condition remains true, the statements are repeated. The following loop is written in C++:

```
while( val1 < val2 )
{
    val1++;
    val2--;
}
```

When coding this structure in assembly language, it is convenient to reverse the loop condition and jump to **endwhile** when the condition becomes true. Assuming that **val1** and **val2** are variables, we must move one of them to a register at the beginning, and restore the variable at the end:

```
        mov   eax,val1              ; copy variable to eax
while:
        cmp   eax,val2              ; if not (val1 < val2)
        jnl   endwhile             ;    exit the loop
        inc   eax                  ; val1++;
        dec   val2                 ; val2--;
        jmp   while                ; repeat the loop
endwhile:
        mov   val1,eax             ; save new value for val1
```

EAX is a proxy (substitute) for **val1** inside the loop. Any references to **val1** must be through EAX. Also, note that JNL was used, implying that **val1** and **val2** are signed integers.

6.5.3.1 Example: IF statement Nested in a Loop

High-level structured languages are particularly good at representing nested control structures. In the following C++ example, an IF statement is nested inside a WHILE loop:

```
while( op1 < op2 )
{
    op1++;
    if( op2 == op3 )
      X = 2;
    else
      X = 3;
}
```

Before we code this loop in assembly language, let's use the flowchart in Figure 6-2 to describe the logic. To simplify the translation to assembly language, registers have been substituted for variables (EAX = op1, EBX = op2, and ECX = op3), and label names have been added to the shapes.

Assembly Code   The easiest way to generate the assembly code from a flowchart is to implement the code for each shape. Note the direct correlation between the flowchart labels and the labels used in the following source code. The code could be shorter, but there's no denying that it is easy to follow the flowchart:

```
        mov   eax,op1              ; copy variables to registers
        mov   ebx,op2
        mov   ecx,op3
L1: cmp   eax,ebx                  ; EAX < EBX?
        jl    L2                   ; true
        jmp   L7                   ; false
L2: inc   eax
```

```
L3: cmp   ebx,ecx          ; EBX == ECX?
    je    L4               ; true
    jmp   L5               ; false
L4: mov   X,2              ; X = 2
    jmp   L6
L5: mov   X,3              ; X = 3
L6: jmp   L1               ; repeat the loop
L7: mov   op1,eax          ; update op1
```

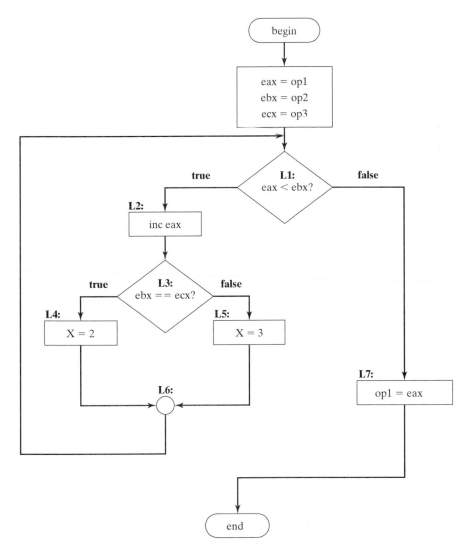

Figure 6-2   Loop Containing IF Statement.

6.5.4 Table-Driven Selection

Table-driven selection is a way of using a table lookup to replace a multiway selection structure. To use it, you must create a table containing lookup values and the offsets of labels or procedures, and use a loop to search the table. This works best when a large number of comparisons are made.

For example, the following is part of a table containing single-character lookup values and addresses of procedures:

```
.data
CaseTable BYTE    'A'                ; lookup value
    DWORD Process_A                  ; address of procedure
    BYTE  'B'
    DWORD Process_B
    (etc.)
```

Let's assume that Process_A, Process_B, Process_C, and Process_D are located at addresses 120h, 130h, 140h, and 150h, respectively. The table would be arranged in memory as shown in Figure 6-3.

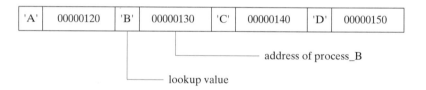

Figure 6-3 Table of Procedure Offsets.

Example Program   In the following example program (*ProcTble.asm*), the user inputs a character from the keyboard. Using a loop, the character is compared to each entry in the table. The first match found in the table causes a call to the procedure offset stored immediately after the lookup value. Each procedure loads EDX with the offset of a different string, which is displayed during the loop:

```
TITLE Table of Procedure Offsets            (ProcTble.asm)

; This program contains a table with offsets of procedures.
; It uses the table to execute indirect procedure calls.

INCLUDE Irvine32.inc
.data
CaseTable  BYTE    'A'                ; lookup value
           DWORD   Process_A          ; address of procedure
EntrySize = ($ - CaseTable)
           BYTE    'B'
           DWORD   Process_B
           BYTE    'C'
           DWORD   Process_C
```

```
            BYTE    'D'
            DWORD     Process_D
NumberOfEntries = 4
prompt BYTE "Press capital A,B,C,or D: ",0
```

Define a separate message string for each procedure:

```
msgA BYTE "Process_A",0
msgB BYTE "Process_B",0
msgC BYTE "Process_C",0
msgD BYTE "Process_D",0

.code
main PROC
    mov   edx,OFFSET prompt          ; ask user for input
    call WriteString
    call ReadChar                    ; read character into AL
    mov   ebx,OFFSET CaseTable       ; point EBX to the table
    mov   ecx,NumberOfEntries        ; loop counter
L1:
    cmp   al,[ebx]                   ; match found?
    jne   L2                         ; no: continue
    call NEAR PTR [ebx + 1]          ; yes: call the procedure
```

This CALL instruction calls the procedure whose address is stored in the memory location referenced by EBX+1. An indirect call such as this requires the NEAR PTR operator.

```
    call WriteString                 ; display message
    call Crlf
    jmp   L3                         ; exit the search
L2:
    add   ebx,EntrySize              ; point to the next entry
    loop L1                          ; repeat until ECX = 0

L3:
    exit
main ENDP
```

Each of the following procedures moves a different string offset to EDX:

```
Process_A PROC
    mov   edx,OFFSET msgA
    ret
Process_A ENDP
```

```
Process_B PROC
    mov   edx,OFFSET msgB
    ret
Process_B ENDP

Process_C PROC
    mov   edx,OFFSET msgC
    ret
Process_C ENDP

Process_D PROC
    mov   edx,OFFSET msgD
    ret
Process_D ENDP
END main
```

The table-driven selection method involves some initial overhead, but it can reduce the amount of code you must write. A table can handle a large number of comparisons, and it can be more easily modified than a long series of compare, jump, and CALL instructions. An table can even be reconfigured at runtime.

6.5.5 Section Review

Notes: In all compound expressions, use short-circuit evaluation. Assume that **X, val1**, **val2**, and **val3** are 16-bit variables.

1. Implement the following pseudocode in assembly language:

    ```
    if ( bx > cx )
       X = 1;
    ```

2. Implement the following pseudocode in assembly language:

    ```
    if ( dx <= cx )
       X = 1;
    else
       X = 2;
    ```

3. Implement the following pseudocode in assembly language:

    ```
    if ( val1 > cx AND cx > dx )
       X = 1;
    else
       X = 2;
    ```

4. Implement the following pseudocode in assembly language:

    ```
    if ( bx > cx OR bx > val1 )
       X = 1;
    else
       X = 2;
    ```

5. Implement the following pseudocode in assembly language:

```
if ( bx > cx AND bx > dx) OR ( dx > ax )
   X = 1;
else
   X = 2;
```

6. *Challenge:* Rewrite the following code (from Section 6.5.3.1) so that it is functionally equivalent, but uses fewer instructions:

```
        mov   eax,op1              ; copy variables to registers
        mov   ebx,op2
        mov   ecx,op3
L1: cmp   eax,ebx              ; EAX < EBX?
    jl    L2                   ; true
    jmp   L7                   ; false
L2: inc   eax
L3: cmp   ebx,ecx              ; EBX == ECX?
    je    L4                   ; true
    jmp   L5                   ; false
L4: mov   X,2                  ; X = 2
    jmp   L6
L5: mov   X,3                  ; X = 3
L6: jmp   L1                   ; repeat the loop
L7: mov   op1,eax              ; update op1
```

6.6   Application: Finite-State Machines

A *finite-state machine* (FSM) is a machine or program that changes state based on some input. It is fairly simple to use a graph to represent an FSM, which contains squares (or circles) called *nodes* and lines with arrows between the circles called *edges* (or *arcs*).

A simple example is shown in Figure 6-4. Each node represents a program state, and each edge represents a transition from one state to another. One node is designated as the *start state*, shown in our diagram with an incoming arrow. The remaining states can be labeled with numbers or letters. One or more states are designated as *terminal states*, notated by a thick border around the square. A terminal state represents a state in which the program might stop without producing an error. A finite-state machine is a specific instance of a more general type of structure called a *directed graph* (or *diagraph*). The latter is a set of nodes connected by edges having specific directions.

> Directed graphs have many useful applications in computer science, related to dynamic data structures and advanced searching techniques.

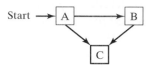

Figure 6-4   Simple Finite-State Machine.

6.6.1   Validating an Input String

Programs that read input streams often must validate their input by performing a certain amount of error checking. A programming language compiler, for instance, can use a finite-state machine to scan source programs and convert words and symbols into *tokens*, which are objects such as keywords, arithmetic operators, and identifiers.

   When using a finite-state machine to check the validity of an input string, you usually read the input character by character. Each character is represented by an edge (transition) in the diagram. A finite-state machine detects illegal input sequences in one of two ways:

- The next input character does not correspond to any transitions from the current state.
- The end of input is reached and the current state is a nonterminal state.

Character String Example. Let's check the validity of an input string according to the following two rules:

- The string must begin with the letter 'x' and end with the letter 'z.'
- Between the first and last characters, there can be zero or more letters within the range {'a'..'y'}.

   The FSM diagram in Figure 6-5 describes this syntax. Each transition is identified with a particular type of input. For example, the transition from state A to state B can only be accomplished if the letter **x** is read from the input stream. A transition from state B to itself is accomplished by the input of any letter of the alphabet except **z**. A transition from state B to state C occurs only when the letter **z** is read from the input stream.

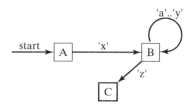

Figure 6-5   FSM for String.

If the end of the input stream is reached while the program is in state A or B, an error condition results because only state C is marked as a terminal state. The following input strings, for example, would be recognized by this FSM:

```
xaabcdefgz
xz
xyyqqrrstuvz
```

6.6.2   Validating a Signed Integer

A finite-state machine for parsing a signed integer is shown in Figure 6-6. Input consists of an optional leading sign followed by a sequence of digits. There is no stated maximum number of digits implied by the diagram.

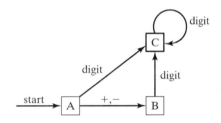

Figure 6-6   Signed Decimal Integer FSM.

Finite-state machines are very easily translated into assembly language code. Each state in the diagram (A, B, C, ...) is represented in the program by a label. The following actions are performed at each label:

- A call to an input procedure reads the next character from input.
- If the state is a terminal state, check to see if the user has pressed the Enter key to end the input.
- One or more compare instructions check for each possible transition leading away from the state. Each comparison is followed by a conditional jump instruction.

For example, at state A, the following code reads the next input character and checks for a possible transition to state B:

```
StateA:
    call  Getnext            ; read next char into AL
    cmp   al,'+'             ; leading + sign?
    je    StateB             ; go to State B
    cmp   al,'-'             ; leading - sign?
```

```
je      StateB                  ; go to State B
call    IsDigit                 ; ZF = 1 if AL contains a digit
jz      StateC                  ; go to State C
call    DisplayErrorMsg         ; invalid input found
jmp     Quit
```

Also in state A, we call **IsDigit**, a link library procedure that sets the Zero flag when a numeric digit is read from input. This makes it possible to look for a transition to state C. Failing that, the program displays an error message and exits. The flowchart in Figure 6-7 represents the code attached to label **StateA**.

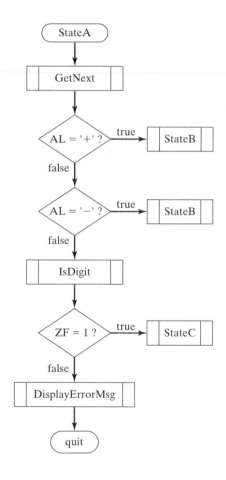

Figure 6-7   Signed Integer FSM Flowchart.

FSM Implementation The following is a complete program that implements the finite-state machine from Figure 6-6 describing a signed integer:

```
TITLE Finite State Machine                (Finite.asm)

INCLUDE Irvine32.inc

.data
ENTER_KEY = 13
InvalidInputMsg BYTE "Invalid input",13,10,0

.code
main PROC
        call Clrscr

StateA:
    call   Getnext                 ; read next char into AL
    cmp    al,'+'                  ; leading + sign?
    je     StateB                  ; go to State B
    cmp    al,'-'                  ; leading - sign?
    je     StateB                  ; go to State B
    call   IsDigit                 ; ZF = 1 if AL contains a digit
    jz     StateC                  ; go to State C
    call   DisplayErrorMsg         ; invalid input found
    jmp    Quit

StateB:
    call   Getnext                 ; read next char into AL
    call   IsDigit                 ; ZF = 1 if AL contains a digit
    jz     StateC
    call   DisplayErrorMsg         ; invalid input found
    jmp    Quit

StateC:
    call   Getnext                 ; read next char into AL
    call   IsDigit                 ; ZF = 1 if AL contains a digit
    jz     StateC
    cmp    AL,ENTER_KEY            ; Enter key pressed?
    je     Quit                    ; yes: quit
    call   DisplayErrorMsg         ; no: invalid input found
    jmp    Quit

Quit:
    call Crlf
    exit
main ENDP

;------------------------------------------------
Getnext PROC
;
; Reads a character from standard input.
```

```
; Receives: nothing
; Returns: AL contains the character
;--------------------------------------------------
     call   ReadChar              ; input from keyboard
     call   WriteChar             ; echo on screen
     ret
Getnext ENDP

;--------------------------------------------------
DisplayErrorMsg PROC
;
; Displays an error message indicating that
; the input stream contains illegal input.
; Receives: nothing.
; Returns: nothing
;--------------------------------------------------
     push   edx
     mov    edx,OFFSET InvalidInputMsg
     call   WriteString
     pop    edx
     ret
DisplayErrorMsg ENDP
END main
```

The **IsDigit** procedure from the book's link library sets the Zero flag if the character in AL is a valid decimal digit. Otherwise, the Zero flag is cleared:

```
;--------------------------------------------------
Isdigit PROC
;
; Determines whether the character in AL is a
; valid decimal digit.
; Receives: AL = character
; Returns: ZF=1 if AL contains a valid decimal
;    digit; otherwise, ZF=0.
;--------------------------------------------------
     cmp    al,'0'
     jb     ID1
     cmp    al,'9'
     ja     ID1
     test   ax,0                          ; set ZF = 1
ID1: ret
Isdigit ENDP
```

6.6.3 Section Review

1. A finite-state machine is a specific application of what type of data structure?
2. In a finite-state machine diagram, what do the nodes represent?

3. In a finite-state machine diagram, what do the edges represent?
4. In the signed integer finite-state machine (Section 6.6.2), which state is reached when the input consists of "+5"?
5. In the signed integer finite-state machine (Section 6.6.2), how many digits can occur after a minus sign?
6. What happens in a finite-state machine when no more input is available, and the current state is a nonterminal state?
7. Would the following simplification of a signed decimal integer finite-state machine work just as well as the one shown in Section 6.6.2? If not, why not?

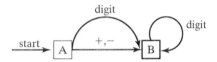

8. *Challenge:* Diagram a finite-state machine that recognizes real numbers without exponents. The decimal point is required. Examples are: +3.5, −4.2342, 5., .2.

6.7   Using the .IF Directive (Optional)

The Microsoft assembler (MASM) provides .IF, a high-level directive that makes programming compound IF statements much easier than if you were to code using CMP and conditional jump instructions. Here is the syntax:

```
.IF condition1
    statements
[.ELSEIF condition2
    statements ]
[.ELSE
    statements ]
.ENDIF
```

The square brackets above show that .ELSEIF and .ELSE are optional, whereas .IF and .ENDIF are required. A *condition* is a boolean expression involving the same operators used in C++ and Java (such as <, >, ==, and !=). The expression is evaluated at runtime. The following are examples of valid conditions:

```
eax > 10000h
val1 <= 100
val2 == eax
val3 != ebx
```

The following are examples of compound conditions. **Val1** and **val2** are assumed to be doubleword variables:

```
(eax > 0) && (eax > 10000h)
(val1 <= 100) || (val2 <= 100)
(val2 != ebx) && !CARRY?
```

A complete list of relational and logical operators is shown in Table 6-6.

Table 6-6   Runtime Relational and Logical Operators.

Operator	Description
expr1 == *expr2*	Returns true when *expression1* is equal to *expr2*.
expr1 != *expr2*	Returns true when *expr1* is not equal to *expr2*.
expr1 > *expr2*	Returns true when *expr1* is greater than *expr2*.
expr1 >= *expr2*	Returns true when *expr1* is greater than or equal to *expr2*.
expr1 < *expr2*	Returns true when *expr1* is less than *expr2*.
expr1 <= *expr2*	Returns true when *expr1* is less than or equal to *expr2*.
! *expr*	Returns true when *expr* is false.
expr1 && *expr2*	Performs logical AND between *expr1* and *expr2*.
expr1 ‖ *expr2*	Performs logical OR between *expr1* and *expr2*.
expr1 & *expr2*	Performs bitwise AND between *expr1* and *expr2*.
CARRY?	Returns true if the Carry flag is set.
OVERFLOW?	Returns true if the Overflow flag is set.
PARITY?	Returns true if the Parity flag is set.
SIGN?	Returns true if the Sign flag is set.
ZERO?	Returns true if the Zero flag is set.

Generating ASM Code   When you use high-level directives such as .IF and .ELSE, the assembler takes on the role of code-writer for you. For example, let's write an .IF directive that compares EAX to the variable **val1**:

```
mov eax,6
.IF eax > val1
  mov result,1
.ENDIF
```

val1 and **result** are assumed to be 32-bit unsigned integers. When the assembler reads the foregoing lines, it expands them into the following assembly language instructions:

```
mov eax,6
cmp eax,val1
jbe @C0001              ; jump on unsigned comparison
mov result,1
@C0001:
```

The label name @C0001 was created by the assembler. This is done in a way that guarantees that all labels within same procedure are unique.

6.7.1   Signed and Unsigned Comparisons

When you use the .IF directive to compare values, you must be aware of how assembler generates conditional jumps. If the comparison involves an unsigned variable, an unsigned conditional jump instruction will be inserted in the generated code. This is a repeat of a previous example that compares EAX to **val1**, an unsigned doubleword:

```
.data
val1 DWORD    5
result DWORD ?
.code
   mov eax,6
   .IF eax > val1
     mov result,1
   .ENDIF
```

The assembler expands this using the JBE (unsigned jump) instruction:

```
   mov eax,6
   cmp eax,val1
   jbe @C0001              ; jump on unsigned comparison
   mov result,1
@C0001:
```

Comparing a Signed Integer   Let's try a similar comparison with **val2**, a signed doubleword:

```
.data
val2 SDWORD -1
.code
   mov eax,6
   .IF eax > val2
     mov result,1
   .ENDIF
```

Now the assembler generates code using the JLE instruction, the jump based on signed comparisons:

```
   mov eax,6
   cmp eax,val2
   jle @C0001              ; jump on signed comparison
   mov result,1
@C0001:
```

Comparing Registers   The question we might then ask is, what happens if two registers are compared? Clearly, the assembler cannot determine whether the values are signed or unsigned:

```
   mov eax,6
   mov ebx,val2
   .IF eax > ebx
```

```
      mov result,1
   .ENDIF
```

It turns out that the assembler defaults to an unsigned comparison, so the .IF directive comparing two registers is implemented using the JBE instruction.

6.7.2 Compound Expressions

Many compound boolean expressions use the logical OR and AND operators. When using the .IF directive, the || symbol is the logical OR operator:

```
.IF expression1 || expression2
   statements
.ENDIF
```

Similarly, the && symbol is the logical AND operator:

```
.IF expression1 && expression2
   statements
.ENDIF
```

6.7.2.1 SetCursorPosition Example

The **SetCursorPosition** procedure, shown in the next example, performs range checking on its two input parameters, DH and DL (see *SetCur.asm*). The y-coordinate (DH) must be between 0 and 24. The x-coordinate (DL) must be between 0 and 79. If either is found to be out of range, an error message is displayed:

```
SetCursorPosition PROC
; Sets the cursor position.
; Receives: DL = X-coordinate, DH = Y-coordinate
; Checks the ranges of DL and DH.
; Returns: nothing
;------------------------------------------------
.data
BadXCoordMsg BYTE "X-Coordinate out of range!",0Dh,0Ah,0
BadYCoordMsg BYTE "Y-Coordinate out of range!",0Dh,0Ah,0
.code
    .IF (DL < 0) || (DL > 79)
        mov   edx,OFFSET BadXCoordMsg
        call  WriteString
        jmp   quit
    .ENDIF
    .IF (DH < 0) || (DH > 24)
        mov   edx,OFFSET BadYCoordMsg
        call  WriteString
        jmp   quit
    .ENDIF
    call Gotoxy
quit:
    ret
SetCursorPosition ENDP
```

6.7.2.2   College Registration Example

Suppose a college student wants to register for courses. We will use two criteria to determine whether or not the student can register: The first is the person's grade average, based on a 0 to 400 scale, where 400 is the highest possible grade. The second is the number of credits the person wants to take. A multiway branch structure can be used, involving .IF, .ELSEIF, and .ENDIF. The following shows an example (see *Regist.asm*):

```
.data
TRUE = 1
FALSE = 0
gradeAverage   WORD 275              ; test value
credits        WORD 12               ; test value
OkToRegister   BYTE ?
.code
    mov OkToRegister,FALSE
    .IF gradeAverage > 350
       mov OkToRegister,TRUE
    .ELSEIF (gradeAverage > 250) && (credits <= 16)
       mov OkToRegister,TRUE
    .ELSEIF (credits <= 12)
       mov OkToRegister,TRUE
    .ENDIF
```

Table 6-7 lists the corresponding code generated by the assembler, which you can view by looking at the *Dissasembly* window of the Microsoft Visual Studio debugger. (It has been cleaned up here a bit to make it easier to read.) MASM-generated code will appear in the source listing file if you use the /Sg command-line option when assembling programs.

Table 6-7   Registration Example, MASM-Generated Code.

```
          mov   byte ptr OkToRegister,0
          cmp   word ptr gradeAverage,350
          jbe   @C0006
          mov   byte ptr OkToRegister,1
          jmp   @C0008
@C0006:
          cmp   word ptr gradeAverage,250
          jbe   @C0009
          cmp   word ptr credits,16
          ja    @C0009
          mov   byte ptr OkToRegister,1
          jmp   @C0008
@C0009:
          cmp   word ptr credits,12
          ja    @C0008
          mov   byte ptr OkToRegister,1
@C0008:
```

6.7.3 .REPEAT and .WHILE Directives

The .REPEAT and .WHILE directives offer alternatives to writing your own loops with CMP and conditional jump instructions. They permit the conditional expressions listed earlier in Table 6-6.

The .REPEAT directive executes the loop body before testing the runtime condition following the .UNTIL directive:

```
.REPEAT
    statements
.UNTIL condition
```

The .WHILE directive tests the condition before executing the loop:

```
.WHILE condition
    statements
.ENDW
```

Examples: The following statements display the values 1 through 10 using the .WHILE directive:

```
mov eax,0
.WHILE eax < 10
    inc eax
    call WriteDec
    call Crlf
.ENDW
```

The following statements display the values 1 through 10 using the .REPEAT directive:

```
mov eax,0
.REPEAT
    inc eax
    call WriteDec
    call Crlf
.UNTIL eax == 10
```

6.7.3.1 Example: Loop Containing an IF Statement

Earlier in this chapter in Section 6.5.3.1, we showed how to write assembly language code for an IF statement nested inside a WHILE loop. Here is the pseudocode:

```
while( op1 < op2 )
{
    op1++;
    if( op2 == op3 )
      X = 2;
    else
      X = 3;
}
```

The following is an implementation of the pseudocode using the .WHILE and .IF directives. Because **op1**, **op2**, and **op3** are variables, they are moved to registers to avoid having two memory operands in any one instruction:

```
.data
op1 DWORD 2                    ; test data
op2 DWORD 4                    ; test data
op3 DWORD 5                    ; test data
.code
    mov eax,op1
    mov ebx,op2
    mov ecx,op3
    .WHILE eax < ebx
      inc eax
      .IF ebx == ecx
          mov X,2
      .ELSE
          mov X,3
      .ENDIF
    .ENDW
```

6.8 Chapter Summary

The AND, OR, XOR, NOT, and TEST instructions are called *bitwise instructions* because they work at the bit level. Each bit in a source operand is matched to a bit in the same position of the destination operand:

- The AND instruction produces 1 when both input bits are 1.
- The OR instruction produces 1 when at least one of the input bits is 1.
- The XOR instruction produces 1 only when the input bits are different.
- The TEST instruction performs an implied AND operation on the destination operand, setting the flags appropriately. The destination operand is not changed.
- The NOT instruction reverses all bits in a destination operand.

The CMP instruction compares a destination operand to a source operand. It performs an implied subtraction of the source from the destination and modifies the CPU status flags accordingly. CMP is usually followed by a conditional jump instruction that may produce a transfer of control to a code label.

Four types of conditional jump instructions are shown in this chapter:

- Table 6-2 contains examples of jumps based on specific flag values, such as JC (jump carry), JZ (jump zero), and JO (jump overflow).
- Table 6-3 contains examples of jumps based on equality, such as JE (jump equal), JNE (jump not equal), and JECXZ (jump if ECX = 0).
- Table 6-4 contains examples of conditional jumps based on comparisons of unsigned integers, such as JA (jump if above), JB (jump if below), and JAE (jump if above or equal).

- Table 6-5 contains examples of signed jumps, such as JL (jump if less) and JG (jump if greater).

The LOOPZ (LOOPE) instruction repeats when the Zero flag is set and ECX is greater than Zero. The LOOPNZ (LOOPNE) instruction repeats when the Zero flag is clear and ECX is greater than zero. (In Real-address mode, LOOPZ and LOOPNZ use the CX register.)

Encryption is a process that encodes data, and *decryption* is a process that decodes data. The XOR instruction can be used to perform simple encryption and decryption, one byte at a time.

Flowcharts are an effective tool for visually representing program logic. You can easily write assembly language code, using a flowchart as a model. It is helpful to attach a label to each flowchart symbol and use the same label in your assembly source code.

A *finite-state machine* (FSM) is an effective tool for validating strings containing recognizable characters such as signed integers. It is quite easy to implement a finite-state machine in assembly language if each state is represented by a label.

The .IF, .ELSE, .ELSEIF, and .ENDIF directives evaluate runtime expressions and greatly simplify assembly language coding. They are particularly useful when coding complex compound boolean expressions. You can also create conditional loops, using the .WHILE and .REPEAT directives.

6.9 Programming Exercises

1. ArrayScan using LOOPZ
Using the ArrayScan program in Section 6.3.4.2 as a model, implement the search using the LOOPZ instruction. *Optional:* draw a flowchart of the program.

2. Loop Implementation
Implement the following C++ code in assembly language, using the block-structured .IF and .WHILE directives. Assume that all variables are 32-bit signed integers:

```
while( op1 < op2 )
{
    op1++;
    if( op2 == op3 )
      X = 2;
    else
      X = 3;
}
```

Optional: draw a flowchart of your code.

3. Test Score Evaluation (1)
Using the following table as a guide, write a program that asks the user to enter an integer test score between 0 and 100. The program should display the appropriate letter grade:

Score Range	Letter Grade
90 to 100	A
80 to 89	B
70 to 79	C
60 to 69	D
0 to 59	F

Optional: draw a flowchart of the program.

4. Test Score Evaluation (2)

Using the solution program from the preceding exercise as a starting point, add the following features:

- Run in a loop so that multiple test scores can be entered.
- Accumulate a counter of the number of test scores.
- Perform range checking on the user's input: display an error message if the test score is less than 0 or greater than 100.

Optional: draw a flowchart of the program.

5. College Registration (1)

Using the College Registration example from Section 6.7.2.2 as a starting point, do the following:

- Recode the logic using CMP and conditional jump instructions (instead of the .IF and .ELSEIF directives).
- Perform range checking on the **credits** value; it cannot be less than 1 or greater than 30. If an invalid entry is discovered, display an appropriate error message.

Optional: draw a flowchart of the program.

6. College Registration (2)

Using the solution program from the preceding exercise as a starting point, write a complete program that does the following:

1. Input **gradeAverage** and **credits** from the user. If the user enters zero for either value, halt the program.
2. Perform range checking on both **credits** and **gradeAverage**. The latter must be between 0 and 400. If either value is out of range, display an appropriate error message.
3. Determine whether or not the person can register (using the existing example) and display an appropriate message.

4. Repeat steps 1 through 3 until the user decides to quit.

Optional: draw a flowchart of the program.

7. Boolean Calculator (1)

Create a program that functions as a simple boolean calculator for 32-bit integers. It should display a menu that asks the user to make a selection from the following list:

1. x AND y
2. x OR y
3. NOT x
4. x XOR y
5. Exit program

When the user makes a choice, call a procedure that displays the name of the operation about to be performed. (We will implement the operations in the exercise following this one.)
Optional: draw a flowchart of the program.

8. Boolean Calculator (2)

Continue the solution program from the preceding exercise by implementing the following procedures:

- AND_op: Prompt the user for two hexadecimal integers. AND them together and display the result in hexadecimal.
- OR_op: Prompt the user for two hexadecimal integers. OR them together and display the result in hexadecimal.
- NOT_op: Prompt the user for a hexadecimal integer. NOT the integer and display the result in hexadecimal.
- XOR_op: Prompt the user for two hexadecimal integers. Exclusive-OR them together and display the result in hexadecimal.

Optional: draw a flowchart of the program.

9. Weighted Probabilities

Write a program that randomly chooses between three different colors for displaying text on the screen. Use a loop to display twenty lines of text, each with a randomly chosen color. The probabilities for each color are to be as follows: white = 30%, blue = 10%, green = 60%. *Hint:* generate a random integer between 0 and 9. If the resulting integer is in the range 0–2, choose white. If the integer equals 3, choose blue. If the integer is in the range 4–9, choose green.

7

Integer Arithmetic

7.1   Introduction

In Chapter 6, you learned how to manipulate individual bits in integers, using boolean operators. We're going to extend that knowledge here by showing you how to move bits around in a
number, using *shift* and *rotate* operations. Operations such as these are particularly useful when
controlling various types of hardware devices. Assembly language programmers are experts
with bits.

The question is, then, why does this chapter also cover multiplication and division? It
turns out that multiplication and division are implemented by the processor as left and right
shift operations, respectively. So when you're learning one of these topics, you're also learning
the other.

Did you ever wonder how computers manage to add and subtract extremely large numbers? By now, you're aware that the largest integer available in C++ is typically 32 bits, which
makes it virtually impossible to do extended arithmetic. In assembly language, on the other
hand, there are simple machine-level instructions (ADC and SBB) that make it easy to add and
subtract integers of virtually any size.

One topic in this chapter that I find particularly useful is on implementing arithmetic
expressions. When I started programming in Pascal and later in C and C++, I wondered how
compilers manage to take complicated expressions apart and break them into discrete machine-
language instructions. In the same way that compilers do, you will learn how to use operator precedence rules and register optimization when translating expressions into assembly language. If
you later take a course in compiler construction, you will explore the same topic in even more
detail than is offered here.

7.2   Shift and Rotate Instructions

Along with the bitwise instructions from the previous chapter, shift instructions are among the
most characteristic of assembly language. *Shifting* means to move bits right and left inside an
operand. All of the following instructions affect the Overflow and Carry flags:

SHL	Shift left
SHR	Shift right
SAL	Shift arithmetic left
SAR	Shift arithmetic right
ROL	Rotate left
ROR	Rotate right
RCL	Rotate carry left
RCR	Rotate carry right

SHLD   Double-precision shift left

SHRD   Double-precision shift right

7.2.1   Logical Shifts versus Arithmetic Shifts

There are two basic ways to shift the bits in a number. The first, called a *logical shift*, fills the newly created bit position with zero. In the following diagram, a byte is logically shifted one position to the right. Note that bit 7 is assigned 0:

For example, if we do a single logical right shift on the binary value 11001111, it becomes 01100111.

The other type of shift is called an *arithmetic shift*. The newly created bit position is filled with a copy of the original number's sign bit:

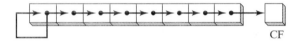

For example the binary value 11001111 has a 1 in the sign bit. When shifted arithmetically one bit to the right, it becomes 11100111.

7.2.2   SHL Instruction

The SHL (shift left) instruction performs a logical left shift on the destination operand, filling the lowest bit with 0. The highest bit is moved to the Carry flag, and the bit that was in the Carry flag is lost:

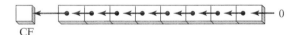

The first operand is the destination, and the second is the shift count:

    SHL destination,count

The following lists the types of operands permitted by this instruction:

    SHL reg,imm8
    SHL mem,imm8
    SHL reg,CL
    SHL mem,CL

The Intel 8086/8088 processors require *imm8* to be equal to 1. From the Intel 80286 processor onward, *imm8* can be any integer. On any Intel processor, CL may contain an integer that is used as a shift counter. The formats shown here also apply to the SHR, SAL, SAR, ROR, ROL, RCR, and RCL instructions.

Example   In the following instructions, BL is shifted once to the left. The highest bit is copied into the Carry flag and the lowest bit position is cleared:

```
mov   bl,8Fh                    ; BL = 10001111b
shl   bl,1                      ; BL = 00011110b, CF = 1
```

Fast Multiplication   One of the best uses of SHL is for performing high-speed multiplication by powers of 2. Shifting any operand left by *n* bits multiplies the operand by 2^n. For example, shifting 5 left 1 bit yields the product 5 * 2:

```
mov dl,5
shl dl,1
```

Before: | 0 0 0 0 0 1 0 1 | = 5

After: | 0 0 0 0 1 0 1 0 | = 10

If we shift 10 left by 2 bits, the result is the same as multiplying 10 by 2^2:

```
mov dl,10
shl dl,2                        ; (10 * 4) = 40
```

7.2.3 SHR Instruction

The SHR (shift right) instruction performs a logical right shift on the destination operand, replacing the highest bit with a 0. The lowest bit is copied into the Carry flag, and the bit that was in the Carry flag is lost:

SHR uses the same instruction formats as SHL. In the following example, the 0 from the lowest bit in AL is copied into the Carry flag, and the highest bit in AL is cleared:

```
mov   al,0D0h                   ; AL = 11010000b
shr   al,1                      ; AL = 01101000b, CF = 0
```

Fast Division   Logically shifting any unsigned operand right by *n* bits divides the operand by 2^n. Here, for example, we divide 32 by 2^1, producing 16:

```
mov dl,32
shr dl,1
```

$$\text{Before:}\quad \boxed{0\;0\;1\;0\;0\;0\;0\;0}\;=32$$

$$\text{After:}\quad \boxed{0\;0\;0\;1\;0\;0\;0\;0}\;=16$$

In the following example, 64 is divided by 2^3:

```
mov   al,01000000b           ; AL = 64
shr   al,3                   ; divide by 8, AL = 00001000b
```

(Division of signed numbers by shifting is accomplished using the SAR instruction because it preserves the number's sign bit.)

7.2.4   SAL and SAR Instructions

SAL (shift arithmetic left) is identical to the SHL instruction. The SAR (shift arithmetic right) instruction performs a right arithmetic shift on its destination operand:

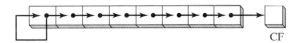

The syntax and operands for SAR and SHR are identical to those for SHL and SHR. The shift may be repeated, based on the counter in the second operand:

```
SAR destination,count
```

The following example shows how SAR duplicates the sign bit. AL is negative before and after it is shifted to the right:

```
mov   al,0F0h                ; AL = 11110000b (-16)
sar   al,1                   ; AL = 11111000b (-8)   CF = 0
```

Signed Division   You can divide a signed operand by a power of 2, using the SAR instruction. In the following example, -128 is divided by 2^3. The quotient is -16:

```
mov   dl,-128                ; DL = 10000000b
sar   dl,3                   ; DL = 11110000b
```

7.2.5   ROL Instruction

The ROL (rotate left) instruction shifts each bit to the left. Also, the highest bit is copied both into the Carry flag and into the lowest bit. The instruction format is the same as for the SHL instruction:

Bit rotation differs from bit shifting in that the former does not lose any bits. A bit that is rotated off one end of a number appears again at the other end. In the following example, the high bit is copied into both the Carry flag and bit position 0:

```
mov   al,40h                 ; AL = 01000000b
rol   al,1                   ; AL = 10000000b, CF = 0
rol   al,1                   ; AL = 00000001b, CF = 1
rol   al,1                   ; AL = 00000010b, CF = 0
```

You can use ROL to exchange the upper (bits 4–7) and lower (bits 0–3) halves of a byte. For example, if 26h is rotated four bits in either direction, it becomes 62h:

```
mov  al,26h
rol  al,4                    ; AL = 62h
```

> Did you know that half a byte is called a *nybble*? (No, I didn't make that up.)

7.2.6   ROR Instruction

The ROR (rotate right) instruction shifts each bit to the right. Also, the lowest bit is copied into the Carry flag and into the highest bit at the same time. The instruction format is the same as for SHL:

In the following example, the lowest bit is copied into the Carry flag and into the highest bit of the result:

```
mov  al,01h                  ; AL = 00000001b
ror  al,1                    ; AL = 10000000b, CF = 1
ror  al,1                    ; AL = 01000000b, CF = 0
```

7.2.7   RCL and RCR Instructions

The RCL (rotate carry left) instruction shifts each bit to the left, copies the Carry flag to the least significant bit (LSB), and copies the most significant bit (MSB) into the Carry flag:

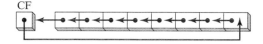

If you think of the Carry flag as just an extra bit added to the high end of the number, then RCL becomes a simple rotate left operation.

In the following example, the CLC instruction clears the Carry flag. The first RCL instruction moves the high bit of BL into the Carry flag, and shifts all other bits to the left. The second

RCL instruction moves the Carry flag into the lowest bit position, and shifts all other bits to the left:

```
clc                           ; CF = 0
mov bl,88h                    ; CF,BL = 0 10001000b
rcl bl,1                      ; CF,BL = 1 00010000b
rcl bl,1                      ; CF,BL = 0 00100001b
```

Recover a Bit from the Carry Flag   RCL can recover a bit that has previously been shifted into the Carry flag. The following example checks the lowest bit of **testval** by shifting its lowest bit into the Carry flag. Then RCL restores the number to its original value:

```
.data
testval  BYTE   01101010b
.code
shr testval,1                 ; shift LSB into Carry flag
jc  quit                      ; exit if Carry flag set
rcl testval,1                 ; else restore the number
```

RCR Instruction.   The RCR (rotate carry right) instruction shifts each bit to the right, copies the Carry flag into the most significant bit, and copies the least significant bit into the Carry flag:

As in the case of RCL, it helps to visualize the integer in this figure as a 9-bit value, with the Carry flag to the right of the least significant bit.

In the following example, STC sets the Carry flag before rotating the Carry flag into the MSB, and rotating the LSB into the Carry flag:

```
stc                           ; CF = 1
mov    ah,10h                 ; CF,AH = 00010000 1
rcr    ah,1                   ; CF,AH = 10001000 0
```

7.2.8   SHLD/SHRD Instructions

The SHLD and SHRD instructions require at least an Intel386 processor. The SHLD (shift left double) instruction shifts a destination operand a given number of bits to the left. The bit positions opened up by the shift are filled by the most significant bits of the source operand. The source operand is not affected, but the Sign, Zero, Auxiliary, Parity, and Carry flags are affected:

```
SHLD destination, source, count
```

The SHRD (shift right double) instruction shifts a destination operand a given number of bits to the right. The bit positions opened up by the shift are filled by the least significant bits of the source operand:

```
SHRD destination, source, count
```

The following instruction formats apply to both SHLD and SHRD. The *destination* operand can be a register or memory operand, and the *source* operand must be a register. The *count* operand can be either the CL register or an 8-bit immediate operand:

```
SHLD  reg16,reg16,CL/imm8
SHLD  mem16,reg16,CL/imm8
SHLD  reg32,reg32,CL/imm8
SHLD  mem32,reg32,CL/imm8
```

Example 1: For example, the following statements shift **wval** to the left 4 bits and insert the high 4 bits of AX into the low 4 bit positions of **wval:**

```
.data
wval WORD 9BA6h
.code
mov   ax,0AC36h
shld  wval,ax,4                      ; wval = BA6Ah
```

The data movement is shown in the following figure:

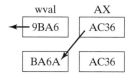

Example 2: In the following example, AX is shifted to the right 4 bits and the low 4 bits of DX are shifted into the high 4 positions of AX:

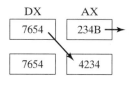

```
mov  ax,234Bh
mov  dx,7654h
shrd ax,dx,4                          ; AX = 4234h
```

SHLD and SHRD can be used to manipulate bit-mapped images, when groups of bits must be shifted left and right to reposition images on the screen. Another potential application is data encryption, in which the encryption algorithm involves the shifting of bits. Finally, the two instructions can be used when performing fast multiplication and division with very long integers.

7.2.9   Section Review

1. Which instruction moves each bit in an operand to the left and copies the highest bit into both the Carry flag and the lowest bit position?
2. Which instruction moves each bit to the right, copies the lowest bit into the Carry flag, and copies the Carry flag into the highest bit position?
3. Which instruction shifts each bit to the right and replicates the sign bit?
4. Which instruction performs the following operation?

```
Before:   CF,AL = 1 11010101
After:    CF,AL = 1 10101011
```

(CF = Carry flag)

5. Suppose there were no rotate instructions. Show how we might use SHR and a conditional jump instruction to rotate AL 1 position to the right.
6. What happens to the Carry flag when the SHR AX,1 instruction is executed?
7. Write a logical shift instruction that multiplies the contents of EAX by 16.
8. Write a logical shift instruction that divides EBX by 4.
9. Write a single rotate instruction that exchanges the high and low halves of the DL register.
10. Write a SHLD instruction that shifts the highest bit in the AX register into the lowest bit position of DX and shifts DX one bit to the left.
11. In the following code sequence, show the value of AL after each shift or rotate instruction has executed:

```
mov al,0D4h
shr al,1            ; a.
mov al,0D4h
sar al,1            ; b.
mov al,0D4h
sar al,4            ; c.
mov al,0D4h
rol al,1            ; d.
```

12. In the following code sequence, show the value of AL after each shift or rotate instruction has executed:

```
mov al,0D4h
ror al,3            ; a.
mov al,0D4h
rol al,7            ; b.
stc
mov al,0D4h
rcl al,1            ; c.
stc
mov al,0D4h
rcr al,3            ; d.
```

13. *Challenge:* Write a series of instructions that shift the lowest bit of AX into the highest bit of BX without using the SHRD instruction. Next, perform the same operation using SHRD.

14. *Challenge:* One way to calculate the parity of a 32-bit number in EAX is to use a loop that shifts each bit into the Carry flag and accumulates a count of the number of times the Carry flag was set. Write a code that does this, and set the Parity flag accordingly.

7.3   Shift and Rotate Applications

7.3.1   Shifting Multiple Doublewords

Programs sometimes need to shift all bits within an array, as one might when moving a bit-mapped graphic image from one screen location to another. Using an array of three double-words, the following steps can be used to shift the array 1 bit to the right:

- Set ESI to the offset of **array**.
- The high-order doubleword at [ESI + 8] is shifted right and its lowest bit is copied into the Carry flag.
- The value at [ESI + 4] is shifted right, its highest bit is filled from the Carry flag, and its lowest bit is copied into the new Carry flag.
- The low-order doubleword at [ESI + 0] is shifted right, its highest bit is filled from the Carry flag, and its lowest bit is copied into the new Carry flag.

The following figure shows the array contents and indirect references:

99999999h	99999999h	99999999h
[esi]	[esi + 4]	[esi + 8]

The program named *MultiShf.asm* implements the following code:

```
.data
ArraySize = 3
array DWORD ArraySize DUP(99999999h)     ; 1001 1001...
.code
    mov esi,0
    shr array[esi + 8],1       ; high dword
    rcr array[esi + 4],1       ; middle dword, include Carry
    rcr array[esi],1           ; low dword, include Carry
```

The program output shows the numbers in binary before and after the shift:

```
1001 1001 1001 1001 1001 1001 1001 1001 1001 1001 ...(etc.)
0100 1100 1100 1100 1100 1100 1100 1100 1100 1100 ...(etc.)
```

7.3.2   Binary Multiplication

As we have already seen, SHL performs unsigned multiplication efficiently when the multiplier is a power of 2. You can factor any binary number into powers of 2. For example, to multiply unsigned EAX by 36, we can factor 36 into $(2^5 + 2^2)$ and use the distributive property of multiplication to carry out the operation:

```
EAX * 36 = EAX * (32 + 4)
         = (EAX * 32) + (EAX * 4)
```

Shifting an unsigned integer n bits to the left multiplies it by 2^n. The following figure shows the multiplication 123 * 36, producing 4428, the product:

```
              01111011        123
       ×      00100100        36
             ─────────
              01111011        123 SHL 2
     +      01111011          123 SHL 5
          ───────────────
          0001000101001100    4428
```

Notice that bits 2 and 5 are set in the multiplier, 36. These are exactly the shift values used in the example. The following code implements this multiplication using 32-bit registers:

```
.code
    mov eax,123
    mov ebx,eax
    shl eax,5              ; mult by 2^5
    shl ebx,2              ; mult by 2^2
    add eax,ebx           ; add the products
```

As a chapter exercise, you will be asked to generalize this example and create a procedure that multiplies any two 32-bit unsigned integers using shifting and addition.

7.3.3   Displaying Binary Bits

A good way to apply the SHL instruction is to display a byte in ASCII binary format. We can take advantage of the fact that the highest bit is copied into the Carry flag each time the byte is shifted to the left. The following program displays each of the bits in EAX:

```
TITLE Displaying Binary Bits              (WriteBin.asm)

; Display a 32-bit integer in binary.

INCLUDE Irvine32.inc

.data
binValue DWORD 1234ABCDh          ; sample binary value
buffer BYTE 32 dup(0),0
```

```
.code
main PROC
    mov eax,binValue                    ; number to display
    mov ecx,32                          ; number of bits in EAX
    mov esi,offset buffer

L1: shl eax,1                           ; shift high bit into Carry flag
    mov BYTE PTR [esi],'0'              ; choose 0 as default digit
    jnc L2                              ; if no Carry, jump to L2
    mov BYTE PTR [esi],'1'              ; else move 1 to buffer

L2: inc esi                             ; next buffer position
    loop L1                             ; shift another bit to left

    mov edx,OFFSET buffer               ; display the buffer
    call WriteString
    call Crlf
    exit
main ENDP
END main
```

7.3.4 Isolating a Bit String

Often a byte or word contains more than one field, making it necessary to extract short sequences of bits called *bit strings*. For example, in Real-address mode, MS-DOS function 57h returns the date stamp of a file in DX. (The date stamp shows the date on which the file was last modified.) Bits 0–4 represent a day number between 1 and 31, bits 5–8 are the month number, and bits 9–15 hold the year number.

Suppose a file was last modified on March 10, 1999. The file's date stamp would appear as follows in the DX register (the year number is relative to 1980):

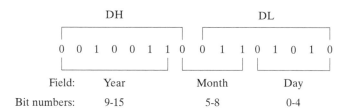

To extract a single field, we can shift its bits into the lowest part of a register and clear the irrelevant bit positions. The following code example extracts the day number by making a copy of DL and masking off all bits not belonging to the field:

```
mov    al,dl                           ; make a copy of DL
and    al,00011111b                    ; clear bits 5-7
mov    day,al                          ; save in day
```

To extract the month number, we move bits 5–8 into the low part of AL before masking off all other bits. AL is then shifted right until the month number is in the lowest five positions:

```
mov    ax,dx              ; make a copy of DX
shr    ax,5               ; shift right 5 bits
and    al,00001111b       ; clear bits 4-7
mov    month,al           ; save in month
```

The year number (bits 9–15) is completely within the DH register. We move this to AL and shift it right 1 bit:

```
mov    al,dh              ; make a copy of DH
shr    al,1               ; shift right one position
mov    ah,0               ; clear AH to zeros
add    ax,1980            ; year is relative to 1980
mov    year,ax            ; save in year
```

7.3.5 Section Review

1. Write a sequence of instructions that shift three memory bytes to the right by 1 bit position. Use the following data definition:

   ```
   byteArray BYTE 81h,20h,33h
   ```

2. Write a sequence of instructions that shift three memory words to the left by 1 bit position. Use the following data definition:

   ```
   wordArray WORD 810Dh,0C064h,93ABh
   ```

3. Write instructions that calculate EAX * 24 using binary multiplication.

4. Write instructions that calculate EAX * 21 using binary multiplication. *Hint:* $21 = 2^4 + 2^2 + 2^0$.

5. What change would be made to the *WriteBin.asm* program in Section 7.3.3 if you wanted to display the binary bits in reverse order?

6. The time stamp of a file uses bits 0–4 for the seconds, bits 5–10 for the minutes, and bits 11–15 for the hours. Write instructions that extract the minutes and copy the value to a byte variable named **bMinutes**.

7.4   Multiplication and Division Instructions

Finally, we can finish all the basic arithmetic operations on binary integers by introducing integer multiplication and division instructions. The Intel instruction set lets you multiply and divide 8-, 16-, and 32-bit integers, using the MUL (unsigned multiply), DIV (unsigned divide), IMUL (signed multiply), and IDIV (signed divide) instructions.

7.4.1 MUL Instruction

The MUL (unsigned multiply) instruction multiplies an 8-, 16-, or 32-bit operand by either AL, AX, or EAX. The instruction formats are:

```
MUL  r/m8
MUL  r/m16
MUL  r/m32
```

The single operand is the multiplier. The following table shows the default multiplicand and product, depending on the size of the multiplier:

Multiplicand	Multiplier	Product
AL	*r/m8*	AX
AX	*r/m16*	DX:AX
EAX	*r/m32*	EDX:EAX

The register(s) holding the product are twice the size of the multiplicand and multiplier, guaranteeing that overflow will never occur. The following illustration shows EAX multiplied by a 32-bit multiplier:

The MUL instruction sets the Carry and Overflow flags if the upper half of the product is not equal to zero. (We will focus on the Carry flag here, since it is normally used for unsigned arithmetic.) For example, when AX is multiplied by a 16-bit operand, the product is stored in DX:AX. If DX is not equal to zero, the Carry flag is set.

Example 1: The following statements perform 8-bit unsigned multiplication (5 * 10h), producing 50h in AX:

```
mov al,5h
mov bl,10h
mul bl                    ; CF = 0
```

The Carry flag is clear because AH (the upper half of the product) equals zero.

Example 2: The following statements perform 16-bit unsigned multiplication (0100h * 2000h), producing 00200000h in DX:AX:

```
.data
val1  WORD  2000h
```

```
val2   WORD   0100h
.code
mov ax,val1
mul val2                        ; CF = 1
```

The Carry flag is set because DX is not equal to zero.

Example 3:   The following statements perform 32-bit unsigned multiplication (12345h * 1000h), producing 0000000012345000h in EDX:EAX:

```
mov eax,12345h
mov ebx,1000h
mul ebx                         ; CF = 0
```

The Carry flag is clear because EDX equals zero.

7.4.2 IMUL Instruction

The IMUL (signed multiply) instruction performs signed integer multiplication. It has the same syntax and uses the same operands as the MUL instruction. What is different is that it preserves the sign of the product.

IMUL sets the Carry and Overflow flags if the high-order product is not a sign extension of the low-order product. (Because the Overflow flag is normally used for signed arithmetic, we will focus on it here.) The following examples help to illustrate:

Example 1:   The following instructions perform 8-bit signed multiplication (48 * 4), producing +192 in AX:

```
mov    al,48
mov    bl,4
imul   bl                       ; AX = 00C0h, OF = 1
```

AH is not a sign extension of AL, so the Overflow flag is set.

Example 2:   The following instructions perform 8-bit signed multiplication (−4 * 4), producing −16 in AX:

```
mov    al,-4
mov    bl,4
imul   bl                       ; AX = FFF0h, OF = 0
```

AH is a sign extension of AL (the signed result fits within AL), so the Overflow flag is clear.

Example 3:   The following instructions perform 16-bit signed multiplication (48 * 4), producing +192 in DX:AX:

```
mov    ax,48
mov    bx,4
imul   bx                       ; DX:AX = 000000C0h, OF = 0
```

DX is a sign extension of AX, so the Overflow flag is clear.

Example 4: The following instructions perform 32-bit signed multiplication (4823424 * −423), producing −2,040,308,352 in EDX:EAX:

```
mov    eax,+4823424
mov    ebx,-423
imul   ebx                    ; EDX:EAX = FFFFFFFF86635D80h, OF = 0
```

EDX is a sign extension of EAX, so the Overflow flag is clear.

7.4.3 DIV Instruction

The DIV (unsigned divide) instruction performs 8-bit, 16-bit, and 32-bit division on unsigned integers. A single operand is supplied (register or memory operand), which is assumed to be the divisor. The instruction formats for DIV are:

```
DIV r/m8
DIV r/m16
DIV r/m32
```

The following table shows the relationship between the dividend, divisor, quotient, and remainder. Everything is determined by the size of the divisor:

Dividend	Divisor	Quotient	Remainder
AX	r/m8	AL	AH
DX:AX	r/m16	AX	DX
EDX:EAX	r/m32	EAX	EDX

The following illustration shows EDX:EAX as the default dividend when a 32-bit divisor is used:

$$\frac{\boxed{\text{EDX} \mid \text{EAX}}}{\boxed{r/m32}} = \boxed{\text{EAX}} \quad \text{(quotient)}$$
$$\boxed{\text{EDX}} \quad \text{(remainder)}$$

Example 1: The following instructions perform 8-bit unsigned division (83h / 2), producing a quotient of 41h and a remainder of 1):

```
mov    ax,0083h              ; dividend
mov    bl,2                  ; divisor
div    bl                    ; AL = 41h,  AH = 01h
```

Example 2: The following instructions perform 16-bit unsigned division (8003h / 100h), producing a quotient of 80h and a remainder of 3. DX contains the high part of the dividend, so it must be cleared before the DIV instruction executes:

```
mov    dx,0                  ; clear dividend, high
mov    ax,8003h              ; dividend, low
```

```
mov    cx,100h              ; divisor
div    cx                   ; AX = 0080h,  DX = 0003h
```

Example 3: The following instructions perform 32-bit unsigned division using a memory operand as the divisor:

```
.data
dividend QWORD 0000000800300020h
divisor  DWORD 00000100h
.code
mov edx,DWORD PTR dividend + 4    ; high doubleword
mov eax,DWORD PTR dividend        ; low doubleword
div divisor                       ; EAX = 08003000h, EDX = 00000020h
```

7.4.4   Signed Integer Division

7.4.4.1   CBW, CWD, CDQ Instructions

Before discussing signed integer division, we need to look at three instructions that perform integer sign-extension. The CBW (convert byte to word) instruction extends the sign bit of AL into the AH register. This preserves the number's sign:

```
.data
byteVal SBYTE -65            ; 9Bh
.code
    mov al,byteVal           ; AL = 9Bh
    cbw                      ; AX = FF9Bh
```

In other words, 9Bh and FF9Bh both equal −65. The only difference between the two is their storage size. (Sign extension was explained in Section 4.1.5.3 along with the MOVSX instruction.)

The CWD (convert word to doubleword) instruction extends the sign bit of AX into the DX register:

```
.data
wordVal SWORD -65            ; FF9Bh
.code
    mov ax,wordVal           ; AX = FF9Bh
    cwd                      ; DX:AX = FFFFFF9Bh
```

The CDQ (convert doubleword to quadword) instruction extends the sign bit of EAX into the EDX register:

```
.data
dwordVal SDWORD -65          ; FFFFFF9Bh
.code
    mov eax,dwordVal
    cdq                      ; EDX:EAX = FFFFFFFFFFFFFF9Bh
```

7.4.4.2   The IDIV Instruction

The IDIV (signed divide) instruction performs signed integer division, using the same operands as the DIV instruction. When doing 8-bit division, you must sign-extend the dividend into AH before IDIV executes. (The CBW instruction can be used.) In the next example, we divide −48 by 5. After IDIV executes, the quotient in AL is −9 and the remainder in AH is −3:

```
.data
byteVal SBYTE -48
.code
    mov  al,byteVal              ; dividend
    cbw                          ; extend AL into AH
    mov  bl,5                    ; divisor
    idiv bl                      ; AL = -9, AH = -3
```

Similarly, 16-bit division requires that AX be sign-extended into DX. In the next example, we divide −5000 by 256:

```
.data
wordVal SWORD -5000
.code
mov  ax,wordVal                  ; dividend, low
cwd                              ; extend AX into DX
mov  bx,256                      ; divisor
idiv bx                          ; quotient AX = -19
                                 ; remainder DX = -136
```

Similarly, 32-bit division requires that EAX be sign-extended into EDX. The next example divides −50000 by 256:

```
.data
dwordVal SDWORD -50000
.code
    mov  eax,dwordVal            ; dividend, low
    cdq                          ; extend EAX into EDX
    mov  ebx,256                 ; divisor
    idiv ebx                     ; quotient EAX = -195
                                 ; remainder EDX = -80
```

> For both DIV and IDIV, all of the arithmetic status flags are undefined after the operation.

7.4.4.3 Divide Overflow

If a division operand produces a quotient that is too large to fit into the destination operand, a *divide overflow* condition results. This causes a CPU interrupt, and the current program halts. The following instructions, for example, generate a divide overflow because the quotient (100h) will not fit into the AL register:

```
        mov ax,1000h
        mov bl,10h
        div bl                   ; AL cannot hold 100h
```

When this code executes under MS-Windows, the following dialog window appears:

A similar dialog window appears when you write instructions that attempt to divide by zero:

```
mov ax,dividend
mov bl,0
div bl
```

At this point in the book, we're not equipped with the proper tools to recover from divide overflow. We'll just let the program terminate, and then use a debugger to find out where the evil deed occurred. One thing you can do is to use a 32-bit divisor to reduce the probability of a divide overflow condition. For example:

```
mov eax,1000h
cdq
mov ebx,10h
div ebx                        ; EAX = 00000100h
```

Prevention of divide by zero is much easier. You can simply test the divisor and jump past the division instruction if it equals zero:

```
mov ax,dividend
mov bl,divisor
cmp bl,0                       ; check the divisor
je  NoDivideZero               ; zero? display error
div bl                         ; not zero: continue
.

.
NoDivideZero:
;(display "Attempt to divide by zero")
```

7.4.5 Implementing Arithmetic Expressions

In Section 4.2.5 we showed how to implement arithmetic expressions using addition and subtraction. Let's expand the possibilities now by including multiplication and division. There are at least three reasons for doing this: First, it's fun to pretend being a C++ or Java compiler, and find out how they would do it. Second, the best way to test your understanding of the multiplication and division instructions presented in this chapter is to implement complete expressions. Third, you can implement better error checking than a typical compiler by checking the size of the product following multiplication operations. Most high-level language compilers ignore the upper 32 bits of the product when multiplying two 32-bit operands. In assembly language, however, you can use the Carry and Overflow flags to tell you when the product does not fit into 32 bits. The use of these flags was explained in Section 7.4.1 and Section 7.4.2.

If you would like to compare your code to that of a compiler, take a look at the assembly code the compiler generates either by opening a debugging window or by generating a source listing file. Most C++ compilers make this easy to do.

Example 1: Implement the following C++ statement in assembly language, using unsigned 32-bit integers:

```
var4 = (var1 + var2) * var3;
```

This is a straightforward problem because we can work from left to right (addition, then multiplication). After the second instruction, EAX contains the sum of **var1** and **var2**. In the third instruction, EAX is multiplied by **var3** and the product is stored in EAX:

```
mov eax,var1
add eax,var2
mul var3                         ; EAX = EAX * var3
jc  tooBig                       ; unsigned overflow?
mov var4,eax
jmp next
tooBig:                          ; display error message
```

If the MUL instruction generates a product larger than 32 bits, the JC instruction jumps to a label that handles the error.

Example 2: Implement the following C++ statement, using unsigned 32-bit integers:

```
var4 = (var1 * 5) / (var2 - 3);
```

In this example, there are two subexpressions within parentheses. The left side can be assigned to EDX:EAX, so it is not necessary to check for overflow. The right side is assigned to EBX, and the final division completes the expression:

```
mov eax,var1                     ; left side
mov ebx,5
mul ebx                          ; EDX:EAX = product
mov ebx,var2                     ; right side
sub ebx,3
div ebx                          ; final division
mov var4,eax
```

Example 3: Implement the following C++ statement, using signed 32-bit integers:

```
var4 = (var1 * -5) / (-var2 % var3);
```

This example is a little trickier than the previous ones. We can begin with the expression on the right side and store its value in EBX. Because the operands are signed, it's important to sign-extend the dividend into EDX and use the IDIV instruction:

```
mov eax,var2              ; begin right side
neg eax
cdq                       ; sign-extend dividend
idiv var3                 ; EDX = remainder
mov ebx,edx               ; EBX = right side
```

Next, we calculate the expression on the left side, storing the product in EDX:EAX:

```
mov eax,-5                ; begin left side
imul var1                 ; EDX:EAX = left side
```

Finally, the left side (EDX:EAX) is divided by the right side (EBX):

```
idiv ebx                  ; final division
mov var4,eax              ; quotient
```

7.4.6   Section Review

1. Explain why there can never be overflow when the MUL and IMUL instructions execute.
2. How is the IMUL instruction different from MUL in the way it generates a multiplication product?
3. What has to happen in order for the IMUL to set the Carry and Overflow flags?
4. When EBX is the operand in a DIV instruction, which register holds the quotient?
5. When BX is the operand in a DIV instruction, which register holds the quotient?
6. When BL is the operand in a MUL instruction, which registers hold the product?
7. Show an example of sign-extension before calling the IDIV instruction with a 16-bit operand.
8. What will be the contents of AX and DX after the following operation?

```
mov    dx,0
mov    ax,222h
mov    cx,100h
mul    cx
```

9. What will be the contents of AX after the following operation?

```
mov    ax,63h
mov    bl,10h
div    bl
```

10. What will be the contents of EAX and EDX after the following operation?

```
mov    eax,123400h
mov    edx,0
mov    ebx,10h
div    ebx
```

11. What will be the contents of AX and DX after the following operation?

```
mov   ax,4000h
mov   dx,500h
mov   bx,10h
div   bx
```

12. Write instructions that multiply −5 by 3 and store the result in a 16-bit variable **val1.**
13. Write instructions that divide −276 by 10 and store the result in a 16-bit variable **val1.**
14. Implement the following C++ expression in assembly language, using 32-bit unsigned operands: val1 = (val2 ∗ val3) / (val4 − 3)
15. Implement the following C++ expression in assembly language, using 32-bit signed operands: val1 = (val2 / val3) ∗ (val1 + val2)

7.5 Extended Addition and Subtraction

Extended addition and subtraction is the adding and subtracting of numbers having an almost unlimited size. Suppose you were asked to write a C++ program that adds two 128-bit integers. The solution would not be easy! But in assembly language, the ADC (add with carry) and SBB (subtract with borrow) instructions are well-suited to this type of problem.

7.5.1 ADC Instruction

The ADC (add with carry) instruction adds both a source operand and the contents of the Carry flag to a destination operand. The instruction formats are the same as for the MOV instruction:

```
ADC  reg,reg
ADC  mem,reg
ADC  reg,mem
ADC  mem,imm
ADC  reg,imm
```

For example, the following instructions add two 8-bit integers (FFh + FFh), producing a 16-bit sum in DL:AL, which is 01FEh:

```
mov dl,0
mov al,0FFh
add al,0FFh                    ; AL = FE
adc dl,0                       ; DL = 01
```

Similarly, the following instructions add two 32-bit integers (FFFFFFFFh + FFFFFFFFh), producing a 64-bit sum in EDX:EAX: 00000001FFFFFFFEh:

```
mov edx,0
mov eax,0FFFFFFFFh
add eax,0FFFFFFFFh
adc edx,0
```

7.5.2   Extended Addition Example

The following **Extended_Add** procedure adds two integers of almost any size. It uses a loop to add each pair of doublewords, save the Carry flag, and include the carry with each subsequent pair of doublewords:

```
;------------------------------------------------------
Extended_Add PROC
;
; Calculates the sum of two extended integers that are
;   stored as an array of doublewords.
; Receives: ESI and EDI point to the two integers,
; EBX points to a variable that will hold the sum, and
; ECX indicates the number of doublewords to be added.
;------------------------------------------------------
    pushad
    clc                          ; clear the Carry flag

L1: mov eax,[esi]                ; get the first integer
    adc eax,[edi]                ; add the second integer
    pushfd                       ; save the Carry flag
    mov [ebx],eax                ; store partial sum
    add esi,4                    ; advance all 3 pointers
    add edi,4
    add ebx,4
    popfd                        ; restore the Carry flag
    loop L1                      ; repeat the loop

    adc word ptr [ebx],0         ; add any leftover carry
    popad
    ret
Extended_Add ENDP
```

(See *ExtAdd.asm* on the sample program disk.)

The following is a program excerpt that calls **Extended_Add**, passing it two 64-bit integers. Notice that we are careful to allocate an extra doubleword in the sum for any carry that may result:

```
.data
op1 QWORD 0A2B2A40674981234h
op2 QWORD 08010870000234502h
sum DWORD 3 dup(?)
.code
main PROC
    mov   esi,OFFSET op1         ; first operand
    mov   edi,OFFSET op2         ; second operand
    mov   ebx,OFFSET sum         ; sum operand
    mov   ecx,2                  ; number of doublewords
    call Extended_Add
    mov   esi,OFFSET sum         ; dump memory
```

```
        mov   ebx,4
        mov   ecx,3
        call  DumpMem
        exit
main ENDP
```

The following output was produced by the program. As we can see, the addition did produce a carry:

```
Dump of offset 00404010
-------------------------------
74BB5736   22C32B06   00000001
```

Because **DumpMem** displays the sum as three separate integers in little endian order, the three doublewords must be rearranged in order to show the actual sum: 0000000122C32B0674BB5736h.

7.5.3   SBB Instruction

The SBB (subtract with borrow) instruction subtracts both a source operand and the value of the Carry flag from a destination operand. The possible operands are the same as for the ADC instruction.

The following example code performs 64-bit subtraction. It sets EDX:EAX to 0000000100000000h and subtracts 1 from this value. The lower 32 bits are subtracted first, setting the Carry flag. Then the upper 32 bits are subtracted, including the Carry flag:

```
mov edx,1                      ; upper half
mov eax,0                      ; lower half
sub eax,1                      ; subtract 1
sbb edx,0                      ; subtract upper half
```

The 64-bit difference in EDX:EAX is 00000000FFFFFFFFh.

7.5.4   Section Review

1. Describe the ADC instruction.
2. Describe the SBB instruction.
3. What will be the values of EDX:EAX after the following instructions execute?

```
mov edx,10h
mov eax,0A0000000h
add eax,20000000h
adc edx,0
```

4. What will be the values of EDX:EAX after the following instructions execute?

```
mov edx,100h
mov eax,80000000h
sub eax,90000000h
sbb edx,0
```

5. What will be the contents of DX after the following instructions execute (STC sets the Carry flag)?

```
mov   dx,5
stc                      ; set Carry flag
mov   ax,10h
adc   dx,ax
```

6. *Challenge:* The following program is supposed to subtract **val1** from **val2**. Find and correct all logic errors (CLC clears the Carry flag):

```
.data
val1   QWORD   20403004362047A1h
val2   QWORD   055210304A2630B2h
result QWORD   0
.code
    mov   cx,8                  ; loop counter
    mov   esi,val1              ; set index to start
    mov   edi,val2
    clc                        ; clear Carry flag
top:
    mov   al,byte ptr [esi]     ; get first number
    sbb   al,byte ptr [edi]     ; subtract second
    mov   byte ptr [esi],al     ; store the result
    dec   esi
    dec   edi
    loop top
```

7.6 ASCII and Packed Decimal Arithmetic (Optional)

The integer arithmetic shown so far in this book has dealt only with binary values. The CPU calculates in binary, but it is also possible to perform arithmetic on ASCII decimal strings.

Suppose that we would like to input two numbers from the user and add them together. The following is a sample of the program's output, in which the user has input 3402 and 1256:

```
Enter first number:    3402
Enter second number:   1256
The sum is:            4658
```

We have two options when calculating and displaying the sum:

1. Convert both operands to binary, add the binary values, and convert the sum from binary to ASCII digit strings.
2. Add the digit strings directly by successively adding each pair of ASCII digits (2 + 6, 0 + 5, 4 + 2, and 3 + 1). The sum is an ASCII digit string, so it can be directly displayed on the screen.

The second option requires specialized instructions that adjust the sum after adding each pair of ASCII digits. The instruction set has four instructions that deal with ASCII addition, subtraction, multiplication, and division:

AAA	(ASCII adjust after addition)
AAS	(ASCII adjust after subtraction)
AAM	(ASCII adjust after multiplication)
AAD	(ASCII adjust before division)

ASCII Decimal and Unpacked Decimal   The high 4 bits of an unpacked decimal integer are always zeros, whereas the same bits in an ASCII decimal number are equal to 0011b. The following example shows how 3,402 is stored using both formats:

ASCII format: | 33 | 34 | 30 | 32 | Unpacked BCD: | 03 | 04 | 00 | 02 |

(all values are in hexadecimal)

In general, ASCII arithmetic is slow because it is performed digit by digit, but it offers an advantage: the ability to process large numbers. For example, the following decimal integer can be represented accurately in ASCII format, but cannot be represented by a 32-bit binary number:

```
2345678000263653834 56
```

When executing ASCII addition and subtraction, operands can be in either ASCII format or in unpacked decimal format. Only unpacked decimal numbers can be used for multiplication and division.

7.6.1 AAA Instruction

The AAA (ASCII adjust after addition) instruction adjusts the binary result of an ADD or ADC instruction. It makes the result in AL consistent with ASCII digit representation. The following example shows how to add the ASCII digits 8 and 2 correctly, using the AAA instruction. We have to clear AH to zero before performing the addition. The last instruction converts both AH and AL to ASCII digits:

```
mov   ah,0
mov   al,'8'          ; AX = 0038h
add   al,'2'          ; AX = 006Ah
aaa                   ; AX = 0100h     (ASCII adjust result)
or    ax,3030h        ; AX = 3130h = '10' (convert to ASCII)
```

7.6.2   AAS Instruction

The AAS (ASCII adjust after subtraction) instruction follows a SUB or SBB instruction that has subtracted one unpacked BCD value from another and stored the result in AL. It makes the result in AL consistent with ASCII digit representation. Adjustment is necessary only when the subtraction generates a negative result. For example, the following statements subtract ASCII 9 from 8:

```
.data
val1 BYTE '8'
val2 BYTE '9'
.code
mov ah,0
mov al,val1                ; AX = 0038h
sub al,val2                ; AX = 00FFh
aas                        ; AX = FF09h
pushf                      ; save the Carry flag
or al,30h                  ; AX = FF39h
popf                       ; restore the Carry flag
```

After the SUB instruction, AX equals 00FFh. The AAS instruction converts AL to 09h and subtracts 1 from AH, setting it to FFh and setting the Carry flag.

7.6.3   AAM Instruction

The AAM (ASCII adjust after multiplication) instruction adjusts the binary result of a MUL instruction. The multiplication must have been performed on unpacked decimal numbers. The multiplication also cannot be performed on ASCII numbers until the highest four bits of each number are cleared. In the following example, we multiply 5 by 6 and adjust the result in AX. After adjusting the result, AX = 0300h, which is the unpacked decimal representation of 30:

```
.data
AscVal BYTE 05h,06h
.code
mov bl,ascVal              ; first operand
mov al,ascVal+1            ; second operand
mul bl                     ; AX = 001Eh
aam                        ; AX = 0300h
```

7.6.4   AAD Instruction

The AAD (ASCII adjust before division) instruction adjusts the unpacked decimal dividend in AX before a division operation. The following example divides unpacked decimal 37 by 5. First, the AAD instruction converts 0307h to 0025h. Then the DIV instruction yields a quotient of 07h in AL and a remainder of 02h in AH:

```
.data
quotient  BYTE ?
```

```
remainder BYTE ?
.code
mov  ax,0307h              ; dividend
aad                        ; AX = 0025h
mov  bl,5                  ; divisor
div  bl                    ; AX = 0207h
mov  quotient,al
mov  remainder,ah
```

7.6.5   Packed Decimal Integers

Packed decimal integers store two decimal digits per byte. Each decimal digit is represented by four bits, as in the storage of 12,345,678.

```
packedBCD DWORD 12345678h
```

Packed decimal format has at least two strengths:

- The numbers can have almost any number of significant digits. This makes it possible to perform calculations with a great deal of accuracy.
- Conversion of packed decimal numbers to ASCII (and vice versa) is relatively fast.

Two instructions, DAA (decimal adjust after addition) and DAS (decimal adjust after subtraction), adjust the result of an addition or subtraction operation on packed decimal numbers. Unfortunately, no such instructions exist for multiplication and division. In those cases, the number must be unpacked, multiplied or divided, and repacked.

7.6.5.1   DAA Instruction

The DAA (decimal adjust after addition) instruction converts the binary result of an ADD or ADC instruction in AL to packed decimal format. For example, the following instructions add packed decimals 35 and 48. The lower digit of the result (7Dh) is greater than 9, and it is adjusted. The upper digit, which is 8 after the first adjustment, is not adjusted:

```
mov  al,35h
add  al,48h                ; AL = 7Dh
daa                        ; AL = 83h (adjusted result)
```

7.6.5.2   DAS Instruction

The DAS (decimal adjust after subtraction) instruction converts the binary result of a SUB or SBB instruction in AL to packed decimal format. For example, the following statements subtract packed decimal 48 from 85 and adjust the result:

```
mov  bl,48h
mov  al,85h
sub  al,bl                 ; AL = 3Dh
das                        ; AL = 37h  (adjusted result)
```

7.7   Chapter Summary

Along with the bitwise instructions from the preceding chapter, shift instructions are among the most characteristic of assembly language. To *shift* a number means to move its bits right or left.

The SHL (shift left) instruction shifts each bit in a destination operand to the left, filling the lowest bit with 0. One of the best uses of SHL is for performing high-speed multiplication by powers of 2. Shifting any operand left by n bits multiplies the operand by 2^n. The SHR (shift right) instruction shifts each bit to the right, replacing the highest bit with a 0. Shifting any operand right by n bits divides the operand by 2^n.

SAL (shift arithmetic left) and SAR (shift arithmetic right) are shift instructions specifically designed for shifting signed numbers.

The ROL (rotate left) instruction shifts each bit to the left and copies the highest bit to both the Carry flag and the lowest bit position. The ROR (rotate right) instruction shifts each bit to the right and copies the lowest bit to both the Carry flag and the highest bit position.

The RCL (rotate carry left) instruction shifts each bit to the left and copies the highest bit into the Carry flag, which is first copied into the lowest bit of the result. The RCR (rotate carry right) instruction shifts each bit to the right and copies the lowest bit into the Carry flag. The Carry flag is copied into the highest bit of the result.

The SHLD (shift left double) instruction shifts a target operand a given number of bits to the left. The SHRD (shift right double) instruction shifts a target operand a given number of bits to the right. Both instructions require an IA-32 family processor.

The MUL instruction multiplies an 8-, 16-, or 32-bit operand by either AL, AX, or EAX. The IMUL instruction performs signed integer multiplication. It has the same syntax and uses the same operands as the MUL instruction.

The DIV instruction performs 8-bit, 16-bit, and 32-bit division on unsigned integers. The IDIV instruction performs signed integer division, using the same operands as the DIV instruction.

The CBW (convert byte to word) instruction extends the sign bit of AL into the AH register. The CDQ (convert doubleword to quadword) instruction extends the sign bit of EAX into the EDX register. The CWD (convert word to doubleword) instruction extends the sign bit of AX into the DX register.

Extended addition and subtraction refers to adding and subtracting very large integers. The ADC (add with carry) instruction adds both a source operand and the contents of the Carry flag to a destination operand. The SBB (subtract with borrow) instruction subtracts both a source operand and the value of the Carry flag from a destination operand.

The following instructions are designed to enable arithmetic using both ASCII decimal integers (strings of digits) and unpacked decimal integers:

- The AAA (ASCII adjust after addition) instruction adjusts the binary result of an ADD or ADC instruction.
- The AAS (ASCII adjust after subtraction) instruction adjusts the binary result of a SUB or SBB instruction.

- The AAM (ASCII adjust after multiplication) instruction adjusts the binary result of a MUL instruction.

- The AAD (ASCII adjust before division) instruction adjusts the unpacked decimal dividend in AX before a division operation.

Two additional instructions are for use with packed decimal integers:

- The DAA (decimal adjust after addition) instruction converts the binary result of an ADD or ADC instruction in AL to packed decimal format.

- The DAS (decimal adjust after subtraction) instruction converts the binary result of a SUB or SBB instruction in AL to packed decimal format.

7.8   Programming Exercises

1. Extended Addition Procedure

Modify the **Extended_Add** procedure in Section 7.5.1 to add two 256-bit (32-byte) integers.

2. Extended Subtraction Procedure

Create and test a procedure named **Extended_Sub** that subtracts two binary integers of arbitrary size. Restrictions: The storage size of the two integers must be the same, and their size must be a multiple of 32 bits.

3. ShowFileTime

Suppose the time field of a file directory entry uses bits 0–4 for the seconds, bits 5–10 for the minutes, and bits 11–15 for the hours (24-hour clock). For example, the following binary value indicates a time of 02:16:07, in *hh:mm:ss* format:

```
00010 010000 00111
```

Write a procedure named **ShowFileTime** that receives a binary file time value in the AX register and displays the time in *hh:mm:ss* format.

4. Shifting Multiple Doublewords

Write a procedure that shifts an array of five 32-bit integers using the SHRD instruction (Section 7.2.8). Write a program that tests your procedure and displays the array.

5. Fast Multiplication

Write a procedure named **FastMultiply** that multiplies any unsigned 32-bit integer by EAX, using only shifting and addition. Pass the integer to the procedure in the EBX register, and return the product in the EAX register. Write a short test program that calls the procedure and displays the product. (We will assume that the product is never larger than 32 bits.)

6. Greatest Common Divisor (GCD)

The greatest common divisor of two integers is the largest integer that will evenly divide both integers. The GCD algorithm involves integer division in a loop, described by the following C++ code:

```
int GCD(int x, int y)
{
    x = abs(x);                  // absolute value
    y = abs(y);
    do {
      int n = x % y;
      x = y;
      y = n;
    } while y > 0;
    return y;
}
```

Implement this function in assembly language and write a test program that calls the function several times, passing it different values. Display all results on the screen.

7. Prime Number Program

Write a procedure that sets the Zero flag if the 32-bit integer passed in the EAX register is prime. (A prime number is evenly divisible by only itself and 1.) Optimize the program's loop to run as efficiently as possible. Your program should prompt the user for a number and then display a message indicating whether or not the number is prime. The program should then ask for another number from the user. Continue the loop in this fashion until the user enters a prearranged value such as −1.

8. Packed Decimal Conversion

Write a procedure named **PackedToAsc** that converts a 4-byte packed decimal number to a string of ASCII decimal digits. Pass the packed number to the procedure in EAX, and pass a pointer to a buffer that will hold the ASCII digits. Write a short test program that demonstrates several conversions and displays the converted numbers on the screen.

8

Advanced Procedures

8.1 Introduction

Originally, this chapter simply explained how to write procedures in assembly language. Somehow, it became much more than that. Perhaps it was because the underlying structures of programming languages seem to have so much in common.

There is a natural tendency to look for universal concepts that make learning easier, so we're going to use this chapter to show you how all procedures work, using assembly language as a low-level programming tool. In other words, what you learn here is often discussed in mid-level programming courses in C++ and Java, and in a core computer science course called *programming languages*. The following topics, discussed in this chapter, are basic programming language concepts:

- Creating and initializing local variables on the stack
- Variable scope and lifetime
- Stack parameters
- Stack frames
- Passing parameters by value and by reference
- Classifying parameters as *input, output,* and *input-output*
- Recursion

A number of other topics in this chapter are designed purely to further your knowledge of assembly language:

- INVOKE, PROC, and PROTO directives
- USES and ADDR operators
- Memory models and language specifiers
- Using indirect addressing to access stack parameters
- Writing multimodule programs

Above all, your knowledge of assembly language makes it possible for you to peek into the mind of the compiler writer, as he or she produces the low-level code that makes a program run.

8.2   Local Variables

A *local variable* is a variable that is created, used, and destroyed within a single procedure. Assuming that you've already programmed in some high-level language, you are familar with local variables.

In preceding chapters, we declared all variables in the data segment. Such variables are called *static global* variables. The term *static* indicates that a variable's lifetime is the same as the duration of the current program. The term *global* indicates a variable's visibility. A global variable is visible from all procedures in the current source code file.

In this chapter, we create and manipulate local variables in assembly language. Local variables have distinct advantages over global variables:

- Restricted access to a local variable helps when you're debugging, because only a limited number of program statements can modify the variable.
- Local variables make efficient use of memory, because their storage space can be released and made available to new variables.

- The same variable name can appear in two or more procedures without creating a name clash.

Local variables are created on the runtime stack. They cannot be given default values at assembly time, but they can be initialized at runtime.

8.2.1   LOCAL Directive

The LOCAL directive declares one or more local variables inside a procedure. It must be placed on the line immediately following a PROC directive. The syntax is:

```
LOCAL varlist
```

varlist is a list of variable definitions, separated by commas, which may span multiple lines. Each variable definition takes the following form:

```
label:type
```

The label may be any valid identifier, and *type* can either be a standard type (WORD, DWORD, etc.) or a user-defined type. (Structures and other user-defined types are explained in Chapter 10.)

Example 1   The **MySub** procedure contains a single local variable named **var1** of type BYTE:

```
MySub PROC
    LOCAL var1:BYTE
```

Example 2   The **BubbleSort** procedure contains a doubleword local variable named **temp** and a BYTE variable named **SwapFlag**:

```
BubbleSort PROC
    LOCAL temp:DWORD, SwapFlag:BYTE
```

Example 3   The **Merge** procedure contains a local variable named **pArray** that points to a memory word:

```
Merge PROC
    LOCAL pArray:PTR WORD
```

Example 4   The local variable **TempArray** is an array of ten doublewords. Note the use of brackets to show the array size:

```
LOCAL TempArray[10]:DWORD
```

Automatic Code Generation   You may be wondering what code is actually generated by the assembler when local variables are used. The answer may be found by looking at the Disassembly window of the Visual Studio debugger. Let's try this by assembling and debugging the following procedure declaration:

```
BubbleSort PROC
    LOCAL temp:DWORD, SwapFlag:BYTE
    ;
```

```
        ret
BubbleSort ENDP
```

The following is a slightly edited copy of the debugger's disassembly of **BubbleSort**:

```
BubbleSort:
    push ebp
    mov  ebp,esp
    add  esp,0FFFFFFF8h              ; add -8 to ESP
    mov  esp,ebp
    pop  ebp
    ret
```

The ADD instruction adds −8 to ESP, moving it downward and creating an opening in the stack between ESP and EBP for the two local variables:

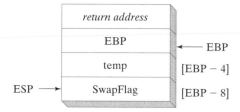

SumOf Procedure Example   In the following example, **tempSum** is a local doubleword variable in the **SumOf** procedure:

```
SumOf PROC
    LOCAL tempSum:DWORD
    mov  tempSum,eax
    add  tempSum,ebx
    add  tempSum,ecx              ; tempsum = eax + ebx + ecx
    mov  eax,tempSum
    ret
SumOf ENDP
```

Reserving Stack Space   If you plan to create arrays of any size as local variables, be sure to reserve (*allocate*) adequate stack space before assembling the program. Inside the *Irvine32.inc* file, for example, the following STACK directive reserves 4096 bytes of stack space:

```
.stack 4096
```

If procedure calls are nested, the stack space must be large enough to hold the sum of all local variables active at any point in the program's execution. For example, suppose **Sub1** calls **Sub2**, and **Sub2** calls **Sub3**. Each might have a local array variable:

```
Sub1 PROC
    LOCAL array1[50]:DWORD            ; 200 bytes
```

```
        .
        .
    Sub2 PROC
        LOCAL array2[80]:WORD            ; 160 bytes
        .
        .
    Sub3 PROC
        LOCAL array3[300]:BYTE           ; 300 bytes
```

When the program enters **Sub3** it will have the combined local variables from **Sub1**, **Sub2**, and **Sub3** on the stack. There will be 660 bytes used by local variables, plus the two procedure return addresses (8 bytes), plus any registers that might have been pushed on the stack within the procedures.

8.2.2 Section Review

1. Name three advantages of local variables over global variables.
2. (*True/False*): Local variables can be assigned default values at assembly time.
3. (*True/False*): A maximum of four local variables may be defined using a single LOCAL directive.
4. (*True/False*): The same name may be used for local variables in two different procedures.
5. Declare a local variable named **pArray** that is a pointer to an array of doublewords.
6. Declare a local variable named **buffer** that is an array of 20 bytes.
7. Declare a local variable named **pwArray** that points to a 16-bit unsigned integer.
8. Declare a local variable named **myByte** that holds an 8-bit signed integer.
9. Declare a local variable named **myArray** that is an array of 20 doublewords.

8.3 Stack Parameters

There are two basic types of procedure parameters: *register parameters* and *stack parameters*. The Irvine32 and Irvine16 libraries use register parameters. In this section, we will show you how to declare and use stack parameters.

> Values passed to a procedure by a calling program are called *arguments*. When the values are received by the called procedure, they are called *parameters*.

Register parameters are optimized for program execution speed. Unfortunately, they tend to create code clutter in calling programs. Existing register contents often must be saved before they can be loaded with argument values. Such is the case when calling **DumpMem**, for example:

```
    pushad
    mov  esi,OFFSET array           ; starting OFFSET
```

```
mov   ecx,LENGTHOF array              ; size, in units
mov   ebx,TYPE array                  ; doubleword format
call DumpMem                          ; display memory
popad
```

Stack parameters are the other option. The required arguments must be pushed on the stack by a calling program. For example, if **DumpMem** used stack parameters, we could call it using the following sequence of instructions:

```
push OFFSET array
push LENGTHOF array
push TYPE array
call DumpMem
```

MASM has a convenient directive named INVOKE that automatically pushes arguments on the stack and calls a procedure. The original four lines of calling statements can be reduced to just one:

```
INVOKE DumpMem,OFFSET array,LENGTHOF array,TYPE array
```

There's another good reason to learn about stack parameters: Nearly all high-level languages use them. If you want to call functions in the MS-Windows library, for example, you must pass arguments on the stack.

8.3.1 INVOKE Directive

The INVOKE directive is a more powerful replacement for Intel's CALL instruction that lets you pass multiple arguments. Here is the general syntax:

INVOKE *procedureName [, argumentList]*

ArgumentList is an optional comma-delimited list of arguments that may be passed to the procedure. Right away, you can see an important difference between INVOKE and CALL: The latter cannot include a list of arguments.

INVOKE permits almost any number of arguments, and the individual arguments can appear on separate source code lines. An argument can be any of the types listed in Table 8-1.

Table 8-1 Argument Types Used with INVOKE.

Type	Examples
immediate value	10, 3000h, OFFSET myList, TYPE array
integer expression	(10 * 20), COUNT
variable name	myList, array, myWord, myDword
address expression	[myList+2], [ebx + esi]

Table 8-1   Argument Types Used with INVOKE. (Continued)

Type	Examples
register name	eax, bl, edi
ADDR *name*	ADDR myList

Example   INVOKE is used here to call a procedure named **AddTwo**, passing it two 32-bit integers:

```
.data
val1 DWORD 12345h
val2 DWORD 23456h
.code
    INVOKE AddTwo,val1,val2
```

The same procedure call could also be accomplished by pushing the parameter values on the stack (in reverse order) before executing the CALL instruction:

```
push val2
push val1
call AddTwo
```

Following is a picture of the stack just prior to the CALL instruction:

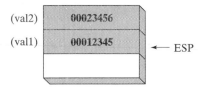

Arguments can be pushed on the stack in different ways, as we will show later in Section 8.4.2.

8.3.1.1   ADDR Operator

The ADDR operator can be used to pass a pointer when calling a procedure with the INVOKE directive. Passing an address as a procedure argument is called *passing by reference*. For example, this INVOKE statement passes the address of **myArray** to the **FillArray** procedure:

```
INVOKE FillArray, ADDR myArray
```

ADDR returns either a near pointer or a far pointer, depending on what is called for by the program's memory model. In Protected mode programs using the flat memory model, ADDR and OFFSET both return a 32-bit offset. (The .MODEL directive in *Irvine32.inc* specifies the flat memory model.)

In Real-address mode, you can create small memory model programs in which ADDR and OFFSET both return 16-bit offsets. We specify the small model in *Irvine16.inc*, the include file used with the Real-address mode programs in this book.

Far pointers, on the other hand, are 32-bit segment/offset combinations. They are primarily used in either system-level programs or Real-address programs having multiple code and data segments.

Example 1   The following code calls the **FillArray procedure**, passing it the address of an array of byte values. Notice that the argument is on a separate line with its own comment:

```
.data
myArray BYTE 50 DUP(?)
.code
    INVOKE FillArray,
      ADDR myArray                  ; points to the array
```

Example 2   The following shows how to call a procedure named **Swap**, passing it the addresses of the first two elements in an array of doublewords:

```
.data
Array DWORD 20 DUP(?)
.code
...
INVOKE Swap,
    ADDR Array
    ADDR Array+4
```

8.3.2 PROC Directive

The PROC directive permits you to declare a procedure name with a list of named parameters, as the following simplified syntax shows:

```
label PROC,
    parameter_1,
    parameter_2,
    .
    .
    parameter_n
```

The list of parameters can also be placed on the same line:

```
label PROC, parameter_1, parameter_2, ..., parameter_n
```

A single parameter has the following syntax:

```
paramName:type
```

ParamName is an arbitrary name you assign to the parameter. Its scope is limited to the current procedure (called *local scope*). The same parameter name can be used in more than one procedure, but it cannot be the name of a global variable or code label. The *type* can be one of the following: BYTE, SBYTE, WORD, SWORD, DWORD, SDWORD, FWORD, QWORD, or TBYTE. It can also be a *qualified type*, which may be a pointer to an existing type. Following are examples of qualified types:

PTR BYTE	PTR SBYTE
PTR WORD	PTR SWORD
PTR DWORD	PTR SDWORD
PTR QWORD	PTR TBYTE

Although it is possible to add NEAR and FAR attributes to these expressions, they are relevant only in more specialized applications. Qualified types can also be created using the TYPEDEF and STRUCT directives, which we will cover in Chapter 10.

8.3.2.1 Examples

Let's look at a few examples of procedure declarations using various types of parameters. Some of the procedure names appeared earlier in the chapter, but their implementations are unimportant for the moment:

Example 1 The following procedure receives two doubleword values:

```
AddTwo PROC,
    val1:DWORD,
    val2:DWORD
    . . .
AddTwo ENDP
```

Example 2 The following procedure receives a pointer to a byte:

```
FillArray PROC,
    pArray:PTR BYTE
    . . .
FillArray ENDP
```

Example 3 The following procedure receives two pointers to doublewords:

```
Swap PROC,
    pValX:PTR DWORD,
    pValY:PTR DWORD
    . . .
Swap ENDP
```

Example 4 The following procedure receives a byte pointer named **pBuffer**. It has a local doubleword variable named **fileHandle**:

```
ReadFile PROC,
    pBuffer:PTR BYTE
    LOCAL fileHandle:DWORD
    . . .
ReadFile ENDP
```

8.3.3 PROTO Directive

The PROTO directive creates a *prototype* for an existing procedure. A prototype declares a procedure's name and parameter list. It allows you to call a procedure before defining it. (If you have programmed in C++, you are already familiar with function prototypes, used in class declarations.)

MASM requires a prototype for each procedure called by an INVOKE statement. PROTO must appear first before INVOKE. In other words, the standard ordering of these directives is as follows:

```
PROTO MySub                    ; procedure prototype

INVOKE MySub                   ; procedure call

MySub PROC                     ; procedure implementation
    .
    .
    .
MySub ENDP
```

An alternative scenario is possible: The procedure implementation can appear in the program prior to the location of the INVOKE statement for that procedure. In that case, PROC acts as its own prototype:

```
MySub PROC                     ; procedure implementation
    .
    .
    .
MySub ENDP

INVOKE MySub                   ; procedure call
```

Assuming that you have already written a particular procedure, you can easily create its prototype by copying the PROC statement and making the following changes:

- Change the word PROC to PROTO.
- Remove the USES operator and its register list, if any.

For example, suppose we have already created the **ArraySum** procedure:

```
ArraySum PROC USES esi ecx,
    ptrArray:PTR DWORD,        ; points to the array
    szArray:DWORD              ; array size
    ; (remaining lines omitted...)
ArraySum ENDP
```

The prototype is quite similar:

```
ArraySum PROTO,
    ptrArray:PTR DWORD,        ; points to the array
    szArray:DWORD              ; array size
```

Recall that the USES operator, covered in Section 5.5.5.1 of Chapter 5, automatically generates push and pop instructions that save and restore selected registers.

8.3.3.1 ArraySum Example

For the example in this section, we will create a new version of **ArraySum**, a procedure from an earlier chapter that calculates the sum of an array of doublewords. In the original version, we passed arguments in registers; now we can use the PROC directive to declare stack parameters:

```
ArraySum PROC USES esi ecx,
     ptrArray:PTR DWORD,     ; points to the array
     szArray:DWORD           ; array size

     mov   esi,ptrArray      ; address of the array
     mov   ecx,szArray       ; size of the array
     cmp   ecx,0             ; length = zero?
     je    L2                ; yes: quit
     mov   eax,0             ; set the sum to zero

L1: add   eax,[esi]         ; add each integer to sum
     add   esi,4             ; point to next integer
     loop  L1                ; repeat for array size
L2: ret                     ; sum is in EAX
ArraySum ENDP
```

The INVOKE directive calls **ArraySum**, passing the address of an array and the number of elements in the array:

```
.data
array DWORD 10000h,20000h,30000h,40000h,50000h
theSum DWORD  ?
.code
main PROC
    INVOKE ArraySum,
       ADDR array,          ; address of the array
       LENGTHOF array       ; number of elements
    mov theSum,eax          ; store the sum
```

The INVOKE directive greatly simplifies the passing of arguments. In general, it is easier to use named parameters than register parameters. Parameter names are self-documenting, and they free up the registers for other uses.

8.3.4 Passing by Value or by Reference

Passing by Value   When a copy of a variable's value is passed to a procedure, we call this *passing by value*. Generally, arguments are passed by value when we want to protect them against being changed by the called procedure. This is how it works when the argument is a variable: A copy of the variable is pushed on the stack by the calling program. The called procedure retrieves the value from the stack and uses it. Even if the procedure modifies the parameter, it has no access to the corresponding argument variable in the calling program.

The following code example shows a simple scenario where **main** passes a copy of **myData** to the **Sub1** procedure. Sub1 receives the input parameter and calls it **someData**. It sets someData to zero, but that has no effect on myData:

```
.data
myData WORD 1000h            ; this never changes
.code
main PROC
    INVOKE Sub1, myData
    exit
main ENDP

Sub1 PROC someData:WORD
    mov someData,0
    ret
Sub1 ENDP
```

There is, of course, no way to prevent **Sub1** from modifying **someData**. In any event, the modification is self-contained within the Sub1 procedure. If a program bug is detected relating to someData, it can easily be found and fixed.

Passing by Reference   When the address of a variable is passed to a procedure, we call this *passing by reference*. The called procedure is given the opportunity to modify the variable's contents, via the address it was given. A good rule of thumb is that you pass by reference only when you expect the procedure to modify the variable.

In the following example, the address of **myData** is passed to the **Sub2** procedure. The Sub2 procedure copies the address to ESI, dereferences it, and assigns a value of zero. myData is immediately assigned zero:

```
.data
myData WORD 1000h
.code
main PROC
    INVOKE Sub2, ADDR myData      ; pass by reference
    exit
main ENDP

Sub2 PROC dataPtr:PTR WORD
    mov esi,dataPtr               ; get the address
    mov WORD PTR[esi],0           ; dereference, assign zero
    ret
Sub2 ENDP
```

Passing Data Structures   There is one important exception to the rule of thumb we just presented regarding passing by reference. When passing a data structure (such as an array), high-level languages pass by reference. It is completely impractical to pass a large amount of data by value, because it would entail pushing the data directly on the stack. This would slow the program down and use up precious stack space. The only disadvantage to passing by reference is that the called procedure has the ability to modify the contents of the array. C++ has a *const* qualifier that prevents this, but such a qualifier does not exist in assembly language.

8.3.5   Parameter Classifications

Procedure parameters are usually classified according to the direction of data transfer between the calling program and the called procedure:

- *Input:* An input parameter is data passed by a calling program to a procedure. The called procedure is not expected to modify the corresponding parameter variable, and even if it does, the modification is confined to the procedure itself.
- *Output:* An output parameter is created by passing a pointer to a variable when a procedure is called. The procedure does not use any existing data from the variable, but it fills in a new value before it returns. For example, the Win32 Console Library has a function named **ReadConsole** that reads a string of characters from standard input into an array of bytes. The calling program passes a pointer to a doubleword variable, which is filled in by ReadConsole with an integer indicating the number of characters read:

```
ReadConsole PROTO,
    handle:DWORD,                       ; input handle
    lpBuffer:PTR BYTE,                  ; pointer to buffer
    nNumberOfBytesToRead:DWORD,         ; num chars to read
    lpNumberOfBytesWritten:PTR DWORD,   ; num bytes read
    lpReserved:DWORD                    ; always zero
```

In this example, *handle, lpReserved,* and *nNumberOfBytesToRead* are input parameters. *lpBuffer* and *lpNumberOfBytesWritten* are output parameters.

- *Input-Output:* An input-output parameter represents a value passed as input to a procedure, which the procedure may modify. The same parameter is then able to return the changed data to the calling program. Whenever the address of a variable is passed to a procedure, it has the potential to be an input-output parameter.

8.3.6   Example: Exchanging Two Integers

The following program contains an implementation of the **Swap** procedure, which exchanges the contents of two 32-bit integers. We display a dump of the array, exchange the array elements, and display the array a second time:

```
TITLE Swap Procedure Example                (Swap.asm)

INCLUDE Irvine32.inc

Swap PROTO,               ; procedure prototype
```

```
        pValX:PTR DWORD,
        pValY:PTR DWORD
    .data
    Array DWORD 10000h,20000h

    .code
    main PROC
        ; Display the array before the exchange:
        mov   esi,OFFSET Array
        mov   ecx,2                ; count = 2
        mov   ebx,TYPE Array
        call DumpMem               ; dump the array values

        INVOKE Swap, ADDR Array, ADDR [Array+4]

        ; Display the array after the exchange:
        call DumpMem
        exit
    main ENDP

;------------------------------------------------------------
Swap PROC USES eax esi edi,
        pValX:PTR DWORD,           ; pointer to first integer
        pValY:PTR DWORD            ; pointer to second integer
;
; Exchange the values of two 32-bit integers
; Returns: nothing
;------------------------------------------------------------
        mov esi,pValX              ; get pointers
        mov edi,pValY
        mov eax,[esi]              ; get first integer
        xchg eax,[edi]             ; exchange with second
        mov [esi],eax              ; replace first integer
        ret
Swap ENDP
END main
```

The two parameters in the Swap procedure, **pValX** and **pValY**, are input-output parameters. Their existing values are *input* to the procedure, and their new values are also *output* from the procedure.

8.3.7 Trouble-Shooting Tips

8.3.7.1 Saving and Restoring Registers

In general, the PUSH and POP instructions perform a valuable service. They make it easy to preserve registers that will be changed by a sequence of instructions, with the purpose of restoring those registers later. There are not very many general-purpose registers, so they tend to be used up quickly.

Suppose ECX has been assigned an important value just before a loop, but ECX must also be used as the loop counter. We can push ECX on the stack before assigning the loop counter, and restore ECX to its original value after the loop:

```
mov  ecx,importantVal
push ecx                    ; save ECX
  .
mov  ecx,LoopCounter        ; set up the loop
L1:
  .
  .
loop L1
pop  ecx                    ; restore ECX
```

But you must be careful to match the PUSH and POP instructions exactly. In the next example, the POP instruction was mistakenly placed inside the loop and it is likely that the loop may not end:

```
mov  ecx,importantVal
push ecx                    ; save ECX
  .
mov  ecx,LoopCounter        ; set up the loop
L1:
  .
  .
pop  ecx                    ; restore ECX ??!
loop L1
```

Multiple values will be popped from the stack, yet ECX was only pushed once. Each POP instruction increments ESP, and soon it no longer points to valid stack data. The stack becomes corrupted, and the next time the program executes a return from a procedure (RET instruction), it branches to an unplanned location in memory. In Protected mode, the code causes a general protection fault.

8.3.7.2   Wrong Operand Sizes

If you use an array, remember that addresses are based on the sizes of the array elements. To address the second element of a doubleword array, for example, you would add 4 to the array's starting address. For example, when we call the **Swap** procedure from Section 8.3.6, we want to pass pointers to the first two elements of **DoubleArray**. Suppose we incorrectly calculate the address of the second element as DoubleArray + 1:

```
.data
DoubleArray DWORD 10000h,20000h
.code
    INVOKE Swap, ADDR [DoubleArray + 0], ADDR [DoubleArray + 1]
```

The resulting hexadecimal values in **DoubleArray** after calling **Swap** will not be what we expect.

8.3.7.3   Passing the Wrong Type of Pointer

When using INVOKE, remember that the assembler does not validate the type of pointer you pass to a procedure. For example, the **Swap** procedure from Section 8.3.6 expects to receive two doubleword pointers. Suppose you inadvertently pass it pointers to bytes:

```
.data
ByteArray BYTE 10h,20h,30h,40h,50h,60h,70h,80h
.code
    INVOKE Swap, ADDR [ByteArray + 0], ADDR [ByteArray + 1]
```

The program will assemble and run, but when ESI and EDI are dereferenced, 32-bit values are exchanged. **ByteArray** ends up with the following values: 20h, 30h, 40h, 50h, 40h, 60h, 70h, and 80h.

8.3.7.4   Passing Immediate Values

If a procedure has a reference parameter, you cannot pass it an immediate argument. Consider the following procedure, which has a single reference parameter:

```
Sub2 PROC dataPtr:PTR WORD
    mov esi,dataPtr          ; get the address
    mov [esi],0              ; dereference, assign zero
    ret
Sub2 ENDP
```

The following INVOKE statement assembles but causes a runtime error. The **Sub2** procedure receives 1000h as a pointer value and dereferences memory location 1000h:

```
    INVOKE Sub2, 1000h
```

When this was tested, it caused a general protection fault because memory location 1000h was not within the program's data segment.

8.3.8   Section Review

1. (*True/False*): The CALL instruction cannot include procedure arguments.
2. (*True/False*): The INVOKE directive can include up to a maximum of three arguments.
3. (*True/False*): The INVOKE directive can only pass memory operands, but not register values.
4. (*True/False*): The PROC directive can contain a USES operator, but the PROTO directive cannot.
5. (*True/False*): When using the PROC directive, all parameters must be listed on the same line.
6. (*True/False*): It is best to pass an array by reference so that it will not have to be copied onto the stack.
7. (*True/False*): Passing an object by value is more secure than passing by reference, because the latter permits the object to be modified by the called procedure.

8. (*True/False*): If you pass a variable containing the offset of an array of bytes to a procedure that expects a pointer to an array of words, the assembler will not catch your error.

9. (*True/False*): If you pass an immediate value to a procedure that expects a reference parameter, you can generate a general-protection fault (in Protected mode).

10. Is the value returned by the ADDR operator different from that of the OFFSET operator when a program is running under the flat memory model?

11. Declare a procedure named **MultArray** that receives two pointers to arrays of doublewords, and a third parameter indicating the number of array elements.

12. Create a PROTO directive for the procedure in the preceding exercise.

13. Did the **Swap** procedure from Section 8.3.6 use input parameters, output parameters, or input-output parameters?

14. In the **ReadConsole** procedure from Section 8.3.5, is **lpBuffer** an input parameter or an output parameter?

15. *Challenge:* Draw a diagram showing the stack parameters created by the following INVOKE statement (running under the flat memory model):

```
.data
count = 10
myArray WORD count DUP(?)
.code
INVOKE SumArray, ADDR myArray, count
```

8.4 Stack Frames

We have already said that INVOKE pushes arguments on the stack and issues a CALL instruction. Although INVOKE is convenient, it generates its own assembly code, which works against one of the major goals of learning assembly language: learning all the details. Let's go a little deeper now and manipulate stack parameters directly, using PUSH and CALL instructions. In the long run, this approach gives you the flexibility to deal with unusual situations. First, it is important to understand memory models and language specifiers.

A *stack frame* (or *activation record*) is the area of the stack set aside for a procedure's return address, passed parameters, any saved registers, and local variables. The stack frame is created by the following sequential steps:

- Arguments are pushed on the stack.
- The procedure is called, causing the return address to be pushed on the stack.
- As the procedure begins to execute, EBP is pushed on the stack.
- EBP is set equal to ESP. From this point on, EBP acts as a base reference for all of the procedure parameters.
- A value can be subtracted from ESP to create space for local variables.

The structure of a stack frame is directly affected by both a program's memory model and its choice of argument passing convention.

8.4.1 Memory Models

MASM uses the .MODEL directive to determine several important characteristics of a program: its memory model type, procedure naming scheme, and parameter passing convention. The latter two are particularly important when assembly language interfaces to other programming languages. The syntax of the .MODEL directive is:

```
.MODEL memorymodel [,modeloptions]
```

MemoryModel   The *memorymodel* field can be one of the models described in Table 8-2. All of the modes, with the exception of flat, are used for programming in 16-bit Real-address mode.

Table 8-2   Memory Models.

Model	Description
tiny	A single segment, containing both code and data. This model is used by .com programs.
small	One code segment and one data segment. All code and data are near, by default.
medium	Multiple code segments and a single data segment.
compact	One code segment and multiple data segments.
large	Multiple code and data segments.
huge	Same as the large model, except that individual data items may be larger than a single segment.
flat	Protected mode. Uses 32-bit offsets for code and data. All data and code (including system resources) are in a single 32-bit segment.

The Real-address mode programs shown so far in this book have all used the small memory model because it keeps all code within a single code segment, and all data (including the stack) within a single segment. As a result, we only have to manipulate code and data offsets, and the segments never change.

Protected mode programs use the flat memory model, where all offsets are 32 bits, and the code and data can be as large as 4GB. The *Irvine32.inc* file, for example, contains the following .MODEL directive:

```
.model flat,stdcall
```

Model Options   The *modeloptions* field (in the .MODEL directive) can contain both a language specifier and a stack distance. The *language specifier* determines calling and naming conventions for procedures and public symbols. We will elaborate on this in Section 8.4.3.1. The *stack distance* can be either NEARSTACK (the default) or FARSTACK. It's use is specialized, so we will omit it from now on.

8.4.2   Language Specifiers

Let's take a closer look at the language specifiers used in the .MODEL directive. The options are C, BASIC, FORTRAN, PASCAL, SYSCALL, and STDCALL. The C, BASIC, FORTRAN, and PASCAL specifiers enable assembly language programmers to create procedures that are compatible with these languages. The SYSCALL and STDCALL specifiers are variations on the other language specifiers.

In this book, we focus on the three most commonly used language specifiers: C, PASCAL, and STDCALL. Each is shown here with the flat memory model:

- .model flat, C
- .model flat, pascal
- .model flat, stdcall

The language specifier used in all of the example programs in this book is STDCALL; it is also the language specifier used when calling MS-Windows functions.

8.4.2.1   STDCALL Specifier

The STDCALL language specifier dictates that procedure arguments must be pushed on the stack in reverse order (last to first). For example, the following INVOKE statement

```
INVOKE AddTwo,5,6
```

would generate the following assembly language code:

```
push 6
push 5
call AddTwo
```

Another important consideration is how procedure arguments are removed from the stack after a procedure call. STDCALL dictates that a constant operand must be supplied to the RET instruction. This constant is added by RET to ESP after the return address is popped from the stack:

```
AddTwo PROC
  .
  .
  ret 8          ; add 8 to ESP after returning
AddTwo ENDP
```

By adding 8 to the stack pointer, we reset it to the value it had before the arguments were pushed on the stack by the calling program.

Finally, STDCALL modifies exported (public) procedure names by storing them in the following format:

```
_name@nn
```

A leading underscore is added to the procedure name, and an integer follows the @ sign indicating the number of bytes used by the procedure parameters (rounded upward to a multiple of 4).

For example, suppose the procedure **MySub** has two doubleword parameters. The name passed by the assembler to the linker is **_MySub@8**.

> It's important to note that the LINK32.EXE program is case-sensitive, so it considers a name such as _MYSUB@8 to be different from _MySub@8. To view all procedure names inside an OBJ file, use the DUMPBIN utility with the /SYMBOLS option.

8.4.2.2   C Specifier

The C language specifier dictates that procedure arguments are pushed on the stack in reverse order, just like STDCALL.

Regarding the removal of procedure arguments from the stack after a procedure call, the C language approach is different: In the calling program, a constant is added to ESP, resetting it to the value it had before the arguments were pushed:

```
push 6                          ; second argument
push 5                          ; first argument
call AddTwo
add  esp,8                      ; clean up the stack
```

The C language specifier handles external procedure names in the same way as STDCALL.

8.4.2.3   PASCAL Specifier

The PASCAL language specifier dictates that procedure arguments be pushed on the stack in forward order (first to last). For example, the following INVOKE statement

```
INVOKE AddTwo,5,6
```

would generate the following assembly language code:

```
push 5                          ; first argument
push 6                          ; second argument
call AddTwo
```

Regarding the removal of procedure arguments from the stack after a procedure call, the PASCAL specifier is the same as STDCALL.

When the assembler passes a procedure name to the linker, the PASCAL specifier causes the procedure name to be converted to all uppercase letters. A procedure name such as **AddTwo** is converted to the name **ADDTWO**.

8.4.3   Explicit Access to Stack Parameters

You have already seen how to access procedure parameters by name in Section 8.3. Alternatively, you can access parameters explicitly, using notation such as [ebp+8]. This gives you a greater amount of control over the stack data, and lets you see exactly what's going on. If you use this approach, you generally do not declare procedure parameters. This will also prevent you from using the INVOKE statement, since it depends on the existence of procedure prototypes. The calling program will have to push arguments directly on the stack.

For example, calling the **AddTwo** procedure requires pushing two integers on the stack. AddTwo returns the sum of the integers in EAX. We can simulate the STDCALL method of passing arguments in reverse order:

```
.data
sum DWORD ?
.code
    push 6                      ; second argument
    push 5                      ; first argument
    call AddTwo                 ; EAX = sum
    mov  sum,eax                ; save the sum
```

The **AddTwo** procedure pushes EBP on the stack to preserve it. This is critical, because EBP might have an important value used by the calling program. We also set EBP to the same value as ESP so EBP can be the base locator for the stack frame:

```
AddTwo PROC
    push ebp
    mov  ebp,esp
```

After the two instructions have executed, the following figure shows the contents of the stack frame:

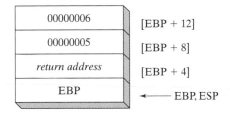

The two arguments, 5 and 6, are located at EBP+8 and EBP+12, respectively. Recall that 6 was pushed before 5, and the stack grows downward in memory. Knowing these locations, the **AddTwo** procedure can add their values and store the sum in EAX:

```
AddTwo PROC
    push ebp
    mov ebp,esp                 ; base of stack frame
    mov eax,[ebp + 12]          ; second argument
    add eax,[ebp + 8]           ; first argument
    pop ebp
    ret 8                       ; clean up the stack
AddTwo ENDP
```

Notice that we emulate the STDCALL language specifier by passing a constant to the RET instruction. This approach is not required, but it is a good idea because it makes **AddTwo** consistent with other procedures that use parameter declarations.

In Protected mode, for a procedure having n parameters named P_i, and $i = \{1, 2 \ldots, n\}$, the expression $[EBP + k_i]$ addresses each parameter on the stack. The value k is calculated as $k = (i + 1) * 4$. For example, $P_1 = [EBP + 8]$, $P_2 = [EBP + 12]$, and $P_3 = [EBP + 16]$. The ordering of i is dependent on the language specifier in the memory model. STDCALL, for example, pushes the parameters in descending order, from P_n down to P_1. When using the small memory model in Real-address mode, the formula for k changes to: $k = (i + 1) * 2$.

8.4.3.1   Saving and Restoring Registers

Procedures often have to push additional registers on the stack immediately after setting EBP to ESP, so the registers can be restored to their original values later. (Recall that in Chapter 5 we explained that a procedure should always restore the state of the registers before returning, so calling programs can use the registers for their own data.)

In the next example, we push EDX inside the **AddTwo** procedure after setting EBP to the base of the stack frame:

```
AddTwo PROC
    push ebp
    mov  ebp,esp                    ; base of stack frame
    push edx                        ; save EDX
      .
      .
    pop  edx                        ; restore EDX
    pop  ebp
    ret  8                          ; clean up the stack
AddTwo ENDP
```

Pushing EDX does not affect the displacement of parameters from EBP because the stack grows downward without affecting EBP:

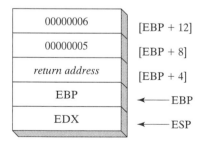

8.4.4   Passing Arguments by Reference

In the examples shown in this section so far, all arguments were passed to procedures by value. There are also occasions when we need to pass the address of a variable, and this is called *passing by reference*.

8.4.4.1 ArrayFill Example

Let's write a procedure named **ArrayFill** that fills an array with 16-bit random integers. It receives two arguments: the first is the offset of an array, and the second is an integer that specifies the array length. The first argument is passed by reference, and the second is passed by value. Calling the procedure is easy. We just push the offset of the array on the stack, followed by the array's size:

```
.data
count = 100
array WORD count DUP(?)
.code
push OFFSET array
push COUNT
call ArrayFill
```

The stack frame is shown here, containing the offset of **array** and the value of **count:**

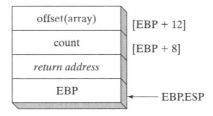

Inside the **ArrayFill** procedure, the following statement copies the array's offset from the stack into ESI:

```
mov    esi,[ebp+12]              ; offset of array
```

Here is the completed **ArrayFill** procedure:

```
ArrayFill PROC
    push ebp
    mov  ebp,esp
    pushad
    mov  esi,[ebp+12]            ; offset of array
    mov  ecx,[ebp+8]             ; array size
    cmp  ecx,0                   ; ECX < 0?
    jle  L2                      ; yes: skip over loop
L1:
    mov  eax,10000h              ; get random 0 - FFFFh
    call Random_Range            ; from the link library
    mov  [esi],eax
    add  esi,TYPE DWORD
    loop L1
L2: popad
    pop ebp
```

```
    ret 8                              ; clean up the stack
ArrayFill ENDP
```

8.4.4.2 LEA Instruction

The LEA instruction returns the offset of any type of indirect operand. Because an indirect operand uses one or more registers, its offset must be calculated at runtime. The assembler OFFSET operator, on the other hand, only returns constant assembly time offsets.

LEA is particularly useful for obtaining the address of a stack parameter. For example, if a procedure has a local array variable, you might want to move its offset into an index register. The following **FillString** procedure does this, so it can fill a string with a random sequence of ASCII digits $0 - 9$:

```
FillString PROC USES eax esi
    LOCAL string[20]:BYTE
; Create and fill a 20-byte string with ASCII digits.

    lea   esi,string               ; load effective address
    mov   ecx,20
L1: mov   eax,10
    call RandomRange               ; AL = 0..9
    add   al,30h                   ; convert to ASCII character
    mov   [esi],al
    add   esi,1
    Loop L1
    ret
FillString ENDP
```

Note that **string** is an indirect operand, so the following instruction would generate an error (MOV..OFFSET only works with direct operands):

```
    mov eax,OFFSET string          ; error
```

8.4.5 Creating Local Variables

We've already seen that local variables have some advantages over global variables. As an alternative to using the LOCAL directive, you can create local variables on the stack in a more direct manner.

C++ Example   The following C++ function declares several local variables named **X, Y, name,** and **Z:**

```
void MySub()
{
    char X = 'X';
    int Y = 10;
    char name[20];
    name[0] = 'B';
    double Z = 1.2;
}
```

The foregoing C++ code can easily be implemented in assembly language if we use Visual C++ as a guide. Each stack entry defaults to 32 bits, so each variable's storage size in bytes is rounded upward to a multiple of 4. As may be seen in the following table, a total of 36 bytes are reserved for the local variables:

Variable	Bytes	Stack Offset
X	4	EBP – 4
Y	4	EBP – 8
name	20	EBP – 28
Z	8	EBP – 36

The following implementation of **MySub** creates the same four local variables, assigns values to them, and destroys them. The constant assigned to **Z** is a 64-bit encoded real:

```
MySub PROC
    push ebp
    mov ebp,esp
    sub esp,36                      ; create variables

    mov BYTE PTR [ebp-4],'X'                        ; X
    mov DWORD PTR [ebp-8],10                        ; Y
    mov BYTE PTR [ebp-20],'Y'                       ; name[0]
    mov DWORD PTR [ebp-32],3ff33333h               ; Z(high)
    mov DWORD PTR [ebp-36],33333333h               ; Z(low)

    mov esp,ebp                     ; destroy variables
    pop ebp
    ret
MySub ENDP
```

8.4.6   ENTER and LEAVE Instructions (Optional)

The ENTER instruction automatically creates a stack frame for a called procedure. It reserves stack space for local variables and saves EBP on the stack. Specifically, it performs three actions:

- Pushes EBP on the stack (*push ebp*)
- Sets EBP to the base of the stack frame (*mov ebp,esp*)
- Reserves space for local variables (*sub esp,numbytes*)

ENTER has two operands: The first is a constant specifying the number of bytes of stack space to reserve for local variables, and the second operand specifies the lexical nesting level of the procedure:

```
ENTER localbytes, nestinglevel
```

The *lexical nesting level* is the depth of a procedure in a hierarchy of procedure calls. Because it is useful only to high-level language compilers, we won't discuss it here.

Example 1   The following example declares a procedure without any local variables:

```
MySub PROC
    enter 0,0
```

It is equivalent to the following instructions:

```
MySub PROC
    push ebp
    mov ebp,esp
```

Example 2   The ENTER instruction reserves 8 bytes of stack space for local variables:

```
MySub PROC
    enter 8,0
```

It is equivalent to the following instructions:

```
MySub PROC
    push ebp
    mov ebp,esp
    sub esp,8
```

> If you use the ENTER instruction, it is strongly advised that you also use the LEAVE instruction at the end of the same procedure. Otherwise, the stack space you create for local variables might never be released. This would cause the RET instruction to pop the wrong return address off the stack.

LEAVE Instruction   The LEAVE instruction terminates the stack frame for a procedure. It reverses the action of a previous ENTER instruction by restoring ESP and EBP to the values they were assigned when the procedure was called. Using the **MySub** procedure example again, we can write the following:

```
MySub PROC
    enter 8,0
    .
    .
    leave
    ret
MySub ENDP
```

The following equivalent set of instructions reserve and discard 8 bytes of space for local variables:

```
MySub PROC
    push ebp
    mov  ebp,esp
    sub  esp,8
```

```
        .
        .
      mov   esp,ebp
      pop   ebp
      ret
   MySub ENDP
```

8.4.7 Section Review

1. (*True/False*): The EBP register is saved by procedures that use stack parameters whenever they modify EBP.
2. (*True/False*): Local variables are created by adding a positive integer to the stack pointer.
3. (*True/False*): In the procedures shown in this chapter, the last argument to be pushed on the stack is addressed as [ebp+8].
4. (*True/False*): Passing by reference requires popping a parameter's offset from the stack inside the called procedure.
5. Describe the small memory model.
6. Describe the flat memory model.
7. How is the C language option (of the .MODEL directive) different from that of PASCAL in regard to passing procedure names to the linker?
8. How does the STDCALL language option handle cleaning up the stack after a procedure call?
9. Here is a calling sequence for a procedure named **AddThree** that adds three doublewords (assume STDCALL):

```
      push 10h
      push 20h
      push 30h
      call AddThree
```

   Draw a picture of the procedure's stack frame immediately after EBP has been pushed on the stack.
10. Write statements in the **AddThree** procedure (from the preceding question) that calculate the sum of the three stack parameters.
11. What special ability does the LEA instruction have that MOV–OFFSET does not?
12. In the C++ example shown in Section 8.4.5, how much stack space was used by a variable of type *char*?
13. *Discussion:* What advantages might the C calling convention have over the Pascal calling convention?

8.5 Recursion

A *recursive* procedure is one that calls itself, either directly or indirectly. *Recursion*, the practice of calling recursive procedures, can be a powerful tool when working with data structures that have repeating patterns. Examples are linked lists and various types of connected graphs where a program must retrace its path.

Endless Recursion The most obvious type of recursion occurs when a procedure calls itself. The following program, for example, has a procedure named **Endless** that calls itself repeatedly without ever stopping:

```
TITLE Endless Recursion                    (Endless.asm)

INCLUDE Irvine32.inc
.data
endlessStr BYTE "This recursion never stops",0
.code
main PROC
    call Endless
    exit
main ENDP
Endless PROC
    mov edx,OFFSET endlessStr
    call WriteString
    call Endless
    ret                         ; never reaches this instruction
Endless ENDP
END main
```

Of course, this example doesn't have any practical value. Each time the procedure calls itself, it uses up 4 bytes of stack space when the CALL instruction pushes the return address. The RET instruction is never reached.

> If you have access to a performance-monitoring utility such as the Windows 2000 Task manager, open it and click on the Performance dialog. Then run the *Endless.exe* program from this chapter's directory. Memory will slowly fill up and the program will consume 100% of the CPU resources. After a few minutes the program's stack will overflow and cause a processor exception (the program will halt).

8.5.1 Recursively Calculating a Sum

It is still practical for a procedure to directly call itself, as long as you provide it a terminating condition. When the terminating condition becomes true, the stack unwinds itself by executing all pending RET instructions. To illustrate, let's create a recursive procedure named **CalcSum** that sums the integers 1 to *n*, where *n* is an input parameter passed in ECX. CalcSum returns the sum in EAX:

```
TITLE Sum of Integers                  (CSum.asm)

INCLUDE Irvine32.inc
.code
```

```
main PROC
    mov   ecx,5                 ; count = 5
    mov   eax,0                 ; holds the sum
    call CalcSum                ; calculate sum
L1: call WriteDec               ; display eax
    call Crlf                   ; new line
    exit
main ENDP

;--------------------------------------------------------
CalcSum PROC
; Calculates the sum of a list of integers
; Receives: ecx = count
; Returns: eax = sum
;--------------------------------------------------------
    cmp   ecx,0                 ; check counter value
    jz    L2                    ; quit if zero
    add   eax,ecx               ; otherwise, add to sum
    dec   ecx                   ; decrement counter
    call CalcSum                ; recursive call
L2: ret
CalcSum ENDP
end Main
```

The first two lines of **CalcSum** check the counter and exit the procedure when ECX – 0. The code bypasses any further recursive calls. When the RET instruction is reached for the first time, it backs up to the previous call to CalcSum, which backs up to *its* previous call, and so on. Table 8-3 shows the return addresses (as labels) pushed on the stack by the CALL instruction, along with the concurrent values of ECX (counter) and EAX (sum).

Table 8-3 Stack Frame for the CalcSum Program.

Pushed On Stack	ECX	EAX
L1	5	0
L2	4	5
L2	3	9
L2	2	12
L2	1	14
L2	0	15

From this example, we see that even the simplest recursive procedure makes ample use of the stack. At the very minimum, 4 bytes of stack space are used up each time a procedure call takes place because the return address must be saved on the stack.

8.5.2   Calculating a Factorial

Most recursive procedures use stack parameters because the stack is perfectly designed to save temporary data during the recursive process. When the recursion unwinds, the data saved on the stack can be useful.

The next example we will look at calculates the factorial of an integer n. The *factorial* algorithm calculates *n!,* where n is an unsigned integer. The first time the **factorial** function is called, the parameter n is the starting number, shown here programmed in C/C++/Java syntax:

```
int function factorial(int n)
{
    if(n == 0)
      return 1;
    else
      return n * factorial(n-1);
}
```

Given any number n, we assume that we can calculate the factorial of $n-1$. If so, we can continue to reduce n until it equals zero. By definition, 0! equals 1. In the process of backing up to the original expression $n!$, we accumulate the product of each multiplication. For example, to calculate 5!, the recursive algorithm descends along the left column of the following figure, and backs up along the right column:

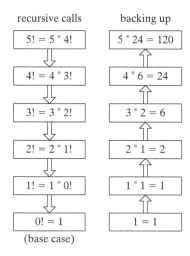

The following assembly language program implements the recursive factorial. We pass n (an unsigned integer between 0 and 12) on the stack to the **Factorial** procedure, and a value is returned in EAX. Because a 32-bit register is used, the largest factorial it can hold is 12! (479,001,600).

```
TITLE Calculating a Factorial                    (Fact.asm)

INCLUDE Irvine32.inc
.code
main PROC
    push 12                        ; calc 12!
    call Factorial                 ; calculate factorial (eax)
ReturnMain:
    call WriteDec                  ; display it
    call Crlf
    exit
main ENDP

;----------------------------------------------------
Factorial PROC
; Calculates a factorial.
; Receives: [ebp+8] = n, the number to calculate
; Returns: eax = the factorial of n
;----------------------------------------------------
    push ebp
    mov  ebp,esp
    mov  eax,[ebp+8]               ; get n
    cmp  eax,0                     ; n > 0?
    ja   L1                        ; yes: continue
    mov  eax,1                     ; no: return 1
    jmp  L2

L1: dec  eax
    push eax                       ; Factorial(n-1)
    call Factorial

; Instructions from this point on execute when each
; recursive call returns.

ReturnFact:
    mov ebx,[ebp+8]                ; get n
    mul ebx                        ; edx:eax = eax * ebx

L2: pop  ebp                       ; return EAX
    ret  4                         ; clean up stack
Factorial ENDP
END main
```

When **Factorial** is called, the offset of the next instruction after the call is pushed on the stack. From **main**, this is the offset of the label **ReturnMain**; from **Factorial**, it is the offset of the label **ReturnFact**. In Figure 8-1, the stack is shown after several recursive calls. You can see that new values for n and EBP are pushed on the stack each time Factorial calls itself.

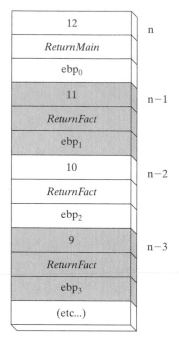

Figure 8-1   Stack usage by the Factorial Program.

Each procedure call in our example uses 12 bytes of stack space. Just before **Factorial** calls itself, $n-1$ is pushed on the stack as the input argument. The procedure returns its own factorial value in EAX, which is then multiplied by the value pushed on the stack before the call.

8.5.3   Section Review

1. (*True/False*): Given the same task to accomplish, a recursive procedure usually uses less memory than a nonrecursive one.
2. In the Factorial function, what condition terminates the recursion?
3. Which statements in the Factorial procedure execute after each recursive call has finished?
4. What will happen to the Factorial program's output when trying to calculate 13!?
5. *Challenge:* In the Factorial program, how many bytes of stack space are used by the Factorial procedure when calculating 12!?
6. *Challenge:* Write the pseudocode for a recursive algorithm that generates the first 20 integers of the Fibonacci series (1,1,2,3,5,8,11,21,...). Why would this be an inefficient way to solve the problem?

8.6   Creating Multimodule Programs

An application program of any size is difficult to manage when all of its source code is in the same file. It is more convenient to break the program up into multiple source code files (called *modules*), making each file easy to view and edit. If you modify a single module, you need only to reassemble it and then re-link the entire program. In general, linking multiple object modules is much faster than assembling a large source code file.

There are a few steps that you must follow when creating a multimodule program:

- Create a main source code module (ASM file) for the program. The main procedure will be in this module.
- If procedures are likely to become large, create a separate source code module for each procedure. If the procedures are small, you might consider grouping related procedures in the same module.
- Use the PROTO directive in the main program to identify the names and parameter lists for the procedures you will be calling.
- Include PROTO directives for all procedures inside each program module. Strictly speaking, each module needs only to have PROTO directives for procedures that it calls. Unused procedure prototypes are just ignored by the assembler.

It's usually easiest to keep track of the various files in a multimodule program by creating a separate disk directory for the files. That's what we did for the *ArraySum* program, to be shown next.

8.6.1   Example: ArraySum Program

The *ArraySum* program, first presented in Chapter 5, is an easy program to separate into modules. We will also use the new tools introduced in this chapter for passing parameters: PROTO and INVOKE. For a quick review of the program's design, let's review the structure chart used in Chapter 5. Recall that the shaded rectangles refer to procedures in the book's link library:

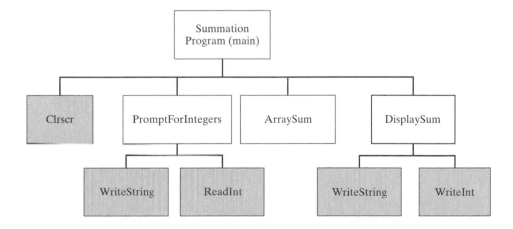

This chart shows, for example, that **main** calls **PromptForIntegers**, which in turn calls **WriteString** and **ReadInt**.

8.6.1.1   Include File: Function Prototypes

The *sum.inc* file is a text file that includes *Irvine32.inc* and three function prototypes for the procedures in this program:

```
Include file for the ArraySum Program       (sum.inc)

INCLUDE Irvine32.inc

PromptForIntegers PROTO,
    ptrPrompt:PTR BYTE,            ; prompt string
    ptrArray:PTR DWORD,            ; points to the array
    arraySize:DWORD                ; size of the array

ArraySum PROTO,
    ptrArray:PTR DWORD,            ; points to the array
    count:DWORD                    ; size of the array

DisplaySum PROTO,
    ptrPrompt:PTR BYTE,            ; prompt string
    theSum:DWORD                   ; sum of the array
```

8.6.1.2   Main Module

First, we will take a look at the program's main module, named *Sum_main.asm*. It contains the program's data and the main procedure. It includes *sum.inc*, which makes all of the function prototypes available to this module:

```
TITLE Integer Summation Program (Sum_main.asm)

; This program inputs multiple integers from the user,
; stores them in an array, calculates the sum of the
; array, and displays the sum.

INCLUDE sum.inc                 ; function prototypes

; modify Count to change the size of the array:
Count = 3
.data
prompt1 BYTE   "Enter a signed integer: ",0
prompt2 BYTE   "The sum of the integers is: ",0
array   DWORD  Count DUP(?)
sum     DWORD  ?

.code
main PROC
    call Clrscr
    INVOKE PromptForIntegers,     ; input the array
      ADDR prompt1,
      ADDR array,
      Count

    INVOKE ArraySum,              ; sum the array
      ADDR array,                 ; returns sum in EAX
```

```
        Count
     mov sum,eax                    ; save in a variable

     INVOKE DisplaySum,            ; display the sum
       ADDR prompt2,
       sum

     call Crlf
     exit
main ENDP
END main
```

8.6.1.3 PromptForIntegers Module

The **PromptForIntegers** procedure is in a module named _prompt.asm_. The leading underscore is not required, but it helps to identify the module as being part of a larger program. This module also has an INCLUDE directive for _sum.inc_:

```
TITLE Prompt For Integers         (_prompt.asm)

INCLUDE sum.inc
.code
;----------------------------------------------------
PromptForIntegers PROC,
  ptrPrompt:PTR BYTE,              ; prompt string
  ptrArray:PTR DWORD,              ; pointer to array
  arraySize:DWORD                  ; size of the array
;
; Prompts the user for an array of integers and fills
; the array with the user's input.
; Returns:  nothing
;----------------------------------------------------
    pushad                        ; save all registers

    mov   ecx,arraySize           ; get the array size
    cmp   ecx,0                   ; array size <= 0?
    jle   L2                      ; yes: quit
    mov   edx,ptrPrompt           ; address of the prompt
    mov   esi,ptrArray            ; address of the array

L1:
    call WriteString              ; display string
    call ReadInt                  ; read integer into EAX
    call Crlf; go to next output line
    mov   [esi],eax               ; store in array
    add   esi,4                   ; next array position
    loop L1                       ; repeat for array size
```

```
L2:
    popad                            ; restore all registers
    ret
PromptForIntegers ENDP
END
```

We are careful to save and restore the general-purpose registers in this procedure, using the PUSHAD and POPAD instructions. The procedures in the Irvine32 and Irvine16 libraries also preserve registers so that calling programs will not have their registers modified in unpredictable ways.

Finally, because *_prompt.asm* is not the program's startup module, the END directive has no operand. The program's entry point has already been specified in the main module.

8.6.1.4   ArraySum Module

The ArraySum procedure is in a module named *_arrysum.asm*:

```
TITLE ArraySum Procedure                      (_arrysum.asm)

INCLUDE sum.inc
.code
;----------------------------------------------------
ArraySum PROC,
    ptrArray:PTR DWORD,        ; pointer to array
    arraySize:DWORD            ; size of array
;
; Calculates the sum of an array of 32-bit integers.
; Returns:  EAX = sum
;----------------------------------------------------
    push ecx                   ; don't push EAX
    push esi

    mov   eax,0                ; set the sum to zero
    mov   esi,ptrArray
    mov   ecx,arraySize
    cmp   ecx,0                ; array size <= 0?
    jle   L2                   ; yes: quit

L1:
    add   eax,[esi]            ; add each integer to sum
    add   esi,4                ; next array position
    loop L1                    ; repeat for array size

L2:
    pop esi
    pop ecx                    ; return sum in EAX
    ret
```

```
ArraySum ENDP
END
```

The **ArraySum** procedure uses EAX, ECX, and ESI, modifying their contents. It pushes ECX and ESI on the stack so they can be restored before the procedure returns. EAX, on the other hand, is assigned the procedure's return value, so we cannot push it on the stack at the beginning of the procedure.

8.6.1.5   DisplaySum Module

The DisplaySum procedure is located in a module named _display.asm_:

```
TITLE DisplaySum Procedure              (_display.asm)

INCLUDE sum.inc
.code
;------------------------------------------------------
DisplaySum PROC,
    ptrPrompt:PTR BYTE,      ; prompt string
    theSum:DWORD             ; the array sum
;
; Displays the sum on the console.
; Returns:  nothing
;------------------------------------------------------
    push eax
    push edx

    mov  edx,ptrPrompt       ; pointer to prompt
    call WriteString
    mov  eax,theSum
    call WriteInt            ; display EAX
    call Crlf

    pop  edx
    pop  eax
    ret
DisplaySum ENDP
END
```

8.6.1.6   Batch File for Assembling and Linking

We use a customized batch file to assemble and link this program. The batch file passes specific source code filenames to the assembler, and specific object filenames to the linker:

```
PATH c:\Masm615
SET INCLUDE=c:\Masm615\include
SET LIB=c:\Masm615\lib

ML -Zi -c -Fl -coff Sum_main.asm _display.asm _arrysum.asm _prompt.asm
if errorlevel 1 goto terminate

LINK32 Sum_main.obj _display.obj _arrysum.obj _prompt.obj
irvine32.lib kernel32.lib /SUBSYSTEM:CONSOLE /DEBUGª
if errorLevel 1 goto terminate

:terminate
pause
```

[a] Although the LINK32 command line appears to wrap around in this text window, it is actually a single line in
    the batch file.

Following is the screen output produced by the batch file:

```
Microsoft (R) Macro Assembler Version 6.15.8803
Copyright (C) Microsoft Corp 1981-2000.  All rights reserved.

 Assembling: Sum_main.asm
 Assembling: _display.asm
 Assembling: _arrysum.asm
 Assembling: _prompt.asm
Microsoft (R) Incremental Linker Version 6.00.8447
Copyright (C) Microsoft Corp 1992-1998. All rights reserved.
```

8.6.2 Section Review

1. (*True/False*): Linking OBJ modules is much faster than assembling ASM source files.
2. (*True/False*): Separating a large program into short modules makes a program more difficult to maintain.
3. (*True/False*): In a multimodule program, the label next to the END statement occurs only once, in the startup module.
4. (*True/False*): PROTO directives use up memory, so you must be careful not to include a PROTO directive for a procedure unless the procedure is actually called.

8.7 Chapter Summary

The LOCAL directive declares one or more local variables inside a procedure. It must be placed on the line immediately following a PROC directive. Local variables have distinct advantages over global variables:

- Access to the name and contents of a local variable can be restricted to its containing procedure. Local variables help when debugging programs, because only a limited number of program statements are capable of modifying the local variables.

- A local variable's lifetime is limited to the execution scope of its enclosing procedure. Local variables make efficient use of memory because the same storage space can be used for other variables.
- The same variable name may be used in more than one procedure without causing a naming clash.

There are two basic types of procedure parameters: register parameters and stack parameters. The Irvine32 and Irvine16 libraries use register parameters, which are optimized for program execution speed. Unfortunately, they tend to create code clutter in calling programs. Stack parameters are the alternative. The procedure arguments must be pushed on the stack by a calling program.

The INVOKE directive is a more powerful replacement for Intel's CALL instruction that lets you pass multiple arguments. The ADDR operator can be used to pass a pointer when calling a procedure with the INVOKE directive.

A stack frame (or activation record) is the area of the stack set aside for a procedure's return address, passed parameters, and local variables. The stack frame is created when the running program begins to execute a procedure.

The PROC directive declares a procedure name with a list of named parameters. The PROTO directive creates a prototype for an existing procedure. A prototype declares a procedure's name and parameter list.

When a copy of a variable's value is passed to a procedure, we call it *passing by value*. When the address of a variable is passed to a procedure, it's called *passing by reference*. The called procedure is given the opportunity to modify the variable's contents, via the address it was given. High-level languages pass arrays to functions by reference, which is exactly what you should do in assembly language.

Following are several trouble-shooting tips:

1. In general, the PUSH and POP instructions perform a valuable service. They make it easy to preserve registers that will be changed by a sequence of instructions, with the purpose of restoring those registers later.
2. When working with an array, remember that addresses are based on the sizes of the array elements.
3. When using INVOKE, remember that the assembler does not validate the type of pointer you pass to a procedure.
4. If a procedure has a reference parameter, you cannot pass it an immediate argument.

MASM uses the .MODEL directive to determine several important characteristics of a program: its memory model type, function naming scheme, and parameter passing convention. The Real-address mode programs shown so far in this book have all used the small memory model because it keeps all code within a single code segment, and all data (including the stack) within a single segment. Protected mode programs use the flat memory model, in which all offsets are 32 bits, and the code and data can be as large as 4GB.

The language specifier used with the .MODEL directive can be C, PASCAL, or STDCALL.

Procedure parameters can be accessed using indirect addressing with the EBP register. Expressions such as [ebp+8] give you a high level of control over stack parameter addressing. The LEA instruction returns the offset of any type of indirect operand. LEA is ideally suited for use with stack parameters.

The ENTER instruction creates a stack frame for a called procedure by reserving stack space for local variables and saving EBP on the stack. The LEAVE instruction terminates the stack frame for a procedure by reversing the action of a preceding ENTER instruction.

A recursive procedure is one that calls itself, either directly or indirectly. Recursion, the practice of calling recursive procedures, can be a powerful tool when working with data structures that have repeating patterns.

An application program of any size is difficult to manage when all of its source code is in the same file. It is more convenient to break the program up into multiple source code files (called modules), making each file easy to view and edit.

8.8   Programming Exercises

The following exercises can be done in either Protected or Real-address mode.

1. Exchanging Integers

Create an array of randomly ordered integers. Using the **Swap** procedure from Section 8.3.6 as a tool, write a loop that exchanges each consecutive pair of integers in the array.

2. DumpMem Procedure

Write a wrapper procedure for the link library's **DumpMem** procedure, using stack parameters. The name can be slightly different, such as **DumpMemory**. The following is an example of how it should be called:

```
INVOKE DumpMemory,OFFSET array,LENGTHOF array,TYPE array
```

Write a test program that calls your procedure several times, using a variety of data types.

3. Nonrecursive Factorial

Write a nonrecursive version of the **Factorial** procedure (Section 8.5.2) that uses a loop. Write a short program that interactively tests your Factorial procedure. Let the user enter the value of *n*. Display the calculated factorial.

4. Factorial Comparison

Write a program that compares the runtime speeds of both the recursive **Factorial** procedure from Section 8.5.2 and the nonrecursive Factorial procedure written for the preceding programming exercise. Use the **GetMseconds** procedure from the book's link library to measure and display the number of milliseconds required to call each Factorial procedure several thousand times in a row.

5. Greatest Common Divisor

Write a recursive implementation of Euclid's algorithm for finding the greatest common divisor (GCD) of two integers. Descriptions of this algorithm are available in algebra books and on the Web. (Note: a nonrecursive version of the GCD problem was given in the programming exercises for Chapter 7.)

9

Strings and Arrays

9.1   Introduction

By now, you just might be convinced that assembly language programmers have an advantage over high-level language programmers when it comes to writing fast code. The ideal part of a program to optimize is the code within loops, and loops are always used when processing arrays and strings. So here we are, in a chapter that shows you how to get the most of string and array processing, and hopefully, shows you how to write better code.

We will begin with a set of highly optimized string primitive instructions built into the Intel instruction set. They are designed for moving, comparing, loading, and storing blocks of data.

Next, we take you through several typical string-handling procedures directly from the Irvine32 (or Irvine16) library. Their implementations are fairly similar to the code you might see in an implementation of the standard C string library.

The third part of the chapter shows how to manipulate two-dimensional arrays, using advanced indirect addressing modes: base-index and base-index-displacement. You may recall that simple indirect addressing was introduced in Section 4.4.

The last part of the chapter, entitled "Searching and Sorting Integer Arrays," is the most interesting. You will see how easy it is to implement two of the most common array processing algorithms in computer science: bubble sort, and binary search. It's a great idea to study these algorithms in Java or C++, as well as assembly language.

9.2   String Primitive Instructions

There are five groups of instructions in the Intel instruction set for processing arrays of bytes, words, and doublewords. Although they are called *string primitives*, they are not limited to character arrays.

Each of the instructions in Table 9-1 uses either ESI, EDI, or both registers to address memory. They are unique in that they use only memory operands. String primitives can automatically repeat, making them especially useful for processing strings and arrays.

Table 9-1   String Primitive Instructions.

Instruction	Description
MOVSB, MOVSW, MOVSD	**Move string data:** Copy an integer from one memory location to another.
CMPSB, CMPSW, CMPSD	**Compare strings:** Compare two memory values.
SCASB, SCASW, SCASD	**Scan string:** Compare an integer to the contents of memory.
STOSB, STOSW, STOSD	**Store string data:** Store an integer into memory.
LODSB, LODSW, LODSD	**Load accumulator from string:** Load an integer from memory into the accumulator (AL, AX, or EAX).

In Protected mode programs, ESI is automatically an offset in the segment addressed by DS, and EDI is automatically an offset in the segment addressed by ES. DS and ES are always set to the same value and you cannot change them. (In Real-address mode, on the other hand, ES and DS are often manipulated by ASM programmers.)

In Real-address mode, the string primitives use the SI and DI registers to address memory. SI is an offset from DS, and DI is an offset from ES. Usually, you will set ES to the same segment value as DS at the beginning of **main**:

```
main PROC
    mov ax,@data                ; get addr of data seg
    mov ds,ax                   ; initialize DS
    mov es,ax                   ; initialize ES
```

Using a Repeat Prefix   By itself, a string primitive instruction processes only a single memory value. If you add a *repeat prefix*, the instruction repeats, using ECX as a counter. In other words, you can process an entire array using only one instruction. The following repeat prefixes are used:

REP	Repeat while ECX > 0
REPZ, REPE	Repeat while the Zero flag is set and ECX > 0
REPNZ, REPNE	Repeat while the Zero flag is clear and ECX > 0

In the following example, MOVSB moves 10 bytes from **string1** to **string2.** The repeat prefix first tests ECX > 0 before executing the MOVSB instruction. If ECX = 0, the instruction is ignored and control passes to the next line in the program. If ECX > 0, ECX is decremented and the instruction repeats:

```
cld                             ; clear direction flag
mov esi,OFFSET string1          ; ESI points to source
mov edi,OFFSET string2          ; EDI points to target
mov ecx,10                      ; set counter to 10
rep movsb                       ; move 10 bytes
```

ESI and EDI are automatically incremented each time MOVSB repeats. This behavior is controlled by the CPU's Direction flag.

Direction Flag   String primitive instructions use the Direction flag to determine whether ESI and EDI will be automatically incremented or decremented by string primitives:

Value of the Direction Flag	Effect on ESI and EDI	Address Sequence
clear	incremented	low-high
set	decremented	high-low

The Direction flag can be explicitly changed using the CLD and STD instructions:

```
CLD                             ; clear Direction flag
STD                             ; set Direction flag
```

Let's now look at each of the string primitive instructions in more detail.

9.2.1   MOVSB, MOVSW, and MOVSD

The MOVSB, MOVSW, and MOVSD instructions copy data from the memory location pointed to by ESI to the memory location pointed to by EDI. The two registers are either incremented or decremented automatically (based on the value of the Direction flag):

MOVSB	move (copy) bytes
MOVSW	move (copy) words
MOVSD	move (copy) doublewords

You can use a repeat prefix with MOVSB, MOVSW, and MOVSD. The Direction flag determines the incrementing or decrementing of ESI and EDI. The size of the increment/decrement is shown in the following table:

Instruction	Value automatically added/subtracted from ESI and EDI
MOVSB	1
MOVSW	2
MOVSD	4

Example: Copy Doubleword Array   Suppose we want to copy twenty integers from **source** to **target**. After we copy the data, ESI and EDI point one position (four bytes) beyond the end of each array:

```
.data
source DWORD 20 DUP(0FFFFFFFFh)
target DWORD 20 DUP(?)

.code
    cld                                 ; direction = forward
    mov ecx,LENGTHOF source             ; set REP counter
    mov esi,OFFSET source               ; ESI points to source
    mov edi,OFFSET target               ; EDI points to target
    rep movsd                           ; copy doublewords
```

9.2.2   CMPSB, CMPSW, and CMPSD

The CMPSB, CMPSW, and CMPSD instructions each compare a memory operand pointed to by ESI to a memory operand pointed to by EDI:

CMPSB	compare bytes
CMPSW	compare words
CMPSD	compare doublewords

You can use a repeat prefix with CMPSB, CMPSW, and CMPSD. The Direction flag determines the incrementing or decrementing of ESI and EDI.

> There is another form of the compare string instruction, called the *explicit form*, in which both operands are supplied. They must be indirect operands, and PTR must be used to make the operand sizes clear. For example:
>
> ```
>     cmps DWORD PTR [esi],[edi]
> ```
>
> But CMPS is tricky because the assembler lets you supply misleading operands:
>
> ```
>     cmps DWORD PTR [eax],[ebx]
> ```
>
> Regardless of which operands are used, CMPS still compares the contents of memory pointed to by ESI to the memory pointed to by EDI. For this reason, it's best to avoid using CMPS and use the specific versions (CMPSB, CMPSW, CMPSD) instead. Also, the order of operands in CMPS is opposite to the more familiar CMP instruction:
>
> ```
>     CMP  target,source
>     CMPS source,target
> ```
>
> Here's another way to remember the difference: CMP implies subtraction of *source* from *target*. CMPS implies subtraction of *target* from *source*.

Example   Suppose we want to compare a pair of doublewords using CMPSD. In the following sample data, we see that **source** is less than **target**. When JA executes, the conditional jump is not taken; the JMP instruction is executed instead:

```
.data
source DWORD 1234h
target DWORD 5678h
.code
    mov esi,OFFSET source
    mov edi,OFFSET target
    cmpsd                        ; compare doublewords
    ja L1                        ; jump if source > target
    jmp L2                       ; jump, since source <= target
```

If we wanted to compare multiple doublewords, it would be necessary to clear the Direction flag (forward), initialize ECX as a counter, and use a repeat prefix with CMPSD:

```
    mov esi,OFFSET source
    mov edi,OFFSET target
    cld                          ; direction = up
    mov ecx,count                ; repetition counter
    repe cmpsd                   ; repeat while equal
```

The REPE prefix repeats the comparison, incrementing ESI and EDI automatically, until either ECX equals zero, or any pair of doublewords is found to be different.

9.2.2.1   Example: Comparing Two Strings

A pair of strings are typically compared by matching each of their characters in sequence, starting at the beginning of both strings. For example, the first three characters of "AABC" and "AABB" are identical. In the fourth position, the ASCII code for "C" (in the first string) is greater than the ASCII code for "B" (in the second string). Thus, the first string is considered greater than the second string.

Similarly, if the strings "AAB" and "AABB" are compared, the second string has a larger value. The first three characters are identical, but one additional character exists in the second string.

The following code uses CMPSB to compare two strings of identical length. The REPE prefix causes CMPSB to continue incrementing ESI and EDI and comparing characters one by one until a difference is found between the two strings:

```
TITLE Comparing Strings                  (Cmpsb.asm)

; This program uses CMPSB to compare two strings
; of equal length.

INCLUDE Irvine32.inc
.data
source BYTE "MARTIN   "
dest   BYTE "MARTINEZ"
str1   BYTE "Source is smaller",0dh,0ah,0
str2   BYTE "Source is not smaller",0dh,0ah,0

.code
main PROC
    cld                      ; direction = forward
    mov   esi,OFFSET source
    mov   edi,OFFSET dest
    mov   cx,LENGTHOF source
    repe  cmpsb
    jb    source_smaller
    mov   edx,OFFSET str2
    jmp   done

source_smaller:
    mov   edx,OFFSET str1

done:
    call WriteString
    exit
main ENDP
END main
```

Using the given test data, the message "Source is smaller" displays on the console. As can be seen below, ESI and EDI are left pointing one position beyond the point where the two strings were found to differ:

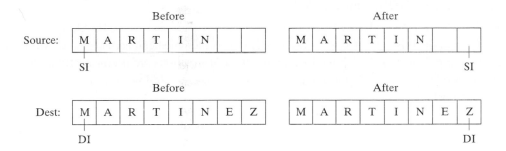

(If the strings had been identical, ESI and EDI would have been left pointing one position beyond the ends of their respective strings.)

It should be emphasized that comparing two strings with CMPSB only works adequately when the strings are of equal length. That is why it was important in the preceding example to pad "MARTIN" with two trailing spaces to make it the same length as "MARTINEZ". Needless to say, this imposes an awkward constraint on string handling, which we can eliminate later in this chapter when showing the **Str_compare** procedure (Section 9.3.1).

9.2.3   SCASB, SCASW, and SCASD

The SCASB, SCASW, and SCASD instructions compare a value in AL/AX/EAX to a byte, word, or doubleword, respectively, addressed by EDI.

These instructions are particularly useful when looking for a single value in a long string or array. Combined with the REPE (or REP) prefix, the string or array is scanned while ECX > 0 and the value in AL/AX/EAX matches each subsequent value in memory. The REPNE prefix scans until either AL/AX/EAX matches a value in memory or ECX = 0.

Scan for a Matching Character   In the following example we search the string **alpha**, looking for the letter F. If the letter is found, EDI points one position beyond the matching character. (If the letter were not found, the JNZ instruction would exit.):

```
.data
alpha BYTE "ABCDEFGH",0
.code
mov edi,OFFSET alpha          ; EDI points to the string
mov al,'F'                    ; search for the letter F
mov ecx,LENGTHOF alpha        ; set the search count
cld                           ; direction = up
repne scasb                   ; repeat while not equal
jnz quit                      ; quit if letter not found
dec edi                       ; found: back up EDI
```

In this example, JNZ was added after the loop to test for the possibility that the loop stopped because ECX = 0 and the letter (F) was not found.

9.2.4 STOSB, STOSW, and STOSD

The STOSB, STOSW, and STOSD instructions store the contents of AL/AX/EAX, respectively, in memory at the offset pointed to by EDI. Also, EDI is incremented/decremented based on the Direction flag. When used with the REP prefix, these instructions are useful for filling all elements of a string or array with a single value. For example, the following code initializes each byte in **string1** to 0FFh:

```
.data
Count = 100
string1 BYTE Count DUP(?)
.code
mov al,0FFh                      ; value to be stored
mov edi,OFFSET string1           ; ES:DI points to target
mov ecx,Count                    ; character count
cld                              ; direction = forward
rep stosb                        ; fill with contents of AL
```

9.2.5 LODSB, LODSW, and LODSD

The LODSB, LODSW, and LODSD instructions load a byte or word from memory at ESI into AL/AX/EAX, respectively. Also, ESI is incremented/decremented based on the Direction flag. The REP prefix is rarely used with LODS because each new value loaded into the accumulator overwrites its previous contents. Instead, it is used to load a single value. For example, LODSB substitutes for the following two instructions (assuming that the Direction flag is clear):

```
mov  al,[esi]          ; move byte into AL
inc  esi               ; point to next byte
```

Array Multiplication Example   The following program multiplies each element of a double-word array by a constant value and stores the product in a new array. LODSD and STOSD work together:

```
TITLE Multiply an Array                   (Mult.asm)

; This program multiplies each element of an array
; of 32-bit integers by a constant value.

INCLUDE Irvine32.inc
.data
array DWORD 1,2,3,4,5,6,7,8,9,10
multiplier DWORD 10

.code
main PROC
    cld                          ; direction = forward
    mov esi,OFFSET array         ; source index
    mov edi,esi                  ; destination index
    mov ecx,LENGTHOF array       ; loop counter
```

```
    L1: lodsd                        ; load [ESI] into EAX
        mul multiplier               ; multiply by a value
        stosd                        ; store EAX into [EDI]
        loop L1

        exit
    main ENDP
    END main
```

9.2.6   Section Review

1. In reference to string primitives, which 32-bit register is known as the *accumulator*?
2. Which instruction compares an integer in the accumulator to the contents of memory, pointed to by EDI?
3. Which index register is used by the STOSD instruction?
4. Which instruction copies data from the memory location addressed by ESI into the accumulator?
5. What does the REPZ prefix do for a CMPSB instruction?
6. Which Direction flag value causes index registers to move backward through memory when executing string primitives?
7. When a repeat prefix is used with STOSW, what value is added to or subtracted from the index register?
8. In what way is the CMPS instruction ambiguous or misleading?
9. *Challenge:* When the Direction flag is clear and SCASB has found a matching character, where does EDI point?
10. *Challenge:* When scanning an array for the first occurrence of a particular character, which repeat prefix would be best?

9.3   Selected String Procedures

In this section, we will create several simple procedures that manipulate null-terminated strings. If you're a C programmer, you will probably notice that these procedures are suspiciously similar to functions in the standard C library. These procedures have been placed in the Irvine32 link library,[1] and the following procedure prototypes can be found in *Irvine32.inc*:

```
; Copy a source string to a target string.
Str_copy PROTO,
    source:PTR BYTE,
    target:PTR BYTE

; Return the length of a string (excluding the null byte) in EAX.
Str_length PROTO,
    pString:PTR BYTE
```

---

[1] For Real-mode programming, the Irvine16 library contains the same procedures.

```
; Compare string1 to string2. Set the Zero and
; Carry flags in the same way as the CMP instruction.
Str_compare PROTO,
    string1:PTR BYTE,
    string2:PTR BYTE

; Trim a given trailing character from a string.
; The second argument is the character to trim.
Str_trim PROTO,
    pString:PTR BYTE,
    char:BYTE

; Convert a string to upper case.
Str_ucase PROTO,
    pString:PTR BYTE
```

9.3.1 Str_compare Procedure

The **Str_compare** procedure compares two strings. The calling format is:

```
INVOKE Str_compare, ADDR string1, ADDR string2
```

The strings are compared byte by byte, using their 8-bit integer ASCII codes. The comparison is case-sensitive because ASCII codes are different for uppercase and lowercase letters. The procedure does not return a value, but the Carry and Zero flags can be interpreted as follows (using the *string1* and *string2* arguments):

Relation	Carry Flag	Zero Flag	Branch if True
string1 < string2	1	0	JB
string1 = string2	0	1	JE
string1 > string2	0	0	JA

(You may recall that back in Chapter 6 we explained how the CMP instruction sets the Carry and Zero flags when comparing unsigned integers.)

The following is a listing of the **Str_compare** procedure. See the *Compare.asm* program for a demonstration:

```
Str_compare PROC USES eax edx esi edi,
    string1:PTR BYTE,
    string2:PTR BYTE
;
; Compare two strings.
; Returns nothing, but the Zero and Carry flags are affected
; exactly as they would be by the CMP instruction.
;----------------------------------------------------
    mov esi,string1
    mov edi,string2
```

```
L1: mov   al,[csi]
    mov   dl,[edi]
    cmp   al,0                    ; end of string1?
    jne   L2                      ; no
    cmp   dl,0                    ; yes: end of string2?
    jne   L2                      ; no
    jmp   L3                      ; yes, exit with ZF = 1
L2: inc   esi                     ; point to next
    inc   edi
    cmp   al,dl                   ; chars equal?
    je    L1                      ; yes: continue loop
                                  ; no: exit with flags set
L3: ret
Str_compare ENDP
```

It might be asked, why wasn't the CMPSB instruction used in this implementation? In order to use CMPSB, we would have to know the length of the longer string. That would require two calls to the **Str_length** procedure (in the next section). In this particular case, it is easier to check for the null terminators in both strings within the same loop.

9.3.2   Str_length Procedure

The **Str_length** procedure returns the length of a string in the EAX register. When you call it, pass the offset of a string. For example:

```
INVOKE Str_length, ADDR myString
```

Here is the procedure implementation:

```
Str_length PROC USES edi,
    pString:PTR BYTE          ; pointer to string
    mov edi,pString
    mov eax,0                 ; character count
L1: cmp byte ptr [edi],0      ; end of string?
    je  L2                    ; yes: quit
    inc edi                   ; no: point to next
    inc eax                   ; add 1 to count
    jmp L1
L2: ret
Str_length ENDP
```

See the *Length.asm* program for a demonstration of this procedure.

9.3.3   Str_copy Procedure

The **Str_copy** procedure copies a null-terminated string from a source location to a target location. Before calling this procedure, you must make sure the target operand is large enough to hold the copied string. The syntax for calling Str_copy is:

```
INVOKE Str_copy, ADDR source, ADDR target
```

No values are returned by the procedure. Here is the implementation:

```
Str_copy PROC USES eax ecx esi edi,
    source:PTR BYTE,                   ; source string
    target:PTR BYTE                    ; target string
;
; Copy a string from source to target.
; Requires: the target string must contain enough
;           space to hold a copy of the source string.
;-----------------------------------------------------
    INVOKE Str_length,source          ; EAX = length source
    mov ecx,eax                       ; REP count
    inc ecx                           ; add 1 for null byte
    mov esi,source
    mov edi,target
    cld                               ; direction = forward
    rep movsb                         ; copy the string
    ret
Str_copy ENDP
```

See the *CopyStr.asm* program for a demonstration of this procedure.

9.3.4   Str_trim Procedure

The **Str_trim** procedure removes all occurrences of a selected trailing character from a null-terminated string. You might use it, for example, to remove all spaces from the end of a string. The logic for this procedure is interesting because you have to check a number of possible cases (shown here with # as the trailing character):

1. The string is empty.
2. The string contains other characters followed by one or more trailing characters, as in "Hello##".
3. The string contains only one character, the trailing character, as in "#".
4. The string contains no trailing character, as in "Hello" or "H".
5. The string contains one or more trailing characters followed by one or more nontrailing characters, as in "#H" or "###Hello".

The easiest way to truncate characters from a string is to insert a null byte just after the characters you want to retain. Any characters after the null byte become insignificant. Here is the procedure's source code. The *Trim.asm* program tests **Str_trim**:

```
Str_trim PROC USES eax ecx edi,
    pString:PTR BYTE,                 ; points to string
    char:BYTE                         ; char to remove
;
; Remove all occurrences of a given character from
; the end of a string.
```

```
; Returns: nothing
;-------------------------------------------------------------
    mov   edi,pString
    INVOKE Str_length,edi          ; returns length in EAX
    cmp   eax,0                     ; zero-length string?
    je    L2                        ; yes: exit
    mov   ecx,eax                   ; no: counter = string length
    dec   eax
    add   edi,eax                   ; EDI points to last char
    mov   al,char                   ; char to trim
    std                             ; direction = reverse
    repe  scasb                     ; skip past trim character
    jne   L1                        ; removed first character?
    dec   edi                       ; adjust EDI: ZF=1 && ECX=0
L1: mov   BYTE PTR [edi+2],0        ; insert null byte
L2: ret
Str_trim ENDP
```

In all cases but one, EDI stops two bytes behind the character that we want to replace with null. Note the following table, which shows various test cases for nonempty strings:

String Definition	EDI, When SCASB Stops	Zero Flag	ECX	Position to Store the Null
str BYTE "Hello##",0	str + 3	0	> 0	[edi + 2]
str BYTE "#",0	str − 1	1	0	[edi + 1]
str BYTE "Hello",0	str + 3	0	> 0	[edi + 2]
str BYTE "H",0	str − 1	0	0	[edi + 2]
str BYTE "#H",0	str + 0	0	> 0	[edi + 2]

Using the first string definition from the foregoing table, the following figure shows the position of EDI when SCASB stops:

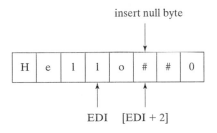

When SCASB ends, a special test is made for the one case in which the string contains a single character, and that character is the one to be trimmed. In this case, EDI points only one byte ahead of the character to replace with null (since the SCASB stopped because ECX=0 and not because ZF=1). To compensate, we decrement EDI once before storing a null byte at [edi+2], as shown in the following figure:

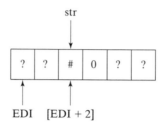

9.3.5 Str_ucase Procedure

The **Str_ucase** procedure converts a string to all uppercase characters. It returns no value. When you call it, pass the offset of a string:

```
INVOKE Str_ucase, ADDR myString
```

Here is the procedure implementation:

```
Str_ucase PROC USES eax esi,
    pString:PTR BYTE
; Convert a null-terminated string to uppercase.
; Returns: nothing
;-----------------------------------------------
    mov esi,pString
L1:
    mov al,[esi]                    ; get char
    cmp al,0                        ; end of string?
    je  L3                          ; yes: quit
    cmp al,'a'                      ; below "a"?
    jb  L2
    cmp al,'z'                      ; above "z"?
    ja  L2
    and BYTE PTR [esi],11011111b    ; convert the char
L2: inc esi                         ; next char
    jmp L1

L3: ret
Str_ucase ENDP
```

(See the *Ucase.asm* program for a demonstration of this procedure.)

9.3.6   Section Review

1. (*True/False*): The **Str_compare** procedure stops when the null terminator of the longer string is reached.
2. (*True/False*): The **Str_compare** procedure does not need to use ESI and EDI to access memory.
3. (*True/False*): The **Str_length** procedure uses SCASB to find the null terminator at the end of the string.
4. (*True/False*): The **Str_copy** procedure prevents a string from being copied into too small a memory area.
5. What Direction flag setting is most appropriate for the **Str_trim** procedure?
6. Why does the **Str_trim** procedure use the JNE instruction?
7. What happens in the **Str_ucase** procedure if the target string contains a digit?
8. *Challenge:* If the **Str_length** procedure used SCASB, which repeat prefix would be most appropriate?
9. *Challenge:* If the **Str_length** procedure used SCASB, how would it calculate and return the string length?

9.4   Two-Dimensional Arrays

Many applications, mathematical and otherwise, involve the processing of two-dimensional arrays. The Intel instruction set includes two operand types, base-index and base-index-displacement, which are well suited to array applications.

9.4.1   Base-Index Operands

A base-index operand adds the values of two registers (called *base* and *index*), producing an offset address. Any two 32-bit general-purpose registers may be used. Here are examples of various combinations:

```
.data
array WORD 1000h,2000h,3000h
.code
    mov   ebx,OFFSET array
    mov   esi,2
    mov   ax,[ebx+esi]          ; AX = 2000h

    mov   edi,OFFSET array
    mov   ecx,4
    mov   ax,[edi+ecx]          ; AX = 3000h

    mov   ebp,OFFSET array
    mov   esi,0
    mov   ax,[ebp+esi]          ; AX = 1000h
```

In Real-address mode, it is possible to use 16-bit registers as base-index operands. In that case, the only permitted combinations are: [bx+si], [bx+di], [bp+si], and [bp+di]. (As always, avoid using BP except when addressing data on the stack.)

Table Example   A base-index operand is very useful when accessing two-dimensional tables. A base register usually contains a row offset, and an index register contains a column offset. To show a simple application of this addressing mode, let's create a data definition for a table that has three rows and five columns:

```
tableB  BYTE  10h,   20h,   30h,   40h,   50h
        BYTE  60h,   70h,   80h,   90h,   0A0h
        BYTE  0B0h,  0C0h,  0D0h,  0E0h,  0F0h
NumCols = 5
```

In memory, this table is simply a continuous stream of bytes as if it were a one-dimensional array. But we prefer to think of it as a two-dimensional table, and say that it has three *logical rows* and five *logical columns*. We are not required to declare each table row on a separate line, but it does help express the table structure. The physical storage of this array is in row-major order, where the last byte in the first row is followed by the first byte in the second row, and so on.

Suppose we want to locate a particular entry in the table using row and column coordinates. Assuming that coordinates are zero-based, we can see that the entry at row 1, column 2 contains 80h. All we have to do is set EBX to the table's offset, add (NumCols * RowNumber) for the row offset, and set ESI to the column number:

```
RowNumber = 1
ColumnNumber = 2
mov ebx,OFFSET tableB
add ebx,NumCols * RowNumber
mov esi,ColumnNumber
mov al,[ebx + esi]              ; AL = 80h
```

Arbitrarily, let's say that the array is located at offset 150. Then the effective address represented by EBX + ESI is 157. The following figure helps to show how EBX and ESI are added to produce the effective address:

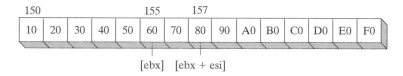

As in the case of the other indirect addressing modes, if the effective address points outside the program's data region, a general protection fault occurs.

Calculating the 16-bit Sum   The following program fragment (from *Table.asm*) calculates the sum of row 1 in our example table. It presents an interesting challenge, to add each byte to a 16-bit accumulator:

```
      RowNumber = 1
      mov   ecx,NumCols              ; loop counter
      mov   ebx,OFFSET tableB
      add   ebx,(NumCols * RowNumber); move to row 1
      mov   esi,0                    ; beginning of row
      mov   ax,0                     ; zero the sum
      mov   dx,0                     ; holds each value

L1: mov   dl,[ebx+esi]              ; get a byte
      add   ax,dx                    ; add to accumulator
      inc   esi                      ; point to next column
      loop L1
```

Clearly, we cannot use AL as the accumulator because it would quickly overflow. The sum, 280h, must be stored in AX, a 16-bit register. As an exercise, you can write code to calculate the sum of a single column in the table.

9.4.2 Base-Index Displacement

A base-index-displacement operand combines a displacement, a base register, and an index register to produce an effective address. Here are the two most common formats:

```
[base + index + displacement]
displacement[base + index]
```

Displacement can be either the name of a variable or a constant expression. Any general-purpose 32-bit registers may be used for the base and index. Because Real-address mode permits 16-bit registers to used as base/index operands, they are subject to the same restrictions as in base-index addressing.

Table Example   As in the case of base-index operands, this type of operand is also well suited to processing two-dimensional tables. The name of a table can be used as the displacement portion of the operand, a base register can contain the offset of a row within the table, and an index register can contain the offset of a column within the row. For example:

```
tableB[ebx + esi]
```

Let's use the same data definition we used in Section 9.4.1:

```
tableB  BYTE   10h,  20h,  30h,  40h,  50h
        BYTE   60h,  70h,  80h,  90h,  0A0h
        BYTE  0B0h, 0C0h, 0D0h, 0E0h, 0F0h
NumCols = 5
```

Suppose we want to locate a particular entry in the table using row and column coordinates. Assuming that coordinates are zero-based, we can see that the entry at row 1, column 2 contains 80h. All we have to do is set EBX to the offset of row 1 and set ESI to column number 2:

```
mov   ebx,NumCols            ; row offset
mov   esi,2                  ; column number
mov   al,tableB[ebx + esi]   ; [150 + 5 + 2] = [157]
                             ; AL = 80h
```

Assuming for the moment that **tableB** begins at offset 150, the following diagram shows the positions of EBX and ESI relative to the array:

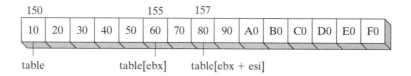

(The *Table2.asm* program on the sample program disk contains the complete implementation of this example.)

9.4.3 Section Review

1. In a base-index operand, which registers can be used?
2. Show an example of a base-index operand.
3. Show an example of a base-index-displacement operand.
4. Suppose a two-dimensional array of doublewords has three logical rows and four logical columns. If ESI is used as the row pointer, what value would be added to ESI to move from one row to the next?
5. Suppose a two-dimensional array of doublewords has three logical rows and four logical columns. Write several instructions using ESI and EDI that would address the third column in the second row. (Numbering for rows and columns starts at zero.)
6. *Challenge:* In Real-address mode, is there any problem with using BP to address an array?
7. *Challenge:* In Protected mode, is there any problem with using EBP to address an array?

9.5 Searching and Sorting Integer Arrays

A great deal of time and energy has been expended by computer scientists in finding better ways to search and sort massive quantities of data. It has been easily proven that choosing the best algorithm for a particular application is far more useful than buying a faster computer. Most students study searching and sorting using high-level languages such as C++ and Java. But it's very possible that assembly language lends a different perspective to the study of algorithms, as we are able to see the low-level implementation details. It's interesting to note that the most famous algorithm author of this century, Donald Knuth, used assembly language for his published program examples.[2]

Searching and sorting also gives us an excellent chance to try out some of the addressing modes introduced in this chapter. In particular, base-indexed addressing turns out to be very useful because we can point one register (such as EBX) to the base of an array, and use another register (such as ESI) to index into any other array location.

9.5.1   Bubble Sort

A bubble sort compares each pair of array values, beginning in positions 0 and 1. If the two values are found to be in reverse order, they are exchanged. The following illustration shows one complete pass through a list of integers:

One Pass (Bubble Sort)

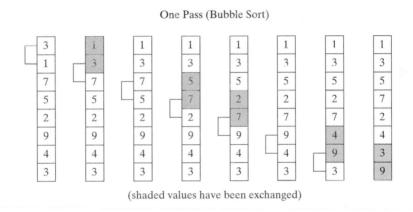

(shaded values have been exchanged)

After one pass, the array is still not sorted, so an outer loop starts another pass through the array. After $n-1$ passes, the array is guaranteed to be sorted.

A bubble sort works well for small-sized arrays, but it becomes tremendously inefficient for larger ones. It is an $O(n^2)$ algorithm, meaning that the sort time increases quadratically in relation to the number of array elements (n). Suppose, for example, that it takes 0.1 second to sort 1000 elements. As the number of elements increases by a factor of 10, the time required to sort the array increases by a factor of 10^2 (100). The following table shows sort times for various array sizes, assuming that 1000 array elements can be sorted in 0.1 seconds:

Array Size	Time (seconds)
1,000	0.1
10,000	10.0

---

[2]   Knuth, Donald. *The Art of Computer Programming,* Volume I: *Fundamental Algorithms.*

Array Size	Time (seconds)
100,000	1000
1,000,000	100,000 (27.78 hours)

A bubble sort would not be a good sort for an array of 1 million integers, as it would take over 27 hours to finish! But it is fine for a few hundred integers.

Pseudocode   It's useful to create a simplified version of the bubble sort, using pseudocode that is similar to assembly language. We will use **N** to represent the size of the array, **cx1** to represent the outer loop counter, and **cx2** to represent the inner loop counter:

```
cx1 = N - 1
while( cx1 > 0 )
{
  esi = addr(array)
  cx2 = cx1
  while( cx2 > 0 )
  {
    if( array[esi] < array[esi+4] )
      exchange( array[esi], array[esi+4] )
    add esi,4
    dec cx2
  }
  dec cx1
}
```

Mechanical concerns, such as saving and restoring the outer loop counter, have purposely been left out. At a glance, it is clear that the inner loop count (**cx2**) is based on the current value of the outer loop count (**cx1**), which in turn, decreases with each pass through the array.

Assembly Language   Once the pseudocode is understood, it becomes a small step to create the final implementation in assembly language, placing it in a procedure with parameters and local variables:

```
;-----------------------------------------------------------
BubbleSort PROC USES eax ecx esi,
    pArray:PTR DWORD,                   ; pointer to array
    Count:DWORD                         ; array size
;
; Sort an array of 32-bit signed integers in ascending
; order, using the bubble sort algorithm.
; Receives: pointer to array, array size
; Returns: nothing
;-----------------------------------------------------------
    mov ecx,Count
    dec ecx                             ; decrement count by 1
```

```
L1: push ecx                    ; save outer loop count
    mov esi,pArray              ; point to first value

L2: mov eax,[esi]              ; get array value
    cmp [esi+4],eax            ; compare a pair of values
    jge L3                     ; if [esi] <= [edi], don't exch
    xchg eax,[esi+4]           ; exchange the pair
    mov [esi],eax

L3: add esi,4                  ; move both pointers forward
    loop L2                    ; inner loop

    pop ecx                    ; retrieve outer loop count
    loop L1                    ; else repeat outer loop

L4: ret
BubbleSort ENDP
```

9.5.2 Binary Search

It is surprising how often a simple array search is necessary in everyday programming applications. For a small array (1000 elements or less), it's easy to do a *sequential search*, where you start at the beginning of the array and examine each element in sequence until a matching one is found. For any array of *n* elements, such a search requires an average of *n* / 2 comparisons. If a small array is involved, one would hardly notice the time taken to perform a sequential search. On the other hand, searching an array of 1 million elements might be impractical.

The *binary search* algorithm was discovered to be particularly effective when searching for a single item in a large array. It has one important precondition: the array elements must be arranged in either ascending or descending order. Here's an informal description of the algorithm: Before beginning the search, ask the user to enter an integer, which we will call *searchVal*.

1. The range of the array to be searched is indicated by the subscripts named *first* and *last*. If *first* > *last*, exit the search, indicating failure to find a match.
2. Calculate the midpoint of the array, between array subscripts *first* and *last*.
3. Compare *searchVal* to the integer at the midpoint of the array:

   • If the values are equal, return from the procedure with the midpoint in EAX. This return value indicates that a match has been found in the array.
   • On the other hand, if *searchVal* is larger than the number at the midpoint, reset the first array subscript to one position higher than the midpoint.
   • Or, if *searchVal* is smaller than the number at the midpoint, reset the last array subscript to one position below the midpoint.

4. Return to Step 1.

The binary search is tremendously efficient because it uses a *divide and conquer* strategy. The range of values is divided in half with each iteration of the loop. In general, it is described as an O(log n) algorithm, meaning that as the number of array elements increases by a factor of n, the average search time increases by only a factor of log n. Because the actual search times are so short, the following table simply records the maximum number of comparisons required for various array sizes:

Array Size (n)	Maximum Number of Comparisons: $(\log_2 n) + 1$
64	7
1,024	11
65,536	17
1,048,576	21
4,294,967,296	33

Following is a C++ implementation of a binary search function that works with signed integers:

```cpp
int BinSearch( int values[], const int searchVal, int count )
{
  int first = 0;
  int last = count - 1;
  while( first <= last )
  {
    int mid = (last + first) / 2;
    if( values[mid] < searchVal )
      first = mid + 1;
    else if( values[mid] > searchVal )
      last = mid - 1;
    else
      return mid;        // success
  }
  return -1;             // not found
}
```

Following is an assembly language implementation of the binary search:

```
;-------------------------------------------------------------------
BinarySearch PROC uses ebx edx esi edi,
    pArray:PTR DWORD,                  ; pointer to array
    Count:DWORD,                       ; array size
    searchVal:DWORD                    ; search value
LOCAL first:DWORD,                     ; first position
    last:DWORD,                        ; last position
    mid:DWORD                          ; midpoint
;
```

```
; Search an array of signed integers for a single value.
; Receives: Pointer to array, array size, search value.
; Returns: If a match is found, EAX = the array position of the
; matching element; otherwise, EAX = -1.
;---------------------------------------------------------------
      mov   first,0                   ; first = 0
      mov   eax,Count                 ; last = (count - 1)
      dec   eax
      mov   last,eax
      mov   edi,searchVal             ; EDI = searchVal
      mov   ebx,pArray                ; EBX points to the array

L1: ; while first <= last
      mov   eax,first
      cmp   eax,last
      jg    L5                        ; exit search

; mid = (last + first) / 2
      mov   eax,last
      add   eax,first
      shr   eax,1
      mov   mid,eax

; EDX = values[mid]
      mov   esi,mid
      shl   esi,2                     ; scale mid value by 4
      mov   edx,[ebx+esi]             ; EDX = values[mid]

; if ( EDX < searchval(EDI) )
;   first = mid + 1;
      cmp   edx,edi
      jge   L2
      mov   eax,mid                   ; first = mid + 1
      inc   eax
      mov   first,eax
      jmp   L4

; else if( EDX > searchVal(EDI) )
;   last = mid - 1;
L2: cmp   edx,edi                     ; optional
      jle   L3
      mov   eax,mid                   ; last = mid - 1
      dec   eax
      mov   last,eax
      jmp   L4

; else return mid
L3: mov   eax,mid                     ; value found
      jmp   L9                        ; return (mid)
```

```
L4: jmp   L1                       ; continue the loop

L5: mov   eax,-1                   ; search failed
L9: ret
BinarySearch ENDP
```

9.5.2.1   Test Program

To demonstrate both the bubble sort and binary search functions presented in this chapter, let's write a short test program that performs the following steps, in sequence:

- Fills an array with random integers
- Displays the array
- Sorts the array using a bubble sort
- Redisplays the array
- Asks the user to enter an integer
- Performs a binary search for the user's integer (in the array)
- Displays the results of the binary search

The various procedures have been placed in separate source files to make it easier to locate and edit source code. Table 9-2 lists each module and its contents. Most professionally written programs are also written in separate modules.

Table 9-2   Modules in the Bubble Sort/Binary Search Program.

Module	Contents
B_main.asm	Main module: Contains the main, **ShowResults**, and **Ask-ForSearchVal** procedures. Contains the program entry point and manages the overall sequence of tasks.
Bsort.asm	**BubbleSort** procedure: Performs a bubble sort on a 32-bit signed integer array.
Bsearch.asm	**BinarySearch** procedure: Performs a binary search on a 32-bit signed integer array.
FillArry.asm	**FillArray** procedure: Fills a 32-bit signed integer array with a range of random values.
PrtArry.asm	**PrintArray** procedure: Writes the contents of a 32-bit signed integer array to standard output.

The procedures in all modules except *B_main* are written in such a way that it would be easy to use them in other programs without making any modifications. This is highly desirable, because we might save time in the future by reusing existing code. The same approach is used in the Irvine32 and Irvine16 link libraries.

Following is an include file (*Bsearch.inc*) containing prototypes of the procedures called from the main module:

```
; Bsearch.inc - prototypes for procedures used in
; the BubbleSort / BinarySearch program.

; Searches for an integer in an array of 32-bit signed
; integers.
BinarySearch PROTO,
    pArray:PTR DWORD,              ; pointer to array
    Count:DWORD,                   ; array size
    searchVal:DWORD                ; search value

; Fills an array with 32-bit signed random integers
FillArray PROTO,
    pArray:PTR DWORD,              ; pointer to array
    Count:DWORD,                   ; number of elements
    LowerRange:SDWORD,             ; lower range
    UpperRange:SDWORD              ; upper range

; Writes a 32-bit signed integer array to standard output
PrintArray PROTO,
    pArray:PTR DWORD,
    Count:DWORD

; Sorts the array in ascending order
BubbleSort PROTO,
    pArray:PTR DWORD,
    Count:DWORD
```

Following is a listing of *B_main.asm*, the main module:

```
TITLE Bubble Sort and Binary Search       B_main.asm)

; Bubble sort an array of 32-bit signed integers,
; and perform a binary search.
; Main module, calls Bsearch.asm, Bsort.asm, FillArry.asm

INCLUDE Irvine32.inc
INCLUDE Bsearch.inc       ; procedure prototypes

LOWVAL = -5000            ; minimum value
HIGHVAL = +5000           ; maximum value
ARRAY_SIZE = 50           ; size of the array

.data
array DWORD ARRAY_SIZE DUP(?)

.code
main PROC
    call Randomize
```

```
    ; Fill an array with random signed integers
    INVOKE FillArray, ADDR array, ARRAY_SIZE, LOWVAL, HIGHVAL

    ; Display the array
    INVOKE PrintArray, ADDR array, ARRAY_SIZE
    call WaitMsg

    ; Perform a bubble sort and redisplay the array
    INVOKE BubbleSort, ADDR array, ARRAY_SIZE
    INVOKE PrintArray, ADDR array, ARRAY_SIZE

    ; Demonstrate a binary search
    call AskForSearchVal                      ; returned in EAX
    INVOKE BinarySearch,
      ADDR array, ARRAY_SIZE, eax
    call ShowResults

    exit
main ENDP

;------------------------------------------------------------
AskForSearchVal PROC
;
; Prompts the user for a signed integer.
; Receives: nothing
; Returns: EAX = value input by user
;------------------------------------------------------------
.data
prompt BYTE "Enter a signed decimal integer "
       BYTE "to find in the array: ",0
.code
    call Crlf
    mov   edx,OFFSET prompt
    call WriteString
    call ReadInt
    ret
AskForSearchVal ENDP

;------------------------------------------------------------
ShowResults PROC
;
; Displays the resulting value from the binary search.
; Receives: EAX = position number to be displayed
; Returns: nothing
;------------------------------------------------------------
.data
msg1 BYTE "The value was not found.",0
msg2 BYTE "The value was found at position ",0
```

```
.code
.IF eax == -1
   mov edx,OFFSET msg1
   call WriteString
.ELSE
   mov edx,OFFSET msg2
   call WriteString
   call WriteDec
.ENDIF
   call Crlf
   call Crlf
   ret
ShowResults ENDP
END main
```

The PrintArray and FillArray procedures, shown next, are each in their own source code modules:

```
;-------------------------------------------------------------
PrintArray PROC USES eax ecx edx esi,
    pArray:PTR DWORD,              ; pointer to array
    Count:DWORD                    ; number of elements
;
; Writes an array of 32-bit signed decimal integers to
; standard output, separated by commas
; Receives: pointer to array, array size
; Returns: nothing
;-------------------------------------------------------------
.data
comma BYTE ", ",0
.code
    mov esi,pArray
    mov ecx,Count
    cld                            ; direction = forward

L1: lodsd                          ; load [ESI] into EAX
    call WriteInt                  ; send to output
    mov  edx,OFFSET comma
    call Writestring               ; display comma
    loop L1

    call Crlf
    ret
PrintArray ENDP

;-------------------------------------------------------------
FillArray PROC USES eax edi ecx edx,
    pArray:PTR DWORD,              ; pointer to array
    Count:DWORD,                   ; number of elements
    LowerRange:SDWORD,             ; lower range
```

```
        UpperRange:SDWORD                    ; upper range
;
; Fills an array with a random sequence of 32-bit signed
; integers between LowerRange and (UpperRange - 1).
; Returns: nothing
;--------------------------------------------------------------
        mov edi,pArray                  ; EDI points to the array
        mov ecx,Count                   ; loop counter
        mov edx,UpperRange
        sub edx,LowerRange              ; EDX = absolute range (0..n)

L1: mov   eax,edx                       ; get absolute range
        call RandomRange
        add   eax,LowerRange            ; bias the result
        stosd                           ; store EAX into [edi]
        Loop L1

        ret
FillArray ENDP
```

9.5.3 Section Review

1. If an array were already in sequential order, how many times would the outer loop of the **BubbleSort** procedure Section 9.5.1 execute?

2. In the **BubbleSort** procedure, how many times does the inner loop execute on the first pass through the array?

3. In the **BubbleSort** procedure, does the inner loop always execute the same number of times?

4. If it were found (through testing) that an array of 500 integers could be sorted in 0.5 seconds, how many seconds would it take to bubble sort an array of 5000 integers?

5. What is the maximum number of comparisons needed by the binary search algorithm when an array contains 128 elements?

6. Given an array of n elements, what is the maximum number of comparisons needed by the binary search algorithm?

7. *Challenge:* In the **BinarySearch** procedure (Section 9.5.2), why is it that the statement at label **L2** could be removed without affecting the outcome?

8. *Challenge:* In the **BinarySearch** procedure, how might the statement at label **L4** be eliminated?

9.6 Chapter Summary

String primitive instructions are unusual in that they require no register operands and are optimized for high-speed memory access. They are:

- MOVS: Move string data

- CMPS: Compare strings
- SCAS: Scan string
- STOS: Store string data
- LODS: Load accumulator from string

Each of these instructions has a suffix of B, W, or D when manipulating bytes, words, and doublewords, respectively.

REP repeats a string primitive instruction, with automatic incrementing or decrementing of index registers. For example, when REPE is used with SCASB, it scans memory bytes until a value in memory pointed to by EDI matches the contents of the AL register. The Direction flag determines whether the index register is incremented or decremented during each iteration of a string primitive instruction.

Strings and arrays are practically the same. Traditionally, a string consisted of an array of single-byte ASCII values, but now strings can also be arrays of 16-bit Unicode characters. The only important difference between a string and an array is that a string is usually terminated by a single null byte (containing zero).

Array manipulation is processor-intensive because it nearly always involves a looping algorithm. Most programs spend a high percentage (80 to 90) of their time executing a small fraction of their overall code. As a result, you can speed up your software by reducing the number and complexity of instructions inside loops. Assembly language is a great tool for code optimization because you can control every detail. For instance, you might choose to use registers rather than memory variables. Or, you might use one of the string-processing instructions shown in this chapter rather than MOV and CMP instructions.

Several useful string-processing procedures were introduced in this chapter: The **Str_copy** procedure copies one string to another. **Str_length** returns the length of a string. **Str_compare** compares two strings. **Str_trim** removes a selected character from the end of a string. **Str_ucase** converts a string to uppercase letters.

Base-index operands make it easier to process two-dimensional arrays (tables). You can set a base register to the address of a table row, and point an index register to the offset of a column within the selected row. Any general-purpose 32-bit registers can be used as base and index registers. Base-index-displacement operands are similar to base-index, except that they also include the name of the array:

```
[ebx + esi]                        ; base-index
array[ebx + esi]                   ; base-index-displacement
```

We presented assembly language implementations of a bubble sort and a binary search. A bubble sort orders the elements of an array in ascending or descending order. It is effective for arrays having no more than a few hundred elements, but inefficient for larger arrays. A binary search permits rapid searching for a single value in an ordered array. It is easy to implement in assembly language.

9.7   Programming Exercises

The following exercises can be done in either Protected mode or Real-address mode. Each of the following procedures assumes the use of null-terminated strings. Be sure to write a short driver program that tests each procedure.

1. Improved Str_copy Procedure

The **Str_copy** procedure shown in this chapter does not limit the number of characters to be copied. Create a new version (named **Str_copyN**) that requires an additional input parameter indicating the maximum number of characters to be copied.

2. Str_concat Procedure

Write a procedure named **Str_concat** that concatenates a source string to the end of a target string. Sufficient space must be available in the target string before this procedure is called. Pass pointers to the source and target strings. Here is a sample call:

```
.data
targetStr BYTE "ABCDE",10 DUP(0)
sourceStr BYTE "FGH",0
.code
INVOKE Str_concat, ADDR targetStr, ADDR sourceStr
```

3. Str_remove Procedure

Write a procedure named **Str_remove** that removes *n* characters from a string. Pass a pointer to the position in the string where the characters are to be removed. Pass an integer specifying the number of characters to remove. The following code, for example, shows how to remove "xxxx" from target:

```
.data
target BYTE "abcxxxxdefghijklmop",0
.code
INVOKE Str_remove, ADDR target + 3, 4
```

4. Str_find Procedure

Write a procedure named **Str_find** that searches for the first matching occurrence of a source string inside a target string and returns the matching position. The input parameters should be a pointer to the source string and a pointer to the target string. If a match is found, the procedure sets the Zero flag and EAX points to the matching position in the target string. Otherwise, the Zero flag is clear. The following code, for example, searches for "ABC" and returns with EAX pointing to the "A" in the target string:

```
.data
target BYTE "123ABC342432",0
source BYTE "ABC",0
pos    DWORD ?
```

```
.code
INVOKE Str_find, ADDR source, ADDR target
jnz notFound
mov pos,eax              ; store the position value
```

5. Str_nextword Procedure

Write a procedure called **Str_nextword** that scans a string for the first occurrence of a certain delimiter character and replaces the delimiter with a null byte. There are two input parameters: a pointer to the string, and the delimiter character. After the call, if the delimiter was found, the Zero flag is set and EAX contains the offset of the next character beyond the delimiter. Otherwise, the Zero flag is clear. For example, we can pass the address of **target** and a comma as the delimiter:

```
.data
target BYTE "Johnson,Calvin",0
.code
INVOKE Str_nextword, ADDR target, ','
jnz notFound
```

After calling **Str_nextword**, EAX would point to the character following the position where the comma was found (and replaced):

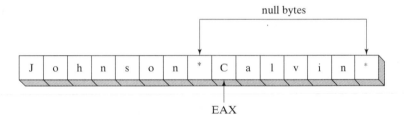

6. Constructing a Frequency Table

Write a procedure named **Get_frequencies** that constructs a character frequency table. Input to the procedure should be a pointer to a string, and a pointer to an array of 256 doublewords. Each array position is indexed by its corresponding ASCII code. When the procedure returns, each entry in the array contains a count of how many times that character occurred in the string. For example:

```
.data
target BYTE "AAEBDCFBBC",0
freqTable DWORD 256 DUP(0)
.code
INVOKE Get_frequencies, ADDR target, ADDR freqTable
```

Following is a picture of the string and entries 41 (hexadecimal) through 48 in the frequency table. Position 41 contains the value 2 because the letter A (ASCII code 41h) occurred twice in the string. Similar counts are shown for the other characters:

Target string:	A	A	E	B	D	C	F	B	B	C	0
ASCII code:	41	41	45	42	44	43	46	42	42	43	0

Frequency table:	2	3	2	1	1	1	0	0	0	0	0
Index:	41	42	43	44	45	46	47	48	49	4A	4B	etc.

Frequency tables are useful in data compression and other applications involving character processing. For example, the *Huffman encoding* algorithm stores the most frequently occurring characters in fewer bits than other characters that occur less often.

7. Sieve of Eratosthenes

The *Sieve of Eratosthenes,* invented by the Greek mathematician having the same name, provides a way to find all the prime numbers within a given range. The algorithm involves creating an array of bytes in which positions are "marked" by inserting 1's in the following manner: Beginning with position 2 (which is a prime number), insert a 1 in each array position that is a multiple of 2. Then do the same thing for multiples of 3, the next prime number. Find the next prime number after 3, which is 5, and mark all positions that are multiples of 5. Proceed in this manner until all multiples of primes have been found. The remaining positions of the array that are unmarked indicate which numbers are prime. For this program, create a 65,000-element array and display all primes between 2 and 65,000.

8. Bubble Sort

Add a variable to the **BubbleSort** procedure in Section 9.5.1 that is set to 1 whenever a pair of values is exchanged within the inner loop. Use this variable to exit the sort before its normal completion if you discover that no exchanges took place during a complete pass through the array. (This variable is commonly known as an *exchange flag.*)

9. Binary Search

Rewrite the binary search procedure shown in this chapter by using registers for mid, first, and last. Add comments to clarify the registers' usage.

10

Structures and Macros

10.1   Structures

A *structure* is a template or pattern given to a logically related group of variables. The individual variables in the structure are called *fields*. Program statements can access the structure as a single entity, or they can access individual fields.

Structures have been around a long time, as long as programming languages themselves. They were essential whenever programs needed to pass a lot of data from one procedure to another. For example, suppose the input to a procedure consisted of twenty different units of data relating to a disk drive. It would not be practical to call the procedure and try to pass all the required arguments in the correct order. Instead, you could place all of the related data in a structure and pass the address of the structure to the procedure. Very little stack space would be used (one address), and it would give the called procedure the opportunity to insert new data into the structure fields.

One bit of good news: structures in assembly language are essentially the same as structures in C and C++. With a small effort at translation, you can take any structure from the MS-Windows API library and make it work in assembly language. A good debugger such as Microsoft Visual Studio will display the names and contents of structure fields at runtime.

COORD Structure   Let's start with a simple example: The COORD structure used by the MS-Windows programming library identifies X and Y screen coordinates. The field named X has an offset of 0 relative to the beginning of the structure, and the field Y's offset equals 2:

```
COORD STRUCT
   X  WORD  ?                      ; offset 00
   Y  WORD  ?                      ; offset 02
COORD ENDS
```

> A *union* also groups together multiple identifiers, but the identifiers overlap the same area in memory. Unions will be covered in Section 10.1.7.

Using a structure involves three sequential steps:

1. Define the structure.
2. Declare one or more variables of the structure type, called *structure variables*.
3. Write runtime instructions that access the structure fields.

10.1.1   Defining Structures

A structure is defined using the STRUCT and ENDS directives. Inside the structure, you define fields using the same syntax as for ordinary variables. The basic syntax is:

```
name STRUCT
    field-declarations
name ENDS
```

Structures can contain virtually any number of fields.

Field Initializers   When you provide initializers for the fields in a structure, they become the default values when structure variables are declared. You can use various types of initializers:

- **Undefined:** Use ? to leave the field contents undefined.
- **Strings:** Use characters enclosed in quotation marks to intialize a field with a string.
- **Integers:** Use either an integer constant or an integer expression to initialize an integer field.
- **Arrays:** Use the DUP operator to initialize array elements when the field is an array.

For example, let's define a structure named **Employee** that describes employee information, with fields such as ID number, last name, years of service, and an array of salary history values. The following structure definition would be inserted in the program prior to the declaration of any variables of type **Employee**:

```
Employee STRUCT
    IdNum     BYTE "000000000"
    LastName BYTE 30 DUP(0)
    Years     WORD 0
    SalaryHistory DWORD 0,0,0,0
Employee ENDS
```

The following figure shows a linear representation of the structure:

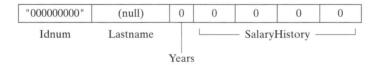

10.1.2   Declaring Structure Variables

You can declare instances of a structure (called *structure variables*) and initialize them with specific values. If empty angle brackets <> are used, the assembler retains a structure's default field initializers. Or, you can insert new values in selected fields. Examples of both approaches are shown here, using the **COORD** and **Employee** structures:

```
.data
point1 COORD <5,10>
point2 COORD <>
worker Employee <>
```

It is possible to override some or all of the default field values. The following example overrides the **IdNum** field of the **Employee** structure:

```
person1 Employee <"555223333">
```

An alternative notational form uses curly braces { ... } rather than angle brackets:

```
person2 Employee {"555223333"}
```

When the initializer for a string field is shorter than the field, the remaining positions are padded with spaces. It's important to note that a null byte is not automatically inserted at the end of a string field. If you plan to call library functions such as **WriteString**, you have to insert the null byte yourself.

You can skip over structure fields by inserting commas as place-markers. For example, the following statement skips the **IdNum** field and initializes the **LastName** field:

```
person3 Employee <,"Jones">
```

If the field contains an array, use the DUP operator to initialize some or all of the array elements. If the initializer is shorter than the field, the remaining positions will be filled with zeros. Here, for example, we initialize the first two **SalaryHistory** values and set the rest to zero:

```
person4 Employee <,,,2 DUP(20000)>
```

Array of Structures   You can declare an array of structures, as is done in the next example. Each element of **AllPoints** is initialized to <0,0>:

```
NumPoints = 3
AllPoints COORD NumPoints DUP(<0,0>)
```

10.1.3 Referencing Structure Variables

References to both structure variables and structure names can be made using the TYPE and SIZEOF operators. For example, let's return to the same **Employee** structure we saw earlier:

```
Employee STRUCT                              ; bytes
    IdNum     BYTE "000000000"               ;  9
    LastName BYTE 30 DUP(0)                  ; 30
    Years     WORD 0                         ;  2
    SalaryHistory DWORD 0,0,0,0              ; 16
Employee ENDS                                ; 57 total
```

Given the following data definition,

```
.data
worker Employee <>
```

each of the following expressions returns the same value:

```
    TYPE Employee                   ; 57
    SIZEOF Employee                 ; 57
    SIZEOF worker                   ; 57
```

> Recall that the TYPE operator returns the number of bytes used by the identifier's storage type (BYTE, WORD, DWORD, etc.) The LENGTHOF operator returns a count of the number of elements in an array. The SIZEOF operator multiplies LENGTHOF by TYPE. These were covered in Section 4.3.

Field References   Direct references to individual fields require a structure variable as a qualifier. The following constant expressions can be generated at assembly time, using the **Employee** structure:

```
TYPE Employee.SalaryHistory      ; 4
LENGTHOF Employee.SalaryHistory  ; 4
TYPE Employee.Years              ; 2
```

The following are runtime references to **worker**, a structure variable:

```
.data
worker Employee <>
.code
mov dx,worker.Years
mov worker.SalaryHistory,20000       ; first salary
mov worker.SalaryHistory+4,30000     ; second salary
mov edx,OFFSET worker.LastName
```

Indirect Operands   Indirect operands permit the use of a register (such as ESI) to address structure data. Such addressing provides flexibility, particularly when passing a structure's address to a procedure, or when using an array of structures. The PTR operator is required when referencing indirect operands:

```
mov esi,OFFSET worker
mov ax,(Employee PTR [esi]).Years
```

Had we written the following statement, it would not assemble because **Years** by itself does not identify a specific structure:

```
mov ax,[esi].Years               ; invalid
```

Looping Through an Array   A loop is often used with indirect or indexed addressing to manipulate an array of structures. The following program (*AllPoints.asm*), assigns coordinates to the **AllPoints** array:

```
TITLE Loop Through Array         (AllPoints.asm)

INCLUDE Irvine32.inc
.data
NumPoints = 3
AllPoints COORD NumPoints DUP(<0,0>)

.code
main PROC
    mov edi,0                ; array index
    mov ecx,NumPoints        ; loop counter
    mov ax,1                 ; starting X, Y values
L1:
    mov (COORD PTR AllPoints[edi]).X,ax
    mov (COORD PTR AllPoints[edi]).Y,ax
    add edi,TYPE COORD
```

```
        inc ax
        loop L1

        exit
main ENDP
END main
```

10.1.4 Example: Displaying the System Time

MS-Windows provides console functions that set the screen cursor position and get the system time. To use these functions, you have to create instances of two predefined structures: COORD and SYSTEMTIME:

```
COORD STRUCT
    X WORD ?
    Y WORD ?
COORD ENDS

SYSTEMTIME STRUCT
    wYear WORD ?
    wMonth WORD ?
    wDayOfWeek WORD ?
    wDay WORD ?
    wHour WORD?
    wMinute WORD ?
    wSecond WORD ?
    wMilliseconds WORD ?
SYSTEMTIME ENDS
```

Both structures are defined in *SmallWin.inc*, a file located in the assembler's INCLUDE directory, and referenced by *Irvine32.inc*

To get the system time (adjusted for your local time zone), call the MS-Windows **GetLocalTime** function and pass it the address of a SYSTEMTIME structure:

```
.data
sysTime SYSTEMTIME <>
.code
INVOKE GetLocalTime, ADDR sysTime
```

Then retrieve the appropriate values from the SYSTEMTIME structure. For example:

movzx eax,sysTime.wYear

call WriteDec

> The *SmallWin.inc* file, created by the author, contains structure definitions and function prototypes adapted from the Microsoft Windows header files for C and C++ programmers. It represents a small subset of the possible functions that can be called by application programs.

When a Win32 program produces screen output, it calls the MS-Windows **GetStdHandle** function to retrieve the standard console output handle (an integer):

```
.data
consoleHandle DWORD ?
.code
INVOKE GetStdHandle, STD_OUTPUT_HANDLE
mov consoleHandle,eax
```

(The constant STD_OUTPUT_HANDLE is defined *SmallWin.inc*.)

To set the cursor position, call the MS-Windows **SetConsoleCursorPosition** function, passing it the console output handle and a COORD structure variable containing X, Y character coordinates:

```
.data
XYPos COORD <10,5>
.code
INVOKE SetConsoleCursorPosition, consoleHandle, XYPos
```

Program Listing   The following program (*ShowTime.asm*) retrieves the system time and displays it at a selected screen location. It runs only in Protected mode:

```
TITLE Structures                        (ShowTime.ASM)

INCLUDE Irvine32.inc
.data
sysTime SYSTEMTIME <>
XYPos COORD <10,5>
consoleHandle DWORD ?
colonStr BYTE ":",0

.code
main PROC
; Get the standard output handle for the Win32 Console.
    INVOKE GetStdHandle, STD_OUTPUT_HANDLE
    mov consoleHandle,eax

; Set the cursor position and get the system time.
    INVOKE SetConsoleCursorPosition, consoleHandle, XYPos
    INVOKE GetLocalTime, ADDR sysTime

; Display the system time (hh:mm:ss).
    movzx eax,sysTime.wHour        ; hours
    call  WriteDec
    mov   edx,offset colonStr      ; ":"
    call  WriteString
    movzx eax,sysTime.wMinute      ; minutes
    call  WriteDec
    mov   edx,offset colonStr      ; ":"
    call  WriteString
    movzx eax,sysTime.wSecond      ; seconds
    call  WriteDec

    call Crlf
    call Crlf
```

```
        call WaitMsg                    ; "Press Enter..."
        exit
main ENDP
END main
```

The following definitions were used by this program from *SmallWin.inc* (automatically included by *Irvine32.inc*):

```
STD_OUTPUT_HANDLE EQU -11

SYSTEMTIME STRUCT . . .

COORD STRUCT . . .

GetStdHandle PROTO,
    nStdHandle:DWORD

GetLocalTime PROTO,
    lpSystemTime:PTR SYSTEMTIME

SetConsoleCursorPosition PROTO,
    nStdHandle:DWORD,
    coords:COORD
```

Following is a snapshot of the screen output, taken at 12:16 p.m.:

```
            12:16:35

Press [Enter] to continue...
```

10.1.5 Nested Structures

You can create *nested structure definitions,* where structures contain other structures. For example, a **Rectangle** can be defined in terms of its upper-left and lower-right corners, both COORD objects:

```
Rectangle STRUCT
    UpperLeft COORD <>
    LowerRight COORD <>
Rectangle ENDS
```

Rectangle variables can be declared either without any overrides, or by overriding the individual COORD fields. Alternative notational forms are used here:

```
rect1 Rectangle < >
rect2 Rectangle { }
```

```
rect3 Rectangle { {10,10}, {50,20} }
rect4 Rectangle < <10,10>, <50,20> >
```

The following is a direct reference to a nested structure field:

```
mov rect1.UpperLeft.X, 10
```

Using an indirect operand, you can access a nested field. In the following example, we move 40 to the Y coordinate of the upper-left corner of the structure pointed to by ESI:

```
mov esi,OFFSET rect1
mov (Rectangle PTR [esi]).UpperLeft.Y, 10
```

The OFFSET operator can be used to return pointers to individual structure fields, including nested fields:

```
mov edi,OFFSET rect2.LowerRight
mov (COORD PTR [edi]).X, 50
mov edi,OFFSET rect2.LowerRight.X
mov WORD PTR [edi], 50
```

10.1.6 Example: Drunkard's Walk

A number of programming textbooks over the years have included a "Drunkard's Walk" exercise, where the program simulates the path taken by a less-than-sober professor on his or her way home. Using a random number generator, you can choose a direction for each step the professor takes. Usually, you have to check to make sure the person hasn't veered off into a campus lake, but we won't bother with that here. Imagine that the person begins at the center of an imaginary grid, in which each square represents a step in a north, south, east, or west direction. The person follows a random path through the grid:

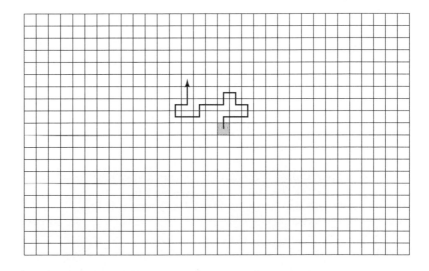

The program that is about to be presented uses a COORD structure to keep track of each step along the path taken by the professor. The steps are stored in an array of COORD objects:

```
WalkMax = 50
DrunkardWalk STRUCT
    path COORD WalkMax DUP(<0,0>)
    pathsUsed WORD 0
DrunkardWalk ENDS
```

Walkmax is a constant that determines the total number of steps taken by the professor in the simulation. The **pathsUsed** field indicates, when the program loop ends, how many steps were taken by the professor. As the professor takes each step, his/her position is stored in a COORD object and inserted in the next available position in the **path** array. The program displays the coordinates on the screen.

Program Listing   Here is the complete program listing:

```
TITLE Drunkard's Walk                  (Walk.asm)

INCLUDE Irvine32.inc
WalkMax = 50
StartX = 25
StartY = 25

DrunkardWalk STRUCT
    path COORD WalkMax DUP(<0,0>)
    pathsUsed WORD 0
DrunkardWalk ENDS

DisplayPosition PROTO currX:WORD, currY:WORD

.data
aWalk DrunkardWalk <>

.code
main PROC
    mov  esi,offset aWalk
    call TakeDrunkenWalk
    exit
main ENDP

;------------------------------------------------------------
TakeDrunkenWalk PROC
LOCAL currX:WORD, currY:WORD
;
; Take a walk in random directions (north, south, east,
; west).
; Receives: ESI points to a DrunkardWalk structure
; Returns:  the structure is initialized with random values
;------------------------------------------------------------
    pushad
```

```
; Point EDI to the array of COORD objects.
    mov edi,esi
    add edi,OFFSET DrunkardWalk.path
    mov ecx,WalkMax              ; loop counter
    mov currX,StartX             ; current X-location
    mov currY,StartY             ; current Y-location

Again:
    ; Insert current location in array.
    mov ax,currX
    mov (COORD PTR [edi]).X,ax
    mov ax,currY
    mov (COORD PTR [edi]).Y,ax

    INVOKE DisplayPosition, currX, currY

    mov  eax,4                   ; choose a direction (0-3)
    call RandomRange

    .IF eax == 0                 ; North
      inc currY
    .ELSEIF eax == 1             ; South
      dec currY
    .ELSEIF eax == 2             ; West
      dec currX
    .ELSE                        ; East (EAX = 3)
      inc currX
    .ENDIF

    add  edi,TYPE COORD          ; point to next COORD
    loop Again

Finish:
    mov (DrunkardWalk PTR [esi]).pathsUsed, WalkMax
    popad
    ret
TakeDrunkenWalk ENDP

;-------------------------------------------------------
DisplayPosition PROC currX:WORD, currY:WORD
; Display the current X and Y positions.
;-------------------------------------------------------
.data
commaStr BYTE ",",0
.code
    pushad
    movzx eax,currX              ; current X position
    call  WriteDec
    mov   edx,OFFSET commaStr    ; "," string
    call  WriteString
```

```
              movzx eax,currY                    ; current Y position
              call  WriteDec
              call  Crlf
              popad
              ret
       DisplayPosition ENDP
       END main
```

(Let us note, for the record, that I have never seen, nor recently heard about, any professors walking home drunk from class.)

TakeDrunkenWalk Procedure   Let's take a closer look at the **TakeDrunkenWalk** procedure. It receives a pointer (ESI) to a **DrunkardWalk** structure. Using the OFFSET operator, it calculates the offset of the **path** array and copies it to EDI:

```
       mov edi,esi
       add edi,OFFSET DrunkardWalk.path
```

The initial X and Y positions (StartX and StartY) of the professor are set to 25, at the center of an imaginary 50-by-50 grid:

```
       mov currX,StartX               ; current X-location
       mov currY,StartY               ; current Y-location
```

At the beginning of the loop, the first two entries in the **path** array are initialized:

```
    Again:
       ; Insert current location in array.
       mov ax,currX
       mov (COORD PTR [edi]).X,ax
       mov ax,currY
       mov (COORD PTR [edi]).Y,ax
```

At the end of the walk, a counter is inserted into the **pathsUsed** field, indicating how many steps were taken:

```
    Finish:
       mov (DrunkardWalk PTR [esi]).pathsUsed, WalkMax
```

In the current version of the program, **pathsUsed** is always equal to **WalkMax**, but that could change if we checked for hazards such as lakes and buildings. Then the loop would terminate before **WalkMax** was reached.

10.1.7   Declaring and Using Unions

Whereas each field in a structure has an offset relative to the first byte of the structure, all the fields in a *union* start at the same offset. The storage size of a union is equal to the length of its longest field. When not part of a structure, a union is declared using the UNION and ENDS directives:

```
unionname UNION
    union-fields
unionname ENDS
```

If the union is nested inside a structure, the syntax is slightly different:

```
structname STRUCT
    structure-fields
    UNION unionname
        union-fields
    ENDS
structname ENDS
```

The field declarations in a union follow the same rules as for structures, except that each field can have only a single initializer. For example, the **Integer** union has three different size attributes for the same data:

```
Integer UNION
    D DWORD 0
    W WORD  0
    B BYTE  0
Integer ENDS
```

You can nest a union inside a structure by using the union name in a declaration, as we have done here for the **FileID** field inside the **FileInfo** structure:

```
FileInfo STRUCT
    FileID Integer <>
    FileName BYTE 64 DUP(?)
FileInfo ENDS
```

Or you can declare a union directly inside the structure, as we have done here for the **FileID** field:

```
FileInfo STRUCT
  UNION FileID
      D DWORD 0
      W WORD  0
      B BYTE  0
  ENDS
  FileName BYTE 64 DUP(?)
FileInfo ENDS
```

Declaring and Using Union Variables   A union variable is declared and initialized in much the same way as a structure variable. There is one important difference: No more than one initializer is permitted. The following are examples of Integer-type variables:

```
val1 Integer <12345678h>
val2 Integer <100h>
val3 Integer <>
```

To use a union variable in an executable instruction, you must supply the name of one of the variant fields. In the following example, we assign register values to the **Integer** union fields. Note the flexibility we have in being able to use different operand sizes:

```
mov val3.B, al
mov val3.W, ax
mov val3.D, eax
```

Unions can also contain structures. The following INPUT_RECORD structure is used by some MS-Windows console input functions. It contains a union named **Event**, which selects between several predefined structure types. The **EventType** field indicates which type of record appears in the union. Each structure has a different layout and size, but only one is used at a time:

```
INPUT_RECORD STRUCT
    EventType WORD ?
    UNION Event
        KEY_EVENT_RECORD <>
        MOUSE_EVENT_RECORD <>
        WINDOW_BUFFER_SIZE_RECORD <>
        MENU_EVENT_RECORD <>
        FOCUS_EVENT_RECORD <>
    ENDS
INPUT_RECORD ENDS
```

A complete definition of INPUT_REC_ STRUCT can be found in the *Microsoft MSDN Platform SDK Reference*. In Chapter 11 we will show how to use the KEY_EVENT_RECORD.

10.1.8 Section Review

1. What is the purpose of the STRUCT directive?
2. Create a structure named **MyStruct** containing two fields: **field1**, a single word, and **field2**, an array of 20 doublewords. The initial values of the fields may be left undefined.

The structure created in Exercise 2 (MyStruct) will be used in Exercises 3 through 11:

3. Declare a **MyStruct** variable with default values.
4. Declare a **MyStruct** variable that initializes the first field to zero.
5. Declare a **MyStruct** variable and initialize the second field to an array containing all zeros.
6. Declare a variable as an array of 20 **MyStruct** objects.
7. Using the **MyStruct** array from the preceding exercise, move **field1** of the first array element to AX.
8. Using the **MyStruct** array from the preceding exercise, use ESI to index to the third array element and move AX to **field1**. *Hint:* Use the PTR operator.
9. What value does the expression **TYPE MyStruct** return?
10. What value does the expression **SIZEOF MyStruct** return?
11. Write an expression that returns the number of bytes in **field2** of **MyStruct**.

The following exercises are not related to MyStruct:

12. Assume that the following structure has been defined:

```
RentalInvoice STRUCT
   invoiceNum BYTE 5 DUP(' ')
   dailyPrice WORD ?
   daysRented WORD ?
RentalInvoice ENDS
```

State whether or not each of the following declarations is valid:

```
a. rentals RentalInvoice <>
b. RentalInvoice rentals <>
c. march RentalInvoice <'12345',10,0>
d. RentalInvoice <,10,0>
e. current RentalInvoice <,15,0,0>
```

13. Write a statement that retrieves the **wHour** field of a SYSTEMTIME structure.

14. Using the following **Triangle** structure, declare a structure variable and initialize its vertices to (0,0), (5, 0), and (7,6):

```
Triangle STRUCT
    Vertex1 COORD <>
    Vertex2 COORD <>
    Vertex3 COORD <>
Triangle ENDS
```

15. Declare an array of **Triangle** structures. Write a loop that initializes **Vertex1** of each triangle to random coordinates in the range (0..10, 0..10).

10.2 Macros

10.2.1 Overview

A *macro procedure* is a named block of assembly language statements. Once defined, it can be invoked (called) as many times in a program as you wish. When you *invoke* a macro procedure, a copy of its statements is inserted directly into the program. It is customary to refer to *calling* a macro procedure, although technically there is no CALL instruction involved.

> The term *macro procedure* is used in the Microsoft Assembler manual to identify macros that do not return a value. There are also *macro functions* that return a value. Among programmers, the word *macro* is usually understood to mean the same thing as *macro procedure*. From this point on, we will use the shorter form.

Location Macros are either coded directly in the source program (usually at the beginning), or they are placed in a separate text file and inserted into the source program during assembly using the INCLUDE directive. A macro definition must be found by the assembler before trying to assemble any calls to the macro. The assembler's preprocessor scans the macros and places them in a buffer. When calls to the macro are found, each macro call is replaced by a copy of the macro. In the following example, a macro named **NewLine** contains a single statement that calls the **Crlf** library procedure:

```
NewLine MACRO
    call Crlf
ENDM
```

This definition would normally be placed just before the data segment. Next, in the code segment, we call the macro:

```
.code
    NewLine
```

When the preprocessor scans this program and discovers the call to **NewLine**, it replaces the macro call with the following statement:

```
    call Crlf
```

All that has taken place is text substitution. This particular example could have been accomplished using the TEXTEQU directive, but we will soon show how to pass arguments to macros, making them far more powerful than TEXTEQU.

10.2.2 Defining Macros

A macro can be defined anywhere in a program's source code, using the MACRO and ENDM directives. The syntax is:

```
macroname MACRO parameter-1, parameter-2...
    statement-list
ENDM
```

There is no set rule regarding indentation, but you should indent statements between *macroname* and ENDM to show that they belong to the macro. For consistency, you may want to use a special prefix character. In this book, we use a lowercase "m" prefix, creating recognizable macro names such as mPutchar, mWriteString, and mGotoxy.

The statements between the MACRO and ENDM directives are not assembled until the macro is invoked. There can be any number of parameters in the macro definition, as long as they are separated by commas.

mPutchar Macro Example   Let's create a macro named **mPutchar** that takes a single input parameter called **char** and displays it on the console by calling **WriteChar** from the book's link library:

```
mPutchar MACRO char
    push eax
    mov  al,char
    call WriteChar
```

```
    pop eax
ENDM
```

Required Parameters   Using the REQ qualifier, you can specify that a macro parameter is required. If the macro is called without an argument to match the required parameter, the assembler displays an error. For example:

```
mPutchar MACRO char:REQ
    push eax
    mov  al,char
    call WriteChar
    pop eax
ENDM
```

If a macro has multiple required parameters, each one must include the REQ qualifier.

Macro Comments   Commented lines in macros usually begin with a double semicolon (;;). The macro comments appear when the macro is defined, but not when the macro is expanded.

> In general, macros execute more quickly than procedures because procedures have the extra overhead of CALL and RET instructions. There is, however, one disadvantage to using macros: repeated use of large macros tends to increase a program's size because each call to a macro inserts a new copy of the macro's statements in the program.

Using the ECHO Directive   The ECHO directive displays a message on the console as the program is assembled. In the following version of **mPutchar**, the message "Expanding the mPutchar macro" appears on the console during assembly:

```
mPutchar MACRO char:REQ
    ECHO Expanding the mPutchar macro
    push eax
    mov al,char
    call WriteChar
    pop eax
ENDM
```

10.2.3 Invoking Macros

A macro is invoked (called) by inserting its name into a program's source code, possibly followed by macro arguments. The syntax for calling a macro is:

```
macroname argument-1, argument-2, ...
```

Macroname must be the name of a macro defined prior to this point in the source code. Each argument is a text value that replaces a parameter in the macro. The order of arguments must correspond to the order of parameters, but the number of arguments does not have to match the number of parameters. If too many arguments are passed, the assembler issues a warning. If too few arguments are passed to a macro, the unfilled parameters are left blank.

Invoking mPutchar   In the previous section, we defined the **mPutChar** macro. When invoking mPutchar, we can pass any character or ASCII code. The following statement invokes mPutchar and passes it the letter A:

```
mPutchar 'A'
```

The assembler's preprocessor automatically expands the statement into the following code, shown in the listing file:

```
1   push eax
1   mov  al,'A'
1   call WriteChar
1   pop  eax
```

The '1' in the left column indicates the macro expansion level, which increases when you call other macros from within a macro. The following loop displays the first twenty letters of the alphabet:

```
        mov al,'A'
        mov ecx,20
L1:
        mPutchar al                 ; macro call
        inc  al
        loop L1
```

This loop is expanded by the preprocessor into the following code (visible in the source listing file). The macro call is shown just before its expansion:

```
        mov  al,'A'
        mov  ecx,20
L1:
        mPutchar al                 ; macro call
1   push eax
1   mov  al,al
1   call WriteChar
1   pop  eax
        inc  al
        loop L1
```

10.2.4 Macro Examples

In this section, we present a number of macros that you might find useful. All of them appear in a file named *Macros.inc*, which can be copied into your programs. Use the following sequence of INCLUDE directives when you test the macros:

```
INCLUDE Irvine32.inc
INCLUDE Macros.inc
```

10.2.4.1   mWriteStr Macro

Let's create a macro named **mWriteStr** that writes a string to standard output by calling **WriteString** from the book's link library. There is one parameter containing the name of the string to be displayed:

```
mWriteStr MACRO string
    push edx
    mov  edx,OFFSET string
    call WriteString
    pop  edx
ENDM
```

mWriteStr takes care of the tedious work of saving EDX on the stack, filling EDX with the string's offset, and popping EDX from the stack after the procedure call. (Recall that we should always save and restore EDX because it might hold other important data.)

If **mWriteStr** were only used once in a program, the savings of coding time would not be dramatic. But when the same macro is used numerous times, a lot of time is saved performing repetitious tasks.

The parameter called **string** is replaced each time the macro is called. For example, to display three different strings, we call the macro three times, passing a different argument each time:

```
.data
msg1 BYTE "This is message 1.",0Dh,0Ah,'$'
msg2 BYTE "This is message 2.",0Dh,0Ah,'$'
msg3 BYTE "This is message 3.",0Dh,0Ah,'$'
.code
mWriteStr msg1
mWriteStr msg2
mWriteStr msg3
```

The following is excerpted from a listing file in which each call to **mWriteStr** is followed by the statements it generates:

```
mWriteStr msg1
1   push edx
1   mov  edx,OFFSET msg1
1   call WriteString
1   pop  edx
mWriteStr msg2
1   push edx
1   mov  edx,OFFSET msg2
1   call WriteString
1   pop  edx
mWriteStr msg3
1   push edx
1   mov  edx,OFFSET msg3
1   call WriteString
1   pop  edx
```

10.2.4.2   mReadStr Macro

The **mReadStr** macro encapsulates a call to the **ReadString** library procedure. It receives the name of an array of characters:

```
mReadStr MACRO varName
    push ecx
    push edx
    mov  edx,OFFSET varName
    mov  ecx,(SIZEOF varName) - 1
    call ReadString
    pop  edx
    pop  ecx
ENDM
```

Following is a sample call to **mReadStr**:

```
.data
firstName BYTE 30 DUP(?)
.code
mReadStr firstName
```

10.2.4.3   mGotoxy Macro

The **mGotoxy** macro locates the cursor at a specific row and column on the screen. Using the REQ qualifier, we can specify that a macro parameter is required. If the macro is called without an argument to match the required parameter, an error message is generated by the assembler:

```
mGotoxy MACRO X:REQ, Y:REQ
    push edx
    mov dh,Y                    ;; row
    mov dl,X                    ;; column
    call Gotoxy
    pop edx
ENDM
```

The macro can be called and passed immediate values, memory operands, or register values, as long as they are 8-bit integers:

```
mGotoxy   10,20                ; immediate values
mGotoxy   row,col              ; memory operands
mGotoxy   ch,cl                ; register values
```

Check for Conflicts   Be sure that register values passed as arguments do not conflict with registers used inside a macro. If we call **mGotoxy** using DH and DL, for instance, the macro does not work properly. To see why, let's inspect the expanded code after the parameters have been substituted:

```
1   push edx
2   mov dh,dl                   ;; row
```

```
3   mov dl,dh                        ;; column
4   call Gotoxy
5   pop edx
```

Assuming that DL is passed as the Y-value and DH is the X-value, line 2 replaces DH before we have a chance to copy the column value to DL on line 3.

10.2.4.4   mDumpMem Macro

As you probably noticed even back in Chapter 5, procedure calls can be awkward when you pass parameters in registers. For example, the **DumpMem** procedure from the book's link library requires passing an address in ESI, the number of displayed units in ECX, and the memory unit size in EBX (1, 2, or 4). In the following example, we display eight doublewords belonging to **array**:

```
push ebx                        ; save registers
push ecx
push esi
mov   esi,OFFSET array          ; addr of the array
mov   ecx,8                     ; item count
mov   ebx,TYPE array            ; display doublewords
call  DumpMem
pop   esi                       ; restore registers
pop   ecx
pop   ebx
```

It might be that ESI, EBX, and ECX were holding other important data before this procedure call, making it necessary to push and pop their values.

It can be useful to write a macro that acts as a wrapper around a procedure call. The macro can save existing register values, place each argument in an appropriate register, call the procedure, and restore the register values. The following **mDumpMem** macro calls the **DumpMem** procedure:

```
mDumpMem MACRO address,          ;; address of variable
    itemCount,                   ;; number of items
    componentSize                ;; size of each item
    push ebx                     ;; save registers
    push ecx
    push esi
    mov esi,address              ;; initialize arguments
    mov ecx,itemCount
    mov ebx,componentSize
    call DumpMem                 ;; call library procedure
    pop esi                      ;; restore registers
    pop ecx
    pop ebx
ENDM
```

The following statement invokes **mDumpMem**:

```
mDumpMem OFFSET array, 8, 4
```

An alternative format for invoking the macro permits you to use a line-continuation character (\) at the end of the first and second lines:

```
mDumpMem OFFSET array,      \          ; array offset
    LENGTHOF array,         \          ; number of units
    TYPE array                         ; size of each unit
```

You can then place a comment on each line, explaining the macro argument.

10.2.4.5   Macros Containing Code and Data

In addition to producing executable instructions, macros can also produce data. The **mWrite** macro, for example, displays a literal string on the console:

```
mWrite MACRO text
    LOCAL string                       ;; local label
    .data
    string BYTE text,0                 ;; define the string
    .code
    push edx
    mov  edx,OFFSET string
    call Writestring
    pop  edx
ENDM
```

Notice that something new was used here. The LOCAL directive instructs the preprocessor to create a unique label name each time the **mWrite** macro is expanded. This avoids the naming conflict that would result if **mWrite** were expanded twice within the same file. The following statements invoke **mWrite** twice, passing it different string literals:

```
mWrite "Please enter your first name"
mWrite "Please enter your last name"
```

The expansion of these two statements by the assembler (copied from the source listing file) shows how each string is declared with a different label:

```
      mWrite "Please enter your first name"
1     .data
1     ??0000 BYTE "Please enter your first name",0
1     .code
1     push edx
1     mov  edx,OFFSET ??0000
1     call Writestring
1     pop  edx
```

```
       mWrite "Please enter your last name"
1    .data
1    ??0001 BYTE "Please enter your last name",0
1    .code
1    push edx
1    mov  edx,OFFSET ??0001
1    call Writestring
1    pop  edx
```

The label names produced by the assembler have the form *??nnnn*, where *nnnn* is a unique integer. The LOCAL directive should also be used for code labels within a macro. Then the macro can be invoked more than once.

10.2.5   Nested Macros

It sometimes helps to use a modular approach when creating macros. Keep each macro short and simple, and use it as a building block to make more elaborate macros. You can (hopefully) minimize the writing of duplicate code. When a macro is invoked from another macro, it is called a *nested* macro. There is really no disadvantage to using nested macros, because the preprocessor expands them as if all statements belonged to the same macro. A parameter passed to the outside macro can be passed directly to the enclosed macro.

mWriteLn Macro   For example, it would be nice to have a macro named **mWriteLn** that not only writes a string literal to the console, but also appends an end of line. The macro can first invoke **mWrite** and then call the **Crlf** function from the link library:

```
mWriteLn MACRO text
    mWrite text
    call Crlf
ENDM
```

The **text** parameter is passed directly to the **mWrite** macro. When the macro is used in a program, it looks like the following:

```
mWriteLn "My Sample Macro Program"
```

In the source listing file, the nesting level (2) next to the statements indicates that a nested macro has been expanded:

```
       mWriteLn "My Sample Macro Program"
2    .data
2    ??0002 BYTE "My Sample Macro Program",0
2    .code
2    push edx
2    mov  edx,OFFSET ??0002
```

```
2    call Writestring
2    pop  edx
1    call Crlf
```

10.2.6 Example Program: Wrappers

Let's create a short program (*Wraps.asm*) that shows off the macros we've already introduced as procedure wrappers. Because each macro hides a lot of tedious parameter passing, the program is surprisingly compact. We will assume that all of the macros shown so far are located inside the *Macros.inc* file:

```
TITLE Procedure Wrapper Macros            (Wraps.asm)

INCLUDE Irvine32.inc
INCLUDE Macros.inc                    ; macro definitions

.data
array DWORD 1,2,3,4,5,6,7,8
firstName BYTE 31 DUP(?)
lastName  BYTE 31 DUP(?)

.code
main PROC
    mGotoxy 20,0
    mWriteLn "Sample Macro Program"

    mGotoxy 0,5
    mWrite "Please enter your first name: "
    mReadStr firstName
    call Crlf
    mWrite "Please enter your last name: "
    mReadStr lastName
    call Crlf

; Display the person's complete name:
    mWrite "Your name is "
    mWriteStr firstName
    mWrite " "
    mWriteStr lastName

    call Crlf
    mDumpMem OFFSET array, LENGTHOF array, TYPE array

    exit
main ENDP
END main
```

Program Output   The following is a sample of the program's output:

```
Sample Macro Program


Please enter your first name: Kip

Please enter your last name: Irvine

Your name is Kip Irvine

Dump of offset 00404000
--------------------------------
00000001  00000002  00000003  00000004  00000005  00000006
00000007  00000008
```

10.2.7   Section Review

1. (*True/False*): When a macro is invoked, the CALL and RET instructions are automatically inserted into the assembled program.
2. (*True/False*): Macro expansion is handled by the assembler's preprocessor.
3. What is the primary advantage to using a macro versus using the TEXTEQU directive?
4. (*True/False*): As long as it is in the code segment, a macro definition may appear either before or after statements that invoke the macro.
5. (*True/False*): Replacing a procedure with a macro containing the procedure's code will increase the compiled code size of a program if the macro is invoked multiple times.
6. (*True/False*): A macro cannot contain data definitions.
7. What is the purpose of the LOCAL directive?
8. Which directive displays a message on the console during the assembly step?
9. Write a macro named **OutChar** that displays a single character on the screen. It should have a single parameter, the character to be displayed.
10. Write a macro named **mGenRandom** that generates a random integer between 0 and $n-1$. Let n be the only parameter.
11. Write a nested macro that invokes the **mWrite** macro from Section 10.2.4.5.
12. Write a nested macro that invokes both the **mGotoxy** macro from Section 10.2.4.3 and the **mWrite** macro from Section 10.2.4.5.
13. Show the expanded code produced by the following statement that invokes the **mWriteStr** macro from Section 10.2.4.1:

    ```
    mWriteStr namePrompt
    ```

14. Show the expanded code produced by the following statement that invokes the **mReadStr** macro from Section 10.2.4.2:

    ```
    mReadStr customerName
    ```

15. *Challenge:* Write a macro named **mDumpMemx** that receives a single parameter, the name of a variable. Your macro must call the **mDumpMem** macro, passing it the variable's offset, number of units, and unit size. Demonstrate a call to the mDumpMemx macro.

10.3 Conditional-Assembly Directives

A number of different conditional-assembly directives can be used in conjunction with macros to make them more flexible. The general syntax for conditional-assembly directives is:

```
IF condition
    statements
[ELSE
    statements]
ENDIF
```

Table 10-1 lists the more common conditional-assembly directives. When the descriptions say that a directive *permits assembly,* it means that any subsequent statements are assembled up to the next ENDIF directive. It must be emphasized that the directives listed in the table are evaluated at assembly time, not at runtime.

Table 10-1   Conditional-Assembly Directives.

IF *expression*	Permits assembly if the value of *expression* is true (nonzero). Possible relational operators are LT, GT, EQ, NE, LE, and GE.
IFB <*argument*>	Permits assembly if *argument* is blank. The argument name must be enclosed in angle brackets (<>).
IFNB <*argument*>	Permits assembly if *argument* is not blank. The argument name must be enclosed in angle brackets (<>).
IFIDN <*arg1*>,<*arg2*>	Permits assembly if the two arguments are equal (identical). Uses a case-sensitive comparison.
IFIDNI <*arg1*>,<*arg2*>	Permits assembly if the two arguments are equal. Uses a case-insensitive comparison.
IFDIF <*arg1*>,<*arg2*>	Permits assembly if the two arguments are unequal. Uses a case-sensitive comparison.
IFDIFI <*arg1*>,<*arg2*>	Permits assembly if the two arguments are unequal. Uses a case-insensitive comparison.
IFDEF *name*	Permits assembly if *name* has been defined.
IFNDEF *name*	Permits assembly if *name* has not been defined.

Table 10-1   Conditional-Assembly Directives. (Continued)

ENDIF	Ends a block that was begun using one of the conditional-assembly directives.
ELSE	Assembles all statements up to ENDIF if the condition specified by a previous conditional directive is false.
EXITM	Exits a macro immediately, preventing any following macro statements from being expanded.

10.3.1   Checking for Missing Arguments

A macro can check to see if any of its arguments are blank. Often, if a blank argument is received by a macro, invalid instructions result when the macro is expanded by the preprocessor. For example, if we invoke the **mWriteStr** macro without passing an argument, the macro expands with an invalid instruction when moving the string offset to EDX. The following are statements generated by the assembler, which detects the missing operand and issues an error message:

```
mWriteStr
1   push edx
1   mov   edx,OFFSET
Macro2.asm(18) : error A2081: missing operand after unary operator
1   call WriteString
1   pop   edx
```

To prevent errors caused by missing operands, you can use the IFB (*if blank*) directive, which returns true if a macro argument is blank. Or you can use the IFNB (*if not blank*) operator, which returns true if a macro argument is not blank. Let's create a new version of **mWriteStr** that displays an error message during assembly:

```
mWriteStr MACRO string
    IFB <string>
        ECHO ----------------------------------------
        ECHO *   Error: parameter missing in mWriteStr
        ECHO *   (no code generated)
        ECHO ----------------------------------------
        EXITM
    ENDIF
    push edx
    mov   edx,OFFSET string
    call WriteString
    pop   edx
ENDM
```

(Recall from Section 10.2.2 that the ECHO directive writes a message to the console while a program is being assembled.) The EXITM directive tells the preprocessor to exit the macro and to not expand any more statements from the macro.

The following shows the screen output when assembling a program with a missing parameter:

```
Assembling: Macro2.asm
------------------------------------------
*   Error: parameter missing in mWriteStr
*   (no code generated)
------------------------------------------
```

10.3.2   Default Argument Initializers

Macros can have default argument initializers. If a macro argument is missing when the macro is called, the default argument is used instead. The syntax is:

```
paramname := < argument >
```

(Spaces before and after the operators are optional.)

For example, the **mWriteLn** macro can supply a string containing a single space as its default argument. If it is called with no arguments, it still prints a space followed by an end of line:

```
mWriteLn MACRO text:=<" ">
    mWrite text
    call Crlf
ENDM
```

The assembler issues an error if a null string ("") is used as the default argument, so we have to insert at least one space between the quotes.

10.3.3   Boolean Expressions

The assembler permits the following relational operators to be used in constant boolean expressions:

LT	Less than
GT	Greater than
EQ	Equal to
NE	Not equal to
LE	Less than or equal to
GE	Greater than or equal to

10.3.4 IF, ELSE, and ENDIF Directives

The IF directive must be followed by a constant boolean expression. The expression can contain integer constants, symbolic constants, or constant macro arguments, but it cannot contain register or variable names. One syntax format uses just IF and ENDIF:

```
IF expression
    statement-list
ENDIF
```

Another format uses IF, ELSE, and ENDIF:

```
IF expression
    statement-list
ELSE
    statement-list
ENDIF
```

Example: mGotoxyConst Macro   The **mGotoxyConst** macro uses the LT and GT operators to perform range checking on the arguments passed to the macro. The arguments X and Y must be constants. Another constant symbol named ERRS counts the number of errors found. Depending on the value of X, we may set ERRS to 1. Depending on the value of Y, we may add 1 to ERRS. Finally, if ERRS is greater than zero, the EXITM directive exits the macro:

```
;-------------------------------------------------------
mGotoxyConst MACRO X:REQ, Y:REQ
;
; Set the cursor position
; This version checks the ranges of X and Y.
; are not used.
;-------------------------------------------------------
    LOCAL ERRS                     ;; local constant
    ERRS = 0
    IF (X LT 0) OR (X GT 79)
        ECHO Warning: First argument to mGotoxy (X) is out of range.
        ECHO ****************************************************
        ERRS = 1
    ENDIF
    IF (Y LT 0) OR (Y GT 24)
        ECHO Warning: Second argument to mGotoxy (Y) is out of range.
        ECHO ****************************************************
        ERRS = ERRS + 1
    ENDIF
    IF ERRS GT 0                   ;; if errors found,
      EXITM                        ;; exit the macro
    ENDIF
    push edx
    mov  dh,Y
```

```
        mov   dl,X
        call  Gotoxy
        pop   edx
ENDM
```

10.3.5   The IFIDN and IFIDNI Directives

The IFIDNI directive performs a case-insensitive match between two symbols (including macro parameter names), and returns true if they are equal. The IFIDN directive performs a case-sensitive match. IFIDNI is particularly useful when you want to make sure the caller of your macro has not used a register argument that might conflict with register usage inside the macro. Its syntax is:

```
IFIDNI <symbol>, <symbol>
    statements
ENDIF
```

The syntax for IFIDN is identical.

In the following **mReadBuf** macro, for example, the second argument cannot be EDX because it will be overwritten when the offset of **buffer** is moved into EDX. The following revised version of the macro displays a warning message if this requirement is not met:

```
;---------------------------------------------------------
mReadBuf MACRO bufferPtr, maxChars
;
; Read from standard input into a buffer.
; The second argument cannot be edx/EDX
;---------------------------------------------------------
    IFIDNI <maxChars>,<EDX>
        ECHO Warning: Second argument to mReadBuf cannot be EDX
        ECHO **************************************************
        EXITM
    ENDIF
    push ecx
    push edx
    mov  edx,bufferPtr
    mov  ecx,maxChars
    call ReadString
    pop  edx
    pop  ecx
ENDM
```

The following statement causes the macro to generate a warning message because EDX is the second argument:

```
mReadBuf OFFSET buffer,edx
```

10.3.6   Special Operators

As shown below, there are four assembler operators that make macros more flexible:

&	Substitution operator
<>	Literal-text operator
!	Literal-character operator
%	Expansion operator

10.3.6.1   Substitution Operator (&)

The *substitution* (&) operator resolves ambiguous references to parameter names within a macro. For example, suppose that a macro named **ShowRegister** displays the name and hexadecimal contents of a 32-bit register. The following would be a sample call:

```
.code
ShowRegister ECX
```

Following is a sample of the output generated by the call to ShowRegister:

```
ECX=00000101
```

A string variable containing the register name could be defined inside the macro:

```
ShowRegister MACRO regName
.data
tempStr BYTE " regName=",0
```

But the preprocessor would assume that **regName** was part of a string literal and would not replace it with the argument value passed to the macro. Instead, if we add the & operator, it forces the preprocessor to insert the macro argument (such as ECX) into the string literal. The following shows how to define **tempStr**:

```
ShowRegister MACRO regName
.data
tempStr BYTE " &regName=",0
```

The following listing contains the complete **ShowRegister** macro. It is defined in the *Macros.inc* file and used by the **DumpRegs** procedure:

```
;----------------------------------------------------
ShowRegister MACRO regName
             LOCAL tempStr
; Display a 32-bit register name and its contents.
;----------------------------------------------------
```

```
.data
tempStr BYTE "   &regName=",0
.code
    push eax
    push edx

; Display the register name
    mov   edx,offset tempStr
    call  WriteString

; Display the register contents in hexadecimal
    mov   eax,regName
    call  WriteHex

    pop   edx
    pop   eax
ENDM
```

10.3.6.2   Expansion Operator (%)

The *expansion* operator (%) expands text macros or converts constant expressions into their text representations. It does this in several different ways. When used with TEXTEQU, the % operator evaluates a constant expression and converts the result to an integer.

In the following example, the % operator evaluates the expression (5 + count) and returns the integer 15 (as text):

```
count = 10
sumVal TEXTEQU %(5 + count)          ; = "15"
```

If a macro requires a constant integer argument, the % operator gives you the flexibility of passing an integer expression. The expression is evaluated to its integer value, which is then passed to the macro. For example, when invoking **mGotoxyConst**, the expressions here evaluate to 50 and 7:

```
mGotoxyConst %(5 * 10), %(3 + 4)
```

The preprocessor produces the following statements:

```
1    push edx
1    mov  dh,7
1    mov  dl,50
1    call Gotoxy
1    pop  edx
```

% at Beginning of Line   When the expansion operator (%) is the first character on a source code line, it instructs the preprocessor to expand all text macros and macro functions found on the same line. Suppose, for example, we wanted to display the size of an array on the screen during assembly. The following attempts would not produce the intended result:

```
.data
array DWORD 1,2,3,4,5,6,7,8
```

```
.code
ECHO The array contains (SIZEOF array) bytes
ECHO The array contains %(SIZEOF array) bytes
```

The screen output would be useless:

```
The array contains (SIZEOF array) bytes
The array contains %(SIZEOF array) bytes
```

Instead, if we use TEXTEQU to create a text macro containing (SIZEOF array), the macro can be expanded on the next line:

```
TempStr TEXTEQU %(SIZEOF array)
%   ECHO The array contains TempStr bytes
```

The following output is produced:

```
The array contains 32 bytes
```

Displaying the Line Number   Let's look at a macro named **Mul32** that multiplies its first two arguments together and returns the product in the third argument. It can handle registers, memory operands, and even immediate operands (except for the product):

```
MUL32 MACRO op1, op2, product
    IFIDNI <op2>,<EAX>
      LINENUM TEXTEQU %(@LINE)
      ECHO --------------------------------------------------
%     ECHO *  Error on line LINENUM: EAX cannot be the second
      ECHO *  argument when invoking the MUL32 macro.
      ECHO --------------------------------------------------
    EXITM
    ENDIF
    push eax
    mov  eax,op1
    mul  op2
    mov  product,eax
    pop  eax
ENDM
```

Mul32 checks one important requirement, that EAX cannot be the second argument. What is interesting about the macro is that it displays the line number from where the macro was called, to make it easier to track down and fix the problem.

The Text macro LINENUM is defined first. It references @LINE, a predefined assembler operator that returns the current source code line number:

```
LINENUM TEXTEQU %(@LINE)
```

Next, the expansion operator (%) in the first column of the line containing the ECHO statement causes LINENUM to be expanded:

```
%       ECHO *   Error on line LINENUM: EAX cannot be the second
```

Suppose the following macro call occurs in a program on line 40:

```
    MUL32 val1,eax,val3
```

Then the following message is displayed during assembly:

```
    ----------------------------------------------------
    *   Error on line 40: EAX cannot be the second
    *   argument when invoking the MUL32 macro.
    ----------------------------------------------------
```

You can view a test of the **Mul32** macro in the program named *Macro3.asm*.

10.3.6.3   Literal-Text Operator (<>)

The *literal-text* operator (<>) groups one or more characters and symbols into a single text literal. It prevents the preprocessor from interpreting members of the list as separate arguments. This operator is particularly useful when a string contains special characters, such as commas, percent signs (%), ampersands (&), and semicolons (;), that would otherwise be interpreted as delimiters or other operators.

For example, the **mWrite** macro presented earlier in this chapter receives a string literal as its only argument. If we were to pass it the following string, the preprocessor would interpret it as three separate macro arguments:

```
    mWrite "Line three", 0dh, 0ah
```

Everything after the first comma would be ignored because the macro expects only one argument. On the other hand, if we surrounded the string with the literal-text operator, the preprocessor would consider it all to be a single macro argument, commas and all:

```
    mWrite <"Line three", 0dh, 0ah>
```

10.3.6.4   Literal-Character Operator (!)

The *literal-character* operator (!) was invented for much the same purpose as the literal-text operator: It forces the preprocessor to treat a predefined operator as an ordinary character. In the following TEXTEQU definition, the ! operator prevents the > symbol from being a text delimiter:

```
    BadYValue TEXTEQU <Warning: Y-coordinate is !> 24>
```

Warning Message Example   The following example helps to show how the %, &, and ! operators work together. Let's assume that we have defined the **BadYValue** symbol. We can create a macro named **ShowWarning** that receives a text argument, encloses it in quotes, and passes the literal to the **mWrite** macro. Note the use of the substitution (&) operator:

```
ShowWarning MACRO message
    mWrite "&message"
ENDM
```

Next, we invoke **ShowWarning**, passing it the expression %BadYValue. The % operator evaluates (dereferences) **BadYValue** and produces its equivalent string:

```
.code
ShowWarning %BadYValue
```

As you might expect, the program runs and displays the warning message:

```
Warning: Y-coordinate is > 24
```

10.3.7   Macro Functions

A macro function is similar to a macro procedure in that it assigns a name to a list of assembly language statements. It is different in that it always returns a constant (integer or string) using the EXITM directive.

In the following example, the **IsDefined** macro returns true (-1) if a given symbol has been defined; otherwise, it returns false (0):

```
IsDefined MACRO symbol
    IFDEF symbol
      EXITM <-1>                   ;; True
    ELSE
      EXITM <0>                    ;; False
    ENDIF
ENDM
```

The EXITM (exit macro) directive halts all further expansion of the macro.

Calling a Macro Function   When you call a macro function, its argument list must be enclosed in parentheses. For example, we can call the **IsDefined** macro, passing it **RealMode**, the name of a symbol which may or may not have been defined:

```
IF IsDefined( RealMode )
  mov ax,@data
  mov ds,ax
ENDIF
```

If the assembler has already encountered a definition of **RealMode** before this point in the assembly process, it assembles the two instructions:

```
mov ax,@data
mov ds,ax
```

The same IF directive can be placed inside a macro named **Startup**:

```
Startup MACRO
    IF IsDefined( RealMode )
      mov ax,@data
      mov ds,ax
    ENDIF
ENDM
```

A macro such as **IsDefined** can be useful when you design programs that are assembled for different memory models. For example, we can use it to determine which include file to use:

```
IF IsDefined( RealMode )
    INCLUDE Irvine16.inc
ELSE
    INCLUDE Irvine32.inc
ENDIF
```

Defining the RealMode Symbol   All that remains is to find a way to define the **RealMode** symbol. One way is to put the following line at the beginning of a program:

```
RealMode = 1
```

Alternatively, the assembler's command line has an option for defining symbols, using the –D switch. The following ML command defines the RealMode symbol and assigns it a value of 1:

```
ML -c -DRealMode=1 myProg.asm
```

The corresponding ML command for Protected mode programs should not define the RealMode symbol:

```
ML -c -coff myProg.asm
```

The HelloNew Program   The following program (*HelloNew.asm*) uses the macros we have just described, displaying a message on the screen:

```
TITLE Macro Functions              (HelloNew.asm)

INCLUDE Macros.inc
IF IsDefined( RealMode )
    INCLUDE Irvine16.inc
ELSE
    INCLUDE Irvine32.inc
ENDIF

.code
main PROC
    Startup
    mWriteLn "This program can be assembled to run "
    mWriteLn "in both Real mode and Protected mode."
    exit
```

```
main ENDP
END main
```

This program can be assembled in either Real-address mode, using *makeHello16.bat*, or in Protected mode using *make32.bat*.

10.3.8   Section Review

1. What is the purpose of the IFB directive?
2. What is the purpose of the IFIDN directive?
3. Which directive stops all further expansion of a macro?
4. How is IFIDNI different from IFIDN?
5. What is the purpose of the IFDEF directive?
6. Which directive marks the end of a conditional block of statements?
7. Show an example of a macro parameter having a default argument initializer.
8. List all the relational operators that can be used in constant boolean expressions.
9. Write a short example that uses the IF, ELSE, and ENDIF directives.
10. Write a statement using the IF directive that checks the value of macro parameter Z; if Z is less than zero, display a message during assembly indicating that Z is invalid.
11. What is the purpose of the & operator in a macro definition?
12. What is the purpose of the ! operator in a macro definition?
13. What is the purpose of the % operator in a macro definition?
14. Write a short macro that demonstrates the use of the & operator when the macro parameter is embedded in a literal string.
15. Assume the following **mLocate** macro definition:

```
mLocate MACRO xval,yval
    IF xval LT 0                          ;; xval < 0?
      EXITM                               ;; if so, exit
    ENDIF
    IF yval LT 0                          ;; yval < 0?
      EXITM                               ;; if so, exit
    ENDIF
    mov bx,0                              ;; video page 0
    mov ah,2                              ;; locate cursor
    mov dh,yval
    mov dl,xval
    int 10h                               ;; call the BIOS
ENDM
```

Show the source code generated by the preprocessor when the macro is expanded by each of the following statements:

```
.data
row BYTE 15
col BYTE 60
```

```
.code
mLocate -2,20
mLocate 10,20
mLocate col,row
```

10.4   Defining Repeat Blocks

MASM has a number of looping directives for generating repeated blocks of statements: WHILE, REPEAT, FOR, and FORC. Unlike the LOOP instruction, these directives work only at assembly time, using constant values as loop conditions and counters:

- The WHILE directive repeats a statement block based on a boolean expression.
- The REPEAT directive repeats a statement block based on the value of a counter.
- The FOR directive repeats a statement block by iterating over a list of symbols.
- The FORC directive repeats a statement block by iterating over a string of characters.

Each is demonstrated in an example program named *Repeat.asm*.

> The constant directives shown in this chapter should not be confused with the run-time directives such as .IF and .ENDIF that were introduced in Section 6.7 of Chapter 6. The latter were able to evaluate expressions based on runtime values such as registers and variables.

10.4.1   WHILE Directive

The WHILE directive repeats a statement block as long as a particular constant expression is true. The syntax is:

```
WHILE constExpression
    statements
ENDM
```

The following code shows how to generate Fibonacci numbers between 1 and F0000000h as a series of assembly-time constants:

```
.data
val1 = 1
val2 = 1
DWORD val1                          ; first two values
DWORD val2
val3 = val1 + val2
WHILE val3 LT 0F0000000h
    DWORD val3
    val1 = val2
    val2 = val3
    val3 = val1 + val2
ENDM
```

The values generated by this code can be viewed in a listing (.LST) file.

10.4.2   REPEAT Directive

The REPEAT directive repeats a statement block a fixed number of times. The syntax is:

```
REPEAT constExpression
    statements
ENDM
```

ConstExpression, an unsigned constant integer expression, determines the number of repetitions. The following REPEAT loop, for example, creates an array of 100 doublewords and initializes their values in the sequence {10,20,30,40,...,1000}:

```
iVal = 10
REPEAT 100
    DWORD iVal
    iVal = iVal + 10
ENDM
```

> In MASM 5, the REPEAT directive was called REP. You can still use the old name.

10.4.3   FOR Directive

The FOR directive repeats a statement block by iterating over a comma-delimited list of symbols. Each symbol in the list causes one iteration of the loop. The syntax is:

```
FOR parameter,<arg1,arg2,arg3,...>
    statements
ENDM
```

On the first loop iteration, *parameter* takes on the value of *arg1*; on the second iteration, *parameter* takes on the value of *arg2*, and so on through the last argument in the list.

> MASM 5 programs used IRP rather than FOR. You can still use IRP.

Student Enrollment Example   Let's create a student enrollment scenario in which we have a COURSE structure containing a course number and number of credits. A SEMESTER structure contains an array of six courses and a counter named **NumCourses**:

```
COURSE STRUCT
    Number  BYTE 9 DUP(?)
    Credits BYTE ?
COURSE ENDS

; A semester contains an array of courses.
SEMESTER STRUC
    Courses COURSE 6 DUP(<>)
    NumCourses WORD ?
SEMESTER ENDS
```

We can use a FOR loop to define four SEMESTER objects, each having a different name selected from the list of symbols between angle brackets:

```
.data
FOR semName,<Fall1999,Spring2000,Summer2000,Fall2000>
    semName SEMESTER <>
ENDM
```

If we inspect the listing file, we find the following variables:

```
.data
Fall1999 SEMESTER <>
Spring2000 SEMESTER <>
Summer2000 SEMESTER <>
Fall2000 SEMESTER <>
```

10.4.4 FORC Directive

The FORC directive repeats a statement block by iterating over a string of characters. Each character in the string causes one iteration of the loop. The syntax is:

```
FORC parameter, <string>
    statements
ENDM
```

On the first loop iteration, *parameter* is equal to the first character in the string; on the second iteration, *parameter* is equal to the second character in the string, and so on, to the end of the string.

The following example creates a character lookup table consisting of several nonalphabetic characters. Note that < and > must be preceded by the literal-character (!) operator to prevent them from violating the syntax of the FORC directive:

```
Delimiters LABEL BYTE
FORC code,<@#$%^&*!<!>>
    BYTE "&code"
ENDM
```

The following data table is generated, which shows in a listing file:

```
00000000  40              1          BYTE "@"
00000001  23              1          BYTE "#"
00000002  24              1          BYTE "$"
00000003  25              1          BYTE "%"
00000004  5E              1          BYTE "^"
00000005  26              1          BYTE "&"
00000006  2A              1          BYTE "*"
00000007  3C              1          BYTE "<"
00000008  3E              1          BYTE ">"
```

10.4.5   Example: Linked List

It is fairly simple to combine a structure declaration with the REPEAT directive to instruct the assembler to create a linked list data structure. Each node in a linked list contains a data area and a link area:

In the data area, one or more variables can hold data that are unique to each node. In the link area, a pointer contains the address of the next node in the list. The link part of the final node usually contains a null pointer.

Let's create a program that creates and displays a simple linked list. First, the program defines a list node having a single integer (data) and a pointer to the next node:

```
ListNode STRUCT
    NodeData DWORD ?              ; the node's data
    NextPtr  DWORD ?              ; pointer to next node
ListNode ENDS
```

Next, the REPEAT directive creates multiple instances of **ListNode** objects. For testing purposes, the **NodeData** field contains an integer constant that ranges from 1 to 15. Inside the loop, we increment the counter and insert values into the ListNode fields:

```
TotalNodeCount = 15
NULL = 0
Counter = 0

.data
LinkedList LABEL DWORD
REPEAT TotalNodeCount
    Counter = Counter + 1
    ListNode <Counter, ($ + Counter * SIZEOF ListNode)>
ENDM
```

The expression ($ + Counter * SIZEOF ListNode) tells the assembler to multiply the counter by the **ListNode** size and add their product to the current location counter. The value is inserted into the **NextPtr** field in the structure. (It's interesting to note that the location counter's value ($) remains fixed at the first node of the list.)

The list is given a *tail node* that marks the end of the list. It can be easily identified because its **NextPtr** field contains NULL (0):

```
ListNode <0,0>
```

When the program traverses the list, it uses the following statements to retrieve the **NextPtr** field and compare it to NULL so the end of the list can be detected:

```
mov  eax,(ListNode PTR [esi]).NextPtr
cmp  eax,NULL
```

Program Listing   The following is a complete listing of the program. In main, it uses a loop to traverse the list and display the data values of all the nodes. Rather than use a fixed counter for the loop, the program checks for the NULL pointer in the tail node and stops looping when it is found:

```
TITLE Creating a Linked List              (List.asm)

INCLUDE Irvine32.inc

ListNode STRUCT
  NodeData DWORD ?
  NextPtr  DWORD ?
ListNode ENDS

TotalNodeCount = 15
NULL = 0
Counter = 0
.data
LinkedList LABEL DWORD
REPEAT TotalNodeCount
    Counter = Counter + 1
    ListNode <Counter, ($ + Counter * SIZEOF ListNode)>
ENDM
ListNode <0,0>                    ; tail node

.code
main PROC
    mov   esi,OFFSET LinkedList

; Display the integers in the NodeData fields.
NextNode:
    ; Check for the tail node.
    mov   eax,(ListNode PTR [esi]).NextPtr
    cmp   eax,NULL
    je    quit

    ; Display the node data.
    mov   eax,(ListNode PTR [esi]).NodeData
    call  WriteDec
    call  Crlf

    ; Get pointer to next node.
    mov   esi,(ListNode PTR [esi]).NextPtr
    jmp   NextNode

quit:
    exit
main ENDP
END main
```

10.4.6   Section Review

1. Briefly describe the WHILE directive.
2. Briefly describe the REPEAT directive.
3. Briefly describe the FOR directive.
4. Briefly describe the FORC directive.
5. Which looping directive would be the best tool to generate a character lookup table?
6. Write the statements generated by the following macro:

```
REPEAT val,<100,20,30>
    BYTE 0,0,0,val
ENDM
```

7. Assume the following **mRepeat** macro has been defined:

```
mRepeat MACRO char,count
    LOCAL L1
    mov   cx,count
L1: mov   ah,2
    mov   dl,char
    int   21h
    loop L1
ENDM
```

Write the code generated by the preprocessor when the **mRepeat** macro is expanded by each of the following statements:

```
mRepeat   'X',50
mRepeat   AL,20
mRepeat   byteVal,countVal
```

8. *Challenge:* In the Linked List example program (Section 10.4.5), what would be the result if the REPEAT loop were coded as follows?

```
REPEAT TotalNodeCount
    Counter = Counter + 1
    ListNode <Counter, ($ + SIZEOF ListNode)>
ENDM
```

10.5   Chapter Summary

A structure is a template or pattern that becomes a user-defined type. Many structures are already defined in the MS-Windows API library, and are used for the transfer of data between application programs and the library. Structures can contain a diverse set of field types. Each field declaration may use a field-initializer, which assigns a default value to the field.

Structures themselves take up no memory. But when a structure variable is declared, it consumes memory. The SIZEOF operator returns the number of bytes used by the variable.

The dot operator (.) references a structure field by using either a structure variable or an indirect operand such as [esi]. When an indirect operand references a structure field, you must use the PTR operator to identify the structure type, as in (COORD PTR [esi]).X.

When a structure contains fields that are themselves structures, we call it a nested structure definition. An example was shown in the Drunkard's Walk program (Section 10.1.6), where the **DrunkardWalk** structure contained an array of COORD structures.

Macros are usually defined at the beginning of a program, before the data and code segments. Then, when calls are made to the macros, the preprocessor inserts a copy of each macro's code into the program at the calling location.

Macros can be effectively used as *wrappers* around procedure calls, so they can simplify the passing of parameters and preserving of registers. Macros such as **mGotoxy, mDumpMem**, and **mWriteStr** call procedures from the book's link library.

A *macro procedure* (or *macro*) is a named block of assembly language statements. A *macro function* is similar, except that it also returns a constant value.

Conditional-assembly directives such as IF, IFNB, and IFIDNI provide a great deal of utility to macros because they can be used to check for arguments that are out of range, missing, or of the wrong type. The ECHO directive displays error messsages during assembly, making it possible to alert the programmer to errors in arguments passed to macros.

The substitution operator (&) resolves ambiguous references to parameter names. The expansion operator (%) expands text macros and converts contant expressions to text. The literal-text operator (< >) groups diverse characters and text into a single literal. The literal-character operator (!) forces the preprocessor to treat predefined operators as ordinary characters.

Repeat block directives can greatly reduce the amount of repetitive coding you must perform:

- The WHILE directive repeats a statement block based on a boolean expression.
- The REPEAT directive repeats a statement block based on the value of a counter.
- The FOR directive repeats a statement block by iterating over a list of symbols.
- The FORC directive repeats a statement block by iterating over a string of characters.

10.6   Programming Exercises

1. mReadkey Macro

This exercise requires reading Section 15.2.2. The program must run in Real-address mode. Create a macro that waits for a keystroke and returns the key that was pressed. The macro should include parameters for the ASCII code and keyboard scan code. For example, the following code waits for a key; when it returns, the two arguments contain the ASCII code and scan code:

```
.data
ascii BYTE ?
scan BYTE ?
.code
mReadkey ascii, scan
```

2. mWritestringAttr Macro

Create a macro that writes a null-terminated string to the console with a given text color. The macro parameters should include the string name and the color. For example:

```
.data
myString BYTE "Here is my string",0
.code
mWriteStringAttr myString, (white * 16) + blue
```

3. mMove32 Macro

Write a macro named **mMove32** that receives two 32-bit memory operands. The macro should move the source operand to the destination operand.

4. mMult32 Macro

Create a macro named **mMult32** that multiplies two unsigned 32-bit memory operands and produces a 32-bit product.

5. mReadInt Macro

Create a macro named **mReadInt** that reads a 16- or 32-bit signed integer from standard input and returns the value in an argument. Use conditional operators to allow the macro to adapt to the size of the desired result. Write a program that calls the macro, passing it operands of various sizes.

6. mWriteInt Macro

Create a macro named **mWriteInt** that writes a signed integer to standard output by calling the **WriteInt** library procedure. The argument passed to the macro can be a byte, word, or double-word. Use conditional operators in the macro so it adapts to the size of the argument. Write a program that demonstrates the macro, passing it arguments of different sizes.

7. mScroll Macro

(Requires reading Section 15.3.3.5) Create a macro named **mScroll** that displays a color rectangle on the screen. Include the following parameters in the macro definition:

ULrow	Upper-left window row
ULcol	Upper-left window column
LRrow	Lower-right window row
LRcol	Lower-right window column
attrib	Color of scrolled lines

If **attrib** is blank, assume a color of light gray characters on a black background.

8. Drunkard's Walk

When testing the Drunkard Walk program, you may have noticed that the professor doesn't seem to wander very far from the starting point. This is no doubt caused by the fact that there is an equal probability of the professor moving in each direction. Modify the program so that there is a 60% probability that the professor will continue to walk in the same direction as he/she did when taking the previous step. *Hint:* You will have to assign a default starting direction before the loop begins. Also, recall that a programming exercise in Chapter 6 dealt with weighted probabilities.

11

32-Bit Windows Programming

11.1 Win32 Console Programming

Hopefully, some of the following questions have been in the back of your mind while reading this book:

- How do 32-bit programs handle text input-output?
- How are colors handled in 32-bit console mode?
- How does the Irvine32 link library work?
- How are times and dates handled in MS-Windows?
- How can I use MS-Windows functions to read and write data files?

- Is it possible to write a graphical Windows application in assembly language?
- How do Protected mode programs translate segments and offsets to physical addresses?
- I've heard that virtual memory is good. But why is that so?

This chapter will answer these questions and more, as we show you the basics of 32-bit programming under Microsoft Windows. Most of the information here is oriented toward 32-bit console mode text applications because they are reasonably easy to program, given a knowledge of structures and procedure parameters. The Irvine32 link library is completely built on Win32 console functions, so you can compare its source code to the information in this chapter.

Why not write the type of graphical applications you usually see running under MS-Windows? The main reason is that they tend to be *extremely* long and detailed. For years, C and C++ programmers have labored over technical details such as graphical device handles, message posting, font metrics, device bitmaps, and mapping modes, with the help of excellent authors. In fact, there is a devoted group of assembly language programmers on the Web who are quite good at Windows programming. I have links to many of their Web sites from my own, named *Assembly Language Sources* (http://www.nuvisionmiami.com/kip/asm.htm).

So that graphical programmers are not completely disappointed, Section 11.2 does introduce 32-bit graphical programming in a generic sort of way. It's only a start, but you might be inspired to go further into the topic. A list of recommended books for futher study is given in the summary at the end of this chapter.

On the surface, 32-bit console mode programs look and behave like 16-bit MS-DOS programs running in text mode. Both types of programs read from standard input and write to standard output. They both support command-line redirection, and they can both display text in color. Beneath the surface, however, 32-bit console programs and MS-DOS programs are quite different. The former runs in 32-bit Protected mode, whereas MS-DOS programs run in Real-address mode. By necessity, they use completely different function libraries. Win32 programs call functions from the same function library used by graphical Windows applications. MS-DOS programs use BIOS and MS-DOS interrupts that have existed since the introduction of the IBM-PC.

An *Application Programming Interface* (API) is a collection of types, constants, and functions that provide a way to directly manipulate objects through programming. Therefore, the Win32 API lets you tap into the objects that make up the 32-bit version of MS-Windows.

Closely related to the Win32 API is the Microsoft *Platform SDK*. The letters SDK stand for *software development kit*, which is a collection of tools, libraries, sample code, and documentation that helps programmers create applications. A *platform* is an operating system or a group of closely related operating systems.

If you really fall in love with MS-Windows programming, you're going to want a lot more information than is supplied in this chapter. The best reference of all is the Microsoft MSDN Web site, currently located at **www.msdn.microsoft.com**.

11.1.1   Background Information

When a Windows application starts, it creates either a console window or a graphical window. We have been using the following option with the LINK command in the *make32.bat* batch file that tells the linker to create a console-based application:

```
/SUBSYSTEM:CONSOLE
```

A console program looks and behaves like an MS-DOS window, with some enhancements, which we will see later. Consoles read from standard input and write either to standard output or to the standard error output. The console has a single input buffer and one or more screen buffers:

- The *input buffer* contains a queue of *input records*, each containing data about an input event. Examples of input events are keyboard input, mouse clicks, and the user's resizing of the console window.
- A *screen buffer* is a two-dimensional array of character and color data that affects the appearance of text in the console window.

Throughout this section, we can only introduce you to a number of MS-Windows functions and provide a few simple examples. There are many details which cannot be covered here because of space limitations. To find out more, install the MSDN Library CD supplied with Microsoft Visual Studio, or visit the Microsoft MSDN Web site (currently located at www.msdn.microsoft.com).

Character Sets and Windows API Functions   There are two types of character sets that can be used when calling functions in the Win32 API. The 8-bit ASCII/ANSI character set, and the 16-bit Unicode set (available in Windows NT, 2000, and XP). Windows API functions dealing with text are usually supplied in two versions, one ending in the letter A (for 8-bit ANSI characters), and the other ending in W (for *wide* character sets, including Unicode). One of these is WriteConsole:

- WriteConsoleA
- WriteConsoleW

Function names ending in W are not supported by Windows 95 or 98. In Windows NT, 2000, and XP, on the other hand, Unicode is the native character set. When you call a function such as **WriteConsoleA**, the operating system first converts the characters from ANSI to Unicode, and then calls **WriteConsoleW**.

In the Microsoft MSDN Library documentation for functions such as WriteConsole, the trailing A or W is omitted from the name. In the include file for the programs in this book, we redefine function names such as **WriteConsoleA**:

```
WriteConsole EQU <WriteConsoleA>
```

This definition makes it possible to call WriteConsole using its generic name.

High-Level and Low-Level Access   There are two levels of access to the console, permitting tradeoffs between simplicity and complete control:

- High-level console functions read a stream of characters from the console's input buffer. They write character data to the console's screen buffer. Both input and output can be redirected to read from or write to text files.
- Low-level console functions retrieve detailed information about keyboard and mouse events, and user interactions with the console window (dragging, resizing, etc.). These functions also permit detailed control of the window size and position, as well as text colors.

11.1.1.1 Windows Data Types

Microsoft Windows API functions are documented using function declarations for C/C++ programmers. In these declarations, the types of all function parameters are based either on standard C types or on one of the MS-Windows predefined types (listed in Table 11-1). It is important to distinguish data values from pointers to values. A type name that begins with the letters LP is a *long pointer* to some other object.

Table 11-1   Translating MS-Windows Types to MASM.

MS-Windows Type	MASM Type	Description
BOOL	BYTE	A boolean value
BSTR	PTR BYTE	A 32-bit character pointer
BYTE	BYTE	An 8-bit unsigned integer
COLORREF	DWORD	A 32-bit value used as a color value
DWORD	DWORD	A 32-bit unsigned integer or the address of a segment and its associated offset
HANDLE	DWORD	A 32-bit unsigned integer
LONG	SDWORD	A 32-bit signed integer
LPARAM	DWORD	A 32-bit value passed as a parameter to a window procedure or callback function (may be a pointer)
LPCSTR	PTR BYTE	A 32-bit pointer to a constant character string
LPSTR	PTR BYTE	A 32-bit pointer to a character string
LPCTSTR	DWORD	A 32-bit pointer to a constant character string that is portable for Unicode and double-byte character sets
LPTSTR	DWORD	A 32-bit pointer to a character string that is portable for Unicode and double-byte character sets

Table 11-1   Translating MS-Windows Types to MASM. (Continued)

MS-Windows Type	MASM Type	Description
LPVOID	DWORD	A 32-bit pointer to an unspecified type
LRESULT	DWORD	A 32-bit value returned from a window procedure or callback function
UINT	DWORD	A 32-bit unsigned integer
WNDPROC	DWORD	A 32-bit pointer to a window procedure
WORD	WORD	A 16-bit unsigned integer
WPARAM	DWORD	A 32-bit value passed as a parameter to a window procedure or callback function
LPCRECT	PTR RECT	A 32-bit pointer to a constant (nonmodifiable) RECT structure

11.1.1.2   Console Handles

Nearly all Win32 console functions require you to pass a handle as the first argument. A *handle* is a 32-bit unsigned integer that uniquely identifies an object such as a bitmap, drawing pen, or any input/output device. We will use the following handles:

```
STD_INPUT_HANDLE              standard input
STD_OUTPUT_HANDLE             standard output
STD_ERROR_HANDLE             standard error output
```

The latter two handles are used when writing to the console's active screen buffer.

> The *SmallWin.inc* file supplied with this book contains all of the symbolic constants, function proto-types, and related definitions shown in this chapter. You can find it in MASM's INCLUDE directory.

The **GetStdHandle** function returns a handle to a console stream: input, output, or error output. You need a handle in order to do any input/output in a console-based program. Here is the function prototype:

```
GetStdHandle PROTO,
   nStdHandle:DWORD                    ; handle type
```

nStdHandle can be STD_INPUT_HANDLE, STD_OUTPUT_HANDLE, or STD_ERROR_HANDLE. The function returns the handle in EAX, which should be copied into a variable for safekeeping. Here is a sample call:

```
.data
inputHandle DWORD ?
```

```
.code
    INVOKE GetStdHandle, STD_INPUT_HANDLE
    mov inputHandle,eax
```

11.1.2   Win32 Console Functions

Table 11-2 contains a quick reference to the complete set of Win32 console functions.[1] You can find a complete description of each function in the MSDN library either on CD-ROM or at www.msdn.microsoft.com.

Table 11-2   Win32 Console Functions.

Function	Description
AllocConsole	Allocates a new console for the calling process.
CreateConsoleScreenBuffer	Creates a console screen buffer.
FillConsoleOutputAttribute	Sets the text and background color attributes for a specified number of character cells.
FillConsoleOutputCharacter	Writes a character to the screen buffer a specified number of times.
FlushConsoleInputBuffer	Flushes the console input buffer.
FreeConsole	Detaches the calling process from its console.
GenerateConsoleCtrlEvent	Sends a specified signal to a console process group that shares the console associated with the calling process.
GetConsoleCP	Retrieves the input code page used by the console associated with the calling process.
GetConsoleCursorInfo	Retrieves information about the size and visibility of the cursor for the specified console screen buffer.
GetConsoleMode	Retrieves the current input mode of a console's input buffer or the current output mode of a console screen buffer.
GetConsoleOutputCP	Retrieves the output code page used by the console associated with the calling process.
GetConsoleScreenBufferInfo	Retrieves information about the specified console screen buffer.
GetConsoleTitle	Retrieves the title bar string for the current console window.

---

[1]   Source: Microsoft MSDN Documentation, January 2001. Reprinted with permission from Microsoft Corporation.

Table 11-2   Win32 Console Functions. (Continued)

Function	Description
GetConsoleWindow	Retrieves the window handle used by the console associated with the calling process.
GetLargestConsoleWindowSize	Retrieves the size of the largest possible console window.
GetNumberOfConsoleIn-putEvents	Retrieves the number of unread input records in the console's input buffer.
GetNumberOfConsoleMouse-Buttons	Retrieves the number of buttons on the mouse used by the current console.
GetStdHandle	Retrieves a handle for the standard input, standard output, or standard error device.
HandlerRoutine	An application-defined function used with the SetConsoleCtrlHandler function.
PeekConsoleInput	Reads data from the specified console input buffer without removing it from the buffer.
ReadConsole	Reads character input from the console input buffer and removes it from the buffer.
ReadConsoleInput	Reads data from a console input buffer and removes it from the buffer.
ReadConsoleOutput	Reads character and color attribute data from a rectangular block of character cells in a console screen buffer.
ReadConsoleOutputAttribute	Copies a specified number of foreground and background color attributes from consecutive cells of a console screen buffer.
ReadConsoleOutputCharacter	Copies a number of characters from consecutive cells of a console screen buffer.
ScrollConsoleScreenBuffer	Moves a block of data in a screen buffer.
SetConsoleActiveScreenBuffer	Sets the specified screen buffer to be the currently displayed console screen buffer.
SetConsoleCP	Sets the input code page used by the console associated with the calling process.
SetConsoleCtrlHandler	Adds or removes an application-defined HandlerRoutine from the list of handler functions for the calling process.

Table 11-2   Win32 Console Functions. (Continued)

Function	Description
SetConsoleCursorInfo	Sets the size and visibility of the cursor for the specified console screen buffer.
SetConsoleCursorPosition	Sets the cursor position in the specified console screen buffer.
SetConsoleMode	Sets the input mode of a console's input buffer or the output mode of a console screen buffer.
SetConsoleOutputCP	Sets the output code page used by the console associated with the calling process.
SetConsoleScreenBufferSize	Changes the size of the specified console screen buffer.
SetConsoleTextAttribute	Sets the foreground (text) and background color attributes of characters written to the screen buffer.
SetConsoleTitle	Sets the title bar string for the current console window.
SetConsoleWindowInfo	Sets the current size and position of a console screen buffer's window.
SetStdHandle	Sets the handle for the standard input, standard output, or standard error device.
WriteConsole	Writes a character string to a console screen buffer beginning at the current cursor location.
WriteConsoleInput	Writes data directly to the console input buffer.
WriteConsoleOutput	Writes character and color attribute data to a specified rectangular block of character cells in a console screen buffer.
WriteConsoleOutputAttribute	Copies a number of foreground and background color attributes to consecutive cells of a console screen buffer.
WriteConsoleOutputCharacter	Copies a number of characters to consecutive cells of a console screen buffer.

11.1.3   Console Input

By now, you have used the **ReadString** and **ReadChar** procedures from the book's link library quite a few times. They were designed to be simple and straightforward, so you could concentrate on other issues. Both procedures are wrappers around **ReadConsole**, a Win32 function. (A *wrapper* procedure hides some of the details of another procedure.)

Console Input Buffer   The Win32 console has an input buffer containing an array of input event records. Each input event, such as a keystroke, mouse movement, or mouse-button click, creates an input record in the console's input buffer. High-level input functions such as **ReadConsole** filter and process the input data, returning only a stream of characters.

11.1.3.1   ReadConsole Function

The **ReadConsole** function provides a convenient way to read text input and put it in a buffer. Here is the prototype:

```
ReadConsole PROTO,
    handle:DWORD,                       ; input handle
    pBuffer:PTR BYTE,                   ; pointer to buffer
    maxBytes:DWORD,                     ; number of chars to read
    pBytesRead:PTR DWORD,               ; ptr to num bytes read
    notUsed:DWORD                       ; (not used)
```

The *handle* argument is a valid console input handle returned by the **GetStdHandle** function. The *pBuffer* parameter is the offset of a character array. The *maxBytes* parameter is a 32-bit integer specifying the maximum number of characters to read. The *pBbytesRead* parameter is a pointer to a doubleword that permits the function to fill in, when it returns, a count of the number of characters placed in the buffer. The last parameter is not used, but you must still pass it a value (zero, for example).

Example Program   Suppose we want to write a program to read characters entered by the user. First, we call **GetStdHandle** to get the console's standard input handle. Then we call **ReadConsole**, using the same input handle:

```
TITLE Read From the Console          (ReadConsole.asm)

; This program reads a line of input from standard input.

INCLUDE Irvine32.inc

BufSize = 80

.data
buffer BYTE BufSize DUP(?),0,0
stdInHandle DWORD ?
bytesRead   DWORD ?

.code
main PROC
    ; Get handle to standard input
    INVOKE GetStdHandle, STD_INPUT_HANDLE
    mov stdInHandle,eax

    ; Wait for user input
    INVOKE ReadConsole, stdInHandle, ADDR buffer,
      BufSize - 2, ADDR bytesRead, 0
```

```
      ; Display the buffer
      mov   esi,OFFSET buffer
      mov   ecx,16              ; 16 bytes
      mov   ebx,TYPE buffer
      call  DumpMem

      exit
main ENDP
END main
```

We can test this program by entering "abcdefg" from the keyboard. Note the hexadecimal dump of **buffer**:

```
Dump of offset 00404000
-------------------------------
61 62 63 64 65 66 67 0D 0A 00 00 00 00 00 00 00
```

Notice that nine bytes are inserted in the buffer ("abcdefg", plus 0Dh and 0Ah, the end-of-line characters inserted when the user pressed the Enter key). The **bytesRead** variable will be equal to 9.

When writing your own programs, be sure to include two extra bytes in your input buffer for the end-of-line characters. If you want the buffer to contain a null-terminated string, replace the byte containing 0Dh with a null byte. This is exactly what is done by the **ReadString** procedure from Irvine32.lib.

11.1.3.2   Single-Character Input

Single-character input in console mode is a little tricky. You have to do the following steps, in order:

1. Get a copy of the current console flags by calling **GetConsoleMode**. Save the flags in a variable.
2. Change the console flags by calling **SetConsoleMode**.
3. Input a character by calling **ReadConsole**.
4. Restore the previous values of the console flags by calling **SetConsoleMode.**

The **GetConsoleMode** function gets the current flag mode values of a console's input buffer, or the current output mode of a console screen buffer, and copies the flags to a double-word variable:

```
GetConsoleMode PROTO,
    hConsoleHandle:DWORD,             ; input or output handle
    lpMode:PTR DWORD                  ; points to DWORD variable
```

The **SetConsoleMode** function sets the current input mode of a console's input buffer, or the current output mode of a console screen buffer:

```
SetConsoleMode PROTO,
    hConsoleHandle:DWORD,              ; console handle
    dwMode:DWORD                       ; console mode flags
```

The set of possible values for *dwMode* is somewhat large, so you will need to look up the **SetConsoleMode** function in the Microsoft MSDN online library. For now, we can say that a value of zero clears all flags and enables single-character input.

Example   The following statements, taken from the link library's **ReadChar** procedure, input a single keyboard character:

```
.data
saveFlags DWORD ?                 ; backup copy of flags
.code
; Get & save the current console input mode flags
INVOKE GetConsoleMode,
    consoleInHandle,
    ADDR saveFlags

; Clear all console flags
INVOKE SetConsoleMode,
    consoleInHandle,
    0                             ; new flag values

; Read a single character from input
INVOKE ReadConsole,
    consoleInHandle,              ; console input handle
    ADDR buffer,                  ; pointer to buffer
    1,                            ; max characters to read
    ADDR bytesRead,0              ; return value

; Restore the previous flags state
INVOKE SetConsoleMode,
    consoleInHandle,
    saveFlags
```

Aren't you glad you didn't have to write your own **ReadChar** procedure in the first week of class?

A final comment on **ReadChar**: If no characters are waiting in the input stream, the program waits for a key to be pressed. Extended keyboard keys such as function keys and arrow keys are ignored. (Look on the book's Web site for an example that deals with input of extended keyboard keys.)

11.1.4 Console Output

In earlier chapters, it was important to make console output as simple as possible. As far back as Chapter 5, the **WriteString** procedure in the Irvine32 link library required only a single argument, the offset of a string in EDX. It turns out that WriteString is actually a wrapper around a more detailed call to a Win32 function named **WriteConsole**.

In this chapter, however, you learn how to make direct calls to Win32 functions such as **WriteConsole** and **WriteConsoleOutputCharacter**. Direct calls involve more detailed knowledge, but they also offer you more flexibility than the Irvine32 library procedures.

11.1.4.1 Data Structures

Several of the Win32 console functions use predefined data structures, including COORD and SMALL_RECT. The COORD structure specifies X and Y screen coordinates in character measurements, which default to 0–79 and 0–24:

```
COORD STRUCT
    X WORD ?
    Y WORD ?
COORD ENDS
```

The SMALL_RECT structure specifies a window's location in character measurements:

```
SMALL_RECT STRUCT
  Left    WORD ?
  Top     WORD ?
  Right   WORD ?
  Bottom WORD ?
SMALL_RECT ENDS
```

11.1.4.2 WriteConsole Function

The **WriteConsole** function writes a string to the screen, using the console output handle. It is the simplest to use, and it acts upon standard ASCII control characters such as *tab*, *carriage return*, and *line feed*. Here is the function prototype:

```
WriteConsole PROTO,
    handle:DWORD,                ; output handle
    pBuffer:PTR BYTE,            ; pointer to buffer
    bufsize:DWORD,               ; size of buffer
    pCount:PTR DWORD,            ; output count
    lpReserved:DWORD             ; (not used)
```

The first parameter is a console output handle. The second, *pBuffer*, is a pointer to an array of characters. The third parameter is a 32-bit integer equal to the length of the string. The fourth parameter points to an integer holding the number of bytes actually written when the function returns. The fifth parameter, which is not used, should be set to zero when calling the function.

11.1.4.3 Example Program: Console1

The following program, *Console1.asm*, demonstrates the **GetStdHandle, ExitProcess,** and **WriteConsole** functions by writing a string to the console window:

```
TITLE Win32 Console Example #1                        (Console1.asm)

; This program calls the following Win32 Console functions:
; GetStdHandle, ExitProcess, WriteConsole
```

```
INCLUDE Irvine32.inc

.data
endl EQU <0dh,0ah>           ; end of line sequence
message \
BYTE "-------------------- Console1.asm ----------------------"
BYTE endl,endl
BYTE "This program is a simple demonstration of console ",endl
BYTE "mode output, using the GetStdHandle and WriteConsole ",endl
BYTE "functions.",endl
BYTE "-------------------------------------------------------"
BYTE endl,endl,endl
messageSize = ($-message)

consoleHandle DWORD 0        ; handle to standard output device
bytesWritten  DWORD ?        ; number of bytes written

.code
main PROC
  ; Get the console output handle:
    INVOKE GetStdHandle, STD_OUTPUT_HANDLE
    mov consoleHandle,eax

  ; Write a string to the console:
    INVOKE WriteConsole,
       consoleHandle,                ; console output handle
       ADDR message,                 ; string pointer
       messageSize,                  ; string length
       ADDR bytesWritten,            ; returns num bytes written
       0                             ; not used

    INVOKE ExitProcess,0
main ENDP
END main
```

The program produces the following output:

```
------------------------ Console1.asm ----------------------

This program is a simple demonstration of console
mode output, using the GetStdHandle and WriteConsole
functions.
-------------------------------------------------------------
```

11.1.4.4   WriteConsoleOutputCharacter Function

The **WriteConsoleOutputCharacter** function copies an array of characters to consecutive cells of the console screen buffer, beginning at a specified location. Here is the prototype:

```
WriteConsoleOutputCharacter PROTO,
   handleScreenBuf:DWORD,             ; console output handle
```

```
    pBuffer:PTR BYTE,              ; pointer to buffer
    bufsize:DWORD,                 ; size of buffer
    xyPos:COORD,                   ; first cell coordinates
    pCount:PTR DWORD               ; output count
```

If the text reaches the end of a line, it wraps around. The attribute values in the screen buffer are not changed. If the function cannot write the character, it returns zero. ASCII control codes such as *tab*, *carriage return*, and *line feed* are ignored.

11.1.5   Reading and Writing Files

11.1.5.1   CreateFile Function

The **CreateFile** function either creates a new file or opens an existing file. If successful, it returns a handle to the open file; otherwise, it returns a special constant named INVALID_HANDLE_VALUE. Here is the prototype:

```
CreateFile PROTO,
    pFilename:PTR BYTE,            ; ptr to filename
    desiredAccess:DWORD,          ; access mode
    shareMode:DWORD,              ; share mode
    lpSecurity:DWORD,             ; ptr to security attributes
    creationDisposition:DWORD,    ; file creation options
    flagsAndAttributes:DWORD,     ; file attributes
    htemplate:DWORD               ; handle to template file
```

The first parameter is a pointer to a null-terminated string containing either a partial or fully qualified filename (*drive:\path\filename*). The *desiredAccess* parameter specifies how the file will be accessed (reading or writing). The *shareMode* parameter controls the ability for multiple programs to access the file while it is open. The *lpSecurity* parameter is a pointer to a security structure that controls security rights under Windows NT, 2000, and XP. The *creation-Disposition* parameter lets you specify what action to take when a file already exists, or does not exist. The *flagsAndAttributes* parameter consists of bit flags that specify file attributes such as archive, encrypted, hidden, normal, system, and temporary. The *htemplate* parameter contains an optional handle to a template file that supplies file attributes and extended attributes for the file being created; although we do not use this parameter, it must be passed to the function with a value of zero.

DesiredAccess   By setting the *desiredAccess* parameter, you can obtain read access, write access, read/write access, or device query access to the file. You can use any combination of the values listed in Table 11-3, plus a large set of specific flag values not listed here.

Table 11-3   DesiredAccess Parameter Options.

Value	Meaning
0	Specifies device query access to the object. An application can query device attributes without accessing the device.
GENERIC_READ	Specifies read access to the object. Data can be read from the file and the file pointer can be moved. Combine with GENERIC_WRITE for read/write access.
GENERIC_WRITE	Specifies write access to the object. Data can be written to the file and the file pointer can be moved. Combine with GENERIC_READ for read/write access.

CreationDisposition   The *creationDisposition* parameter specifies which action to take on files that exist, and which action to take when files do not exist. It must be one of the values shown in Table 11-4.

Table 11-4   CreationDisposition Parameter Options.

Value	Meaning
CREATE_NEW	Creates a new file. The function fails if the file already exists.
CREATE_ALWAYS	Creates a new file. If the file exists, the function overwrites the file, clears the existing attributes, and combines the file attributes and flags specified by the *attributes* parameter with the predefined constant FILE_ATTRIBUTE_ARCHIVE.
OPEN_EXISTING	Opens the file. The function fails if the file does not exist.
OPEN_ALWAYS	Opens the file if it exists. If the file does not exist, the function creates the file as if *CreationDisposition* were CREATE_NEW.
TRUNCATE_EXISTING	Opens the file. Once opened, the file is truncated to size zero. You must open the file with at least GENERIC_WRITE access. This function fails if the file does not exist.

Table 11-5 lists the more commonly used values permitted in the *flagsAndAttributes* parameter. (For a complete list, see the **CreateFile** entry in the Microsoft MSDN documentation.) Any combination of the attributes is acceptable, except that all other file attributes override FILE_ATTRIBUTE_NORMAL.

Table 11-5   Selected FlagsAndAttributes Values.

Attribute	Meaning
FILE_ATTRIBUTE_ARCHIVE	The file should be archived. Applications use this attribute to mark files for backup or removal.
FILE_ATTRIBUTE_HIDDEN	The file is hidden. It is not to be included in an ordinary directory listing.
FILE_ATTRIBUTE_NORMAL	The file has no other attributes set. This attribute is valid only if used alone.
FILE_ATTRIBUTE_READONLY	The file is read only. Applications can read the file but cannot write to it or delete it.
FILE_ATTRIBUTE_TEMPORARY	The file is being used for temporary storage.

Examples   The following examples are for illustrative purposes only, to show how you might create and open files. See the online Microsoft MSDN documentation for **CreateFile** to learn about the many available options:

- Open an existing file for reading:

```
INVOKE CreateFile,
    ADDR filename,              ; ptr to filename
    GENERIC_READ,               ; access mode
    DO_NOT_SHARE,               ; share mode
    NULL,                       ; ptr to security attributes
    OPEN_EXISTING,              ; file creation options
    FILE_ATTRIBUTE_NORMAL,      ; file attributes
    0                           ; handle to template file
```

- Open an existing file for writing:

```
INVOKE CreateFile,
    ADDR filename,
    GENERIC_WRITE,              ; access mode
    DO_NOT_SHARE,
    NULL,
    OPEN_EXISTING,
    FILE_ATTRIBUTE_NORMAL,
    0
```

- Create a new file with normal attributes, erasing any existing file by the same name:

```
INVOKE CreateFile,
    ADDR filename,
    GENERIC_WRITE,
    DO_NOT_SHARE,
```

```
        NULL,
        CREATE_ALWAYS,                  ; overwrite existing file
        FILE_ATTRIBUTE_NORMAL,
        0
```

- Create a new file only if the file does not already exist:

```
INVOKE CreateFile,
    ADDR filename,
    GENERIC_WRITE,
    DO_NOT_SHARE,
    NULL,
    CREATE_NEW,                     ; don't erase existing file
    FILE_ATTRIBUTE_NORMAL,
    0
```

(The constants named DO_NOT_SHARE and NULL are defined in the include file used by programs in this chapter. See the latest documentation for all our include files and link libraries on the book's Web site.)

11.1.5.2 CloseHandle Function

The **CloseHandle** function closes an open file handle. Its prototype is:

```
CloseHandle PROTO, handle:DWORD
```

11.1.5.3 ReadFile Function

The **ReadFile** function reads text from an input file. ReadFile can optionally run in asynchronous mode, meaning that the program does not wait for the operation to finish. Here is the prototype:

```
ReadFile PROTO,                     ; read buffer from input file
    handle:DWORD,                   ; handle to file
    pBuffer:PTR BYTE,               ; ptr to buffer
    nBufsize:DWORD,                 ; num bytes to read
    pBytesRead:PTR DWORD,           ; bytes actually read
    pOverlapped:PTR DWORD           ; ptr to asynchronous info
```

The *handle* parameter is an open file handle returned by **CreateFile**. The *pBuffer* parameter points to a buffer that will receive data read from the file. The *nBufsize* parameter indicates the maximum number of bytes to read from the file. The *pBytesRead* parameter points to an integer variable that indicates the number of bytes actually read when the function returns. The *pOverlapped* parameter is optional; it points to a structure that specifies how the function can read the file asynchronously. For synchronous operation (the default), pass a null pointer (0) as the *pOverlapped* value.

11.1.5.4 WriteFile Function

The **WriteFile** function writes data to a file, using an output handle. The handle can be the screen buffer handle, or it can be one assigned to a text file. The function starts writing data to the file at the position indicated by the file's internal position pointer. After the write operation has been completed, the file's position pointer is adjusted by the number of bytes actually written. Here is the function prototype:

```
WriteFile PROTO,
    fileHandle:DWORD,                 ; output handle
    pBuffer:PTR BYTE,                 ; pointer to buffer
    nBufsize:DWORD,                   ; size of buffer
    pBytesWritten:PTR DWORD,          ; num bytes written
    pOverlapped:PTR DWORD             ; ptr to asynchronous info
```

11.1.5.5   Example WriteFile Program

The following program (*Writefile.asm*) creates a new file and writes some text to the file. It uses the CREATE_ALWAYS option, so any existing file is erased:

```
TITLE Using WriteFile                          (WriteFile.asm)

INCLUDE Irvine32.inc

.data
buffer BYTE "This text is written to an output file.",0dh,0ah
bufSize = ($-buffer)
errMsg BYTE "Cannot create file",0dh,0ah,0
filename      BYTE "output.txt",0
fileHandle    DWORD ?            ; handle to output file
bytesWritten DWORD ?            ; number of bytes written

.code
main PROC
    INVOKE CreateFile,
      ADDR filename, GENERIC_WRITE, DO_NOT_SHARE, NULL,
      CREATE_ALWAYS, FILE_ATTRIBUTE_NORMAL, 0

    mov fileHandle,eax              ; save file handle
    .IF eax == INVALID_HANDLE_VALUE
      mov  edx,OFFSET errMsg        ; display error message
      call WriteString
      jmp  QuitNow
    .ENDIF

    INVOKE WriteFile,               ; write text to file
       fileHandle,                  ; file handle
       ADDR buffer,                 ; buffer pointer
       bufSize,                     ; number of bytes to write
       ADDR bytesWritten,           ; number of bytes written
       0                            ; overlapped execution flag

    INVOKE CloseHandle, fileHandle
```

```
QuitNow:
    INVOKE ExitProcess,0           ; end program
main ENDP
END main
```

11.1.5.6   Moving the File Pointer

The **SetFilePointer** function moves the position pointer of an open file. This function can be used to append data to a file or to perform random-access record processing:

```
SetFilePointer PROTO,
   handle:DWORD,                   ; file handle
   nDistanceLo:SDWORD,             ; bytes to move pointer
   pDistanceHi:PTR SDWORD,         ; ptr to bytes to move, high
   moveMethod:DWORD                ; starting point
```

The *moveMethod* parameter specifies the starting point for moving the file pointer. There are three possible values: FILE_BEGIN, FILE_CURRENT, and FILE_END. The distance itself is a 64-bit signed integer value, divided into two parts:

* *nDistanceLo* – the lower 32 bits
* *pDistanceHi* – a pointer to a variable containing the upper 32 bits.

If *pDistanceHi* is null, only the value in *nDistanceLo* will be used to move the file pointer. The following is a sample call that prepares to append to the end of a file:

```
INVOKE SetFilePointer,
   fileHandle,             ; file handle
   0,                      ; distance low
   0,                      ; distance high
   FILE_END                ; move method
```

On the samples disk, the *AppendFile.asm* program appends data to an existing file.

11.1.5.7   Example ReadFile Program

The *ReadFile.asm* program opens the text file created by the *WriteFile.asm* program, reads the data, closes the file, and displays the buffer:

```
TITLE Using ReadFile                            (ReadFile.asm)

INCLUDE Irvine32.inc

.data
buffer BYTE 500 DUP(?)
bufSize = ($-buffer)
errMsg BYTE "Cannot open file",0dh,0ah,0
filename    BYTE "output.txt",0
fileHandle  DWORD ?                  ; handle to output file
byteCount   DWORD ?                  ; number of bytes written
```

```
    .code
main PROC
    INVOKE CreateFile,                 ; open file for input
        ADDR filename, GENERIC_READ,
        DO_NOT_SHARE, NULL, OPEN_EXISTING,
        FILE_ATTRIBUTE_NORMAL, 0

    mov fileHandle,eax                 ; save file handle
    .IF eax == INVALID_HANDLE_VALUE
        mov   edx,OFFSET errMsg        ; display error message
        call WriteString
        jmp   QuitNow
    .ENDIF

    INVOKE ReadFile,                   ; read file into buffer
        fileHandle, ADDR buffer,
        bufSize, ADDR byteCount, 0

    INVOKE CloseHandle,                ; close the file
        fileHandle

    mov esi,byteCount                  ; insert null terminator
    mov buffer[esi],0                  ; into buffer
    mov edx,OFFSET buffer              ; display the buffer
    call WriteString

QuitNow:
    INVOKE ExitProcess,0               ; end program
main ENDP
END main
```

(Recall that the .IF and .ENDIF directives were explained in Section 6.7.)

11.1.6   Console Window Manipulation

The Win32 API gives you some limited control over the console window, as well as the screen buffer that holds data displayed by the window. Figure 11-1 shows that the screen buffer can be larger than the number of lines currently displayed in the console window. The console window acts as a "viewport," showing only part of the buffer contents.

There are several functions that affect the console window and its position relative to the screen buffer. **SetConsoleWindowInfo** sets the size and position of the console window relative to the screen buffer. The **GetConsoleScreenBufferInfo** function returns (among other things) the rectangle coordinates of the console window relative to the screen buffer. **SetConsoleCursorPosition** sets the cursor position to any location within the screen buffer; if that area is not visible, the console window is shifted to make the cursor visible.

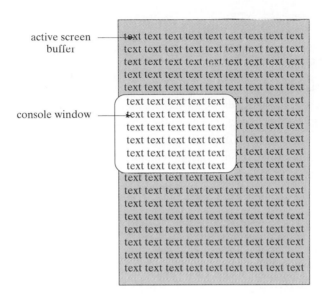

Figure 11-1   Screen Buffer and Console Window.

The **ScrollConsoleScreenBuffer** function moves some or all of the text within the screen buffer, which can affect the displayed text in the console window.

11.1.6.1   SetConsoleTitle

The **SetConsoleTitle** function lets you change the console window's title. An example is:

```
.data
titleStr BYTE "Console title",0
.code
INVOKE SetConsoleTitle, ADDR titleStr
```

11.1.6.2   GetConsoleScreenBufferInfo

The **GetConsoleScreenBufferInfo** function returns information about the current state of the console window. It has two parameters: a handle to the console screen, and a pointer to a structure that is filled in by the function:

```
GetConsoleScreenBufferInfo PROTO,
    outHandle:DWORD,                    ; handle to screen buffer
    pBufferInfo:PTR CONSOLE_SCREEN_BUFFER_INFO
```

The following is the CONSOLE_SCREEN_BUFFER_INFO structure:

```
CONSOLE_SCREEN_BUFFER_INFO STRUCT
  dwSize            COORD <>
  dwCursorPos       COORD <>
```

```
    wAttributes        WORD ?
    srWindow           SMALL_RECT <>
    maxWinSize         COORD <>
CONSOLE_SCREEN_BUFFER_INFO ENDS
```

dwSize returns the size of the screen buffer, in character columns and rows. *dwCursorPos* returns the location of the cursor. Both fields are COORD structures. *wAttributes* returns the foreground and background colors of characters written to the console by functions such as **WriteConsole**. *srWindow* returns the coordinates of the console window relative to the screen buffer. *maxWinSize* returns the maximum size of the console window, based on the current screen buffer size, font, and video display size. The following is a sample call to the function:

```
.data
consoleInfo CONSOLE_SCREEN_BUFFER_INFO <>
.code
    INVOKE GetConsoleScreenBufferInfo, outHandle,
      ADDR consoleInfo
```

Here is a sample of the structure data, shown by the Microsoft Visual Studio debugger:

11.1.6.3   SetConsoleWindowInfo Function

The **SetConsoleWindowInfo** function lets you set the size and position of the console window relative to its screen buffer. Following is its function prototype:

```
SetConsoleWindowInfo PROTO,          ; set position of console window
    nStdHandle:DWORD,                ; screen buffer handle
    bAbsolute:DWORD,                 ; coordinate type
    pConsoleRect:PTR SMALL_RECT      ; ptr to window rectangle
```

The *bAbsolute* parameter indicates how the coordinates in the structure pointed to by *pConsoleRect* are to be used. If *bAbsolute* is true, the coordinates specify the new upper-left and lower-right corners of the console window. If *bAbsolute* is false, the coordinates will be added to the current window coordinates.

The following *Scroll.asm* program writes fifty lines of text to the screen buffer. It then resizes and repositions the console window, effectively scrolling the text backwards. It uses the **SetConsoleWindowInfo** function:

```
TITLE Scrolling the Console Window                  (Scroll.asm)

INCLUDE Irvine32.inc

.data
message BYTE ":  This line of text was written "
        BYTE "to the screen buffer",0dh,0ah
messageSize = ($-message)

outHandle DWORD 0           ; standard output handle
bytesWritten  DWORD ?       ; number of bytes written
lineNum DWORD 0
windowRect SMALL_RECT <0,0,60,11>    ; left,top,right,bottom

.code
main PROC
    INVOKE GetStdHandle, STD_OUTPUT_HANDLE
    mov outHandle,eax

.REPEAT
    mov  eax,lineNum
    call WriteDec               ; display each line number
    INVOKE WriteConsole,
      outHandle,                ; console output handle
      ADDR message,             ; string pointer
      messageSize,              ; string length
      ADDR bytesWritten,        ; returns num bytes written
      0                         ; not used
    inc  lineNum                ; next line number
.UNTIL lineNum > 50

; Resize and reposition the console window relative to the
; screen buffer.
    INVOKE SetConsoleWindowInfo,
      outHandle,
      TRUE,
      ADDR windowRect       ; window rectangle

    call Readchar             ; wait for a key
    call Clrscr               ; clear the screen buffer
    call Readchar             ; wait for a second key
```

```
        INVOKE ExitProcess,0
main ENDP
END main
```

It is best to run this program directly from MS-Windows Explorer rather than an integrated editor environment. The editor may affect the behavior and appearance of the console window. Note that you must press a key twice at the end: once to clear the screen buffer, and a second time to end the program. (This was added for testing purposes.)

11.1.6.4   SetConsoleScreenBufferSize Function

The **SetConsoleScreenBufferSize** function lets you set the screen buffer size to X columns by Y rows. Here is the prototype:

```
SetConsoleScreenBufferSize PROTO,
    outHandle:DWORD,            ; handle to screen buffer
    dwSize:COORD               ; new screen buffer size
```

11.1.7   Controlling the Cursor

The Win32 API provides functions to set the cursor size, visibility, and screen location. An important data structure related to these functions is CONSOLE_CURSOR_INFO, which contains information about the console's cursor size and visibility:

```
CONSOLE_CURSOR_INFO STRUCT
    dwSize    DWORD ?
    bVisible BYTE ?
CONSOLE_CURSOR_INFO ENDS
```

dwSize is the percentage (1 to 100) of the character cell filled by the cursor. *bVisible* equals TRUE if the cursor is visible.

11.1.7.1   GetConsoleCursorInfo Function

The **GetConsoleCursorInfo** function returns the size and visibility of the console cursor. Pass it a pointer to a CONSOLE_CURSOR_INFO structure:

```
GetConsoleCursorInfo PROTO,
    outHandle:DWORD,                              ; output handle
    pCursorInfo:PTR CONSOLE_CURSOR_INFO          ; cursor information
```

By default, the cursor size is 25, indicating that the character cell is 25% filled by the cursor.

11.1.7.2   SetConsoleCursorInfo Function

The **SetConsoleCursorInfo** function sets the size and visibility of the cursor. Pass it a pointer to a CONSOLE_CURSOR_INFO structure:

```
SetConsoleCursorInfo PROTO,
    outHandle:DWORD,                              ; output handle
    pCursorInfo:PTR CONSOLE_CURSOR_INFO          ; cursor information
```

11.1.7.3   SetConsoleCursorPosition

The **SetConsoleCursorPosition** function sets the X, Y position of the cursor. Pass it a COORD structure and the console output handle:

```
SetConsoleCursorPosition PROTO,
    outHandle:DWORD,                ; input mode handle
    coords:COORD                    ; screen X,Y coordinates
```

11.1.8   Controlling the Text Color

There are two ways to control the color of text in a console window. You can change the current text color by calling **SetConsoleTextAttribute**, which affects all subsequent text output to the console. Alternatively, you can set the attributes of specific cells by calling **WriteConsoleOutputAttribute**.

11.1.8.1   SetConsoleTextAttribute Function

The **SetConsoleTextAttribute** function lets you set the foreground and background colors for all subsequent text output to the console window. Here is its prototype:

```
SetConsoleTextAttribute PROTO,
    outHandle:DWORD,                ; console output handle
    nColor:DWORD                    ; color attribute
```

The color value is stored in the low-order byte of the *nColor* parameter. Colors are created using the same method as for the video BIOS, shown in Section 15.3.2.

11.1.8.2   WriteConsoleOutputAttribute Function

The **WriteConsoleOutputAttribute** function copies an array of attribute values to consecutive cells of the console screen buffer, beginning at a specified location. Here is the prototype:

```
WriteConsoleOutputAttribute PROTO,
    outHandle:DWORD,                ; output handle
    pAttribute:PTR WORD,            ; write attributes
    nLength:DWORD,                  ; number of cells
    xyCoord:COORD,                  ; first cell coordinates
    lpCount:PTR DWORD               ; number of cells written
```

pAttribute points to an array of attributes in which the low-order byte of each contains the color. *nLength* is the length of the array. *xyCoord* is the starting screen cell to receive the attributes, and *lpCount* points to a variable that will hold the number of cells written when the function returns.

11.1.8.3   Example WriteColors Program

To demonstrate the use of colors and attributes, the *WriteColors.asm* program creates an array of characters and an array of attributes, one for each character. It calls **WriteConsoleOutputAttribute** to copy the attributes to the screen buffer, and **WriteConsoleOutputCharacter** to copy the characters to the same screen buffer cells:

```
TITLE Writing Text Colors                  (WriteColors.asm)
```

```
INCLUDE Irvine32.inc
.data
outHandle    DWORD ?
cellsWritten DWORD ?
xyPos COORD <10,2>

; Array of character codes:
buffer BYTE 1,2,3,4,5,6,7,8,9,10,11,12,13,14,15
       BYTE 16,17,18,19,20
BufSize = ($ - buffer)
; Array of attributes:
attributes WORD 0Fh,0Eh,0Dh,0Ch,0Bh,0Ah,9,8,7,6
           WORD 5,4,3,2,1,0F0h,0E0h,0D0h,0C0h,0B0h
.code
main PROC
; Get the Console standard output handle:
    INVOKE GetStdHandle,STD_OUTPUT_HANDLE
    mov outHandle,eax

; Set the colors of adjacent cells:
    INVOKE WriteConsoleOutputAttribute,
        outHandle, ADDR attributes,
        BufSize, xyPos,
        ADDR cellsWritten

; Write character codes 1 through 20:
    INVOKE WriteConsoleOutputCharacter,
        outHandle, ADDR buffer, BufSize,
        xyPos, ADDR cellsWritten

    INVOKE ExitProcess,0              ; end program
main ENDP
END main
```

Here is a snapshot of the program's output, which shows that character codes 1–20 are displayed as graphic characters. Each character is in a different color, although the colors do not appear on the printed page:

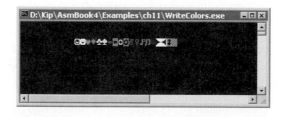

11.1.9   Time and Date Functions

The Win32 API provides a fairly large selection of time and date functions. For starters, you can get and set the current date and time. We only show a small subset of such functions in the current section, but you might also want to look at the Win32 functions listed in Table 11-6.

Table 11-6   Win32 DateTime Functions.[a]

Function	Description
CompareFileTime	Compares two 64-bit file times.
DosDateTimeToFileTime	Converts MS-DOS date and time values to a 64-bit file time.
FileTimeToDosDateTime	Converts a 64-bit file time to MS-DOS date and time values.
FileTimeToLocalFileTime	Converts a UTC (*universal coordinated time*) file time to a local file time.
FileTimeToSystemTime	Converts a 64-bit file time to system time format.
GetFileTime	Retrieves the date and time that a file was created, last accessed, and last modified.
GetLocalTime	Retrieves the current local date and time.
GetSystemTime	Retrieves the current system date and time in UTC format.
GetSystemTimeAdjustment	Determines whether the system is applying periodic time adjustments to its time-of-day clock.
GetSystemTimeAsFileTime	Retrieves the current system date and time in UTC format.
GetTickCount	Retrieves the number of milliseconds that have elapsed since the system was started.
GetTimeZoneInformation	Retrieves the current time-zone parameters.
LocalFileTimeToFileTime	Converts a local file time to a file time based on UTC.
SetFileTime	Sets the date and time that a file was created, last accessed, or last modified.
SetLocalTime	Sets the current local time and date.
SetSystemTime	Sets the current system time and date.
SetSystemTimeAdjustment	Enables or disables periodic time adjustments to the system's time-of-day clock.
SetTimeZoneInformation	Sets the current time-zone parameters.

Table 11-6   Win32 DateTime Functions.[a] (Continued)

Function	Description
SystemTimeToFileTime	Converts a system time to a file time.
SystemTimeToTzSpecificLocal-Time	Converts a UTC time to a specified time zone's corresponding local time.

[a]   Source: Microsoft MSDN Windows SDK documentation.

SYSTEMTIME Structure   The SYSTEMTIME structure is used by date- and time-related Windows API functions:

```
SYSTEMTIME STRUCT
    wYear WORD ?                    ; year (4 digits)
    wMonth WORD ?                   ; month (1-12)
    wDayOfWeek WORD ?               ; day of week (0-6)
    wDay WORD ?                     ; day (1-31)
    wHour WORD ?                    ; hours (0-23)
    wMinute WORD ?                  ; minutes (0-59)
    wSecond WORD ?                  ; seconds (0-59)
    wMilliseconds WORD ?            ; milliseconds (0-999)
SYSTEMTIME ENDS
```

The *wDayOfWeek* field value begins with Sunday = 0, Monday = 1, and so on. The value in *wMilliseconds* is not exact because the computer's internal clock is modified over time.

11.1.9.1   GetLocalTime and SetLocalTime

The **GetLocalTime** function returns the date and current time of day, according to the system clock. The time is adjusted for the local time zone. When calling it, pass a pointer to a SYSTEMTIME structure:

```
GetLocalTime PROTO,
    pSystemTime:PTR SYSTEMTIME
```

The **SetLocalTime** function sets the system's local date and time. When calling it, pass a pointer to a SYSTEMTIME structure:

```
SetLocalTime PROTO,
    pSystemTime:PTR SYSTEMTIME
```

If the function executes successfully, it returns a nonzero integer; if it fails, it returns zero.

The following is a sample call to **GetLocalTime**:

```
.data
sysTime SYSTEMTIME <>
.code
INVOKE GetLocalTime,ADDR sysTime
```

11.1.9.2   GetTickCount Function

The **GetTickCount** function returns the number of milliseconds that have elapsed since the system was started:

```
GetTickCount PROTO              ; return value in EAX
```

Because the returned value is a doubleword, the time will wrap around to zero if the system is run continuously for 49.7 days. You can use this function to monitor the elapsed time in a loop, and break out of the loop when a certain time limit has been reached. The following program, for example, displays a dot on the screen every 100 milliseconds, and checks the elapsed time until 5000 milleseconds have been reached. Its code could be used in a variety of programs:

```
TITLE Calculate Elapsed Time            (TimingLoop.asm)

; This program uses GetTickCount to calculate the number
; of milliseconds that have elapsed since the program
; started.

INCLUDE Irvine32.inc
TIME_LIMIT = 5000
.data
startTime DWORD ?
dot BYTE ".",0

.code
main PROC
    INVOKE GetTickCount             ; get milliseconds
    mov startTime,eax

L1:mov  edx,OFFSET dot              ; display a dot
    call WriteString

    INVOKE Sleep,100                ; sleep for 100 ms

    INVOKE GetTickCount
    sub  eax,startTime              ; check the elapsed time
    cmp  eax,TIME_LIMIT
    jb   L1

L2:exit
main ENDP
END main
```

11.1.9.3   Sleep Function

The **Sleep** function suspends the current program to pause for a specified number of milliseconds:

```
Sleep PROTO,
    dwMilliseconds:DWORD
```

11.1.9.4   GetDateTime Procedure

The **GetDateTime** procedure in the Irvine32 library returns a 64-bit integer holding the number of 100-nanosecond time intervals that have elapsed since January 1, 1601. This may seem a little odd, in that computers were completely unknown at the time. In any event, Microsoft uses this value to keep track of file dates and times. The following steps are recommended by the Win32 SDK when you want to prepare a system date/time value for date arithmetic:

1. Call a function such as **GetLocalTime** that fills in a SYSTEMTIME structure.
2. Convert the SYSTEMTIME structure to a FILETIME structure by calling the **SystemTimeToFileTime** function.
3. Copy the resulting FILETIME structure to a 64-bit quadword.

A FILETIME structure divides a 64-bit quadword into two doublewords:

```
FILETIME STRUCT
    loDateTime DWORD ?
    hiDateTime DWORD ?
FILETIME ENDS
```

The following **GetDateTime** procedure receives a pointer to a 64-bit quadword variable. It stores the current date and time in the variable, in Win32 FILETIME format:

```
;---------------------------------------------------
GetDateTime PROC,
    pStartTime:PTR QWORD
    LOCAL sysTime:SYSTEMTIME, flTime:FILETIME
;
; Gets and saves the current local date/time as a
; 64-bit integer (in the Win32 FILETIME format).
;---------------------------------------------------
; Get the system local time
    INVOKE GetLocalTime,
      ADDR sysTime

; Convert the SYSTEMTIME to FILETIME
    INVOKE SystemTimeToFileTime,
      ADDR sysTime,
      ADDR flTime

; Copy the FILETIME to a 64-bit integer
    mov esi,pStartTime
    mov eax,flTime.loDateTime
    mov DWORD PTR [esi],eax
    mov eax,flTime.hiDateTime
    mov DWORD PTR [esi+4],eax
    ret
GetDateTime ENDP
```

11.1.9.5   Creating a Stopwatch Timer

We can use the **GetTickCount** function as a tool to create two procedures that together act as a simple stopwatch timer. One procedure, named **TimerStart**, records the current time. The second procedure, **TimerStop**, returns the number of milliseconds that have elapsed since the last call to **TimerStart**.

The following *Timer.asm* program calls both procedures and creates an intentional delay by calling the **Sleep** function:

```
TITLE Calculate Elapsed Time                    (Timer.asm)

; Demonstrate a simple stopwatch timer, using
; the Win32 GetTickCount function.

INCLUDE Irvine32.inc

TimerStart PROTO,
    pSavedTime: PTR DWORD

TimerStop PROTO,
    pSavedTime: PTR DWORD

.data
msg BYTE " milliseconds have elapsed",0dh,0ah,0
timer1 DWORD ?

.code
main PROC
    INVOKE TimerStart,        ; start the timer
      ADDR timer1

    INVOKE Sleep, 5000        ; sleep for 5 seconds

    INVOKE TimerStop,         ; EAX = elapsed milliseconds
      ADDR timer1

    call WriteDec             ; display elapsed time
    mov   edx,OFFSET msg
    call WriteString

    exit
main ENDP

;----------------------------------------------------
TimerStart PROC uses eax esi,
    pSavedTime: PTR DWORD
; Starts a stopwatch timer.
; Receives: pointer to a variable that will hold
;     the current time.
; Returns: nothing
;----------------------------------------------------
    INVOKE GetTickCount
    mov    esi,pSavedTime
```

```
    mov     [esi],eax
    ret
TimerStart ENDP

;----------------------------------------------------
TimerStop PROC uses esi,
    pSavedTime: PTR DWORD
;
; Stops the current stopwatch timer.
; Receives: pointer to a variable holding the
;           saved time
; Returns: EAX = number of elapsed milliseconds
; Remarks: Accurate to about 10ms
;----------------------------------------------------
    INVOKE GetTickCount
    mov esi,pSavedTime
    sub  eax,[esi]

    ret
TimerStop ENDP
END main
```

The **TimerStart** procedure receives a pointer to a doubleword, into which it saves the current time. The **TimerStop** procedure receives a pointer to the same doubleword, and returns the difference (in milliseconds) between the current time and the previously recorded time. Because of slight inaccuracies in the system time functions, the timer shown here is only accurate to 10 milliseconds.

11.1.10   Section Review

1. What linker command specifies that the target program is for the Win32 console?
2. *(True/False):* A function ending with the letter W (such as **WriteConsoleW**) is designed to work with a wide (16-bit) character set such as Unicode.
3. *(True/False):* Unicode is the native character set for Windows 98.
4. *(True/False):* The **ReadConsole** function reads mouse information from the input buffer.
5. *(True/False):* Win32 console input functions can detect when the user has resized the console window.
6. Name the MASM data type that matches each of the following standard MS-Windows types:

   ```
   BOOL
   COLORREF
   HANDLE
   LPSTR
   WPARAM
   ```

7. Which Win32 function returns a handle to standard input?

8. Which high-level Win32 function reads text input and places the characters in a buffer?
9. Show an example call to the **ReadConsole** function.
10. Describe the COORD structure.
11. Show an example call to the **WriteConsole** function.
12. Show an example call to the **CreateFile** function that will open an existing file for reading.
13. Show an example call to the **CreateFile** function that will create a new file with normal attributes, erasing any existing file by the same name.
14. Show an example call to the **ReadFile** function.
15. Show an example call to the **WriteFile** function.
16. Which function moves the file pointer?
17. Which function changes the title of the console window?
18. Which function lets you change the dimensions of the screen buffer?
19. Which function lets you change the size of the cursor?
20. Which function lets you change the color of subsequent text output?
21. Which function lets you copy an array of attribute values to consecutive cells of the console screen buffer?
22. Which function lets you pause a program for a selected number of milliseconds?

11.2   Writing a Graphical Windows Application

In this section, we will show how to write a simple graphical application for Microsoft Windows. The program creates and displays a main window, displays message boxes, and responds to mouse events. The information provided here is only a brief introduction; it would require at least an entire chapter to describe the workings of even the simplest MS-Windows application. If you want more information, see the Microsoft MSDN Library CD (supplied with Visual Studio), and look in the section entitled "Platform SDK, Win32 API." Another great source is Charles Petzold's book, *Programming in Windows: The Definitive Guide to the Win32 API.*

Required Files   You must have the following files available when assembling and running the example program shown in this section:

Filename	Description
make32.bat	Batch file specifically for building this program.
WinApp.asm	Program source code
GraphWin.inc	Include file containing structures, constants, and function prototypes used by the program
kernel32.lib	Same MS-Windows API library used earlier in this chapter
user32.lib	Additional MS-Windows API functions

The *make32.bat* file contains assembling and linking commands that are nearly identical to the ones we've been using throughout the book:

```
ML -c -coff %1.asm
LINK %1.obj kernel32.lib user32.lib /SUBSYSTEM:WINDOWS
```

Note that /SUBSYSTEM:WINDOWS replaces the /SUBSYSTEM:CONSOLE we used in previous chapters. The program calls functions from two standard MS-Windows libraries: kernel32.lib and user32.lib.

Display Window   The program displays a main window which fills the screen. It is reduced in size here to make it fit on the printed page:

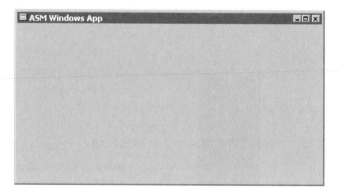

11.2.1 Necessary Structures

The **POINT** structure specifies the X and Y coordinates of a point on the screen, measured in pixels. It can be used, for example, to locate graphic objects, windows, and mouse clicks:

```
POINT STRUCT
  ptX  DWORD ?
  ptY  DWORD ?
POINT ENDS
```

The **RECT** structure defines the boundaries of a rectangle. The **left** member contains the X-coordinate of the left side of the rectangle. The **top** member contains the Y-coordinate of the top of the rectangle. Similar values are stored in the **right** and **bottom** members:

```
RECT STRUCT
  left                DWORD ?
  top                 DWORD ?
  right               DWORD ?
  bottom              DWORD ?
RECT ENDS
```

The **MSGStruct** structure defines the data needed for a MS-Windows message:

```
MSGStruct STRUCT
   msgWnd            DWORD ?
   msgMessage        DWORD ?
   msgWparam         DWORD ?
   msgLparam         DWORD ?
   msgTime           DWORD ?
   msgPt  POINT <>
MSGStruct ENDS
```

The **WNDCLASS** structure defines a window class. Each window in a program must belong to a class, and each program must define a window class for its main window. This class is registered with the operating system before the main window can be shown:

```
WNDCLASS STRUC
   style             DWORD ?        ; window style options
   lpfnWndProc       DWORD ?        ; pointer to WinProc function
   cbClsExtra        DWORD ?        ; shared memory
   cbWndExtra        DWORD ?        ; number of extra bytes
   hInstance         DWORD ?        ; handle to current program
   hIcon             DWORD ?        ; handle to icon
   hCursor           DWORD ?        ; handle to cursor
   hbrBackground     DWORD ?        ; handle to background brush
   lpszMenuName      DWORD ?        ; pointer to menu name
   lpszClassName     DWORD ?        ; pointer to WinClass name
WNDCLASS ENDS
```

Here's a quick summary of the parameters:

- *style* is a combination of different style options, such as WS_CAPTION and WS_BORDER, that control the window's appearance and behavior.
- *lpfnWndProc* is a pointer to a function (in our program) that receives and processes event messages triggered by the user.
- *cbClsExtra* refers to shared memory used by all windows belonging to the class. Can be null.
- *cbWndExtra* specifies the number of extra bytes to allocate following the window instance.
- *hInstance* holds a handle to the current program instance.
- *hIcon* and *hCursor* hold handles to icon and cursor resources for the current program.
- *hbrBackground* holds a background (color) brush.
- *lpszMenuName* points to a menu string.
- *lpszClassName* points to a null-terminated string containing the window's class name.

11.2.2   The MessageBox Function

The easiest way for a program to display text is to put it in a message box that pops up and waits for the user to click on a button. The **MessageBox** function from the Win32 API library displays a simple message box. Its prototype is:

```
MessageBox PROTO,
    hWnd:DWORD,
    pText:PTR BYTE,
    pCaption:PTR BYTE,
    style:DWORD
```

hWnd is a handle to the current window. *pText* points to a null-terminated string that will appear inside the box. *pCaption* points to a null-terminated string that will appear in the box's caption bar. *style* is an integer that describes both the dialog box's icon (optional) and the buttons (required). Buttons are identified by constants such as MB_OK and MB_YESNO. Icons are also identified by constants such as MB_ICONQUESTION. When a message box is displayed, you can add together the constants for the icon and buttons:

```
INVOKE MessageBox, hWnd, ADDR QuestionText,
       ADDR QuestionTitle, MB_OK + MB_ICONQUESTION
```

11.2.3   The WinMain Procedure

Every Windows application needs a startup procedure, usually named **WinMain**, which is responsible for the following tasks:

- Get a handle to the current program.
- Load the program's icon and mouse cursor.
- Register the program's main window class and identify the procedure that will process event messages for the window.
- Create the main window.
- Show and update the main window.
- Begin a loop that receives and dispatches messages.

11.2.4   The WinProc Procedure

The **WinProc** procedure receives and processes all event messages relating to a window. Most events are initiated by the user by clicking and dragging the mouse, pressing keyboard keys, and so on. This procedure's job is to decode each message, and if the message is recognized, to carry out application-oriented tasks relating to the message. Here is the declaration:

```
WinProc PROC,
    hWnd:DWORD,                    ; handle to the window
    localMsg:DWORD,                ; message ID
    wParam:DWORD,                  ; parameter 1 (varies)
    lParam:DWORD                   ; parameter 2 (varies)
```

The content of the third and fourth parameters will vary, depending on the specific message ID. When the mouse is clicked, for example, *lParam* contains the X and Y coordinates of the point clicked.

In the example program that we will be looking at soon, the **WinProc** procedure handles three specific messages:

- WM_LBUTTONDOWN, generated when the user presses the left mouse button
- WM_CREATE, indicates that the main window was just created
- WM_CLOSE, indicates that the application's main window is about to close

For example the following lines (from the procedure) handle the WM_LBUTTONDOWN message by calling **MessageBox** to display a popup message to the user:

```
.IF eax == WM_LBUTTONDOWN
  INVOKE MessageBox, hWnd, ADDR PopupText,
    ADDR PopupTitle, MB_OK
  jmp WinProcExit
```

Here is the resulting message seen by the user:

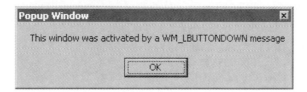

Any other messages that we don't wish to handle are passed on to **DefWindowProc**, the default message handler for MS-Windows.

11.2.5   The ErrorHandler Procedure

The **ErrorHandler** procedure, which is optional, is called if the system reports an error during the registration and creation of the program's main window. For example, the **RegisterClass** function returns a nonzero value if the program's main window was successfully registered. But if it returns zero, we call **ErrorHandler** (to display a message) and quit the program:

```
INVOKE RegisterClass, ADDR MainWin
.IF eax == 0
  call ErrorHandler
  jmp Exit Program
.ENDIF
```

The **ErrorHandler** procedure has several important tasks to perform:

- Call **GetLastError** to retrieve the system error number
- Call **FormatMessage** to retrieve the appropriate system-formatted error message string
- Call **MessageBox** to display a popup message box containing the error message string
- Call **LocalFree** to free the memory used by the error message string

11.2.6   Program Listing

Don't be distressed by the length of this program. Much of it is code that would be identical in any MS-Windows application:

```
TITLE Windows Application                 (WinApp.asm)

; This program displays a resizable application window and
; several popup message boxes. Special thanks to Tom Joyce
; for the first version of this program.

.386
.model flat,STDCALL
INCLUDE GraphWin.inc

;=================== DATA =======================
.data

AppLoadMsgTitle BYTE "Application Loaded",0
AppLoadMsgText  BYTE "This window displays when the WM_CREATE "
                BYTE "message is received",0

PopupTitle BYTE "Popup Window",0
PopupText  BYTE "This window was activated by a "
           BYTE "WM_LBUTTONDOWN message",0

GreetTitle BYTE "Main Window Active",0
GreetText  BYTE "This window is shown immediately after "
           BYTE "CreateWindow and UpdateWindow are called.",0

CloseMsg   BYTE "WM_CLOSE message received",0

ErrorTitle  BYTE "Error",0
WindowName  BYTE "ASM Windows App",0
className   BYTE "ASMWin",0

; Define the Application's Window class structure.
MainWin WNDCLASS <NULL,WinProc,NULL,NULL,NULL,NULL,NULL, \
    COLOR_WINDOW,NULL,className>

msg        MSGStruct <>
winRect    RECT <>
hMainWnd   DWORD ?
hInstance  DWORD ?

;=================== CODE =========================
.code
WinMain PROC
; Get a handle to the current process.
    INVOKE GetModuleHandle, NULL
    mov hInstance, eax
    mov MainWin.hInstance, eax
```

```
; Load the program's icon and cursor.
    INVOKE LoadIcon, NULL, IDI_APPLICATION
    mov MainWin.hIcon, eax
    INVOKE LoadCursor, NULL, IDC_ARROW
    mov MainWin.hCursor, eax

; Register the window class.
    INVOKE RegisterClass, ADDR MainWin
    .IF eax == 0
      call ErrorHandler
      jmp Exit_Program
    .ENDIF

; Create the application's main window.
    INVOKE CreateWindowEx, 0, ADDR className,
      ADDR WindowName,MAIN_WINDOW_STYLE,
      CW_USEDEFAULT,CW_USEDEFAULT,CW_USEDEFAULT,
      CW_USEDEFAULT,NULL,NULL,hInstance,NULL

; If CreateWindowEx failed, display a message and exit.
    .IF eax == 0
      call ErrorHandler
      jmp  Exit_Program
    .ENDIF

; Save the window handle, show and draw the window.
    mov hMainWnd,eax
    INVOKE ShowWindow, hMainWnd, SW_SHOW
    INVOKE UpdateWindow, hMainWnd

; Display a greeting message.
    INVOKE MessageBox, hMainWnd, ADDR GreetText,
      ADDR GreetTitle, MB_OK

; Begin the program's message-handling loop.
Message_Loop:
    ; Get next message from the queue.
    INVOKE GetMessage, ADDR msg, NULL,NULL,NULL

    ; Quit if no more messages.
    .IF eax == 0
      jmp Exit_Program
    .ENDIF

    ; Relay the message to the program's WinProc.
    INVOKE DispatchMessage, ADDR msg
    jmp Message_Loop

Exit_Program:
    INVOKE ExitProcess,0
WinMain ENDP
```

In the previous loop, the **msg** structure is passed to the **GetMessage** function. It fills in the structure, which is then passed to the MS-Windows **DispatchMessage** function.

```
;----------------------------------------------------------
WinProc PROC,
    hWnd:DWORD, localMsg:DWORD, wParam:DWORD, lParam:DWORD
; The application's message handler, which handles
; application-specific messages. All other messages
; are forwarded to the default Windows message
; handler.
;----------------------------------------------------------
    mov eax, localMsg

    .IF eax == WM_LBUTTONDOWN      ; mouse button?
      INVOKE MessageBox, hWnd, ADDR PopupText,
        ADDR PopupTitle, MB_OK
      jmp WinProcExit
    .ELSEIF eax == WM_CREATE       ; create window?
      INVOKE MessageBox, hWnd, ADDR AppLoadMsgText,
        ADDR AppLoadMsgTitle, MB_OK
      jmp WinProcExit
    .ELSEIF eax == WM_CLOSE        ; close window?
      INVOKE MessageBox, hWnd, ADDR CloseMsg,
        ADDR WindowName, MB_OK
      INVOKE PostQuitMessage,0
      jmp WinProcExit
    .ELSE                          ; other message?
      INVOKE DefWindowProc, hWnd, localMsg, wParam, lParam
      jmp WinProcExit
    .ENDIF

WinProcExit:
    ret
WinProc ENDP

;----------------------------------------------------------
ErrorHandler PROC
; Display the appropriate system error message.
;----------------------------------------------------------
.data
pErrorMsg  DWORD ?          ; ptr to error message
messageID  DWORD ?
.code
    INVOKE GetLastError     ; Returns message ID in EAX
    mov messageID,eax

    ; Get the corresponding message string.
    INVOKE FormatMessage, FORMAT_MESSAGE_ALLOCATE_BUFFER + \
```

```
          FORMAT_MESSAGE_FROM_SYSTEM,NULL,messageID,NULL,
          ADDR pErrorMsg,NULL,NULL

     ; Display the error message.
     INVOKE MessageBox,NULL, pErrorMsg, ADDR ErrorTitle,
       MB_ICONERROR+MB_OK

     ; Free the error message string.
     INVOKE LocalFree, pErrorMsg
     ret
ErrorHandler ENDP
END WinMain
```

11.2.6.1   Running the Program

When the program first loads, the following message box displays:

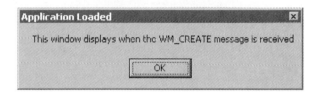

When the user clicks on OK to close the **Application Loaded** message box, another message box displays:

When the user closes the **Main Window Active** message box, the program's main window displays:

When the user clicks the mouse anywhere inside the main window, the following message box displays:

When the user closes this message box and then clicks on the X in the upper-right corner of the main window, the following message displays just before the window closes:

When the user closes this message box, the program ends.

11.2.7 Section Review

1. Describe a **POINT** structure.
2. How is the **WNDCLASS** structure used?
3. In a **WNDCLASS** structure, what is the meaning of the *lpfnWndProc* field?
4. In a **WNDCLASS** structure, what is the meaning of the *style* field?
5. In a **WNDCLASS** structure, what is the meaning of the *hInstance* field?
6. When **CreateWindowEx** is called, how is the window's appearance information transmitted to the function?
7. Show an example of calling the **MessageBox** function.
8. Name two button constants that can be used when calling the **MessageBox** function.
9. Name two icon constants that can be used when calling the **MessageBox** function.
10. Name at least three tasks performed by the **WinMain** (startup) procedure.
11. Describe the role of the **WinProc** procedure in the example program.
12. Which messages are processed by the **WinProc** procedure in the example program?
13. Describe the role of the **ErrorHandler** procedure in the example program.
14. Does the message box activated immediately after calling **CreateWindow** appear before or after the application's main window?
15. Does the message box activated by WM_CLOSE appear before or after the main window closes?

11.3   IA-32 Memory Management

When MS-Windows 3.0 was first released, there was a great deal of interest among program-mers about the switch from Real mode to Protected mode. (Anyone who wrote programs for Windows 2.x will recall how difficult it was to stay within 640K in Real-address mode!) With Windows Protected mode (and soon after, Virtual mode), whole new possibilities seemed to open up. One must not forget that it was the Intel386 processor (the first of the IA-32 family) that made all of this possible. What we now take for granted was a gradual 10-year evolution from the unstable Windows 3.0 to the sophisticated (and stable) versions of Windows and Linux offered today.

This section of the chapter will focus on two primary aspects of memory management:

- Translating logical addresses into linear addresses
- Translating linear addresses into physical addresses (paging)

Let's briefly review some of the IA-32 memory-management terms introduced in Chapter 2, beginning with the following:

- *Multitasking* permits multiple programs (or tasks) to run at the same time. The processor divides up its time between all of the running programs.
- *Segments* are variable-sized areas of memory used by a program containing either code or data.
- *Segmentation* provides a way to isolate memory segments from each other. This permits multiple programs to run simultaneously without interfering with each other.
- A *segment descriptor* is a 64-bit value that identifies and describes a single memory seg-ment: it contains information about the segment's base address, access rights, size limit, type, and usage.

Now we will add two new terms to the list:

- A *segment selector* is a 16-bit value stored in a segment register (CS, DS, SS, ES, FS, or GS).
- A *logical address* is a combination of a segment selector and a 32-bit offset.

Segment registers have been ignored throughout this book because they are never modi-fied directly by user programs. We have only been concerned with 32-bit offsets. From a sys-tem programmer's point of view, however, segment registers are important because they contain indirect references to memory segments.

11.3.1   Linear Addresses

11.3.1.1   Translating Logical Addresses to Linear Addresses

A multitasking operating system allows several programs (tasks) to run in memory at the same time. Each program has its own unique area for data. Suppose three programs each had a variable at offset 200h; how could the three variables be separate from each other without being shared? The answer to this is that the IA-32 processor uses a one- or two-step process to convert each variable's offset into a unique memory location.

The first step combines a segment value with a variable's offset to create a *linear address*. This linear address could be the variable's physical address. But operating systems such as MS-Windows and Linux employ an IA-32 feature called *paging* to permit programs to use more linear memory than is physically available in the computer. They must use a second step called *page translation* to convert a linear address to a physical address. We will explain page translation in Section 11.3.2.

First, let's look at the way the processor uses a segment and offset to determine the linear address of a variable. Each segment selector points to a segment descriptor (in a descriptor table), which contains the base address of a memory segment. The 32-bit offset in the logical address is added to the segment's base address, generating the linear address, as shown in Figure 11-2.

Linear Address A *linear address* is a 32-bit integer ranging between 0 and FFFFFFFFh, which refers to a memory location. The linear address may also be the physical address of the target data, if a feature called *paging* is disabled.

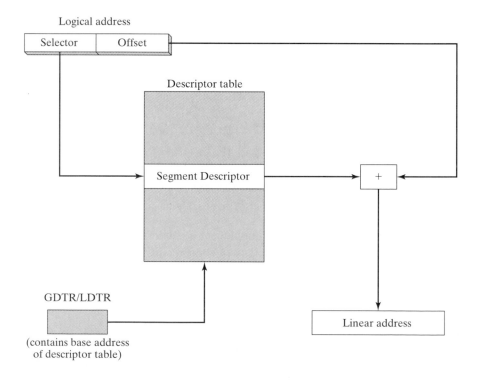

Figure 11-2   Converting a Logical Address Into a Linear Address.

11.3.1.2   Paging

Paging is an important feature of the IA-32 processor that makes it possible for a computer to run a combination of programs that would not otherwise fit into memory. The processor does this by initially loading only part of a program in memory, while the remaining parts are kept on disk. The memory used by the program is divided into small units called *pages*, typically 4 KB each. As each program runs, the processor selectively unloads inactive pages from memory and loads other pages that are immediately required.

The operating system maintains a *page directory* and a set of *page tables* to keep track of the pages used by all programs currently in memory. When a program attempts to access an address somewhere in the linear address space, the processor automatically converts the linear address into a physical address. This conversion is called *page translation*. If the requested page is not currently in memory, the processor interrupts the program and issues a *page fault*. The operating system copies the required page from disk into memory before the program can resume. From the point of view of an application program, page faults and page translation happen automatically.

In Windows 2000, for example, you can activate a utility named *Task Manager* and see the difference between physical memory and virtual memory. The following example shows a computer with 256 MB of physical memory:

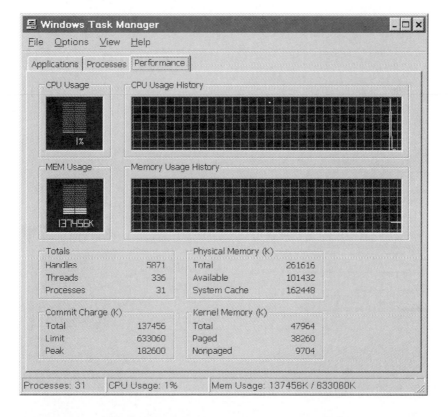

The total amount of virtual memory currently in use is in the *Commit Charge* frame of the Task Manager. Notice in the figure that the virtual memory limit is 633 MB, considerably larger than the computer's physical memory size.

11.3.1.3   Descriptor Tables

Segment descriptors can be found in two types of tables: *global descriptor tables* (GDT), and *local descriptor tables* (LDT).

Global Descriptor Table (GDT)   There is only one global descriptor table, which is created when the operating system switches the processor into Protected mode. Its base address is held in the GDTR (global descriptor table register). The table contains entries (called *segment descriptors*) that point to segments. The operating system has the option of storing the segments used by all programs in the GDT.

Local Descriptor Tables (LDT)   In a multitasking operating system, each task or program is usually assigned its own table of segment descriptors, called a *local descriptor table* (LDT). The LDTR register contains the address of the program's LDT.

Each segment descriptor contains the base address of a segment within the linear address space. This segment is usually distinct from all other segments, as is the case in Figure 11-3. Three different logical addresses are shown, each selecting a different entry in the LDT. In this figure we assume that paging is disabled, so the linear address space is also the physical address space.

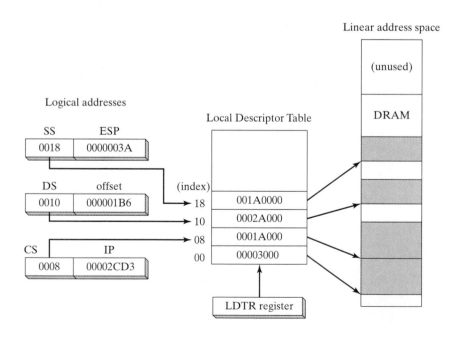

Figure 11-3   Indexing into a Local Descriptor Table.

11.3.1.4   Segment Descriptor Details

A segment descriptor contains bit-mapped fields that specify the segment limit, as well as the segment type. A code segment is automatically designated read-only, for example. If a program tries to modify a code segment, a processor fault is generated. Segment descriptors can contain protection levels that protect operating system data from access by application programs. The following are descriptions of individual selector fields:

Base address: 32-bit integer that defines the starting location of the segment in the 4 GB linear address space.

Privilege level: Each segment can be assigned a privilege level between 0 and 3, where 0 is the most privileged, usually for operating system kernel code. If a program with a higher-numbered privilege level tries to access a segment having a lower-numbered privilege level, a processor fault is generated.

Segment type: Indicates the type of segment and specifies the type of access that can be made to the segment, and the direction the segment can grow (up or down). Data (including Stack) segments can be read-only or read/write, and can grow either up or down. Code segments can be execute-only or execute/read-only.

Segment present flag: This bit indicates whether the segment is currently present in physical memory.

Granularity flag: Determines the interpretation of the Segment limit field. If the bit is clear, the segment limit is interpreted in byte units. If the bit is set, the segment limit is interpreted in 4,096-byte units.

Segment limit: 20-bit integer that specifies the size of the segment. It is interpreted in one of two ways, depending on the Granularity flag:

- Segment size of 1 byte to 1 MB.
- Segment size of 4096 bytes to 4 GB.

11.3.2   Page Translation

When paging is enabled, the processor must translate a 32-bit linear address into a 32-bit physical address.[2] There are three structures used in the process:

- Page directory: An array of up to 1024 32-bit page-directory entries.
- Page table: An array of up to 1024 32-bit page-table entries.
- Page: A 4-K or 4-MB address space.

To simplify the following discussion, we will assume that 4-KB pages are used:

A linear address is divided into three fields: a pointer to a page directory entry, a pointer to a page table entry, and an offset into a page frame. Control register (CR3) contains the starting

---

[2] The Pentium Pro and later processors permit a 36-bit address option, but it will not be covered here.

address of the page directory. The following steps are carried out by the processor when translating a linear address to a physical address, as shown in Figure 11-4:

1. The *linear address* references a location in the linear address space.
2. The 10-bit *directory* field in the linear address is an index to a page directory entry. The page directory entry contains the base address of a page table.
3. The 10-bit *table* field in the linear address is an index into the page table identified by the page directory entry. The page table entry at that position contains the base location of a *page* in physical memory.
4. The 12-bit *offset* field in the linear address is added to the base address of the page, generating the exact physical address of the operand.

The operating system has the option of using a single page directory for all running programs and tasks, or one page directory per task, or a combination of the two.

11.3.2.1 MS-Windows Virtual Machine Manager

Now that we have a general idea of how the IA-32 manages memory, it might be interesting to see how memory management is handled by MS-Windows. The following passage is paraphrased from the Microsoft Platform SDK documentation for Windows 95 and 98:

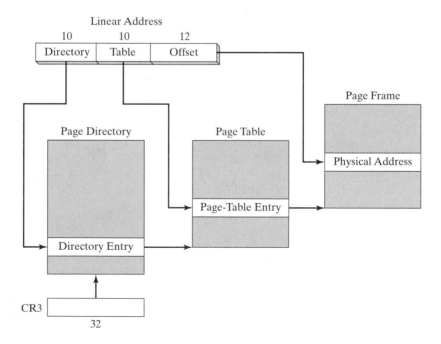

Figure 11-4 Translating Linear Address to Physical Address.

> The Virtual Machine Manager (VMM) is the 32-bit Protected mode operating system at the core of Windows 95 and 98. Its primary responsibility is to create, run, monitor, and terminate virtual machines. The VMM provides services that manage memory, processes, interrupts, and exceptions. It works with virtual devices, 32-bit Protected mode modules, to allow the virtual devices to intercept interrupts and faults to control application programs' access to hardware and installed software.
>
> Both the VMM and the virtual devices run in a single 32-bit flat model address space at privilege level 0. The system creates two global descriptor table entries (segment descriptors), one for code and the other for data. Both segments begin at linear address 0, and never change. The VMM provides multithreaded, preemptive multitasking. It runs multiple applications simultaneously by sharing CPU time between the virtual machines in which the applications run.

In the foregoing passage, we can interpret the term *virtual machine* to be what Intel calls a *process* or *task*. It consists of program code, supporting software, memory, and registers. Each virtual machine is assigned its own address space, I/O port space, interrupt vector table, and local descriptor table. Applications running in virtual-8086 mode run at privilege level 3. Protected-mode programs run at privilege level 1, 2, or 3.

11.3.3   Section Review

1. Define the following terms:

    a. multitasking.
    b. segmentation.

2. Define the following terms:

    a. segment selector
    b. logical address

3. (*True/False*): A segment selector points to an entry in a segment descriptor table.
4. (*True/False*): A segment descriptor contains the base location of a segment.
5. (*True/False*): A segment selector is 32 bits.
6. (*True/False*): A segment descriptor does not contain segment size information.
7. Describe a linear address.
8. How does paging relate to linear memory?
9. If paging is disabled, how does the processor translate a linear address to a physical address?
10. What advantage does paging offer?
11. Which register contains the base location of a local descriptor table?
12. Which register contains the base location of a global descriptor table?
13. How many global descriptor tables can exist?
14. How many local descriptor tables can exist?
15. Name at least four fields in a segment descriptor.

16. Which structures are involved in the paging process?
17. What structure contains the base address of a page table?
18. What structure contains the base address of a page frame?

11.4 Chapter Summary

On the surface, 32-bit console mode programs look and behave like 16-bit MS-DOS programs running in text mode. Both types of programs read from standard input and write to standard output, they support command-line redirection, and they can display text in color. Beneath the surface, however, Win32 consoles and MS-DOS programs are quite different. Win32 runs in 32-bit Protected mode, whereas MS-DOS runs in Real-address mode. Win32 programs can call functions from the same function library used by graphical Windows applications. MS-DOS programs are limited to a smaller set of BIOS and MS-DOS interrupts that have existed since the introduction of the IBM-PC.

There are two types of character sets used in Windows API functions: the 8-bit ASCII/ANSI character set, and the 16-bit wide/Unicode character set.

Standard MS-Windows data types used in the API functions must be translated to MASM data types (see Table 11-1).

Console handles are 32-bit integers used for input/output in console windows. The **GetStdHandle** function retrieves a console handle. For high-level console input, call the **ReadConsole** function; for high-level output, call **WriteConsole**. When creating or opening a file, call **CreateFile**. When reading from a file, call **ReadFile**, and when writing, call **WriteFile**. **CloseHandle** closes a file. To move a file pointer, call **SetFilePointer**.

To manipulate the console screen buffer, call **SetConsoleScreenBufferSize**. To change the text color, call **SetConsoleTextAttribute**. The WriteColors program in this chapter demonstrated the **WriteConsoleOutputAttribute** and **WriteConsoleOutputCharacter** functions.

To get the system time, call **GetLocalTime**; to set the time, call **SetLocalTime**. Both functions use the SYSTEMTIME structure. The **GetDateTime** function example in this chapter returns the date and time as a 64-bit integer, specifying the number of 100-nanosecond intervals that have occurred since January 1, 1601. The **TimerStart** and **TimerStop** functions can be used to create a simple stopwatch timer.

When creating a graphical MS-Windows application, you must fill in a WNDCLASS structure with information about the program's main window class. You must create a **WinMain** procedure that gets a handle to the current process, loads the icon and mouse cursor, registers the program's main window, creates the main window, shows and updates the main windows, and begins a message loop that receives and dispatches messages.

The **WinProc** procedure is responsible for handling incoming Windows messages, often activated by user actions such as a mouse click or keystroke. The example program processes a WM_LBUTTONDOWN message, a WM_CREATE message, and a WM_CLOSE message. It displays popup messages when these events are detected.

The memory management section of this chapter focuses on two main topics: translating logical addresses into linear addresses, and translating linear addresses into physical addresses.

A logical address points to an entry in a segment descriptor table, which in turn points to a segment in linear memory. The segment descriptor contains information about the segment, including its size and type of access. There are two types of descriptor tables: a single global descriptor table (GDT) and one or more local descriptor tables (LDT).

Paging is an important feature of the IA-32 processor that makes it possible for a computer to run a combination of programs that would not otherwise fit into memory. The processor does this by initially loading only part of a program in memory, while the remaining parts are kept on disk. The processor uses a page directory, page table, and page frame to generate the physical location of data. A page directory contains pointers to page tables. A page table contains pointers to pages.

Reading   For further reading about Windows programming, the following books may be helpful:

- Kauler, Barry. *Windows Assembly Language and System Programming*. R & D Books, 1997.
- Petzold, Charles. *Programming Windows: The Definitive Guide to the Win32 API*.

11.5   Programming Exercises

1. ReadString
Implement your own version of the **ReadString** procedure, using stack parameters. Pass it a pointer to a string and an integer indicating the maximum number of characters to be entered. Return a count (in EAX) of the number of characters actually entered. The procedure must input a string from the console and insert a null byte at the end of the string (in the position occupied by 0Dh). See Section 11.1.3.1 for details on the Win32 **ReadConsole** function. Write a short program that tests your procedure.

2. String Input/Output
Write a program that inputs the following information from the user, using the Win32 **ReadConsole** function: First name, last name, age, phone number. Redisplay the same information with labels and attractive formatting, using the Win32 **WriteConsole** function. Do not use any procedures from the Irvine32 library.

3. Clearing the Screen
Write your own version of the link library's **Clrscr** procedure that clears the screen.

4. Random Screen Fill
Write a program that fills each screen cell with a random character, in a random color. *Extra:* assign a 50% probability that the color of any character will be red.

5. DrawBox
Draw a box on the screen using line-drawing characters from the character set listed on the inside back cover of your book. *Hint:* Use the **WriteConsoleOutputCharacter** function.

6. Student Records

Write a program that creates a new text file. Prompt the user for a student identification number, last name, first name, and date of birth. Write this information to the file. Input several more records in the same manner and close the file.

7. Scrolling Text Window

Write a program that writes 50 lines of text to the console screen buffer. Number each line. Move the console window to the top of the buffer, and begin scrolling the text upward at a steady rate (two lines per second). Stop scrolling when the console window reaches the end of the buffer.

8. Block Animation

Write a program that draws a small square on the screen using several blocks (ASCII code DBh) in color. Move the square around the screen in randomly generated directions. Use a fixed delay value of 100 ms. *Extra:* Use a randomly generated delay value between 10 ms and 100 ms.

12

High-Level Language Interface

12.1 Introduction

Most programmers do not write large-scale applications in assembly language, simply because it takes too long. High-level languages are designed to relieve the programmer of details that would otherwise slow down a project's development. But assembly language is still used widely to configure hardware devices and optimize both the speed and code size of programs.

In this chapter, we focus on the *interface*, or connection, between assembly language and high-level programming languages. In the first section, we will show how to write inline assembly code in C++. In the next section, we will link separate assembly language modules to C++ programs. Examples are shown for both Protected mode and Real-address mode.

12.1.1 General Conventions

There are a number of general considerations that must be addressed when calling assembly language procedures from high-level languages:

First, the *naming convention* used by a language refers to the rules or characteristics regarding the naming of variables and procedures. For example, we have to answer an important question: Does the assembler or compiler alter the names of identifiers placed in object files, and if so, how?

Second, the *memory model* used by a program (tiny, small, compact, medium, large, huge, or flat) determines the segment size (16 or 32 bits), and whether calls and references will be near (within the same segment) or far (between different segments).

Calling Convention   The *calling convention* refers to the low-level details about how procedures are called. The following details must be considered:

- Which registers must be preserved by called procedures.
- The method used to pass arguments: in registers, on the stack, in shared memory, or by some other method.
- The order in which arguments are passed by calling programs to procedures.
- Whether arguments are passed by value or by reference.
- How the stack pointer is restored after a procedure call.
- How functions return values to calling programs.

External Identifiers   When calling an assembly language procedure from a program written in another language, external identifiers must have compatible naming conventions. *External identifiers* are names that have been placed in a module's object file in such a way that the linker can make the names available to other program modules. The linker resolves references to external identifiers, but can only do so if the naming conventions being used are consistent.

For example, suppose a C program named *main.cpp* calls an external procedure named **ArraySum**. As illustrated below, the C compiler automatically preserves case and appends a leading underscore to the external name, changing it to **_ArraySum**:

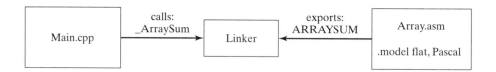

The *Array.asm* module, written in assembly language, exports the **ArraySum** procedure name as ARRAYSUM, because the module uses the Pascal language option in its. MODEL directive. The linker fails to produce an executable program because the two exported names are different.

Compilers for older programming languages such as COBOL and PASCAL usually convert identifiers to all uppercase letters. More recent languages such as C, C++, and Java preserve the case of identifiers. In addition, languages that support function overloading (such as C++) use a technique known as *name decoration* that adds additional characters to function names. A function named *MySub(int n, double b),* for example, might be exported as *MySub#int#double*.

In an assembly language module, you can control case sensitivity by choosing one of the language specifiers in the .MODEL directive (see Section 8.4.2 for details).

Segment Names   When linking an assembly language procedure to a program written in a high-level language, segment names must be compatible. In this chapter, we use Microsoft simplified segment directives such as .CODE and .DATA because they are compatible with segment names produced by most C++ compilers.

Memory Models   A calling program and a called procedure must both use the same memory model. In Real-address mode, for example, you can choose from the small, medium, compact, large, and huge models. In Protected mode, you must use the flat model. We show examples of both modes in this chapter.

12.1.2   Section Review

1. What is meant by the *naming convention* used by a language?
2. Which memory models are available in Real-address mode?
3. Will an assembly language procedure that uses the Pascal language specifier link to a C++ program?
4. When a procedure written in assembly language is called by a high-level language program, must the calling program and the procedure use the same memory model?
5. Why is case-sensitivity important when calling assembly language procedures from C and C++ programs?
6. Does a language's calling convention include the preserving of certain registers by procedures?

12.2   Inline Assembly Code

12.2.1   __asm Directive in Microsoft Visual C++

Inline assembly code is assembly language source code that is inserted directly into high-level language programs. Most C/C++ compilers support this feature, as do Borland C++, Pascal, and Delphi.

In this section, we demonstrate how to write inline assembly code for Microsoft Visual C++ running in 32-bit Protected mode with the flat memory model. Other high-level language compilers support inline assembly code, but the exact syntax varies. See the book's Web site for any changes to inline assembly code in Visual C++.NET.

Inline assembly code is a straightforward alternative to writing assembly code in external modules. The primary advantage to writing inline code is simplicity, because there are no external linking issues, naming problems, and parameter passing protocols to worry about.

The primary disadvantage to using inline assembly code is its lack of portability. This is an issue when a high-level language program must be compiled for different target platforms. Inline assembly code that runs on an Intel Pentium processor will not run on a RISC processor, for example. To some extent, the problem can be solved by inserting conditional definitions in the program's source code to enable different versions of functions for different target systems. But it is easy to see that maintenance is still a problem. A link library of external assembly language procedures, on the other hand, could easily be replaced by a similar link library designed for a different target machine.

The __asm Directive   In Visual C++, the **__asm** directive can be placed at the beginning of a single statement, or it can mark the beginning of a block of assembly language statements (called an *asm block*). The syntax is:

```
__asm  statement

__asm {
  statement-1
  statement-2
  . . .
  statement-n
}
```

(There are two underline characters before "asm.")

Comments   Comments can be placed after any statements in the asm block, using either assembly language syntax or C/C++ syntax. The Visual C++ manual suggests that you avoid assembler-style comments because they might interfere with C macros, which expand on a single logical line. Here are examples of permissible comments:

```
mov  esi,buf    ; initialize index register
mov  esi,buf    // initialize index register
mov  esi,buf    /* initialize index register */
```

Features   Here is what you can do when writing inline assembly code:

- Use any instruction from the Intel instruction set.
- Use register names as operands.
- Reference function parameters by name.
- Reference code labels and variables that were declared outside the *asm* block. (This is important, because local function variables must be declared outside the asm block.)
- Use numeric literals that incorporate either assembler-style or C-style radix notation. For example, 0A26h and 0xA26 are equivalent and can both be used.
- Use the PTR operator in statements such as **inc BYTE PTR [esi]**.
- Use the EVEN and ALIGN directives.

Limitations   You cannot do the following when writing inline assembly code:

- Use data definition directives such as DB (BYTE) and DW (WORD).
- Use assembler operators (other than PTR).
- Use STRUCT, RECORD, WIDTH, and MASK.
- Use macro directives, including MACRO, REPT, IRC, IRP, and ENDM, or macro operators (<>, !, &, %, and .TYPE).
- Reference segments by name. (You can, however, use segment register names as operands.)

Register Values   You cannot make any assumptions about register values at the beginning of an asm block. The registers may have been modified by code that executed just before the asm block. The __**fastcall** keyword in Microsoft Visual C++ causes the compiler to use registers to pass parameters. To avoid register conflicts, do not use __**fastcall** and __**asm** together.

In general, you can modify EAX, EBX, ECX, and EDX in your inline code, because the compiler does not expect these values to be preserved between statements. If you modify too many registers, however, you may make it impossible for the compiler to fully optimize the C++ code in the same procedure because optimization requires the use of registers.

Although you cannot use the OFFSET operator, you can still retrieve the offset of a variable using the LEA instruction. For example, the following instruction moves the offset of **buffer** to ESI:

```
lea esi,buffer
```

Length, Type, and Size   You can use the LENGTH, SIZE, and TYPE operators with the inline assembler. The LENGTH operator returns the number of elements in an array. The TYPE operator returns one of the following, depending on its target:

- The number of bytes used by a C or C++ type or scalar variable
- The number of bytes used by a structure
- For an array, the size of a single array element

The SIZE operator returns LENGTH * TYPE. The following program excerpt demonstrates the values returned by the inline assembler for various C++ types.

> Microsoft Visual C++ 6.0's inline assembler does not support the SIZEOF and LENGTHOF operators that were introduced in MASM 6.0.

12.2.1.1   Using the LENGTH, TYPE, and SIZE Operators

The following program contains inline assembly code that uses the LENGTH, TYPE, and SIZE operators to evaluate C++ variables. The value returned by each expression is shown as a comment on the same line:

```
struct Package {
    long originZip;              // 4
    long destinationZip;        // 4
    float shippingPrice;        // 4
};
    char myChar;
    bool myBool;
    short myShort;
    int myInt;
    long myLong;
    float myFloat;
```

```
    double myDouble;
    Package myPackage;

    long double myLongDouble;
    long myLongArray[10];

__asm {
    mov eax,myPackage.destinationZip;

    mov eax,LENGTH myInt;           // 1
    mov eax,LENGTH myLongArray;     // 10

    mov eax,TYPE myChar;            // 1
    mov eax,TYPE myBool;            // 1
    mov eax,TYPE myShort;           // 2
    mov eax,TYPE myInt;             // 4
    mov eax,TYPE myLong;            // 4
    mov eax,TYPE myFloat;           // 4
    mov eax,TYPE myDouble;          // 8
    mov eax,TYPE myPackage;         // 12
    mov eax,TYPE myLongDouble;      // 8
    mov eax,TYPE myLongArray;       // 4

    mov eax,SIZE myLong;            // 4
    mov eax,SIZE myPackage;         // 12
    mov eax,SIZE myLongArray;       // 40
}
```

12.2.2 File Encryption Example

Let's write a short program that reads a file, encrypts it, and writes the output to another file. The **TranslateBuffer** function uses an __**asm** block to define statements that loop through a character array and XOR each character with a predefined value. The inline statements can refer to function parameters, local variables, and code labels. Because this example was compiled under Microsoft Visual C++ as a Win32 Console application, the unsigned integer data type is 32 bits:

```
void TranslateBuffer( char * buf,
    unsigned count, unsigned char encryptChar )
{
    asm {
    mov esi,buf
    mov ecx,count
    mov al,encryptChar
L1:
    xor [esi],al
    inc  esi
    loop L1
    }               // asm
}
```

In main(), **TranslateBuffer** is called from a loop that reads blocks of data from a file, encrypts it, and writes the translated buffer to a new file:

```cpp
// ENCODE.CPP - Copy and encrypt a file

#include <iostream>
#include <fstream>
#include "translat.h"
using namespace std;

int main()
{
  const int BUFSIZE = 200;
  char buffer[BUFSIZE];
  unsigned int count;

  unsigned short encryptCode;
  cout << "Encryption code [0-255]? ";
  cin >> encryptCode;

  ifstream infile( "infile.txt", ios::binary );
  ofstream outfile( "outfile.txt", ios::binary );

  while (!infile.eof() )
  {
    infile.read(buffer, BUFSIZE );
    count = infile.gcount();
    TranslateBuffer(buffer, count, encryptCode);
    outfile.write(buffer, count);
  }
  return 0;
}
```

The *translat.h* header file contains a single function prototype for **TranslateBuffer**:

```cpp
void TranslateBuffer( char * buf, unsigned count,
                      unsigned char eChar );
```

12.2.2.1   Procedure Call Overhead

If you view the Disassembly window while debugging this program in a debugger, it is interesting to see exactly how much overhead can be involved in calling and returning from a procedure. The following statements push the arguments on the stack and call **TranslateBuffer:**

```
const EncryptCode = 0F1h
.code
push EncryptCode
mov  ecx,dword ptr [count]
push ecx
push OFFSET buffer
call TranslateBuffer
add  esp,0Ch
```

The following is the assembly language code for **TranslateBuffer**. Note that a number of statements were automatically inserted by the compiler, to set up EBP and save a standard set of registers that are always preserved whether or not they are actually modified by the procedure:

```
    push   ebp
    mov    ebp,esp
    push   ebx
    push   esi
    push   edi
    mov    esi,buf              ; inline code starts here
    mov    ecx,count
    mov    al,eChar
L1:
    xor    [esi],al
    inc    esi
    loop   L1                   ; inline code ends here
    pop    edi
    pop    esi
    pop    ebx
    pop    ebp
    ret
```

> The compiler was instructed to generate a *Debug* target, which is non-optimized code suitable for interactive debugging. If we had selected a *Release* target, the compiler would have generated more efficient (but harder to read) code. In Section 12.3.4.2 we will show you fully optimized compiler-generated code.

The six inline instructions in the **TranslateBuffer** function shown at the beginning of this section turned out to require a total of 22 instructions to execute. If the function were called thousands of times, the execution speed loss might be measurable. To avoid this, we can insert the inline code directly in the loop that called TranslateBuffer, creating a much more efficient program:

```
encryptChar = unsigned char (encryptCode);
while (!infile.eof() )
{
   infile.read(buffer, BUFSIZE );
   count = infile.gcount();
   __asm {
       lea esi,buffer
       mov ecx,count
       mov al,encryptChar
   L1:
       xor [esi],al
       inc  esi
```

```
        Loop L1
    } // asm
     outfile.write(buffer, count);
}
```

Notice that we had to cast **encryptCode** from an unsigned short integer into an *unsigned char* and store it in **encryptChar,** because short integers are 2 bytes and characters are 1 byte.

12.2.3 Section Review

1. How is inline assembly code different from an inline C++ procedure?
2. What advantage does inline assembly code offer over the use of external assembly language procedures?
3. Show at least two ways of placing comments in inline assembly code.
4. (*Yes/no*): Can an inline statement refer to code labels outside the __asm block?
5. (*Yes/no*): Can both the EVEN and ALIGN directives be used in inline assembly code?
6. (*Yes/no*): Can the OFFSET operator be used in inline assembly code?
7. (*Yes/no*): Can variables be defined with both DW and the DUP operator in inline assembly code?
8. When using the __**fastcall** calling convention, what might happen if your inline assembly code modifies registers?
9. Rather than using the OFFSET operator, is there another way to move a variable's offset into an index register?
10. What value is returned by the LENGTH operator when applied to an array of 32-bit integers?
11. What value is returned by the SIZE operator when applied to an array of long integers?

12.3 Linking to C++ Programs

We want to show how to write external procedures in assembly language that can be called from C and C++ programs. Such programs consist of at least two modules: the first, written in assembly language, contains the external procedure; the second module contains the C/C++ code that starts and ends the program. There are a few specific requirements and features of C/C++ that affect the way you write assembly code.

Arguments   Arguments are passed by C/C++ programs from right to left, as they appear in the argument list. After the procedure returns, the calling program is responsible for cleaning up the stack. This can be done by either adding a value to the stack pointer equal to the size of the arguments or popping an adequate number of values from the stack.

External Names   C/C++ automatically appends an underscore (_) to the beginning of each external identifier. For example, if we call a procedure named **ReadSector** from a C/C++ program, the procedure name must begin with an underscore in the ASM module:

```
    public _ReadSector        Public declaration
    _ReadSector PROC          Procedure name
```

When assembling a module containing an external procedure, you must use a command line option that preserves case-sensitive names. Otherwise, a name such as _ReadSector would be automatically converted to _READSECTOR by the assembler. Then, when linking this module to a C/C++ program, the linker would not be able to match up the procedure name being called by the C++ program. To assure case sensitivity for public names, use MASM's **/Cx** command line option.

Declaring the Function   In a C language program, use the **extern** qualifier when declaring an external assembly language function. For example, this is how to declare **ReadSector**:

```
extern ReadSector( char buffer[], long startSector,
        int driveNum, int numSectors );
```

If the function is called from a C++ program, you must also add a "C" qualifier that prevents name decoration:

```
extern "C" ReadSector( char buffer[], long startSector,
            int driveNum, int numSectors );
```

Name decoration is a standard C++ compiler technique that involves modifying a function name with extra characters that indicate the exact type of each function parameter. It is required in any language that supports function overloading (two functions having the same name, with different parameter lists). From the assembly language programmer's point of view, the problem with name decoration is that the C++ compiler tells the linker to look for the decorated name rather than the original one when producing the executable file.

12.3.1   Linking to Borland C++

In this section of the chapter we will use the 16-bit version of Borland C++ 5.01 and select MS-DOS as the target operating system with a small memory model. We use Borland TASM 4.0 as the assembler for these examples, because most users of Borland C++ are likely to use Turbo Assembler rather than MASM. We will also create 16-bit real mode applications using Borland C++ 5.01, and demonstrate both small and large memory model programs, showing how to call both near and far procedures.

Function Return Values   In Borland C++, functions return 16-bit values in AX and 32-bit values in DX:AX. Larger data structures (structure values, arrays, etc.) are stored in a static data location, and a pointer to the data is returned in AX. (In medium, large, and huge memory model programs, a 32-bit pointer is returned in DX:AX.)

Setting Up a Project   In the Borland C++ integrated development environment (IDE), create a new project. Create a source code module (CPP file) and enter the code for the main C++ program. Create the ASM file containing the procedure you plan to call. Use TASM to assemble the program into an object module, either from the DOS command line or from the Borland C++ IDE, using its transfer capability.

If you have assembled the ASM module separately, add the object file created by the assembler to the C++ project. Invoke the MAKE or BUILD command from the menu. It compiles the CPP file, and if there are no errors, it links the two object modules to produce an executable program. Suggestion: limit the name of the CPP source file to eight characters, or the Turbo Debugger for DOS will not be able to find it when you debug the program.

Debugging   The Borland C++ compiler does not allow the DOS debugger to be run from the IDE. Instead, you need to run Turbo Debugger for DOS either from the DOS prompt or from the Windows desktop. Using the debugger's File/Open menu command, select the executable file created by the C++ linker. The C++ source code file should immediately display, and you can begin tracing and running the program.

Saving Registers   Assembly procedures called by Borland C++ must preserve the values of BP, DS, SS, SI, DI, and the Direction flag.

Storage Sizes   A 16-bit Borland C++ program uses specific storage sizes for all its data types. These are unique to this particular implementation and must be adjusted for every C++ compiler. Refer to Table 12-1.

Table 12-1   Borland C++ Data Types in 16-Bit Applications.

C++ Type	Storage Bytes	ASM Type
char, unsigned char	1	byte
int, unsigned int, short int	2	word
enum	2	word
long, unsigned long	4	dword
float	4	dword
double	8	qword
long double	10	tbyte
near pointer	2	word
far pointer	4	dword

12.3.2   ReadSector Example

Let's begin with a Borland C++ program that calls an external assembly language procedure named **ReadSector**. C++ compilers generally do not include library functions for reading disk sectors, because such details are too hardware-dependent, and it would be impractical to implement libraries for all possible computers. Assembly language programs can easily read disk sectors by calling INT 21h Function 7305h (see Section 14.4 for details). Our present task, then, is to create the interface between assembly language and C++ that combines the strengths of both languages.

The **ReadSector** example requires the use of a 16-bit compiler because it involves calling MS-DOS interrupts. (Calling 16-bit interrupts from 32-bit programs is possible, but it is beyond the scope of this book.)[1] The last version of Visual C++ to produce 16-bit programs was version 1.5. Other compilers that produce 16-bit code are Turbo C and Turbo Pascal, both by Borland.

Program Execution   First, we will demonstrate the program's execution. When the C++ program starts up, the user selects the drive number, starting sector, and number of sectors to read. For example, this user wants to read sectors 0–19 from drive A:

```
Sector display program.

Enter drive number [1=A, 2=B, 3=C, 4=D, 5=E,...]: 1
Starting sector number to read: 0
Number of sectors to read: 20
```

This information is passed to the assembly language procedure, which reads the sectors into a buffer. The C++ program begins to display the buffer, one sector at a time. As each sector is displayed, non-ASCII characters are replaced by dots. For example, the following is the program's display of sector 0 from drive A:

```
Reading sectors 0 - 20 from Drive 1

Sector 0 -----------------------------------------------------------
.<.(P3j2IHC........@.................)Y...MYDISK     FAT12    .3.
....{...x..v..V.U."..~..N..........|.E...F..E.8N$}"....w.r...:f..
|f;..W.u.....V....s.3..F...f..F..V..F....v.`.F..V.. ....^...H...F
..N.a....#.r98-t.`....}..at9Nt... ;.r.....}.......t.<.t..........
..}....}.....^.f......}.}..E..N....F..V......r....p..B.-`fj.RP.Sj
.j...t...3..v...v.B...v.............V$...d.ar.@u.B.^.Iuw....'..I
nvalid system disk...Disk I/O error...Replace the disk, and then
press any key....IOSYSMSDOS   SYS...A....~...@...U.
```

Sectors continue to be displayed, one by one, until the entire buffer has been displayed.

12.3.2.1   Main C++ Program That Calls ReadSector

We can now show the complete C++ program that calls the **ReadSector** procedure:

```
// main.cpp - Calls the ReadSector Procedure
#include <iostream.h>
#include <conio.h>
```

---

[1] See Barry Kauler's book, mentioned at the end of Chapter 11.

```cpp
#include <stdlib.h>
const int SECTOR_SIZE = 512;

extern "C" ReadSector( char * buffer, long startSector,
            int driveNum, int numSectors );

void DisplayBuffer( const char * buffer, long startSector,
      int numSectors )
{
  int n = 0;
  long last = startSector + numSectors;
  for(long sNum = startSector; sNum < last; sNum++)
  {
    cout << "\nSector " << sNum
         << " --------------------------"
         << "--------------------------\n";
    for(int i = 0; i < SECTOR_SIZE; i++)
    {
      char ch = buffer[n++];
      if( unsigned(ch) < 32 || unsigned(ch) > 127)
        cout << '.';
      else
        cout << ch;
    }
    cout << endl;
    getch();
  }
}

int main()
{
  char * buffer;
  long startSector;
  int driveNum;
  int numSectors;

system("CLS");
  cout << "Sector display program.\n\n"
  << "Enter drive number [1=A, 2=B, 3=C, 4=D, 5=E,...]: ";
  cin >> driveNum;
  cout << "Starting sector number to read: ";
  cin >> startSector;
  cout << "Number of sectors to read: ";
  cin >> numSectors;
  buffer = new char[numSectors * SECTOR_SIZE];

cout << "\n\nReading sectors " << startSector << " - "
        << (startSector + numSectors) << " from Drive "
        << driveNum << endl;
```

```
ReadSector( buffer, startSector, driveNum, numSectors );
  DisplayBuffer( buffer, startSector, numSectors );
  system("CLS");
  return 0;
}
```

At the top of the listing, we find the declaration, or prototype, of the **ReadSector** function:

```
extern "C" ReadSector( char *buffer, long startSector,
            int driveNum, int numSectors );
```

The first parameter, *buffer*, points to the sector data after it has been read from the disk. The second parameter, *startSector*, is the starting sector number to read. The third parameter, *driveNum*, is the disk drive number. The fourth parameter, *numSectors*, specifies the number of sectors to read. The first parameter is passed by reference and all other parameters are passed by value.

In **main**, the user is prompted for the drive number, starting sector, and number of sectors. The program also dynamically allocates storage for the buffer that holds the sector data:

```
cout << "Sector display program.\n\n"
  << "Enter drive number [1=A, 2=B, 3=C, 4=D, 5=E,...]: ";
cin >> driveNum;
cout << "Starting sector number to read: ";
cin >> startSector;
cout << "Number of sectors to read: ";
cin >> numSectors;
buffer = new char[numSectors * SECTOR_SIZE];
```

This information is passed to the external **ReadSector** procedure, which fills the buffer with sectors from the disk:

```
ReadSector( buffer, startSector, driveNum, numSectors );
```

The buffer is passed to **DisplayBuffer**, a function in the C++ program that displays each sector in ASCII text format:

```
DisplayBuffer( buffer, startSector, numSectors );
```

12.3.2.2   Assembly Language Module

The assembly language module containing the **ReadSector** procedure is shown here. Note that because this is a Real-mode application, the .386 directive must appear after the .MODEL directive to tell the assembler to create 16-bit segments:

```
TITLE Reading Disk Sectors              (ReadSec.asm)

; The ReadSector procedure is called from a 16-bit
; Real-mode application written in Borland C++ 5.01.
; It can read FAT12, FAT16, and FAT32 disks under
; MS-DOS, Windows 95, Windows 98, and Windows Me.
```

```
Public _ReadSector
.model small
.386

DiskIO STRUC
    strtSector  DD ?                ; starting sector number
    nmSectors   DW 1                ; number of sectors
    bufferOfs   DW ?                ; buffer offset
    bufferSeg   DW ?                ; buffer segment
DiskIO ENDS

.data
diskStruct DiskIO <>

.code
;-------------------------------------------------------------
_ReadSector PROC NEAR C
 ARG bufferPtr:WORD, startSector:DWORD, driveNumber:WORD, \
     numSectors:WORD
;
; Read n sectors from a specified disk drive.
; Receives: pointer to buffer that will hold the sector,
;    data, starting sector number, drive number,
;    and number of sectors.
; Returns: nothing
;-------------------------------------------------------------
    enter 0,0
    pusha
    mov  eax,startSector
    mov  diskStruct.strtSector,eax
    mov  ax,numSectors
    mov  diskStruct.nmSectors,ax
    mov  ax,bufferPtr
    mov  diskStruct.bufferOfs,ax
    push ds
    pop  diskStruct.bufferSeg
    mov  ax,7305h                   ; ABSDiskReadWrite
    mov  cx,0FFFFh                  ; must be 0FFFFh
    mov  dx,driveNumber             ; drive number
    mov  bx,OFFSET diskStruct       ; sector number
    mov  si,0                       ; read mode
    int  21h                        ; read disk sector
    popa
    leave
    ret
_ReadSector ENDP
END
```

Because Borland Turbo Assembler was used to code this example, it uses the Borland ARG keyword to specify the procedure arguments. Note that the ARG directive allows us to specify the arguments in the same order as the corresponding C++ function declaration:

```
ASM:          _ReadSector PROC near C
              ARG bufferPtr:word, startSector:dword, \
                  driveNumber:word, numSectors:word

C++:          extern "C" ReadSector( char *buffer,
                  long startSector, int driveNum,
                  int numSectors );
```

The arguments are pushed on the stack in reverse order, which is the standard C calling convention. Farthest away from EBP is **numSectors**, the first parameter pushed on the stack, as shown by the following stack frame:

[BP + 12]	numSectors
[BP + 10]	driveNum
[BP + 06]	startSector
[BP + 04]	ofs(buffer)
[BP + 02]	(return addr)
SP, BP ⟶	BP

Note that **startSector** is a 32-bit doubleword and occupies locations [bp+6] through [bp+09] on the stack. This program was compiled for the small memory model, so **buffer** is passed as a 16-bit near pointer.

12.3.3 Example: Large Random Integers

To show a useful example of calling an external function from Borland C++, we can call **LongRand,** an assembly language function that returns a pseudorandom unsigned 32-bit integer. This is useful because the standard rand() function in the Borland C++ library only returns an integer between 0 and RAND_MAX (32,767). Our procedure returns an integer between 0 and 4,294,967,295.

This program is compiled in the large memory model, allowing the data to be larger than 64K, and requiring that 32-bit values be used for the return address and data pointer values. The external function declaration in C++ is:

```
extern "C" unsigned long LongRandom();
```

The listing of the main program is shown here. The program allocates storage for an array called **rArray**. It uses a loop to call **LongRandom**, inserts each number in the array, and writes the number to standard output:

```cpp
// main.cpp
// Calls the external LongRandom function, written in
// assembly language, that returns an unsigned 32-bit
// random integer. Compile in the Large memory model.

#include <iostream.h>
extern "C" unsigned long LongRandom();
const int ARRAY_SIZE = 500;

int main()
{
  // Allocate array storage, fill with 32-bit
  // unsigned random integers, and display:

  unsigned long * rArray = new unsigned long[ARRAY_SIZE];

  for(unsigned i = 0; i < ARRAY_SIZE; i++)
  {
    rArray[i] = LongRandom();
    cout << rArray[i] << ',';
  }
  cout << endl;
  return 0;
}
```

The LongRandom Function   The assembly language module containing the **LongRandom** function is a simple adaptation of the **Random32** procedure from the book's link library:

```asm
; LongRandom module        (longrand.asm)

.model large
.386
Public _LongRandom
.data
seed  DWORD 12345678h

; Return an unsigned pseudo-random 32-bit integer
; in DX:AX,in the range 0 - FFFFFFFFh.
.code
_LongRandom  PROC far, C
      mov    eax, 343FDh
      imul   seed
      add    eax, 269EC3h
      mov    seed, eax     ; save the seed for the next call
      ror    eax,8         ; rotate out the lowest digit
      ret
_LongRandom  ENDP
end
```

Borland C++ expects the 32-bit function return value to be in the DX:AX registers, so we copy the high 16-bits from EAX into DX with the SHLD instruction, which seems conveniently designed for this task:

```
shld edx,eax,16
```

12.3.4   Using Assembly Language to Optimize C++ Code

One of the ways you can use assembly language to optimize programs written in other languages is to look for speed bottlenecks. Loops are good candidates for optimization because any extra statements in a loop may be repeated enough times to have a noticeable effect on your program's performance.

Most C/C++ compilers have a command-line option that automatically generates an assembly language listing of the C/C++ program. In Microsoft Visual C++, for example, the listing file can contain any combination of C++ source code, assembly code, and machine code, shown by the options in Table 12-2. Perhaps the most useful is **/FAs**, which shows how C++ statements are translated into assembly language.

Table 12-2   Visual C++ Command-Line Options for ASM Code Generation.

Command Line	Contents of Listing File
/FA	Assembly-Only Listing
/FAc	Assembly with Machine Code
/FAs	Assembly with Source Code
/FAcs	Assembly, Machine Code, and Source

The following C++ procedure named **FindArray** searches for a single value in an array of long integers. The function returns true if the search is successful, or false if it is not:

```
#include "findarr.h"

bool FindArray( long searchVal, long array[], long count )
{
   for(int i = 0; i < count; i++)
     if( searchVal == array[i] )
       return true;
   return false;
}
```

The header file *findarr.h* contains the function prototype for **FindArray**. This identifies it as an external procedure that is called in the manner of a C language procedure, without any name decoration:

```
extern "C" {
   bool FindArray( long searchVal, long array[], long count );
}
```

12.3.4.1 FindArray Code Generated by Visual C++

Let's look at the assembly language source code generated by Visual C++ for the **FindArray** function, alongside the function's C++ source code. This procedure was compiled to a *Win32 Debug* target, which automatically turns off the compiler's code optimization feature. The flat memory model is selected:

```
TITLE findArr.cpp
.386P
.model FLAT
PUBLIC _FindArray
_TEXTSEGMENT

_searchVal$ = 8
_array$ = 12
_count$ = 16
_i$ = -4

_FindArray PROC NEAR
; 29   : {
   push ebp
   mov  ebp, esp
   push ecx                 ; create local variable i

; 30   :   for(int i = 0; i < count; i++)
   mov  DWORD PTR _i$[ebp], 0
   jmp  SHORT $L174

$L175:
   mov  eax, DWORD PTR _i$[ebp]
   add  eax, 1
   mov  DWORD PTR _i$[ebp], eax

$L174:
   mov  ecx, DWORD PTR _i$[ebp]
   cmp  ecx, DWORD PTR _count$[ebp]
   jge  SHORT $L176

; 31   : if( searchVal == array[i] )
   mov  edx, DWORD PTR _i$[ebp]
   mov  eax, DWORD PTR _array$[ebp]
   mov  ecx, DWORD PTR _searchVal$[ebp]
   cmp  ecx, DWORD PTR [eax+edx*4]
   jne  SHORT $L177

; 32   : return true;
   mov  al, 1
   jmp  SHORT $L172

$L177:
; 33   :
; 34   : return false;
   jmp  SHORT $L175
```

```
$L176:
    xor   al, al

$L172:
; 35   : }
    mov   esp, ebp                    ; restore stack pointer
    pop   ebp
    ret   0
_FindArray ENDP
_TEXT ENDS
END
```

(The C++ compiler uses the .386P directive, which enables the assembly of both privileged and nonprivileged Intel386 instructions. All instructions in our examples, are nonprivileged, since privileged instructions are only for advanced system programming.)

Three 32-bit arguments were pushed on the stack in the following order: **count, array,** and **searchVal**. Of these three, **array** is the only one passed by reference, because in C/C++, an array name is an implicit pointer to the array's first element. The procedure saves EBP on the stack and creates space for the local variable **i** by pushing an extra doubleword on the stack:

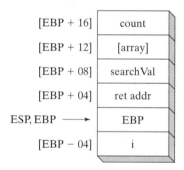

Inside the procedure, the compiler reserves local stack space for the variable **i** by pushing ECX (line 29). The same storage is released at the end when EBP is copied back into ESP (line 35).

There are 14 assembly code statements between the labels $L175 and $L176, which constitute the main body of the loop. We can easily write an assembly language procedure that is more efficient than the code shown here.

12.3.4.2   Linking MASM to Visual C++

Let's create a hand-optimized version of **FindArray**. A few basic principles can be applied to the optimization of this procedure:

- Move as much processing out of the repeated loop as possible.
- Move stack parameters and local variables to registers.
- Take advantage of specialized instructions (in this case, SCASD).

For the current application, we will use Microsoft Visual C++ to compile the calling C++ program, and Microsoft MASM to assemble the called procedure. Visual C++ generates 32-bit applications that run only in Protected mode. We choose Win32 Console as the target application type for the examples shown here, although there is no reason why the same procedures would not work in ordinary MS-Windows applications. In Visual C++, functions return 8-bit values in AL, 16-bit values in AX, 32-bit values in EAX, and 64-bit values in EDX:EAX. Larger data structures (structure values, arrays, etc.) are stored in a static data location, and a pointer to the data is returned in EAX.

Our **FindArray** code is slightly more readable than the code generated by the C++ compiler because we can use meaningful label names and define constants that simplify the use of stack parameters. Here is the complete program listing:

```
TITLE The FindArray Procedure              (Scasd.asm)

; This version uses hand-optimized assembly
; language code, with the SCASD instruction.

.386
.model flat
public  _FindArray
true = 1
false = 0

; Stack parameters:
srchVal    equ  [ebp+08]
arrayPtr   equ  [ebp+12]
count      equ  [ebp+16]

.code
_FindArray PROC near
     push   ebp
     mov    ebp,esp
     push   edi

     mov    eax, srchVal        ; search value
     mov    ecx, count          ; number of items
     mov    edi, arrayPtr       ; pointer to array

     repne scasd                ; do the search
     jz     returnTrue          ; ZF = 1 if found

returnFalse:
     mov    al, false
     jmp    short exit

returnTrue:
     mov    al, true

exit:
     pop    edi
```

```
        pop     ebp
        ret
_FindArray ENDP
end
```

Code Optimization by the C++ Compiler   Before we develop an overblown sense of superiority over the C++ compiler, let's ask the compiler to try again, this time optimizing its code for speed. The new version of **FindArray** is shown here:

```
_searchVal$ = 8
_array$ = 12
_count$ = 16

_FindArray PROC NEAR
        mov     edx, DWORD PTR _count$[esp-4]
        xor     eax, eax
        push    esi
        test    edx, edx
        jle     SHORT $L176
        mov     ecx, DWORD PTR _array$[esp]
        mov     esi, DWORD PTR _searchVal$[esp]

$L174:
        cmp     esi, DWORD PTR [ecx]
        je      SHORT $L182
        inc     eax
        add     ecx, 4
        cmp     eax, edx
        jl      SHORT $L174
        xor     al, al
        pop     esi
        ret     0
$L182:
        mov     al, 1
        pop     esi
        ret     0
$L176:
        xor     al, al
        pop     esi
        ret     0
_FindArray ENDP
```

The improvement of this version over the compiler's nonoptimized version is dramatic. Variables have been moved to registers, and the loop portion has been reduced from twelve instructions to six. In fact, the timed execution of this new version is roughly the same as the hand-optimized code we showed earlier.

Dangers of Leaving Out EBP   You may have noticed that the C++ compiler eliminated all references to EBP, shaving off a few more clock cycles. It took advantage of the fact that ESP can be used as an indirect operand, so stack parameters can be accessed without the need of EBP. **Count**, for example, located at stack offset ESP + 12, is assigned to EDX. The stack offset is calculated in a roundabout sort of way as **_count\$ + (ESP − 4),** where **_count\$** is equal to 16:

```
mov   edx, DWORD PTR _count$[esp-4]
```

Here is a picture of the revised stack frame used by the program in Example 10:

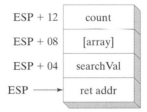

Before you get the idea that all stack parameters should be handled this way, think again. For instance, without EBP, the procedure cannot push any registers on the stack without adjusting the offsets between ESP and the stack parameters. Suppose we had the following statements at the beginning of **FindArray**:

```
arrayPtr   equ [esp+10]

_FindArray PROC near
    push esi
    mov   esi, arrayPtr              ; esi = arrayPtr
```

This code doesn't work, of course, because as soon as ESI is pushed, the predefined stack offset of **arrayPtr** changes. And yet, if we don't push ESI before modifying it, we violate the Microsoft rule that says ESI must be preserved in high-level language procedures. The C++ compiler compensates for this by adjusting the stack offsets after any PUSH instructions have taken place. This is fine for a compiler, but not easy for humans to do accurately.

Pointers Versus Subscripts   It's not unusual for C/C++ programmers to assert that processing arrays with pointers is more efficient than using subscripts. For example, the following version of **FindArray** uses a pointer:

```
bool FindArray( long searchVal, long array[], long count )
{
  long * p = array;
  for(i = 0; i < count; i++, p++)
    if( n == *p )
      return true;
  return false;
}
```

Running this version of **FindArray** through the C++ compiler produced virtually the same assembly language code as the earlier version using subscripts. At least in this instance, using a pointer variable was no more efficient than using a subscript. Here is the loop from the **FindArray** target code that was produced by the C++ compiler:

```
$L176:
    cmp     esi, DWORD PTR [ecx]
    je      SHORT $L184
    inc     eax
    add     ecx, 4
    cmp     eax, edx
    jl      SHORT $L176
```

In closing, let us say that most high-level language compilers do a very effective job of code optimization. Your time would be well spent studying the output produced by a C++ compiler, to learn about optimization techniques, parameter passing, and object code implementation. In fact, many computer science students take a compiler-writing course that includes such topics. It is also important to realize that compilers take the general case, as they usually have no specific knowledge about individual applications or installed hardware. Some compilers provide specialized optimization for a particular processor such as the Pentium, which can significantly improve the speed of compiled programs.

Hand-coded assembly language can also take full advantage of specialized hardware features that might be found in a computer system. Some examples are video cards, sound cards, and data acquisition boards.

12.3.5 Section Review

1. When the following C language function is called, will the argument x be pushed on the stack first or last?

   ```
   void MySub( x, y, z );
   ```

2. What is the purpose of the "C" specifier in the *extern* declaration in procedures called from C++?
3. Why is name decoration important when calling external assembly language procedures from C++?
4. Which registers and flags must be preserved by assembly language procedures called from Borland C++?
5. In Borland C++, how many bytes are used by the following types? 1) int, 2) enum, 3) float, 4) double.
6. In the **ReadSector** module in this section, if the ARG directive were not used, how would you code the following statement?

   ```
   mov  eax,startSector
   ```

7. In the **LongRandom** Function shown in this section, if the SHLD instruction were not available, which sequence of instructions could be used instead?

8. In this chapter, when an optimizing C++ compiler was used, what differences in code generation occurred between the loop coded with array subscripts and the loop coded with pointer variables?

12.4   Chapter Summary

Assembly language is the perfect tool for optimizing selected parts of a large application written in some high-level language. Assembly language is also a good tool for customizing certain procedures for specific hardware. These techniques require one of two approaches:

- Write inline assembly code embedded within high-level language code.
- Link assembly language procedures to high-level language code.

Both approaches have their merits and their limitations. In this chapter, we presented both approaches.

The naming convention used by a language refers to the way segments and modules are named, as well as rules or characteristics regarding the naming of variables and procedures. The memory model used by a program determines whether calls and references will be near (within the same segment) or far (between different segments).

When calling an assembly language procedure from a program written in another language, any identifiers that are shared between the two languages must be compatible. You must also use segment names in the procedure that are compatible with the calling program. The writer of a procedure uses the high-level language's calling convention to determine how to receive parameters. The calling convention also affects whether the stack pointer must be restored by the called procedure or by the calling program.

In Visual C++, the **__asm** directive is used for writing inline assembly code in a C++ source program. In this chapter, a File Encryption program was used to demonstrate inline assembly language.

This chapter showed how to link assembly language procedures to both Microsoft Visual C++ programs and Borland C++ programs. Visual C++ uses only Protected mode, whereas Borland C++ can generate programs in either Real-address mode or Protected mode. Aside from this, the two languages have similar interfaces to assembly language.

The ReadSector program showed a useful combination of Borland C++ running in Real-address mode, calling an assembly language procedure that reads individual sectors from a disk.

A procedure named **FindArray** was written in assembly language and called from a Visual C++ program running in Protected mode. We compared the assembly language source file generated by the compiler to hand-assembled code, in our efforts to learn more about code optimization techniques.

12.5   Programming Exercises

1. ReadSector, Large Model
Convert the **ReadSector** procedure (Section 12.3.2) to the large memory model, and call it from the same C++ program. Remember that the buffer parameter will now be passed as a 32-bit pointer, containing a segment and offset. Compile the C++ program under the large memory model.

2. ReadSector, Hexadecimal Display
Add a new procedure to the C++ program in Section 12.3.2 that calls the **ReadSector** procedure. This new procedure should display each sector in hexadecimal. Be sure to use the setfillchar manipulator from the istream class to pad each byte with a leading zero.

3. LongRandomArray Procedure
Using the **LongRandom** procedure in Section 12.3.3 as a starting point, create a procedure called **LongRandomArray** that fills an array with 32-bit unsigned random integers. Pass an array pointer from a C or C++ program, along with a count indicating the number of array elements to be filled:

```
extern "C" void LongRandomArray( unsigned long * buffer,
        unsigned count );
```

4. External TranslateBuffer Procedure
Write an external procedure in assembly language that performs the same type of encryption shown in the **TranslateBuffer** inline procedure that appeared in Section 12.2.2. Run the compiled program in the debugger, and judge whether this version runs any faster than the Encode.cpp program from Section 12.2.2.

5. Prime Number Program
Write an assembly language procedure that returns a value of 1 if the 32-bit integer passed in the EAX register is prime, or 0 if EAX is nonprime. Call this procedure from a high-level language program. Let the user input some very large numbers, and have your program display a message for each one indicating whether or not it is prime.

6. FindBitString Procedure
Modify the FindArray example from Section 12.3.4.2. Name your function **FundRevArray** and let it begin searching at the end of the array. Search in the reverse direction for the first matching value and return the index position of the matching element. If no match is found, return −1.

13

16-Bit MS-DOS Programming

13.1   MS-DOS and the IBM-PC

IBM's PC-DOS was the first operating system to implement Real-address mode on the IBM Personal Computer, using the Intel 8088 processor. Later, it evolved into Microsoft MS-DOS. Because of this history, it makes sense to use MS-DOS as the environment for explaining all about Real-mode programming. Real-address mode is frequently called *16-bit mode* because addresses are constructed from 16-bit values.

In this chapter, you will learn the basic memory organization of MS-DOS, how to activate MS-DOS function calls (called *interrupts*), and how to perform basic input-output operations at the operating system level. All of the programs in this chapter run in Real-address mode because they use the INT instruction. Interrupts were originally designed to run under MS-DOS in Real-address mode. It is possible to call interrupts in Protected mode, but the techniques for doing so are beyond the scope of this book.

Real-address mode programs have the following characteristics:

- They can only address 1 megabyte of memory.
- Only one program can run at once (single tasking) in a single session.
- No memory boundary protection is possible, so any application program can overwrite memory used by the operating system.
- Offsets are 16 bits

When it first appeared, the IBM PC had a strong appeal because it was affordable, and it ran Lotus 1-2-3, the electronic spreadsheet program that was instrumental in the PC's adoption by businesses. Computer hobbyists loved the PC because it was an ideal tool for learning how computers work. It should be noted that Digital Research CP/M, the most popular 8-bit operating system before PC-DOS, was only capable of addressing 64K of RAM. From this point of view, PC-DOS's 640K seemed like a gift from heaven.

Because of the obvious memory and speed limitations of the early Intel microprocessors, the IBM-PC was a single-user computer. There was no built-in protection against memory corruption by application programs. In contrast, the minicomputer systems available at the time could handle multiple users, and prevented application programs from overwriting each other's data. Over time, more robust operating systems for the PC have become available, making it a viable alternative to minicomputer systems, particularly when PCs are networked together.

13.1.1 Memory Organization

In Real-address mode, the lowest 640K of memory is used by both the operating system and application programs. Following this is video memory and reserved memory for hardware controllers. Finally, locations C0000 to FFFFF are reserved for system ROM (read-only memory). Figure 13-1 shows a simple memory map. Within the operating system area of memory, the lowest 1,024 bytes of memory (addresses 00000 - 003FF) contain a table of 32-bit addresses named the *interrupt vector table*. These addresses, called *interrupt vectors*, are used by the CPU when processing hardware and software interrupts.

Just above the vector table is the *BIOS and MS-DOS data area*. Next is the *software BIOS*, which includes procedures that manage most I/O devices, including the keyboard, disk drive, video display, serial and printer ports. BIOS procedures are loaded from a hidden system file on an MS-DOS system (boot) disk. The MS-DOS kernel is a collection of procedures (called *services*) that are also loaded from a file on the system disk.

Grouped with the MS-DOS kernel are the file buffers and installable device drivers. Next highest in memory, the resident part of the *command processor* is loaded from an executable file named *command.com*. The command processor interprets commands typed at the MS-DOS prompt, and loads and executes programs stored on disk. A second part of the command processor sits in high memory just below location A0000.

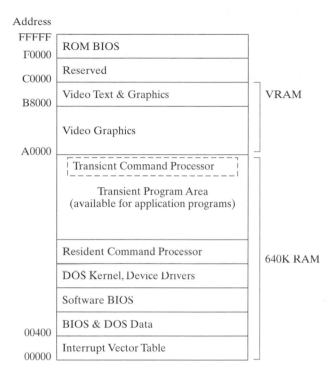

Figure 13-1   MS-DOS Memory Map.

Application programs can load into memory at the first address above the resident part of the command processor, and can use memory all the way up to address 9FFFF. If the currently running program overwrites the transient command processor area, the latter is reloaded from the boot disk when the program exits.

Video Memory   The video memory area (VRAM) on an IBM-PC begins at location A0000, which is used when the video adapter is switched into graphics mode. When the video is in color text mode, memory location B8000 holds all text currently displayed on the screen. The screen is memory-mapped, so that each row and column on the screen corresponds to a 16-bit word in memory. When a character is copied into video memory, it immediately appears on the screen.

ROM BIOS   The *ROM BIOS*, at memory locations F0000 to FFFFF, is an important part of the computer's operating system. It contains system diagnostic and configuration software, as well as low-level input-output procedures used by application programs. The BIOS is stored in a static memory chip on the system board. Most systems follow a standardized BIOS specification modeled after IBM's original BIOS.

13.1.2 Redirecting Input-Output

Throughout this chapter, references will be made to the *standard input device* and the *standard output device*. Both are collectively called the *console,* which involves the keyboard for input and the video display for output.

When running programs from the command prompt, you can redirect standard input so that it is read from a file or hardware port rather than the keyboard. Standard output can be redirected to a file, printer, or other I/O device. Without this capability, programs would have to be substantially revised before their input-output could be changed. For example, the operating system has a program named *sort.exe* that sorts an input file. The following command sorts a file named *myfile.txt* and displays the output:

```
sort < myfile.txt
```

The following command sorts *myfile.txt* and sends the output to *outfile.txt:*

```
sort < myfile.txt > outfile.txt
```

You can use the pipe (|) symbol to copy the output from the DIR command to the input of the *sort.exe* program. The following command sorts the current disk directory and displays the output on the screen:

```
dir | sort
```

The following command sends the output of the sort program to the default (non-networked) printer (identified by PRN):

```
dir | sort > prn
```

The complete set of device names is shown in Table 13-1.

Table 13-1 Standard MS-DOS Device Names.

Device Name	Description
CON	Console (video display or keyboard)
LPT1 or PRN	First parallel printer
LPT2, LPT3	Parallel ports 2 and 3
COM1, COM2	Serial ports 1 and 2
NUL	Nonexistent or dummy device

13.1.3   Software Interrupts

A *software interrupt* is a call to an operating system procedure. Most of these procedures, called *interrupt handlers*, provide input-output capability to application programs. They are used for such tasks as:

- Displaying characters and strings
- Reading characters and strings from the keyboard
- Displaying text in color
- Opening and closing files
- Reading data from files
- Writing data to files
- Setting and retrieving the system time and date

13.1.4   INT Instruction

The INT (*call to interrupt procedure*) instruction pushes the CPU flags on the stack and calls an interrupt handler. Before the INT instruction is executed, one or more parameters must be inserted in registers. At the very least, a number identifying the particular procedure must be moved to the AH register. Depending on the function, other values may have to be passed to the interrupt in registers. The syntax is

```
INT number
```

Where *number* is an integer in the range 0 – FF hexadecimal.

13.1.4.1   Interrupt Vectoring

The CPU processes the INT instruction using the interrupt vector table, which we've already mentioned, is a table of addresses in the lowest 1,024 bytes of memory. Each entry in this table is a 32-bit segment-offset address that points to an interrupt handler. The actual addresses in this table vary from one machine to another. Figure 13-2 illustrates the steps taken by the CPU when the INT instruction is invoked by a program:

- **Step 1:** The number following the INT mnemonic tells the CPU which entry to locate in the interrupt vector table. In the illustration, the INT 10h instruction executes.
- **Step 2:** The CPU pushes the flags on the stack, disables hardware interrupts, and executes a call to the address stored in the interrupt vector table (F000:F065).
- **Step 3:** The interrupt handler at F000:F065 begins execution and finishes when the IRET instruction is reached.
- **Step 4:** The IRET (interrupt return) instruction causes the program to resume execution at the next instruction after INT 10h in the calling program.

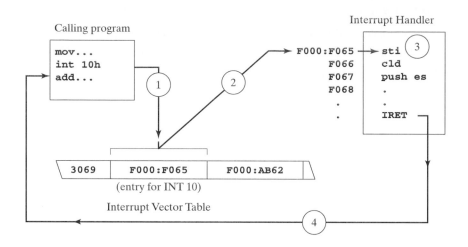

Figure 13-2   Interrupt Vectoring Process.

13.1.4.2   Common Interrupts

Software interrupts call *interrupt service routines* (ISRs) either in the BIOS or in DOS. Some frequently used interrupts are:

- *INT 10h Video Services.* Procedures that display routines that control the cursor position, write text in color, scroll the screen, and display video graphics.
- *INT 16h Keyboard Services.* Procedures that read the keyboard and check its status.
- *INT 17h Printer Services.* Procedures that initialize, print, and return the printer status.
- *INT 1Ah Time of Day.* Procedure that gets the number of clock ticks since the machine was turned on or sets the counter to a new value.
- *INT 1Ch User Timer Interrupt.* An empty procedure that is executed 18.2 times per second.
- *INT 21h MS-DOS Services.* Procedures that provide input-output, file handling, and memory management. Also known as *MS-DOS function calls*.

13.1.5   Section Review

1. What is the highest memory location into which you can load an application program?
2. What occupies the lowest 1,024 bytes of memory?
3. What is the starting location of the BIOS and MS-DOS data area?
4. What is the name of the memory area containing low-level procedures used by the computer for input-output?
5. Show an example of redirecting a program's output to the printer.
6. What is the MS-DOS device name for the first parallel printer?
7. What is an interrupt service routine?

8. When the INT instruction executes, what is the first task carried out by the CPU?

9. What four steps are taken by the CPU when an INT instruction is invoked by a program? *Hint:* See Figure 13-2.

10. When an interrupt service routine finishes, how does an application program resume execution?

11. Which interrupt number is used for video services?

12. Which interrupt number is used for the time of day?

13.2   MS-DOS Function Calls (INT 21h)

The first program I ever wrote in Intel assembly language displayed a "*" on the screen, using the following three instructions:

```
mov ah,2
mov dl,'*'
int 21h
```

I was excited, at least for a few minutes. I had heard that assembly language was difficult, but this was encouraging. Of course, I didn't know what lay ahead, which you have already learned by reading the first twelve chapters of this book.

It turns out that MS-DOS provides a lot of easy-to-use functions for displaying text on the console. They are all part of a group typically called *INT 21h MS-DOS Function calls*. There are some 90 or so different functions supported by this interrupt, identified by a function number placed in the AH register. An excellent, if somewhat outdated source is Ray Duncan's book, *Advanced MS-DOS Programming*. A more comprehensive and up-to-date list is available on the Web, named *Ralf Brown's Interrupt List*.

For each INT 21h function described in this chapter, we will list the necessary input parameters, return values, notes about its use, and include a short code example that calls the function.

A number of functions require that the 32-bit address of an input parameter be stored in the DS:DX registers. DS, the data segment register, is usually set to your program's data area. If for some reason this is not the case, use the SEG operator to set DS to the segment containing the data passed to INT 21h. The following statements do this:

```
.data
inBuffer BYTE 80 DUP(?)
.code
mov ax,SEG inBuffer
mov ds,ax
mov dx,OFFSET inBuffer
```

INT 21h Function 4Ch: Terminate Process   INT 21h Function 4Ch terminates the current program (called a *process*). In the Real-address mode programs presented in this book, we have relied on a macro definition in the Irvine16 library named **exit**. It is defined as:

```
exit TEXTEQU <.EXIT>
```

In other words, we redefine **exit** as .EXIT (a MASM directive that ends a program). This was done to make the programs as similar as possible to our 32-bit Protected mode programs, which also use an **exit** macro. The code generated by **.EXIT** is:

```
mov ah,4Ch              ; terminate process
int 21h
```

If you supply an optional return code argument to the .EXIT macro, the assembler generates one more instruction that moves the return code to AL:

```
.EXIT 0                 ; macro call
```

Generated code:

```
mov ah,4Ch              ; terminate process
mov al,0                ; return code
int 21h
```

The value in AL, called the *process return code*, is received by the calling process (including a batch file) to indicate the returns status of your program. By convention, a return code of zero is considered successful completion. Other return codes between 1 and 255 can be used to indicate additional outcomes that have specific meaning for your program.

13.2.1   Selected Output Functions

In this section we present some of the most common INT 21h functions for writing characters and text. None of these functions alter the default current screen colors, so output will only be in color if you have previously set the screen color by other means. (For example, you can call the link library's **SetTextColor** procedure, or you can call video BIOS functions from Chapter 15.)

Filtering Control Characters   All of the functions in this section *filter*, or interpret ASCII control characters. If you write a backspace character to standard output, for example, the cursor moves one column to the left. Table 13-2 contains a list of control characters that you are likely to encounter.

Table 13-2   ASCII Control Characters.

ASCII Code	Description
08h	Backspace (moves one column to the left)
09h	Horizontal tab (skips forward *n* columns)
0Ah	Line feed (moves to next output line)
0Ch	Form feed (moves to next printer page)

Table 13-2 ASCII Control Characters. (Continued)

ASCII Code	Description
0Dh	Carriage return (moves to leftmost output column)
1Bh	Escape character

Appendix C contains a fairly extensive list of BIOS and MS-DOS interrupts.

The next several tables describe the important features of INT 21h Functions 2, 5, 6, 9, and 40h. INT 21h Function 2 writes a single character to standard output. INT 21h Function 5 writes a single character to the printer. INT 21h Function 6 writes a single unfiltered character to standard output. INT 21h Function 9 writes a string (terminated by a $ character) to standard output. INT 21h Function 40h writes an array of bytes to a file or device.

INT 21h Function 2	
Description	Write a single character to standard output and advance the cursor one column forward
Receives	AH = 2 DL = character value
Returns	nothing

Sample call	`mov ah,2`
	`mov dl,'A'`
	`int 21h`

INT 21h Function 5	
Description	Write a single character to the printer
Receives	AH = 5 DL = character value
Returns	nothing

Sample call	`mov   ah,5      ; select printer output`
	`mov   dl,"Z"     ; character to be printed`
	`int   21h       ; call MS-DOS`

Notes	MS-DOS waits until the printer is ready to accept the character. You can terminate the wait by pressing the Ctrl Break keys. The default output is to the printer port for LPT1.

INT 21h Function 6	
Description	Write a character to standard output
Receives	AH = 6 DL = character value
Returns	If ZF = 0, AL contains the character's ASCII code.

Sample call	```mov ah,6```
	```mov dl,"A"```
	```int 21h```

Notes	Unlike other INT 21h Functions, this one does not filter (interpret) ASCII control characters.

INT 21h Function 9	
Description	Write a $-terminated string to standard output
Receives	AH = 9 DS:DX = segment/offset of the string
Returns	nothing

Sample call	```.data```
	```string BYTE "This is a string$"```
	```.code```
	```mov ah,9```
	```mov dx,OFFSET string```
	```int 21h```

Notes	The string must be terminated by a dollar-sign character ($).

INT 21h Function 40h	
Description	Write an array of bytes to a file or device
Receives	AH = 40h BX = file or device handle (console = 1) CX = number of bytes to write DS:DX = address of array
Returns	AX = number of bytes written

INT 21h Function 40h	

Sample call	```
	.data
	message "Hello, world"
	.code
	mov ah,40h
	mov bx,1
	mov cx,LENGTHOF message
	mov dx,OFFSET message
	int 21h
	``

13.2.2   Hello World Program Example

The following is a simple program that displays a string on the screen using an MS-DOS function call:

```
TITLE Hello World Program        (Hello.asm)

INCLUDE Irvine16.inc
.data
message BYTE "Hello, world!",0dh,0ah

.code
main PROC
    mov ax,@data                 ; initialize DS
    mov ds,ax

    mov   ah,40h                 ; write to file/device
    mov   bx,1                   ; output handle
    mov   cx,SIZEOF message      ; number of bytes
    mov   dx,OFFSET message      ; addr of buffer
    int   21h

    exit
main ENDP
END main
```

13.2.3   Selected Input Functions

In this section, we describe a few of the most commonly used MS-DOS functions that read from standard input. For a more complete list, see Appendix C. As shown in the following table, INT 21h Function 1 reads a single character from standard input:

INT 21h Function 1	
Description	Read a single character from standard input
Receives	AH = 1

INT 21h Function 1	
Returns	AL = character (ASCII code)
| **Sample call** | ```
mov ah,1
int 21h
mov char,al
``` |
| **Notes** | If no character is present in the input buffer, the program waits. This function echoes the character to standard output. |

INT 21h Function 6 reads a character from standard input if the character is already waiting in the input buffer. If the buffer is empty, the function returns with the Zero flag set and no other action is taken:

INT 21h Function 6	
Description	Read a character from standard input without waiting
Receives	AH = 6 DL = FFh
Returns	If ZF = 0, AL contains the character's ASCII code.
| **Sample call** | ```
mov ah,6
mov dl,0FFh
int 21h
jz skip
mov char,AL
skip:
``` |
| **Notes** | The interrupt only returns a character if one is already waiting in the input buffer. Does not echo the character to standard output, and does not filter control characters. |

INT 21h Function 0Ah reads a buffered string from standard input, terminated by the Enter key. If you call this function, you must pass a pointer to an input structure having the following format (**count** can be between 0 and 128):

```
count = 80
KEYBOARD STRUCT
    maxInput BYTE count                    ; max chars to input
    inputCount BYTE ?                      ; actual input count
    buffer BYTE count DUP(?)               ; holds input chars
KEYBOARD ENDS
```

The *maxInput* field specifies the maximum number of characters the user can input, including the Enter key. The backspace key can be used to erase characters and back up the cursor. The user terminates the input either by pressing the Enter key or by pressing Ctrl-Break. All non-ASCII keys, such as PageUp and F1, are filtered out and are not stored in the buffer. After the function returns, the *inputCount* field indicates how many characters were input, not counting the Enter key. The following table describes Function 0Ah:

INT 21h Function 0Ah	
Description	Read an array of buffered characters from standard input
Receives	AH = 0Ah DS:DX = address of keyboard input structure
Returns	The structure is initialized with the input characters.
| **Sample call** | ```
.data
kybdData KEYBOARD <>
.code
    mov ah,0Ah
    mov dx,OFFSET kybdData
    int 21h
``` |

INT 21h Function 0Bh gets the status of the standard input buffer:

INT 21h Function 0Bh	
Description	Get the status of the standard input buffer
Receives	AH = 0Bh
Returns	If a character is waiting, AL = 0FFh; otherwise, AL = 0.
| **Sample Call** | ```
    mov ah,0Bh
    cmp al,0
    je skip
    ; (input the character)
skip:
``` |
| **Notes** | Does not remove the character. |

13.2.3.1   Example: String Encryption Program

INT 21h Function 6 has the unique ability to read characters from standard input without pausing the program or filtering control characters. This can be put to good use if we run a program from the command prompt and redirect the input. That is, the input will come from a text file rather than the keyboard.

The following program (*Encrypt.asm*) reads each character from standard input, uses the XOR instruction to alter the character, and writes the altered character to standard output:

```
TITLE Encryption Program                     (Encrypt.asm)

; This program uses MS-DOS function calls to
; read and encrypt a file. Run it from the
; command prompt, using redirection:
;    Encrypt < infile.txt > outfile.txt
; Function 6 is also used for output, to avoid
; filtering ASCII control characters.

INCLUDE Irvine16.inc
XORVAL = 239                    ; any value between 0-255
.code
main PROC
    mov   ax,@data
    mov   ds,ax

L1:
    mov   ah,6                  ; direct console input
    mov   dl,0FFh               ; don't wait for character
    int   21h                   ; AL = character
    jz    L2                    ; quit if ZF = 1 (EOF)
    xor   al,XORVAL
    mov   ah,6                  ; write to output
    mov   dl,al
    int   21h
    jmp   L1                    ; repeat the loop

L2: exit
main ENDP
END   main
```

The choice of 239 as the encryption value is completely arbitrary. You can use any value between 0 and 255 in this context. The encryption is weak, of course, but it might be enough to discourage the average user from trying to defeat the encryption. When you run the program at the command prompt, indicate the name of the input file (and output file, if any). The following are two examples:

| `encrypt < infile.txt` | Input from file (infile.txt), output to console |
| `encrypt < infile.txt > outfile.txt` | Input from file (infile.txt), output to file (outfile.txt) |

13.2.3.2   Int 21h Function 3Fh

INT 21h Function 3Fh, as shown in the following table, reads an array of bytes from a file or device. It can be used for keyboard input when the device handle in BX is equal to zero:

INT 21h Function 3Fh	
Description	Read an array of bytes from a file or device
Receives	AH = 3Fh BX = file/device handle (0 = keyboard) CX = maximum bytes to read DS:DX = address of input buffer
Returns	AX = number of bytes actually read
| **Sample Call** | ```
.data
inputBuffer BYTE 127 dup(0)
bytesRead WORD ?
.code
mov   ah,3Fh
mov   bx,0                  ; keyboard handle
mov   cx,LENGTHOF inputBuffer
mov   dx,OFFSET inputBuffer
int   21h
mov   bytesRead,ax
``` |
| **Notes** | If reading from the keyboard, input terminates when the Enter key is pressed, and the 0Dh, 0Ah, characters are appended to the input buffer. |

If the user enters more characters than were requested by the function call, excess characters remain in the MS-DOS input buffer. If the function is called anytime later in the program, execution may not pause and wait for user input, because the buffer already contains data (including the 0Dh, 0Ah, marking the end of the line). This can even occur between separate instances of program execution. To be absolutely sure your program works as intended, you need to flush the input buffer, one character at a time, after calling Function 3Fh. The following code does this (see the *Keybd.asm* program for a complete demonstration):

```
;-------------------------------------------
FlushBuffer PROC
; Flush the standard input buffer.
; Receives: nothing. Returns: nothing
;-------------------------------------------
.data
oneByte BYTE ?
.code
   pusha
L1:
   mov ah,3Fh                   ; read file/device
   mov bx,0                     ; keyboard handle
```
```

```
          mov cx,1                      ; one byte
          mov dx,OFFSET oneByte         ; save it here
          int 21h                       ; call MS-DOS
          cmp oneByte,0Ah               ; end of line yet?
          jne L1                        ; no: read another
          popa
          ret
FlushBuffer ENDP
```

13.2.4 Date/Time Functions

Many popular software applications display the current date and time. Others retrieve the date and time and use it in their internal logic. A scheduling program, for example, can use the current date to verify that a user is not accidentally scheduling an appointment in the past.

As shown in the next series of tables, INT 21h Function 2Ah gets the system date, and INT 21h Function 2Bh sets the system date. INT 21h Function 2Ch gets the system time, and INT 21h Function 2Dh sets the system time.

INT 21h Function 2Ah	
Description	Get the system date
Receives	AH = 2Ah
Returns	CX = year DH, DL = month, day AL = day of week (Sunday = 0, Monday = 1, etc.)

Sample Call	`mov ah,2Ah`
	`int 21h`
	`mov year,cx`
	`mov month,dh`
	`mov day,dl`
	`mov dayOfWeek,al`

INT 21h Function 2Bh	
Description	Set the system date
Receives	AH = 2Bh CX = year DH = month DL = day

INT 21h Function 2Bh	
Returns	If the change was successful, AL = 0; otherwise, AL = FFh.
| **Sample Call** | ```
mov ah,2Bh
mov cx,year
mov dh,month
mov dl,day
int 21h
cmp al,0
jne failed
``` |
| **Notes** | Probably will not work if you are running Windows NT, 2000, or XP with a restricted user profile. |

INT 21h Function 2Ch	
Description	Get the system time
Receives	AH = 2Ch
Returns	CH = hours (0 − 23) CL = minutes (0 − 59) DH = seconds (0 − 59) DL = hundredths of seconds (usually not accurate)
| **Sample Call** | ```
mov ah,2Ch
int 21h
mov hours,ch
mov minutes,cl
mov seconds,dh
``` |

INT 21h Function 2Dh	
Description	Set the system time
Receives	AH = 2Dh CH = hours (0 − 23) CL = minutes (0 − 59) DH = seconds (0 − 59)
Returns	If the change was successful, AL = 0; otherwise, AL = FFh

INT 21h Function 2Dh	
| **Sample Call** | ```
mov   ah,2Dh
mov   ch,hours
mov   cl,minutes
mov   dh,seconds
int   21h
cmp   al,0
jne   failed
``` |
| **Notes** | Probably will not work if you are running Windows NT, 2000, or XP with a restricted user profile. |

13.2.4.1 Example: Displaying the Time and Date

The following program (*DateTime.asm*) displays the system date and time. The code is a little longer than one would expect, because the program inserts leading zeros before the hours, minutes, and seconds:

```
TITLE Display the Date and Time       (DateTime.asm)

Include Irvine16.inc
Write PROTO char:BYTE
.data
str1 BYTE "Date: ",0
str2 BYTE ",  Time: ",0

.code
main PROC
    mov   ax,@data
    mov   ds,ax

; Display the date:
    mov   dx,OFFSET str1
    call  WriteString
    mov   ah,2Ah                  ; get system date
    int   21h
    movzx eax,dh                  ; month
    call  WriteDec
    INVOKE Write,'-'
    movzx eax,dl                  ; day
    call  WriteDec
    INVOKE Write,'-'
    movzx eax,cx                  ; year
    call  WriteDec

; Display the time:
    mov   dx,OFFSET str2
```
```

```
        call    WriteString
        mov     ah,2Ch                  ; get system time
        int     21h
        movzx   eax,ch                  ; hours
        call    WritePaddedDec
        INVOKE  Write,':'
        movzx   eax,cl                  ; minutes
        call    WritePaddedDec
        INVOKE  Write,':'
        movzx   eax,dh                  ; seconds
        call    WritePaddedDec
        call    Crlf

        exit
main ENDP

;-----------------------------------------------
Write PROC char:BYTE
; Display a single character.
;-----------------------------------------------
        push    eax
        push    edx
        mov     ah,2                    ; character output function
        mov     dl,char
        int     21h
        pop     edx
        pop     eax
        ret
Write ENDP

;-----------------------------------------------
WritePaddedDec PROC
; Display unsigned integer in EAX, padding
; to two digit positions with a leading zero.
;-----------------------------------------------
        .IF eax < 10
           push    eax
           push    edx
           mov     ah,2                 ; display leading zero
           mov     dl,'0'
           int     21h
           pop     edx
           pop     eax
        .ENDIF

        call WriteDec                   ; write unsigned decimal
        ret                             ; using value in EAX
WritePaddedDec ENDP
END main
```

Sample output:

```
Date: 12-8-2001,   Time: 23:01:23
```

13.2.5 Section Review

1. Which register holds the function number when calling INT 21h?
2. Which INT 21h function terminates a program?
3. Which INT 21h function writes a single character to standard output?
4. Which INT 21h function writes a string terminated by a $ character to standard output?
5. Which INT 21h function writes a block of data to a file or device?
6. Which INT 21h function reads a single character from standard input?
7. Which INT 21h function reads a block of data from the standard input device?
8. If you want to get the system date, display it, and then change it, which INT 21h functions are required?
9. Which INT 21h functions shown in this chapter probably will not work under Windows NT, 2000, or XP with a restricted user profile?
10. Which INT 21h function would you use to check the standard input buffer to see if a character is waiting to be processed?

13.3 Standard MS-DOS File I/O Services

INT 21h provides such an enormous number of file and directory I/O services that it would be impossible to even come close to showing them here. Table 13-3 shows a few of the functions that you are likely to use.

Table 13-3 File- and Directory-Related INT 21h Functions.

Function	Description
716Ch	Create or open a file
3Eh	Close file handle
42h	Move file pointer
5706h	Get file creation date and time

File/Device Handles   Both MS-DOS and MS-Windows use 16-bit integers called *handles* to identify files and I/O devices. There are five predefined device handles. Each, except handle 2 (error output), supports redirection at the command prompt. These handles are available all the time:

0   Keyboard (standard input)

1   Console (standard output)

2   Error output

3   Auxiliary device (asynchronous)

4   Printer

Each I/O function has a common characteristic: if it fails, the Carry flag is set and an error code is returned in AX. You can use this error code to display an appropriate message. Table 13-4 contains a list of the error codes and their descriptions.

Table 13-4   MS-DOS Extended Error Codes.

Error Code	Description
01	Invalid function number
02	File not found
03	Path not found
04	Too many open files (no handles left)
05	Access denied
06	Invalid handle
07	Memory control blocks destroyed
08	Insufficient memory
09	Invalid memory block address
0A	Invalid environment
0B	Invalid format
0C	Invalid access code
0D	Invalid data
0E	Reserved
0F	Invalid drive was specified
10	Attempt to remove the current directory
11	Not same device
12	No more files

Table 13-4   MS-DOS Extended Error Codes. (Continued)

Error Code	Description
13	Diskette write-protected
14	Unknown unit
15	Drive not ready
16	Unknown command
17	Data error (CRC)
18	Bad request structure length
19	Seek error
1A	Unknown media type
1B	Sector not found
1C	Printer out of paper
1D	Write fault
1E	Read fault
1F	General failure

13.3.0.1   Create or Open File (716Ch)

INT 21h Function 716Ch can either create a new file or open an existing file. It permits the use of extended filenames and file sharing. As shown below, the filename may optionally include a directory path.

INT 21h Function 716Ch	
Description	Create new file or open existing file
Receives	AX = 716Ch BX = access mode (0 = read, 1 = write, 2 = read/write) CX = attributes (0 = normal, 1 = read only, 2 = hidden, 3 = system, 8 = volume ID, 20h = archive) DX = action (1 = open, 2 = truncate, 10h = create) DS:SI = segment/offset of filename DI = alias hint (optional)
Returns	If the create/open was successful, CF = 0, AX = file handle, and CX = action taken. If create/open failed, CF = 1.

INT 21h Function 716Ch	
| **Sample Call** | ```
mov    ax,716Ch          ; extended open/create
mov    bx,0               ; read-only
mov    cx,0               ; normal attribute
mov    dx,1               ; open existing file
mov    si,OFFSET Filename
int    21h
jc     failed
mov    handle,ax          ; file handle
mov    actionTaken,cx     ; action taken to open file
``` |
| **Notes** | The access mode in BX can optionally be combined with one of the following sharing mode values: 0 = share_compatible, 10h = share_denyreadwrite, 20h = share_denywrite, 30h = share_denyread, 40h = share_denynone. For details about the sharing modes and optional *alias hint* field (in DI), consult the Microsoft Platform SDK documentation. |

Additional Examples   The following code either creates a new file or truncates an existing file having the same name:

```
mov   ax,716Ch             ; extended open/create
mov   bx,2                 ; read-write
mov   cx,0                 ; normal attribute
mov   dx,10h + 02h         ; action: create + truncate
mov   si,OFFSET Filename
int   21h
jc    failed
mov   handle,ax            ; file handle
mov   actionTaken,cx       ; action taken to open file
```

The following code attempts to create a new file. It fails (with the Carry flag set) if the file already exists:

```
mov   ax,716Ch             ; extended open/create
mov   bx,2                 ; read-write
mov   cx,0                 ; normal attribute
mov   dx,10h               ; action: create
mov   si,OFFSET Filename
int   21h
jc    failed
mov   handle,ax            ; file handle
mov   actionTaken,cx       ; action taken to open file
```

13.3.1   Close File Handle (3Eh)

INT 21h Function 3Eh closes a file handle. This function flushes the file's write buffer by copying any remaining data to disk, as shown in the following table.
```

INT 21h Function 3Eh	
Description	Close file handle
Receives	AH = 3Eh BX = file handle
Returns	If the file was closed successfully, CF = 0; otherwise, CF = 1

Sample Call	```.data```
	 ```filehandle WORD ?```
	 ```.code```
	 ```mov ah,3Eh```
	 ```mov bx,filehandle```
	 ```int 21h```
	 ```jc failed```

Notes	If the file has been modified, its time stamp and date stamp are updated.

13.3.2 Move File Pointer (42h)

INT 21h Function 42h, as can be seen in the following table, moves the position pointer of an open file to a new location. When calling this function, the *method code* in AL identifies how the pointer will be set:

0	Offset from the beginning of the file
1	Offset from the current location
2	Offset from the end of the file

INT 21h Function 42h	
Description	Move file pointer
Receives	AH = 42h AL = method code BX = file handle CX:DX = 32-bit offset value
Returns	If the file pointer was moved successfully, CF = 0 and DX:AX returns the new file pointer offset; otherwise, CF = 1.

INT 21h Function 42h	
| Sample Call | ```
mov    ah,42h
mov    al,0        ; method: offset from beginning
mov    bx,handle
mov    cx,offsetHi
mov    dx,offsetLo
int    21h
``` |
| Notes | The returned file pointer offset in DX:AX is always relative to the beginning of the file. |

13.3.2.1   Get File Creation Date and Time

INT 21h Function 5706h, shown in the following table, obtains the date and time when a file was created. This is not necessarily the same date and time when the file was last modified, or even accessed.

INT 21h Function 5706h	
Description	Get file creation date and time
Receives	AX = 5706h BX = file handle
Returns	If the function call was successful, CF = 0, DX = date, CX = time, and SI = milliseconds. If the function failed, CF = 1.
| Sample Call | ```
mov ax,5706h              ; Get creation date/time
mov bx,handle
int 21h
jc  error                 ; quit if failed
mov date,dx
mov time,cx
mov milliseconds,si
``` |
| Notes | The file must already be open. The *milliseconds* value indicates the number of 10-millisecond intervals to add to the MS-DOS time. Range is 0 to 199, indicating that the field can add as many as 2 seconds to the overall time. |

13.3.3   Selected Library Procedures

Two procedures from the Irvine16 link library are shown here: **ReadString** and **WriteString**. **ReadString** is the trickiest of the two, since it must read one character at a time until it encounters the end of line sequence (0Dh, 0Ah). It reads these two characters from standard input without copying them to the buffer.

13.3.3.1   ReadString

The **ReadString** procedure reads a string from standard input, and places the characters in an
input buffer. It reads past the end of line and removes the carriage-return linefeed characters
from the string:

```
;----------------------------------------------------------
ReadString PROC
; Receives: DS:DX points to the input buffer,
;           CX = maximum input size
; Returns:  AX = size of the input string
; Comments: Stops when the Enter key (0Dh) is pressed.
;----------------------------------------------------------
    push cx                          ; save registers
    push si
    push cx                          ; save digit count again
    mov  si,dx                       ; point to input buffer
L1: mov  ah,1                        ; function: keyboard input
    int  21h                         ; returns character in AL
    cmp  al,0Dh                      ; end of line?
    je   L2                          ; yes: exit
    mov  [si],al                     ; no: store the character
    inc  si                          ; increment buffer pointer
    loop L1                          ; loop until CX=0
L2: mov  byte ptr [si],0             ; end with a null byte
    pop  ax                          ; original digit count
    sub  ax,cx                       ; AX = size of input string
    pop  si                          ; restore registers
    pop  cx
    ret
ReadString ENDP
```

13.3.3.2   WriteString

The **WriteString** procedure writes a null-terminated string to standard output. It calls a helper
procedure named **Str_length** that returns the number of bytes in a string:

```
;----------------------------------------------------------
WriteString PROC
; Writes a null-terminated string to standard output
; Receives: DS:DX = address of string
; Returns: nothing
;----------------------------------------------------------
    pusha
    push ds                          ; set ES to DS
    pop  es
    mov  di,dx                       ; ES:DI = string ptr
    call Str_length                  ; AX = string length
    mov  cx,ax                       ; CX = number of bytes
```

```
        mov   ah,40h              ; write to file or device
        mov   bx,1               ; standard output handle
        int   21h                ; call MS-DOS
        popa
        ret
WriteString ENDP
```

13.3.4   Example: Read and Copy a Text File

We presented INT 21h Function 3Fh earlier in this chapter, in the context of reading from standard input. This function can also be used to read a file, if the handle in BX identifies a file that has been opened for input. When Function 3Fh returns, AX indicates the number of bytes actually read from the file. When the end of the file is reached, the value returned in AX is less than the number of bytes requested (in CX).

We also presented INT 21h Function 40h earlier in this chapter in the context of writing to standard output (device handle 1). Instead, the handle in BX can refer to an open file. The function automatically updates the file's position pointer, so the next call to Function 40h begins writing where the previous call left off.

The *Readfile.asm* program we're about to show you demonstrates several INT 21h functions presented in this section:

- Function 716Ch: Create new file or open existing file
- Function 3Fh: Read from file or device
- Function 40h: Write to file or device
- Function 3Eh: Close file handle

The following program opens a text file for input, reads no more than 5,000 bytes from the file, displays it on the console, creates a new file, and copies the data to a new file:

```
TITLE Read a text file            (Readfile.asm)

; Read, display, and copy a text file.
INCLUDE Irvine16.inc

.data
BufSize = 5000
infile     BYTE "my_text_file.txt",0
outfile    BYTE "my_output_file.txt",0
inHandle   WORD ?
outHandle  WORD ?
buffer     BYTE BufSize DUP(?)
bytesRead  WORD ?

.code
main PROC
    mov   ax,@data
    mov   ds,ax
```

```
; Open the input file
   mov ax,716Ch                         ; extended create or open
   mov bx,0                             ; mode = read-only
   mov cx,0                             ; normal attribute
   mov dx,1                             ; action: open
   mov si,OFFSET infile
   int 21h                              ; call MS-DOS
   jc  quit                             ; quit if error
   mov inHandle,ax

; Read the input file
   mov ah,3Fh                           ; read file or device
   mov bx,inHandle                      ; file handle
   mov cx,BufSize                       ; max bytes to read
   mov dx,OFFSET buffer                 ; buffer pointer
   int 21h
   jc  quit                             ; quit if error
   mov bytesRead,ax

; Display the buffer
   mov ah,40h                           ; write file or device
   mov bx,1                             ; console output handle
   mov cx,bytesRead                     ; number of bytes
   mov dx,OFFSET buffer                 ; buffer pointer
   int 21h
   jc  quit                             ; quit if error

; Close the file
   mov  ah,3Eh                          ; function: close file
   mov  bx,inHandle                     ; input file handle
   int  21h                             ; call MS-DOS
   jc  quit                             ; quit if error

; Create the output file
   mov ax,716Ch                         ; extended create or open
   mov bx,1                             ; mode = write-only
   mov cx,0                             ; normal attribute
   mov dx,12h                           ; action: create/truncate
   mov si,OFFSET outfile
   int 21h                              ; call MS-DOS
   jc  quit                             ; quit if error
   mov outHandle,ax                     ; save handle

; Write buffer to new file
   mov ah,40h                           ; write file or device
   mov bx,outHandle                     ; output file handle
   mov cx,bytesRead                     ; number of bytes
   mov dx,OFFSET buffer                 ; buffer pointer
   int 21h
   jc  quit                             ; quit if error
```

```
; Close the file
    mov   ah,3Eh                    ; function: close file
    mov   bx,outHandle              ; output file handle
    int   21h                       ; call MS-DOS
quit:
    call  Crlf
    exit
main ENDP
END main
```

13.3.5 Reading the MS-DOS Command Tail

In the programs that follow, we will often pass information to programs on the command line. Suppose we needed to pass the name *file1.doc* to a program named *attr.exe*. The MS-DOS command line would be

```
attr FILE1.DOC
```

When a program runs, any additional text on its command line is automatically stored in the 128-byte MS-DOS command tail area, at offset 80h in an area named the *program segment prefix* (PSP). The first byte contains a count of the number of characters typed on the command line. Using our example of the *attr.exe* program, the hexadecimal contents of the command tail are as follows:

Offset:	80	81	82	83	84	85	86	87	88	89	8A	8B
Contents:	0A	20	46	49	4C	45	31	2E	44	4F	43	0D
			F	I	L	E	1	.	D	O	C	

You can see the command tail bytes using CodeView, if you load the program and set the command-line arguments before running the program.

> To set command-line parameters in CodeView, choose *Set Runtime Arguments...* from the *Run* menu. To view the parameters, press F10 to execute the first program instruction, open a memory window, select *Memory* from the *Options* menu, and enter ES:0x80 into the *Address Expression* field.

There is one exception to the rule that MS-DOS stores all characters after the command or program name: It doesn't keep the file and device names used when redirecting input-output. For example, MS-DOS does not save any text in the command tail when the following command is typed because both *infile.txt* and PRN are used for redirection:

```
prog1 < infile.txt > prn
```

The **Get_Commandtail** procedure from the book's link library returns a copy of the command tail. When calling this procedure, set DX to the offset of the buffer where the command tail will be copied. It skips over leading spaces with SCASB and sets the Carry flag if the command tail is empty. This makes it easy for the calling program to execute a JC (*jump carry*) instruction if nothing is typed on the command line:

```
.data
buffer BYTE 129 DUP(?)
.code
    mov  ax,@data
    mov  ds,ax
    mov  dx,OFFSET buffer              ; point to buffer
    call Get_Commandtail
```

The following is a listing of **Get_Commandtail**:

```
Get_Commandtail PROC
;
; Gets a copy of the MS-DOS command tail at PSP:80h.
; Receives: DX contains the offset of the buffer
;    that receives a copy of the command tail.
; Returns: CF=1 if the buffer is empty; otherwise,
;    CF=0.
;----------------------------------------------------
    push es
    pusha                         ; save general registers

    mov  ah,62h                   ; get PSP segment address
    int  21h                      ; returned in BX
    mov  es,bx                    ; copied to ES

    mov  si,dx                    ; point to buffer
    mov  di,81h                   ; PSP offset of command tail
    mov  cx,0                     ; byte count
    mov  cl,es:[di-1]             ; get length byte
    cmp  cx,0                     ; is the tail empty?
    je   L2                       ; yes: exit
    cld                           ; no: scan forward
    mov  al,20h                   ; space character
    repz scasb                    ; scan for non-space
    jz   L2                       ; all spaces found
    dec  di                       ; non space found
    inc  cx
```

> By default, the assembler assumes that DI is an offset from the segment address in DS. The segment override (es:[di]) tells the CPU to use the segment address in ES instead.

```
L1: mov   al,es:[di]              ; copy tail to buffer
    mov   [si],al                 ; pointed to by DS:SI
    inc   si
    inc   di
    loop  L1
    clc                           ; CF=0 means tail found
    jmp   L3

L2: stc                           ; set CF: no command tail
L3: mov byte ptr [si],0           ; store null byte
    popa                          ; restore registers
    pop es
    ret
Get_Commandtail ENDP
```

INT 21h Function 62h returns the segment portion of the program segment prefix's address. The following statements from the example program call this function:

```
    mov   ah,62h                  ; get PSP segment address
    int   21h                     ; returned in BX
    mov   es,bx                   ; copied to ES
```

It is necessary to set ES to the PSP segment before using SCASB to scan for the first nonblank character in the command tail.

13.3.6   Example: Creating a Binary File

A *binary file* is given its name because the data stored in the file is simply a binary image of program data. Suppose, for example, that your program created and filled an array of doublewords:

```
myArray DWORD 50 DUP(?)
```

If you wanted to write this array to a text file, you would have to convert each integer to a string and write it separately. A more efficient way to store this data would be to just write a binary image of **myArray** to a file. An array of 50 doublewords uses 200 bytes of memory, and that is exactly the amount of disk space the file would use.

The following *Binfile.asm* program fills an array with random integers, displays the integers on the screen, writes the integers to a binary file, and closes the file. It reopens the file, reads the integers, and displays them on the screen:

```
TITLE Binary File Program              (Binfile.asm)

; This program creates a binary file containing
; an array of doublewords.
INCLUDE Irvine16.inc

.data
myArray DWORD 50 DUP(?)
```

```
fileName    BYTE "binary array file.bin",0
fileHandle WORD ?
commaStr    BYTE ", ",0

; Set CreateFile to zero if you just want to
; read and display the existing binary file.
CreateFile = 1

.code
main PROC
    mov  ax,@data
    mov  ds,ax

.IF CreateFile EQ 1
    call FillTheArray
    call DisplayTheArray
    call CreateTheFile
    call WaitMsg
    call Crlf
.ENDIF
    call ReadTheFile
    call DisplayTheArray

quit:
    call Crlf
    exit
main ENDP

;-------------------------------------------------------
ReadTheFile PROC
;
; Open and read the binary file.
; Receives: nothing.  Returns: nothing
;-------------------------------------------------------
    mov ax,716Ch            ; extended file open
    mov bx,0                ; mode: read-only
    mov cx,0                ; attribute: normal
    mov dx,1                ; open existing file
    mov si,OFFSET fileName  ; filename
    int 21h                 ; call MS-DOS
    jc  quit                ; quit if error
    mov fileHandle,ax       ; save handle

; Read the input file, then close the file.
    mov ah,3Fh              ; read file or device
    mov bx,fileHandle       ; file handle
    mov cx,SIZEOF myArray   ; max bytes to read
    mov dx,OFFSET myArray   ; buffer pointer
    int 21h
    jc  quit                ; quit if error
```

```
        mov ah,3Eh                  ; function: close file
        mov bx,fileHandle           ; output file handle
        int 21h                     ; call MS-DOS
quit:
    ret
ReadTheFile ENDP

;------------------------------------------------------
DisplayTheArray PROC
;
; Display the doubleword array.
; Receives: nothing.  Returns: nothing
;------------------------------------------------------
    mov   cx,LENGTHOF myArray
    mov   si,0
L1:
    mov   eax,myArray[si]           ; get a number
    call  WriteHex                  ; display the number
    mov   edx,OFFSET commaStr       ; display a comma
    call  WriteString
    add   si,TYPE myArray           ; next array position
    loop  L1
    ret
DisplayTheArray ENDP

;------------------------------------------------------
FillTheArray PROC
;
; Fill the array with random integers.
; Receives: nothing.  Returns: nothing
;------------------------------------------------------
    mov   CX,LENGTHOF myArray
    mov   si,0
L1:
    mov   eax,1000h                 ; generate random integers
    call  RandomRange               ; between 0 - 999 in EAX
    mov   myArray[si],eax           ; store in the array
    add   si,TYPE myArray           ; next array position
    loop  L1
    ret
FillTheArray ENDP

;------------------------------------------------------
CreateTheFile PROC
;
; Create a file containing binary data.
; Receives: nothing.  Returns: nothing
;------------------------------------------------------
    mov ax,716Ch                    ; create file
```

```
        mov bx,1                    ; mode: write only
        mov cx,0                    ; normal file
        mov dx,12h                  ; action: create/truncate
        mov si,OFFSET fileName      ; filename
        int 21h                     ; call MS-DOS
        jc  quit                    ; quit if error
        mov fileHandle,ax           ; save handle

    ; Write the integer array to the file.
        mov ah,40h                  ; write file or device
        mov bx,fileHandle           ; output file handle
        mov cx,SIZEOF myArray       ; number of bytes
        mov dx,OFFSET myArray       ; buffer pointer
        int 21h
        jc  quit                    ; quit if error

    ; Close the file.
        mov  ah,3Eh                 ; function: close file
        mov  bx,fileHandle          ; output file handle
        int  21h                    ; call MS-DOS
quit:
    ret
CreateTheFile ENDP
END main
```

It is worth noting that the writing of the entire array can be done with a single call to INT 21h Function 40h. There is no need for a loop:

```
        mov ah,40h                  ; write file or device
        mov bx,fileHandle           ; output file handle
        mov cx,SIZEOF myArray       ; number of bytes
        mov dx,OFFSET myArray       ; buffer pointer
        int 21h
```

The same is true when reading the file back into the array. A single call to INT 21h Function 3Fh does the job:

```
        mov ah,3Fh                  ; read file or device
        mov bx,fileHandle           ; file handle
        mov cx,SIZEOF myArray       ; max bytes to read
        mov dx,OFFSET myArray       ; buffer pointer
        int 21h
```

13.3.7   Section Review

1. Name the five standard MS-DOS device handles.
2. After calling an MS-DOS I/O function, which flag indicates that an error has occurred?
3. When you call Function 716Ch to create a file, what arguments are required?

4. Show an example of opening an existing file for input.
5. When you call Function 716Ch to read a binary array from a file that is already open, what argument values are required?
6. How do you check for end of file when reading an input file using INT 21h Function 3Fh?
7. When calling Function 3Fh, how is reading from a file different from reading from the keyboard?
8. If you wanted to read a random-access file, which INT 21h function would permit you to jump directly to a particular record in the middle of the file?
9. Write a short code segment that positions the file pointer 50 bytes from the beginning of a file. Assume that the file is already open, and BX contains the file handle.

13.4 Chapter Summary

In this chapter, you learned the basic memory organization of MS-DOS, how to activate MS-DOS function calls, and how to perform basic input-output operations at the operating system level.

The standard input device and the standard output device are collectively called the *console*, which involves the keyboard for input and the video display for output.

A *software interrupt* is a call to an operating system procedure. Most of these procedures, called *interrupt handlers*, provide input-output capability to application programs.

The INT (call to interrupt procedure) instruction pushes the CPU flags on the stack and calls an interrupt handler. The CPU processes the INT instruction using the *interrupt vector table*, a table containing 32-bit segment-offset addresses of interrupt handlers.

When a program runs, any additional text on its command line is automatically stored in the 128-byte MS-DOS command tail area, at offset 80h in an area named the *program segment prefix* (PSP). The **Get_Commandtail** procedure from the book's link library returns a copy of the command tail.

Some frequently used interrupts are:

- INT 10h Video Services: Procedures that display routines that control the cursor position, write text in color, scroll the screen, and display video graphics.
- INT 16h Keyboard Services: Procedures that read the keyboard and check its status.
- INT 17h Printer Services: Procedures that initialize, print, and return the printer status.
- INT 1Ah Time of Day: A procedure that gets the number of clock ticks since the machine was turned on or sets the counter to a new value.
- INT 1Ch User Timer Interrupt: An empty procedure that is executed 18.2 times per second.

A number of important INT 21h functions were presented in this chapter:

- INT 21h MS-DOS Services. Procedures that provide input-output, file handling, and memory management. Also known as MS-DOS function calls.
- INT 21h is usually called an MS-DOS function call. There are some 90 or so different functions supported by this interrupt, identified by a function number placed in the AH register.
- INT 21h Function 4Ch terminates the current program (called a process).

- INT 21h Functions 2 and 6 write a single character to standard output.
- INT 21h Function 5 writes a single character to the printer.
- INT 21h Function 9 writes a string to standard output.
- INT 21h Function 40h writes an array of bytes to a file or device.
- INT 21h Function 1 reads a single character from standard input.
- INT 21h Function 6 reads a character from standard input without waiting.
- INT 21h Function 0Ah reads a buffered string from standard input.
- INT 21h Function 0Bh gets the status of the standard input buffer
- INT 21h Function 3Fh reads an array of bytes from a file or device.
- INT 21h Function 2Ah gets the system date.
- INT 21h Function 2Bh sets the system date.
- INT 21h Function 2Ch gets the system time.
- INT 21h Function 2Dh sets the system time.
- INT 21h Function 716Ch either creates a file or opens an existing file.
- INT 21h Function 3Eh closes a file handle.
- INT 21h Function 42h moves a file's position pointer.
- INT 21h Function 5706h obtains a file's creation date and time.
- INT 21h Function 62h returns the segment portion of the program segment prefix address.

The following sample programs showed how to apply MS-DOS functions:

- The *DateTime.asm* program displays the system date and time.
- The *Readfile.asm* program opens a text file for input, reads the file, displays it on the console, creates a new file, and copies the data to a new file.
- The *Binfile.asm* program fills an array with random integers, displays the integers on the screen, writes the integers to a binary file, and closes the file. It reopens the file, reads the integers, and displays them on the screen.

A binary file is given its name because the data stored in the file is a binary image of program data.

13.5   Chapter Exercises

The following exercises must be done in Real-address mode. Do not use any functions from the Irvine16 library. Use INT 21h function calls for all input-output, unless an exercise specifically says to do otherwise.

1. Read a Text File
Open a file for input, read the file, and display its contents on the screen in hexadecimal. Make the input buffer smaller than the file and use a loop to repeat the call to Function 3Fh as many times as necessary until the entire file has been processed.

2. Copy a Text File

Modify the **Readfile** program in Section 13.3.4 so that it can read a file of any size. Assuming that the buffer is smaller than the input file, use a loop to read all data. Display appropriate error messages if the Carry flag is set after any INT 21h function calls.

3. Setting the Date

Write a program that displays the current date and prompts the user for a new date. If a non-blank date is entered, use it to update the system date.

4. Upper Case Conversion

Write a program that uses INT 21h to input lower case letters from the keyboard and convert them to upper case. Display only the upper case letters.

5. File Creation Date

Write a procedure that displays the date when a file was created, along with its filename. Write a test program that demonstrates the procedure with several different filenames, including extended filenames. If a file cannot be found, display an appropriate error message.

6. Text Matching Program

Write a program that opens a text file containing up to 60K bytes and performs a case-insensitive search for a string. The string and the filename can be input by the user. Display each line from the file on which the string appears and prefix each line with a line number. Review the **Str_find** procedure from Section 9.7, but note that your program must run in Real-address mode.

7. File Encryption Using XOR

Enhance the file encryption program from Section 6.3.4.3 as follows:

- Prompt the user for the name of a plain text file and a cipher text file.
- Open the plain text file for input, and open the cipher text file for output.
- Let the user enter a single integer encryption code (0–255).
- Read the input file into a buffer, and exclusive-OR each byte with the encryption code.
- Write the buffer to the cipher text file.

The only procedure you may call from the book's link library is **ReadInt**. All other input/output must be performed using INT 21h.

8. CountWords Procedure

Write a program that counts the words in a text file. Prompt the user for a file name, and display the word count on the screen. The only procedure you may call from the book's link library is **WriteDec**. All other input/output must be performed using INT 21h.

14

Disk Fundamentals

14.1   Disk Storage Systems

As a well-rounded programmer and/or computer scientist, you should know something about the whole disk storage picture. Your interests might be in the areas of runtime efficiency, or system-level access to data, data security and integrity, or just a general understanding of what goes on inside the computer. With such interests in mind, we will begin this chapter with a discussion of basic disk hardware, show how it relates to the BIOS-level disk storage, and finally show how the operating system interacts with application programs to provide access to files and directories. (Recall that BIOS stands for *Basic Input-Output System*, discussed in Chapter 2.)

As always, the interaction between a computer's virtual layers is apparent. At the operating system level, it is not useful to know the exact disk geometry (physical locations) or brand-specific disk information. The BIOS, which in this case amounts to disk controller firmware, acts as a broker between the disk hardware and the operating system. Similarly, application programs are not concerned with the particular choice of file storage system. They depend on the operating system to provide straightforward access to files and directories.

Using assembly language, you can bypass the operating system completely when accessing data. This can be useful: you might have to store and retrieve data stored in an unconventional format, to recover lost data, or to perform diagnostics on disk hardware. In this chapter, for example, we show how to read one disk sector at a time. At the end of the chapter, as an illustration of typical OS-level access to data, we include a number of MS-DOS functions used for drive and directory manipulation.

14.1.1 Tracks, Cylinders, and Sectors

Disk storage systems all have certain common characteristics: They have physical partitioning of data, they allow direct access to data, and they have a way of mapping filenames to physical storage. At the hardware level of a disk storage system are platters, sides, tracks, cylinders, and sectors, all of which describe the physical layout of a disk. At the software level are clusters and files, which MS-DOS uses to locate data.

A typical hard drive, shown in Figure 14-1, is made up of multiple platters attached to a spindle that rotates at constant speed. Above the surface of each platter is a read/write head that records magnetic pulses. The read/write heads move in toward the center and out toward the rim as a group, in small steps.

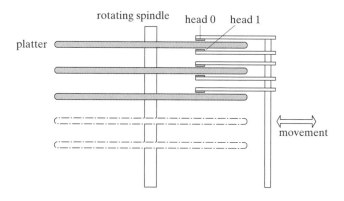

Figure 14-1 Physical Elements of a Hard Drive.

The surface of a disk is formatted into invisible concentric bands called *tracks,* on which data are stored magnetically. A typical 3.5" hard drive may contain thousands of tracks. Moving the read/write heads from one track to another is called *seeking*. The *average seek time* is one type of disk speed measurement. Another measurement is RPM (revolutions per minute), typically 7,200. The outside track of a disk is track 0, and the track numbers increase as you move towards the center.

A *cylinder* refers to all tracks accessible from a single position of the read/write heads. A file is initially stored on a disk using adjacent cylinders. This reduces the amount of movement by the read-write heads.

A *sector* is a 512-byte portion of a track, as shown in Figure 14-2. Physical sectors are magnetically (invisibly) marked on the disk by the manufacturer, using what is called a *low-level format*. Sector sizes never change, regardless of the installed operating system. A hard disk may have 63 or more sectors per track.

Physical disk geometry is a way of describing the disk's structure to make it readable by the system BIOS. It consists of the number of cylinders per disk, the number of read/write heads per cylinder, and the number of sectors per track.

Fragmentation   Over time, as files become more spread out around a disk, they become fragmented. A *fragmented* file is one whose sectors are no longer located in contiguous areas of the disk. When this happens, the read-write heads have to skip across tracks when reading the file's data. This slows down the reading and writing of files, and makes the data more susceptible to errors.

Translation to Logical Sector Numbers   Hard disk controllers perform a process called *translation*, the conversion of physical disk geometry to a logical structure that is understood by the operating system. The controller is usually embedded in firmware, either on the drive itself or on a separate controller card. After translation, the operating system can work with what are called *logical sector numbers*. Logical sector numbers are always numbered sequentially, starting at zero.

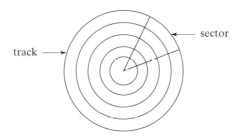

Figure 14-2   Disk Tracks and Sectors.

14.1.2 Disk Partitions (Volumes)

A single physical hard drive is divided into one or more logical units named *partitions,* or *volumes.* Each formatted partition is represented by a separate drive letter such as C, D, or E, and it can be formatted using one of several file systems.

A drive may contain two types of partitions: primary and extended. Two configurations are possible, depending on whether you want an extended partition:

- Up to three primary partitions and one extended partition.
- Up to four primary partitions and no extended partition.

An *extended partition* can be divided into an unlimited number of *logical partitions.* Each logical partition appears as a separate drive letter. Primary partitions can be made bootable, whereas logical partitions cannot. It is possible to format each system or logical partition with a different file system.

Suppose for example, that a 20 GB hard drive was assigned a primary 10 GB partition (drive C), and on it, we installed the operating system. Its extended partition would be 10 GB. Arbitrarily, we could divide the latter into two logical partitions of 2 GB and 8 GB, and format them with various file systems such as FAT16, FAT32, or NTFS. (We will discuss the details of these file systems in the next section of this chapter.) Assuming that no other hard drives were already installed, the two logical partitions would be assigned drive letters D and E.

Multi-Boot Systems   It is quite common to create multiple primary partitions, each capable of booting (loading) a different operating system. This makes it possible to test software in different environments, and to take advantage of security features in the more advanced systems. Many software developers use one primary partition to create a test environment for software under development. Then they have another primary partition that holds production software that has already been tested and is ready for use by customers.

Logical partitions, on the other hand, are primarily intended for data. It is possible for different operating systems to share data stored in the same logical partition. For example, all recent versions of MS-Windows and Linux can read FAT32 disks. A computer can boot from any of these operating systems and read the same data files in a shared logical partition.

> ***Tools:*** You can use the FDISK.EXE program under MS-DOS and Windows 98 to create and remove partitions, but it does not preserve data. Better yet, Windows 2000 and XP have a Disk Manager utility that provides the ability to create, delete, and resize partitions without destroying data. There are also third-party partitioning programs such as *PartitionMagic* by Power-Quest that permit nondestructive resizing and moving partitions.

Dual-Boot Example   In the following example, the Windows 2000 *Disk Management* tool displays all six partitions on a single hard drive:

Volume	Layout	Type	File System	Status	Capacity	Free Space	% Free
⊜	Partition	Basic		Healthy	5.13 GB	5.13 GB	100 %
⊜	Partition	Basic		Healthy	2.01 GB	2.01 GB	100 %
⊜ BACKUP (E:)	Partition	Basic	FAT32	Healthy	7.80 GB	4.84 GB	62 %
⊜ DATA_1 (D:)	Partition	Basic	FAT32	Healthy	7.80 GB	2.68 GB	34 %
⊜ SYSTEM 98	Partition	Basic	FAT32	Healthy	1.95 GB	1.12 GB	57 %
⊜ WIN2000-A (C:)	Partition	Basic	NTFS	Healthy (System)	3.91 GB	1.43 GB	36 %
⊜ ZIP-100 (G:)	Partition	Basic	FAT	Healthy (Active)	95 MB	85 MB	89 %

The displayed figure is for a system that boots under both Windows 98 and Windows 2000. There are two primary partitions, arbitrarily named SYSTEM 98 and WIN2000-A. Only one primary partition can be active at one time. When active, a primary partition is called the *system partition*.

In the figure, the system partition is currently WIN2000-A, assigned to drive C. Note that the inactive system partition has no drive letter. If we should restart the computer and boot from SYSTEM 98, it would become drive C, and the WIN2000-A partition would be inactive.

The extended partition, meanwhile, has been divided into four logical partitions, two of which are unformatted, and the remaining two, named BACKUP and DATA_1, are formatted using the FAT32 file system.

Master Boot Record   The Master Boot Record (MBR), created when the first partition is created on a hard disk, is located in the drive's first logical sector. The MBR contains the following:

- The disk *partition table*, which describes the sizes and locations of all partitions on the disk.
- A small program that locates the partition's boot sector and transfers control to a program in the sector that loads the operating system.

14.1.3   Section Review

1. (*True/False*): A track is divided into multiple units called *sectors*.
2. (*True/False*): A sector consists of multiple tracks.
3. A _____ consists of all tracks accessible from a single position of the read/write heads of a hard drive.
4. (*True/False*): Physical sectors are always 512 bytes because the sectors are marked on the disk by the manufacturer.
5. Under FAT32, how many bytes are used by a logical sector?
6. Why are files initially stored in adjacent cylinders?
7. When a file's storage becomes fragmented, what does this mean in terms of cylinders and *seek* operations performed by the drive?
8. Another name for a drive partition is a drive _____.
9. What does a drive's *average seek time* measure?
10. What is a *low-level format*?
11. How many primary partitions can there be on a hard drive?
12. How many extended partitions can there be on a hard drive?

13. What is contained in the *master boot record*?
14. How many primary partitions can be active at the same time?
15. When a primary partition is active, it is called the _____ partition.

14.2   File Systems

Every operating system has some type of disk management system. At the lowest level, it manages partitions. At the next-highest level, it manages files and directories. A file system must keep track of the location, sizes, and attributes of each disk file. Let's take a look at the FAT-type file systems commonly used on IA-32 systems. Each provides the following connections:

- A mapping of logical sectors to *clusters*, the basic unit of storage for all files and directories.
- A mapping of file and directory names to sequences of clusters.

A *cluster* is the smallest unit of space used by a file; it consists of one or more adjacent disk sectors. A file system stores each file as a linked sequence of clusters. The size of a cluster depends on both the type of file system in use and the size of its disk partition. The following shows a file made up of two 2,048-byte clusters, each containing four 512-byte sectors:

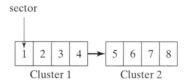

A chain of clusters is referenced by a *file allocation table* (FAT) that keeps track of all clusters used by a file. A pointer to the first cluster entry in the FAT is stored in each file's directory entry. Section 14.3.3 explains the FAT in greater detail.

Wasted Space   Even a small file requires at least one cluster of disk storage, which can result in wasted space. The following shows an 8,200 byte file, which completely fills two 4,096-byte clusters and uses only 8 bytes of a third cluster. This leaves 4,088 bytes of wasted disk space in the third cluster:

File size: 8,200 bytes

| | | 8 bytes used, |
| 4,096 used | 4,096 used | 4,088 empty |

Cluster 1   Cluster 2   Cluster 3

Actually, a cluster size of 4,096 (4 KB) is considered an efficient way to store small files. Imagine what would result if our 8,200-byte file were stored on a volume having 32 KB clusters. In that case, 24,568 bytes (32,768 − 8,200) would be wasted. On volumes having a large number of small files, small cluster sizes are best.

Standard cluster sizes and file system types for hard drives are shown in Table 14-1. These values have changed slightly with each new Microsoft operating system. The values shown here apply to Windows 2000 and XP.

Table 14-1   Partition and Cluster Sizes (over 1 GB).

Volume Size	FAT16 Cluster	FAT32 Cluster	NTFS Cluster[a]
1.25 GB – 2 GB	32 KB	4 KB	2 KB
2 GB – 4 GB	64 KB[b]	4 KB	4 KB
4 GB – 8 GB	ns (*not supported*)	4 KB	4 KB
8 GB – 16 GB	ns	8 KB	4 KB
16 GB – 32 GB	ns	16 KB	4 KB
32 GB – 2 TB	ns	ns[c]	4 KB

[a]   Default sizes under NTFS. Can be changed when disk is formatted.
[b]   64KB clusters with FAT16 are only supported by Windows 2000 and XP.
[c]   A software patch is available that permits Windows 98 to format drives over 32 GB.

14.2.1   FAT12

The FAT12 file system was first used on IBM-PC diskettes. It is still supported by all versions of MS-Windows and Linux. The cluster size is only 512 bytes, so it is ideal for storing small files. Each entry in its File Allocation Table is 12 bits long. A FAT12 volume holds fewer than 4,087 clusters.

14.2.2   FAT16

The FAT16 file system is the only available format for hard drives formatted under MS-DOS. It is supported by all versions of MS-Windows and Linux. There are some drawbacks to FAT16:

- Storage is inefficient on volumes over 1 GB because FAT16 uses large cluster sizes.
- Each entry in the File Allocation Table is 16 bits long, limiting the total number of clusters.
- The volume can hold between 4,087 and 65,526 clusters.
- The boot sector is not backed up, so a single sector read error can be catastrophic.
- There is no built-in file system security or individual user permissions.

14.2.3   FAT32

The FAT32 file system was introduced with the OEM2 release of Windows 95, and was refined under Windows 98. It has a number of improvements over FAT16:

- It supports long filenames.
- A single file can be as large as 4 GB minus 2 bytes.

- Each entry in the File Allocation Table is 32 bits long.
- A volume can hold up to 268,435,456 clusters.
- The root folder can be located anywhere on the disk, and it can be almost any size.
- Volumes can hold up to 32 GB.
- It uses a smaller cluster size than FAT16 on volumes holding 1–8 GB, resulting in less wasted space.
- The boot record includes a backup copy of critical data structures. This means that FAT32 drives are less susceptible to a single point of failure than FAT16 drives.

14.2.4   NTFS

The NTFS file system is supported by Windows NT, 2000, and XP. It has significant improvements over FAT32:

- NTFS handles very large volumes, which can be either on a single hard drive or spanned across multiple hard drives.
- The default cluster size is 4 KB for disks over 2 GB.
- Supports Unicode filenames (non-ANSI characters) up to 255 characters long.
- Allows the setting of permissions on files and folders. Access can be by individual users or groups of users. Different levels of access are possible (read, write, modify, etc.)
- Provides built-in data encryption and compression on files, folders, and volumes.
- Can track individual changes to files over time in a *change journal*.
- Disk quotas can be set for individual users or groups of users.
- Provides robust recovery from data errors. Automatically repairs errors by keeping a transaction log.
- Supports disk mirroring, in which the same data are simultaneously written to multiple drives.

Table 14-2 lists each of the different file systems commonly used on Intel-based computers, showing their support by various operating systems.

Table 14-2   Operating System Support for File Systems.

File System	MS-DOS	Linux	Win 95/ 98	Win NT 4	Win 2000/ XP
FAT12	X	X	X	X	X
FAT16	X	X	X	X	X
FAT32		X	X		X
NTFS				X	X

14.2.5   Primary Disk Areas

FAT12 and FAT16 volumes have specific locations reserved for the boot record, file allocation table, and root directory. (The root directory on a FAT32 drive is not stored in a fixed location.) The size of each area is determined when the volume is formatted. For example, a 3.5-inch, 1.44 MB diskette is divided into the following areas:

Logical Sector	Contents
0	Boot record
1–18	File allocation table (FAT)
19–32	Root directory
33–2,879	Data area

The *boot record* contains both a table holding volume information, and a short boot program that loads MS-DOS into memory. The boot program checks for the existence of certain operating system files and loads them into memory. Table 14-3 shows a representative list of fields in a typical boot record. It should be noted that the exact arrangement of fields varies between different versions of the operating system.

Table 14-3   MS-DOS Boot Record Layout.

Offset	Length	Description
00	3	Jump to boot code (JMP instruction)
03	8	Manufacturer name, version number
0B	2	Bytes per sector
0D	1	Sectors per cluster (power of 2)
0E	2	Number of reserved sectors (preceding FAT #1)
10	1	Number of copies of FAT
11	2	Maximum number of root directory entries
13	2	Number of disk sectors for drives under 32MB
15	1	Media descriptor byte
16	2	Size of FAT, in sectors
18	2	Sectors per track
1A	2	Number of drive heads
1C	4	Number of hidden sectors
20	4	Number of disk sectors for drives over 32MB
24	1	Drive number (modified by MS-DOS)
25	1	Reserved

Table 14-3   MS-DOS Boot Record Layout. (Continued)

Offset	Length	Description
26	1	Extended boot signature (always 29h)
27	4	Volume ID number (binary)
2B	11	Volume label
36	8	File-system type (ASCII)
3E	—	Start of boot program and data

The *root directory* is a disk volume's main directory. Each entry in the root directory contains information about a file, including its name, size, attribute, and starting cluster number. The *data area* of the disk is where files are stored. The data area can contain both files and subdirectories.

14.2.6 Section Review

1. (*True/False*): A file system maps logical sectors to clusters.
2. (*True/False*): The starting cluster number of a file is stored in the *disk parameter table*.
3. (*True/False*): All file systems except NTFS require the use of at least one cluster to store a file.
4. (*True/False*): The FAT32 file system allows the setting of individual user permissions for directories, but not files.
5. (*True/False*): Linux does not support the FAT32 file system.
6. Under Windows 98, what is the largest permitted FAT16 volume?
7. Suppose your disk volume's boot record was corrupted. Which file system(s) would provide support for a backup copy of the boot record?
8. Which file system(s) support 16-bit Unicode filenames?
9. Which file system(s) support *disk mirroring*, where the same data are simultaneously written to multiple drives?
10. Suppose you need to keep a record of the last ten changes to a file. Which file system(s) support this feature?
11. If you have a 20 GB disk volume and you wish to have a cluster size <= 8 KB (to avoid wasted space), which file system(s) could you use?
12. What is the largest FAT32 disk volume that supports 4 KB clusters?
13. Describe the four areas (in order) of a 1.44MB diskette.
14. On a disk drive formatted with MS-DOS, how might one find out how many sectors are used by each cluster?
15. *Challenge:* If a disk has a cluster size of 8 KB, how many bytes of wasted space will there be when storing an 8,200-byte file?

16. *Challenge:* Explain how NTFS stores sparse files. (To answer this question, you will have to visit the Microsoft MSDN Web site and look for the information.)

14.3 Disk Directory

Every disk has a *root directory,* which is the primary list of files on the disk. The root directory may also contain the names of other directories, called *subdirectories.* A subdirectory may be thought of as a directory whose name appears in some other directory—the latter is known as the *parent directory.* Each subdirectory can contain filenames and additional directory names. The result is a treelike structure with the root directory at the top, branching out to other directories at lower levels. An example is shown in the following figure:

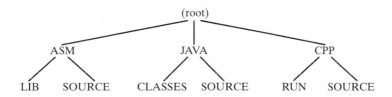

Each directory name and each file within a directory is qualified by the names of the directories above it, called the *path*. For example, the path for the file PROG1.ASM in the SOURCE directory below ASM is

```
C:\ASM\SOURCE\PROG1.ASM
```

Generally, the drive letter can be omitted from the path when an input-output operation is carried out on the current disk drive. A complete list of the directory names in our sample directory tree follows:

```
C:\
\ASM
\ASM\LIB
\ASM\SOURCE
\JAVA
\JAVA\CLASSES
\JAVA\SOURCE
\CPP
\CPP\RUN
\CPP\SOURCE
```

Thus, a *file specification* can take the form of an individual filename or a directory path followed by a filename. It can also be preceded by a drive specification.

14.3.1 MS-DOS Directory Structure

If we tried to explain all the various directory formats available today on Intel-based computers, we would at least have to include Linux, MS-DOS, and all the versions of MS-Windows.

Instead, let's use MS-DOS as a basic example and examine its structure more closely. Then we will follow with a description of the extended filename structure available in MS-Windows.

Each MS-DOS directory entry is 32 bytes long and contains the fields shown in Table 14-4. The *filename* field holds the name of a file, a subdirectory, or the disk volume label. The first byte may indicate the file's status, or it may be the first character of a filename. The possible status values are shown in Table 14-5. The 16-bit *starting cluster number* field refers to the number of the first cluster allocated to the file, as well as its starting entry in the file allocation table (FAT). The *file size* field is a 32-bit number that indicates the file size, in bytes.

Table 14-4   MS-DOS Directory Entry.

Hexadecimal Offset	Field Name	Format
00-07	Filename	ASCII
08-0A	Extension	ASCII
0B	Attribute	8-bit binary
0C-15	Reserved by MS-DOS	
16-17	Time stamp	16-bit binary
18-19	Date stamp	16-bit binary
1A-1B	Starting cluster number	16-bit binary
1C-1F	File size	32-bit binary

Table 14-5   Filename Status Byte.

Status Byte	Description
00h	The entry has never been used.
01h	If the attribute byte = 0Fh and the status byte = 01h, this is the last long filename entry.
05h	The first character of the filename is actually the E5h character (rare).
E5h	The entry contains a filename, but the file has been erased.
2Eh	The entry (.) is for a directory name. If the second byte is also 2Eh (..), the cluster field contains the cluster number of this directory's parent directory.
4*n*h	First long filename entry: If the attribute byte = 0Fh, this marks the first of multiple entries containing a single long filename. The digit *n* indicates the number of entries used by the filename.

Attribute   The *attribute* field identifies the type of file. The field is bit-mapped and usually contains a combination of one of the values shown in Figure 14-3. The two *reserved* bits should always be 0. The *archive* bit is set when a file is modified. The *subdirectory* bit is set if the entry contains the name of a subdirectory. The *volume label* identifies the entry as the name of a disk volume. The *system file* bit indicates that the file is part of the operating system. The *hidden file* bit makes the file hidden; its name does not appear in a display of the directory. The *read-only* bit prevents the file from being deleted or modified in any way. Finally, an attribute value of 0Fh indicates that the current directory entry is for an extended filename.

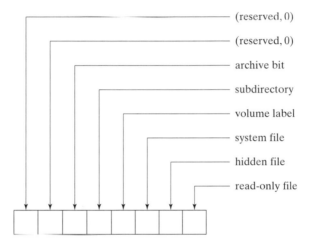

Figure 14-3   File Attribute Byte Fields.

Date and Time   The *date stamp* field indicates the date when the file was created or last changed, expressed as a bit-mapped value:

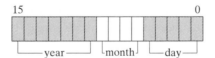

The year value is between 0 and 119, and is automatically added to 1980 (the year the IBM-PC was released). The month value is between 1 and 12, and the day value is between 1 and 31.

The *time stamp* field indicates the time when the file was created or last changed, expressed as a bit-mapped value. The hours may be 0–23, the minutes 0–59, and the seconds 0–29, stored as a count of 2-second increments:

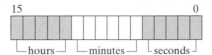

For example, a value of 10100 equals 40 seconds. The following indicates a time of 14:02:40:

$$0\ \ 1\ \ 1\ \ 1\ \ 0\ \ \ 0\ \ 0\ \ 0\ \ 0\ \ 1\ \ 0\ \ \ 1\ \ 0\ \ 1\ \ 0\ \ 0$$
$$\underbrace{\hspace{1.5cm}}_{\text{hours}}\quad\underbrace{\hspace{2cm}}_{\text{minutes}}\quad\underbrace{\hspace{1.5cm}}_{\text{seconds}}$$

Let's examine the entry for a file named MAIN.CPP, shown in the following figure. This file has a normal attribute and its archive bit (20h) has been set, showing that the file was modified. Its starting cluster number is 0020h, its size is 000004EEh bytes, the *Time* field equals 4DBDh (9:45:58), and the *Date* field equals 247Ah (March 26, 1998):

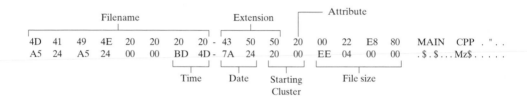

In this figure, the time, date, and starting cluster number are 16-bit values, stored in little endian order (low byte, followed by high byte). The *File size* field is a doubleword, also stored in little endian order.

14.3.2 Long Filenames in MS-Windows

In MS-Windows, any filename longer than 8 + 3 characters, or any filename using both uppercase and lowercase letters is assigned multiple directory entries. If the attribute byte equals 0Fh, the system looks at the byte at offset 0. If the upper digit = 4, this entry begins a series of long filename entries. The lower digit indicates the number of directory entries to be used by the long filename. Subsequent entries count downward from $n-1$ to 1, where n = the number of entries. For example, if a filename requires three entries, the first status byte will be 43h. The subsequent entries will be status bytes equal to 02h and 01h, as may be seen in the following table:

Status Byte	Description
43	Indicates that three entries are used for the long filename, total, and this entry holds the last part of the filename.
02	Holds the second part of the filename.
01	Holds the first part of the filename.

To illustrate, let's use a file having the 26-character filename ABCDEFGHIJKLM-NOPQRSTUV.TXT and save it as a text file in the root directory of drive A. Next, we run DEBUG..EXE from the Command prompt and load the directory sectors into memory at offset 100. This is followed by the D (dump command):[1]

```
L 100 0 13 5                (load sectors 13h - 17h)
D 100                       (dump offset 100 on the screen)
```

Windows creates three directory entries for this file, as shown in Figure 14-4.

Let's start with the entry at 01C0h. The first byte, containing 01, marks this entry as the last of a sequence of long filename entries. It is followed by the first 13 characters of the filename "ABCDEFGHIJKLM". Each Unicode character is 16-bits, stored in little endian order. Note that the attribute byte at offset 0B equals 0F, indicating that this is an extended filename entry (any filename having this attribute is automatically ignored by MS-DOS).

The entry at 01A0h contains the final 13 characters of the long filename, which are "NOPQRSTUV.TXT."

At offset 01E0h, the auto-generated short filename is built from the first six letters of the long filename, followed by ~1, followed by the first three characters after the last period in the original name. These characters are 1-byte ASCII codes. The short filename entry also contains the file creation date and time, the last access date, the last modified date and time, the starting cluster number, and the file size. Here is the information displayed by the Windows *Explorer Property* dialog, which matches the raw directory data:

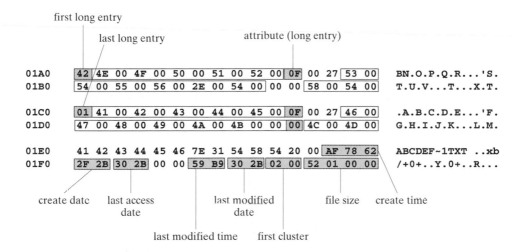

Figure 14-4   Sample Disk Directory.

---

[1]   See the DEBUG tutorial on this book's Web site.

Size:	338 bytes (338 bytes)
Size on disk:	512 bytes (512 bytes)
Created:	Yesterday, September 15, 2001, 12:19:49 PM
Modified:	Today, September 16, 2001, 11:10:50 PM
Accessed:	Today, September 16, 2001
Attributes:	☐ Read-only ☐ Hidden ☑ Archive

14.3.3   File Allocation Table (FAT)

As we've mentioned before, the FAT12, FAT16, and FAT32 file systems use a table called the *file allocation table* (FAT) to keep track of each file's location on the disk. The FAT is a map of all clusters on the disk, showing their ownership by specific files. Each entry corresponds to a cluster number, and each cluster contains one or more sectors. In other words, the 10th FAT entry identifies the 10th cluster on the disk, the 11th entry identifies the 11th cluster, and so on.

Each file is represented in the FAT as a linked list, called a *cluster chain*. Each FAT entry contains an integer that identifies the next entry. Two cluster chains are shown in the following diagram, one for **File1**, and another for **File2**:

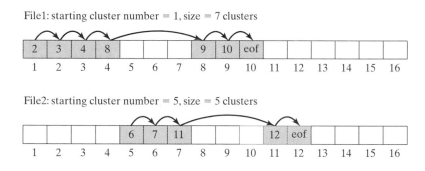

From this diagram, we see that **File1** occupies clusters 1, 2, 3, 4, 8, 9, and 10. **File2** occupies clusters 5, 6, 7, 11, and 12. The **eof** in the last FAT entry for a file is a predefined integer value that tells the OS that the final cluster in the chain has been reached.

When a file is created, the operating system looks for the first available cluster entry in the FAT. Gaps often occur because there are not enough contiguous clusters to hold the entire file. In the preceding diagram, this happened to both **File1** and **File2**. When a file is modified and saved back to disk, its cluster chain often becomes increasingly fragmented. If many files become fragmented, the disk's performance begins to degrade because the read/write heads must jump between different tracks to locate all of a file's clusters. You can run a utility such as *Scandisk* to rebuild the FAT and defragment all files. (Scandisk is a utility supplied with MS-DOS and Windows.)

14.3.4 Section Review

1. (*True/False*): A file specification includes both a file path and a file name.
2. (*True/False*): The primary list of files on a disk is called the *base directory*.
3. (*True/False*): A file's directory entry contains the file's starting sector number.
4. (*True/False*): The MS-DOS date field in a directory entry must be added to 1980.
5. How many bytes are used by an MS-DOS directory entry?
6. Name the seven basic fields of an MS-DOS directory entry (do not include the *reserved* field).
7. In an MS-DOS filename entry, identify the six possible status byte values.
8. Show the format of the time stamp field in an MS-DOS directory entry.
9. When a long filename is stored in a volume directory (under MS-Windows), how is the first long filename entry identified?
10. If a filename has 18 characters, how many long filename entries are required?
11. MS-Windows added two new date fields to the original MS-DOS file directory entry. What are their names?
12. *Challenge:* Illustrate the file allocation table links for a file that uses clusters 2, 3, 7, 6, 4, 8, in that order.

14.4 Reading and Writing Disk Sectors (7305h)

INT 21h, Function 7305h (absolute disk read and write) lets you read and write logical disk sectors. Like all INT instructions, it is designed to run only in 16-bit Real-address mode. We will not atttempt to call INT 21h (or any other interrupt) from Protected mode because of the complexities involved.

Function 7305h works on FAT12, FAT16, and FAT32 file systems, under Windows 95, 98, and Windows Me. It does not work under Windows NT, 2000, or XP, because of their tighter security. Any program permitted to read and write disk sectors could easily bypass file and directory sharing permissions. When calling function 7305h, pass the following arguments:

AX	7305h
DS:BX	Segment/offset of a DISKIO structure variable
CX	0FFFFh
DL	Drive number (0 = default, 1 = A, 2 = B, 3 = C, etc.)
SI	Read/write flag

A DISKIO structure contains the starting sector number, the number of sectors to read or write, and the segment/offset address of the sector buffer:

```
DISKIO STRUCT
    startSector DWORD 0          ; starting sector number
    numSectors  WORD 1           ; number of sectors
    bufferOfs   WORD buffer      ; buffer offset
    bufferSeg   WORD @DATA        ; buffer segment
DISKIO ENDS
```

The following are examples of an input buffer to hold the sector data, along with a DISKIO structure variable:

```
.data
buffer BYTE 512 DUP(?)
diskStruct DISKIO <>
```

When calling Function 7305h, the argument passed in SI determines whether you want to read or write sectors. To read, clear bit 0; to write, set bit 0. In addition, bits 13, 14, and 15 are configured when writing sectors using the following scheme:

Bits 13–15	Type of Sector
000	Other/unknown
001	FAT data
010	directory data
011	normal file data

The remaining bits (1 through 12) must always be clear.

Example 1:   The following statements read one or more sectors from drive C:

```
mov ax,7305h                 ; absolute Read/Write
mov cx,0FFFFh                ; always this value
mov dl,3                     ; drive C
mov bx,OFFSET diskStruct     ; DISKIO structure
mov si,0                     ; read sector
int 21h
```

Example 2:   The following statements write one or more sectors to drive A:

```
mov ax,7305h                 ; absolute Read/Write
mov cx,0FFFFh                ; always this value
mov dl,1                     ; drive A
mov bx,OFFSET diskStruct     ; DISKIO structure
mov si,6001h                 ; write normal sector(s)
int 21h
```

14.4.1   Sector Display Program

Let's put what we've learned about sectors to good use by writing a program that reads and displays individual disk sectors in ASCII format. The pseudocode is listed here:

```
Display heading
Ask for starting sector number and drive number
do while (keystroke <> ESC)
  Read one sector
  If MS-DOS error then exit
  Display one sector
  Wait for keystroke
  Increment sector number
end do
```

Program Listing   Here is a complete listing of the *Sector16.asm* program. It works under Windows 95, 98, and Me, but not under Windows NT, 2000, or XP because of their tighter security relating to disk access:

```
TITLE Sector Display Program                     (Sector32.asm)

; Demonstrates INT 21h function 7305h (ABSDiskReadWrite)
; This Real-mode program reads and displays disk sectors.

INCLUDE Irvine16.inc
Setcursor PROTO, row:BYTE, col:BYTE
EOLN EQU <0dh,0ah>
ESC_KEY = 1Bh
DATA_ROW = 5
DATA_COL = 0
SECTOR_SIZE = 512
READ_MODE = 0                      ; for Function 7505h

DISKIO STRUCT
    startSector DWORD ?            ; starting sector number
    numSectors  WORD 1             ; number of sectors
    bufferOfs   WORD buffer        ; buffer offset
    bufferSeg   WORD @DATA         ; buffer segment
DISKIO ENDS

.data
driveNumber BYTE ?
diskStruct DISKIO <>
buffer BYTE SECTOR_SIZE DUP(0),0     ; one sector

curr_row    BYTE    ?
curr_col    BYTE    ?
; String resources
strLine        BYTE   EOLN,79 DUP(0C4h),EOLN,0
strHeading     BYTE "Sector Display Program (Sector32.exe)"
               BYTE EOLN,EOLN,0
```

```
strAskSector   BYTE "Enter starting sector number: ",0
strAskDrive    BYTE "Enter drive number (1=A, 2=B, "
               BYTE "3=C, 4=D, 5=E, 6=F): ",0
strCannotRead BYTE EOLN,"*** Cannot read the sector. "
               BYTE "Press any key...", EOLN, 0
strReadingSector \
    BYTE "Press Esc to quit, or any key to continue..."
    BYTE EOLN,EOLN,"Reading sector: ",0
.code
main PROC
    mov    ax,@data
    mov    ds,ax
    call   Clrscr
    mov    dx,OFFSET strHeading          ; display greeting
    call   Writestring                   ; ask user for...
    call   AskForSectorNumber

L1: call   Clrscr
    call   ReadSector                    ; read a sector
    jc     L2                            ; quit if error
    call   DisplaySector
    call   ReadChar
    cmp    al,ESC_KEY                    ; Esc pressed?
    je     L3                            ; yes: quit
    inc    diskStruct.startSector        ; next sector
    jmp    L1                            ; repeat the loop

L2: mov    dx,OFFSET strCannotRead        ; error message
    call   Writestring
    call   ReadChar

L3: call   Clrscr
    exit
main ENDP

;------------------------------------------------------
AskForSectorNumber PROC
;
; Prompts the user for the starting sector number
; and drive number. Initializes the startSector
; field of the DISKIO structure, as well as the
; driveNumber variable.
;------------------------------------------------------
    pusha
    mov   dx,OFFSET strAskSector
    call  WriteString
    call  ReadInt
    mov   diskStruct.startSector,eax
    call  Crlf
```

```
        mov   dx,OFFSET strAskDrive
        call  WriteString
        call  ReadInt
        mov   driveNumber,al
        call  Crlf
        popa
        ret
AskForSectorNumber ENDP

;-------------------------------------------------------
ReadSector PROC
;
; Reads a sector into the input buffer.
; Receives: DL = Drive number
; Requires: DiskIO structure must be initialized.
; Returns:  If CF=0, the operation was successful;
;           otherwise, CF=1 and AX contains an
;           error code.
;-------------------------------------------------------
        pusha
        mov   ax,7305h               ; ABSDiskReadWrite
        mov   cx,-1                  ; always -1
        mov   dl,driveNumber         ; drive number
        mov   bx,OFFSET diskStruct   ; sector number
        mov   si,READ_MODE           ; read mode
        int   21h                    ; read disk sector
        popa
        ret
ReadSector ENDP

;-------------------------------------------------------
DisplaySector PROC
;
; Display the sector data in <buffer>, using INT 10h
; BIOS function calls. This avoids filtering of ASCII
; control codes.
; Receives: nothing. Returns: nothing.
; Requires: buffer must contain sector data.
;-------------------------------------------------------
        mov   dx,OFFSET strHeading    ; display heading
        call  WriteString
        mov   eax,diskStruct.startSector ; display sector number
        call  WriteDec
        mov   dx,OFFSET strLine       ; horizontal line
        call  Writestring
        mov   si,OFFSET buffer        ; point to buffer
        mov   curr_row,DATA_ROW       ; set row, column
        mov   curr_col,DATA_COL
        INVOKE SetCursor,curr_row,curr_col
```

```
        mov    cx,SECTOR_SIZE            ; loop counter
        mov    bh,0                      ; video page 0
    L1: push   cx                        ; save loop counter
        mov    ah,0Ah                    ; display character
        mov    al,[si]                   ; get byte from buffer
        mov    cx,1                      ; display it
        int    10h
        call   MoveCursor
        inc    si                        ; point to next byte
        pop    cx                        ; restore loop counter
        loop   L1                        ; repeat the loop
        ret
    DisplaySector ENDP

    ;-------------------------------------------------
    MoveCursor PROC
    ;
    ; Advance the cursor to the next column,
    ; check for possible wraparound on the screen.
    ;-------------------------------------------------
        cmp    curr_col,79               ; last column?
        jae    L1                        ; yes: go to next row
        inc    curr_col                  ; no: increment column
        jmp    L2
    L1: mov    curr_col,0                ; next row
        inc    curr_row
    L2: INVOKE Setcursor,curr_row,curr_col
        ret
    MoveCursor ENDP

    ;-------------------------------------------------------
    Setcursor PROC USES dx,
        row:BYTE, col:BYTE
    ;
    ; Set the screen cursor position
    ;-------------------------------------------------------
        mov   dh, row
        mov   dl, col
        call Gotoxy
        ret
    Setcursor ENDP
    END main
```

The core of the program is the **ReadSector** procedure, which reads each sector from the disk using INT 21h Function 7305h. The sector data are placed in a buffer, and the buffer is displayed by the **DisplaySector** procedure.

DisplaySector Procedure   Most sectors contain binary data, and if INT 21h were used to display them, ASCII control characters would be filtered. Tab and Newline characters, for example, would cause the display to become disjointed. Instead, it's better to use INT 10h Function 9 (see Section 15.3.3), which displays ASCII codes 0–31 as graphics characters. Since INT 10h Function 9 does not advance the cursor, additional code must be written to move the cursor one column to the right after displaying each character. The **SetCursor** procedure simplifies the calling of **Gotoxy** from the Irvine16 library.

Variations   There are many interesting variations that could be created from the *Sector32.asm* program. For example, you could prompt the user for a range of sector numbers to be displayed. Each sector could also be displayed in hexadecimal. You could also let the user scroll forward and backward through the sectors using the PageUp and PageDown keys.

14.4.2   Section Review

1. (*True/False*): You can read sectors from a hard drive using INT 21h Function 7305h under Windows Me, but not under Windows XP.
2. (*True/False*): INT 21h Function 7305h reads one or more disk sectors only in Protected mode.
3. Which input parameters are required by INT 21h Function 7305h?
4. In the Sector Display Program (Section 14.4.1), why is Interrupt 10h used to display characters?
5. *Challenge:* In the Sector Display Program (Section 14.4.1), what would happen if the starting sector number was out of range?

14.5   System-Level File Functions

In Real-address mode, INT 21h provides many useful functions (Table 14-6) that create and change directories, change file attributes, find matching files, and so forth. These functions tend to be less available in high-level languages. When calling any of these services, the function number is placed in AH or AX. Other registers contain additional values passed to MS-DOS.

Table 14-6   Selected INT 21h Disk Services.

Function Number	Function Name
0Eh	Set default drive
19h	Get default drive
7303h	Get disk free space
39h	Create subdirectory
3Ah	Remove subdirectory
3Bh	Set current directory
41h	Delete file
43h	Get/set file attribute
47h	Get current directory path

Table 14-6   Selected INT 21h Disk Services. (Continued)

Function Number	Function Name
4Eh	Find first matching file
4Fh	Find next matching file
56h	Rename file
57h	Get/set file date and time
59h	Get extended error information

Let's take a detailed look at a few commonly used functions. A more detailed list of MS-DOS interrupts and their descriptions can be found in Appendix C.

14.5.1   Get Disk Free Space (7303h)

INT 21h Function 7303h can be used to find both the size of a disk volume and how much free disk space is available. The information is returned in a standard structure named **ExtGetDskFreSpcStruc**, as shown below:

```
ExtGetDskFreSpcStruc STRUC
     StructSize               WORD   ?
     Level                    WORD   ?
     SectorsPerCluster        DWORD  ?
     BytesPerSector           DWORD  ?
     AvailableClusters        DWORD  ?
     TotalClusters            DWORD  ?
     AvailablePhysSectors     DWORD  ?
     TotalPhysSectors         DWORD  ?
     AvailableAllocationUnits DWORD  ?
     TotalAllocationUnits     DWORD  ?
     Rsvd                     DWORD  2 DUP (?)
ExtGetDskFreSpcStruc ENDS
```

(A copy of this structure is in the *Irvine16.inc* file.) The following list contains a short description of each field:

- **StructSize**: A return value that represents the size of the **ExtGetDskFreSpcStruc** structure, in bytes. When INT 21h Function 7303h (Get_ExtFreeSpace) executes, it places the structure size in this member.
- **Level**: An input and return level value. This field must be initialized to zero.
- **SectorsPerCluster**: The number of sectors inside each cluster.
- **BytesPerSector**: The number of bytes in each sector.
- **AvailableClusters**: The number of available clusters.
- **TotalClusters**: The total number of clusters on the volume.

- **AvailablePhysSectors**: The number of physical sectors available on the volume, without adjustment for compression.
- **TotalPhysSectors**: The total number of physical sectors on the volume, without adjustment for compression.
- **AvailableAllocationUnits**: The number of available allocation units on the volume, without adjustment for compression.
- **TotalAllocationUnits**: The total number of allocation units on the volume, without adjustment for compression.
- **Rsvd**: Reserved member.

Calling the Function   When calling INT 21h Function 7303h, the following input parameters are required:

- AX must equal 7303h.
- ES:DI must point to a **ExtGetDskFreSpcStruc** variable.
- CX must contain the size of the **ExtGetDskFreSpcStruc** variable.
- DS:DX must point to a null-terminated string containing the drive name. You can use the MS-DOS type of drive specification such as ("C:\"), or you can use a universal naming convention volume specification such as ("\\Server\Share").

If the function executes successfully, it clears the Carry flag and fills in the structure. Otherwise, it sets the Carry flag. After calling the function, the following types of calculations might be useful:

- To find out how large the volume is in kilobytes, use the following formula: (TotalClusters * SectorsPerCluster * BytesPerSector) / 1024.
- To find out how much free space exists in the volume, in kilobytes, the formula should be: (AvailableClusters * SectorsPerCluster * BytesPerSector) / 1024.

14.5.1.1   Disk Free Space Program

The following program uses INT 21h Function 7303h to get free space information on a FAT-type drive volume. It displays both the volume size and free space:

```
TITLE Disk Free Space              (DiskSpc.asm)

; This program produces meaningful output under Windows
; 95, 98, and Me, but not under Windows NT, 2000,
; or XP.

INCLUDE Irvine16.inc
.data
buffer ExtGetDskFreSpcStruc <>
driveName BYTE "C:\",0
str1 BYTE "Volume size (KB): ",0
str2 BYTE "Free space (KB):  ",0
str3 BYTE "Function call failed.",0dh,0ah,0
```

```
    .code
main PROC
    mov   ax,@data
    mov   ds,ax
    mov   es,ax                    ; ES must point to data segment

    mov   buffer.Level,0           ; must be zero
    mov   di, OFFSET buffer        ; ES:DI points to buffer
    mov   cx, SIZEOF buffer        ; buffer size
    mov   dx, OFFSET DriveName     ; ptr to drive name
    mov   ax, 7303h                ; Get disk free space
    int   21h
    jc    error                    ; Failed if CF = 1

    mov   dx,OFFSET str1           ; volume size
    call  WriteString
    call  CalcVolumeSize
    call  WriteDec
    call  Crlf

    mov   dx,OFFSET str2           ; free space
    call  WriteString
    call  CalcVolumeFree
    call  WriteDec
    call  Crlf
    jmp   quit
error:
    mov   dx,OFFSET str3           ; function call failed
    call  WriteString
quit:
    exit
main ENDP

;----------------------------------------------------------------
CalcVolumeSize PROC
; Calculate and return the disk volume size, in kilobytes.
; Receives: buffer variable, a ExtGetDskFreSpcStruc structure
; Returns:  EAX = volume size
; Remarks:  (SectorsPerCluster * 512 * TotalClusters) / 1024
;----------------------------------------------------------------
    mov eax,buffer.SectorsPerCluster
    shl eax,9                      ; mult by 512
    mul buffer.TotalClusters
    mov ebx,1024
    div ebx                        ; return kilobytes
    ret
CalcVolumeSize ENDP

;----------------------------------------------------------------
CalcVolumeFree PROC
```

```
; Calculate and return the number of available kilobytes on the
;           given volume.
; Receives: buffer variable, a ExtGetDskFreSpcStruc structure
; Returns:  EAX = available space, in kilobytes
; Remarks:  (SectorsPerCluster * 512 * AvailableClusters) / 1024
;--------------------------------------------------------------
    mov eax,buffer.SectorsPerCluster
    shl eax,9                     ; mult by 512
    mul buffer.AvailableClusters
    mov ebx,1024
    div ebx                       ; return kilobytes
    ret
CalcVolumeFree ENDP
END main
```

14.5.2   Create Subdirectory (39h)

INT 21h Function 39h creates a new subdirectory. It receives a pointer in DS:DX to a null-terminated string containing a path specification. The following example shows how to create a new subdirectory called ASM off the root directory of the default drive:

```
.data
pathname BYTE "\ASM",0
.code
    mov ah,39h                    ; create subdirectory
    mov dx,OFFSET pathname
    int 21h
    jc display_error
```

The Carry flag is set to 1 if the function fails. The possible error return codes are 3 and 5. Error 3 (*path not found*) means that some part of the pathname does not exist. Suppose we have asked MS-DOS to create the directory ASM\PROG\NEW, but the path ASM\PROG does not exist. This would generate the error 3. Error 5 (*access denied*) indicates that the proposed subdirectory already exists or the first directory in the path is the root directory and it is already full.

14.5.3   Remove Subdirectory (3Ah)

INT 21h Function 3Ah removes a directory. It receives a pointer to the desired drive and path in DS:DX. If the drive name is left out, the default drive is assumed. The following code removes the \ASM directory from drive C:

```
.data
pathname  BYTE   'C:\ASM',0
.code
    mov ah,3Ah                    ; remove subdirectory
    mov dx,OFFSET pathname
    int 21h
    jc display_error
```

The Carry flag is set if the function fails. The possible error codes are 3 (*path not found*), 5 (*access denied: the directory contains files*), 6 (*invalid handle*), and 16 (*attempt to remove the current directory*).

14.5.4 Set Current Directory (3Bh)

INT 21h Function 3Bh sets the current directory. It receives a pointer in DS:DX to a null-terminated string containing the target drive and path. For example, the following statements set the current directory to C:\ASM\PROGS:

```
.data
pathname  BYTE "C:\ASM\PROGS",0
.code
    mov ah,3Bh                     ; set current directory
    mov dx,OFFSET pathname
    int 21h
    jc display_error
```

14.5.5 Get Current Directory (47h)

INT 21h Function 47h returns a string containing the current directory. It receives a drive number in DL (0 = default, 1 = A, 2 = B, etc.), and a pointer in DS:SI to a 64-byte buffer. In this buffer, MS-DOS places a null-terminated string with the full pathname from the root directory to the current directory (the drive letter and leading backslash are omitted). If the Carry flag is set when the function returns, the only possible error return code in AX is 0Fh (*invalid drive specification*).

In the following example, MS-DOS returns the current directory path on the default drive. Assuming that the current directory is C:\ASM\PROGS, the string returned by MS-DOS is "ASM\PROGS":

```
.data
pathname  BYTE 64 dup(0)               ; path stored here by MS-DOS
.code
    mov ah,47h                         ; get current directory path
    mov dl,0                           ; on default drive
    mov si,OFFSET pathname
    int 21h
    jc display_error
```

14.5.6 Section Review

1. Which INT 21h function would you use to get the cluster size of a disk drive?
2. Which INT 21h function would you use to find out how many clusters are free on drive C?
3. Which INT 21h functions would you call if you wanted to create a directory named D:\apps and make it the current directory?
4. Which INT 21h function would you call if you wanted to make a file read-only?

14.6 Chapter Summary

At the operating system level, it is not useful to know the exact disk geometry (physical locations) or brand-specific disk information. The BIOS, which in this case amounts to disk controller firmware, acts as a broker between the disk hardware and the operating system.

The surface of a disk is formatted into invisible concentric bands called tracks, on which data are stored magnetically. The average seek time is one type of disk speed measurement. Another measurement is RPM (revolutions per minute).

A cylinder refers to all tracks accessible from a single position of the read/write heads. Over time, as files become more spread out around a disk, they become fragmented and are no longer stored on adjacent cylinders.

A sector is a 512-byte portion of a track. Physical sectors are magnetically (invisibly) marked on the disk by the manufacturer, using what is called a low-level format.

Physical disk geometry describes a disk's structure to make it readable by the system BIOS.

A single physical hard drive is divided into one or more logical units named partitions, or volumes. A drive may have as many as four main partitions. If one is an extended partition, the remaining three must be primary partitions. The extended partition can be subdivided into an unlimited number of logical partitions. Each logical partition appears as a separate drive letter, and may have a different file system than other partitions. The primary partitions can each hold a bootable operating system.

The master boot record (MBR), created when the first partition is created on a hard disk, is located in the drive's first logical sector. The MBR contains the following:

- The disk partition table, which describes the sizes and locations of all partitions on the disk.
- A small program that locates the partition's boot sector and transfers control to a program in the boot sector, which in turn loads the operating system.

A file system keeps track of the location, size and attributes of each disk file. It provides a mapping of logical sectors to clusters, the basic unit of storage for all files and directories, and a mapping of file and directory names to sequences of clusters.

A cluster is the smallest unit of space used by a file; it consists of one or more adjacent disk sectors. A chain of clusters is referenced by a file allocation table (FAT) that keeps track of all clusters used by a file.

The following file systems are used in IA-32 Systems:

- The FAT12 file system was first used on IBM-PC diskettes.
- The FAT16 file system is the only available format for hard drives formatted under MS-DOS.
- The FAT32 file system was introduced with the OEM2 release of Windows 95, and was refined under Windows 98.
- The NTFS file system is supported by Windows NT, 2000, and XP.

Every disk has a root directory, which is the primary list of files on the disk. The root directory may also contain the names of other directories, called subdirectories.

MS-DOS and Windows use a table called the file allocation table (FAT) to keep track of each file's location on the disk. The FAT is a map of all clusters on the disk, showing their ownership by specific files. Each entry corresponds to a cluster number, and each cluster is associated with one or more sectors.

In Real-address mode, INT 21h provides many useful functions (Table 14-6) that create and change directories, change file attributes, find matching files, and so forth. These functions tend to be less available in high-level languages.

The Sector Display program reads and displays selected sectors from a disk volume.

The Disk Free Space program displays both the size of the selected disk volume and the amount of free space.

14.7   Programming Exercises

The following exercises must be done in Real-address mode. Many of the programs suggested here will alter your disk or directory. Be sure to make a backup copy of any disk affected by these programs, or create a temporary scratch disk to be used while testing them. *Under no circumstances should you run the programs on a fixed disk until you have debugged them carefully!*

1. Set Default Disk Drive

Write a procedure that prompts the user for a disk drive letter (*A, B, C,* or *D*), and then sets the default drive to the user's choice. (See Appendix C.)

2. Disk Space

Write a procedure named **Get_DiskSize** that returns the amount of total data space on a selected disk drive. *Input:* AL = drive number (0 = A, 1 = B, 2 = C, ...). *Output:* DX:AX = data space, in bytes.

3. Disk Free Space

Write a procedure named **Get_DiskFreespace** that returns the amount of free space on a selected disk drive. *Input:* DS:DX points to a string containing the drive specifier. *Output:* EDX:EAX = disk free space, in bytes. Write a program that tests the procedure and displays the 64-bit result in hexadecimal.

4. Create a Hidden Directory

Write a procedure that creates a hidden directory named \temp. Use the DIR command to verify its hidden status.

5. Disk Free Space, in Clusters

Modify the Disk Free Space program from Section 14.5.1.1 so that it displays the following information:

```
        Drive specification:              "C:\"
        Bytes per sector:                 512
```

```
Sectors per cluster:            8
Total Number of clusters:       999999
Number of available clusters:   99999
```

> The following group of exercises are all variations on the Sector Display program pre-
> sented earlier in this chapter. Most of these exercises can be done either individually or in
> clusters of exercises.

6. Displaying the Sector Number

Using the Sector Display program (Section 14.4.1) as a starting point, display a string at the top
of the screen that indicates the drive specifier and current sector number (in hexadecimal).

7. Hexadecimal Sector Display

Using the Sector Display program as a starting point, add code that lets the user press F2 to display the current sector in hexadecimal, with 24 bytes on each line. The offset of the first byte in
each line should be displayed at the beginning of the line. The display will be 22 lines high with
a partial line at the end. The following is a sample of the first two lines, to show the layout:

```
0000 17311625 25425B75 279A4909 200D0655 D7303825 4B6F9234
0018 273A4655 25324B55 273A4959 293D4655 A732298C FF2323DB
(etc.)
```

15

BIOS-Level Programming

15.1   Introduction

As soon as the first IBM-PC appeared, droves of programmers (including myself) wanted to know how to get inside the box and work directly with the computer hardware. Peter Norton was quick to discover all sorts of useful and secret information, leading to his landmark book entitled *Inside the IBM-PC*. In a fit of generosity, IBM actually published all the assembly language source code for the IBM PC/XT BIOS (I still have a copy). Important game designers such as

Michael Abrash (author of *Quake & Doom*) learned how to optimize graphics and sound software, using their knowledge of PC hardware.[1] Now you can join this esteemed group, and work behind the scenes, below DOS and Windows, at the BIOS (*basic input-output system*) level.

In this chapter, you're going to learn such useful things as:

- What happens when a keyboard key is pressed, and where all the characters end up.
- How to check the keyboard buffer to see if characters are waiting, and how to clear old keystrokes out of the buffer.
- How to read non-ASCII keyboard keys such as function keys and cursor arrows.
- How to display color text, and why colors are based on the video display's RGB color mixing system.
- How to divide up the screen into color panels, and scroll each one separately.
- How to draw bit-mapped graphics in 256 colors.
- How to detect mouse movements and mouse clicks.

15.1.1 BIOS Data Area

The BIOS data area, shown in Table 15-1, contains system data used by the ROM BIOS service routines. For example, the keyboard typeahead buffer (at offset 001Eh) contains the ASCII codes and keyboard scan codes of keys waiting to be processed by the BIOS.

Table 15-1 BIOS Data Area, at Segment 0040h.

Hex Offset	Description
0000 – 0007	Port addresses, COM1 – COM4
0008 – 000F	Port addresses, LPT1 – LPT4
0010 – 0011	Installed hardware list
0012	Initialization flag
0013 – 0014	Memory size, in Kbytes
0015 – 0016	Memory in I/O channel
0017 – 0018	Keyboard status flags
0019	Alternate key entry storage
001A – 001B	Keyboard buffer pointer (head)
001C – 001D	Keyboard buffer pointer (tail)

---

[1] Michael Abrash's book, entitled *The Zen of Code Optimization*, is a prime example.

Table 15-1   BIOS Data Area, at Segment 0040h. (Continued)

Hex Offset	Description
001E – 003D	Keyboard typeahead buffer
003E – 0048	Diskette data area
0049	Current video mode
004A – 004B	Number of screen columns
004C – 004D	Regen buffer length, in bytes
004E – 004F	Regen buffer starting offset
0050 – 005F	Cursor positions, video pages 1 – 8
0060	Cursor end line
0061	Cursor start line
0062	Currently displayed video page number
0063 – 0064	Active display base address
0065	CRT mode register
0066	Register for color graphics adapter
0067 – 006B	Cassette data area
006C – 0070	Timer data area

15.2   Keyboard Input with INT 16h

You may recall that in Section 2.5 we differentiated the various levels of input-output available to assembly language programs. In this chapter, you are given the opportunity to work directly at the BIOS level by calling functions that were (for the most part) installed by the computer manufacturer. At this level, you are only one level above the hardware itself, and you have a great deal of flexibility and control over the computer. One major restriction to our approach is that all programs must run either in Real-address mode or Virtual-8086 mode. That does not present a problem, as you can easily run them from MS-Windows or from a DOS emulator running under Linux.

In the current chapter, we introduce keyboard input using the BIOS keyboard handler, INT 16h. It does not permit redirection, but it is the best way to read extended keyboard keys such as function keys, arrow keys, PgUp, and PgDn. Each one of these extended keys generates an 8-bit *scan code*, shown on the inside cover of this book. The scan codes are unique to IBM-compatible computers.

In fact, all keyboard keys generate scan codes, but we don't usually pay attention to scan codes for ASCII characters because the ASCII codes are universal. When an extended key is pressed, its ASCII code is either 00h or E0h, shown in the following table:

Keys	ASCII code
Ins, Del, PageUp, PageDown, Home, End, Up arrow, Down arrow, Left arrow, Right arrow	E0h
Function keys (F1 – F12)	00h

15.2.1   How the Keyboard Works

Keyboard input follows an event path beginning with the keyboard controller chip and ending with characters being placed in a 30-byte array called the *keyboard typeahead buffer* (see Figure 15-1). Up to fifteen keystrokes can be held there at any given moment, because each keystroke generates two bytes (ASCII code + scan code). The following events occur when the user presses a key:

- The keyboard controller chip sends an 8-bit numeric scan code (sc) to the PC's keyboard input port.
- The input port is designed so that it triggers an *interrupt*, which is a predefined signal to the CPU that an input-output device needs attention. The CPU responds by executing the INT 9h service routine.
- The INT 9h service routine retrieves the keyboard scan code (sc) from the input port and looks up the corresponding ASCII code (ac), if any. It inserts both the scan code and the ASCII code into a buffer called the *typeahead buffer*. (If the scan code has no matching ASCII code, the ASCII code in the typeahead buffer is set to zero.)

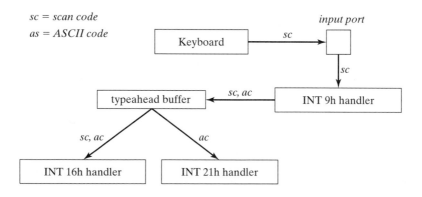

Figure 15-1   Keystroke Processing Sequence.

Once the scan code and ASCII code are safely in the typeahead buffer, they stay there until the currently running program retrieves them. There are two ways to do this:

- Call a BIOS-level function using INT 16h that retrieves both the scan code and ASCII code from the keyboard typeahead buffer. This is useful when processing extended keys such as function keys and cursor arrows, which have no ASCII codes.
- Call an MS-DOS-level function using INT 21h that retrieves the ASCII code from the input buffer. If an extended key has been pressed, INT 21h must be called a second time to retrieve the scan code. INT 21h keyboard input was explained in Section 13.2.3.

15.2.2   INT 16h Functions

INT 16h has some clear advantages over INT 21h when it comes to keyboard handling. First, INT 16h can retrieve both the scan code and ASCII code in a single step. Second, INT 16h has additional operations such as setting the typematic rate and retrieving the state of the keyboard flags. The *typematic rate* is the rate at which a keyboard key repeats when you hold it down. When you don't know whether the user will press an ordinary key or an extended key, INT 16h is usually the best function to call.

15.2.2.1   Set Typematic Rate (03h)

INT 16h Function 03h lets you set the keyboard typematic repeat rate, as illustrated in the following table. When you hold down a key, there is a delay of 250–1000 milliseconds before the key starts to repeat. The repeat rate can be between 1Fh (slowest) and 0 (fastest).

INT 16h Function 03h	
Description	Set typematic repeat rate
Receives	AH = 3 AL = 5 BH = repeat delay (0 = 250 ms; 1 = 500 ms; 2 = 750 ms; 3 = 1000 ms) BL = repeat rate (0 = fastest, 1Fh = slowest)
Returns	nothing

Sample Call	```mov ax,0305h```
	```mov bh,1 ; 500 ms repeat delay```
	```mov bl,0Fh ; repeat rate```
	```int 16h```

15.2.2.2   Push Key into Keyboard Buffer (05h)

As shown in the next table, INT 16h Function 05h lets you push a key into the keyboard typeahead buffer. A key consists of two 8-bit integers: the ASCII code and the keyboard scan code.

INT 16h Function 05h	
Description	Push key into keyboard buffer
Receives	AH = 5 CH = scan code CL = ASCII code
Returns	If typeahead buffer is full, CF = 1 and AL = 1; otherwise, CF = 0, AL = 0.

Sample Call	```mov ah,5```
	```mov ch,3Bh ; scan code for F1 key```
	```mov cl,0 ; ASCII code```
	```int 16h```

15.2.2.3   Wait for Key (10h)

INT 16h Function 10h removes the next available key from the keyboard typeahead buffer. If none is waiting, the keyboard handler waits for the user to press a key, as shown in the following table:

INT 16h Function 10h	
Description	Wait for key
Receives	AH = 10h
Returns	AH = keyboard scan code AL = ASCII code

Sample Call	```mov ah,10h```
	```int 16h```
	```mov scanCode,ah```
	```mov ASCIICode,al```

Notes	If no key is already in the buffer, the function waits for a key.

Sample Program   The following keyboard display program uses a loop with INT 16h to input keystrokes and display both the ASCII code and scan code of each key. It terminates when the Esc key is pressed:

```
TITLE Keyboard Display          (Keybd.asm)

; This program displays keyboard scan codes
; and ASCII codes, using INT 16h.

INCLUDE Irvine16.inc
.code
```

```
main PROC
    mov ax,@data
    mov ds,ax
    call ClrScr                 ; clear screen

L1: mov ah,10h                  ; keyboard input
    int 16h                     ; using BIOS
    call DumpRegs               ; AH = scan, AL = ASCII
    cmp al,1Bh                  ; ESC key pressed?
    jne L1                      ; no: repeat the loop

    call ClrScr                 ; clear screen
    exit
main ENDP
END main
```

The call to **DumpRegs** displays all the registers, but you need only look at AH (scan code) and AL (ASCII code). When the user presses the F1 function key, for example, this is the resulting display (3B00h):

```
EAX=00003B00   EBX=00000000   ECX=000000FF   EDX=000005D6
ESI=00000000   EDI=00002000   EBP=0000091E   ESP=00002000
EIP=0000000F   EFL=00003202   CF=0   SF=0   ZF=0   OF=0
```

15.2.2.4   Check Keyboard Buffer (11h)

INT 16h Function 11h lets you peek into the keyboard typeahead buffer to see if any keys are waiting. It returns the ASCII code and scan code of the next available key, if any. You can use this function inside a loop that carries out other program tasks. Note that the function does not remove the key from the typeahead buffer. See the following table for details:

INT 16h Function 11h	
Description	Check keyboard buffer
Receives	AH = 11h
Returns	If a key is waiting, ZF = 0, AH = scan code, AL = ASCII code; otherwise, ZF = 1.

Sample Call	`mov ah,11h`
	`int 16h`
	`jz  NoKeyWaiting        ; no key in buffer`
	`mov scanCode,ah`
	`mov ASCIICode,al`

Notes	Does not remove the key (if any) from the buffer.

15.2.2.5   Get Keyboard Flags

INT 16h Function 12h, as demonstrated below, returns valuable information about the current state of the keyboard flags. Perhaps you have noticed that word-processing programs often display flags or notations at the bottom of the screen when keys such as *CapsLock*, *NumLock*, and *Insert* are pressed. They do this by continually examining the keyboard status flag, watching for any changes.

INT 16h Function 12h	
Description	Get keyboard flags
Receives	AH = 12h
Returns	AX = copy of the keyboard flags

Sample Call	`mov ah,12h`
	`int 16h`
	`mov keyFlags,ax`

Notes	The keyboard flags are located at addresses 00417h - 00418h, in the BIOS data area.

The keyboard flags, shown in Table 15-2, are particularly interesting because they tell you a great deal about what the user is doing with the keyboard. Is the user holding down the left shift key or the right shift key? Is he or she also holding down the Alt key? Questions of this type can only be answered using INT 16h. Each bit is a 1 when its matching key is currently held down.

Table 15-2   Keyboard Flag Values.[a]

Bit	Description
0	Right Shift key is down
1	Left Shift key is down
2	Either Ctrl key is down
3	Either Alt key is down
4	Scroll Lock toggle is on
5	Num Lock toggle is on
6	Caps Lock toggle is on
7	Insert toggle is on
8	Left Ctrl key is down

Table 15-2   Keyboard Flag Values.[a] (Continued)

Bit	Description
9	Left Alt key is down
10	Right Ctrl key is down
11	Right Alt key is down
12	Scroll key is down
13	Num Lock key is down
14	Caps Lock key is down
15	SysReq key is down

[a] Source: Ray Duncan, *Advanced MSDOS*, 2nd ed. (1988), pp. 586-587.

15.2.2.6   Clearing the Keyboard Buffer

Programs often involve a looping operation that can only be interrupted by certain keys. Game programs, for example, often must check for keyboard arrow keys and other special keys while repeating a graphic animation. The user might press any number of irrelevant keys that only fill up the keyboard typeahead buffer. But when the right key is pressed, the program is expected to immediately respond to the command.

Using the INT 16h functions, we know how to check the keyboard buffer to see if any keys are waiting (Function 11h), and we know how to remove a key from the buffer (Function 10h). The following program demonstrates a procedure named **ClearKeyboard** that uses a loop to clear the keyboard buffer, while checking for a particular keyboard scan code. For testing purposes, the program checks for the ESC key, but the procedure can check for any key:

```
TITLE Testing ClearKeyboard        (ClearKbd.asm)

; This program shows how to clear the keyboard
; buffer while waiting for a particular key.
; To test it, rapidly press random keys to fill
; up the buffer. Then press Esc and note that the
; program ends immediately.

INCLUDE Irvine16.inc
ClearKeyboard PROTO, scanCode:BYTE
ESC_key = 1                        ; scan code

.code
main PROC
L1:
    ; Display a dot, to show program's progress
    mov ah,2
```

```
        mov dl,'.'
        int 21h
        mov eax,300                      ; delay for 300 ms
        call Delay

        INVOKE ClearKeyboard,ESC_key     ; check for Esc key
        jnz L1                           ; continue loop if ZF=0
quit:
        call Clrscr
        exit
main ENDP

;----------------------------------------------------
ClearKeyboard PROC,
        scanCode:BYTE
;
; Clears the keyboard while checking for a
; particular scan code.
; Receives: keyboard scan code
; Returns: Zero flag set if the ASCII code is
; found; otherwise, Zero flag is clear.
;----------------------------------------------------
        push ax
L1:
        mov ah,11h               ; check keyboard buffer
        int 16h                  ; any key pressed?
        jz  noKey                ; no: exit now
        mov ah,10h               ; yes: remove from buffer
        int 16h
        cmp ah,scanCode          ; was it the exit key?
        je  quit                 ; yes: exit now (ZF=1)
        jmp L1                   ; no: check buffer again

noKey:                           ; no key pressed
        or al,1                  ; clear zero flag
quit:
        pop ax
        ret
ClearKeyboard ENDP
END main
```

The program displays a dot on the screen once every 300 milliseconds. When testing it, press any number of random keys, which are both ignored and removed from the typeahead buffer. Note that as soon as ESC is pressed, the program stops immediately.

15.2.3   Section Review

1. Which interrupt (16h or 21h) is best for reading user input that includes function keys and other extended keys?
2. Where in memory are keyboard input characters kept while waiting to be processed by application programs?
3. What operations are performed by the INT 9h service routine?
4. Which INT 16h function pushes keys into the keyboard buffer?
5. Which INT 16h function removes the next available key from the keyboard buffer?
6. Which INT 16h function examines the keyboard buffer and returns the scan code and ASCII code of the first available input?
7. *(yes/no):* Does INT 16h function 11h remove a character from the keyboard buffer?
8. Which INT 16h function gives you the value of the keyboard flag byte?
9. Which bit in the keyboard flag byte indicates that the ScrollLock key has been pressed?
10. Write statements that input the keyboard flag byte and repeat a loop until the Ctrl key is pressed.
11. *Challenge:* The **ClearKeyboard** procedure in Section 15.2.2.6 checks for only a single keyboard scan code. Suppose your program had to check for multiple scan codes (the four cursor arrows, for example). Without writing actual code, suggest modifications you could make to the procedure to make this possible.

15.3   VIDEO Programming with INT 10h

15.3.1   Basic Background

15.3.1.1   Three Levels of Access

When an application program needs to write characters on the screen in text mode, it can choose between three types of video output:

- **MS-DOS-level access:** Any computer running or emulating MS-DOS can use INT 21h to write text to the video display. Input/output can easily be redirected to other devices such as a printer or disk. Output is quite slow and you cannot control the text color.
- **BIOS-level access:** Characters are output using INT 10h function, known as *BIOS services*. This executes more quickly than INT 21h, and permits the control of text color. When filling large screen areas, a slight delay can usually be detected. Output cannot be redirected.
- **Direct video access:** Characters are moved directly to video RAM, so the execution is instantaneous. Output cannot be redirected. During the MS-DOS era, word processors and electronic spreadsheet programs all used this method. (Usage of this method is restricted to full-screen mode under Windows NT, 2000, and XP.)

Application programs vary in their choice of which level of access to use. Those requiring the highest performance choose direct video access; others choose BIOS-level access. MS-DOS-level access is used when the output may have to be redirected, or when the screen is shared with other programs. It should be mentioned that MS-DOS interrupts use BIOS-level routines to do their work, and BIOS routines use direct video access to produce their output.

15.3.1.2   Running Programs in Full-Screen Mode
Programs that draw graphics using the Video BIOS should be executed in one of the following environments:

- Pure MS-DOS
- A DOS emulator under Linux
- Under MS-Windows in full-screen mode.

In MS-Windows, there are two ways to switch into full-screen mode:

- Create a shortcut to the program's EXE file. Then open the Properties dialog for the short-cut, select the *Screen* properties, and select *Full-screen mode*.
- Open a Command window from the Start menu, then press Alt-Enter to switch to full screen mode. Using the CD (change directory) command, navigate to your EXE file's directory, and run the program by typing its name. Alt-Enter is a *toggle*, so if you press it again, it will return the program to Window mode.

15.3.1.3   Understanding Video Text
There are two general types of video modes: text mode and graphics mode. When a computer is booted in MS-DOS, the video controller is set to Video Mode 3 (color text, 80 columns by 25 rows). There are a number of graphics modes, some of which are listed in Table 15-6 in Section 15.4.

In text mode, rows are numbered from the top of the screen, row 0. Each row is the height of a character cell, using the currently active font. Columns are numbered from the left side of the screen, column 0. Each column is the width of a character cell.

Fonts   Characters are generated from a memory-resident table of character fonts. Originally, the table was in ROM, but later versions of the BIOS permitted programmers to rewrite the character tables at run time. This makes it possible to create custom fonts in text mode.

Video Text Pages   Text mode video memory is divided into multiple separate video pages, each with the ability to hold a full screen of text. Programs can display one page while writing text to other hidden pages, and they can rapidly flip back and forth between pages. In the days of high-performance MS-DOS applications, it was often necessary to keep several text screens in memory at the same time. With the current popularity of graphical interfaces, this text page feature is no longer so important. The default video page is Page 0.

Attributes   As illustrated below, each screen character is assigned an attribute byte that controls both the color of the character (called the *foreground*) and the screen color behind the character (called the *background*).

Each position on the video display holds a single character, along with its own *attribute* (color). The attribute is stored in a separate byte, following the character in memory. In the following figure, three positions on the screen contain the letters ABC:

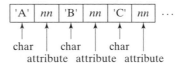

Blinking   Characters on the video display can blink. The video controller does this by reversing the foreground and background colors of a character at a predetermined rate. By default, when a PC boots into MS-DOS mode, blinking is enabled. It is possible to turn blinking off using a video BIOS function. Also, blinking is off by default when you open up an MS-DOS emulation window under MS-Windows.

15.3.2   Controlling the Color

15.3.2.1   Mixing Primary Colors

Each color pixel on a video display is generated using three separate electron beams: red, green, and blue. A fourth channel controls the overall intensity, or brightness of the pixel. All available text colors can therefore be represented by 4-bit binary values, in the following form (I = intensity, R = red, G = green, B = blue). The following diagram shows the composition of a white pixel:

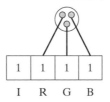

By mixing three primary colors, new colors can be generated, as can be seen in the following diagram. Further, by turning on the intensity bit, the mixed colors have a brighter shade:

Mix these primary colors . . .	To get this color	Add the Intensity bit
red + green + blue	light gray	white
green + blue	cyan	light cyan
red + blue	magenta	light magenta

Mix these primary colors . . .	To get this color	Add the Intensity bit
red + green	brown	yellow
(no colors)	black	dark gray

The primary colors and mixed colors are compiled into a list of all possible 4-bit colors, shown in Table 15-3. Each color in the right-hand column has its intensity bit set.

Table 15-3   Four-Bit Color Text Encoding.

IRGB	Color	IRGB	Color
0000	black	1000	gray
0001	blue	1001	light blue
0010	green	1010	light green
0011	cyan	1011	light cyan
0100	red	1100	light red
0101	magenta	1101	light magenta
0110	brown	1110	yellow
0111	light gray	1111	white

15.3.2.2   Attribute Byte

In color text mode, each character is assigned an attribute byte, which consists of two 4-bit color codes: background and foreground:

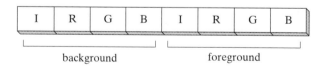

Blinking   There is one complication to this simple color scheme. If the video adapter currently has blinking enabled, the high bit of the background color controls the character blinking. When this bit is set, the character blinks:

When blinking is enabled, only the low-intensity colors in the left-hand column of Table 15-3 are available as background colors (black, blue, green, cyan, red, magenta, brown, and light gray). The default color when MS-DOS boots is 00000111 binary (light gray on black background).

Constructing Attribute Bytes   To construct a video attribute byte from two colors (foreground and background), use the assembler's SHL operator to shift the background color bits four positions to the left, and OR it with the foreground color. For example, the following statements create an attribute of light gray text on a blue background:

```
BLUE = 1
LIGHT_GRAY = 111b
mov bh,(BLUE SHL 4) OR LIGHT_GRAY             ; 00010111
```

The following creates white characters on a red background:

```
WHITE = 1111b
RED = 100b
mov bh,(RED SHL 4) OR WHITE                   ; 01001111
```

The following lines produce blue letters on a brown background:

```
BLUE = 1
BROWN = 110b
mov  bh,((BROWN SHL 4) OR BLUE)               ; 01100001
```

> Fonts and colors may appear slightly different when running the same program under different operating systems. For example, in Windows 2000, blinking is disabled unless you switch to full-screen mode.

15.3.3   INT 10h Video Functions

Table 15-4 lists the most frequently used INT 10h functions. Each will be discussed separately, with its own short example. The discussion of functions 0Ch and 0Dh will be deferred until the graphics section of this chapter (Section 15.4).

Table 15-4   Selected INT 10h Functions.

Function Number	Description
0	Set the video display to one of the text or graphics modes.
1	Set cursor lines, controlling the cursor shape and size.
2	Position the cursor on the screen.
3	Get the cursor's screen position and size.

Table 15-4   Selected INT 10h Functions. (Continued)

Function Number	Description
6	Scroll a window on the current video page upward, replacing scrolled lines with blanks.
7	Scroll a window on the current video page downward, replacing scrolled lines with blanks.
8	Read the character and its attribute at the current cursor position.
9	Write a character and its attribute at the current cursor position.
0Ah	Write a character only (no attribute) at the current cursor position.
0Ch	Write a graphics pixel on the screen in graphics mode.
0Dh	Read the color of a single graphics pixel at a given location.
0Fh	Get video mode information.
10h	Toggle blinking and intensity modes.
1Eh	Write a string to the screen in teletype mode.

> It's a good idea to preserve the general-purpose registers (using PUSH) before calling INT 10h, because the different BIOS versions are not consistent in the way they affect registers.

15.3.3.1   Set Video Mode (00h)

INT 10h Function 0 lets you set the current video mode to one of the text or graphics modes. The text modes are listed in Table 15-5:

Table 15-5   Video Text Modes Recognized by INT 10h.

Mode	Resolution (columns X rows, in pixels)	Number of Colors
0	40 X 25	1
1	40 X 25	16
2	80 X 25	2
3	80 X 25	16
7	80 X 25	2
14h	132 X 25	16

It's a good idea to get the current video mode (INT 10h Function 0Fh) and save it in a variable before setting it to a new value. Then you can restore the original video mode when your program exits. The following table shows how to set the video mode:

INT 10h Function 0	
Description	Set the video mode
Receives	AH = 0 AL = video mode
Returns	nothing

Sample Call	`mov ah,0`
	`mov al,3      ; video mode 3 (color text)`
	`int 10h`

Notes	The screen is cleared automatically unless the high bit in AL is set before calling this function.

15.3.3.2 Set Cursor Lines (01h)

INT 10h Function 01h, as shown in the next table, sets the text cursor size. The text cursor is displayed using starting and ending scan lines, which make it possible to control its size. Application programs can do this in order to show the current status of an operation. For example, a text editor might increase the cursor size when the NumLock key is toggled on; when it is pressed again, the cursor returns to its original size.

INT 10h Function 01h	
Description	Set cursor lines
Receives	AH = 01h CH = top line CL = bottom line
Returns	nothing

Sample Call	`mov ah,1`
	`mov cx,0607h   ; default color cursor size`
	`int 10h`

Notes	The monochrome display uses 12 lines for its cursor, while all other displays use 8 lines.

The cursor is described as a sequence of horizontal lines, where line 0 is at the top. The default color cursor starts at line 6 and ends at line 7, as shown in the following figure:

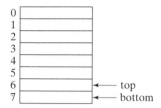

15.3.3.3   Set Cursor Position (02h)

INT 10h Function 2 locates the cursor at a specific row and column on the video page of your choice, as seen in the following table.

INT 10h Function 02h	
Description	Set cursor position
Receives	AH = 2 DH, DL = row, column values BH = video page
Returns	nothing
Sample Call	```mov ah,2\nmov dh,10 ; row 10\nmov dl,20 ; column 20\nmov bh,0 ; video page 0\nint 10h```

15.3.3.4   Get Cursor Position and Size (03h)

INT 10h Function 3, shown in the next table, returns the row/column position of the cursor as well as the starting and ending lines that determine the cursor size. This function can be quite useful in programs where the user is moving the cursor around a menu. Depending on where the cursor is, you know which menu choice has been selected.

INT 10h Function 03h	
Description	Get cursor position and size
Receives	AH = 3 BH = video page

INT 10h Function 03h	
Returns	CH, CL = starting, ending cursor scan lines DH, DL = row, column of cursor's location

Sample Call	`mov ah,3`
	 `mov bh,0                     ; video page 0`
	 `int 10h`
	 `mov cursor,CX`
	 `mov position,DX`

Showing and Hiding the Cursor   It is useful to be able to temporarily hide the cursor when displaying menus, writing continuously to the screen, or reading mouse input. To hide the cursor, you can set its top line value to an illegal (large) value. To redisplay the cursor, return the cursor lines to their defaults (lines 6 and 7):

```
HideCursor PROC
    mov   ah,3               ; get cursor size
    int   10h
    or    ch,30h             ; set upper row to illegal value
    mov   ah,1               ; set cursor size
    int   10h
    ret
HideCursor ENDP

ShowCursor PROC
    mov   ah,3               ; get cursor size
    int   10h
    mov   ah,1               ; set cursor size
    mov   cx,0607h           ; default size
    int   10h
    ret
ShowCursor ENDP
```

Of course, we're ignoring the possibility that the user might have set the cursor to a different size before hiding the cursor. Here's an alternate version of **ShowCursor** that simply clears the high 4 bits of CH without touching the lower 4 bits where the cursor lines are stored:

```
ShowCursor PROC
    mov   ah,3               ; get cursor size
    int   10h
    mov   ah,1               ; set cursor size
    and   ch,0Fh             ; clear high 4 bits
    int   10h
    ret
ShowCursor ENDP
```

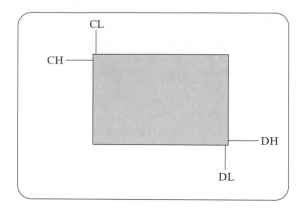

Figure 15-2   Defining a Window Using INT 10h.

Unfortunately, this method of hiding the cursor does not always work. An alternative method is to use INT 10h Function 02h to position the cursor off the edge of the screen (row 25, for example).

15.3.3.5   Scroll Window Up (06h)

INT 10h Functions 6 scrolls all text within a rectangular area of the screen (called a *window*) upward. A *window* is defined using row and column coordinates for its upper-left and lower-right corners. The default MS-DOS screen has rows numbered 0-24 from the top, and columns numbered 0–79 from the left. Therefore, a window covering the entire screen would be from 0,0 to 24,79. In Figure 15-2, the CH/CL registers define the row and column of the upper-left corner, and DH/DL define the row and column of the lower right corner.

As a window is scrolled up, its bottom line is replaced by a blank line. If all lines are scrolled, the window is cleared (made blank). Lines scrolled out of the window cannot be recovered. The following table describes INT 10h Function 6.

INT 10h Function 06h	
Description	Scroll window up
Receives	AH = 6 AL = number of lines to scroll (0 = all) BH = video attribute for blanked area CH, CL = row, column of upper left window corner DH, DL = row, column of lower right window corner
Returns	nothing

INT 10h Function 06h			
Sample Call	mov	ah,6	; scroll window up
	mov	al,0	; entire window
	mov	ch,0	; upper left row
	mov	cl,0	; upper left column
	mov	dh,24	; lower right row
	mov	dl,79	; lower right column
	mov	bh,7	; attribute for blanked area
	int	10h	; call BIOS

15.3.3.6   Example: Writing Text to a Window

When INT 10h Function 6 (or 7) scrolls a window, it sets the attributes of the scrolled lines inside the window. If you subsequently write text inside the window using a DOS function call, the text will use the same foreground and background colors. The following program (*TextWin.asm*) demonstrates this technique:

```
TITLE Color Text Window                (TextWin.asm)

; Display a color window and write text inside.
INCLUDE Irvine16.inc
.data
message BYTE "Message in Window", 0

.code
main PROC
    mov ax,@data
    mov ds,ax

; Scroll a window.
    mov ax,0600h              ; scroll window
    mov bh,(blue SHL 4) OR yellow   ; attribute
    mov cx,050Ah              ; upper-left corner
    mov dx,0A30h              ; lower-right corner
    int 10h

; Position the cursor inside the window.
    mov ah,2                  ; set cursor position
    mov dx,0714h              ; row 7, col 20
    mov bh,0                  ; video page 0
    int 10h

; Write some text in the window.
    mov  dx,OFFSET message
    call WriteString
```

```
; Wait for a keypress.
    mov ah,10h
    int 16h
    exit
main ENDP
END main
```

15.3.3.7 Scroll Window Down (07h)

The scroll window down function is identical to Function 06h, except that the text inside the window moves downward. It uses the same input parameters.

15.3.3.8 Read Character and Attribute (08h)

INT 10h Function 8 returns the character and its attribute at the current cursor position, as shown below. This is used by programs to read text directly off the screen (a technique known as *screen scraping*). Programs that scan the contents of a text screen and convert the text to spoken sounds for hearing-impaired users can use this function.

INT 10h Function 08h	
Description	Read character and attribute
Receives	AH = 8 BH = video page
Returns	AL = ASCII code of the character AH = attribute of the character

Sample Call	```mov ah,8```
	```mov bh,0 ; video page 0```
	```int 10h```
	```mov char,al ; save the character```
	```mov attrib,ah ; save the attribute```

15.3.3.9 Write Character and Attribute (09h)

INT 10h Function 9 writes a character in color at the current cursor position. As can be seen in the following table, this function can display any ASCII character, including the special IBM graphics characters matching ASCII codes 1 to 31.

INT 10h Function 09h	
Description	Write character and attribute

INT 10h Function 09h	
Receives	AH = 9 AL = ASCII code of character BH = video page BL = attribute CX = repetition count
Returns	nothing

Sample Call	```
	mov ah,9
	mov al,'A' ; ASCII character
	mov bh,0 ; video page 0
	mov bl,71h ; attribute (blue on white)
	mov cx,1 ; repetition count
	int 10h
	``

Notes	Does not advance the cursor after writing the character.

The *repetition count* in CX specifies how many times the character is to be repeated. (The character should not be repeated beyond the end of the current screen line.) After a character is written, you must call INT 10h Function 2 to advance the cursor if more characters will be written on the same line.

15.3.3.10   Write Character (0Ah)

INT 10h Function 0Ah writes a character to the screen at the current cursor position without changing the current screen attribute. As shown in the next table, it is identical to Function 9 except that the attribute is not specified.

INT 10h Function 0Ah	
Description	Write character
Receives	AH = 0Ah AL = character BH = video page CX = repetition count
Returns	nothing

Sample Call	```
	mov ah,0Ah
	mov al,'A' ; ASCII character
	mov bh,0 ; video page 0
	mov cx,1 ; repetition count
	int 10h
	``

INT 10h Function 0Ah	
Notes	Does not advance the cursor.

15.3.3.11   Toggle Blinking and Intensity Modes

INT 10h Function 10h has a number of useful subfunctions, including number 03h that permits the highest bit of a color attribute to either control the color intensity or blink the character. See the following table for details:

INT 10h Function 10h, Subfunction 03h	
Description	Toggle blinking/intensity Bit
Receives	AX = 10h AL = 3 BL = blink mode (0 = enable intensity, 1 = enable blinking)
Returns	nothing
| Sample Call | ```
mov ah,10h
mov al,3
mov bl,1                    ; enable blinking
int 10h
``` |
| Notes | Under MS-Windows, the video display must still be running in a full-screen window. |

15.3.3.12   Get Video Mode Information (0Fh)

INT 10h Function 0Fh returns information about the current video mode, including the mode number, the number of display columns, and the active video page number, as seen below.

INT 10h Function 0Fh	
Description	Get current video mode information
Receives	AH = 0Fh
Returns	AL = current display mode AH = number of columns (characters or pixels) BH = active video page
```

INT 10h Function 0Fh	
| **Sample Call** | ```
mov  ah,0Fh
int  10h
mov  vmode,al        ; save the mode
mov  columns,ah      ; save the columns
mov  page,bh         ; save the page
``` |
| **Notes** | Works in both text and graphics modes. |

15.3.3.13   Write String in Teletype Mode (13h)

INT 10h Function 13h, shown in the following table, writes a string to the screen at a given row and column location. The string can optionally contain both characters and attribute values. (See the *Colorst2.asm* program on the book's Web site for a working example.)

INT 10h Function 13h	
Description	Write string in teletype mode
Receives	AH = 13h AL = write mode (see notes) BH = video page BL = attribute (if AL = 00h or 01h) CX = string length (character count) DH, DL = screen row, column ES:BP = segment:offset of string
Returns	nothing
| **Sample Call** | ```
.data
colorString BYTE 'A',1Fh,'B',1Ch,'C',1Bh,'D',1Ch
row     BYTE   10
column BYTE    20
.code
mov   ax,SEG colorString        ; set ES segment
mov   es,ax
mov   ah,13h                    ; write string
mov   al,2                      ; write mode
mov   bh,0                      ; video page
mov   cx,(SIZEOF colorString) / 2  ; string length
mov   dh,row                    ; start row
mov   dl,column                 ; start column
mov   bp,OFFSET colorString     ; string offset
int   10h
``` |

INT 10h Function 13h	
Notes	Write mode values: • 00h = string contains only character codes; cursor not updated after write, and attribute is in BL. • 01h = string contains only character codes; cursor is updated after write, and attribute is in BL. • 02h = string contains alternating character codes and attribute bytes; cursor position not updated after write. • 03h = string contains alternating character codes and attribute bytes; cursor position is updated after write.

15.3.3.14   Example: Displaying a Color String

The following program (*ColorStr.asm*) displays a string on the console, using a different color for each character. It must be run in full screen mode if you want to see characters blink. By default, blinking is enabled, but you can remove the call to **EnableBlinking** and see the same string on a dark gray background:

```
TITLE Color String Example              (ColorStr.asm)

INCLUDE Irvine16.inc
.data
ATTRIB_HI = 10000000b
string BYTE "ABCDEFGHIJKLMOP"
color  BYTE (black SHL 4) OR blue

.code
main PROC
    mov  ax,@data
    mov  ds,ax

    call ClrScr
    call EnableBlinking      ; this is optional
    mov  cx,SIZEOF string
    mov  si,OFFSET string

L1: push cx                  ; save loop counter
    mov  ah,9                ; write character/attribute
    mov  al,[si]             ; character to display
    mov  bh,0                ; video page 0
    mov  bl,color            ; attribute
    or   bl,ATTRIB_HI        ; set blink/intensity bit
    mov  cx,1                ; display it one time
    int  10h
    mov  cx,1                ; advance cursor to
    call AdvanceCursor       ; next screen column
    inc  color               ; next color
```

```
        inc   si                          ; next character
        pop   cx                          ; restore loop counter
        Loop L1

        call Crlf
        exit
main ENDP

;--------------------------------------------------
EnableBlinking PROC
;
; Enable blinking (using the high bit of color
; attributes). In MS-Windows, this only works if
; the program is running in full screen mode.
; Receives: nothing. Returns: nothing
;--------------------------------------------------
        push ax
        push bx
        mov ax,1003h                      ; toggle blink/intensity
        mov bl,1                          ; blinking is enabled
        int 10h
        pop bx
        pop ax
        ret
EnableBlinking ENDP
```

The AdvanceCursor procedure can be used in any program
that writes to the console using INT 10h.

```
;--------------------------------------------------
AdvanceCursor PROC
;
; Advances the cursor n columns to the right.
; Receives: CX = number of columns
; Returns: nothing
;--------------------------------------------------
        pusha
L1:
        push cx                           ; save loop counter
        mov   ah,3                        ; get cursor position
        mov   bh,0                        ; into DH, DL
        int   10h                         ; changes CX register!
        inc   dl                          ; increment column
        mov   ah,2                        ; set cursor position
        int   10h
        pop   cx                          ; restore loop counter
        loop L1                           ; next column
```

```
        popa
        ret
AdvanceCursor ENDP
END main
```

15.3.4   Library Procedure Examples

Let's take a look at two useful, but simple procedures from the Irvine16 link library, **Gotoxy** and **Clrscr**.

15.3.4.1   Gotoxy Procedure

The **Gotoxy** procedure sets the cursor position on video page 0:

```
;----------------------------------------------------
Gotoxy PROC
;
; Sets the cursor position on video page 0.
; Receives: DH,DL = row, column
; Returns: nothing
;----------------------------------------------------
    pusha
    mov ah,2                    ; set cursor position
    mov bh,0                    ; video page 0
    int 10h
    popa
    ret
Gotoxy ENDP
```

15.3.4.2   Clrscr Procedure

The **Clrscr** procedure clears the screen and locates the cursor at row 0, column 0 on video page 0:

```
;------------------------------------------------------
Clrscr PROC
;
; Clears the screen (video page 0) and locates the cursor
; at row 0, column 0.
; Receives: nothing
; Returns:  nothing
;------------------------------------------------------
    pusha
    mov ax,0600h                ; scroll window up
    mov cx,0                    ; upper left corner (0,0)
    mov dx,184Fh                ; lower right corner (24,79)
    mov bh,7                    ; normal attribute
    int 10h                     ; call BIOS
    mov ah,2                    ; locate cursor at 0,0
    mov bh,0                    ; video page 0
    mov dx,0                    ; row 0, column 0
```

```
        int 10h
        popa
        ret
   Clrscr ENDP
```

15.3.5   Section Review

1. What are the three levels of access to the video display mentioned in the beginning of this section?
2. Which level of access produces the fastest output?
3. How do you run a program in full-screen mode?
4. When a computer is booted in MS-DOS, what is the default video mode?
5. Each position on the video display holds what information for a single character?
6. Which electron beams are required to generate any color on a video display?
7. Show the mapping of foreground and background colors in the video attribute byte.
8. Which INT 10h function positions the cursor on the screen?
9. Which INT 10h function scrolls text in a rectangular window upward?
10. Which INT 10h function writes a character and attribute at the current cursor position?
11. Which INT 10h function sets the cursor size?
12. Which INT 10h function gets the current video mode?
13. What parameters are required when setting the cursor position with INT 10h?
14. How is it possible to hide the cursor?
15. Which parameters are required when scrolling text in a window upward?
16. Which parameters are required when writing a character and attribute at the current cursor position?
17. Which INT 10h function toggles the blinking and intensity mode bit?
18. Which values should be moved to AH and AL when clearing the screen using INT 10h function 6?
19. *Challenge:* If you have a dog, why do you think he/she might be surprised that you spend hours at a time staring at a blank computer screen?

15.4   Drawing Graphics Using INT 10h

It's fairly easy to draw graphics points and lines using INT 10h Function 0Ch. (We will start with this function and later show how to draw graphics by writing data directly to video RAM.) Before drawing pixels, you have to put the video adapter into one of the standard graphics modes, shown in Table 15-6. Each mode can be set using INT 10h function 0 (set video mode).

Table 15-6 Video Graphics Modes Recognized by INT 10h.

Mode	Resolution (columns X rows, in pixels)	Number of Colors
6	640 X 200	2
0Dh	320 X 200	16
0Eh	640 X 200	16
0Fh	640 X 350	2
10h	640 X 350	16
11h	640 X 480	2
12h	640 X 480	16
13h	320 X 200	256
6Ah	800 X 600	16

Coordinates   For each video mode, the resolution is expressed as *XMax*, *YMax*. The screen coordinates range from x = 0, y = 0 in the upper-left corner of the screen, to x = *XMax−1*, y = *YMax−1* in the lower-right corner of the screen.

15.4.1 INT 10h Pixel-Related Functions

15.4.1.1 Write Graphics Pixel (0Ch)

INT 10h Function 0Ch, as shown in the next table, draws a pixel on the screen when the video controller is in graphics mode. Function 0Ch executes rather slowly, particularly when drawing a lot of pixels. (Most graphics applications write directly into video memory, after calculating the number of colors per pixel, the horizontal resolution, and so on.)

INT 10h Function 0Ch	
Description	Write graphics pixel
Receives	AH = 0Ch AL = pixel value BH = video page CX = x-coordinate DX = y-coordinate
Returns	nothing

INT 10h Function 0Ch	

Sample Call	```
	mov ah,0Ch
	mov al,pixelValue
	mov bh,videoPage
	mov cx,x_coord
	mov dx,y_coord
	int 10h
	``

Notes	The video display must be in graphics mode. The pixel value is (0 − 1) in two-color mode, and (0 − 15) in 16-color mode. If bit 7 is set in AL, the new pixel will be XORed with the current contents of the pixel (allowing the pixel to be erased).

15.4.1.2   Read Graphics Pixel (0Dh)

Function 0Dh, shown below, reads a graphics pixel from the screen at a given row and column position, and returns the pixel value in AL.

INT 10h Function 0Dh	
Description	Read graphics pixel
Receives	AH = 0Dh BH = video page CX = x-coordinate DX = y-coordinate
Returns	AL = pixel value

Sample Call	```
	mov ah,0Dh
	mov bh,0 ; video page 0
	mov cx,x_coord
	mov dx,y_coord
	int 10h
	mov pixelValue,al
	``

Notes	The video display must be in graphics mode. The pixel value is 0 or 1 in 2-color mode, and (0-15) in 16-color mode.

15.4.2   DrawLine Program

The *DrawLine* program switches into graphics mode using INT 10h and draws a straight horizontal line. You can try out different graphics modes by modifying a single program statement that currently selects video Mode 11h:

```
mov   ah,0                        ; set video mode
mov   al,Mode_11                  ; modify for different modes
int   10h                         ; call BIOS routine
```

In MS-Windows, this program should be run in full-screen mode.[2] Following is the complete program listing:

```
TITLE DrawLine Program              (Pixel1.asm)

; This program draws a straight line, using INT 10h
; function calls.
INCLUDE Irvine16.inc

;------------ Video Mode Constants -------------------
Mode_06 = 6                      ; 640 X 200,  2 colors
Mode_0D = 0Dh                    ; 320 X 200, 16 colors
Mode_0E = 0Eh                    ; 640 X 200, 16 colors
Mode_0F = 0Fh                    ; 640 X 350,  2 colors
Mode_10 = 10h                    ; 640 X 350, 16 colors

Mode_11 = 11h                    ; 640 X 480,  2 colors
Mode_12 = 12h                    ; 640 X 480, 16 colors
Mode_13 = 13h                    ; 320 X 200, 256 colors
Mode_6A = 6Ah                    ; 800 X 600, 16 colors

.data
saveMode  BYTE  ?                ; save the current video mode
currentX  WORD 100               ; column number (X-coordinate)
currentY  WORD 100               ; row number (Y-coordinate)
color     BYTE 1                 ; default color

; In 2-color modes, white = 1
; In 16-color modes, blue = 1

.code
main PROC
    mov ax,@data
    mov ds,ax

; Save the current video mode
    mov   ah,0Fh
    int   10h
    mov   saveMode,al

; Switch to a graphics mode
    mov   ah,0                    ; set video mode
    mov   al,Mode_11
    int   10h

; Draw a straight line
    LineLength = 100
```

---

[2] You may have trouble running *Pixel1.asm* and *Pixel2.asm* under MS-Windows on computers having a relatively low amount of video RAM. If this is a problem, switch to mode 11h or boot into pure MS-DOS mode.

```
    mov   dx,currentY
    mov   cx,LineLength        ; loop counter
L1:
    push  cx
    mov   ah,0Ch               ; write pixel
    mov   al,color             ; pixel color
    mov   bh,0                 ; video page 0
    mov   cx,currentX
    int   10h
    inc   currentX
    ;inc  color        ; try this for multi-color modes
    pop   cx
    Loop L1

; Wait for a keystroke
    mov   ah,0
    int   16h

; Restore the starting video mode
    mov   ah,0                 ; set video mode
    mov   al,saveMode          ; saved video mode
    int   10h
    exit
main ENDP
END main
```

15.4.3   Cartesian Coordinates Program

The *Cartesian Coordinates* program draws the X and Y axes of a Cartesian coordinate system, with the intersection point at screen locations X = 400 and Y = 300. There are two important procedures, **DrawHorizLine** and **DrawVerticalLine**, which could easily be inserted in other graphics programs. The program sets the video adapter to Mode 6A (800 x 600, 16 colors).

```
TITLE Cartesian Coordinates                  (Pixel2.asm)

; This program switches into 800 X 600 graphics mode and
; draws the X and Y axes of a Cartesian coordinate system.
; Switch to full-screen mode before running this program.
; Color constants are defined in Irvine16.inc.

INCLUDE Irvine16.inc

Mode_6A = 6Ah                ; 800 X 600, 16 colors
X_axisY = 300
X_axisX = 50
X_axisLen = 700

Y_axisX = 400
Y_axisY = 30
Y_axisLen = 540
```

```
.data
saveMode BYTE ?

.code
main PROC
    mov ax,@data
    mov ds,ax

; Save the current video mode
    mov   ah,0Fh               ; get video mode
    int   10h
    mov   saveMode,al

; Switch to a graphics mode
    mov   ah,0                 ; set video mode
    mov   al,Mode_6A           ; 800 X 600, 16 colors
    int   10h

; Draw the X-axis
    mov   cx,X_axisX           ; X-coord of start of line
    mov   dx,X_axisY           ; Y-coord of start of line
    mov   ax,X_axisLen         ; length of line
    mov   bl,white             ; line color (see IRVINE16.inc)
    call  DrawHorizLine        ; draw the line now

; Draw the Y-axis
    mov   cx,Y_axisX           ; X-coord of start of line
    mov   dx,Y_axisY           ; Y-coord of start of line
    mov   ax,Y_axisLen         ; length of line
    mov   bl,white             ; line color
    call  DrawVerticalLine     ; draw the line now

; Wait for a keystroke
    mov   ah,10h               ; wait for key
    int   16h

; Restore the starting video mode
    mov   ah,0                 ; set video mode
    mov   al,saveMode          ; saved video mode
    int   10h

    exit
main endp

;------------------------------------------------------------
DrawHorizLine PROC
;
; Draws a horizontal line starting at position X,Y with
; a given length and color.
; Receives: CX = X-coordinate, DX = Y-coordinate,
;           AX = length, and BL = color
; Returns: nothing
;------------------------------------------------------------
```

```
        .data
        currX WORD ?

        .code
            pusha
            mov   currX,cx              ; save X-coordinate
            mov   cx,ax                 ; loop counter

        DHL1:
            push  cx                    ; save loop counter
            mov   al,bl                 ; color
            mov   ah,0Ch                ; draw pixel
            mov   bh,0                  ; video page
            mov   cx,currX              ; retrieve X-coordinate
            int   10h
            inc   currX                 ; move 1 pixel to the right
            pop   cx                    ; restore loop counter
            Loop  DHL1

            popa
            ret
        DrawHorizLine ENDP

        ;-----------------------------------------------------
        DrawVerticalLine PROC
        ;
        ; Draws a vertical line starting at position X,Y with
        ; a given length and color.
        ; Receives: CX = X-coordinate, DX = Y-coordinate,
        ;           AX = length, BL = color
        ; Returns: nothing
        ;-----------------------------------------------------
        .data
        currY WORD ?

        .code
            pusha
            mov   currY,dx              ; save Y-coordinate
            mov   currX,cx              ; save X-coordinate
            mov   cx,ax                 ; loop counter

        DVL1:
            push  cx                    ; save loop counter
            mov   al,bl                 ; color
            mov   ah,0Ch                ; function: draw pixel
            mov   bh,0                  ; set video page
            mov   cx,currX              ; set X-coordinate
            mov   dx,currY              ; set Y-coordinate
            int   10h                   ; draw the pixel
            inc   currY                 ; move down 1 pixel
```

```
        pop   cx                       ; restore loop counter
        Loop DVL1

        popa
        ret
DrawVerticalLine ENDP
END main
```

15.4.4 Converting Cartesian Coordinates to Screen Coordinates

Points on a Cartesian graph do not correspond to the absolute coordinates used by the BIOS graphics system. In the preceding two program examples, it was clear that screen coordinates begin at $sx = 0$, $sy = 0$ in the upper left corner of the screen. sx values grow to the right, and sy values grow toward the bottom of the screen. You can use the following formulas to convert Cartesian X, Y to screen coordinates sx, sy:

$$sx = (sOrigX + X) \qquad sy = (sOrigY - Y)$$

where $sOrigX$ and $sOrigY$ are the screen coordinates of the origin of the Cartesian coordinate system. In the Cartesian Coordinates Program (Section 15.4.3), we used $sOrigX = 400$, and $sOrigY = 300$, placing the origin in the middle of the screen. Let's use the following four points to test our formulas:

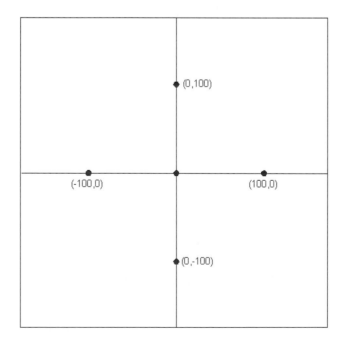

The following table summarizes the conversions of the four points:

Cartesian (X, Y)	(400 + X, 300 – Y)	Screen (sx, sy)
(0, 100)	(400 + 0, 300 – 100)	(400, 200)
(100, 0)	(400 + 100, 300 – 0)	(500, 300)
(0, –100)	(400 + 0, 300 – (–100))	(400, 400)
(–100, 0)	(400 + (–100), 300 – 0)	(300, 300)

15.4.5   Section Review

1. Which INT 10h function draws a single pixel on the video display?
2. When using INT 10h to draw a single pixel, what values must be placed in the AL, BH, CX, and DX registers?
3. What is the main disadvantage to drawing pixels using INT 10h?
4. Write ASM statements that set the video adapter to Mode 11h.
5. Which video mode is 800 x 600 pixels, in 16 colors?
6. What is the formula to convert a Cartesian X coordinate to screen pixel coordinates? (Use the variable sx for the screen column, and use $sOrigX$ for the screen column where the Cartesian origin point (0,0) is located.)
7. If a Cartesian origin point is located at screen coordinates $sy = 250$, $sx = 350$, convert the following Cartesian points in the form (X, Y) into screen coordinates (sx, sy):

```
a. (0, 100)
b. (25, 25)
c. (-200, -150)
```

15.5   Memory-Mapped Graphics

In the preceding section we showed how to draw pixels and lines using Interrupt 10h. The primary disadvantage to that approach was the slow speed, because so much OS code had to be executed every time a pixel was drawn. In the current section, we can draw graphics more efficiently by placing graphics values directly in VRAM, a technique commonly called *memory-mapped graphics*.

15.5.1   Mode 13h: 320 X 200, 256 Colors

Video Mode 13h is the easiest to use when using direct memory. The screen pixels are mapped as a two-dimensional array of bytes, with a separate byte for each pixel. The array begins with the pixel in the upper-left corner of the screen, and continues across the top of the screen for 320 bytes. The next byte maps to the first pixel in the second screen line, and so on. The last byte in the array is mapped to the pixel in the lower-right corner of the screen. Why use a whole byte for each pixel? Because you need 256 different integer values to represent each of the available colors.

OUT Instruction   Pixel and color values are transmitted to the video adapter using the OUT (output to port) instruction. A 16-bit port address is assigned to DX, and the value sent to the port is placed in AL. For example, the video color palette is located at port address 3C8h. The following instructions send the value 20h to the port:

```
mov dx,3C8h              ; port address
mov al,20h               ; value to be output
out dx,al                ; send value to port
```

Color Indexes   The interesting thing about colors in Mode 13h is that each color integer does not directly indicate a color. Instead, it represents an index into a table of colors called a *palette*. Each entry in the palette consists of three separate integer values (0–63) known as *RGB* (red, green, blue). Entry 0 in the color palette controls the screen's background color.

You can create 262,144 different colors (64^3) with this scheme. Only 256 different colors can be displayed at a given time, but your program can easily modify the palette at run time to vary the colors.

RGB Colors   RGB colors are based on the additive mixing of light, as opposed to the subtractive method one uses when mixing liquid paint. With additive mixing, for example, you create the color black by keeping all color intensity levels at zero. White, on the other hand, is created by setting all color levels at 63 (the maximum). In fact, as the following table demonstrates, when all three levels are equal, you get varying shades of gray:

Red	Green	Blue	Color
0	0	0	black
20	20	20	dark gray
35	35	35	medium gray
50	50	50	light gray
63	63	63	white

Pure colors are created by setting all but one color level to zero. To get a light color, increase the other two colors in equal amounts. Here are variations on the color red:

Red	Green	Blue	Color
63	0	0	bright red
10	0	0	dark red
30	0	0	medium red
63	40	40	pink

Bright blue, dark blue, light blue, bright green, dark green, and light green are created in a similar manner. Of course, you can mix pairs of colors in other amounts to create colors such as magenta and lavender. Following are examples:

Red	Green	Blue	Color
0	30	30	cyan
30	30	0	yellow
30	0	30	magenta
40	0	63	lavender

15.5.2 Memory-Mapped Graphics Program

The *Memory Mapped Graphics* program draws a row of 10 pixels on the screen using direct memory mapping in Mode 13h. Following is the program listing:

```
; Memory Mapped Graphics, Mode 13         (Mode13.asm)

INCLUDE Irvine16.inc
.data
saveMode BYTE ?                 ; saved video mode
xVal WORD ?                     ; x-coordinate
yVal WORD ?                     ; y-coordinate
```

> The main procedure sets the video mode to Mode 13h, sets the screen's background color, draws several color pixels, and restores the video adapter to its starting mode.

```
.code
main PROC
    mov ax,@data
    mov ds,ax

    call SetVideoMode
    call SetScreenBackground
    call Draw_Some_Pixels
    call RestoreVideoMode
    exit
main ENDP

;------------------------------------------------------------
SetScreenBackground PROC
;
; This procedure sets the screen's background color.
; Video palette index 0 is the background color.
;------------------------------------------------------------
```

```
    mov dx,3c8h              ; video palette port (3C8h)
    mov al,0                 ; set palette index
    out dx,al
```

Two output ports control the video color palette. The value sent to port 3C8h indicates which video palette entry you plan to change. Then, the color values themselves are sent to port 3C9h.

```
; Set screen background color to dark blue.
    mov dx,3c9h              ; colors go to port 3C9h
    mov al,0                 ; red
    out dx,al
    mov al,0                 ; green
    out dx,al
    mov al,35                ; blue (intensity 35/63)
    out dx,al
    ret
SetScreenBackground ENDP

;------------------------------------------------------------
SetVideoMode PROC
;
; This procedure saves the current video mode, switches to
; a new mode, and points ES to the video segment.
;------------------------------------------------------------
    mov  ah,0Fh              ; get current video mode
    int  10h
    mov  saveMode,al         ; save it

    mov ah,0                 ; set new video mode
    mov al,13h               ; to mode 13h
    int 10h

    push 0A000h              ; video segment address
    pop es                   ; ES = A000h (video segment).
    ret
SetVideoMode ENDP

;------------------------------------------------------------
RestoreVideoMode PROC
;
; This procedure waits for a key to be pressed and
; restores the video mode to its original value.
;------------------------------------------------------------
    mov ah,10h               ; wait for keystroke
    int 16h
    mov ah,0                 ; reset video mode
    mov al,saveMode          ; to saved mode
    int 10h
```

```
        ret
RestoreVideoMode ENDP

;------------------------------------------------------------
Draw_Some_Pixels PROC
;
; This procedure sets individual palette colors and
; draws several pixels.
;------------------------------------------------------------

; Change color at index 1 to white (63,63,63)
        mov dx,3c8h             ; video palette port (3C8h)
        mov al,1                ; set palette index 1
        out dx,al

        mov dx,3c9h             ; colors go to port 3C9h
        mov al,63               ; red
        out dx,al
        mov al,63               ; green
        out dx,al
        mov al,63               ; blue
        out dx,al

        ; Calculate the video buffer offset of the first pixel.
        ; Specific to mode 13h, which is 320 X 200.
        mov xVal,160            ; middle of screen
        mov yVal,100
        mov ax,320              ; 320 for video mode 13h
        mul yVal                ; y-coordinate
        add ax,xVAl             ; x-coordinate

        ; Place the color index into the video buffer.
        mov cx,10               ; draw 10 pixels
        mov di,ax               ; AX contains buffer offset

        ; Draw the 10 pixels now.
DP1:
        mov BYTE PTR es:[di],1  ; store color index
```

> By default, the assembler assumes that DI is an offset from the segment
> address in DS. The segment override (es:[di]) tells the CPU to use the seg-
> ment address in ES instead. (ES currently points to VRAM.)

```
        add di,5                ; move 5 pixels to the right
        Loop DP1
        ret
Draw_Some_Pixels ENDP
END main
```

This program is fairly easy to implement because the pixels happen to be on the same screen line. To draw a vertical line, on the other hand, you could add 320 to each value of DI to move to the next row of pixels. Or, a diagonal line with slope −1 could be drawn by adding 361 to DI. Drawing arbitrary lines between any two points is best handled by *Bresenham's Algorithm*, which is well-documented on many Web sites.

15.5.3 Section Review

1. (*True/False*): Video mode 13h maps screen pixels as a two-dimensional array of bytes, where each byte corresponds to two pixels.
2. (*True/False*): In video mode 13h, each screen row uses 320 bytes of storage.
3. In one sentence, explain how video mode 13h sets the colors of pixels.
4. How is the color index used in video mode 13h?
5. In video mode 13h, what is contained in each element of the color palette?
6. What are the three RGB values for dark gray?
7. What are the three RGB values for white?
8. What are the three RGB values for bright red?
9. *Challenge:* Show how to set the screen background color in video mode 13h to green.
10. *Challenge:* Show how to set the screen background color in video mode 13h to white.

15.6 Mouse Programming

The mouse is usually connected to the computer's motherboard through an RS-232 serial port, a PS-2 mouse port, or a wireless connection. Before detecting the mouse, MS-DOS requires a device driver program to be installed in memory. MS-Windows also has built-in mouse drivers, but for now we will concentrate on functions provided by MS-DOS.

Mouse movements are tracked in a unit of measure called *mickeys* (guess how they came up with that name?). One mickey represents approximately 1/200 of an inch of mouse travel. The mickeys to pixels ratio can be set for the mouse, which defaults to 8 mickeys for each horizontal pixel, and 16 mickeys for each vertical pixel.[3]

15.6.1 Mouse INT 33h Functions

INT 33h provides information about the mouse, including its current position, last button clicked, speed, and so on. You can also use it to display or hide the mouse cursor. In this section, we cover a few of the more essential mouse functions. INT 33h receives the function number in the AX register rather than AH (which is the norm for BIOS interrupts).

15.6.1.1 Reset Mouse and Get Status

INT 33h Function 0 resets the mouse and confirms that it is available. The mouse (if found) is centered on the screen, its display page is set to video page 0, its pointer is hidden, and its

---

[3] From Ray Duncan, *Advanced MS-DOS Programming* (1988), p. 601.

mickeys to pixels ratios and speed are set to default values. The mouse's range of movement is set to the entire screen area. Details are shown in the following table:

INT 33h Function 0	
Description	Reset mouse and get status
Receives	AX = 0
Returns	If mouse support is available AX = FFFFh and BX = number of mouse buttons; otherwise, AX = 0.

Sample Call	```
	mov ax,0
	int 33h
	cmp ax,0
	je MouseNotAvailable
	``

Notes	If the mouse was visible before this call, it is hidden by this function.

15.6.1.2   Showing and Hiding the Mouse Pointer

INT 33h Functions 1 and 2, shown in the next two tables, display and hide the mouse pointer, respectively. The mouse driver keeps an internal counter, which is incremented (if nonzero) by calls to Function 1 and decremented by calls to Function 2. When the counter is zero, the mouse pointer is displayed. Function 0 (reset mouse pointer) sets the counter to −1.

INT 33h Function 1	
Description	Show mouse pointer
Receives	AX = 1
Returns	nothing

Sample Call	```
	mov ax,1
	int 33h
	``

Notes	The mouse driver keeps a count of the number of times this function is called.

INT 33h Function 2	
Description	Hide mouse pointer
Receives	AX = 2
Returns	nothing

INT 33h Function 2	
Sample Call	`mov ax,2` `int 33h`
Notes	The mouse driver continues to track the mouse position.

15.6.1.3 Get Mouse Position and Status

INT 33h Function 3 gets the mouse position and mouse status, as can be seen in the following table:

INT 33h Function 3	
Description	Get mouse position and status
Receives	AX = 3
Returns	BX = mouse button status CX = X-coordinate (in pixels) DX = Y-coordinate (in pixels)

Sample Call	`mov ax,3`
	`int 33h`
	`test bx,1`
	`jne Left_Button_Down`
	`test bx,2`
	`jne Right_Button_Down`
	`test bx,4`
	`jne Middle_Button_Down`

Notes	The mouse button status is returned in BX as follows: If bit 0 is set, the left button is down; if bit 1 is set, the right button is down; if bit 2 is set, the middle button is down.

Converting Pixel to Character Coordinates Standard text fonts in MS-DOS are 8 pixels wide and 8 pixels high, so you can convert pixel coordinates to character coordinates by dividing the former by the character size. Assuming that both pixels and characters start numbering at zero, the following formula converts a pixel-coordinate P to a character-coordinate C, using character-dimension D:

$$C = int(P / D)$$

For example, let's assume that characters are 8 pixels wide. If the X-coordinate returned by INT 33 Function 3 is 100 (pixels), the coordinate would fall within character position 12: C = *int*(100 / 8).

15.6.1.4   Set Mouse Position

INT 33h Function 4, shown in the following table, moves the mouse position to specified X and Y pixel coordinates.

INT 33h Function 4	
Description	Set mouse position
Receives	AX = 4 CX = X-coordinate (in pixels) DX = Y-coordinate (in pixels)
Returns	nothing

Sample Call	```mov ax,4```
	```mov cx,200 ; X-position```
	```mov dx,100 ; Y-position```
	```int 33h```

Notes	If the position lies within an exclusion area, the mouse is not displayed.

Converting Character to Pixel Coordinates   You can convert a screen character coordinate to a pixel coordinate using the following formula, where C = character coordinate, P = pixel coordinate, and D = character dimension:

```
P  =  C  x  D
```

In the horizontal direction, P will be the pixel coordinate of the left side of the character cell. In the vertical direction, P will be the pixel coordinate of the top of the character cell. If characters are 8 pixels wide, and you want to put the mouse in character cell 12, for example, the X-coordinate of the leftmost pixel of that cell is 96.

15.6.1.5   Get Button Presses and Releases

Function 5 returns the status of all mouse buttons, as well as the position of the last button press. In an event-driven programming environment, a *drag* event always begins with a button press. Once a call is made to this function for a particular button, the button's state is reset, and a second call to the function returns nothing:

INT 33h Function 5	
Description	Get button press information
Receives	AX = 5 BX = button ID (0 = left, 1 = right, 2 = center)

INT 33h Function 5	
Returns	AX = button status BX = button press counter CX = X-coordinate of last button press DX = Y-coordinate of last button press

Sample Call	```mov ax,5```
	```mov bx,0 ; button ID```
	```int 33h```
	```test ax,1 ; left button?```
	```jz skip ; no - skip```
	```mov X_coord,cx ; yes: save coordinates```
	```mov Y_coord,dx```

Notes	The mouse button status is returned in AX as follows: If bit 0 is set, the left button is down; if bit 1 is set, the right button is down; if bit 2 is set, the middle button is down.

Function 6 gets button release information from the mouse, as shown in the following table. In event-driven programming, a mouse *click* even occurs only when a mouse button is released. Similarly, a *drag* event ends when the mouse button is released.

INT 33h Function 6	
Description	Get button release information
Receives	AX = 6 BX = button ID (0 = left, 1 = right, 2 = center)
Returns	AX = button status BX = button release counter CX = X-coordinate of last button release DX = Y-coordinate of last button release

Sample Call	```mov ax,6```
	```mov bx,0 ; button ID```
	```int 33h```
	```test ax,1 ; left button?```
	```jz skip ; no - skip```
	```mov X_coord,cx ; yes: save coordinates```
	```mov Y_coord,dx```

Notes	The mouse button status is returned in AX as follows: If bit 0 is set, the left button was released; if bit 1 is set, the right button was released; if bit 2 is set, the middle button was released.

15.6.1.6   Setting Horizontal and Vertical Limits

INT 33h Functions 7 and 8, as illustrated in the next two tables, let you set limits on where the mouse pointer can go on the screen. You do this by setting minimum and maximum coordinates for the mouse cursor. If necessary, the mouse pointer is moved so it lies within the new limits.

INT 33h Function 7	
Description	Set horizontal limits
Receives	AX = 7 CX = minimum X-coordinate (in pixels) DX = maximum X-coordinate (in pixels)
Returns	nothing

Sample Call	```mov ax,7```
	```mov cx,100 ; set X-range to```
	```mov dx,700 ; (100,700)```
	```int 33h```

INT 33h Function 8	
Description	Set vertical limits
Receives	AX = 7 CX = minimum Y-coordinate (in pixels) DX = maximum Y-coordinate (in pixels)
Returns	nothing

Sample Call	```mov ah,```
	```int 33h```
	```mov cx,100 ; set Y-range to```
	```mov dx,500 ; (100,500)```
	```int 33h```

15.6.1.7   Miscellaneous Mouse Functions

A number of other INT 33h functions are useful for configuring the mouse and controlling its behavior. We don't have the space to elaborate on these functions, but they are listed in Table 15-7.

Table 15-7   Miscellaneous Mouse Functions.

Function	Description	Input/Output Parameters
AX = 0Fh	Set mickeys to 8 pixels ratio	Receives: CX = horizontal mickeys, DX = vertical mickeys. The defaults are CX = 8, DX = 16.

Table 15-7   Miscellaneous Mouse Functions. (Continued)

Function	Description	Input/Output Parameters
AX = 10h	Set mouse exclusion area (prevents mouse from entering a rectangle)	Receives: CX, DX = X, Y coordinates of upper-left corner. SI, DI = X, Y coordinates of lower-right corner
AX = 13h	Set double speed threshold	Receives: DX = threshold speed in mickeys per second (the default is 64)
AX = 1Ah	Set mouse sensitivity	Receives: BX = horizontal speed (mickeys per second), CX = vertical speed (mickeys per second), DX = double speed threshold in mickeys per second
AX = 1Bh	Get mouse sensitivity	Returns: BX = horizontal speed, CX = vertical speed, DX = double speed threshold
AX = 1Fh	Disable mouse driver	Returns: If unsuccessful, AX = FFFFh
AX = 20h	Enable mouse driver	none
AX = 24h	Get mouse information	Returns FFFFh on error; otherwise, returns: BH = major version number, BL = minor version number, CH = mouse type (1 = bus, 2 = serial, 3 = InPort, 4 = PS/2, 5 = HP); CL = IRQ number (0 for PS/2 mouse)

15.6.2   Mouse Tracking Program

The *Mouse Tracking* program presented in this section tracks the movement of the text mouse cursor. The X and Y coordinates are continually updated in the lower-right corner of the screen, and when the user clicks the left button, the mouse's position is displayed in the lower-left corner of the screen. Following is the program listing:

```
TITLE Tracking the Mouse                          (mouse.asm)

INCLUDE Irvine16.inc

.data
ESCkey = 1Bh
GreetingMsg BYTE "Press Esc to quit",0dh,0ah,0
```

```
StatusLine  BYTE "Left button:                              "
            BYTE "Mouse position: ",0
blanks      BYTE "                    ",0
Xcoordinate WORD 0                 ; current X-position
Ycoordinate WORD 0                 ; current Y-position
Xclick      WORD 0                 ; X-pos of last button press
Yclick      WORD 0                 ; Y-pos of last button press

.code
main PROC
    mov  ax,@data
    mov  ds,ax

; Hide the text cursor and display the mouse.
    call HideCursor
    mov  dx,OFFSET GreetingMsg
    call WriteString
    call ShowMousePointer

; Display a status line on line 24.
    mov  dh,24
    mov  dl,0
    call Gotoxy
    mov  dx,OFFSET StatusLine
    call Writestring

; Loop: show mouse coordinates, check for left mouse
; button click, or for a keypress (Esc key).
L1: call ShowMousePosition
    call LeftButtonClick      ; check for button click
    mov  ah,11h               ; key pressed already?
    int  16h
    jz   L2                   ; no, continue the loop
    mov  ah,10h               ; remove key from buffer
    int  16h
    cmp  al,ESCkey            ; yes. Is it the ESC key?
    je   quit                 ; yes, quit the program
L2: jmp  L1                   ; no, continue the loop

; Hide the mouse, restore the text cursor, clear
; the screen, and display "Press any key to continue."
quit:
    call HideMousePointer
    call ShowCursor
    call Clrscr
    call WaitMsg
    exit
main ENDP
```

```
;------------------------------------------------------------
GetMousePosition PROC
;
; Return the current mouse position and button status.
; Receives: nothing
; Returns:  BX = button status (0 = left button down,
;              (1 = right button down, 2 = center button down)
;              CX = X-coordinate
;              DX = Y-coordinate
;------------------------------------------------------------
    push ax
    mov  ax,3
    int  33h
    pop  ax
    ret       .
GetMousePosition ENDP

;------------------------------------------------------------
HideCursor proc
;
; Hide the text cursor by setting its top line
; value to an illegal value.
;------------------------------------------------------------
    mov  ah,3                  ; get cursor size
    int  10h
    or   ch,30h                ; set upper row to illegal value
    mov  ah,1                  ; set cursor size
    int  10h
    ret
HideCursor ENDP

ShowCursor PROC
    mov  ah,3                  ; get cursor size
    int  10h
    mov  ah,1                  ; set cursor size
    mov  cx,0607h              ; default size
    int  10h
    ret
ShowCursor ENDP

;------------------------------------------------------------
HideMousePointer PROC
;------------------------------------------------------------
    push ax
    mov  ax,2                  ; hide mouse cursor
    int  33h
    pop  ax
    ret
HideMousePointer ENDP
```

```
;------------------------------------------------------------
ShowMousePointer PROC
;------------------------------------------------------------
    push ax
    mov  ax,1                      ; make mouse cursor visible
    int  33h
    pop  ax
    ret
ShowMousePointer ENDP

;------------------------------------------------------------
LeftButtonClick PROC
;
; Check for the most recent left mouse button press,
; and display its location.
; Receives: BX = button number (0=left, 1=right, 2=middle)
; Returns:  BX = button press counter
;           CX = X-coordinate
;           DX = Y-coordinate
;------------------------------------------------------------
    pusha
    mov  ah,0                      ; get mouse status
    mov  al,5                      ; (button press information)
    mov  bx,0                      ; specify the left button
    int  33h

; Exit proc if the coordinates have not changed.
    cmp  cx,Xclick
    jne  LBC1
    cmp  dx,Yclick
    je   LBC_exit

LBC1:
; Save the mouse coordinates.
    mov  Xclick,cx
    mov  Yclick,dx

; Position the cursor, clear the old numbers.
    mov  dh,24                     ; screen row
    mov  dl,15                     ; screen column
    call Gotoxy
    push dx
    mov  dx,OFFSET blanks
    call WriteString
    pop  dx

; Show the mouse click coordinates.
    call Gotoxy
    mov  ax,Xcoordinate
    call WriteDec
```

```
        mov  dl,20                   ; screen column
        call Gotoxy
        mov  ax,Ycoordinate
        call WriteDec
LBC_exit:
    popa
    ret
LeftButtonClick ENDP

;------------------------------------------------------------
SetMousePosition PROC
;
; Set the mouse's position on the screen.
; Receives: CX = X-coordinate
;           DX = Y-coordinate
; Returns:  nothing
;------------------------------------------------------------
    mov  ax,4
    int  33h
    ret
SetMousePosition ENDP

;------------------------------------------------------------
ShowMousePosition PROC
;
; Get and show the mouse coordinates at the
; bottom of the screen.
; Receives: nothing
; Returns:  nothing
;------------------------------------------------------------
    pusha
    call GetMousePosition

; Exit proc if the coordinates have not changed.
    cmp  cx,Xcoordinate
    jne  SMP1
    cmp  dx,Ycoordinate
    je   SMP_exit

SMP1:
    mov  Xcoordinate,cx
    mov  Ycoordinate,dx

; Position the cursor, clear the old numbers.
    mov  dh,24                   ; screen row
    mov  dl,60                   ; screen column
    call Gotoxy
    push dx
    mov  dx,OFFSET blanks
```

```
        call  WriteString
        pop   dx

; Show the mouse coordinates.
        call  Gotoxy                ; (24,60)
        mov   ax,Xcoordinate
        call  WriteDec
        mov   dl,65                 ; screen column
        call  Gotoxy
        mov   ax,Ycoordinate
        call  WriteDec

    SMP_exit:
        popa
        ret
    ShowMousePosition ENDP
    END main
```

15.6.3   Section Review

1. Which INT 33h function resets the mouse and gets the mouse status?
2. Write ASM statements that reset the mouse and get the mouse status.
3. Which INT 33h function shows and hides the mouse pointer?
4. Write ASM statements that hide the mouse pointer.
5. Which INT 33h function gets the mouse position and status?
6. Write ASM statements that get the mouse position and store it in the variables **mouseX** and **mouseY**.
7. Which INT 33h function sets the mouse position?
8. Write ASM statements that set the mouse pointer to $X = 100$ and $Y = 400$.
9. Which INT 33h function gets mouse button press information?
10. Write ASM statements that jump to label **Button1** when the left mouse button has been pressed.
11. Which INT 33h function gets mouse button release information?
12. Write ASM statements that get the mouse position at the point when the right button was released, and store the position in the variables **mouseX** and **mouseY**.
13. Write ASM statements that set the vertical limits of the mouse to 200 and 400.
14. Write ASM statements that set the horizontal limits of the mouse to 300 and 600.
15. *Challenge:* Suppose you want the mouse pointer to point to the upper-left corner of the character cell located at row 10, column 20 in text mode. What X and Y values will you have to pass to INT 33h Function 4?
16. *Challenge:* Suppose you want the mouse pointer to point to the middle of the character cell located at row 15, column 22 in text mode. What X and Y values will you have to pass to INT 33h Function 4?

15.7   Chapter Summary

Working at the BIOS level gives you more control over the computer's input-output devices than you would have at the MS-DOS level. This chapter shows how to program the keyboard using INT 16h, the video display using INT 10h, and the mouse, using INT 33h.

INT 16h is particularly useful for reading extended keyboard keys such as function keys and cursor arrow keys.

Keyboard hardware works with the INT 9h, INT 16h, and INT 21h handlers to make keyboard input available to programs. The chapter contains a program that polls the keyboard and breaks out of a loop.

Colors are produced on the video display using additive synthesis of primary colors. The color pixels are mapped to the video attribute byte.

There are a wide range of useful INT 10h functions that control the video display at the BIOS level. The chapter contains an example program that scrolls a color window and writes text in the middle.

You can draw color graphics using INT 10h. The chapter contains two example programs that show how to do this. A simple formula can be used to convert logical coordinates to screen coordinates (pixel locations).

An example program with documentation shows how to draw high-speed color graphics by writing directly to video memory.

Numerous INT 33h functions manipulate and read the mouse. An example program tracks both mouse movements and mouse button clicks.

For More Information   Digging up information on BIOS functions is not easy, because many of the good reference books have gone out of print. Here are my favorites:

- Brown, Ralf, and Jim Kyle. *PC Interrupts, A Programmer's Reference to BIOS, DOS, and Third-Party Calls*, Addison-Wesley, 1991.
- Duncan, Ray. *IBM ROM BIOS*, Microsoft Press, 1998.
- Duncan, Ray. *Advanced MS-DOS Programming*, 2nd ed. Microsoft Press, 1988.
- Gilluwe, Frank van. *The Undocumented PC: A Programmer's Guide to I/O, CPUs, and Fixed Memory Areas*, Addison-Wesley, 1996.
- Hogan, Thom. *Programmer's PC Sourcebook : Reference Tables for IBM PCs and Compatibles, Ps/2 Systems, Eisa-Based Systems, Ms-DOS Operating System Through Version*, Microsoft Press, 1991.
- Kyle, Jim. *DOS 6 Developer's Guide*, SAMS, 1993.
- Mazidi, Muhammad Ali, and Janice Gillispie Mazidi. *The 80x86 IBM PC & Compatible Computers,* Volumes I & II, Prentice-Hall, 1995.

15.8   Chapter Exercises

The following exercises must be done in Real-address mode:

1. ASCII Table

Using INT 10h, display all 256 characters from the IBM Extended ASCII character set (inside back cover of the book). Display 40 columns per line, with a space following each character.

2. Scrolling Text Window

Define a text window that is approximately 3/4 of the size of the video display. Let the program carry out the following actions, in sequence:

- Draw a string of random characters on the top line of the window. (You can call Random_range from the Irvine16 library.)
- Scroll the window down one line.
- Pause the program for approximately 500 milliseconds. (You can call the **Delay** function from the Irvine16 library.)
- Draw another line of random text.
- Continue scrolling and drawing until 50 lines have been displayed.

> This program and its various enhancements were given a nickname by my assembly language students based on a popular movie where characters interact in a virtual world. (We can't mention the name of the movie here, but you will probably figure it out by the time you complete the programs.)

3. Scrolling Color Columns

Using the **Scrolling Text Window** exercise as a starting point, make the following changes:

- The random string should only have characters in columns 0, 3, 6, 9, ..., 78. The other columns should be blank. This will create the effect of columns as it scrolls downward.
- Each column should be in a different color.

4. Scrolling Columns in Different Directions

Using the **Scrolling Color Columns** exercise as a starting point, make the following change: Before the loop starts, randomly choose each column to scroll either up or down. It should continue in the same direction for the duration of the program. *Hint:* Define each column as a separately scrolling window.

5. Drawing a Rectangle Using INT 10h

Using the pixel-drawing capabilities of INT 10h, create a procedure named **DrawRectangle** that takes input parameters specifying the location of the upper-left corner and the lower-right corner, and the color. Write a short test program that uses the INVOKE directive to draw several rectangles of different sizes and colors.

6. Plotting a Function Using INT 10h

Using the pixel-drawing capabilities of INT 10h, plot the line determined by the equation $Y = 2(X^2)$.

7. Mode 13 Line

Modify the Memory Mapped Graphics program in Section 15.5.2 so that it draws a single vertical line.

8. Mode 13, Multiple Lines

Modify the Memory Mapped Graphics program in Section 15.5.2 so that it draws a series of 10 vertical lines, each in a different color.

9. Box-Drawing Program

Write a procedure that draws a single-line frame anywhere on the screen. Use the following extended ASCII codes: C0h, BFh, B3h, C4h, D9h, and DAh, from the table on the inside back cover of this book. The procedure's only input parameter should be a pointer to a FRAME structure:

```
FRAME STRUCT
    Left BYTE ?                ; left side
    Top  BYTE ?                ; top line
    Right BYTE ?               ; right side
    Bottom BYTE ?              ; bottom line
    FrameColor BYTE ?          ; box color
FRAME ENDS
```

Write a program that tests your procedure, passing it pointers to various FRAME objects.

16

Expert MS-DOS Programming

16.1   Introduction

This is a good chapter to read if you're planning to be an engineer who works at the hardware level on Intel processors. It's also a good chapter if you want to understand the amazing things MS-DOS experts were able to do with very limited resources a few years ago. It will give you some useful background if you plan to become a systems-level programmer. It is a chapter on MS-DOS system resources and programming. Here's what we're going to do:

- Show you how to get as much flexibility as possible from the .MODEL, .CODE, .STACK and related directives.
- Show you how to define segments from scratch, using explicit segment directives.
- Demonstrate a large memory model program that has multiple code and data segments.
- Explain the runtime structure of COM and EXE programs, including EXE headers.
- Map out the Program Segment Prefix (PSP) and show how you can find the MS-DOS environment string.

- Show you how to replace existing interrupt handlers with your own. We will demonstrate this by writing a Ctrl-Break interrupt handler (also called an *interrupt service routine*, or ISR).
- Explain how hardware interrupts work and list the various *interrupt request* (IRQ) levels used by the Intel 8259 Programmable Interrupt Controller (PIC).
- Write a *terminate and stay resident* (TSR) program that intercepts the Ctrl-Alt-Del key combination. If you learn to this, you can join the ranks of MS-DOS experts.

If you've been around experienced programmers for a few years, you've probably heard a lot of the terms from the foregoing list. Notice how the old-time experts seem to drop terms like IRQ, TSR, PSP, and 8259 into their conversations? Now you can find out what they've been talking about.

16.2   Defining Segments

Programs written for the early versions of MASM had to create rather elaborate definitions for code, data, and stack segments. Instructors all breathed a sigh of relief when simplified segment directives (.code, .stack, .data) came along, because they made the first week of class go much more smoothly. But it was also clear that expert programmers would probably prefer flexibility over simplicity, and stick with the traditional way of doing things. If you've reached this chapter (and understood all preceding chapters), you are now ready to master the arcane details of explicit segment directives.

First, however, we're going to explore the various ways the simplified directives can be used, just in case they satisfy your needs.

16.2.1   Simplified Segment Directives

When you use the .MODEL SMALL directive, the assembler automatically defines DGROUP for your near data segment. The segments in DGROUP hold near data, which can normally be accessed directly through DS or SS. Recall that memory models were explained in Section 8.4.1.

The .DATA and .DATA? directives each create a near data segment, which can be as large as 64 kilobytes when running in Real-address mode. It is placed in a special group identified as DGROUP, which is also limited to 64K.

When you use .FARDATA or .FARDATA? in the small and medium memory models, the assembler creates far data segments FAR_DATA and FAR_BSS, respectively. DS must point to a variable's enclosing segment before the variable can be accessed. Use the SEG operator to set DS:

```
mov ax, SEG farvar2
mov ds, ax
```

Code Segments   Code segments are defined, as you know, by the .CODE directive. In a small memory model program, the .CODE directive causes the assembler to generate a segment named _TEXT. You can see this in the Segments and Groups section of a listing file:

```
 _TEXT . . . . .16 Bit 0009 Word Public 'CODE'
```

(This entry indicates that a 16-bit segment named _TEXT is 9 bytes long. It is aligned on an even word boundary, it is a public segment, and its segment class is 'CODE'.)

In medium, large, and huge model programs, each source code module is assigned a different segment name. The name consists of the module name followed by _TEXT. For example, in a program named *MyProg.asm* that uses the .MODEL LARGE directive, the listing file generates the following code segment entry:

```
MYPROG_TEXT  . . . . .16 Bit 0009 Word Public 'CODE'
```

You can also declare multiple code segments within the same module, regardless of the memory model. Do this by adding an optional segment name to the .CODE directive:

```
.code MyCode
```

There is, however, something you should keep in mind: You can only call the book's 16-bit link library procedures from procedures in segments named _TEXT because the library uses the small memory model. The following statements, for example, cause the linker to generate *fixup overflow* message:

```
.code MyCode
    mov dx,OFFSET msg
    call Writestring
```

Multiple Code Segment Program   The following *MultCode.asm* program contains two code segments. By not including the *Irvine16.inc* file, we can show you all the MASM directives being used in the program:

```
TITLE Multiple Code Segments      (MultCode.asm)

; This small model program contains multiple
; code segments.

.model small,stdcall
.stack 100h
WriteString PROTO

.data
msg1 db "First Message",0dh,0ah,0
msg2 db "Second Message",0dh,0ah,"$"

.code
main PROC
    mov ax,@data
    mov ds,ax
    mov dx,OFFSET msg1
    call WriteString                ; NEAR call
    call Display                    ; FAR call
    .exit
main ENDP
```

```
.code OtherCode
Display PROC FAR
    mov ah,9
    mov dx,offset msg2
    int 21h
    ret
Display ENDP
END main
```

In the foregoing example, the **_TEXT** segment contains the **main** procedure, and the **OtherCode** segment contains the **Display** procedure. Notice that the **Display** procedure must have a FAR modifier, to tell the assembler to generate the type of call instruction that saves both the current segment and offset on the stack. For confirmation, we can see the names of the two code segments in the *MultCode.lst* listing file:

```
OtherCode . . . .16 Bit 0008 Word Public 'CODE'
_TEXT . . . . . .16 Bit 0014 Word Public 'CODE'
```

16.2.2 Explicit Segment Definitions

There are a few occasions when you may prefer to create explicit segment definitions. You may want to define multiple data segments with extra memory buffers, for instance. Or, you may be linking your program to an object library that uses its own proprietary segment names. Finally, you may be writing a procedure to be called from a high-level language compiler that does not use Microsoft's segment names.

A program with explicit segment definitions has two tasks to perform: First, a segment register (DS, ES, or SS) must be set to the location of each segment before it may be used. Second, the assembler must be told how to calculate the offsets of labels within the correct segments.

The SEGMENT and ENDS directives define the beginning and end of a segment. A program may contain almost any number of segments, each with a unique name. Segments can also be grouped together (combined). The syntax is:

```
name SEGMENT [align] [combine] ['class']
    statements
name ENDS
```

- *name* identifies the segment; it can be unique or it can be the name of an existing segment.
- *align* can be BYTE, WORD, DWORD, PARA, or PAGE.
- *combine* can be PRIVATE, PUBLIC, STACK, COMMON, MEMORY, or AT *address*.
- *class* is an identifier enclosed in single quotes that is used when identifying a particular type of segment such as CODE or STACK.

For example, this is how a segment called **ExtraData** could be defined:

```
ExtraData SEGMENT PARA PUBLIC 'DATA'
  var1 BYTE 1
  var2 WORD 2
ExtraData ENDS
```

16.2.2.1   Align Type

When two or more segments are combined, their *align types* tell the linker how to align their starting addresses. The default is PARA, which indicates that each segment must begin on an even 16-byte boundary. Here are examples of 20-bit hexadecimal addresses that fall on paragraph boundaries. Note that the last digit is always zero:

```
    0A150              81B30              07460
```

To create the specified alignment, the assembler inserts bytes at the end of any existing segment until the correct starting address for the each segment is reached. The extra bytes are called *slack bytes*. This only affects segments that are joined to an existing segment, because the first segment in a group always begins on a paragraph boundary. (Recall from Chapter 2 that segment addresses always contain four implied low-order zero bits.) The following align types are available:

- The BYTE align type starts the segment on the next byte following the preceding segment.
- The WORD align type starts the segment at the next 16-bit boundary.
- DWORD starts the segment at the next 32-bit boundary.
- PARA starts the segment at the next 16-byte boundary.
- PAGE starts the segment at the next 256-byte boundary.

If a program will likely be run on either an 8086 or 80286 processor, a WORD align type (or larger) is best for data segments because the processors have a 16-bit data bus. Such processors always move two bytes, the first of which has an even-numbered address. Therefore, a variable on an even boundary requires one memory fetch, while a variable on an odd boundary requires two. An IA-32 processor, on the other hand, fetches 32 bits at a time, and should use the DWORD align type.

16.2.2.2   Combine Type

The combine type tells the linker how to combine segments having the same name. The default type is PRIVATE, indicating that such a segment will not be combined with any other segment.

The PUBLIC and MEMORY combine types cause a segment to be combined with all other public or memory segments by the same name; in effect, they become a single segment. The offsets of all labels are adjusted so they are relative to the start of the same segment.

The STACK combine type resembles the PUBLIC type, in that all other stack segments will be combined with it. MS-DOS automatically initializes SS to the start of the first segment that it finds with a combine type of STACK; MS-DOS sets SP to the segment's length (minus 1) when the program is loaded. In an EXE program, there should be at least one segment with a STACK combine type; otherwise, the linker displays a warning message.

The COMMON combine type makes a segment begin at the same address as any other COMMON segments with the same name. In effect, the segments overlay each other. All offsets are calculated from the same starting address, and variables can overlap.

The AT *address* combine type lets you create a segment at an absolute address; it is often used for data whose location is predefined by the hardware or operating system. No variables or data may be initialized, but you can create variable names that refer to specific offsets. For example:

```
bios SEGMENT AT 40h
  ORG 17h
  keyboard_flag  BYTE ?              ; MS-DOS keyboard flag
bios ENDS

.code
    mov ax,bios                      ; point to BIOS segment
    mov ds,ax
    and ds:keyboard_flag,7Fh         ; clear high bit
```

In this example, a segment override (DS:) was required because **keyboard_flag** is not in the standard data segment. We will explain segment overrides in Section 16.2.3.

16.2.2.3   Class Type
A segment's class type provides another way of combining segments, in particular, those with different names. The class type is simply a string (case-insensitive) enclosed in single quotes. Segments with the same class type are loaded together, although they may be in a different order in the original program. One standard type, CODE, is recognized by the linker and should be used for segments containing instructions. You must include this type label if you plan to use a debugger.

16.2.2.4   ASSUME Directive
The ASSUME directive makes it possible for the assembler to calculate the offsets of labels and variables at assembly time. It is usually placed directly after the SEGMENT directive in the code segment, but you can have as many additional ASSUMEs as you like. If a new one is encountered, the assembler modifies the way it calculates addresses.

ASSUME does not actually change the value of a segment register. You still must set segment registers at run time to the addresses of the desired segments. For example, the following ASSUME tells the assembler to use DS as the default register for the **data1** segment:

```
ASSUME ds:data1
```

The following statement associates CS with **cseg** and SS is associated with **mystack**:

```
ASSUME cs:cseg, ss:mystack
```

16.2.2.5   Example: Multiple Data Segments
Earlier in this section we showed a program having two code segments. Let's now create a program (*MultData.asm*) containing two data segments named **data1** and **data2**. Both are declared with class name DATA. The ASSUME directive associates DS with **data1**, and ES with **data2**:

```
ASSUME cs:cseg, ds:data1, es:data2, ss:mystack
data1 SEGMENT 'DATA'
data2 SEGMENT 'DATA'
```

The following is a complete program listing:

```
TITLE Multiple Data Segments                  (MultData.asm)

; This program shows how to explicitly declare
; multiple data segments.
cseg  SEGMENT 'CODE'
      ASSUME cs:cseg, ds:data1, es:data2, ss:mystack
main PROC
    mov   ax,data1             ; point DS to data1 segment
    mov   ds,ax
    mov   ax,SEG val2          ; point ES to data2 segment
    mov   es,ax

    mov   ax,val1              ; data1 segment assumed
    mov   bx,val2              ; data2 segment assumed
    mov   ax,4C00h             ; exit program
    int   21h
main ENDP
cseg  ENDS

data1 SEGMENT 'DATA'
   val1 WORD 1001h
data1 ENDS

data2 SEGMENT 'DATA'
   val2 WORD 1002h
data2 ENDS

mystack SEGMENT para STACK 'STACK'
   BYTE 100h DUP('S')
mystack ENDS
END main
```

If we examine the listing file created by the assembler, we can see that the two variables **val1** and **val2** have the same values (offsets), but different segment attributes:

```
Name                        Type  Value Attr
val1 . . . . . . . . . . . Word  0000  data1
val2 . . . . . . . . . . . Word  0000  data2
```

16.2.3 Segment Overrides

A *segment override* instructs the processor to use a different segment register from the default (created by the ASSUME directive) when calculating the effective address. It can be used, for example, to access a variable in a segment other than the one currently referenced by DS:

```
mov   al,cs:var1             ; segment pointed to by CS
mov   al,es:var2             ; segment pointed to by ES
```

The following instruction obtains the offset of a variable in a segment not currently ASSUME'd by DS or ES:

```
mov  bx,OFFSET AltSeg:var2
```

Multiple references to variables should be handled by inserting an ASSUME to change the default segment references:

```
ASSUME ds:AltSeg              ; use AltSeg for a while
mov    ax,AltSeg
mov    ds,ax
mov    al,var1
       .
       .
ASSUME ds:data               ; use the default data segment
mov    ax,data
mov    ds,ax
```

16.2.4 Combining Segments

We have shown in several places earlier in this book that larger programs can be effectively divided into separate modules, to simplify editing and debugging. It is possible to combine the segments by giving them the same name and specifying a PUBLIC combine type. This is what happens when you link a 16-bit asm program with the book's Irvine16 link library, using simplified segment directives.

If you use a BYTE align type, each segment will immediately follow the preceding one. If a WORD align type is used, the segments will follow at the next even word boundary. The align type defaults to PARA, in which each segment follows at the next paragraph boundary.

Program Example   Let's look at two program modules with two code segments, two data segments, and one stack segment, which combine to form three segments (CSEG, DSEG, and SSEG). The main module contains all three segments; CSEG and DSEG have a PUBLIC combine type. A BYTE align type is used for CSEG to avoid creating a gap between the two code segments when they are combined. The EXTRN directive in the main program identifies **var2** as a variable existing in a module other than the current one (see the *Seg2a.asm* file).

Main Module

```
TITLE Segment Example              (main module, Seg2.asm)

EXTRN var2:WORD
subroutine_1 PROTO

cseg SEGMENT BYTE PUBLIC 'CODE'
ASSUME cs:cseg,ds:dseg, ss:sseg

main PROC
   mov  ax,dseg                    ; initialize DS
   mov  ds,ax
```

```
        mov   ax,var1                  ; local variable
        mov   bx,var2                  ; external variable
        call subroutine_1             ; external procedure

        mov   ax,4C00h                 ; exit to OS
        int   21h
main ENDP
cseg ENDS

dseg SEGMENT WORD PUBLIC 'DATA'  ; local data segment
    var1 WORD 1000h
dseg ends

sseg SEGMENT STACK'STACK'        ; stack segment
    BYTE 100h dup('S')
sseg ENDS
END main
```

Submodule:

```
TITLE Segment Example            (submodule, Seg2a.ASM)

PUBLIC subroutine_1, var2

cseg SEGMENT BYTE PUBLIC 'CODE'
ASSUME cs:cseg, ds:dseg

subroutine_1 PROC                ; called from MAIN
    mov ah,9
    mov dx,OFFSET msg
    int 21h
    ret
subroutine_1 ENDP
cseg ENDS

dseg SEGMENT WORD PUBLIC 'DATA'

var2 WORD 2000h                  ; accessed by MAIN
msg  BYTE 'Now in Subroutine_1'
     BYTE 0Dh,0Ah,'$'

dseg ENDS
END
```

The following MAP file was created by the linker. showing one code segment, one data segment, and one stack segment:

```
Start   Stop    Length Name                Class
 00000H 0001BH 0001CH CSEG                 CODE
 0001CH 00035H 0001AH DSEG                 DATA
 00040H 0013FH 00100H SSEG                 STACK

Program entry point at 0000:0000
```

16.2.5 Section Review

1. What is the purpose of the SEGMENT directive?
2. What value does the SEG operator return?
3. Explain the function of the ASSUME directive.
4. In a segment definition, what are the possible align types?
5. In a segment definition, what are the possible combine types?
6. Which *align type* is most efficient for an IA-32 processor?
7. What is the purpose of the combine type in a segment definition?
8. How do you define a segment at an absolute address such as 40h?
9. What is the purpose of the class type option in a segment definition?
10. Write an instruction that uses a segment override.
11. In the following example, assume that **segA** begins at address 1A060h. What will be the starting address of the *third* segment, also called **segA**?

```
segA SEGMENT COMMON
  var1  WORD  ?
  var2  BYTE  ?
segA ENDS

stack SEGMENT STACK
  BYTE 100h DUP(0)
stack ENDS

segA SEGMENT COMMON
  var3  WORD  3000h
  var4  BYTE  40h
segA ENDS
```

16.3 Runtime Program Structure

An effective assembly language programmer needs to know a lot about MS-DOS. This section describes COMMAND.COM, the Program Segment Prefix, and the structure of COM and EXE programs.

The COMMAND.COM program supplied with MS-DOS and Windows[1] is called the command processor. It interprets each command typed at a prompt. The following sequence takes place when you type a command:

1. MS-DOS checks to see if the command is internal, such as DIR, REN, or ERASE. If it is, the command is immediately executed by a memory-resident MS-DOS routine.
2. MS-DOS looks for a matching file with an extension of COM. If the file is in the current directory, it is executed.

---

[1] Windows 2000 and XP use CMD.EXE.

3. MS-DOS looks for a matching file with an extension of EXE. If the file is in the current directory, it is executed.

4. MS-DOS looks for a matching file with an extension of BAT. If the file is in the current directory, it is executed. A file with an extension of BAT is called a batch file, which is a text file containing MS-DOS commands to be executed as if the commands had been typed at the console.

5. If MS-DOS is unable to find a matching COM, EXE, or BAT file in the current directory, it searches the first directory in the current path. If it fails to find a match there, it proceeds to the next directory in the path and continues this process until either a matching file is found or the path search is exhausted.

Application programs with extensions of COM and EXE are called *transient programs*. In general, they are loaded into memory long enough to be executed; when they finish, the memory they occupy is released. Transient programs can, if needed, leave a portion of their code in memory when they exit; these are called *memory-resident* programs.

Program Segment Prefix   MS-DOS creates a special 256-byte block at the beginning of a program as it is loaded into memory, called the *program segment prefix*. The structure of the Program Segment Prefix (PSP) is shown in Table 16-1.

Table 16-1   The Program Segment Prefix (PSP).

Offset	Comments
00–15	MS-DOS pointers and vector addresses
16–2B	Reserved by MS-DOS
2C–2D	Segment address of the current environment string
2E–5B	Reserved by MS-DOS
5C–7F	File control blocks 1 and 2, used mainly by pre–MS-DOS 2.0 programs
80–FF	Default disk transfer area and a copy of the current MS-DOS command tail

16.3.1   COM Programs

There are two types of transient programs, depending on the extension used (COM or EXE). A COM program is an unmodified binary image of a machine-language program. It is loaded into memory by MS-DOS at the lowest available segment address, and a PSP is created at offset 0. The code, data, and stack are all stored in the same physical (and logical) segment. The program may be as large as 64K, minus the size of the PSP and two reserved bytes at the end of the stack. As illustrated below, all segment registers are set to the base address of the PSP. The code area begins at offset 100h, and the data area immediately follows the code. The stack area is at the end of the segment because MS-DOS initializes SP to FFFEh:

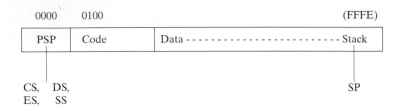

Let's look at a simple program written in COM format. MASM requires a COM program to use the *tiny* memory model. Also, the ORG directive must be used to set the starting location counter for program code to offset 100h. This leaves 100h bytes available for the PSP, which occupies locations 0 through 0FFh:

```
TITLE Hello Program in COM format    (HelloCom.asm)

.model tiny
.code
org 100h                    ; must be before main
main PROC
    mov   ah,9
    mov   dx,OFFSET hello_message
    int   21h
    mov   ax,4C00h
    int   21h
main ENDP

hello_message BYTE 'Hello, world!',0dh,0ah,'$'

END main
```

Variables are usually located after the main procedure, because there is no separate segment for data. If we put the data at the top of the program, the CPU would try to execute the data. An alternative is to place a JMP instruction at the beginning that jumps over the data to the first actual instruction:

```
TITLE Hello Program in COM format       (HelloCom.asm)

.model tiny
.code
org 100h                    ; must be before entry point
main proc
    jmp start               ; skip over the data
hello_message BYTE 'Hello, world!',0dh,0ah,'$'

start:
    mov   ah,9
```

```
      mov   dx,OFFSET hello_message
      int   21h
      mov   ax,4C00h
      int   21h
main ENDP
END main
```

The Microsoft linker requires the /T parameter to tell it to create a COM file rather than an EXE file. COM programs are always smaller than their EXE counterparts—*HelloCom.asm*, for example, is only 17 bytes long when stored on disk. When in memory, however, a COM program eats up an entire 64K memory segment, whether it needs the space or not. COM programs were not designed to run in a multitasking environment.

16.3.2   EXE Programs

An EXE program is stored on disk with an EXE header followed by a load module containing the program itself. The program header is not actually loaded into memory; instead, it contains information used by MS-DOS to load and execute the program.

When MS-DOS loads an EXE program, a program segment prefix (PSP) is created at the first available address, and the program is placed in memory just above it. As MS-DOS decodes the program header, it sets DS and ES to the program's load address. CS and IP are set to the entry point of the program code, where the program begins executing. SS is set to the beginning of the stack segment, and SP is set to the stack size. Here is a diagram showing overlapping code, data, and stack segments:

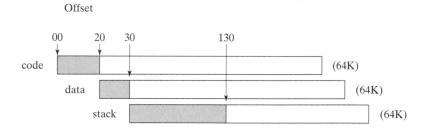

In this program, the code area is 20h bytes, the data area is 10h bytes, and the stack area is 100h bytes.

An EXE program may contain up to 65,535 segments, although it would be unusual to have that many. If a program has multiple data segments, the programmer usually has to manually set DS or ES to each new segment.

16.3.2.1   Memory Usage

The amount of memory an EXE program uses is determined by its program header—in particular, the values for the minimum and maximum number of paragraphs (16 bytes each) needed above the program. By default, the linker sets the maximum value to 65,535 paragraphs, which is more memory than could be available under MS-DOS. When the program is loaded, therefore, MS-DOS automatically allocates whatever memory is available.

The maximum allocation may be set when a program is linked, using the /CP option. This is shown here for a program named *prog1.obj*. The number 1,024 refers to the number of 16-byte paragraphs, expressed in decimal:

```
link/cp:1024 prog1;
```

These values can also be modified after an EXE program is compiled, using the EXEMOD program supplied with the Microsoft assembler. For example, the command to set the maximum allocation to 400h paragraphs (16,384 bytes) for a program named *prog1.exe* is

```
exemod prog1/max 400
```

The EXEMOD program can also display important statistics about a program. Sample output is shown here describing the *prog1.exe* program after it was linked with the maximum allocation set at 1,024 paragraphs:

```
PROG1                            (Hex)                (Dec)
EXE size (bytes)                  876                 2166
Minimum load size (bytes)         786                 1926
Overlay number                      0                    0
Initial CS:IP                0000:0010                  16
Initial SS:SP                0068:0100                 256
Minimum allocation (para)          11                   17
Maximum allocation (para)         400                 1024
Header size (para)                 20                   32
Relocation table offset            1E                   30
Relocation entries                  1                    1
```

16.3.2.2   EXE Header

The header area of an EXE program is used by MS-DOS to correctly calculate the addresses of segments and other components. The header contains information such as the following:

- A relocation table, containing addresses to be calculated when the program is loaded.
- The file size of the EXE program, measured in 512-byte units.
- Minimum allocation: the minimum number of paragraphs needed above the program. Some of this storage might be used for a runtime heap that holds dynamic data. In C++, for example, the *new* operator creates dynamic data.
- Maximum allocation: the maximum number of paragraphs needed above the program.
- Starting values to be given to the IP and SP registers.
- *Displacement* (measured in 16-byte paragraphs) of the stack and code segments from the beginning of the load module.

- A *checksum* of all words in the file, used in catching data errors when loading the program into memory.

16.3.3   Section Review

1. When a command is typed at the MS-DOS prompt, what happens if the command is not an internal MS-DOS command?
2. (*yes/no*): Does MS-DOS look for BAT files before EXE files in the current directory when executing a command?
3. What are transient programs?
4. What is the name of the 256-byte area at the beginning of a transient program?
5. Where does a transient program keep the segment address of the current environment string?
6. What is a COM program?
7. Which memory model(s) are used by COM programs?
8. Which linker command-line switch is required when creating a COM program?
9. What is the memory limitation of a COM program?
10. When running, how efficient is a COM program's use of memory?
11. How many segments can a COM program contain?
12. What are the starting values of all segment registers in a COM program?
13. What is the purpose of the ORG directive?
14. When stored on disk, the two main parts of an EXE program are the *header* and the _____ module.
15. Where do DS and ES point when an EXE program is loaded?
16. What determines the amount of memory allocated to an EXE program?
17. What is the purpose of the EXEMOD program?
18. If you wanted to know the number of relocation entries in an EXE file, where would you look?

16.4   Interrupt Handling

In this section we discuss ways to customize the BIOS and MS-DOS by installing *interrupt handlers* (*interrupt service routines*). As we have seen in earlier chapters, the BIOS and MS-DOS contain interrupt handlers that simplify input/output as well as basic system tasks. We have seen many of these so far—the INT 10h routines for video manipulation, the INT 16h keyboard routines, the INT 21h disk services, and so on. But an equally important part of the operating system is its set of interrupt handlers that respond to hardware interrupts. MS-DOS allows you to replace any of these service routines with one of your own.

> The interrupt handlers presented in this chapter work only when your computer is booted to MS-DOS mode. You can do this using Windows 95 and 98, but not Windows NT, 2000, or XP. The latter operating systems mask the system hardware from application programs to achieve greater system stability and security. If the OS were to allow two simultaneously running programs to modify internal settings on the same hardware device, the results would be unpredictable at best.

An interrupt handler might be written for a variety of reasons. You might want your own program to activate when a hot key is pressed, even when the user is running another application. Borland's SideKick™, for example, was one of the first programs that was able to pop up a note-pad or calculator whenever a special combination of hot keys was pressed.

You can also replace one of MS-DOS's default interrupt handlers in order to provide more complete services. For example, the *divide by zero* interrupt activates when the CPU tries to divide a number by zero, but there is no standard way for a program to recover.

You can replace the MS-DOS critical error handler or the Ctrl-Break handler with one of your own. MS-DOS's default critical error handler causes a program to abort and return to MS-DOS. Your own handler could recover from an error and let the user continue to run the current application program.

A user-written interrupt service routine can handle hardware interrupts more effectively than MS-DOS. For example, the PC's asynchronous communication handler (INT 14h) performs no input/output buffering. This means that an input character is lost if it is not copied from the port before another character arrives. A memory-resident program can wait for an incoming character to generate a hardware interrupt, input the character from the port, and store it in a circular buffer. This frees an application program from having to take valuable time away from other tasks to repeatedly check the serial port.

Interrupt Vector Table   The key to MS-DOS's flexibility lies in the interrupt vector table located in the first 1,024 bytes of RAM (locations 0:0 through 0:03FF). Table 16-2 contains a short sample of vector table entries. Each entry in the table (called an interrupt vector) is a 32-bit segment-offset address that points to one of the existing service routines.

Table 16-2   Interrupt Vector Table Example.

Interrupt Number	Offset	Interrupt Vectors
00-03	0000	02C1:5186 0070:0C67 0DAD:2C1B 0070:0C67
04-07	0010	0070:0C67 F000:FF54 F000:837B F000:837B
08-0B	0020	0D70:022C 0DAD:2BAD 0070:0325 0070:039F
0C-0F	0030	0070:0419 0070:0493 0070:050D 0070:0C67
10-13	0040	C000:0CD7 F000:F84D F000:F841 0070:237D

On any given computer, the vector values will vary because of different versions of the BIOS and MS-DOS. Each interrupt vector corresponds to an interrupt number. In the table, the address of the INT 0 handler (divide by zero) is 02C1:5186h. The offset of any interrupt vector may be found by multiplying its interrupt number by 4. Thus, the offset of the vector for INT 9h is 9 * 4, or 0024 hexadecimal.

Executing Interrupt Handlers   An interrupt handler may be executed in one of two ways: An application program containing an INT instruction automatically calls the handler, executing what is known as a *software interrupt*. Another way for an interrupt handler to be executed is via a *hardware interrupt*, when a hardware device (asynchronous port, keyboard, timer, and so on) sends a signal to the Programmable Interrupt Controller chip.

16.4.1   Hardware Interrupts

A hardware interrupt is generated by the Intel 8259 *Programmable Interrupt Controller* (PIC), which signals the CPU to suspend execution of the current program and execute an interrupt service routine. For example, a keyboard character waiting at the input port would be lost if not saved by the CPU, or characters received from the serial port would be lost if not for an interrupt-driven routine that stores them in a buffer.

Occasionally, programs must disable hardware interrupts when performing sensitive operations on segment registers and the stack. The CLI (*clear interrupt flag*) instruction disables interrupts and the STI (*set interrupt flag*) instruction enables interrupts.

IRQ Levels   Interrupts can be triggered by a number of different devices on a PC, including those listed in Table 16-3. Each device has a priority, based on its *interrupt request level* (IRQ). Level 0 has the highest priority, and level 15 has the lowest. A lower-level interrupt cannot interrupt a higher-level one still in progress. For instance, if communications port 1 (COM1) tried to interrupt the keyboard interrupt handler, it would have to wait until the latter was finished. Also, two or more simultaneous interrupt requests are processed according to their priority levels. The scheduling of interrupts is handled by the 8259 PIC.

Table 16-3   IRQ Assignments (ISA Bus).

IRQ	Interrupt Number	Description
0	8	System timer (18.2 times/second)
1	9	Keyboard
2	0Ah	Programmable Interrupt Controller
3	0Bh	COM2 (serial port 2)
4	0Ch	COM1 (serial port 1)
5	0Dh	LPT2 (parallel port 2)

Table 16-3 IRQ Assignments (ISA Bus). (Continued)

IRQ	Interrupt Number	Description
6	0Eh	Floppy disk controller
7	0Fh	LPT1 (parallel port 1)
8	70h	CMOS real-time clock
9	71h	(redirected to INT 0Ah)
10	72h	(available) Sound card
11	73h	(available) SCSI card
12	74h	PS/2 mouse
13	75h	Math coprocessor
14	76h	Hard disk controller
15	77h	(available)

Let's use the keyboard as an example: When a key is pressed, the 8259 PIC sends an INTR signal to the CPU, passing it the interrupt number; if external interrupts are not currently disabled, the CPU does the following, in sequence:

1. Pushes the Flags register on the stack.
2. Clears the Interrupt flag, preventing any other hardware interrupts.
3. Pushes the current CS and IP on the stack.
4. Locates the interrupt vector table entry for INT 9 and places this address in CS and IP.

Next, the BIOS routine for INT 9 executes, and it does the following in sequence:

1. Reenables hardware interrupts so the system timer is not affected.
2. Inputs a character from the keyboard port and stores it in the keyboard buffer, a 32-byte circular buffer in the BIOS data area.
3. Executes an IRET (interrupt return) instruction, which pops IP, CS, and the Flags register off the stack. Control returns to the program that was executing when the interrupt occurred.

16.4.2 Interrupt Control Instructions

The CPU has a flag called the *Interrupt flag* (IF) that controls the way the CPU responds to external (hardware) interrupts. If the Interrupt flag is set (IF = 1), we say that interrupts are *enabled*; if the flag is clear (IF = 0), then interrupts are *disabled*.

STI Instruction The STI instruction enables external interrupts. For example, the system responds to keyboard input by suspending a program in progress and doing the following: It calls INT 9, which stores the keystroke in a buffer and then returns to the current program. Normally, the Interrupt flag is enabled. Otherwise, the system timer would not calculate the time and date properly, and input keystrokes would be lost.

CLI Instruction   The CLI instruction disables external interrupts. It should be used sparingly—only when a critical operation is about to be performed, one that cannot be interrupted. When changing the value of SS and SP on the 8086/8088, for example, it is advisable to disable interrupts by clearing the Interrupt flag. Otherwise, the correct values of SS and SP could be lost if a hardware interrupt should occur between transfers:

```
cli                             ; disable interrupts
mov     ax,mystack              ; reset SS
mov     ss,ax
mov     sp,100h                 ; reset SP
sti                             ; reenable interrupts
```

Interrupts should never be disabled for more than a few milliseconds at a time, or you may lose keystrokes and slow down the system timer. When the CPU acknowledges either a software or a hardware interrupt, other interrupts are disabled. One of the first things the MS-DOS and BIOS interrupt service routines do is to reenable interrupts.

16.4.3   Writing a Custom Interrupt Handler

One might ask why the interrupt vector table exists at all. We could, of course, call specific procedures in ROM to process interrupts. The designers of the IBM-PC wanted to be able to make modifications and corrections to the BIOS routines without having to replace the ROM chips. By having an interrupt vector table, it was possible to replace addresses in the interrupt vector table so they would point to procedures in RAM.

Application programs can replace an address in the table with one that points to a new interrupt handler. For example, we could write a custom keyboard interrupt handler. There would have to be a compelling reason to do so, because of the effort involved. A more likely alternative would be for an interrupt handler to directly call the default INT 9 keyboard to read a keystroke from the keyboard port. Once the key was placed in the keyboard typeahead buffer, we could manipulate its contents.

INT 21h Functions 25h and 35h make it possible to install interrupt handlers. Function 35h (get interrupt vector) returns the segment-offset address of an interrupt vector. Call the function with the desired interrupt number in AL. The 32-bit vector is returned by MS-DOS in ES:BX. The following statements would retrieve the INT 9 vector, for example:

```
.data
int9Save LABEL WORD
DWORD ?                         ; store old INT 9 address here

.code
mov     ah,35h                  ; get interrupt vector
mov     al,9                    ; for INT 9
```

```
int  21h                      ; call MS-DOS
mov  int9Save,BX              ; store the offset
mov  int9Save+2,ES           ; store the segment
```

INT 21h Function 25h (set interrupt vector) lets you replace an existing interrupt handler with a new handler. Call it with the interrupt number in AL and the segment-offset address of your own interrupt handler in DS:DX. For example:

```
mov ax,SEG kybd_rtn         ; keyboard handler
mov ds,ax                    ; segment
mov dx,OFFSET kybd_rtn      ; offset
mov ah,25h                   ; set Interrupt vector
mov al,9h                    ; for INT 9h
int 21h
 .
 .
kybd_rtn PROC        ; (new INT 9 interrupt handler begins here)
```

16.4.3.1 Ctrl-Break Handler Example

If Ctrl-Break is pressed by the user when an MS-DOS program is waiting for input, control passes to the default INT 23h interrupt handler procedure. The default Ctrl-Break handler terminates the currently running program. This can leave the current program in an unstable state, since files might be left open, memory not released, and so on. It is possible, however, to substitute your own code into the INT 23h handler and prevent the program from halting. The following program installs a simple Ctrl-Break handler:

```
TITLE Control-Break Handler                (Ctrlbrk.asm)

; This program installs its own Ctrl-Break handler and
; prevents the user from using Ctrl-Break (or Ctrl-C)
; to halt the program. The program inputs and echoes
; keystrokes until the Esc key is pressed.

INCLUDE Irvine16.inc

.data
breakMsg BYTE "BREAK",0
msg BYTE "Ctrl-Break demonstration."
    BYTE  0dh,0ah
    BYTE "This program disables Ctrl-Break (Ctrl-C). Press any"
    BYTE  0dh,0ah
    BYTE "keys to continue, or press ESC to end the program."
    BYTE  0dh,0ah,0

.code
main PROC
    mov   ax,@data
    mov   ds,ax

    mov   dx,OFFSET msg      ; display greeting message
    call  Writestring
```

```
install_handler:
    push  ds                 ; save DS
    mov   ax,@code           ; initialize DS to code segment
    mov   ds,ax
    mov   ah,25h             ; set interrupt vector
    mov   al,23h             ; for interrupt 23h
    mov   dx,OFFSET break_handler
    int   21h
    pop   ds                 ; restore DS

L1: mov   ah,1               ; wait for a key, echo it
    int   21h
    cmp   al,1Bh             ; ESC pressed?
    jnz   L1                 ; no: continue

    exit
main ENDP

; The following procedure executes when Ctrl-Break is
; pressed. All registers must be preserved.

break_handler PROC
    push  ax
    push  dx
    mov   dx,OFFSET breakMsg
    call  WriteString
    pop   dx
    pop   ax
    iret
break_handler ENDP
END main
```

The **main** procedure initializes the interrupt vector for INT 23h. The required input parameters for INT 21h function 25h are:

- AH = 25h
- AL = interrupt vector to be handled (23h)
- DS:DX = segment/offset address of the new Ctrl-Break handler

The program's main loop simply inputs and echoes keystrokes until the Esc key is pressed.

> On some systems, you may have to press Ctrl-C rather than Ctrl-Break to activate the Ctrl-Break handler message.

The **break_handler** procedure executes when Ctrl-Break is pressed; it displays a message by calling **WriteString**. When IRET (return from interrupt) executes at the end of break_handler, control returns to the main program. Whichever MS-DOS function was in progress when Ctrl-Break was pressed is restarted. In general, you can call any MS-DOS interrupts from inside a Ctrl-Break handler. You must preserve all registers in an interrupt handler.

You do not have to restore the INT 23h vector because MS-DOS automatically does this when a program ends. The original vector is stored by MS-DOS at offset 000Eh in the program segment prefix.

16.4.4 Terminate and Stay Resident Programs

A *terminate and stay resident* (TSR) program is one that is installed in memory and stays there either until it is removed by special utility software or the computer is rebooted. Such a program can remain hidden and then be activated by some event such as pressing a key.

In the early days of TSRs, compatibility problems would arise when two or more programs replaced the same interrupt vector. Older programs would make the vector point to their own program and provide no forward chain to other programs using the same vector. Later, to remedy this problem, TSR authors would save the existing vector for the interrupt they were replacing, and would forward-chain to the original interrupt handler after their own procedure was finished dealing with the interrupt. This, of course, was an improvement over the old method, but it meant that the last TSR to be installed automatically had top priority in handling the interrupt. It meant that users sometimes had to be careful to load TSR programs in a particular order. There are now commercial programming tools you can use to manage multiple memory-resident programs.

16.4.4.1 Keyboard Example

Suppose we write an interrupt service routine that can inspect each character typed at the keyboard and store it at location 10B2:0020. To install the ISR, we fetch the current INT 9 vector from the interrupt vector table, save it, and replace the table entry with the address of our ISR.

When a keyboard key is pressed, a single byte is transferred by the keyboard controller to the computer's keyboard port, and a hardware interrupt is triggered. The 8259 PIC passes the interrupt number to the CPU, and the latter jumps to the INT 9 address in the interrupt vector table, the address of our ISR. Our procedure gets an opportunity to inspect the keyboard byte. When our keyboard handler exits, it executes a jump to the original BIOS keyboard handler procedure.

This chaining process is shown in Figure 16-1. The addresses are hypothetical. When the BIOS INT 9h routine finishes, the IRET instruction pops the Flags register from the stack and returns control to the program that was executing when the character was pressed.

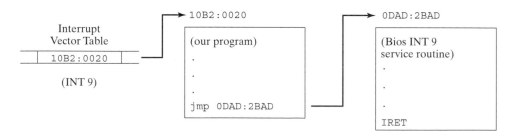

Figure 16-1 Vectoring an Interrupt.

16.4.5   Application: The No_Reset Program

A simple type of memory-resident program is one that prevents the system from being rebooted by the Ctrl-Alt-Delete keys. Once our program is installed in memory, the system may only be rebooted by pressing a special combination of keys: Ctrl-Alt-RightShift-Del. (The only other way to deactivate the program is to turn off and restart the computer.) This program only works if you boot the computer in MS-DOS. Microsoft Windows NT, 2000, and XP prevent a TSR program from intercepting keyboard keys.

The MS-DOS Keyboard Status Byte. One bit of information we need before we start is the location of the keyboard status byte kept by MS-DOS in low memory, shown in Figure 16-2. Our program will inspect this flag to see if the Ctrl, Alt, Del, and RightShift keys are held down. The keyboard status flag is stored in RAM at location 0040:0017h. An additional keyboard status byte, located at 0040:0018h, duplicates the preceding flags, except that bit 3 shows when Ctrl-NumLock is currently active.

Installing the Program. The memory resident code must be installed in memory before it will work. From that point on, all keyboard input is filtered through the program. If the routine has any bugs, the keyboard will probably lock up and require you to cold-start the machine. Keyboard interrupt handlers are particularly hard to debug because we use the keyboard constantly when debugging programs. Professionals who regularly write TSR programs usually invest in hardware-assisted debuggers that maintain a trace buffer in protected memory. Often the most elusive bugs appear only when a program is running in real time, not when you are single-stepping through it. *Note: you must boot the computer in MS-DOS mode before installing this program.*

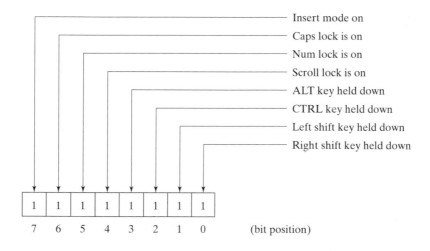

Figure 16-2   Keyboard Status Flag Byte.

Program Listing   In the following program listing, the installation code is located at the end because it will not remain resident in memory. The resident portion, beginning with the label **int9_handler**, is left in memory and pointed to by the INT 9h vector:

```
TITLE Reset-Disabling program                    (No_Reset.asm)

; This program disables the usual DOS reset command
; (Ctrl-Alt-Del), by intercepting the INT 9 keyboard
; hardware interrupt.  It checks the shift status bits
; in the MS-DOS keyboard flag and changes any Ctrl-Alt-Del
; to Alt-Del. The computer can only be rebooted by
; typing Ctrl+Alt+Right shift+Del.  Assemble, link,
; and convert to a COM program by including the /T
; command on the Microsoft LINK command line.
; Boot into pure MS-DOS mode before running this program.

.model tiny
.code
    rt_shift     EQU 01h             ; Right shift key: bit 0
    ctrl_key     EQU 04h             ; CTRL key: bit 2
    alt_key      EQU 08h             ; ALT key: bit 3
    del_key      EQU 53h             ; scan code for DEL key
    kybd_port    EQU 60h             ; keyboard input port

    ORG    100h                      ; this is a COM program
start:
    jmp    setup                     ; jump to TSR installation

;    Memory-resident code begins here
int9_handler PROC FAR
    sti                              ; enable hardware interrupts
    pushf                            ; save regs & flags
    push   es
    push   ax
    push   di

;    Point ES:DI to the DOS keyboard flag byte:
L1: mov    ax,40h                    ; DOS data segment is at 40h
    mov    es,ax
    mov    di,17h                    ; location of keyboard flag
    mov    ah,es:[di]                ; copy keyboard flag into AH

;    Test for the CTRL and ALT keys:
L2: test   ah,ctrl_key               ; CTRL key held down?
    jz     L5                        ; no: exit
    test   ah,alt_key                ; ALT key held down?
    jz     L5                        ; no: exit

;    Test for the DEL and Right-shift keys:
L3: in     al,kybd_port              ; read keyboard port
    cmp    al,del_key                ; DEL key pressed?
```

```
        jne    L5                      ; no: exit
        test   ah,rt_shift             ; right shift key pressed?
        jnz    L5                      ; yes: allow system reset

L4: and    ah,NOT ctrl_key             ; no: turn off bit for CTRL
    mov    es:[di],ah                  ; store keyboard_flag

L5: pop    di                          ; restore regs & flags
    pop    ax
    pop    es
    popf
    jmp    cs:[old_interrupt9]         ; jump to INT 9 routine

old_interrupt9 DWORD ?

int9_handler ENDP
end_ISR label BYTE

; --------------- (end of TSR program) ------------------
;    Save a copy of the original INT 9 vector, and set up
;    the address of our program as the new vector.  Terminate
;    this program and leave the int9_handler procedure in memory.

setup:
    mov ax,3509h                ; get INT 9 vector
    int 21h
    mov word ptr old_interrupt9,bx      ; save INT 9 vector
    mov word ptr old_interrupt9+2,es

    mov ax,2509h                ; set INT 9 vector
    mov dx,offset int9_handler
    int 21h

    mov ax,3100h                ; terminate and stay resident
    mov dx,OFFSET end_ISR       ; point to end of resident code
    shr dx,4                    ; divide by 16
    inc dx                      ; round upward to next paragraph
    int 21h                     ; execute MS-DOS function
END start
```

First let's look at the instructions that install the program. At the label called **setup**, we call INT 21h Function 35h to get the current INT 9h vector, which is then stored in **old_interrupt9**. This is done so the program will be able to forward-chain to the existing keyboard handler procedure. In the same part of the program, INT 21h Function 25h sets interrupt vector 9h to the address of the resident portion of this program. At the end of the program, the call to INT 21h Function 31h exits to MS-DOS, leaving the resident program in memory. The function automatically saves everything from the beginning of the PSP to the offset placed in DX.

The Resident Program   The memory-resident interrupt handler begins at the label named
int9_handler. It is executed every time a keyboard key is pressed. We reenable interrupts as
soon as the handler gets control, because the 8259 PIC has automatically disabled interrupts:

```
int9_handler PROC far
    sti                      ; enable hardware interrupts
    pushf                    ; save registers and status flags
    (etc...)
```

Bear in mind that a keyboard interrupt often occurs while another program is executing. If we
modified the registers or status flags here, we would cause unpredictable results in an application program.

The following statements locate the keyboard flag byte stored at address 0040:0017 and
copy it into AH. The byte must be tested to see which keys are currently being held down:

```
L1: mov ax,40h               ; MS-DOS data segment is at 40h
    mov es,ax
    mov di,17h               ; location of keyboard flag
    mov ah,es:[di]           ; copy keyboard flag into AH
```

The following statements check for both the Ctrl and Alt keys. If both are not currently
held down, we exit:

```
L2: test ah,ctrl_key         ; CTRL key held down?
    jz L5                    ; no: exit
    test ah,alt_key          ; ALT key held down?
    jz L5                    ; no: exit
```

If the Ctrl and Alt keys are both held down, someone may be trying to boot the computer.
To find out which character was pressed, we input the character from the keyboard port and
compare it to the Del key:

```
L3: in    al,kybd_port       ; read keyboard port
    cmp   al,del_key         ; Del key pressed?
    jne   L5                 ; no: exit
    test  ah,rt_shift        ; Right-Shift key pressed?
    jnz   L5                 ; yes: allow system reset
```

If the user has not pressed the Del key, we simply exit and let INT 9h process the keystroke. If the Del key is held down, we know that Ctrl-Alt-Del was pressed; we only allow the
system to be reset if the user is also holding down the Right Shift key. Otherwise, the Ctrl key
bit in the keyboard flag byte is cleared, effectively disabling the user's attempt to reboot the
computer:

```
L4: and ah,NOT ctrl_key          ; no: turn off bit for CTRL
    mov es:[di],ah               ; store keyboard_flag
```

Finally, we execute a far jump to the existing BIOS INT 9h routine, stored in the variable **old_interrupt9**. This allows all normal keystrokes to be processed, which is vital to the computer's basic operation:

```
jmp cs:[old_interrupt9]            ; jump to INT 9 routine
```

16.4.6　Section Review

1. What default action is carried out by the *critical error handler*?
2. What is contained in each entry of the interrupt vector table?
3. At which address is the interrupt vector for INT 10h stored?
4. Which controller chip generates hardware interrupts?
5. Which instruction disables hardware interrupts?
6. Which instruction enables hardware interrupts?
7. Which IRQ level has the highest priority, 0 or 15?
8. Based on what you know about IRQ levels, if a program is in the process of creating a disk file and you press a key on the keyboard, when do you think the key will be placed in the keyboard buffer—before or after the file has been created?
9. When a key is pressed on the keyboard, which hardware interrupt is executed?
10. When an interrupt handler finishes, how does the CPU resume execution wherever it was before the interrupt was triggered?
11. Which MS-DOS functions get and set interrupt vectors?
12. Explain the difference between an interrupt handler and a memory-resident program.
13. Describe a TSR program.
14. How can a TSR program be removed from memory?
15. If a memory resident program replaces one of the interrupt vectors, how can it still take advantage of some functions in the interrupt's existing handler?
16. Which MS-DOS function terminates a program and leaves part of the program resident in memory?
17. In the No_reset program, what key combination will actually boot the computer?

16.5　Chapter Summary

There are a few occasions when programmers need to create explicit segment definitions, particularly when adapting to existing code libraries that use their own segment names. The SEGMENT and ENDS directives define the beginning and end of a segment. When the segment being defined is combined with another segment, its align type tells the linker how many bytes to skip. The combine type tells the linker how to combine segments having the same name. A segment's class type provides yet another way of combining segments. Multiple segments may be combined by giving them the same name and specifying a PUBLIC combine type.

The ASSUME directive makes it possible for the assembler to calculate the offsets of labels and variables at assembly time. A segment override instruction instructs the processor to use a different segment register from the default segment.

The MS-DOS command processor interprets each command typed at a command prompt. Programs with extensions of COM and EXE are called *transient programs*. They are loaded into memory, executed, and then the memory they occupy is released. MS-DOS creates a special 256-byte block at the beginning of a transient program named the *program segment prefix*.

There are two types of transient programs, depending on the extension used: COM and EXE. A COM program is an unmodified binary image of a machine-language program. An EXE program is stored on disk with an EXE header followed by a load module containing the program itself. The header area of an EXE program is used by MS-DOS to correctly calculate the addresses of segments and other components.

Interrupt handlers (interrupt service routines) simplify input/output as well as basic system tasks. You can also replace the default interrupt handlers with your own code in order to provide more complete or customized services. The interrupt vector table is located in the first 1,024 bytes of RAM (locations 0:0 through 0:03FF). Each entry in the table is a 32-bit segment-offset address that points to an interrupt service routine.

A hardware interrupt is generated by the 8259 Programmable Interrupt Controller (PIC), which signals the CPU to suspend execution of the current program and execute an interrupt service routine. Hardware interrupts allow important events in the background to be noticed by the CPU before essential data are lost. Interrupts can be triggered by a number of different devices, each having a priority based on its interrupt request level (IRQ).

The Interrupt flag controls the way the CPU responds to external (hardware) interrupts. If the Interrupt flag is set, interrupts are enabled; if the flag is clear, interrupts are disabled. The STI (set interrupt) instruction enables interrupts; the CLI (clear interrupt) instruction disables interrupts.

A terminate and stay resident (TSR) program leaves part of itself in memory. The most common use for TSR programs is for installed interrupt handlers that remain in memory until the computer is rebooted or the TSR is removed by a special uninstaller.

The No_reset program presented at the end of this chapter is a TSR program that prevents the system from being rebooted by the usual Ctrl-Alt-Delete keys.

A

Installing and Using the Assembler

A.1   Installing the Book's CD-ROM

To install the book's CD-ROM, run **setup** from the root directory. The CD-ROM attached to this book contains the following software:

- *Microsoft Macro Assembler*, version 6.15. By default, this is installed in the C:\Masm615 directory.
- Microsoft 16-bit and 32-bit linkers (*link.exe* and *link32.exe*). By default, they are installed in the C:\Masm615 subdirectory.
- Evaluation copy of the **TextPad** editor, by Helios Software. To install TextPad, run the *TextPad4.exe* program in the \TextPad directory.
- All examples programs from this book. By default, they are installed in the Examples subdirectory.
- Chapter 17, a supplemental chapter, stored as an Adobe Acrobat file, located on the CD-ROM with this book.
- Batch files for assembling, linking, and debugging. By default, they are installed in the same directory as MASM. Following is a list:

make32.bat	Assembles and links 32-bit Protected mode programs.
make16.bat	Assembles and links 16-bit Real-address mode programs.
runCV.bat	Runs the Microsoft CodeView 16-bit debugger.
runQH.bat	Runs the Microsoft QuickHelp utility, which displays help information for the assembler, linker, CodeView, and other utilities.

- Link libraries for use with the sample programs. By default, they are installed in the LIB subdirectory. They include *kernel32.lib, user32.lib, irvine32.lib,* and *irvine16.lib*.

- Include files for use with the sample programs. By default, they are installed in the INCLUDE subdirectory. *Irvine32.inc, Irvine16.inc, SmallWin.inc, GraphWin.inc, macros.inc,* and *win.inc*.
- Various utility programs supplied with the Microsoft assembler, such as *cref.exe, cvpack.exe,* and *nmake.exe*. They are in the same directory as MASM.

A.2   Assembling and Linking 32-Bit Protected Mode Programs

Use the *make32.bat* batch file to assemble and link Protected mode assembly language programs. Following is the syntax, which is not case-sensitive:

```
make32 progname
```

Progname is the name of an assembly language source file, minus the extension. The following command assembles and links a source file named *AddSub.asm*:

```
make32 AddSub
```

Assuming that no errors were generated, the following files would be created in the current directory:

AddSub.obj	Object file
AddSub.lst	Listing file
AddSub.exe	Executable file

You must have a copy of *make32.bat* in the same directory as your source file before you run the **make32** command. You can copy *make32.bat* from the assembler's install directory.

There are two ways to execute the **make32** command:

1. Change to the directory where your source file (such as *AddSub.asm*) is located, and type the following at the command prompt:

   ```
   make32 AddSub
   ```

2. Alternatively, you can use an editor such as **Helios TextPad** to edit and assemble your source file. An evaluation copy of TextPad is provided on the book's CD-ROM. See our Web site for details on setting up TextPad.

A.2.1   Debugging Protected Mode Programs

The Microsoft Assembler package does not include a 32-bit debugger, but you can use either the Microsoft Developer Studio debugger (msdev.exe) supplied with Microsoft Visual C++ 6.0, or you can download **Windows Debugger** from the Microsoft Web site. Look for specific information on the topic: **Debugging 32-bit Programs** on our Web site for more details.

A.2.2   The make32.bat File

A *batch file* is a text file that contains commands that execute as if they were typed at the MS-DOS command prompt. It must have a BAT filename extension, and it can be executed either from the command prompt or from another program.

Table A-1 contains an annotated listing of *make32.bat*. Two of the commands in the left column of the table (REM and LINK32) wrap around in the table because of their length. In the batch file, however, they each occupy a single line.

Table A-1   Batch File Description (*make32.bat*).

Batch File Command	Description
REM Make32.bat, for assembling and linking Protected mode programs	Any line beginning with REM is a comment line that documents the batch file. REM does not execute.
PATH C:\Masm615	Set environment path to the C:\Masm615 directory. This enables the operating system to locate the ML and LINK32 programs.
SET INCLUDE=C:\Masm615\INCLUDE	Set the INCLUDE environment variable. This allows the INCLUDE directive in assembly language programs to locate certain files. For example, we use the *Irvine32.inc* file.
SET LIB=C:\Masm615\LIB	Set the LIB environment variable. This enables the linker to locate the library files used by our programs, such as *Irvine32.lib*.
ML -Zi -c -Fl -coff %1.asm	Invoke the Microsoft assembler (ML.EXE).
IF errorlevel 1 goto terminate	If the previous command generated an error, jump to the label named **terminate** (last line of the file).
LINK32 %1.obj Irvine32.lib kernel32.lib /SUBSYSTEM:CONSOLE /DEBUG	Invoke the Microsoft 32-bit linker (LINK32.EXE). Two library files are specified here: *Irvine32.lib* and *kernel32.lib*.
IF errorLevel 1 goto terminate	If the previous command generated an error, jump to the label named **terminate**.
DIR %1.*	Display a list of all files produced by the assembler and linker, as well as the source file being assembled.
:terminate	This label acts as a place marker for GOTO commands.

Your copy of *make32.bat* may have a different directory name for the assembler and linker because of the setup requirements in your computer laboratory. For example, if the assembler were located in the D:\Apps\Masm615 directory, the following three batch file commands would be changed accordingly:

```
SET PATH=D:\Apps\Masm615
SET INCLUDE=D:\Apps\Masm615\include
SET LIB=D:\Apps\Masm615\lib
```

A.3   Assembling and Linking 16-Bit Real-Address Mode Programs

To assemble and link a 16-bit Real-address mode program, use the *make16* command. For example, if your program is named *AddSub.asm*, use the following command at the MS-DOS prompt:

```
make16 AddSub
```

> You must have a copy of *make16.bat* in the same directory as your source file before you run the make16 command. You can copy the file from the assembler's install directory.

You can run the Microsoft **CodeView** debugger with the *AddSub* program by typing the following command at the MS-DOS prompt:

```
C:\Masm615\runCV AddSub
```

CodeView will load *AddSub.exe* into memory, display its source code (from *AddSub.asm*), and let you trace and debug the program's execution. Be sure to check the book's Web site for a tutorial on using CodeView.

> The 16-bit linker only recognizes filenames having eight or fewer characters (not including the extension). Also, none of the directory names along your program's path can be more than eight characters long.

Table A-2 contains an annotated listing of *make16.bat*. Two of the commands in the left column of the table (REM and LINK) wrap around in the table because of their length. In the batch file, however, they occupy a single line. For a detailed description of the command line arguments passed to the assembler and linker, refer to Appendix D.

Table A-2   Batch File Description (*make16.bat*).

Batch File Command	Description
REM Make16.bat, for assembling and linking Real-address mode programs	Any line beginning with REM is a comment line that documents the batch file. REM does not execute.

Table A-2   Batch File Description (*make16.bat*). (Continued)

Batch File Command	Description
`PATH C:\Masm615`	Set environment path to the C:\Masm615 directory. This enables the operating system to locate the ML and LINK programs.
`SET INCLUDE=C:\Masm615\INCLUDE`	Set the INCLUDE environment variable. This allows the INCLUDE directive in assembly language programs to locate include files. For example, we use the *Irvine16.inc* file.
`SET LIB=C:\Masm615\LIB`	Set the LIB environment variable. This enables the linker to locate the library files used by our programs, such as *Irvine16.lib*.
`ML /nologo -c -Fl -Zi %1.asm`	Invoke the Microsoft assembler (ML.EXE).
`IF errorlevel 1 goto terminate`	If the previous command generated an error, jump to the label named **terminate** (last line of the file).
`LINK /nologo /CODEVIEW %1,,NUL,Irvine16;`	Invoke the Microsoft 16-bit linker. A single library file is specified here: *Irvine16.lib*.
`IF errorLevel 1 goto terminate`	If the previous command generated an error, jump to the label named **terminate**.
`DIR %1.*`	Display a list of all files produced by the assembler and linker, as well as the source file being assembled.
`:terminate`	Label acts as a place marker for GOTO commands.

B

The Intel Instruction Set

B.1 Introduction

This appendix is a quick guide to all real-mode instructions in the Intel IA-32 processor family.

B.1.1 Flags

Each instruction description contains a series of boxes that describe how the instruction will affect the CPU status flags. Each flag is identified by a single letter:

O	Overflow	S	Sign	P	Parity
D	Direction	Z	Zero	C	Carry
I	Interrupt	A	Auxiliary Carry		

Inside the boxes, the following notation shows how each instruction will affect the flags:

1	Sets the flag.
0	Clears the flag.
?	May change the flag to an undetermined value.
(blank)	The flag is not changed.
*	Changes the flag according to specific rules associated with the flag.

For example, the following diagram of the CPU flags is taken from one of the instruction descriptions:

O	D	I	S	Z	A	P	C
?			?	?	*	?	*

From the diagram, we see that the Overflow, Sign, Zero, and Parity flags will be changed to unknown values. The Auxiliary Carry and Carry flags will be modified according to rules associated with the flags. The Direction and Interrupt flags will not be changed.

B.1.2 Instruction Descriptions and Formats

When a reference to source and destination operands is made, we use the natural order of operands in all Intel 80x86 instructions, in which the first operand is the destination and the second is the source. In the MOV instruction, for example, the destination will be assigned a copy of the data in the source operand:

```
MOV destination, source
```

There may be several formats available for a single instruction. Table B-1 contains a list of symbols used in instruction formats. In the descriptions of individual instructions, we use the notation "(IA-32)" to indicate that an instruction or one of its variants is only available on processors in the IA-32 family (Intel386 onward). Similarly, the notation "(80286)" indicates that at least an 80286 processor must be used.

Register notations such as (E)CX, (E)SI, (E)DI, (E)SP, (E)BP, and (E)IP differentiate between IA-32 processors that use the 32-bit registers and all earlier processors that used 16-bit registers.

Table B-1 Symbols Used in Instruction Formats.

Symbol	Description
reg	An 8-, 16-, or 32-bit general register from the following list: AH, AL, BH, BL, CH, CL, AX, BX, CX, DX, SI, DI, BP, SP, EAX, EBX, ECX, EDX, ESI, EDI, EBP, and ESP.
reg8, reg16, reg32	A general register, identified by its number of bits.
segreg	A 16-bit segment register (CS, DS, ES, SS, FS, GS).
accum	AL, AX, or EAX.
mem	A memory operand, using any of the standard memory addressing modes.
mem8, mem16, mem32	A memory operand, identified by its number of bits.
shortlabel	A location in the code segment within −128 to +127 bytes of the current location.
nearlabel	A location in the current code segment, identified by a label.
farlabel	A location in an external code segment, identified by a label.
imm	An immediate operand.
imm8, imm16, imm32	An immediate operand, identified by its number of bits.
instruction	An Intel assembly language instruction.

B.2   The Instruction Set

AAA	**ASCII Adjust After Addition**
	O D I S Z A P C ? ? ? * ? *
	Adjusts the result in AL after two ASCII digits have been added together. If AL > 9, the high digit of the result is placed in AH, and the Carry and Auxiliary Carry flags are set. Instruction Format: AAA

AAD	**ASCII Adjust Before Division**
	O D I S Z A P C ? * * ? * ?
	Converts unpacked BCD digits in AH and AL to a single binary value in preparation for the DIV instruction. Instruction Format: AAD

AAM	**ASCII Adjust After Multiply**
	O D I S Z A P C ? * * ? * ?
	Adjusts the result in AX after two unpacked BCD digits have been multiplied together. Instruction Format: AAM

AAS	**ASCII Adjust After Subtraction**
	O D I S Z A P C ? ? ? * ? *
	Adjusts the result in AX after a subtraction operation. If AL > 9, AAS decrements AH and sets the Carry and Auxiliary Carry flags. Instruction Format: AAS

		ADC	**Add Carry**

O	D	I	S	Z	A	P	C
*			*	*	*	*	*

Adds both the source operand and the Carry flag to the destination operand. Operands must be the same size.

Instruction Formats:

```
ADC   reg,reg              ADC   reg,imm
ADC   mem,reg              ADC   mem,imm
ADC   reg,mem              ADC   accum,imm
```

ADD   **Add**

O	D	I	S	Z	A	P	C
*			*	*	*	*	*

A source operand is added to a destination operand, and the sum is stored in the destination. Operands must be the same size.

Instruction Formats:

```
ADD   reg,reg              ADD   reg,imm
ADD   mem,reg              ADD   mem,imm
ADD   reg,mem              ADD   accum,imm
```

AND   **Logical AND**

O	D	I	S	Z	A	P	C
*			*	*	?	*	0

Each bit in the destination operand is ANDed with the corresponding bit in the source operand.

Instruction Formats:

```
AND   reg,reg              ADD   reg,imm
AND   mem,reg              ADD   mem,imm
AND   reg,mem              ADD   accum,imm
```

BOUND	**Check Array Bounds (80286)**
	O D I S Z A P C

Verifies that a signed index value is within the bounds of an array. On the 80286 processor, the destination operand can be any 16-bit register containing the index to be checked. The source operand must be a 32-bit memory operand in which the high and low words contain the upper and lower bounds of the index value. On the IA-32, the destination can be a 32-bit register and the source can be a 64-bit memory operand.

Instruction Formats:

```
BOUND   reg16,mem32          BOUND   reg32,mem64
```

BSF, BSR	**Bit Scan (IA-32)**
	O D I S Z A P C
	*

Scans an operand to find the first set bit. If the bit is found, the Zero flag is cleared and the destination operand is assigned the bit number (index) of the first set bit encountered. If no set bit is found, ZF = 1. BSF scans from bit 0 to the highest bit, and BSR starts at the highest bit and scans toward bit 0.

Instruction Formats (apply to both BSF and BSR):

```
BSF reg16,r/m16          BSF reg32,r/m32
```

BSWAP	**Byte Swap (IA-32)**
	O D I S Z A P C

Reverses the byte order of a 32-bit destination register.

Instruction Format:

```
BSWAP reg32
```

BT, BTC, BTR, BTS

Bit Tests (IA-32)

O	D	I	S	Z	A	P	C
							*

Copies a specified bit (*n*) into the Carry flag. The destination operand contains the value in which the bit is located, and the source operand indicates the bit's position within the destination. BT copies bit *n* to the Carry flag. BTC copies bit *n* to the Carry flag and complements bit *n* in the destination operand. BTR copies bit *n* to the Carry flag and clears bit *n* in the destination. BTS copies bit *n* to the Carry flag and sets bit *n* in the destination.

Instruction Formats:

```
BT  r/m16,imm8              BT  r/m16,r16
BT  r/m32,imm8              BT  r/m32,r32
```

CALL

Call a Procedure

O	D	I	S	Z	A	P	C

Pushes the location of the next instruction on the stack and transfers to the destination location. If the procedure is *near* (in the same segment), only the offset of the next instruction is pushed; otherwise, both the segment and the offset are pushed.

Instruction Formats:

```
CALL   nearlabel            CALL   mem16
CALL   farlabel             CALL   mem32
CALL   reg
```

CBW

Convert Byte to Word

O	D	I	S	Z	A	P	C

Extends the sign bit in AL throughout the AH register.

Instruction Format:

```
CBW
```

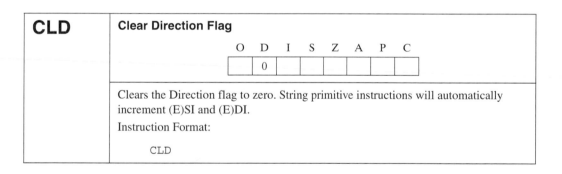

CDQ | **Convert Doubleword to Quadword (IA-32)**

O	D	I	S	Z	A	P	C

Extends the sign bit in EAX throughout the EDX register.
Instruction Format:

    CDQ

CLC | **Clear Carry Flag**

O	D	I	S	Z	A	P	C
							0

Clears the Carry flag to zero.
Instruction Format:

    CLC

CLD | **Clear Direction Flag**

O	D	I	S	Z	A	P	C
	0						

Clears the Direction flag to zero. String primitive instructions will automatically
increment (E)SI and (E)DI.
Instruction Format:

    CLD

CLI | **Clear Interrupt Flag**

O	D	I	S	Z	A	P	C
		0					

Clears the Interrupt flag to zero. This disables maskable hardware interrupts until an
STI instruction is executed.
Instruction Format:

    CLI

| CMC | **Complement Carry Flag** |

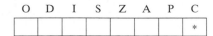

O	D	I	S	Z	A	P	C
							*

Toggles the current value of the Carry flag.

Instruction Format:

```
CMC
```

| CMP | **Compare** |

O	D	I	S	Z	A	P	C
*			*	*	*	*	*

Compares the destination to the source by performing an implied subtraction of the source from the destination.

Instruction Formats:

```
CMP    reg,reg              CMP    reg,imm
CMP    mem,reg              CMP    mem,imm
CMP    reg,mem              CMP    accum,imm
```

| CMPS, CMPSB, CMPSW, CMPSD | **Compare Strings** |

O	D	I	S	Z	A	P	C
*			*	*	*	*	*

Compares strings in memory addressed by DS:(E)SI and ES:(E)DI. Carries out an implied subtraction of the destination from the source. CMPSB compares bytes, CMPSW compares words, and CMPSD compares doublewords (on IA-32 processors). (E)SI and (E)DI are increased or decreased according to the operand size and the status of the direction flag. If the Direction flag is set, (E)SI and (E)DI are decreased; otherwise (E)SI and (E)DI are increased.

Instruction Formats (formats using explicit operands have intentionally been omitted):

```
CMPSB                       CMPSW
CMPSD
```

CMPXCHG	**Compare and Exchange**
	O D I S Z A P C
	* * * * * *

Compares the destination to the accumulator (AL, AX, or EAX). If they are equal, the source is copied to the destination. Otherwise, the destination is copied to the accumulator.

Instruction Formats:

    CMPXCHG reg,reg   CMPXCHG mem,reg

CWDE	**Convert Word to Extended Double (IA-32)**
	O D I S Z A P C

Extends the sign bit in AX into the upper word of the EAX register.

Instruction Format:

    CWDE

DAA	**Decimal Adjust After Addition**
	O D I S Z A P C
	? * * * * *

Adjusts the binary sum in AL after two packed BCD values have been added. Converts the sum to two BCD digits in AL.

Instruction Format:

    DAA

DAS	**Decimal Adjust After Subtraction**
	O D I S Z A P C
	? * * * * *

Converts the binary result of a subtraction operation to two packed BCD digits in AL.

Instruction Format:

    DAS

DEC

Decrement

O	D	I	S	Z	A	P	C
*			*	*	*	*	

Subtracts 1 from an operand. Does not affect the Carry flag.

Instruction Formats:

```
DEC   reg                         DEC   mem
```

DIV

Unsigned Integer Divide

O	D	I	S	Z	A	P	C
?			?	?	?	?	?

Performs either 8-, 16-, or 32-bit unsigned integer division. If the divisor is 8 bits, the dividend is AX, the quotient is AL, and the remainder is AH. If the divisor is 16 bits, the dividend is DX:AX, the quotient is AX, and the remainder is DX. If the divisor is 32 bits, the dividend is EDX:EAX, the quotient is EAX, and the remainder is EDX.

Instruction Formats:

```
DIV   reg                         DIV   mem
```

ENTER

Make Stack Frame (80286)

O	D	I	S	Z	A	P	C
?			*	*	*	*	*

Creates a stack frame for a procedure that receives stack parameters and uses local stack variables. The first operand indicates the number of bytes to reserve for local stack variables. The second operand indicates the procedure nesting level (must be set to 0 for C, Basic, and FORTRAN).

Instruction Format:

```
ENTER imm16,imm8
```

HLT

Halt

O	D	I	S	Z	A	P	C

Stops the CPU until a hardware interrupt occurs. (*Note:* The Interrupt flag must be set with the STI instruction before hardware interrupts can occur.)

Instruction Format:

```
HLT
```

IDIV	**Signed Integer Divide**

O	D	I	S	Z	A	P	C
?			?	?	?	?	?

Performs a signed integer division operation on EDX:EAX, DX:AX, or AX. If the divisor is 8 bits, the dividend is AX, the quotient is AL, and the remainder is AH. If the divisor is 16 bits, the dividend is DX:AX, the quotient is AX, and the remainder is DX. If the divisor is 32 bits, the dividend is EDX:EAX, the quotient is EAX, and the remainder is EDX. Usually the IDIV operation is prefaced by either CBW or CWD to sign-extend the dividend.

Instruction Formats:

```
    IDIV  reg                          IDIV  mem
```

IMUL	**Signed Integer Multiply**

O	D	I	S	Z	A	P	C
*			?	?	?	?	*

Performs a signed integer multiplication on AL, AX, or EAX. If the multiplier is 8 bits, the multiplicand is AL and the product is AX. If the multiplier is 16 bits, the multiplicand is AX and the product is DX:AX. If the multiplier is 32 bits, the multiplicand is EAX and the product is EDX:EAX. The Carry and Overflow flags are set if a 16-bit product extends into AH, or a 32-bit product extends into DX, or a 64-bit product extends into EDX.

Instruction Formats:

Single operand:

```
    IMUL  r/m8                         IMUL  r/m16
    IMUL  r/m32
```

Two operands:

```
    IMUL  r16,r/m16                    IMUL  r16,imm8
    IMUL  r32,r/m32                    IMUL  r32,imm8
    IMUL  r16,imm16                    IMUL  r32,imm32
```

Three operands:

```
    IMUL  r16,r/m16,imm8               IMUL  r16,r/m16,imm16
    IMUL  r32,r/m32,imm8               IMUL  r32,r/m32,imm32
```

IN — Input from Port

O	D	I	S	Z	A	P	C

Inputs a byte or word from a port into AL or AX. The source operand is a port address, expressed as either an 8-bit constant or a 16-bit address in DX. On the IA-32, a doubleword can be input from a port into EAX.

Instruction Formats:

```
IN   accum,imm                 IN   accum,DX
```

INC — Increment

O	D	I	S	Z	A	P	C
*			*	*	*	*	

Adds 1 to a register or memory operand.

Instruction Formats:

```
INC   reg                      INC   mem
```

INS, INSB, INSW, INSD — Input from Port to String (80286)

O	D	I	S	Z	A	P	C

Inputs a string pointed to by ES:(E)DI from a port. The port number is specified in DX. For each value received, (E)DI is adjusted in the same way as LODSB and similar string primitive instructions. The REP prefix may be used with this instruction.

Instruction Formats:

```
INS  dest,DX                   REP  INSB dest,DX
REP  INSW dest,DX              REP  INSD dest,DX
```

INT — Interrupt

O	D	I	S	Z	A	P	C
		0					

Generates a software interrupt, which in turn calls an operating system subroutine. Clears the Interrupt flag and pushes the flags, CS, and IP on the stack before branching to the interrupt routine.

Instruction Formats:

```
INT   imm                      INT   3
```

INTO	**Interrupt on Overflow**
	O D I S Z A P C □ □ * * □ □ □ □
	Generates internal CPU Interrupt 4 if the Overflow flag is set. No action is taken by MS-DOS if INT 4 is called, but a user-written routine may be substituted instead. Instruction Format: `INTO`

IRET	**Interrupt Return**
	O D I S Z A P C * * * * * * * *
	Returns from an interrupt handling routine. Pops the stack into (E)IP, CS, and the flags. Instruction Format: `IRET`

Jcondition	**Conditional Jump**
	O D I S Z A P C □ □ □ □ □ □ □ □
	Jumps to a label if a specified flag condition is true. Prior to the IA-32 processor, the label must be in the range of −128 to +127 bytes from the current location. On IA-32 processors, the label must be in the range of −32,768 to +32,767 bytes from the current location. See Table B-2 for a list of mnemonics. Instruction Format: *Jcondition label*

Table B-2 Conditional Jump Mnemonics.

Mnemonic	Comment	Mnemonic	Comment
JA	jump if above	JE	jump if equal
JNA	jump if not above	JNE	jump if not equal
JAE	jump if above or equal	JZ	jump if zero
JNAE	jump if not above or equal	JNZ	jump if not zero
JB	jump if below	JS	jump if sign

Table B-2   Conditional Jump Mnemonics. (Continued)

Mnemonic	Comment	Mnemonic	Comment
JNB	jump if not below	JNS	jump if not sign
JBE	jump if below or equal	JC	jump if carry
JNBE	jump if not below or equal	JNC	jump if no carry
JG	jump if greater	JO	jump if overflow
JNG	jump if not greater	JNO	jump if no overflow
JGE	jump if greater or equal	JP	jump if parity
JNGE	jump if not greater or equal	JPE	jump if parity equal
JL	jump if less	JNP	jump if no parity
JNL	jump if not less	JPO	jump if parity odd
JLE	jump if less or equal	JNLE	jump if not less than or equal

JCXZ, JECXZ	**Jump If CX Is Zero**
	O D I S Z A P C

	Jump to a short label if the CX register is equal to zero. The short label must be in the range −128 to +127 bytes from the next instruction. On the IA-32 processor, JECXZ jumps if ECX equals zero.
	Instruction Formats:
	`    JCXZ   label              JECXZ label`

JMP	**Jump Unconditionally to Label**
	O D I S Z A P C
	Jump to a code label. A short jump is within −127 to +127 bytes from the current location. A near jump is within the same code segment, and a far jump is outside the current segment.
	Instruction Formats:

	`    JMP   shortlabel          JMP   reg16`
	`    JMP   nearlabel           JMP   mem16`
	`    JMP   farlabel            JMP   mem32`

LAHF	**Load AH from Flags**
	O D I S Z A P C
	☐ ☐ ☐ ☐ ☐ ☐ ☐ ☐
	The lowest 8 bits of the flags are transferred, but not the Trap, Interrupt, Overflow, Direction, or Sign flags.
	Instruction Format:
	`LAHF`

LDS, **LES,** **LFS,** **LGS,** **LSS**	**Load Far Pointer**
	O D I S Z A P C
	☐ ☐ ☐ ☐ ☐ ☐ ☐ ☐
	Loads the contents of a doubleword memory operand into a segment register and the specified destination register. Prior to the IA-32 processor, LDS loads into DS, LES loads into ES. On the IA-32 processor, LFS loads into FS, LGS loads into GS, and LSS loads into SS.
	Instruction Format (same for LDS, LES, LFS, LGS, LSS):
	`LDS    reg,mem`

LEA	**Load Effective Address**
	O D I S Z A P C
	☐ ☐ ☐ ☐ ☐ ☐ ☐ ☐
	Calculates and loads the 16-bit or 32-bit effective address of a memory operand. Similar to MOV..OFFSET, except that only LEA can obtain an address that is calculated at run time.
	Instruction Format:
	`LEA    reg,mem`

LEAVE	**High-Level Procedure Exit**
	O D I S Z A P C
	☐ ☐ ☐ ☐ ☐ ☐ ☐ ☐
	Terminates the stack frame of a procedure. This reverses the action of the ENTER instruction at the beginning of a procedure by restoring (E)SP and (E)BP to their original values.
	Instruction Format:
	`LEAVE`

LOCK	**Lock the System Bus**
	O D I S Z A P C
	Prevents other processors from executing during the next instruction.This instruction is used when another processor might modify a memory operand that is currently being accessed by the CPU.
	Instruction Format:
	``` LOCK instruction ```

LODS, LODSB, LODSW, LODSD	**Load Accumulator from String**
	O D I S Z A P C
	Loads a memory byte or word addressed by DS:(E)SI into the accumulator (AL, AX, or EAX). If LODS is used, the memory operand must be specified. LODSB loads a byte into AL, LODSW loads a word into AX, and LODSD on the IA-32 loads a doubleword into EAX. (E)SI is increased or decreased according to the operand size and the status of the direction flag. If the Direction flag (DF) = 1, (E)SI is decreased; if DF = 0, (E)SI is increased.
	Instruction Formats:
	``` LODS mem LODSB LODS segreg:mem LODSW LODSD ```

LOOP, LOOPW	**Loop**
	O D I S Z A P C
	Decrements (E)CX and jumps to a short label if (E)CX is greater than zero. The destination must be −128 to +127 bytes from the current location. On IA-32 processors, ECX is used as the default loop counter.
	Instruction Format:
	``` LOOP shortlabel LOOPW shortlabel ```

LOOPD

Loop (IA-32)

O	D	I	S	Z	A	P	C

Decrements ECX and jumps to a short label if ECX is greater than zero. The destination must be –128 to +127 bytes from the current location.

Instruction Format:

```
LOOPD shortlabel
```

LOOPE, LOOPZ

Loop If Equal (Zero)

O	D	I	S	Z	A	P	C

Decrements (E)CX and jumps to a short label if (E)CX > 0 and the Zero flag is set.

Instruction Formats:

```
LOOPE shortlabel          LOOPZ shortlabel
```

LOOPNE, LOOPNZ

Loop If Not Equal (Zero)

O	D	I	S	Z	A	P	C

Decrements (E)CX and jumps to a short label if (E)CX > 0 and the Zero flag is clear.

Instruction Formats:

```
LOOPNE shortlabel          LOOPNZ shortlabel
```

MOV

Move

O	D	I	S	Z	A	P	C

Copies a byte or word from a source operand to a destination operand.

Instruction Formats:

```
MOV reg,reg              MOV reg,imm
MOV mem,reg              MOV mem,imm
MOV reg,mem              MOV mem16,segreg
MOV reg16,segreg         MOV segreg,mem16
MOV segreg,reg16
```

MOVS, MOVSB, MOVSW, MOVSD

Move String

O	D	I	S	Z	A	P	C

Copies a byte or word from memory addressed by DS:(E)SI to memory addressed by ES:(E)DI. MOVS requires both operands to be specified. MOVSB copies a byte, MOVSW copies a word, and on the IA-32, MOVSD copies a doubleword. (E)SI and (E)DI are increased or decreased according to the operand size and the status of the direction flag. If the Direction flag (DF) = 1, (E)SI and (E)DI are decreased; if DF = 0, (E)SI and (E)DI are increased.

Instruction Formats:

```
MOVSB
MOVSW
MOVSD
MOVS dest,source
MOVS ES:dest,segreg:source
```

MOVSX

Move with Sign-Extend

O	D	I	S	Z	A	P	C

Copies a byte or word from a source operand to a destination register and sign-extends into the upper half of the destination. This instruction is used to copy an 8-bit or 16-bit operand into a larger destination.

Instruction Formats:

```
MOVSX reg32,reg16          MOVSX reg32,mem16
MOVSX reg16,reg8           MOVSX reg16,m8
```

MOVZX

Move with Zero-Extend

O	D	I	S	Z	A	P	C

Copies a byte or word from a source operand to a destination register and zero-extends into the upper half of the destination. This instruction is used to copy an 8-bit or 16-bit operand into a larger destination.

Instruction Formats:

```
MOVZX reg32,reg16          MOVZX reg32,mem16
MOVZX reg16,reg8           MOVZX reg16,m8
```

MUL

Unsigned Integer Multiply

O	D	I	S	Z	A	P	C
*			?	?	?	?	*

Multiplies AL, AX, or EAX by a source operand. If the source is 8 bits, it is multiplied by AL and the product is stored in AX. If the source is 16 bits, it is multiplied by AX and the product is stored in DX:AX. If the source is 32 bits, it is multiplied by EAX and the product is stored in EDX:EAX.

Instruction Formats:

```
MUL reg                        MUL mem
```

NEG

Negate

O	D	I	S	Z	A	P	C
*			*	*	*	*	*

Calculates the twos complement of the destination operand, and stores the result in the destination.

Instruction Formats:

```
NEG reg                        NEG mem
```

NOP

No Operation

O	D	I	S	Z	A	P	C

This instruction does nothing, but it may be used inside a timing loop or to align a subsequent instruction on a word boundary.

Instruction Format:

```
NOP
```

NOT

Not

O	D	I	S	Z	A	P	C

Performs a logical NOT operation on an operand by reversing each of its bits.

Instruction Formats:

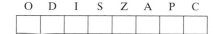

```
NOT  reg                        NOT  mem
```

OR	**Inclusive OR**

O	D	I	S	Z	A	P	C
0			*	*	?	*	0

Performs a boolean (bitwise) OR operation between each matching bit in the destination operand and each bit in the source operand.

Instruction Formats:

```
OR   reg,reg              OR   reg,imm
OR   mem,reg              OR   mem,imm
OR   reg,mem              OR   accum,imm
```

OUT	**Output to Port**

O	D	I	S	Z	A	P	C

Prior to the IA-32, this instruction outputs a byte or word from the accumulator to a port. The port address may be a constant if in the range 0–FFh, or DX may contain a port address between 0 and FFFFh. On an IA-32 processor, a doubleword can be output to a port.

Instruction Formats:

```
OUT   imm8,accum              OUT   DX,accum
```

OUTS, OUTSB, OUTSW, OUTSD	**Output String to Port (80286)**

O	D	I	S	Z	A	P	C

Outputs a string pointed to by ES:(E)DI to a port. The port number is specified in DX. For each value output, (E)DI is adjusted in the same way as LODSB and similar string primitive instructions. The REP prefix may be used with this instruction.

Instruction Formats:

```
OUTS dest,DX              REP OUTSB dest,DX
REP OUTSW dest,DX         REP OUTSD dest,DX
```

POP	**Pop from Stack**
	O D I S Z A P C 
	Copies a word or doubleword at the current stack pointer location into the destination operand, and adds 2 (or 4) to (E)SP.
	Instruction Formats:
	``` POP reg16/reg32 POP segreg POP mem16/mem32 ```

POPA, POPAD	**Pop All Flags from Stack**
	O D I S Z A P C 
	Pops 16 bytes from the top of the stack into the eight general-purpose registers, in the following order: DI, SI, BP, SP, BX, DX, CX, AX. The value for SP is discarded, so SP is not reassigned. POPA pops into 16-bit registers, and POPAD on the IA-32 pops into 32-bit registers.
	Instruction Formats:
	``` POPA POPAD ```

POPF, POPFD	**Pop Flags from Stack**
	O D I S Z A P C
	* * * * * * * *
	POPF pops the top of the stack into the 16-bit FLAGS register. POPFD on the IA-32 pops the top of the stack into the 32-bit EFLAGS register.
	Instruction Formats:
	``` POPF POPFD ```

PUSH	**Push on Stack**
	O D I S Z A P C 
	Subtracts 2 from (E)SP and copies the source operand into the stack location pointed to by (E)SP. From the 80186 onward, an immediate value can be pushed on the stack.
	Instruction Formats:
	``` PUSH reg16/reg32 PUSH segreg PUSH mem16/mem32 PUSH imm16/imm32 ```

PUSHA, PUSHAD

Push All (80286)

O	D	I	S	Z	A	P	C

Pushes the following 16-bit registers on the stack, in order: AX, CX, DX, BX, SP, BP, SI, and DI. The PUSHAD instruction for the IA-32 pushes EAX, ECX, EDX, EBX, ESP, EBP, ESI, and EDI.

Instruction Formats:

```
PUSHA                      PUSHAD
```

PUSHF, PUSHFD

Push Flags

O	D	I	S	Z	A	P	C

PUSHF pushes the 16-bit FLAGS register onto the stack. PUSHFD pushes the 32-bit EFLAGS onto the stack (IA-32).

Instruction Formats:

```
PUSHF                      PUSHFD
```

PUSHW, PUSHD

Push on Stack

O	D	I	S	Z	A	P	C

PUSHW pushes a 16-bit word on the stack, and on the IA-32, PUSHD pushes a 32-bit doubleword on the stack.

Instruction Formats:

```
PUSH    reg16/reg32           PUSH    segreg
PUSH    mem16/mem32           PUSH    imm16/imm32
```

RCL

Rotate Carry Left

O	D	I	S	Z	A	P	C
*							*

Rotates the destination operand left, using the source operand to determine the number of rotations. The Carry flag is copied into the lowest bit, and the highest bit is copied into the Carry flag. The *imm8* operand must be a 1 when using the 8086/8088 processor.

Instruction Formats:

```
RCL    reg,imm8              RCL    mem,imm8
RCL    reg,CL                RCL    mem,CL
```

RCR

Rotate Carry Right

```
O   D   I   S   Z   A   P   C
*                           *
```

Rotates the destination operand right, using the source operand to determine the number of rotations. The Carry flag is copied into the highest bit, and the lowest bit is copied into the Carry flag. The *imm8* operand must be a 1 when using the 8086/8088 processor.

Instruction Formats:

```
RCR   reg, imm8            RCR   mem, imm8
RCR   reg, CL              RCR   mem, CL
```

REP

Repeat String

```
O   D   I   S   Z   A   P   C
```

Repeats a string primitive instruction, using (E)CX as a counter. (E)CX is decremented each time the instruction is repeated, until (E)CX = 0.

Format (shown with MOVS):

```
REP MOVS dest, source
```

REP*condition*

Repeat String Conditionally

```
O   D   I   S   Z   A   P   C
                *
```

Repeats a string primitive instruction until (E)CX = 0 and while a flag condition is true. REPZ (REPE) repeats while the Zero flag is set, and REPZ (REPNE) repeats while the Zero flag is clear. Only SCAS and CMPS should be used with REP*condition,* because they are the only string primitives that modify the Zero flag.

Formats used with SCAS:

```
REPZ    SCAS    dest       REPNE   SCAS    dest
REPZ    SCASB              REPNE   SCASB
REPE    SCASW              REPNZ   SCASW
```

RET, RETN, RETF

Return from Procedure

O	D	I	S	Z	A	P	C

Pops a return address from the stack. RETN (return near) pops only the top of the stack into (E)IP. In Real-address mode, RETF (return far) pops the stack first into (E)IP, and then into CS. RET may be either near or far, depending on the attribute specified or implied by the PROC directive. An optional 8-bit immediate operand tells the CPU to add a value to (E)SP after popping the return address.

Instruction Formats:

```
RET                             RET     imm8
RETN                            RETN    imm8
RETF                            RETF    imm8
```

ROL

Rotate Left

O	D	I	S	Z	A	P	C
*							*

Rotates the destination operand left, using the source operand to determine the number of rotations. The highest bit is copied into the Carry flag and moved into the lowest bit position. The *imm8* operand must be a 1 when using the 8086/8088 processor.

Instruction Formats:

```
ROL   reg,imm8                  ROL   mem,imm8
ROL   reg,CL                    ROL   mem,CL
```

ROR

Rotate Right

O	D	I	S	Z	A	P	C
*							*

Rotates the destination operand right, using the source operand to determine the number of rotations. The lowest bit is copied into both the Carry flag and the highest bit position. The *imm8* operand must be a 1 when using the 8086/8088 processor.

Instruction Formats:

```
ROR   reg,imm8                  ROR   mem,imm8
ROR   reg,CL                    ROR   mem,CL
```

SAHF	**Store AH into Flags**

O	D	I	S	Z	A	P	C
			*	*	*	*	*

Copies AH into bits 0 through 7 of the Flags register.

Instruction Format:

```
SAHF
```

SAL	**Shift Arithmetic Left**

O	D	I	S	Z	A	P	C
*			*	*	?	*	*

Shifts each bit in the destination operand to the left, using the source operand to determine the number of shifts. The highest bit is copied into the Carry flag, and the lowest bit is filled with a zero. The *imm8* operand must be a 1 when using the 8086/8088 processor.

Instruction Formats:

```
SAL    reg,imm8          SAL    mem,imm8
SAL    reg,CL            SAL    mem,CL
```

SAR	**Shift Arithmetic Right**

O	D	I	S	Z	A	P	C
*			*	*	?	*	*

Shifts each bit in the destination operand to the right, using the source operand to determine the number of shifts. The lowest bit is copied into the Carry flag, and the highest bit retains its previous value. This shift is often used with signed operands, because it preserves the number's sign. The *imm8* operand must be a 1 when using the 8086/8088 processor.

Instruction Formats:

```
SAR    reg,imm8          SAR    mem,imm8
SAR    reg,CL            SAR    mem,CL
```

SBB	**Subtract with Borrow**
	O D I S Z A P C
	* * * * * *

Subtracts the source operand from the destination operand and then subtracts the Carry flag from the destination.

Instruction Formats:

```
SBB    reg,reg              SBB    reg,imm
SBB    mem,reg              SBB    mem,imm
SBB    reg,mem
```

SCAS,	**Scan String**
SCASB,	
SCASW,	O D I S Z A P C
	* * * * * *
SCASD	

Scans a string in memory pointed to by ES:(E)DI for a value that matches the accumulator. SCAS requires the operands to be specified. SCASB scans for an 8-bit value matching AL, SCASW scans for a 16-bit value matching AX, and SCASD scans for a 32-bit value matching EAX. (E)DI is increased or decreased according to the operand size and the status of the direction flag. If DF = 1, (E)DI is decreased; if DF = 0, (E)DI is increased.

Instruction Formats:

```
SCASB                        SCASW
SCASD                        SCAS ES:dest
SCAS dest
```

SET*condition*	**Set Conditionally**
	O D I S Z A P C

If the given flag condition is true, the byte specified by the destination operand is assigned the value 1. If the flag condition is false, the destination is assigned a value of 0. The possible values for *condition* are listed in Table B-2, earlier in this appendix.

Instruction Formats:

```
SETcond reg8            SETcond mem8
```

SHL — Shift Left

O	D	I	S	Z	A	P	C
*			*	*	?	*	*

Shifts each bit in the destination operand to the left, using the source operand to determine the number of shifts. The highest bit is copied into the Carry flag, and the lowest bit is filled with a zero (identical to SAL). The *imm8* operand must be a 1 when using the 8086/8088 processor.

Instruction Formats:

```
SHL   reg, imm8          SHL   mem, imm8
SHL   reg, CL            SHL   mem, CL
```

SHLD — Double-Precision Shift Left (IA-32)

O	D	I	S	Z	A	P	C
*			*	*	?	*	*

Shifts the bits of the second operand into the first operand. The third operand indicates the number of bits to be shifted. The positions opened by the shift are filled by the most significant bits of the second operand. The second operand must always be a register, and the third operand may be either an immediate value or the CL register.

Instruction Formats:

```
SHLD reg16, reg16, imm8          SHLD mem16, reg16, imm8
SHLD reg32, reg32, imm8          SHLD mem32, reg32, imm8
SHLD reg16, reg16, CL            SHLD mem16, reg16, CL
SHLD reg32, reg32, CL            SHLD mem32, reg32, CL
```

SHR — Shift Right

O	D	I	S	Z	A	P	C
*			*	*	?	*	*

Shifts each bit in the destination operand to the right, using the source operand to determine the number of shifts. The highest bit is filled with a zero, and the lowest bit is copied into the Carry flag. The *imm8* operand must be a 1 when using the 8086/8088 processor.

Instruction Formats:

```
SHR   reg, imm8          SHR   mem, imm8
SHR   reg, CL            SHR   mem, CL
```

SHRD — Double-Precision Shift Right (IA-32)

O	D	I	S	Z	A	P	C
*			*	*	?	*	*

Shifts the bits of the second operand into the first operand. The third operand indicates the number of bits to be shifted. The positions opened by the shift are filled by the least significant bits of the second operand. The second operand must always be a register, and the third operand may be either an immediate value or the CL register.

Instruction Formats:

```
SHRD reg16,reg16,imm8        SHRD mem16,reg16,imm8
SHRD reg32,reg32,imm8        SHRD mem32,reg32,imm8
SHRD reg16,reg16,CL          SHRD mem16,reg16,CL
SHRD reg32,reg32,CL          SHRD mem32,reg32,CL
```

STC — Set Carry Flag

O	D	I	S	Z	A	P	C
							1

Sets the Carry flag.

Instruction Format:

```
STC
```

STD — Set Direction Flag

O	D	I	S	Z	A	P	C
	1						

Sets the Direction flag, causing (E)SI and/or (E)DI to be decremented by string primitive instructions. Thus, string processing will be from high addresses to low addresses.

Instruction Format:

```
STD
```

STI	**Set Interrupt Flag**

Sets the Interrupt flag, which enables maskable interrupts. Interrupts are automatically disabled when an interrupt occurs, so an interrupt handler procedure immediately reenables them, using STI.

Instruction Format:

```
STI
```

STOS, STOSB, STOSW, STOSD	**Store String Data**

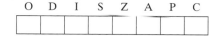

Stores the accumulator in the memory location addressed by ES:(E)DI. If STOS is used, a destination operand must be specified. STOSB copies AL to memory, STOSW copies AX to memory, and STOSD for the IA-32 copies EAX to memory. (E)DI is increased or decreased according to the operand size and the status of the

direction flag. If DF = 1, (E)DI is decreased; if DF = 0, (E)DI is increased.

Instruction Formats:

```
STOSB                          STOSW
STOSD                          STOS ES:mem
STOS mem
```

SUB	**Subtract**

O D I S Z A P C

Subtracts the source operand from the destination operand.

Instruction Formats:

```
SUB    reg,reg               SUB    reg,imm
SUB    mem,reg               SUB    mem,imm
SUB    reg,mem               SUB    accum,imm
```

TEST

Test

O	D	I	S	Z	A	P	C
*			*	*	?	*	0

Tests individual bits in the destination operand against those in the source operand. Performs a logical AND operation that affects the flags but not the destination operand.

Instruction Formats:

```
TEST    reg,reg              TEST    reg,imm
TEST    mem,reg              TEST    mem,imm
TEST    reg,mem              TEST    accum,imm
```

WAIT

Wait for Coprocessor

O	D	I	S	Z	A	P	C

Suspends CPU execution until the coprocessor finishes its current instruction.

Instruction Format:

```
WAIT
```

XADD

Exchange and Add (Intel486)

O	D	I	S	Z	A	P	C
*			*	*	*	*	*

Adds the source operand to the destination operand. At the same time, the original destination value is moved to the source operand.

Instruction Formats:

```
XADD    reg,reg              XADD    mem,reg
```

XCHG

Exchange

O	D	I	S	Z	A	P	C

Exchanges the contents of the source and destination operands.

Instruction Formats:

```
XCH     reg,reg              XCH     mem,reg
XCH     reg,mem
```

XLAT, XLATB	**Translate Byte**

Uses the value in AL to index into a table pointed to by DS:BX. The byte pointed to by the index is moved to AL. An operand may be specified in order to provide a segment override. XLATB may be substituted for XLAT.

Instruction Formats:

```
XLAT                          XLAT  segreg:mem
XLAT  mem                     XLATB
```

XOR	**Exclusive OR**

O	D	I	S	Z	A	P	C
*			*	*	?	*	0

Each bit in the source operand is exclusive ORed with its corresponding bit in the destination. The destination bit is a 1 only when the original source and destination bits are different.

Instruction Formats:

```
XOR  reg,reg                  XOR  reg,imm
XOR  mem,reg                  XOR  mem,imm
XOR  reg,mem                  XOR  accum,imm
```

BIOS and MS-DOS Interrupts

C.1   Introduction

In this appendix, we list some of the more commonly used interrupt numbers, in four groups:

- General list of PC interrupts. These interrupt numbers correspond to the Interrupt vector table stored in the first 1,024 bytes of memory.
- INT 10h Video BIOS functions
- INT 16h Keyboard BIOS functions
- INT 21h MS-DOS functions

In fact, documenting PC interrupts is a huge task, due to the many different versions of MS-DOS, as well as various DOS extenders and PC hardware controllers. The definitive source for interrupts is Ralf Brown's Interrupt List, available in various forms on the Web. Of course, information about Web sites changes almost daily, so check my own Web site for reasonably up-to-date links to the Ralf Brown Interrupt List and other assembly Web sites:

> http://www.nuvisionmiami.com/asmsources

C.2   PC Interrupts

Table C-1   General List of PC Interrupt Numbers.[a]

Number	Description
0	*Divide Error*. CPU-generated: activated when attempting to divide by zero.
1	*Single Step*. CPU-generated: active when the CPU Trap flag is set.
2	*Nonmaskable Interrupt*. External hardware: activated when a memory error occurs.
3	*Breakpoint*. CPU-generated: activated when the 0CCh (INT 3) instruction is executed.

Table C-1   General List of PC Interrupt Numbers.[a] (Continued)

Number	Description
4	*INTO Detected Overflow.* CPU-generated: Activated when the INTO instruction is executed and the Overflow flag is set.
5	*Print Screen.* Activated either by the INT 5 instruction or pressing the Shift-PrtSc keys.
6	*Invalid OpCode* (80286+)
7	*Processor Extension Not Available* (80286+)
8	IRQ0: *System Timer Interrupt.* Updates the BIOS clock 18.2 times per second. For your own programming, see INT 1Ch.
9	IRQ1: *Keyboard Hardware Interrupt.* Activated when a key is pressed. Reads the key from the keyboard port and stores it in the keyboard typeahead buffer.
0A	IRQ2: *Programmable Interrupt Controller*
0B	IRQ3: Serial Communications (COM2)
0C	IRQ4: Serial Communications (COM1)
0D	IRQ5: Fixed Disk
0E	IRQ6: *Diskette Interrupt.* Activated when a disk seek is in progress.
0F	IRQ7: *Parallel Printer*
10	*Video Services.* Routines for manipulating the video display (see the complete list in Table C-3).
11	*Equipment Check.* Return a word showing all the peripherals attached to the system.
12	*Memory Size.* Return the amount of memory (in 1,024-byte blocks) in AX.
13	*Floppy Disk Services.* Reset the disk controller, get the status of the most recent disk access, read and write physical sectors, and format a disk.
14	*Asynchronous (Serial) Port Services.* Initialize and read or write the asynchronous communications port, and return the port's status.
15	*Cassette Controller.*
16	*Keyboard Services.* Read and inspect keyboard input (see the complete list in Table C-4).
17	*Printer Services.* Initialize, print, and return the status of the printer.
18	*ROM BASIC.* Execute cassette BASIC in ROM.
19	*Bootstrap Loader.* Reboot MS-DOS.
1A	*Time of Day.* Get the number of timer ticks since the machine was turned on, or set the counter to a new value. Ticks occur 18.2 times per second.

Table C-1   General List of PC Interrupt Numbers.[a] (Continued)

Number	Description
1B	*Keyboard Break.* This interrupt handler is executed by INT 9h when CTRL-BREAK is pressed.
1C	*User Timer Interrupt.* Empty routine, executed 18.2 times per second. May be used by your own program.
1D	*Video Parameters.* Point to a table containing initialization and information for the video controller chip.
1E	*Diskette Parameters.* Point to a table containing initialization information for the diskette controller.
1F	*Graphics Table.* 8 X 8 Graphics font. Table kept in memory of all extended graphics characters with ASCII codes higher than 127.
20	*Terminate Program.* Terminate a COM program (INT 21h Function 4Ch should be used instead).
21	*MS-DOS Services* (see the complete list in Table C-2).
22	*MS-DOS Terminate Address.* Point to the address of the parent program or process. When the current program ends, this will be the return address.
23	*MS-DOS Break Address.* MS-DOS jumps here when CTRL-BREAK is pressed.
24	*MS-DOS Critical Error Address.* MS-DOS jumps to this address when there is a critical error in the current program, such as a disk media error.
25	*Absolute Disk Read* (obsolete).
26	*Absolute Disk Write* (obsolete).
27	*Terminate and Stay Resident* (obsolete).
28-FF	(Reserved)
33	*Microsoft Mouse.* Functions that track and control the mouse.
34 - 3E	*Floating-Point Emulation.*
3F	*Overlay manager.*
40-41	*Fixed Disk Services.* Fixed disk controller.
42-5F	Reserved: specialized uses
60-6B	Available for application programs to use.
6C-7F	Reserved: specialized uses

Table C-1   General List of PC Interrupt Numbers.[a] (Continued)

Number	Description
80-F0	Reserved: used by ROM BASIC.
F1-FF	Available for application programs.

[a]   Sources: Ray Duncan, *Advanced MS-DOS* 2nd ed, 1998. *Ralf Brown's Interrupt List*, available on the Web.

C.3   Interrupt 21H Functions (MS-DOS Services)

There are so many MS-DOS services available through INT 21h that we could not possibly document them all here. Instead, Table C-2 is simply a brief overview of functions that are commonly used.

Table C-2   Interrupt 21h Functions (MS-DOS Services).

Function	Description
1	*Read character from standard input.* If no character is ready, wait for input. Returns: AL = character.
2	*Write character to standard output.* Receives: DL = character.
3	*Read character from standard auxiliary input* (serial port).
4	*Write character to standard auxiliary output* (serial port).
5	*Write character to printer.* Receives: DL = character.
6	*Direct console input/output.* If DL = FFh, read a waiting character from standard input. If DL is any other value, write the character in DL to standard output.
7	*Direct character input without echo.* Wait for a character from standard input. Returns: AL = character.
8	*Character input without echo.* Wait for a character from the standard input device. Returns: AL = character. Character not echoed. May be terminated by Ctrl-Break.
9	*Write string to standard output.* Receives: DS:DX = address of string.
0A	*Buffered keyboard input.* Read a string of characters from the standard input device. Receives: DS:DX points to a predefined keyboard structure.
0B	*Check standard input status.* Check to see if an input character is waiting. Returns: AL = 0FFh if the character is ready; otherwise, AL = 0.
0C	*Clear keyboard buffer and invoke input function.* Clear the console input buffer, and then execute an input function. Receives: AL = desired function (1, 6, 7, 8, or 0Ah).
0E	*Select default drive.* Receives: DL = drive number (0 = A, 1 = B, etc.).
0F-18	FCB file functions (obsolete).

Table C-2   Interrupt 21h Functions (MS-DOS Services). (Continued)

Function	Description
19	*Get current default drive.* Returns: AL = drive number (0 = A, 1 = B, ...).
1A	*Set disk transfer address.* Receives: DS:DX contains address of disk transfer area.
25	*Set interrupt vector.* Set an entry in the Interrupt Vector Table to a new address. Receives: DS:DX points to the interrupt-handling routine that is inserted in the table; AL = the interrupt number.
26	*Create new program segment prefix.* Receives: DX = segment address for new PSP.
27-29	FCB file functions (obsolete).
2A	*Get system date.* Returns: AL = Day of the week (0–6, where Sunday = 0), CX = year, DH = month, and DL = day.
2B	*Set system date.* Receives: CX = year, DH = month, and DL = day. Returns: AL = 0 if the date is valid.
2C	*Get system time.* Returns: CH = hour, CL = minutes, DH = seconds, and DL = hundredths of seconds.
2D	*Set system time.* Receives: CH = hour, CL = minutes, DH = seconds, and DL = hundredths of seconds. Returns: AL = 0 if the time is valid.
2E	*Set Verify flag.* Receives: AL = new state of MS-DOS Verify flag (0 = off, 1 = on), DL = 00h.
2F	*Get disk transfer address* (DTA). Returns: ES:BX = address.
30	*Get MS-DOS version number.* Returns: AL = major version number, AH = minor version number, BH = OEM serial number, BL:CX = 24-bit user serial number.
31	*Terminate and stay resident.* Terminate the current program or process, leaving part of itself in memory. Receives: AL = return code, and DX = requested number of paragraphs.
32	*Get MS-DOS drive parameter block.* Receives: DL = drive number. Returns: AL = status; DS:BX points to drive parameter block.
33	*Extended break checking.* Indicates whether or not MS-DOS is checking for Ctrl-Break.
34	*Get address of INDOS flag.* (undocumented)
35	*Get interrupt vector.* Receives: AL = interrupt number. Returns: ES:BX = segment/offset of the interrupt handler.
36	*Get disk free space.* (FAT16 only) Receives: DL = drive number (0 = default, 1 = A, etc.). Returns: AX = sectors per cluster, or FFFFh if the drive number is invalid; BX = number of available clusters, CX = bytes per sector, and DX = clusters per drive.
37	*Get switch character.* (undocumented)
38	*Get or set country information.* (See Duncan or Brown for details.)

Table C-2   Interrupt 21h Functions (MS-DOS Services). (Continued)

Function	Description
39	*Create subdirectory.* Receives: DS:DX points to an ASCIIZ string with the path and directory name. Returns: AX = error code if the Carry flag is set.
3A	*Remove subdirectory.* Receives: DS:DX points to an ASCIIZ string with the path and directory name. Returns: AX = error code if the Carry flag is set.
3B	*Change current directory.* Receives: DS:DX points to an ASCIIZ string with the new directory path. Returns: AX = error code if the Carry flag is set.
3C	*Create or truncate file.* Create a new file or truncate an old file to zero bytes. Open the file for output. Receives: DS:DX points to an ASCIIZ string with the file name, and CX = file attribute. Returns: AX = error code if the Carry flag is set; otherwise AX = the new file handle.
3D	*Open existing file.* Open a file for input, output, or input-output. Receives: DS:DX points to an ASCIIZ string with the filename, and AL = the access code (0 = read, 1 = write, 2 = read/write). Returns: AX = error code if the Carry flag is set, otherwise AX = the new file handle.
3E	*Close file handle.* Close the file or device specified by a file handle. Receives: BX = file handle from previous open or create. Returns: If the Carry Flag is set, AX = error code.
3F	*Read from file or device.* Read a specified number of bytes from a file or device. Receives: BX = file handle, DS:DX points to an input buffer, and CX = number of bytes to read. Returns: If the Carry flag is set, AX = error code; otherwise, AX = number of bytes read.
40	*Write to file or device.* Write a specified number of bytes to a file or device. Receives: BX = file handle, DS:DX points to an output buffer, and CX = the number of bytes to write. Returns: If the Carry flag is set, AX = error code; otherwise, AX = number of bytes written.
41	*Delete file.* Remove a file from a specified directory. Receives: DS:DX points to an ASCIIZ string with the filename. Returns: AX = error code if the Carry flag is set.
42	*Move file pointer.* Move the file read/write pointer according to a specified method. Receives: CX:DX = distance (bytes) to move the file pointer, AL = method code, BX = file handle. The method codes are as follows: 0 = move from beginning of file, 1 = move to the current location plus an offset, and 2 = move to the end of file plus an offset. Returns: AX = error code if the Carry flag is set.
43	*Get/Set file attribute.* Get or set the attribute of a file. Receives: DS:DX = pointer to an ASCIIZ path and filename, CX = attribute, and AL = function code (1 = set attribute, 0 = get attribute). Returns: AX = error code if the Carry flag is set.
44	*I/O control for devices.* Get or set device information associated with an open device handle, or send a control string to the device handle, or receive a control string from the device handle.

Table C-2   Interrupt 21h Functions (MS-DOS Services). (Continued)

Function	Description
45	*Duplicate file handle.* Return a new file handle for a file that is currently open. Receives: BX = file handle. Returns: AX = error code if the Carry flag is set.
46	*Force duplicate file handle.* Force the handle in CX to refer to the same file at the same position as the handle in BX. Receives: BX = existing file handle, and CX = second file handle. Returns: AX = error code if the Carry flag is set.
47	*Get current directory.* Get the full path name of the current directory. Receives: DS:SI points to a 64-byte area to hold the directory path, and DL = drive number. Returns: a buffer at DS:SI is filled with the path, and AX = error code if the Carry flag is set.
48	*Allocate memory.* Allocate a requested number of paragraphs of memory, measured in 16-byte blocks. Receives: BX = number of paragraphs requested. Returns: AX = segment of the allocated block, and BX = size of the largest block available (in paragraphs), and AX = error code if the Carry flag is set.
49	*Free allocated memory.* Free memory that was previously allocated by Function 48h. Receives: ES = segment of the block to be freed. Returns: AX = error code if the Carry flag is set.
4A	*Modify memory blocks.* Modify allocated memory blocks to contain a new block size. The block will shrink or grow. Receives: ES = segment of the block, and BX = requested number of paragraphs. Returns: AX = error code if the Carry flag is set, and BX = maximum number of available blocks.
4B	*Load or execute program.* Create a program segment prefix for another program, load it into memory, and execute it. Receives: DS:DX points to an ASCIIZ string with the drive, path, and filename of the program; ES:BX points to a parameter block, and AL = function value. Function values in AL:0 = load and execute the program; 3 = load but do not execute (overlay program). Returns: AX = error code if the Carry flag is set.
4C	*Terminate process.* Usual way to terminate a program and return to either MS-DOS or a calling program. Receives: AL = 8-bit return code, which can be queried by DOS function 4Dh or by the ERRORLEVEL command in a batch file.
4D	*Get return code of process.* Get the return code of a process or program, generated by either function call 31h or function call 4Ch. Returns: AL = 8-bit code returned by the program, AH = type of exit generated: 0 = normal termination, 1 = terminated by CTRL-BREAK, 2 = terminated by a critical device error, and 3 = terminated by a call to function call 31h.
4E	*Find first matching file.* Find the first filename that matches a given file specification. Receives: DS:DX points to an ASCIIZ drive, path, and file specification; CX = File attribute to be used when searching. Returns: AX = error code if the Carry flag is set; otherwise, the current DTA is filled with the filename, attribute, time, date, and size. DOS function call 1Ah (set DTA) is usually called before this function.

Table C-2   Interrupt 21h Functions (MS-DOS Services). (Continued)

Function	Description
4F	*Find next matching file.* Find the next filename that matches a given file specification. This is always called after DOS function 4Eh. Returns: AX = error code if the Carry flag is set; otherwise, the current DTA is filled with the file's information.
54	*Get Verify flag.* Returns: AH = Verify flag for disk I/O (0 = off. 1 = on).
56	*Rename/move file.* Rename a file or move it to another directory. Receives: DS:DX points to an ASCIIZ string that specifies the current drive, path, and filename; ES:DI points to the new path and filename. Returns: AX = error code if the Carry flag is set.
57	*Get/Set file date/time.* Get or set the date and time stamp for a file. Receives: AL = 0 to get the date/time, or AL = 1 to set the date/time; BX = file handle, CX = new file time, and DX = new file date. Returns: AX = error code if the Carry flag is set; otherwise, CX = current file time, and DX = current file date.
58	*Get or set memory allocation strategy.* (See Duncan or Brown for details)
59	*Get extended error information.* Return additional information about an MS-DOS error, including the error class, locus, and recommended action. Receives: BX = MS-DOS version number (zero for version 3.xx). Returns: AX = extended error code, BH = error class, BL = suggested action, and CH = locus.
5A	*Create temporary file.* Generate a unique filename in a specified directory. Receives: DS:DX points to an ASCIIZ pathname, ending with a backslash (\); CX = desired file attribute. Returns: AX = error code if the Carry flag is set; otherwise, DS:DX points to the path with the new filename appended.
5B	*Create new file.* Try to create a new file, but fail if the filename already exists. This prevents you from overwriting an existing file. Receives: DS:DX points to an ASCIIZ string with the path and filename. Returns: AX = error code if the Carry flag is set.
5C-61	Omitted.
62	*Get program segment prefix (PSP) address.* Returns: BX = the segment value of the current program's PSP.
7303h	*Get disk free space.* Fills a structure containing detailed disk space information. Receives: AX = 17303h, ES:DI points to a ExtGetDskFreSpcStruc structure, CX = size of the ExtGetDskFreSpcStruc structure, DS:DX points to a null-terminated string containing the drive name. Returns: The ExtGetDskFreSpcStruc is filled in with disk information. See Section 14.5.1 for details.
7305h	*Absolute disk read and write.* Reads individual disk sectors or groups of sectors. Does not work under Windows NT, 2000, or XP. Receives: AX = 7305h, DS:BX = segment/offset of a DISKIO structure variable, CX = 0FFFFh, DL = drive number (0 = default, 1 = A, 2 = B, 3 = C, etc.), SI = Read/write flag. See Section 14.4 for details.

C.4   Interrupt 10H Functions (Video BIOS)

Table C-3   Interrupt 10h Functions (Video BIOS).

Function	Description
0	*Set video mode.* Set the video display to monochrome, text, graphics, or color mode. Receives: AL = display mode.
1	*Set cursor lines.* Identify the starting and ending scan lines for the cursor. Receives: CH = cursor starting line, and CL = cursor ending line.
2	*Set cursor position.* Position the cursor on the screen. Receives: BH = video page, DH = row, and DL = column.
3	*Get cursor position.* Get the cursor's screen position and its size. Receives: BH = video page. Returns: CH = cursor starting line, CL = cursor ending line, DH = cursor row, and DL = cursor column.
4	*Read light pen.* Read the position and status of the light pen. Returns: CH = pixel row, BX = pixel column, DH = character row, and DL = character column.
5	*Set display page.* Select the video page to be displayed. Receives: AL = desired page number.
6	*Scroll window up.* Scroll a window on the current video page upward, replacing scrolled lines with blanks. Receives: AL = number of lines to scroll, BH = attribute for scrolled lines, CX = upper-left corner row and column, and DX = lower-right row and column.
7	*Scroll window down.* Scroll a window on the current video page downward, replacing scrolled lines with blanks. Receives: AL = number of lines to scroll, BH = attribute for scrolled lines, CX = upper-left corner row and column, and DX = lower-right row and column.
8	*Read character and attribute.* Read the character and its attribute at the current cursor position. Receives: BH = display page. Returns: AH = attribute byte, and AL = ASCII character code.
9	*Write character and attribute.* Write a character and its attribute at the current cursor position. Receives: AL = ASCII character, BH = video page, and CX = repetition factor.
0A	*Write character.* Write a character only (no attribute) at the current cursor position. Receives: AL = ASCII character, BH = video page, BL = attribute, and CX = replication factor.
0B	*Set color palette.* Select a group of available colors for the color or EGA adapter. Receives: AL = display mode, and BH = active display page.
0C	*Write graphics pixel.* Write a graphics pixel when in color graphics mode. Receives: Al = pixel value, CX = x coordinate, and DX = y coordinate.
0D	*Read graphics pixel.* Read the color of a single graphics pixel at a given location. Receives: CX = x coordinate, and DX = y coordinate.

Table C-3   Interrupt 10h Functions (Video BIOS). (Continued)

Function	Description
0E	*Write character.* Write a character to the screen, and advance the cursor. Receives: AL = ASCII character code, BH = video page, BL = attribute or color.
0F	*Get current video mode.* Get the current video mode. Returns: AL = video mode, and BH = active video page.
10	*Set video palette.* (EGA and PCjr only) Set the video palette register, border color, or blink/intensity bit. Receives: AL = function code (00 = set palette register, 01 = set border color, 02 = set palette and border color, 03 = set/reset blink/intensity bit), BH = color, BL = palette register to set. If AL = 2, ES:DX points to a color list.
11	*Character generator.* Select the character size for the EGA display. For example, an 8 by 8 font is used for the 43-line display, and an 8 by 14 font is used for the 25-line display.
12	*Alternate select function.* Return technical information about the EGA display.
13	*Write string.* (PC/AT only) Write a string of text to the video display. Receives: AL = mode, BH = page, BL = attribute, CX = length of string, DH = row, DL = column, and ES:BP points to the string (will not work on the IBM-PC or PC/XT).

C.5   Keyboard BIOS INT 16h Functions

Table C-4   Keyboard BIOS Interrupt 16h Functions.

Function	Description
03h	*Set typematic repeat rate.* Receives: AH = 03h, AL = 5, BH = repeat delay, BL = repeat rate. The delay values in BH are: (0 = 250 ms; 1 = 500 ms; 2 = 750 ms; 3 = 1000 ms). The repeat rate in BL varies from 0 (fastest) to 1Fh (slowest). Returns: nothing.
05h	*Push key into buffer.* Pushes a keyboard character and corresponding scan code into the keyboard typeahead buffer. Receives: AH = 05h, CH = scan code, and CL = character code. If the typeahead buffer is already full, the Carry flag will be set, and AL = 1. Returns: nothing
10	*Wait for key.* Wait for an input character and keyboard scan code. Receives: AH = 10h. Returns: AH = scan code, AL = ASCII character. (Function 00h duplicates this function, using an older type of keyboard.)
11	*Check keyboard buffer.* Find out if a character is waiting in the keyboard typeahead buffer. Receives: AH = 01h. Returns: If a key is waiting, its scan code is returned in AH and its ASCII code is returned in AL, and the Zero flag is cleared (the character will remain in the input buffer). If no key is waiting, the Zero flag is set. (Function 01h duplicates this function, using an older type of keyboard.)

Table C-4   Keyboard BIOS Interrupt 16h Functions. (Continued)

Function	Description
12	*Get keyboard flags.* Return the Keyboard Flag byte stored in low RAM. Receives: AH = 12h. Returns: Keyboard flags in AX. (Function 02h duplicates this function, using an older type of keyboard.)

C.6   Mouse Functions (INT 33h)

INT 33h mouse functions receive their function number in the AX register. For more information about these functions, see Section 15.6. For additional mouse functions, see Table 15-7 on page 605.

Table C-5   INT 33h Mouse Functions.

Function	Description
0000h	*Reset mouse and get status.* Receives: AX = 0000h. resets the mouse and confirms that it is available. The mouse (if found) is centered on the screen, its display page is set to video page 0, its pointer is hidden, and its mickeys-to-pixels ratios and speed are set to default values. The mouse's range of movement is set to the entire screen area.
0001h	*Show mouse pointer.* Receives: AX = 0001h. Returns: nothing. The mouse driver keeps a count of the number of times this function is called.
0002h	*Hide mouse pointer.* Receives: AX = 0002h. Returns: nothing. The mouse position is still tracked when it is invisible.
0003h	*Get mouse position and status.* Receives: AX = 0003h. Returns: BX = mouse button status, CX = X-coordinate (in pixels), DX = Y-coordinate (in pixels).
0004h	*Set mouse position.* Receives: AX = 0004h, CX = X-coordinate (in pixels), DX = Y-coordinate (in pixels). Returns: nothing
0005h	*Get button press information.* Receives: AX = 0005h, BX = button ID (0 = left, 1 = right, 2 = center). Returns: AX = button status, BX = button press counter, CX = X-coordinate of last button press, DX = Y-coordinate of last button press.
0006h	*Get button release information.* Receives: AX = 0006h, BX = button ID (0 = left, 1 = right, 2 = center). Returns: AX = button status, BX = button release counter, CX = X-coordinate of last button release, DX = Y-coordinate of last button release.
0007h	*Set horizontal limits.* Receives: AX = 0007h, CX = minimum X-coordinate (in pixels), DX = maximum X-coordinate (in pixels). Returns: nothing.
0008h	*Set vertical limits.* Receives: AX = 0008h, CX = minimum Y-coordinate (in pixels), DX = maximum Y-coordinate (in pixels). Returns: nothing.

D

MASM Reference

D.1   Introduction

The Microsoft MASM 6.11 manuals were last printed in 1992, and consisted of three volumes:

- *Programmers Guide*
- *Reference*
- *Environment and Tools*

Unfortunately, the printed manuals have not been available for many years, but Microsoft supplies electronic copies of the manuals (MS-Word files) in its *Platform SDK* package. The printed manuals are definitely collectors' items.

The information in this chapter was excerpted from Chapters 1–3 of the *Reference* manual, with updates from the MASM 6.14 *readme.txt* file. The Microsoft license agreement supplied with this book entitles the reader to a single copy of the software and acompanying documentation, which we have, in part, printed here.

Syntax Notation   Throughout this appendix, a consistent syntax notation is used. Words in all capital letters indicate a MASM reserved word that may appear in your program in either uppercase or lowercase letters. In the following example, DATA is a reserved word:

.DATA

Words in italics indicate a defined term or category. In the following example, *number* refers to an integer constant:

ALIGN [[*number*]]

When double brackets ⟦ .. ⟧ surround an item, the item is optional. In the following example, *text* is optional:

⟦ *text* ⟧

When a vertical separator | appears between items in a list of two or more items, you must select one of the items. The following example indicates a choice between NEAR and FAR:

NEAR | FAR

An ellipsis (. . .) indicates repetition of the last item in a list. In the next example, the comma followed by an *initializer* may repeat multiple times:

⟦ *name* ⟧ BYTE *initializer* ⟦ , *initializer* ⟧ . . .

D.2   MASM Reserved Words

The following are operands to various MASM directives. They are also reserved words, meaning that they cannot be used as identifiers (labels, constants, etc.).

$	PARITY?
?	PASCAL
@B	QWORD
@F	REAL4
ADDR	REAL8
BASIC	REAL10
BYTE	SBYTE
C	SDWORD
CARRY?	SIGN?
DWORD	STDCALL
FAR	SWORD
FAR16	SYSCALL
FORTRAN	TBYTE
FWORD	VARARG
NEAR	WORD
NEAR16	ZERO?
OVERFLOW?	

D.3   Register Names

AH	CR0	DR1	EBX	SI
AL	CR2	DR2	ECX	SP
AX	CR3	DR3	EDI	SS
BH	CS	DR6	EDX	ST
BL	CX	DR7	ES	TR3
BP	DH	DS	ESI	TR4
BX	DI	DX	ESP	TR5
CH	DL	EAX	FS	TR6
CL	DR0	EBP	GS	TR7

D.4   Microsoft Assembler (ML)

The ML program (*ML.EXE*) assembles and links one or more assembly language source files. The command-line options are case sensitive. The syntax is:

ML [[*options*]] *filename* [[[[*options*]] *filename*]] . . . [[**/link** *linkoptions*]]

The only required parameter is at least one *filename*, the name of a source file written in assembly language. The following command, for example, assembles the source file **AddSub.asm** and produces the object file *AddSub.obj*:

```
ML -c AddSub.asm
```

The *options* parameter consists of zero or more command-line options, each starting with a slash (/) or dash (−). Multiple options must be separated by at least one space. Table D-1 lists the complete set of command-line options. The command-line options are case-sensitive.

Table D-1   ML Command-Line Options.

Option	Action
/AT	Enables tiny-memory-model support. Enables error messages for code constructs that violate the requirements for .COM format files. Note that this is not equivalent to the .MODEL TINY directive.
/Bl*filename*	Selects an alternate linker.
/c	Assembles only. Does not link.

Table D-1   ML Command-Line Options. (Continued)

Option	Action
/Cp	Preserves case of all user identifiers.
/Cu	Maps all identifiers to uppercase.
/Cx	Preserves case in public and external symbols (default).
/D*symbol* [[*=value*]]	Defines a text macro with the given name. If *value* is missing, it is blank. Multiple tokens separated by spaces must be enclosed in quotation marks.
/EP	Generates a preprocessed source listing (sent to STDOUT). See /Sf.
/F *hexnum*	Sets stack size to *hexnum* bytes (this is the same as /link /STACK:*number*). The value must be expressed in hexadecimal notation. There must be a space between /F and *hexnum*.
/Fe*filename*	Names the executable file.
/Fl[[*filename*]]	Generates an assembled code listing. See /Sf.
/Fm[[*filename*]]	Creates a linker map file.
/Fo*filename*	Names an object file.
/FPi	Generates emulator fixups for floating-point arithmetic (mixed-language only).
/Fr[[*filename*]]	Generates a Source Browser .SBR file.
/FR[[*filename*]]	Generates an extended form of a Source Browser .SBR file.
/Gc	Specifies use of FORTRAN- or Pascal-style function calling and naming conventions. Same as OPTION LANGUAGE:PASCAL.
/Gd	Specifies use of C-style function calling and naming conventions. Same as OPTION LANGUAGE:C.
/H *number*	Restricts external names to *number* significant characters. The default is 31 characters.
/help	Calls QuickHelp for help on ML.
/I *pathname*	Sets path for include file. A maximum of 10 /I options is allowed.
/nologo	Suppresses messages for successful assembly.
/Sa	Turns on listing of all available information.
/Sc	Adds instruction timings to listing file.

Table D-1 ML Command-Line Options. (Continued)

Option	Action
/Sf	Adds first-pass listing to listing file.
/Sg	Turns on listing of assembly-generated code.
/Sl *width*	Sets the line width of source listing in characters per line. Range is 60 to 255 or 0. Default is 0. Same as PAGE *width*.
/Sn	Turns off symbol table when producing a listing.
/Sp *length*	Sets the page length of source listing in lines per page. Range is 10 to 255 or 0. Default is 0. Same as PAGE *length*.
/Ss *text*	Specifies text for source listing. Same as SUBTITLE *text*.
/St *text*	Specifies title for source listing. Same as TITLE *text*.
/Sx	Turns on false conditionals in listing.
/Ta *filename*	Assembles source file whose name does not end with the .ASM extension.
/w	Same as /W0.
/W*level*	Sets the warning level, where *level* = 0, 1, 2, or 3.
/WX	Returns an error code if warnings are generated.
/Zd	Generates line-number information in object file.
/Zf	Makes all symbols public.
/Zi	Generates CodeView information in object file.
/Zm	Enables M510 option for maximum compatibility with MASM 5.1.
/Zp[[*alignment*]]	Packs structures on the specified byte boundary. The *alignment* may be 1, 2, or 4.
/Zs	Performs a syntax check only.
/?	Displays a summary of ML command-line syntax.

D.5 LINK

The following information applies to the 16-bit linker supplied with the Microsoft assembler. The LINK utility combines object files into a single executable file or dynamic-link library. The syntax is:

LINK *options objfiles*[[, [[*exefile*]] [[,[[*mapfile*]] [[,[[*libraries*]] [[,[[*deffile*]]]]]]]]]] [[;]]

Options   Table D-2 describes the LINK command options, with the exception of several rarely used options that are described in Help.

Table D-2   LINK Command Options.

Option	Action
/A:*size*	Option name: /A[[LIGNMENT]]. Directs LINK to align segment data in a segmented-executable file along the boundaries specified by size bytes, where size must be a power of two.
/B	Option name: /B[[ATCH]]. Suppresses prompts for library or object files not found.
/CO	Option name: /CO[[DEVIEW]]. Adds symbolic data and line numbers needed by the Microsoft CodeView debugger. This option is incompatible with the /EXEPACK option.
/CP:*number*	Option name: /CP[[ARMAXALLOC]]. Sets the program's maximum memory allocation to number of 16-byte paragraphs.
/DO	Option name: /DO[[SSEG]]. Orders segments in the default order used by Microsoft high-level languages.
/DS	Option name: /DS[[ALLOCATE]]. Directs LINK to load all data starting at the high end of the data segment. The /DSALLOC option is for assembly-language programs that create MS-DOS .EXE files.
/E	Option name: /E[[XEPACK]]. Packs the executable file. The /EXEPACK option is incompatible with /INCR and /CO. Do not use /EXEPACK on a Windows-based application.
/F	Option name: /F[[ARCALLTRANSLATION]]. Optimizes far calls. The /FARCALL option is automatically on when using /TINY. The /PACKC option is not recommended with /FARCALL when linking a Windows-based program.
/HE	Option name: /HE[[LP]]. Calls QuickHelp for help on LINK.
/HI	Option name: /HI[[GH]]. Places the executable file as high in memory as possible. Use /HIGH with the /DSALLOC option. This option is for assembly-language programs that create MS-DOS .EXE files.
/INC	Option name: /INC[[REMENTAL]]. Prepares for incremental linking with ILINK. This option is incompatible with /EXEPACK and /TINY.
/INF	Option name: /INF[[ORMATION]]. Displays to the standard output the phase of linking and names of object files being linked.

Table D-2 LINK Command Options. (Continued)

Option	Action
/LI	Option name: /LI[[NENUMBERS]]. Adds source file line numbers and associated addresses to the map file. The object file must be created with line numbers. This option creates a map file even if mapfile is not specified.
/M	Option name: /M[[AP]]. Adds public symbols to the map file.
/NOD[[:*libraryname*]]	Option name: /NOD[[EFAULTLIBRARYSEARCH]]. Ignores the specified default library. Specify without *libraryname* to ignore all default libraries.
/NOE	Option name: /NOE[[XTDICTIONARY]]. Prevents LINK from searching extended dictionaries in libraries. Use /NOE when redefinition of a symbol causes error L2044.
/NOF	Option name: /NOF[[ARCALLTRANSLATION]]. Turns off far-call optimization.
/NOI	Option name: /NOI[[GNORECASE]]. Preserves case in identifiers.
/NOL	Option name: /NOL[[OGO]]. Suppresses the LINK copyright message.
/NON	Option name: /NON[[ULLSDOSSEG]]. Orders segments as with the /DOSSEG option, but with no additional bytes at the beginning of the _TEXT segment (if defined). This option overrides /DOSSEG.
/NOP	Option name: /NOP[[ACKCODE]]. Turns off code segment packing.
/PACKC[[:*number*]]	Option name: /PACKC[[ODE]]. Packs neighboring code segments together. Specify number bytes to set the maximum size for physical segments formed by /PACKC.
/PACKD[[:*number*]]	Option name: /PACKD[[ATA]]. Packs neighboring data segments together. Specify number bytes to set the maximum size for physical segments formed by /PACKD. This option is for Windows only.
/PAU	Option name: /PAU[[SE]]. Pauses during the link session for disk changes.
/PM:*type*	Option name: /PM[[TYPE]]. Specifies the type of Windows-based application where *type* is one of the following: PM (or WINDOWAPI), VIO (or WINDOWCOMPAT), or NOVIO (or NOTWINDOWCOMPAT).
/ST:*number*	Option name: /ST[[ACK]]. Sets the stack size to *number* bytes, from 1 byte to 64K.
/T	Option name: /T[[INY]]. Creates a tiny-model MS-DOS program with a .COM extension instead of .EXE. Incompatible with /INCR.
/?	Option name: /?. Displays a summary of LINK command-line syntax.

Environment Variables

Variable	Description
INIT	Specifies path for the TOOLS.INI file.
LIB	Specifies search path for library files.
LINK	Specifies default command-line options.
TMP	Specifies path for the VM.TMP file.

D.6   CodeView Debugger

The Microsoft CodeView debugger runs the assembled or compiled program while simultaneously displaying the program source code, program variables, memory locations, processor registers, and other pertinent information. The syntax is:

   CV [*options*] *executablefile* [*arguments*]

Table D-3 lists the command-line options for the version of CodeView that runs under MS-DOS.

Table D-3   CodeView Command-Line Options.

Option	Action
/2	Permits the use of two monitors.
/25	Starts in 25-line mode.
/43	Starts in 43-line mode.
/50	Starts in 50-line mode.
/B	Starts in black-and-white mode.
/C*commands*	Executes *commands* on startup.
/F	Exchanges screens by flipping between video pages.
/G	Eliminates refresh snow on CGA monitors.
/I[[0 | 1]]	Turns nonmaskable-interrupt and 8259-interrupt trapping on (/I1) or off (/I0).
/K	Disables installation of keyboard monitors for the program being debugged.
/M	Disables CodeView use of the mouse. Use this option when debugging an application that supports the mouse under Windows 3.x.
/N[[0 | 1]]	/N0 tells CodeView to trap nonmaskable interrupts; /N1 tells it not to trap.

Table D-3   CodeView Command-Line Options. (Continued)

Option	Action
/R	Enables 80386/486 debug registers.
/S	Exchanges screens by changing buffers (primarily for use with graphics programs).
/TSF	Toggles TOOLS.INI entry to read/not read the CURRENT.STS file.

D.7   MASM Directives

name = expression

Assigns the numeric value of *expression* to *name*. The symbol may be redefined later.

.186

Enables assembly of instructions for the 80186 processor; disables assembly of instructions introduced with later processors. Also enables 8087 instructions.

.286

Enables assembly of nonprivileged instructions for the 80286 processor; disables assembly of instructions introduced with later processors. Also enables 80287 instructions.

.286P

Enables assembly of all instructions (including privileged) for the 80286 processor; disables assembly of instructions introduced with later processors. Also enables 80287 instructions.

.287

Enables assembly of instructions for the 80287 coprocessor; disables assembly of instructions introduced with later coprocessors.

.386

Enables assembly of nonprivileged instructions for the 80386 processor; disables assembly of instructions introduced with later processors. Also enables 80387 instructions.

.386P

Enables assembly of all instructions (including privileged) for the 80386 processor; disables assembly of instructions introduced with later processors. Also enables 80387 instructions.

.387

Enables assembly of instructions for the 80387 coprocessor.

.486

Enables assembly of nonprivileged instructions for the 80486 processor.

.486P

Enables assembly of all instructions (including privileged) for the 80486 processor.

.586

Enables assembly of nonprivileged instructions for the Pentium processor.

.586P

Enables assembly of all instructions (including privileged) for the Pentium processor.

.686

Enables assembly of nonprivileged instructions for the Pentium Pro processor.

.686P

Enables assembly of all instructions (including privileged) for the Pentium Pro processor.

.8086

Enables assembly of 8086 instructions (and the identical 8088 instructions); disables assembly of instructions introduced with later processors. Also enables 8087 instructions. This is the default mode for processors.

.8087

Enables assembly of 8087 instructions; disables assembly of instructions introduced with later coprocessors. This is the default mode for coprocessors.

ALIAS <alias> = <actual-name>

Maps an old function name to a new name. *Alias* is the alternate or alias name, and *actual-name* is the actual name of the function or procedure. The angle brackets are required. The ALIAS directive can be used for creating libraries that allow the linker (LINK) to map an old function to a new function.

ALIGN [[*number*]]

Aligns the next variable or instruction on a byte that is a multiple of *number*.

.ALPHA

Orders segments alphabetically.

ASSUME *segregister*:*name* [[, *segregister*:*name*]]. . .
ASSUME *dataregister*:*type* [[, *dataregister*:*type*]]. . .
ASSUME *register*:ERROR [[, *register*:ERROR]]. . .
ASSUME [[*register*:]] NOTHING [[, *register*:NOTHING]]. . .

Enables error-checking for register values. After an **ASSUME** is put into effect, the assembler watches for changes to the values of the given registers. **ERROR** generates an error if the register is used. **NOTHING** removes register error-checking. You can combine different kinds of assumptions in one statement.

.BREAK [[.IF *condition*]]

Generates code to terminate a **.WHILE** or **.REPEAT** block if *condition* is true.

[[*name*]] BYTE *initializer* [[, *initializer*]] . . .

Allocates and optionally initializes a byte of storage for each *initializer*. Can also be used as a type specifier anywhere a type is legal.

name **CATSTR** [[*textitem1* [[, *textitem2*]] . . .]]

Concatenates text items. Each text item can be a literal string, a constant preceded by a %, or the string returned by a macro function.

.CODE [[*name*]]

When used with **.MODEL**, indicates the start of a code segment called *name* (the default segment name is _TEXT for tiny, small, compact, and flat models, or *module*_TEXT for other models).

COMM *definition* [[, *definition*]] . . .

Creates a communal variable with the attributes specified in *definition*. Each *definition* has the following form:

[[*langtype*]] [[**NEAR** | **FAR**]] *label:type*[[*:count*]]

The *label* is the name of the variable. The *type* can be any type specifier (**BYTE**, **WORD**, and so on) or an integer specifying the number of bytes. The *count* specifies the number of data objects (one is the default).

COMMENT *delimiter* [[*text*]]

[[*text*]]

[[*text*]] *delimiter* [[*text*]]

Treats all *text* between or on the same line as the delimiters as a comment.

.CONST

When used with **.MODEL**, starts a constant data segment (with segment name CONST). This segment has the read-only attribute.

.CONTINUE [[**.IF** *condition*]]

Generates code to jump to the top of a **.WHILE** or **.REPEAT** block if *condition* is true.

.CREF

Enables listing of symbols in the symbol portion of the symbol table and browser file.

.DATA

When used with **.MODEL**, starts a near data segment for initialized data (segment name _DATA).

.DATA?

When used with **.MODEL**, starts a near data segment for uninitialized data (segment name _BSS).

.DOSSEG

Orders the segments according to the MS-DOS segment convention: CODE first, then segments not in DGROUP, and then segments in DGROUP. The segments in DGROUP follow this order: segments not in BSS or STACK, then BSS segments, and finally STACK segments. Primarily used for ensuring CodeView support in MASM stand-alone programs. Same as **DOSSEG**.

DOSSEG

Identical to **.DOSSEG**, which is the preferred form.

DB

Can be used to define data like **BYTE**.

DD

Can be used to define data like **DWORD**.

DF

Can be used to define data like **FWORD**.

DQ

Can be used to define data like **QWORD**.

DT

Can be used to define data like **TBYTE**.

DW

Can be used to define data like **WORD**.

[[*name*]] **DWORD** *initializer* [[*, initializer*]]. . .

Allocates and optionally initializes a doubleword (4 bytes) of storage for each *initializer*. Can also be used as a type specifier anywhere a type is legal.

ECHO *message*

Displays *message* to the standard output device (by default, the screen). Same as **%OUT**.

.ELSE

See **.IF**.

ELSE

Marks the beginning of an alternate block within a conditional block. See **IF**.

ELSEIF

Combines **ELSE** and **IF** into one statement. See **IF**.

ELSEIF2

ELSEIF block evaluated on every assembly pass if **OPTION:SETIF2** is **TRUE**.

END [[*address*]]

Marks the end of a module and, optionally, sets the program entry point to *address*.

.ENDIF

See **.IF**.

ENDIF

See **IF**.

ENDM

Terminates a macro or repeat block. See **MACRO**, **FOR**, **FORC**, **REPEAT**, or **WHILE**.

name **ENDP**

Marks the end of procedure *name* previously begun with **PROC**. See **PROC**.

name **ENDS**

Marks the end of segment, structure, or union *name* previously begun with **SEGMENT**, **STRUCT**, **UNION**, or a simplified segment directive.

.ENDW

See **.WHILE**.

name **EQU** *expression*

Assigns numeric value of *expression* to *name*. The *name* cannot be redefined later.

name **EQU** *<text>*

Assigns specified *text* to *name*. The *name* can be assigned a different *text* later. See **TEXTEQU**.

.ERR [[*message*]]

Generates an error.

.ERR2 [[*message*]]

.ERR block evaluated on every assembly pass if **OPTION:SETIF2** is **TRUE**.

.ERRB *<textitem>* [[, *message*]]

Generates an error if *textitem* is blank.

.ERRDEF *name* [[, *message*]]

Generates an error if *name* is a previously defined label, variable, or symbol.

.ERRDIF[[**I**]] *<textitem1>*, *<textitem2>* [[, *message*]]

Generates an error if the text items are different. If **I** is given, the comparison is case-insensitive.

.ERRE *expression* [[, *message*]]

Generates an error if *expression* is false (0).

.ERRIDN[[**I**]] *<textitem1>*, *<textitem2>* [[, *message*]]

Generates an error if the text items are identical. If **I** is given, the comparison is case-insensitive.

.ERRNB *<textitem>* [[, *message*]]

Generates an error if *textitem* is not blank.

.ERRNDEF *name* [[, *message*]]

Generates an error if *name* has not been defined.

.ERRNZ *expression* [[, *message*]]

Generates an error if *expression* is true (nonzero).

EVEN

Aligns the next variable or instruction on an even byte.

.EXIT [[*expression*]]

Generates termination code. Returns optional *expression* to shell.

EXITM [[*textitem*]]

Terminates expansion of the current repeat or macro block and begins assembly of the next statement outside the block. In a macro function, *textitem* is the value returned.

EXTERN [[*langtype*]] *name* [[(*altid*)]] :*type* [[, [[*langtype*]] *name* [[(*altid*)]] :*type*]]...

Defines one or more external variables, labels, or symbols called *name* whose type is *type*. The *type* can be **ABS**, which imports *name* as a constant. Same as **EXTRN**.

EXTERNDEF [[*langtype*]] *name*:*type* [[, [[*langtype*]] *name*:*type*]]...

Defines one or more external variables, labels, or symbols called *name* whose type is *type*. If *name* is defined in the module, it is treated as **PUBLIC**. If *name* is referenced in the module, it is treated as **EXTERN**. If *name* is not referenced, it is ignored. The *type* can be **ABS**, which imports *name* as a constant. Normally used in include files.

EXTRN

See **EXTERN**.

.FARDATA [[*name*]]

When used with **.MODEL**, starts a far data segment for initialized data (segment name FAR_DATA or *name*).

.FARDATA? [[*name*]]

When used with **.MODEL**, starts a far data segment for uninitialized data (segment name FAR_BSS or *name*).

FOR parameter [[:**REQ** | :=**default**]] **, <argument** [[**, argument**]]**...>**
   statements
   ENDM

Marks a block that will be repeated once for each *argument*, with the current *argument* replacing *parameter* on each repetition. Same as **IRP**.

FORC
   parameter, *<string> statements*
   ENDM

Marks a block that will be repeated once for each character in *string*, with the current character replacing *parameter* on each repetition. Same as **IRPC**.

[[*name*]] **FWORD** *initializer* [[, *initializer*]]...

Allocates and optionally initializes 6 bytes of storage for each *initializer*. Also can be used as a type specifier anywhere a type is legal.

GOTO *macrolabel*

Transfers assembly to the line marked :*macrolabel*. **GOTO** is permitted only inside **MACRO**, **FOR**, **FORC**, **REPEAT**, and **WHILE** blocks. The label must be the only directive on the line and must be preceded by a leading colon.

name **GROUP** *segment* [[, *segment*]]. . .

Add the specified *segments* to the group called *name*. This directive has no effect when used in 32-bit flat-model programming, and will result in error when used with the /coff command-line option.

.IF *condition1*

statements

[[.**ELSEIF** condition2

statements]]

[[.**ELSE**

statements]]

.ENDIF

Generates code that tests *condition1* (for example, AX > 7) and executes the *statements* if that condition is true. If an **.ELSE** follows, its statements are executed if the original condition was false. Note that the conditions are evaluated at run time.

IF **expression1**

ifstatements

[[**ELSEIF** *expression2*

elseifstatements]]

[[**ELSE**

elsestatements]]

ENDIF

Grants assembly of *ifstatements* if *expression1* is true (nonzero) or *elseifstatements* if *expression1* is false (0) and *expression2* is true. The following directives may be substituted for **ELSEIF**: **ELSEIFB, ELSEIFDEF, ELSEIFDIF, ELSEIFDIFI, ELSEIFE, ELSEIFIDN, ELSEIFIDNI, ELSEIFNB,** and **ELSEIFNDEF.** Optionally, assembles *elsestatements* if the previous expression is false. Note that the expressions are evaluated at assembly time.

IF2 *expression*

IF block is evaluated on every assembly pass if **OPTION:SETIF2** is **TRUE.** See **IF** for complete syntax.

IFB *textitem*

Grants assembly if *textitem* is blank. See **IF** for complete syntax.

IFDEF *name*

Grants assembly if *name* is a previously defined label, variable, or symbol. See **IF** for complete syntax.

IFDIF[[**I**]] *textitem1, textitem2*

Grants assembly if the text items are different. If **I** is given, the comparison is case insensitive. See **IF** for complete syntax.

IFE *expression*

Grants assembly if *expression* is false (0). See **IF** for complete syntax.

IFIDN[[**I**]] *textitem1*, *textitem2*

Grants assembly if the text items are identical. If **I** is given, the comparison is case insensitive. See **IF** for complete syntax.

IFNB *textitem*

Grants assembly if *textitem* is not blank. See **IF** for complete syntax.

IFNDEF *name*

Grants assembly if *name* has not been defined. See **IF** for complete syntax.

INCLUDE *filename*

Inserts source code from the source file given by *filename* into the current source file during assembly. The *filename* must be enclosed in angle brackets if it includes a backslash, semicolon, greater-than symbol, less-than symbol, single quotation mark, or double quotation mark.

INCLUDELIB *libraryname*

Informs the linker that the current module should be linked with *libraryname*. The *libraryname* must be enclosed in angle brackets if it includes a backslash, semicolon, greater-than symbol, less-than symbol, single quotation mark, or double quotation mark.

name **INSTR** [[*position*,]] *textitem1*, *textitem2*

Finds the first occurrence of *textitem2* in *textitem1*. The starting *position* is optional. Each text item can be a literal string, a constant preceded by a **%**, or the string returned by a macro function.

INVOKE *expression* [[, *arguments*]]

Calls the procedure at the address given by *expression*, passing the arguments on the stack or in registers according to the standard calling conventions of the language type. Each argument passed to the procedure may be an expression, a register pair, or an address expression (an expression preceded by **ADDR**).

IRP

See **FOR**.

IRPC

See **FORC**.

name **LABEL** *type*

Creates a new label by assigning the current location-counter value and the given *type* to *name*.

name **LABEL** [[**NEAR** | **FAR** | **PROC**]] **PTR** [[*type*]]

Creates a new label by assigning the current location-counter value and the given *type* to *name*.

.K3D

Enables assembly of K3D instructions.

.LALL

See **.LISTMACROALL**.

.LFCOND

See **.LISTIF**.

.LIST

Starts listing of statements. This is the default.

.LISTALL

Starts listing of all statements. Equivalent to the combination of **.LIST**, **.LISTIF**, and **.LISTMACROALL**.

.LISTIF

Starts listing of statements in false conditional blocks. Same as **.LFCOND**.

.LISTMACRO

Starts listing of macro expansion statements that generate code or data. This is the default. Same as **.XALL**.

.LISTMACROALL

Starts listing of all statements in macros. Same as **.LALL**.

LOCAL *localname* [[, *localname*]]. . .

Within a macro, **LOCAL** defines labels that are unique to each instance of the macro.

LOCAL *label* [[[*count*]]] [[:*type*]] [[, *label* [[[*count*]]] [[*type*]]]]. . .

Within a procedure definition (**PROC**), **LOCAL** creates stack-based variables that exist for the duration of the procedure. The *label* may be a simple variable or an array containing *count* elements.

name **MACRO** [[*parameter* [[:**REQ** | :=*default* | :**VARARG**]]]]. . .

   statements

   ENDM [[*value*]]

   Marks a macro block called *name* and establishes *parameter* placeholders for arguments passed when the macro is called. A macro function returns *value* to the calling statement.

.MMX

Enables assembly of MMX instructions.

.MODEL *memorymodel* [[, *langtype*]] [[, *stackoption*]]

Initializes the program memory model. The *memorymodel* can be **TINY**, **SMALL**, **COMPACT**, **MEDIUM**, **LARGE**, **HUGE**, or **FLAT**. The *langtype* can be **C**, **BASIC**, **FORTRAN**, **PASCAL**, **SYSCALL**, or **STDCALL**. The *stackoption* can be **NEARSTACK** or **FARSTACK**.

NAME *modulename*

Ignored.

.NO87

Disallows assembly of all floating-point instructions.

.NOCREF [[*name*[[, *name*]]. . .]]

Suppresses listing of symbols in the symbol table and browser file. If names are specified, only the given names are suppressed. Same as **.XCREF**.

.NOLIST

Suppresses program listing. Same as **.XLIST.**

.NOLISTIF

Suppresses listing of conditional blocks whose condition evaluates to false (0). This is the default. Same as **.SFCOND.**

.NOLISTMACRO

Suppresses listing of macro expansions. Same as **.SALL**.

OPTION *optionlist*

Enables and disables features of the assembler. Available options include **CASEMAP, DOT-NAME, NODOTNAME, EMULATOR, NOEMULATOR, EPILOGUE, EXPR16, EXPR32, LANGUAGE, LJMP, NOLJMP, M510, NOM510, NOKEYWORD, NOSIGN-EXTEND, OFFSET, OLDMACROS, NOOLDMACROS, OLDSTRUCTS, NOOLD-STRUCTS, PROC, PROLOGUE, READONLY, NOREADONLY, SCOPED, NOSCOPED, SEGMENT,** and **SETIF2**.

ORG *expression*

Sets the location counter to *expression*.

%OUT

See **ECHO**.

[[*name*]] **OWORD** *initializer* [[, *initializer*]]. . .

Allocates and optionally initializes an octalword (16 bytes) of storage for each *initializer*. Can also be used as a type specifier anywhere a type is legal. This data type is used primarily by Streaming SIMD instructions; it holds an array of four 4-byte reals.

PAGE [[[[*length*]], *width*]]

Sets line *length* and character *width* of the program listing. If no arguments are given, generates a page break.

PAGE $^+$

Increments the section number and resets the page number to 1.

POPCONTEXT *context*

Restores part or all of the current *context* (saved by the **PUSHCONTEXT** directive). The *context* can be **ASSUMES, RADIX, LISTING, CPU,** or **ALL**.

label **PROC** [[*distance*]] [[*langtype*]] [[*visibility*]] [[*<prologuearg>*]]

   [[**USES** *reglist*]] [[*, parameter* [[*:tag*]]]]. . .

   statements

label **ENDP**

Marks start and end of a procedure block called *label*. The statements in the block can be called with the **CALL** instruction or **INVOKE** directive.

label **PROTO** [[*distance*]] [[*langtype*]] [[*, [[parameter]]:tag*]]. . .

Prototypes a function.

PUBLIC [[*langtype*]] *name* [[*, [[langtype]] name*]]. . .

Makes each variable, label, or absolute symbol specified as *name* available to all other modules in the program.

PURGE *macroname* [[*, macroname*]]. . .

Deletes the specified macros from memory.

PUSHCONTEXT *context*

Saves part or all of the current *context*: segment register assumes, radix value, listing and cref flags, or processor/coprocessor values. The *context* can be **ASSUMES**, **RADIX**, **LISTING**, **CPU**, or **ALL**.

[[*name*]] **QWORD** *initializer* [[*, initializer*]]. . .

Allocates and optionally initializes 8 bytes of storage for each *initializer*. Also can be used as a type specifier anywhere a type is legal.

.RADIX *expression*

Sets the default radix, in the range 2 to 16, to the value of *expression*.

name **REAL4** *initializer* [[*, initializer*]]. . .

Allocates and optionally initializes a single-precision (4-byte) floating-point number for each *initializer*.

name **REAL8** *initializer* [[*, initializer*]]. . .

Allocates and optionally initializes a double-precision (8-byte) floating-point number for each *initializer*.

name **REAL10** *initializer* [[*, initializer*]]. . .

Allocates and optionally initializes a 10-byte floating-point number for each *initializer*.

recordname **RECORD** *fieldname:width* [[*= expression*]]

   [[*, fieldname:width* [[*= expression*]]]]. . .

Declares a record type consisting of the specified fields. The *fieldname* names the field, *width* specifies the number of bits, and *expression* gives its initial value.

.REPEAT

   statements

.UNTIL *condition*

Generates code that repeats execution of the block of *statements* until *condition* becomes true. **.UNTILCXZ**, which becomes true when CX is zero, may be substituted for **.UNTIL**. The *condition* is optional with **.UNTILCXZ**.

REPEAT *expression*

statements

ENDM

Marks a block that is to be repeated *expression* times. Same as **REPT**.

REPT

See **REPEAT**.

.SALL

See **.NOLISTMACRO**.

name **SBYTE** *initializer* [[, *initializer*]]. . .

Allocates and optionally initializes a signed byte of storage for each *initializer*. Can also be used as a type specifier anywhere a type is legal.

name **SDWORD** *initializer* [[, *initializer*]]. . .

Allocates and optionally initializes a signed doubleword (4 bytes) of storage for each *initializer*. Also can be used as a type specifier anywhere a type is legal.

name **SEGMENT** [[**READONLY**]] [[*align*]] [[*combine*]] [[*use*]] [[*'class'*]]

statements

name **ENDS**

Defines a program segment called *name* having segment attributes *align* (**BYTE**, **WORD, DWORD, PARA, PAGE**), *combine* (**PUBLIC, STACK, COMMON, MEMORY, AT** *address*, **PRIVATE**), *use* (**USE16, USE32, FLAT**), and *class*.

.SEQ

Orders segments sequentially (the default order).

.SFCOND

See **.NOLISTIF**.

name **SIZESTR** *textitem*

Finds the size of a text item.

.STACK [[*size*]]

When used with **.MODEL**, defines a stack segment (with segment name STACK). The optional *size* specifies the number of bytes for the stack (default 1,024). The **.STACK** directive automatically closes the stack statement.

.STARTUP

Generates program start-up code.

STRUC

See **STRUCT**.

name **STRUCT** [[*alignment*]] [[, **NONUNIQUE**]]

fielddeclarations

name **ENDS**

Declares a structure type having the specified *fielddeclarations*. Each field must be a valid data definition. Same as **STRUC**.

name **SUBSTR** *textitem, position* [[, *length*]]

Returns a substring of *textitem*, starting at *position*. The *textitem* can be a literal string, a constant preceded by a %, or the string returned by a macro function.

SUBTITLE *text*

Defines the listing subtitle. Same as **SUBTTL**.

SUBTTL

See **SUBTITLE**.

name **SWORD** *initializer* [[, *initializer*]]. . .

Allocates and optionally initializes a signed word (2 bytes) of storage for each *initializer*. Can also be used as a type specifier anywhere a type is legal.

[[*name*]] **TBYTE** *initializer* [[, *initializer*]]. . .

Allocates and optionally initializes 10 bytes of storage for each *initializer*. Can also be used as a type specifier anywhere a type is legal.

name **TEXTEQU** [[*textitem*]]

Assigns *textitem* to *name*. The *textitem* can be a literal string, a constant preceded by a %, or the string returned by a macro function.

.TFCOND

Toggles listing of false conditional blocks.

TITLE *text*

Defines the program listing title.

name **TYPEDEF** *type*

Defines a new type called *name*, which is equivalent to *type*.

name **UNION** [[*alignment*]] [[, **NONUNIQUE**]]

fielddeclarations

[[*name*]] **ENDS**

Declares a union of one or more data types. The *fielddeclarations* must be valid data definitions. Omit the **ENDS** *name* label on nested **UNION** definitions.

.UNTIL

See **.REPEAT**.

.UNTILCXZ

See **.REPEAT**.

.WHILE *condition*

   statements

.ENDW

  Generates code that executes the block of *statements* while *condition* remains true.

WHILE *expression*

   statements

ENDM

  Repeats assembly of block *statements* as long as *expression* remains true.

[[*name*]] **WORD initializer** [[, *initializer*]]. . .

  Allocates and optionally initializes a word (2 bytes) of storage for each *initializer*. Can also be used as a type specifier anywhere a type is legal.

.XALL

See **.LISTMACRO**.

.XCREF

See **.NOCREF**.

.XLIST

See **.NOLIST**.

.XMM

  Enables assembly of Internet Streaming SIMD Extension instructions.

D.8   Predefined Symbols

$

  The current value of the location counter.

?

  In data declarations, a value that the assembler allocates but does not initialize.

@@:

  Defines a code label recognizable only between *label1* and *label2*, where *label1* is either start of code or the previous @@: label, and *label2* is either end of code or the next @@: label. See **@B** and **@F**.

@B

  The location of the previous @@: label.

@CatStr(*string1* [[, *string2*. . .]] **)**

  Macro function that concatenates one or more strings. Returns a string.

@code

  The name of the code segment (text macro).

@CodeSize

0 for **TINY, SMALL, COMPACT,** and **FLAT** models, and 1 for **MEDIUM, LARGE,** and **HUGE** models (numeric equate).

@Cpu

A bit mask specifying the processor mode (numeric equate).

@CurSeg

The name of the current segment (text macro).

@data

The name of the default data group. Evaluates to DGROUP for all models except **FLAT.** Evaluates to **FLAT** under the **FLAT** memory model (text macro).

@DataSize

0 for **TINY, SMALL, MEDIUM,** and **FLAT** models, 1 for **COMPACT** and **LARGE** models, and 2 for **HUGE** model (numeric equate).

@Date

The system date in the format mm/dd/yy (text macro).

@Environ(*envvar*)

Value of environment variable *envvar* (macro function).

@F

The location of the next @@: label.

@fardata

The name of the segment defined by the **.FARDATA** directive (text macro).

@fardata?

The name of the segment defined by the **.FARDATA?** directive (text macro).

@FileCur

The name of the current file (text macro).

@FileName

The base name of the main file being assembled (text macro).

@InStr([[*position*]], *string1*, *string2*)

Macro function that finds the first occurrence of *string2* in *string1*, beginning at *position* within *string1*. If *position* does not appear, search begins at start of *string1*. Returns a position integer or 0 if *string2* is not found.

@Interface

Information about the language parameters (numeric equate).

@Line

The source line number in the current file (numeric equate).

@Model

　　1 for **TINY** model, 2 for **SMALL** model, 3 for **COMPACT** model, 4 for **MEDIUM** model, 5 for **LARGE** model, 6 for **HUGE** model, and 7 for **FLAT** model (numeric equate).

@SizeStr(*string* **)**

　　Macro function that returns the length of the given string. Returns an integer.

@stack

　　DGROUP for near stacks or STACK for far stacks (text macro).

@SubStr(*string, position* [[*, length*]] **)**

　　Macro function that returns a substring starting at *position*.

@Time

　　The system time in 24-hour hh:mm:ss format (text macro).

@Version

　　610 in MASM 6.1 (text macro).

@WordSize

　　Two for a 16-bit segment or 4 for a 32-bit segment (numeric equate).

D.9 Operators

expression1 + expression2

　　Returns *expression1* plus *expression2*.

expression1 − expression2

　　Returns *expression1* minus *expression2*.

*expression1 * expression2*

　　Returns *expression1* times *expression2*.

expression1 / expression2

　　Returns *expression1* divided by *expression2*.

−expression

　　Reverses the sign of *expression*.

expression1 [expression2]

　　Returns *expression1* plus [*expression2*].

segment: expression

　　Overrides the default segment of *expression* with *segment*. The *segment* can be a segment register, group name, segment name, or segment expression. The *expression* must be a constant.

expression. field [[*. field*]] *. . .*

　　Returns *expression* plus the offset of *field* within its structure or union.

[register]. field [[*. field*]] *. . .*

　　Returns value at the location pointed to by *register* plus the offset of *field* within its structure or union.

<*text*>

Treats *text* as a single literal element.

"*text*"

Treats "*text*" as a string.

'*text*'

Treats '*text*' as a string.

!*character*

Treats *character* as a literal character rather than as an operator or symbol.

;*text*

Treats *text* as a comment.

;;*text*

Treats *text* as a comment in a macro that appears only in the macro definition. The listing does not show *text* where the macro is expanded.

%*expression*

Treats the value of *expression* in a macro argument as text.

&*parameter*&

Replaces *parameter* with its corresponding argument value.

ABS

See the **EXTERNDEF** directive.

ADDR

See the **INVOKE** directive.

expression1* AND *expression2

Returns the result of a bitwise AND operation for *expression1* and *expression2*.

***count* DUP (*initialvalue* [[, *initialvalue*]]. . .)**

Specifies *count* number of declarations of *initialvalue*.

expression1* EQ *expression2

Returns true (−1) if *expression1* equals *expression2*, or returns false (0) if it does not.

expression1* GE *expression2

Returns true (−1) if *expression1* is greater than or equal to *expression2*, or returns false (0) if it is not.

expression1* GT *expression2

Returns true (−1) if *expression1* is greater than *expression2*, or returns false (0) if it is not.

HIGH *expression*

Returns the high byte of *expression*.

HIGHWORD *expression*

Returns the high word of *expression*.

expression1 **LE** *expression2*

Returns true (−1) if *expression1* is less than or equal to *expression2*, or returns false (0) if it is not.

LENGTH *variable*

Returns the number of data items in *variable* created by the first initializer.

LENGTHOF *variable*

Returns the number of data objects in *variable*.

LOW *expression*

Returns the low byte of *expression*.

LOWWORD *expression*

Returns the low word of *expression*.

LROFFSET *expression*

Returns the offset of *expression*. Same as **OFFSET**, but it generates a loader resolved offset, which allows Windows to relocate code segments.

expression1 **LT** *expression2*

Returns true (−1) if *expression1* is less than *expression2*, or returns false (0) if it is not.

MASK { *recordfieldname* | *record* }

Returns a bit mask in which the bits in *recordfieldname* or *record* are set and all other bits are cleared.

expression1 **MOD** *expression2*

Returns the integer value of the remainder (modulo) when dividing *expression1* by *expression2*.

expression1 **NE** *expression2*

Returns true (−1) if *expression1* does not equal *expression2*, or returns false (0) if it does.

NOT *expression*

Returns *expression* with all bits reversed.

OFFSET *expression*

Returns the offset of *expression*.

OPATTR *expression*

Returns a word defining the mode and scope of *expression*. The low byte is identical to the byte returned by **.TYPE**. The high byte contains additional information.

expression1 **OR** *expression2*

Returns the result of a bitwise OR operation for *expression1* and *expression2*.

type **PTR** *expression*

Forces the *expression* to be treated as having the specified *type*.

[[*distance*]] **PTR** *type*

Specifies a pointer to *type*.

SEG *expression*

Returns the segment of *expression*.

expression **SHL** *count*

Returns the result of shifting the bits of *expression* left *count* number of bits.

SHORT *label*

Sets the type of *label* to short. All jumps to *label* must be short (within the range −128 to +127 bytes from the jump instruction to *label*).

expression **SHR** *count*

Returns the result of shifting the bits of *expression* right *count* number of bits.

SIZE *variable*

Returns the number of bytes in *variable* allocated by the first initializer.

SIZEOF {*variable* | *type*}

Returns the number of bytes in *variable* or *type*.

THIS *type*

Returns an operand of specified *type* whose offset and segment values are equal to the current location-counter value.

.TYPE *expression*

See **OPATTR**.

TYPE *expression*

Returns the type of *expression*.

WIDTH {*recordfieldname* | *record*}

Returns the width in bits of the current *recordfieldname* or *record*.

expression1 **XOR** *expression2*

Returns the result of a bitwise XOR operation for *expression1* and *expression2*.

D.10   Runtime Operators

The following operators are used only within **.IF**, **.WHILE**, or **.REPEAT** blocks and are evaluated at run time, not at assembly time:

expression1 == *expression2*

Is equal to.

expression1 != *expression2*

Is not equal to.

expression1 > *expression2*

Is greater than.

expression1 >= expression2

    Is greater than or equal to.

expression1 < expression2

    Is less than.

expression1 <= expression2

    Is less than or equal to.

expression1 || expression2

    Logical OR.

expression1 && expression2

    Logical AND.

expression1 & expression2

    Bitwise AND.

!expression

    Logical negation.

CARRY?

    Status of Carry flag.

OVERFLOW?

    Status of Overflow flag.

PARITY?

    Status of Parity flag.

SIGN?

    Status of Sign flag.

ZERO?

    Status of Zero flag.

Index

T

Microsoft License Agreement

Microsoft MASM Version 6.11 and 6.15
Licenses: 1

IMPORTANT—READ CAREFULLY BEFORE OPENING SOFTWARE PACKETS(S). Unless a separate multilingual license booklet is included in your product package, the following License Agreement applies to you. By opening the sealed packet(s) containing the software, you indicate your acceptance of the following Microsoft License Agreement.

Single-User Products This is a legal agreement between you (either an individual or an entity) and Microsoft Corporation. By opening the sealed software packages and / or by using the software you agree to be bound by the terms of this Agreement. If you do not agree to the terms of this Agreement, promptly return the unopened software packet(s) and the accompanying items (including printed materials and binders or other containers) to the place from which you obtained them for a full refund.

Microsoft Software License

1. Grant of License. This License Agreement ("License") permits you to use one copy of the specified version of the Microsoft software product identified above, which may include "online" or electronic documentation (the "Software") on a single computer. If this package is a License Pak, you may make and use additional copies of the Software up to the number of Licensed Copies authorized above. The Software is in "use" on a computer when it is loaded into temporary memory (i.e., RAM) or installed into permanent memory (e.g., hard disk, CD-ROM, or other storage device) of that computer except that a copy installed on a network server for the sole purpose of distribution to other computers is not "in use."

2. Upgrades. If the Software is an upgrade you may use or transfer the Software only in conjunction with the prior version(s) of the Software.

3. Copyright. The Software (including any images, "applets," photographs, animations, video, audio, music, and text incorporated into the Software is owned by Microsoft or its suppliers and is protected by United States copyright laws and international treaty provisions. Therefore, you must treat the Software like any other copyrighted material (e.g., a book or musical recording) except that you may either (a) make one copy of the Software solely for backup or archival purposes, or (b) transfer the Software to a single hard disk provided you keep the original solely for backup or archival purposes. You may not copy the printed materials accompanying the Software.

4. Other Restrictions. You may not rent or lease the Software, but you may transfer the Software and accompanying written materials on a permanent basis provided you retain no copies and the recipient agrees to the terms of this Agreement. If the Software is an upgrade, any transfer must included the most recent upgrade and all prior versions. You may not reverse engineer, decompile, or disassemble the Software, except to the extent such foregoing restriction is expressly prohibited by applicable law.

5. Dual Media Software. You may receive the Software on more than one medium. Regardless of the type or size of medium you receive, you may use only the medium appropriate for your single use computer. You may not use the other medium on another computer or load, rent, lease, or transfer the disks to another user except as part of the permanent transfer as provided above of all Software and printed materials, not print copies of any user documentation provided in "online" or electronic form.

6. Language Software. If the Software is a Microsoft language product, then you have a royalty-free right to reproduce and distribute executable files created using the Software. If the language product is a Basic or COBOL product, then Microsoft grants you a royalty-free right to reproduce and distribute the run-time modules of the Software *provided* that you (a) distribute the run-time modules only in conjunction with and as a part of your software product; (b) do not use Microsoft's name, logo, or trademark to market your software product; (c) include a valid copyright notice on your software product; and (d) agree to indemnify, hold harmless, and defend Microsoft and its suppliers from any against any claims or lawsuits, including attorney's fees, that arise or result from the use or distribution of your software product. The "run-time modules" are those files in the Software that are identified in the accompanying printed materials as required during execution of your software program. The run-time modules are limited to run-time files and ISAM and REMOLD files. If required in the Software documentation, you agree to display the designated patent notices on the packaging and in the README file in your software product.

Miscellaneous

If you acquired the product in the United States, this EULA is governed by the laws of the State of Washington.

If you acquired this product in Canada, this EULA is governed by the laws of the Province of Ontario, Canada. Each of the parties hereto irrevocably attorns to the jurisdiction of the courts of the Province of Ontario and further agrees to commence any litigation which may arise hereunder in the courts located in the Judicial District of York, Province of Ontario.

If this product was acquired outside the United States, then local laws may apply.

Should you have any questions concerning the EULA, or if you desire to contact Microsoft for any reason, please contract the Microsoft subsidiary serving your country, or write: Microsoft Sales Information Center/One Microsoft Way/Redmond, WA 9805-6399.

Limited Warranty

No Warranties. Microsoft expressly disclaims any warranty for the Software Product. The Software Product and any related documentation is provided "as is" without warranty of any kind, either express or implied, including, without limitation, the implied warranties or merchantability, fitness for a particular purpose, or noninfringement. The entire risk arising out of use or performance of the Software Product remains with you.

No Liability For Damages. In no event shall Microsoft or its suppliers be liable for any damages whatsoever (including, without limitation, damages for loss of business profits, business interruption, loss of business information, or any other pecuniary loss) arising out of the use of or inability to use this Microsoft product, even if Microsoft has been advised of the possibility of such damages. Because some states/jurisdictions do not allow the exclusion or limitation of liability for consequential or incidental damages, the above limitations may not apply to you.

decimal ⇨	hexa-decimal	1	16	32	46	64	80	96	112
⇩		0	1	2	3	4	5	6	7
0	0	null	▶	space	0	@	P	`	p
1	1	☺	◀	!	1	A	Q	a	q
2	2	☻	↕	"	2	B	R	b	r
3	3	♥	‼	#	3	C	S	c	s
4	4	♦	Π	$	4	D	T	d	t
5	5	♣	§	%	5	E	U	e	u
6	6	♠	▬	&	6	F	V	f	v
7	7	•	↨	'	7	G	W	g	w
8	8	◘	^	(	8	H	X	h	x
9	9	○	↓	)	9	I	Y	i	y
10	A	◉	→	*	:	J	Z	j	z
11	B	♂	←	+	;	K	[	k	{
12	C	♀	∟	,	<	L	\	l	|
13	D	♪	↔	-	=	M	]	m	}
14	E	♫	▲	.	>	N	^	n	~
15	F	☼	▼	/	?	O	_	o	Δ